ATLA BIBLIOGRAPHY SERIES
edited by Dr. Kenneth E. Rowe

1. *A Guide to the Study of the Holiness Movement,* by Charles Edwin Jones. 1974.
2. *Thomas Merton: A Bibliography,* by Marquita E. Breit. 1974.
3. *The Sermon on the Mount: A History of Interpretation and Bibliography,* by Warren S. Kissinger. 1975.
4. *The Parables of Jesus: A History of Interpretation and Bibliography,* by Warren S. Kissinger. 1979.
5. *Homosexuality and the Judeo-Christian Tradition: An Annotated Bibliography,* by Thom Horner. 1981.
6. *A Guide to the Study of the Pentecostal Movement,* by Charles Edwin Jones. 1983.
7. *The Genesis of Modern Process Thought: A Historical Outline with Bibliography,* by George R. Lucas, Jr. 1983.
8. *A Presbyterian Bibliography,* by Harold B. Prince. 1983.
9. *Paul Tillich: A Comprehensive Bibliography . . .,* by Richard C. Crossman. 1983.
10. *A Bibliography of the Samaritans,* by Alan David Crown. 1984 (see no. 32).
11. *An Annotated and Classified Bibliography of English Literature Pertaining to the Ethiopian Orthodox Church,* by Jon Bonk. 1984.
12. *International Meditation Bibliography, 1950 to 1982,* by Howard R. Jarrell. 1984.
13. *Rabindranath Tagore: A Bibliography,* by Katherine Henn. 1985.
14. *Research in Ritual Studies: A Programmatic Essay and Bibliography,* by Ronald L. Grimes, 1985.
15. *Protestant Theological Education in America,* by Heather F. Day. 1985.
16. *Unconscious: A Guide to Sources,* by Natalino Caputi. 1985.
17. *The New Testament Apocrypha and Pseudepigrapha,* by James H. Charlesworth. 1987.
18. *Black Holiness,* by Charles Edwin Jones. 1987.
19. *A Bibliography on Ancient Ephesus,* by Richard Oster. 1987.
20. *Jerusalem, the Holy City: A Bibliography,* by James D. Purvis. 1988; Vol. II, 1991.

An Index to
English Periodical Literature
on the Old Testament
and
Ancient Near Eastern Studies

Volume VI

Compiled and Edited by

William G. Hupper

ATLA Bibliography Series, No. 21

The terrible thing about the quest for truth is that you find it.
...Remy de Gourmont

The American Theological Library Association, and
The Scarecrow Press, Inc.
Metuchen, N.J., & London 1994

Illustration is of an Ammonite figurine head found by the Madaba Plains Project. Used by permission of Andrews University.

British Library Cataloguing-in-Publication data available

Library of Congress Cataloging-in-Publication Data
(Revised for volume 6)

Hupper, William G
  An index to English periodical literature on the Old
Testament and ancient Near Eastern studies.

  (ATLA bibliography series no. 21)
  1. Bible. O.T.—Periodicals—Indexes. 2. Middle
East—Periodicals—Indexes. I. American Theological
Library Association. II. Title. III. Series.
Z 7772.A1H86 1987 [BS1171.2] 016.221 86-31448
ISBN 0-8108-1984-8 (v. 1)
ISBN 0-8108-2126-5 (v. 2)
ISBN 0-8108-2319-5 (v. 3)
ISBN 0-8108-2393-4 (v. 4)
ISBN 0-8108-2618-6 (v. 5)
ISBN 0-8108-2822-7 (v. 6)

Table of Contents

iii

Table of Contents

iv

Table of Contents

Table of Contents

Table of Contents

Table of Contents

Table of Contents

Table of Contents

Table of Contents

Table of Contents

Table of Contents

Table of Contents

Table of Contents

Table of Contents

Table of Contents

Table of Contents

Table of Contents

Preface

This completes the third major division within this index. Since this volume is mainly composed of "Exegetical Articles" it is perhaps prudent to reproduce a small section of the Introduction from Volume I. Articles within this division "are arranged according to the Hebrew Bible (i.e., The Pentateuch; The Prophets; and The Hagiographa). Entries are then subdivided by chapter and verse under each book of the Old Testament in an inverted pyramid fashion: articles dealing with larger blocks of passages being first and narrowing ultimately to a single verse or portion of a verse, e.g.:

Multiple Mixed Texts
Chapters 1-10
Chapters 1-3
Chapters 1:1-3:5
Chapter 1
vss 1-15 of Chapter 1
v. 3 of Chapter 1
Chapters 2:1-3:8
etc.

The scope of articles covered under this section may actually cross over into 'Literary Criticism' (found in Volume IV) but are placed here for convenience since they make reference to specific Old Testament passages."[1]

Additionally, this volume contains articles on the Apocrypha and Pseudepigrapha, though the arrangement found in R. H. Charles' great work has been only loosely followed.[2]

Many thanks are again extended to my proofreader, Mrs. Florence Hall, and to Dr. Frederick E. Greenspahn for the assistance in the preparation of sections 805-816 dealing with Rabbinic material.

Melrose, MA
Autumnal Equinox, 1993

---

1. See Volume I, p. xxii.
2. R. H. Charles, ed., *The Apocrypha and Pseudepigrapha of the Old Testament in English* (London: Oxford University Press, 1913) *Two Volumes*

Periodical Abbreviations*

A

A&A   *Art and Archaeology; the arts throughout the ages*
(Washington, DC, Baltimore, MD, 1914-1934)

A/R   *Action/Reaction* (San Anselmo, CA, 1967ff.)

A&S   *Antiquity and Survival* (The Hague, 1955-1962)

A(A)   *Anadolu (Anatolia)* (Ankara, 1956ff.) [Subtitle varies;
Volume 1-7 as: *Anatolia: Revue Annuelle
d'Archeologie*]

AA   *Acta Archaeologica* (Copenhagen, 1930ff.)

AAA   *Annals of Archaeology and Anthropology* (Liverpool,
1908-1948; Suspended, 1916-1920)

AAAS   *Annales archéologiques arabes Syriennes. Revue
d'Archéologie et d'Histoire* (Damascus, 1951ff.)
[Volumes 1-15 as: *Les Annales archéologiques de Syrie*
- Title Varies]

AAASH   *Acta Antiqua Academiae Scientiarum Hungaricae*
(Budapest, 1951ff.)

AAB   *Acta Archaeologica* (Budapest, 1951ff.)

AAI   *Anadolu Araştirmalari Istanbul Üniversitesi Edebiyat Fakültesi
eski Önasya Dilleri ve Kültürleri Kürsüsü Tarafindan
Čikarilir* (Istanbul, 1955ff.) [Supersedes: *Jahrbuch für
Kleinasiatische Forschungen*]

AAOJ   *American Antiquarian and Oriental Journal* (Cleveland,
Chicago 1878-1914)

AASCS   *Antichthon. The Australian Society for Classical Studies*
(Sydney, 1967ff.)

ABBTS   *The Alumni Bulletin [of] Bangor Theological Seminary*
(Bangor, ME; 1926ff.)

ABenR   *The American Benedictine Review* (St. Paul, 1950ff.)

ABR   *Australian Biblical Review* (Melbourne, 1951ff.)

Abr-N   *Abr-Nahrain, An Annual Published by the Department of
Middle Eastern Studies, University of Melbourne*
(Melbourne, 1959ff.)

ACM   *The American Church Monthly* (New York, 1917-1939)
[Volumes 43-45 as: *The New American Church Monthly*]

*All the journals indexed are listed in the Periodical Abbreviations even though no specific citation may appear in the present volume. Although the titles of many foreign language journals have been listed, only English Language articles are included in this index (except as noted). Articles from Modern Hebrew Language Journals are referred to by their English summary page.

ACQ   *American Church Quarterly* (New York, 1961ff.)
       [Volume 7 on as: *Church Theological Review*]

ACQR   *The American Catholic Quarterly Review* (Philadelphia, 1876-1929)

ACR   *The Australasian Catholic Record* (Sydney, 1924ff.)

ACSR   *American Catholic Sociological Review* (Chicago, 1940ff.)
       [From Volume 25 on as: *Sociological Analysis*]

ADAJ   *Annual of the Department of Antiquities of Jordan* (Amman, 1957ff.) [Volume 14 not published—destroyed by fire at the publishers]

AE   *Annales d'Ethiopie* (Paris, 1955ff.)

AEE   *Ancient Egypt and the East* (New York, London, Chicago, 1914-1935; Suspended, 1918-1919)

Aeg   *Aegyptus: Rivista Italiana di Egittologia e di Papirologia* (Milan,1920ff.)

AER   *American Ecclesiastical Review* (Philadelphia, New York, Cincinnati, Baltimore, 1889ff.) [Volumes 11-19 as: *Ecclesiastical Review*]

AfER   *African Ecclesiastical Review: A Quarterly for Priests in Africa* (Masaka, Uganda, 1959ff.)

Aff   *Affirmation* (Richmond, VA, 1966ff.) [Volume 1 runs from 1966 to 1980 inclusive]

AfO   *Archiv für Orientforschung; Internationale Zeitschrift für Wissenschaft vom Vorderen Orient* (Berlin, 1923ff.)

AfRW   *Archiv für Religionswissenschaft* (Leipzig, 1898-1941)

AHDO   *Archives d'histoire du droit oriental et Revue internationale des droits de l'antiquité* (Brussels, 1937-38, 1947-1951, *N.S.,* 1952-53)

AIPHOS   *Annuaire de l'institut de philologie et d'histoire orientales et slaves* (Brussels, 1932ff.)

AJ   *The Antiquaries Journal. Being the Journal of the Society of Antiquaries of London* (London, 1921ff.)

AJA   *The American Journal of Archaeology* (Baltimore, 1885ff.) [Original Series, 1885-1896 shown with *O. S;* Second Series shown without notation]

AJBA   *The Australian Journal of Biblical Archaeology* (Sydney, 1968ff.) [Volume 1 runs from 1968 to 1971 inclusive]

AJP   *The American Journal of Philology* (Baltimore, 1880ff.)

AJRPE   *The American Journal of Religious Psychology and Education* (Worcester, MA, 1904-1911)

AJSL   *The American Journal of Semitic Languages and Literatures* (Chicago, 1884-1941) [Volumes 1-11 as: *Hebraica*]

AJT   *American Journal of Theology* (Chicago, 1897-1920)

AL   *Archivum Linguisticum: A Review of Comparative Philology and General Linguistics* (Glasgow, 1949-1962)

ALUOS	*The Annual of the Leeds University Oriental Society* (Leiden,1958ff.)
Amb	*The Ambassador* (Wartburg Theological Seminary, Dubuque, IA, 1952ff.)
AmHR	*American Historical Review* (New York, Lancaster, PA, 1895ff.)
AmSR	*American Sociological Review* (Washington, DC, 1936ff.)
Anat	*Anatolica: Annuaire International pour les Civilisations de l'Asie Anterieure* (Leiden, 1967ff.)
ANQ	*Newton Theological Institute Bulletin* (Newton, MA, 1906ff.) [Title varies as: *Andover-Newton Theological Bulletin; Andover-Newton Quarterly, New Series,* beginning 1960ff.]
Anthro	*Anthropos; ephemeris internationalis ethnologica et linguistica* (Salzburg, Vienna, 1906ff.)
Antiq	*Antiquity: A Quarterly Review of Archaeology* (Gloucester, England, 1927ff.)
Anton	*Antonianum. Periodicum Philosophico-Theologicum Trimestre* (Rome, 1926ff.)
AO	*Acta Orientalia ediderunt Societates Orientales Bœtava Donica, Norvegica* (Lugundi Batavorum, Havniæ, 1922ff.)
AOASH	*Acta Orientalia Academiae Scientiarum Hungaricae* (Budapest, 1950ff.)
AOL	*Annals of Oriental Literature* (London, 1820-21)
APST	*Aberdeen Philosophical Society, Transactions* (Aberdeen, Scotland, 1840-1931)
AQ	*Augustana Quarterly* (Rock Island, IL, 1922-1948)
AQW	*Anthropological Quarterly* (Washington, DC, 1928ff.) [Volumes1-25 as: *Primitive Man*]
AR	*The Andover Review* (Boston, 1884-1893)
Arch	*Archaeology* (Cambridge, MA, 1948ff.)
Archm	*Archaeometry. Bulletin of the Research Laboratory for Archaeology and the History of Art, Oxford University* (Oxford,1958ff.)
ARL	*The Archæological Review* (London, 1888-1890)
ArOr	*Archiv Orientální. Journal of the Czechoslovak Oriental Institute, Prague* (Vlašska, Czechoslovakia, 1929ff.)
AS	*Anatolian Studies: Journal of the British Institute of Archaeology at Ankara* (London, 1951ff.)
ASAE	*Annales du service des antiquités de l'Égypte* (Cairo, 1899ff.)
ASBFE	*Austin Seminary Bulletin. Faculty Edition* (Austin, TX; begins with volume 71*[sic]*, 1955ff.)

ASR	*Augustana Seminary Review* (Rock Island, IL, 1949-1967) [From volume 12 on as: *The Seminary Review*]
ASRB	*Advent Shield and Review* (Boston, 1844-45)
ASRec	*Auburn Seminary Record* (Auburn, NY, 1905-1932)
ASSF	*Acta Societatis Scientiarum Fennicae* (Helsinki, 1842-1926) [Suomen tideseura]
ASTI	*Annual of the Swedish Theological Institute (in Jerusalem)* (Jerusalem, 1962ff.)
ASW	*The Asbury Seminarian* (Wilmore, KY, 1946ff.)
AT	*Ancient Times: A Quarterly Review of Biblical Archaeology* (Melbourne, 1956-1961)
ATB	*Ashland Theological Bulletin* (Ashland, OH, 1968ff.)
ATG	*Advocate for the Testimony of God* (Richmond, VA, 1834-1839)
AThR	*The American Theological Review* (New York, 1859-1868) [*New Series* as: *American Presbyterian and Theological Review*, 1863-1868]
'Atiqot	*'Atiqot: Journal of the Israel Department of Antiquities* (Jerusalem, 1955ff.)
ATJ	*Africa Theological Journal* (Usa River, Tanzania, 1968ff.)
ATR	*Anglican Theological Review* (New York, Lancaster, PA; 1918ff.)
AubSRev	*Auburn Seminary Review* (Auburn, NY, 1897-1904)
Aug	*Augustinianum* (Rome, 1961ff.)
AULLUÅ	*Acta Universitatis Lundensis. Lunds Universitets Årsskrift. Första Avdelningen. Teologi, Juridik och Humanistika Ämnen* (Lund, 1864-1904; *N. S.,* 1905-1964)
AUSS	*Andrews University Seminary Studies* (Berrien Springs, MI, 1963ff.)
AusTR	*The Australasian Theological Review* (Highgate, South Australia, 1930-1966)

B

B	*Biblica* (Rome, 1920ff.)
BA	*The Biblical Archaeologist* (New Haven; Cambridge, MA; 1938ff.)
Baby	*Babyloniaca Etudes de Philologie Assyro-Babylonienne* (Paris, 1906-1937)
BASOR	*Bulletin of the American Schools of Oriental Research* (So. Hadley, MA; Baltimore, New Haven, Philadelphia, Cambridge, MA;1919ff.)
BASP	*Bulletin of the American Society of Papyrologists* (New Haven, 1963ff.)

BAVSS   *Beiträge zur Assyriologie und vergleichenden semitischen*
          Sprachwissenschaft (Leipzig, 1889-1927)
BBC   *Bulletin of the Bezan Club* (Oxford, 1925-1936)
BC   *Bellamire Commentary* (Oxon., England; 1956-1968)
BCQTR   *British Critic, Quarterly Theological Review and Ecclesiastical*
          Record (London, 1793-1843) [Superseded by: *English*
          Review]
BCTS   *Bulletin of the Crozer Theological Seminary* (Upland, PA,
          1908-1934)
Bery   *Berytus. Archaeological Studies* (Copenhagen, 1934ff.)
BETS   *Bulletin of the Evangelical Theological Society* (Wheaton, IL,
          1958ff.)
BFER   *British and Foreign Evangelical Review, and Quarterly Record*
          of Christian Literature (Edinburgh, London, 1852-1888)
BH   *Buried History. Quarterly Journal of the Australian Institute*
          of Archaeology (Melbourne, 1964-65; 1967ff.)
BibR   *Biblical Repertory* (Princeton, NJ; New York, 1825-1828)
BibT   *The Bible Today* (Collegeville, MN, 1962ff.)
BIES   *Bulletin of the Israel Exploration Society* (Jerusalem,
          1937-1967) [*Yediot-* ידיעות בחקידת

          ארץ־ישראל ועתיקותיה-Begun as: *Bulletin of the*
          Jewish Palestine Exploration Society through volume
          15. English summaries discontinued from volume 27 on
          as translations published in: *Israel Exploration Journal*]
BIFAO   *Bulletin de l'institut français d'archéologie orientale au Caire*
          (Cairo, 1901ff.)
BJ   *Biblical Journal* (Boston, 1842-1843)
BJRL   *Bulletin of the John Rylands Library* (Manchester, 1903ff.)
BM   *Bible Magazine* (New York, 1913-1915)
BMB   *Bulletin du Musée de Byrouth* (Paris, 1937ff.)
BN   *Bible Numerics: a Periodical Devoted to the Numerical*
          Study of the Scriptures (Grafton, MA; 1904)
BO   *Bibliotheca Orientalis* (Leiden, 1944ff.)
BofT   *Banner of Truth* (London, 1955ff.)
BOR   *The Babylonian and Oriental Record: A Monthly Magazine of*
          the Antiquities of the East (London, 1886-1901)
BQ   *Baptist Quarterly* (Philadelphia, 1867-1877)
BQL   *Baptist Quarterly* (London, 1922ff.)
BQR   *Baptist Quarterly Review* (Cincinnati, New York,
          Philadelphia, 1879-1892)
BQRL   *The British Quarterly Review* (London, 1845-1886)
BR   *Biblical Review* (New York, 1916-1932)
BRCM   *The Biblical Review and Congregational Magazine* (London,
          1846-1850)

BRCR   *The Biblical Repository and Classical Review* (Andover, MA, 1831-1850) [Title varies as: *Biblical Repository; The Biblical Repository and Quarterly Observer; The American Biblical Repository*]

BRec   *Bible Record* (New York, 1903-1912) [Volume 1, #1-4 as: *Bible Teachers Training School, New York City, Bulletin*]

BRes   *Biblical Research: Papers of the Chicago Society of Biblical Research* (Amsterdam, Chicago, 1956ff.)

BS   *Bibliotheca Sacra* (New York, Andover, Oberlin, OH; St. Louis, Dallas, 1843, 1844ff.)

BSAJB   *British School of Archaeology in Jerusalem, Bulletin* (Jerusalem, 1922-1925)

BSOAS   *Bulletin of the School of Oriental and African Studies. University of London* (London, 1917ff.)

BSQ   *Bethel Seminary Quarterly* (St. Paul, MN; 1952ff.) [From Volume 13 on as: *Bethel Seminary Journal*]

BT   *Biblical Theology* (Belfast, 1950ff.)

BTF   *Bangalore Theological Forum* (Bangalore, India, 1967ff.)

BTPT   *Bijdragen Tijdschrift voor philosophie en theologie* (Maastricht, 1938ff.) [Title varies as: *Bijdragen. Tijdschrift voor filosofie en theologie*]

BTr   *Bible Translator* (London, 1950ff.)

BUS   *Bucknell University Studies* (Lewisburg, PA; 1941ff.) [From Volume 5 on as: *Bucknell Review*]

BVp   *Biblical Viewpoint* (Greenville, SC, 1967ff.)

BW   *Biblical World* (Chicago, 1893-1920)

BWR   *Bible Witness and Review* (London, 1877-1881)

BWTS   *The Bulletin of the Western Theological Seminary* (Pittsburgh, 1908-1931)

BZ   *Biblische Zeitschrift* (Paderborn, 1903-1939; *New Series,* 1957ff.) [*N.S.* shown without notation]

C

C&C   *Cross and Crown. A Thomistic Quarterly of Spiritual Theology* (St. Louis, 1949ff.)

CAAMA   *Cahiers archéologiques fin de l'antiquité et moyen age* (Paris, 1961ff.)

CAAST   *Connecticut Academy of Arts and Sciences, Transactions* (New Haven, 1866ff.)

Carm   *Carmelus. Commentarii ab instituto carmelitano editi* (Rome, 1954ff.)

CBQ   *Catholic Biblical Quarterly* (Washington, DC; 1939ff.)

CC   *Cross Currents* (West Nyack, NY; 1950ff.)

CCARJ	*Central Conference of American Rabbis Journal* (New York,1953ff.)
CCBQ	*Central Conservative Baptist Quarterly* (Minneapolis, 1958ff.) [From volume 9, #2 on as: *Central Bible Quarterly*]
CCQ	*Crisis Christology Quarterly* (Dubuque, IA; 1943-1949) [Volume 6 as: *Trinitarian Theology*]
CD	*Christian Disciple* (Boston, 1813-1823) [Superseded by: *Christian Examiner*]
CdÉ	*Chronique d'Égypte* (Brussels, 1925ff.)
CE	*Christian Examiner* (Boston, New York, 1824-1869)
Cent	*Centaurus. International Magazine of the History of Science and Medicine* (Copenhagen, 1950ff.)
Center	*The Center* (Atlanta, 1960-1965)
CFL	*Christian Faith and Life* (Columbia, SC, 1897-1939) [Title varies: Original Series as: *The Bible Student and Religious Outlook,* volumes 1 & 2 as: *The Religious Outlook;* New Series as: *The Bible Student;* Third Series as: *The Bible Student and Teacher;* several volumes as: *Bible Champion*]
ChgoS	*Chicago Studies* (Mundelein, IL; 1962ff.)
CJ	*Conservative Judaism* (New York, 1945ff.)
CJL	*Canadian Journal of Linguistics* (Montreal, 1954ff.)
CJRT	*The Canadian Journal of Religious Thought* (Toronto, 1924-1932)
CJT	*Canadian Journal of Theology* (Toronto, 1955ff.)
ClR	*Clergy Review* (London, 1931ff.)
CM	*The Clergyman's Magazine* (London, 1875-1897)
CMR	*Canadian Methodist Review* (Toronto, 1889-1895) [Volumes 1-5 as: *Canadian Methodist Quarterly*]
CNI	*Christian News from Israel* (Jerusalem, 1949ff.)
CO	*Christian Opinion* (New York, 1943-1948)
Coll	*Colloquium. The Australian and New Zealand Theological Review* (Auckland, 1964ff.) [Volume 1 through Volume 2, #1 as: *The New Zealand Theological Review*]
CollBQ	*The College of the Bible Quarterly* (Lexington, KY, 1909-1965) [Break in sequence between 1927 and 1937, resumes in 1938 with volume 15 duplicated in number]
ColTM	*Columbus Theological Magazine* (Columbus, OH; 1881-1910)
CongL	*The Congregationalist* (London, 1872-1886)
CongML	*The Congregational Magazine* (London, 1818-1845)
CongQB	*The Congregational Quarterly* (Boston, 1859-1878)
CongQL	*The Congregational Quarterly* (London, 1923-1958)
CongR	*The Congregational Review* (Boston, Chicago, 1861-1871) [Volumes 1-6 as: *The Boston Review*]

CongRL	*The Congregational Review* (London, 1887-1891)
ConstrQ	*The Constructive Quarterly. A Journal of the Faith, Work, and Thought of Christendom* (New York, London, 1913-1922)
Cont	*Continuum* (St. Paul, 1963-1970)
ContextC	*Context (Journal of the Lutheran School of Theology at Chicago)* (Chicago, 1967-1968)
ContR	*Contemporary Review* (London, New York, 1866ff.)
CovQ	*The Covenant Quarterly* (Chicago, 1941ff.) [Volume 1, #1 as: *Covenant Minister's Quarterly*]
CQ	*Crozer Quarterly* (Chester, PA; 1924-1952)
CQR	*Church Quarterly Review* (London, 1875-1968)
CR	*The Church Review* (New Haven, 1848-1891) [Title varies; Volume 62 not published]
CraneR	*The Crane Review* (Medford, MA; 1958-1968)
CRB	*The Christian Review* (Boston, Rochester; 1836-1863)
CRDSB	*Colgate-Rochester Divinity School Bulletin* (Rochester, NY; 1928-1967)
Crit	*Criterion* (Chicago, 1962ff.)
CRP	*The Christian Review: A Quarterly Magazine* (Philadelphia, 1932-1941)
CS	*The Cumberland Seminarian* (McKenzie, TN; Memphis; 1953-1970)
CSQ	*Chicago Seminary Quarterly* (Chicago, 1901-1907)
CSQC	*The Culver-Stockton Quarterly* (Canton, MO; 1925-1931)
CSSH	*Comparative Studies in Society and History: An International Quarterly* (The Hague, 1958ff.)
CT	*Christian Thought* (New York, 1883-1894)
CTJ	*Calvin Theological Journal* (Grand Rapids, 1966ff.)
CTM	*Concordia Theological Monthly* (St. Louis, 1930ff.)
CTPR	*The Christian Teacher [and Chronicle]* (London, 1835-1838; N.S., 1838-1844 as: *A Theological and Literary Journal*) [Continues as: *The Prospective Review; A Quarterly Journal of Theology and Literature*]
CTSB	*Columbia Theological Seminary Bulletin* (Columbia, SC; Decatur, GA; 1907ff.) [Title varies]
CTSP	*Catholic Theological Society, Proceedings* (Washington, DC; Yonkers, NY; 1948ff.)
CTSQ	*Central Theological Seminary Quarterly* (Dayton, OH; 1923-1931)
CUB	*Catholic University Bulletin* (Washington, DC; 1895-1914) [Volumes 1-20 only]

D

DDSR	*Duke Divinity School Review* (Durham, NC; 1936ff.) [Volumes 1-20 as: *The Duke School of Religion Bulletin;* Volumes 21-29 as: *Duke Divinity School Bulletin*]
DG	*The Drew Gateway* (Madison, NJ; 1930ff.)
DI	*Diné Israel. An Annual of Jewish Law and Israeli Family Law* דיני ישראל, שנתון למשפט עברי ולדיני משפחה בישראל (Jerusalem, 1969ff.)
DJT	*Dialogue: A Journal of Theology* (Minneapolis, 1962ff.)
DownsR	*Downside Review* (Bath, 1880ff.)
DQR	*Danville Quarterly Review* (Danville, KY; Cincinnati; 1861-1864)
DR	*Dublin Review* (London, 1836-1968) [Between 1961 and 1964 as: *Wiseman Review*]
DS	*Dominican Studies. A Quarterly Review of Theology and Philosophy* (Oxford, 1948-1954)
DSJ	*The Dubuque Seminary Journal* (Dubuque, IA; 1966-1967)
DSQ	*Dubuque Seminary Quarterly* (Dubuque, IA; 1947-1949) [Volume 3, #3 not published]
DTCW	*Dimension: Theology in Church and World* (Princeton, NJ; 1964-1969) [Volumes 1 & 2 as: *Dimension* ; New format beginning in 1966 with full title, beginning again with Volume 1]
DTQ	*Dickinson's Theological Quarterly* (London, 1875-1883) [Superseded by *John Lobb's Theological Quarterly*]
DUJ	*The Durham University Journal* (Durham, 1876ff.; *N.S.,* 1940ff.) [Volume 32 of *O.S.* = Volume 1 of *N.S.*]
DUM	*Dublin University Magazine* (Dublin, London, 1833-1880)
DunR	*The Dunwoodie Review* (Yonkers, NY; 1961ff.)

E

EgR	*Egyptian Religion* (New York, 1933-1936)
EI	*Eretz-Israel. Archaeological, Historical and Geographical Studies* (Jerusalem, 1951ff.) ארץ־ישראל, מחקרים בידיעת הארץ ועתיקותיה [English Summaries from Volume 3 on]

EJS   *Archives européennes de Sociologie / European Journal of Sociology / Europäisches Archiv für Soziologie* (Paris, 1960ff.)

EN   *The Everlasting Nation* (London, 1889-1892)

EQ   *Evangelical Quarterly* (London, 1929ff.)

ER   *Evangelical Review* (Gettysburg, PA; 1849-1870) [From Volume 14 on as: *Evangelical Quarterly Review*]

ERCJ   *Edinburgh Review, or Critical Journal* (Edinburgh, London, 1802-1929)

ERG   *The Evangelical Repository: A Quarterly Magazine of Theological Literature* (Glasgow, 1854-1888)

ERL   *The English Review, or Quarterly Journal of Ecclesiastical and General Literature* (London, 1844-1853) [Continues *British Critic*]

ESS   *Ecumenical Study Series* (Indianapolis, 1955-1960)

ET   *The Expository Times* (Aberdeen, Edinburgh, 1889ff.)

ETL   *Ephemerides Theologicae Lovanienses* (Notre Dame, 1924ff.)

Eud   *Eudemus. An International Journal Devoted to the History of Mathematics and Astronomy* (Copenhagen, 1941)

Exp   *The Expositor* (London, 1875-1925)

Exped   *Expedition* (Philadelphia, 1958ff.) [Continues: *The University Museum Bulletin*]

F

F&T   *Faith and Thought* (London, 1958ff.) [Supersedes: *Journal of the Transactions of the Victoria Institute, or Philosophical Society of Great Britain*]

FBQ   *The Freewill Baptist Quarterly* (Providence, London, Dover, 1853-1869)

FDWL   *Friends of Dr.Williams's Library (Lectures)* (Cambridge, Oxford, 1948ff.)

FLB   *Fuller Library Bulletin* (Pasadena, CA; 1949ff.)

FO   *Folia Orientalia* (Kraków, 1960ff.)

Focus   *Focus. A Theological Journal* (Willowdale, Ontario, 1964-1968)

Folk   *Folk-Lore: A Quarterly Review of Myth, Tradition, Institution & Custom being The Transactions of the Folk-Lore Society And Incorporating the Archæological Review and the Folk-Lore Journal* (London, 1890ff.)

Found   *Foundations (A Baptist Journal of History and Theology)* (Rochester, NY; 1958ff.)

FUQ   *Free University Quarterly* (Amsterdam-Centrum, 1950-1965)

G

GBT	*Ghana Bulletin of Theology* (Legon, Ghana; 1957ff.)
GJ	*Grace Journal* (Winona Lake, IN; 1960ff.)
GOTR	*Greek Orthodox Theological Review* (Brookline, MA; 1954ff.)
GR	*Gordon Review* (Boston; Beverly Farms, MA; Wenham, MA; 1955ff.)
GRBS	*Greek, Roman and Byzantine Studies* (San Antonio; Cambridge, MA; University, MS; Durham, NC; 1958ff.) [Volume1 as: *Greek and Byzantine Studies*]
Greg	*Gregorianum; Commentarii de re theologica et philosophica* (Rome, 1920ff.) [Volume 1 as: *Gregorianum; rivista trimestrale di studi teologici e filosofici*]
GUOST	*Glasgow University Oriental Society, Transactions* (Glasgow, 1901ff.)

H

H&T	*History and Theory: Studies in the Philosophy of History* (The Hague, 1960ff.)
HA	*Hebrew Abstracts* (New York, 1954ff.)
HDSB	*Harvard Divinity School Bulletin* (Cambridge, MA; 1935-1969)
Herm	*Hermathena; a Series of Papers on Literature, Science and Philosophy by Members of Trinity College, Dublin* (Dublin, 1873ff.) [Volumes 1-20; changes to issue number from #46 on]
HeyJ	*The Heythrop Journal* (New York, 1960ff.)
HJ	*Hibbert Journal* (London, Boston, 1902-1968)
HJAH	*Historia. Zeitschrift für alte Geschichte / Revue d'Histoire Ancienne / Journal of Ancient History / Rivista di Storia Antica* (Baden, 1950ff.)
HJud	*Historia Judaica. A Journal of Studies in Jewish History Especially in the Legal and Economic History of the Jews* (New York, 1938-1961)
HQ	*The Hartford Quarterly* (Hartford, CT; 1960-1968)
HR	*Homiletic Review* (New York, 1876-1934)
HRel	*History of Religions* (Chicago, 1961ff.)
HS	*Ha Sifrut. Quarterly for the Study of Literature* הספרות, רבעון למדע הספרות (Tel-Aviv, 1968ff.)
HSR	*Hartford Seminary Record* (Hartford, CT; 1890-1913)
HT	*History Today* (London, 1951ff.)

HTR	*Harvard Theological Review* (Cambridge, MA; 1908ff.)
HTS	*Hervormde Teologiese Studien* (Pretoria, 1943ff.)
HUCA	*Hebrew Union College Annual* (Cincinnati, 1904, 1924ff.)

I

IA	*Iranica Antiqua* (Leiden, 1961ff.)
IALR	*International Anthropological and Linguistic Review* (Miami, 1953-1957)
IAQR	*Asiatic Quarterly Review* (London, 1886-1966) [1st Series as: *Asiatic Quarterly Review,* (1886-1890); 2nd Series as: *The Imperial and Asiatic Quarterly and Oriental and Colonial Record,* (1891-1895); 3rd Series, (1896-1912); New Series, Volumes 1 & 2 as: *The Asiatic Quarterly Review* (1913); Volumes 3-48 (1914-1952) as: *Asiatic Review, New Series;* Volumes 49-59 (1953-1964) as: *Asian Review, New Series;* continued as: *Asian Review, Incorporating Art and Letters [and] the Asiatic Review, New Series,* Volumes 1-3 (1964-1966)]
ICHR	*Indian Church History Review* (Serampore, West Bengal, 1967ff.)
ICMM	*The Interpreter. A Church Monthly Magazine* (London, 1905-1924)
IEJ	*Israel Exploration Journal* (Jerusalem, 1950ff.)
IER	*Irish Ecclesiastical Record (A Monthly Journal under Episcopal Sanction)* (Dublin, 1864-1968)
IES	*Indian Ecclesiastical Studies* (Bangalore, India, 1962ff.)
IJA	*International Journal of Apocrypha* (London, 1905-1917) [Issues #1-7 as: *Deutero-Canonica,* pages unnumbered]
IJT	*Indian Journal of Theology* (Serampore, West Bengal, 1952ff.)
ILR	*Israel Law Review* (Jerusalem, 1966ff.)
Inter	*Interchange: Papers on Biblical and Current Questions* (Sydney, 1967ff.)
Interp	*Interpretation; a Journal of Bible and Theology* (Richmond, 1947ff.)
IPQ	*International Philosophical Quarterly* (New York, 1961ff.)
IR	*The Iliff Review* (Denver, 1944ff.)
Iran	*Iran: Journal of the British Institute of Persian Studies* (London, 1963ff.)
Iraq	*Iraq. British School of Archaeology in Iraq* (London, 1934ff.)
IRB	*International Reformed Bulletin* (London, 1958ff.)

IRM	*International Review of Missions* (Edinburgh, London, Geneva, 1912ff.)
Isis	*Isis. An International Review devoted to the History of Science and Civilization* (Brussels; Cambridge, MA; 1913ff.)
ITQ	*Irish Theological Quarterly* (Dublin, Maynooth, 1906ff.)

J

JAAR	*Journal of the American Academy of Religion* (Wolcott, NY; Somerville, NJ; Baltimore; Brattleboro, VT) [Volumes 1-4 as: *Journal of the National Association of Biblical Instructors;* Volumes 5-34 as: *Journal of Bible and Religion*]
JANES	*Journal of the Ancient Near Eastern Society of Columbia University* (New York, 1968ff.)
Janus	*Janus; Archives internationales pour l'Histoire de la Médecine et pour la Géographie Médicale* (Amsterdam; Haarlem; Leiden; 1896ff.)
JAOS	*Journal of the American Oriental Society* (Baltimore, New Haven, 1843ff.)
JAOSS	*Journal of the American Oriental Society, Supplements* (Baltimore, New Haven, 1935-1954)
JARCE	*Journal of the American Research Center in Egypt* (Gluckstadt, Germany; Cambridge, MA; 1962ff.)
JASA	*Journal of the American Scientific Affiliation* (Wheaton, IL, 1949ff.)
JBL	*Journal of Biblical Literature* (Middletown, CT; New Haven; Boston; Philadelphia; Missoula, MT; 1881ff.)
JC&S	*The Journal of Church and State* (Fresno, CA; 1965ff.)
JCE	*Journal of Christian Education* (Sydney, 1958ff.)
JCP	*Christian Philosophy Quarterly* (New York, 1881-1884) [From Volume 2 on as: *The Journal of Christian Philosophy*]
JCS	*Journal of Cuneiform Studies* (New Haven; Cambridge, MA;1947ff.)
JCSP	*Journal of Classical and Sacred Philology* (Cambridge, England, 1854-1857)
JEA	*Journal of Egyptian Archaeology* (London, 1914ff.)
JEBH	*Journal of Economic and Business History* (Cambridge, MA;1928-1932)
JEOL	*Jaarbericht van het Vooraziatisch-Egyptisch Gezelschap Ex Oriente Lux* (Leiden, 1933ff.)
JES	*Journal of Ethiopian Studies* (Addis Ababa, 1963ff.)

Periodical Abbreviations

JESHO   *Journal of the Economic and Social History of the Orient* (Leiden, 1958ff.)

JHI   *Journal of the History of Ideas. A Quarterly Devoted to Intellectual History* (Lancaster, PA; New York;1940ff.

JHS   *The Journal of Hebraic Studies* (New York; 1969ff.)

JIQ   *Jewish Institute Quarterly* (New York, 1924-1930)

JJLP   *Journal of Jewish Lore and Philosophy* (Cincinnati, 1919)

JJP   *Rocznik Papirologii Prawniczej-Journal of Juristic Papyrology* (New York, Warsaw, 1946ff.) [Suspended 1947 & 1959-60]

JJS   *Journal of Jewish Studies* (London, 1948ff.)

JKF   *Jahrbuch für Kleinasiatische Forschungen* (Heidelberg, 1950-1953) [Superseded by *Anadolu Araştirmalari Istanbul Üniversitesi Edebiyat Fakültesi eski Önasya Dilleri ve Kültürleri Kürsüsü Tarafindan Čikarilir*]

JLTQ   *John Lobb's Theological Quarterly* (London, 1884)

JMTSO   *Journal of the Methodist Theological School in Ohio* (Delaware, OH; 1962ff.)

JMUEOS   *Journal of the Manchester Egyptian and Oriental Society* (Manchester, 1911-1953) [Issue #1 as: *Journal of the Manchester Oriental Society*]

JNES   *Journal of Near Eastern Studies* (Chicago, 1942ff.)

JP   *The Journal of Philology* (Cambridge, England; 1868-1920)

JPOS   *Journal of the Palestine Oriental Society* (Jerusalem, 1920-1948) [Volume 20 consists of only one fascicle]

JQR   *Jewish Quarterly Review* (London, 1888-1908; *N.S., Philadelphia*, 1908ff.) [Includes 75th Anniversary Volume as: *JQR, 75th*]

JR   *Journal of Religion* (Chicago, 1921ff.)

JRAI   *Journal of the Royal Anthropological Institute of Great Britain and Ireland* (London, 1872-1965) [Volumes 1-69 as: *Journal of the Anthropological Institute* Continued as: *Man, N.S.*]

JRAS   *Journal of the Royal Asiatic Society of Great Britain and Ireland* (London, 1827ff.) [*Transactions,* 1827-1835 as *TRAS; Journal* from 1834 on: (Shown without volume numbers)]

JRelH   *Journal of Religious History* (Sydney, 1960ff.)

JRH   *Journal of Religion and Health* (Richmond, 1961ff.)

JRT   *Journal of Religious Thought* (Washington, DC; 1943ff.)

JSL   *Journal of Sacred Literature and Biblical Record* (London,1848-1868)

JSOR   *Journal of the Society of Oriental Research* (Chicago, 1917-1932)

JSP   *The Journal of Speculative Philosophy* (St. Louis, 1868-1893)

JSS	*Journal of Semitic Studies* (Manchester, 1956ff.)
JTALC	*Journal of Theology of the American Lutheran Conference* (Minneapolis, 1936-1943) [Volumes 1-5 as: *American Lutheran Conference Journal;* continued from volume 8, #3 as: *Lutheran Outlook* (not included)]
JTC	*Journal for Theology and the Church* (New York, 1965ff.)
JTLC	*Journal of Theology: Church of the Lutheran Confession* (Eau Claire, WI; 1961ff.)
JTS	*Journal of Theological Studies* (Oxford, 1899-1949; *N.S.,* 1950ff.)
JTVI	*Journal of the Transactions of the Victoria Institute, or Philosophical Society of Great Britain* (London, 1866-1957) [Superseded by *Faith & Thought*]
Jud	*Judaism. A Quarterly Journal of Jewish Life and Thought* (New York, 1952ff.)
JWCI	*Journal of the Warburg and Courtauld Institutes* (London,1937ff.)
JWH	*Journal of World History-Cahiers d'Histoire Mondiale -Cuadernos de Historia Mundial* (Paris, 1953ff.)

K

Kêmi	*Kêmi. Revue de philologie et d'archéologie égyptiennes et coptes* (Paris, 1928ff.)
Klio	*Klio. Beiträge zur alten Geschichte* (Leipzig, 1901ff.)
Kobez	*Kobez (Qobeṣ);* קובץ החברה העברית לחקירת ארץ־ישראל ועתיקתיה (Jerusalem, 1921-1945)
KSJA	*Kedem; Studies in Jewish Archaeology* (Jerusalem, 1942, 1945)
Kuml	*Kuml. Årbog for Jysk Arkæologisk Selskab* (Århus, 1951ff.)
Kush	*Kush. Journal of the Sudan Antiquities Service* (Khartoum, Sudan, 1953-1968)
KZ	*Kirchliche Zeitschrift* (St. Louis; Waverly, IA; Chicago; Columbus; 1876-1943)
KZFE	*Kadmos. Zeitschrift für vor-und frühgriechische Epigraphik* (Berlin, 1962ff.)

L

L	*Levant (Journal of the British School of Archaeology in Jerusalem)* (London, 1969ff.)
Lang	*Language. Journal of the Linguistic Society of America* (Baltimore, 1925ff.)
LCQ	*Lutheran Church Quarterly* (Gettysburg, PA; 1928-1949)
LCR	*Lutheran Church Review* (Philadelphia, 1882-1927)
Lĕš	*Lĕšonénu. Quarterly for the Study of the Hebrew Language and Cognate Subjects* לשוננו (Jerusalem, 1925ff.) [English Summaries from Volume 30 onward]
LIST	*Lown Institute. Studies and Texts* (Brandeis University. Lown School of Near Eastern and Judaic Studies. Cambridge, MA; 1963ff.)
Listen	*Listening* (Dubuque, IA; 1965ff.) [Volume numbers start with "zero"]
LofS	*Life of the Spirit* (London, 1946-1964)
LQ	*The Quarterly Review of the Evangelical Lutheran Church* (Gettysburg, PA; 1871-1927; revived in1949ff.) [From 1878 on as: *The Lutheran Quarterly*]
LQHR	*London Quarterly and Holborn Review* (London, 1853-1968)
LS	*Louvain Studies* (Louvain, 1966ff.)
LSQ	*Lutheran Synod Quarterly* (Mankato, MN, 1960ff.) [Formerly *Clergy Bulletin* (Volume 1 of *LSQ* as *Clergy Bulletin,* Volume 20, #1 & #2)]
LTJ	*Lutheran Theological Journal* (North Adelaide, South Australia, 1967ff.)
LTP	*Laval Theologique et Philosophique* (Quebec, 1945ff.)
LTQ	*Lexington Theological Quarterly* (Lexington, KY; 1966ff.)
LTR	*Literary and Theological Review* (New York; Boston, 1834-1839)
LTSB	*Lutheran Theological Seminary Bulletin* (Gettysburg, PA; 1921ff.)
LTSR	*Luther Theological Seminary Review* (St. Paul, MN; 1962ff.)
LWR	*The Lutheran World Review* (Philadelphia, 1948-1950)

M

Man	*Man. A Monthly Record of Anthropological Science* (London,1901-1965; *N. S.,* 1966ff.) [Articles in original series referred to by *article* number not by *page* number - New Series subtitled: *The Journal of the Royal Anthropological Institute*]
ManSL	*Manuscripta* (St. Louis, 1957ff.)
MB	*Medelhavsmuseet Bulletin* (Stockholm, 1961ff.)
MC	*The Modern Churchman* (Ludlow, England; 1911ff.)
McQ	*McCormick Quarterly* (Chicago, 1947ff.) [Volumes 1-13 as: *McCormick Speaking*]
MCS	*Manchester Cuneiform Studies* (Manchester, 1951-1964)
MDIÄA	*Mitteilungen des deutsches Instituts für ägyptische Altertumskunde in Kairo* (Cairo, 1930ff.)
Mesop	*Mesopotamia* (Torino, Italy, 1966ff.)
MH	*The Modern Humanist* (Weston, MA; 1944-1962)
MHSB	*The Mission House Seminary Bulletin* (Plymouth, WI; 1954-1962)
MI	*Monthly Interpreter* (Edinburgh, 1884-1886)
MidS	*Midstream (Council on Christian Unity)* (Indianapolis, 1961ff.)
Min	*Ministry. A Quarterly Theological Review for South Africa* (Morija, Basutolan, 1960ff.)
Minos	*Minos. Investigaciones y Materiales Para el Estudio de los Textos Paleocretenses Publicados Bajo la Dirección de Antonio Tovar y Emilio Peruzzi* (Salamanca, 1951ff.) [From Volume 4 on as: *Minos Revista de Filología Egea*]
MIO	*Mitteilungen des Instituts für Orientforschung [Deutsche Akademie der Wissenschaften zu Berlin Institut für Orientforschung]* (Berlin, 1953ff.)
Miz	*Mizraim. Journal of Papyrology, Egyptology, History of Ancient Laws, and their Relations to the Civilizations of Bible Lands* (New York, 1933-1938)
MJ	*The Museum Journal. Pennsylvania University* (Philadelphia,1910-1935)
MMBR	*The Monthly Magazine and British Register* (London, 1796-1843) [*1st Ser.,* 1796-1826, Volumes 1-60; *N.S.,* 1826-1838, Volumes 1-26; *3rd Ser.,* 1839-1843, Volumes 1-9, however, Volumes 7-9 are marked 95-97*[sic]*]

ModR	*The Modern Review* (London, 1880-1884)
Monist	*The Monist. An International Quarterly Journal of General Philosophical Inquiry* (Chicago; La Salle, IL; 1891ff.)
Mosaic	*Mosaic* (Cambridge, MA; 1960ff.)
MQ	*The Minister's Quarterly* (New York, 1945-1966)
MQR	*Methodist Quarterly Review (South)* (Louisville, Nashville, 1847-1861; 1879-1886; 1886-1930) [*3rd Ser.* as: *Southern Methodist Review;* Volume 52 (1926) misnumbered as 53; Volume 53 (1927) misnumbered as 54; and the volume for 1928 is also marked as 54]
MR	*Methodist Review* (New York, 1818-1931) [Volume 100 not published]
MTSB	*Moravian Theological Seminary Bulletin* (Bethlehem, PA; 1959-1970) [Volume for 1969 apparently not published]
MTSQB	*Meadville Theological School Quarterly Bulletin* (Meadville, PA;1906-1933) [From Volume 25 on as: *Meadville Journal*]
Muséon	*Le Muséon. Revue d'Études Orientales* (Louvain, 1882-1915;1930/32ff.)
MUSJ	*Mélanges de l'Université Saint-Joseph. Faculté orientale* (Beirut, 1906ff.) [Title varies]
Mwa-M	*Milla wa-Milla. The Australian Bulletin of Comparative Religion* (Parkville, Victoria, 1961ff.)

N

NB	*Blackfriars. A Monthly Magazine* (Oxford, 1920ff.) [From Volume 46 on as: *New Blackfriars*]
NBR	*North British Review* (Edinburgh, 1844-1871)
NCB	*New College Bulletin* (Edinburgh, 1964ff.)
NEAJT	*Northeast Asia Journal of Theology* (Kyoto, Japan, 1968ff.)
NEST	*The Near East School of Theology Quarterly* (Beirut, 1952ff.)
Nexus	*Nexus* (Boston, 1957ff.)
NGTT	*Nederduitse gereformeerde teologiese tydskrif* (Kaapstad, N.G., Kerk-Uitgewers, 1959ff.)
NOGG	*Nihon Orient Gakkai geppo* (Tokyo, 1955-1959) [Being the *Bulletin of the Society for Near Eastern Studies in Japan*-Continued as: *Oriento*]
NOP	*New Orient* (Prague, 1960-1968)

Periodical Abbreviations

NPR	*The New Princeton Review* (New York, 1886-1888)
NQR	*Nashotah Quarterly Review* (Nashotah, WI; 1960ff.)
NT	*Novum Testamentum* (Leiden, 1955ff.)
NTS	*New Testament Studies* (Cambridge, England; 1954ff.)
NTT	*Nederlandsch Theologisch Tijdschrift* (Wageningen, 1946ff.)
NTTO	*Norsk Teologisk Tidsskrift* (Oslo, 1900ff.)
Numen	*Numen; International Review for the History of Religions* (Leiden, 1954ff.)
NW	*The New World. A Quarterly Review of Religion, Ethics and Theology* (Boston, 1892-1900)
NYR	*The New York Review. A Journal of The Ancient Faith and Modern Thought (St. John's Seminary)* (New York, 1905-1908)
NZJT	*New Zealand Journal of Theology* (Christchurch, 1931-1935)

O

OA	*Oriens Antiquus* (Rome, 1962ff.)
OBJ	*The Oriental and Biblical Journal* (Chicago, 1880-1881)
OC	*Open Court* (Chicago, 1887-1936)
ONTS	*The Hebrew Student* (Morgan Park, IL; New Haven; Hartford; 1881-1892) [Volumes 3-8 as: *The Old Testament Student;* Volume 9 onwards as: *The Old and New Testament Student*]
OOR	*Oriens: The Oriental Review* (Paris, 1926)
OQR	*The Oberlin Quarterly Review* (Oberlin, OH; 1845-1849)
Or	*Orientalia commentarii de rebus Assyri-Babylonicis, Arabicis, and Aegyptiacis, etc.* (Rome 1920-1930)
Or, N.S.	*Orientalia: commentarii, periodici de rebus orientis antiqui* (Rome, 1932ff.)
Oriens	*Oriens. Journal of the International Society of Oriental Research* (Leiden, 1948ff.)
Orient	*Orient. The Reports of the Society for Near Eastern Studies in Japan* (Tokyo, 1960ff.)
Orita	*Orita. Ibadan Journal of Religious Studies* (Ibadan, Nigeria, 1967ff.)
OrS	*Orientalia Suecana* (Uppsala, 1952ff.)
OSHTP	*Oxford Society of Historical Theology, Abstract of Proceedings* (Oxford, 1891-1968) [Through 1919 as: *Society of Historical Theology, Proceedings*]
Osiris	*Osiris* (Bruges, Belgium; 1936-1968) *[Subtitle varies]*
OTS	*Oudtestamentische Studiën* (Leiden, 1942ff.)

OTW   *Ou-Testamentiese Werkgemeenskap in Suid-Afrika,*
           Proceedings of die (Pretoria, 1958ff.) [Volume 1
           in Volume 14 of: *Hervormde Teologiese Studies*]

P

P	*Preaching: A Journal of Homiletics* (Dubuque, IA; 1965ff.)
P&P	*Past and Present* (London, 1952ff.) *[Subtitle varies]*
PA	*Practical Anthropology* (Wheaton, IL; Eugene, OR; Tarrytown, NY; 1954ff.)
PAAJR	*Proceedings of the American Academy for Jewish Research* (Philadelphia, 1928ff.)
PAOS	*Proceedings of the American Oriental Society* (Baltimore, New Haven; 1842, 1846-50, 1852-1860) [After 1860 all proceedings are bound with *Journal*]
PAPA	*American Philological Association, Proceedings* (Hartford, Boston, 1896ff.) *[Transactions* as: *TAPA. Transactions* and *Proceedings* combine page numbers from volume 77 on]
PAPS	*Proceedings of the American Philosophical Society* (Philadelphia, 1838ff.)
PBA	*Proceedings of the British Academy* (London, 1903ff.)
PEFQS	*Palestine Exploration Fund Quarterly Statement* (London, 1869ff.) [From Volume 69 (1937) on as: *Palestine Exploration Quarterly*]
PEQ	*Palestine Exploration Quarterly* [See: *PEFQS*]
PER	*The Protestant Episcopal Review* (Fairfax, Co., VA; 1886-1900) [Volumes 1-5 as: *The Virginian Seminary Magazine*]
Person	*Personalist. An International Review of Philosophy, Religion and Literature* (Los Angeles, 1920ff.)
PF	*Philosophical Forum* (Boston, 1943-1957; *N.S.,* 1968ff.)
PHDS	*Perspectives. Harvard Divinity School* (Cambridge, MA; 1965-1967)
PIASH	*Proceedings of the Israel Academy of Sciences and Humanities* (Jerusalem, 1967ff.)
PICSS	*Proceedings of the International Conference on Semitic Studies held in Jerusalem, 19-23 July 1965* (Jerusalem, 1969)
PIJSL	*Papers of the Institute of Jewish Studies, London* (Jerusalem,1964)
PJT	*Pacific Journal of Theology* (Western Samoa, 1961ff.)

PJTSA   *Jewish Theological Seminary Association, Proceedings*
              (New York, 1888-1902)
PP   *Perspective* (Pittsburgh, 1960ff.) [Volumes 1-8 as:
              Pittsburgh Perspective]
PQ   *The Presbyterian Quarterly* (New York, 1887-1904)
PQL   *The Preacher's Quarterly* (London, 1954-1969)
PQPR   *The Presbyterian Quarterly and Princeton Review*
              (New York, 1872-1877)
PQR   *Presbyterian Quarterly Review* (Philadelphia,
              1852-1862)
PR   *Presbyterian Review* (New York, 1880-1889)
PRev   *The Biblical Repertory and Princeton Review*
              (Princeton, Philadelphia, New York, 1829-1884)
              [Volume 1 as: *The Biblical Repertory, New
              Series;* Volumes 2-8 as: *The Biblical Repertory
              and Theological Review*]
PRR   *Presbyterian and Reformed Review* (New York,
              Philadelphia, 1890-1902)
PSB   *The Princeton Seminary Bulletin* (Princeton, 1907ff.)
PSTJ   *Perkins School of Theology Journal* (Dallas, 1947ff.)
PTR   *Princeton Theological Review* (Princeton, 1903-1929)
PUNTPS *Proceedings of the University of Newcastle upon Tyne
              Philosophical Society* (Newcastle upon Tyne,
              1964-70)

Q

QCS   *Quarterly Christian Spectator* (New Haven, 1819-1838)
              [1st Series and *New Series* as: *Christian
              Spectator]*
QDAP   *The Quarterly of the Department of Antiquities in
              Palestine* (Jerusalem, 1931-1950)
QRL   *Quarterly Review* (London, 1809-1967)
QTMRP   *The Quarterly Theological Magazine, and Religious
              Repository* (Philadelphia, 1813-1814)

R

R&E   *[Baptist] Review and Expositor* (Louisville, 1904ff.)
R&S   *Religion and Society* (Bangalore, India, 1953ff.)
RAAO   *Revue d'Assyriologie et d'Archéologie Orientale*
              (Paris, 1886ff.)

RChR	The Reformed Church Review (Mercersburg, PA; Chambersburg, PA; Philadelphia; 1849-1926) [Volumes 1-25 as: Mercersburg Review; Volumes 26-40 as: Reformed Quarterly Review; 4th Series on as: Reformed Church Review]
RCM	Reformed Church Magazine (Reading, PA; 1893-1896) [Volume 3 as: Reformed Church Historical Magazine]
RdQ	Revue de Qumran (Paris, 1958ff.)
RDSO	Rivista degli Studi Orientali (Rome, 1907ff.)
RÉ	Revue Égyptologique (Paris, 1880-1896; N.S., 1919-1924)
RefmR	The Reformation Review (Amsterdam, 1953ff.)
RefR	The Reformed Review. A Quarterly Journal of the Seminaries of the Reformed Church in America (Holland, MI; New Brunswick, NJ; 1947ff.) [Volumes 1-9 as: Western Seminary Bulletin]
RÉg	Revue d'Égyptologie (Paris, 1933ff.)
RelM	Religion in the Making (Lakeland, FL; 1940-1943)
Resp	Response—in worship—Music—The arts (St. Paul, 1959ff.)
RestQ	Restoration Quarterly (Austin, TX; Abilene, TX; 1957ff.)
RFEASB	The Hebrew University / Jerusalem: Department of Archaeology. Louis M. Rabinowitz Fund for the Exploration of Ancient Synagogues, Bulletin (Jerusalem, 1949-1960)
RHA	Revue Hittite et Asianique (Paris, 1930ff.)
RIDA	Revue internationale des droits de l'antiquité (Brussels, 1948ff.)
RJ	Res Judicatae. The Journal of the Law Students' Society of Victoria (Melbourne, 1935-1957)
RL	Religion in Life (New York, 1932ff.)
RO	Rocznik Orjentalistyczny. (Wydaje Polskie towarzystwo orjentalisyczne) (Kraków, Warsaw, 1914ff.)
RP	Records of the Past (Washington, DC; 1902-1914)
RR	Review of Religion (New York, 1936-1958)
RS	Religious Studies (London, 1965ff.)
RTP	Review of Theology and Philosophy (Edinburgh, 1905-1915)
RTR	Recueil de travaux relatifs à la philologie et à l'archéologie egyptiennes et assyriennes (Paris, 1870-1923)
RTRM	The Reformed Theological Review (Melbourne, 1941ff.)

S

SAENJ	*Seminar. An Annual Extraordinary Number of the Jurist* (Washington, DC; 1943-1956)
SBAP	*Society of Biblical Archæology, Proceedings* (London, 1878-1918)
SBAT	*Society of Biblical Archæology, Transactions* (London, 1872-1893)
SBE	*Studia Biblica et Ecclesiastica* (Oxford, 1885-1903) [Volume 1 as: *Studia Biblica*]
SBFLA	*Studii (Studium) Biblici Franciscani. Liber Annuus* (Jerusalem, 1950ff.)
SBLP	*Society of Biblical Literature & Exegesis, Proceedings* (Baltimore, 1880)
SBO	*Studia Biblica et Orientalia* (Rome 1959) [Being Volumes 10-12 respectively of *Analecta Biblica. Investigationes Scientificae in Res Biblicas*]
SBSB	*Society for Biblical Studies Bulletin* (Madras, India, 1964ff.)
SCO	*Studi Classici e Orientali* (Pisa, 1951ff.)
Scotist	*The Scotist* (Teutopolis, IL; 1939-1967)
SCR	*Studies in Comparative Religion* (Bedfont, Middlesex, England, 1967ff.)
Scrip	*Scripture. The Quarterly of the Catholic Biblical Association* (London, 1944-1968)
SE	*Study Encounter* (Geneva, 1965ff.)
SEÅ	*Svensk Exegetisk Årsbok* (Uppsala-Lund, 1936ff.)
SEAJT	*South East Journal of Theology* (Singapore, 1959ff.)
Sefunim	*Sefunim (Bulletin)* [היפה] ספונים (Haifa, 1966-1968)
SGEI	*Studies in the Geography of Eretz-Israel* מחקרים בגיאוגרפיה של ארץ־ישראל (Jerusalem, 1959ff.) [English summaries in Volumes 1-3 only; continuing the *Bulletin of the Israel Exploration Society (Yediot)*]
SH	*Scripta Hierosolymitana* (Jerusalem, 1954ff.)
Shekel	*The Shekel* (New York, 1968ff.)
SIR	*Smithsonian Institute Annual Report of the Board of Regents* (Washington, DC; 1846-1964; becomes: *Smithsonian Year* from 1965 on]
SJH	*Seminary Journal* (Hamilton, NY; 1892)
SJT	*Scottish Journal of Theology* (Edinburgh, 1947ff.)
SL	*Studia Liturgica. An International Ecumenical Quarterly for Liturgical Research and Renewal* (Rotterdam, 1962ff.)

SLBR	*Sierra Leone Bulletin of Religion* (Freetown, Sierra Leone; 1959-1966)
SMR	*Studia Montes Regii* (Montreal, 1958-1967)
SMSDR	*Studi e Materiali di Storia Delle Religioni* (Rome, Bologna, 1925ff.
SO	*Studia Orientalia* (Helsinki, 1925ff.)
SOOG	*Studi Orientalistici in Onore di Giorgio Levi Della Vida* (Rome, 1956)
Sophia	*Sophia. A Journal for Discussion in Philosophical Theology* (Parkville, N.S.W., Australia, 1962ff.)
SP	*Spirit of the Pilgrims* (Boston, 1828-1833)
SPR	*Southern Presbyterian Review* (Columbia, SC; 1847-1885)
SQ/E	*The Shane Quarterly* (Indianapolis, 1940ff.) [From Volume 17 on as: *Encounter*]
SR	*The Seminary Review* (Cincinnati, 1954ff.)
SRL	*The Scottish Review* (London, Edinburgh, 1882-1900; 1914-1920)
SS	*Seminary Studies of the Athenaeum of Ohio* (Cincinnati, 1926-1968) [Volumes 1-15 as: *Seminary Studies*]
SSO	*Studia Semitica et Orientalia* (Glasgow, 1920, 1945)
SSR	*Studi Semitici* (Rome, 1958ff.)
ST	*Studia Theologica* (Lund, 1947ff.)
StEv	*Studia Evangelica* (Berlin, 1959ff.) [Being miscellaneous volumes of: *Text und Untersuchungen zur Geschichte der altchristlichen Literatur,* beginning with Volume 73]
StLJ	*The Saint Luke's Journal* (Sewanee, TN; 1957ff.) [Volume 1, #1 as: *St. Luke's Journal of Theology*]
StMR	*St. Marks Review: An Anglican Quarterly* (Canberra, A.C.T., Australia, 1955ff.)
StP	*Studia Patristica* (Berlin, 1957ff.) [Being miscellaneous volumes of: *Text und Untersuchungen zur Geschichte der altchristlichen Literatur,* beginning with Volume 63]
StVTQ	*St. Vladimir's Theological Quarterly* (Crestwood, NY; 1952ff.) [Volumes 1-4 as: *St. Vladimir's Seminary Quarterly*]
Sumer	*Sumer. A Journal of Archaeology in Iraq* (Bagdad, 1945ff.)
SWJT	*Southwestern Journal of Theology* (Fort Worth, 1917-1924; *N.S.,* 1950ff.)
Syria	*Syria, revue d'art oriental et d'archéologie* (Paris, 1920ff.)

T

T&C	*Theology and the Church / SÎN-HÁK kap kàu-Hōe (Tainan Theological College)* (Tainan, Formosa, 1957ff.)
T&L	*Theology and Life* (Lancaster, PA; 1958-1966)
TAD	*Türk tarih, arkeologya ve etnoğrafya dergisi* (Istanbul, 1933-1949; continued as: *Türk arkeoloji Dergisi,* Ankara, 1956ff.)
TAPA	*American Philological Society, Transactions* (See: *PAPA*)
TAPS	*Transactions of the American Philosophical Society* (Philadelphia, 1789-1804; *N.S.,* 1818ff.)
Tarbiẕ	*Tarbiẕ. A quarterly review of the humanities;* תרביץ רבעון למדעי היהדות (Jerusalem, 1929ff.) [English Summaries from Volume 24 on only]
TB	*Tyndale Bulletin* (London, 1956ff.) [Numbers 1-16 as: *Tyndale House Bulletin*]
TBMDC	*Theological Bulletin: McMaster Divinity College* (Hamilton, Ontario, 1967ff.)
TD	*Theology Digest* (St. Mary, KS, 1953ff.)
TE	*Theological Education* (Dayton, 1964ff.)
Tem	*Temenos. Studies in Comparative Religion* (Helsinki, 1965ff.)
TEP	*Theologica Evangelica. Journal of the Faculty of Theology, University of South Africa* (Pretoria, 1968ff.)
Text	*Textus. Annual of the Hebrew University Bible Project* (Jerusalem, 1960ff.)
TF	*Theological Forum* (Minneapolis, 1929-1935)
TFUQ	*Thought. A Quarterly of the Sciences and Letters* (New York, 1926ff.) [From Volume 15 on as: *Thought. Fordham University Quarterly*]
ThE	*Theological Eclectic* (Cincinnati; New York, 1864-1871)
Them	*Themelios, International Fellowship of Evangelical Students* (Fresno, CA; 1962ff.)
Theo	*Theology; A Journal of Historic Christianity* (London, 1920ff.)
ThSt	*Theological Studies* (New York; Woodstock, MD; 1940ff.)
TLJ	*Theological and Literary Journal* (New York, 1848-1861)
TM	*Theological Monthly* (St. Louis, 1921-1929)
TML	*The Theological Monthly* (London, 1889-1891)
TPS	*Transactions of the Philological Society* (London, 1842ff.) [Volumes 1-6 as: *Proceedings*]
TQ	*Theological Quarterly* (St. Louis, 1897-1920)

Tr	*Traditio. Studies in Ancient and Medieval History, Thought and Religion* (New York, 1943ff.)
Trad	*Tradition, A Journal of Orthodox Jewish Thought* (New York, 1958ff.)
TRep	*Theological Repository* (London, 1769-1788)
TRFCCQ	*Theological Review and Free Church College Quarterly* (Edinburgh, 1886-1890)
TRGR	*The Theological Review and General Repository of Religious and Moral Information, Published Quarterly* (Baltimore, 1822)
TRL	*Theological Review: A Quarterly Journal of Religious Thought and Life* (London, 1864-1879)
TT	*Theology Today* (Lansdowne, PA; Princeton, NJ; 1944ff.)
TTCA	*Trinity Theological College Annual* (Singapore, 1964-1969) [Volume 5 apparently never published]
TTD	*Teologisk Tidsskrift* (Decorah, IA; 1899-1907)
TTKB	*Türk Tarih Kurumu Belleten* (Ankara, 1937ff.)
TTKF	*Tidskrift för teologi och kyrkiga frågor (The Augustana Theological Quarterly)* (Rock Island, IL; 1899-1917)
TTL	*Theologisch Tijdschrift* (Leiden, 1867-1919) [English articles from Volume 45 on only]
TTM	*Teologisk Tidsskrift* (Minneapolis, 1917-1928)
TUSR	*Trinity University Studies in Religion* (San Antonio, 1950ff.)
TZ	*Theologische Zeitschrift* (Basel, 1945ff.)
TZDES	*Theologische Zeitschrift (Deutsche Evangelische Synode des Westens, North America)* (St. Louis, 1873-1934) [Continued from Volumes 22 through 26 as: *Magazin für Evangel. Theologie und Kirche;* and from Volume 27 on as: *Theological Magazine*]
TZTM	*Theologische Zeitblätter, Theological Magazine* (Columbus,1911-1919)

U

UC	*The Unitarian Christian* (Boston, 1947ff.) [Volumes 1-4 as: *Our Faith*]
UCPSP	*University of California Publications in Semitic Philology* (Berkeley, 1907ff.)
UF	*Ugarit-Forschungen. Internationales Jahrbuch für die Altertumskunde Syrien-Palästinas* (Neukirchen, West Germany; 1969ff.)
ULBIA	*University of London. Bulletin of the Institute of Archaeology* (London, 1958ff.)

UMB	*The University Museum Bulletin (University of Pennsylvania)* (Philadelphia, 1930-1958)
UMMAAP	*University of Michigan. Museum of Anthropology. Anthropological Papers* (Ann Arbor, 1949ff.)
UnionR	*The Union Review* (New York, 1939-1945)
UPQR	*The United Presbyterian Quarterly Review* (Pittsburgh, 1860-1861)
UQGR	*Universalist Quarterly and General Review* (Boston, 1844-1891)
URRM	*The Unitarian Review and Religious Magazine* (Boston, 1873-1891)
USQR	*Union Seminary Quarterly Review* (New York, 1945ff.)
USR	*Union Seminary Review* (Hampden-Sydney, VA; Richmond; 1890-1946) [Volumes 1-23 as: *Union Seminary Magazine*]
UTSB	*United Theological Seminary Bulletin* (Dayton, 1905ff.) [Including: *The Bulletin of the Evangelical School of Theology; Bulletin of the Union Biblical Seminary,* later, *Bonebrake Theological Bulletin*]
UUÅ	*Uppsala Universitets Årsskrift* (Uppsala, 1861-1960)

V

VC	*Virgiliae Christianae: A Review of Early Christian Life and Language* (Amsterdam, 1947ff.)
VDETF	*Deutsche Vierteljahrsschrift für englisch-theologische Forschung und Kritik / herausgegeben von M. Heidenheim* (Leipzig, Zurich, 1861-1865) [Continued as: *Vierteljahrsschrift für deutsch – englisch- theologische Forschung und Kritik...* 1866-1873]
VDI	*Vestnik Drevnei Istoriĭ. Journal of Ancient History* (Moscow, 1946ff.) [English summaries from 1967 on only]
VDR	*Koinonia* (Nashville, 1957-1968) [Continued as: *Vanderbilt Divinity Review,* 1969-1971]
VE	*Vox Evangelica. Biblical and Historical Essays by the Members of the Faculty of the London Bible College* (London, 1962ff.)
Voice	*The Voice* (St. Paul, 1958-1960) [Subtitle varies]
VR	*Vox Reformata* (Geelong, Victoria, Australia, 1962ff.)
VT	*Vetus Testamentum* (Leiden, 1951ff.)
VTS	*Vetus Testamentum, Supplements* (Leiden, 1953ff.)

xlix

W

Way	*The Way. A Quarterly Review of Christian Spirituality* (London, 1961ff.)
WBHDN	*The Wittenberg Bulletin (Hamma Digest Number)* (Springfield, OH; 1903ff.) [Volumes 40-60 (1943-1963) only contain *Hamma Digest Numbers*]
WesTJ	*Wesleyan Theological Journal. Bulletin of the Wesleyan Theological Society* (Lakeville, IN; 1966ff.)
WLQ	*Wisconsin Lutheran Quarterly* (Wauwatosa, WI; Milwaukee;1904ff.) [Also entitled: *Theologische Quartalschrift*]
WO	*Die Welt des Orients . Wissenschaftliche Beiträge zur Kunde des Morgenlandes* (Göttingen, 1947ff.)
Word	*Word: Journal of the Linguistic Circle of New York* (New York, 1945ff.)
WR	*The Westminster Review* (London, New York, 1824-1914)
WSQ	*Wartburg Seminary Quarterly* (Dubuque, IA; 1937-1960) [Volumes 1-9, #1 as: *Quarterly of the Wartburg Seminary Association*]
WSR	*Wesleyan Studies in Religion* (Buckhannon,WV; 1960-1970) [Volumes 53-62 only*[sic]*]
WTJ	*Westminster Theological Journal* (Philadelphia, 1938ff.)
WW	*Western Watch* (Pittsburgh, 1950-1959) [Superseded by: *Pittsburgh Perspective*]
WZKM	*Wiener Zeitschrift für die Kunde des Morgenlandes* (Vienna, 1886ff.)

Y

YCCAR	*Yearbook of the Central Conference of American Rabbis* (Cincinnati, 1890ff.)
YCS	*Yale Classical Studies* (New Haven, 1928ff.)
YDQ	*Yale Divinity Quarterly* (New Haven, 1904ff.) [Volumes 30-62 as: *Yale Divinity News,* continued as: *Reflections*]
YR	*The Yavneh Review. A Religious Jewish Collegiate Magazine* (New York, 1961ff.) [Volume 2 never published]

Z

Z	*Zygon. Journal of Religion and Science* (Chicago, 1966ff.)
ZA	*Zeitschrift für Assyriologie und verwandte Gebiete* [Volumes 45 on as: *Zeitschrift für Assyriologie und vorderasiatische Archäologie]* (Leipzig, Strassburg, Berlin, 1886ff.)
ZÄS	*Zeitschrift für ägyptische Sprache und Altertumskunde* (Leipzig, Berlin, 1863ff.)
ZAW	*Zeitschrift für die alttestamentliche Wissenschaft* (Giessen, Berlin, 1881ff.)
ZDMG	*Zeitschrift der Deutschen Morgenländischen Gesellschaft* (Leipzig, Wiesbaden, 1847ff.)
ZDPV	*Zeitschrift des Deutschen Palästina-Vereins* (Leipzig, Wiesbaden, 1878ff.) [English articles from Volume 82 on only]
Zion	*Zion. A Quarterly for Research in Jewish History, New Series* ציון, רבעין לחורתולדוה ישראל (Jerusalem, 1935ff.) [English summaries from Volume 3 on only]
ZK	*Zeitschrift für Keilschriftforschung* (Leipzig, 1884-1885)
ZNW	*Zeitschrift für die neutestamentliche Wissenschaft und die Kunde des Urchristentums (...Kunde der älteren Kirche, 1921—)* (Giessen, Berlin, 1900ff.)
ZS	*Zeitschrift für Semitistik und verwandte Gebiete* (Leipzig, 1922-1935)

Sigla[1]

*   Indicates article is additionally listed in other sections of the index.

†   Indicates that title is from the table of contents; from the header; or a composite if title is completely lacking as in early journals.

‡   Indicates a bibliographical article on a specific subject.

---

1.   Complete information may be found in Volume I, page xxiii.

§575 *3.4 Exegetical Studies on the Old Testament - General Studies*

†Anonymous, "Priestley's Notes on the Scriptures," *BCQTR* 30 (1807) 501-510, 610-621. *(Review)* [O.T. Refs. pp. 501-613]

G. R. N[oyes], "Barnes and Bush on the Old Testament," *CE* 38 (1845) 321-347. *(Review)*

*Felix Adler, "On the Exegesis and Criticism of the Old Testament," *JAOS* 10 (1880) lxxxix-xc.

*Philip L. Jones, "The Poetry of the Bible in its Relation to Exegesis," *BQR* 8 (1886) 365-376.

A. R. Fausset, "Exegetical Hints on the Old Testament," *TML* 5 (1891) 26-35; 6 (1891) 145-156. *[Parts I & II]*

A. R. Fausset, "Exegetical Hints on the Old Testament. Part III," *TML* 6 (1891) 396-407.

*Israel Eitan, "The Bearing of Ethiopic on Biblical Exegesis and Lexicography," *JPOS* 3 (1923) 136-143.

*James L. Kelso, "Archaeology's Influence on Old Testament Exegesis," *BS* 94 (1937) 31-36.

*Alexander Sperber, "Biblical Exegesis: Prolegomena to a Commentary and Dictionary to the Bible," *JBL* 64 (1945) 39-140.

*W. H. Morton, "Ras Shamra-Ugarit and Old Testament Exegesis," *R&E* 45 (1948) 63-80.

*James M. Houston, "The Geographical Background in Old Testament Exegesis," *JTVI* 86 (1954) 62-72, 123. (Discussion, pp. 121-122)

*David Weiss, "Halakhic Exegesis," *CJ* 10 (1955-56) #3, 52-58.

*R. Loewe, "The Jewish Midrashim and Patristic Scholastic Exegesis of the Bible," *StP* 1 (1957) 492-514.

D. F. Payne, "Old Testament Exegesis and the Problem of Ambiguity," *ASTI* 5 (1966-67) 48-68.

*Graeme Goldsworthy, "The Old Testament—A Christian Book," *Inter* 2 (1969-70) 24-33. [I. Exegesis; II. Exegesis and miracles; III. Exegesis and ethics; IV. The Authority of the Old Testament; V. Establishing hermeneutics; VI. The application of hermeneutics; Conclusion]

§576 *3.5 Exegetical Studies of Passages in Multiple Books of the Old Testament - General Studies*[1]

Josiah W. Gibbs, "Biblical Criticisms and Remarks: Misapprehensions of the Common English Version of the Bible," *BRCR, N.S.,* 2 (1839) 483-485. [§1. Ex. 32:32; §2. Josh. 24:15; §3. Judg. 9:53; §4. Ps. 1:1; §5. Ps. 17:15; §6. Ps. 84:9; §7. Is. 1:19, 20; §8. Is. 5:18; §9. Dan. 7:9]

Sigma, "Biblical Criticisms and Illustrations," *BRCM* 6 (1849-50) 234-238. [Psa. 9:6; Isa. 38:8; 8:14; 40:6, 7; Psa. 118:22; 121:6]

*H. B. Hackett, "Scripture Facts and Illustrations, Collected During a Journey in Palestine," *CRB* 18 (1853) 405-424, 517-537. [Use of Snow-Water, (Prov. 25:13); Identification of Helbon, (Ezek. 27:18); Salt Deserts, (Jer. 17:6); Turning the Rivers of Water (Prov. 21:1); Dwelling on the House-top (Prov. 21:9); The Tents of Kedar (Psa. 120:5); Grass on the House-tops (Psa. 129:6, 7) & (Isa. 37:27); Pastures in the Desert, (Joel 1:19; 2:22; Psalms 65:12); Use of the word "Brother"; The Ancient Landmark; Skin and Leather Bottles; The Fonts at Tekoa and Jufna; Praying on the House-tops; The Deceitful Brook, (Job 6:15; Jer. 15:18); Valley of Death Shade (Psa. 23:4); Sliding of the Feet (Deut. 22:35; Prov. 3:23; 4:12; Jer. 31:9; 50:32; Psalm 38:17; 66:9); Use of Tents in the East; Thorns; Ancient and Modern Jerusalem; The Smoke of Sodom as Seen from Hebron (Gen. 18:1; 19:28); The Fig-Tree Peeled, (Joel 1:7); Transmission of Scripture Names; Fertility of Palestine]

J. McG., "Bible Difficulties," *JSL, 4th Ser.,* 3 (1863) 172-175. [Psa. 49:3; Job. 32:21; Isa. 21:9; 22:6; 2 Sam. 7:14; Prov. 8:4; Isa. 5:12]

[J.C.(?)], "The Old Testament Text, and its Emendation," *JSL, 4th Ser.,* 4 (1863-64) 328-343. [Gen. 14:15; Nub. 15:1; 2 Kgs. 20:13; Isa. 39:2; Psa. 97:11; 1 Kgs. 1:20; Ezek. 19:10; Gen. 46:28; 1 Kgs. 22:24; Psa. 7:4; Isa. 5:17; Gen. 5:29; Psa. 27:13; Prov. 4:17; Isa. 11:6; 10:25; 41:25; Jer. 9:21; Nah. 2:4; Isa. 5:27; Job 24:3, 4, 9; Psa. 12:6; Prov. 3:14; Psa. 17:3, 4; 38:19; 62:9; 67:9; 25:20; 40:11, 12; Deut. 33:2]

---

1.   This section contains references to more than two books of the Old Testament. Where reference is made to only two books, articles are listed individually *in loc.*

J. C., "The Old Testament Text, and its Emendation," *JSL, 4th Ser.,* 5 (1864) 172-175. [Gen. 14:15; Job. 28:24; Hos. 10:12; Psa. 48:18; 7:4; Gen. 5:29; Psa. 39:5, 6]

Talbot W. Chambers, "Misquoted Scriptures. No. II," *HR* 6 (1881-82) 532-533. [Ex. 11:2; Lev. 16:8; Num. 23:23; Judg. 15:19; Job 11:23]

Talbot W. Chambers, "Misquoted Scriptures. No. III," *HR* 6 (1881-82) 589-590. [Dan. 7:9; Psa. 55:19; II Kgs. 23:6; Psa. 19]

Talbot W. Chambers, "Misquoted Texts. No. IV," *HR* 6 (1881-82) 648-649. [Psa. 110; Isa. 9:5; Hab. 2:4; Hos. 13:9]

Talbot W. Chambers, "Misquoted Scriptures. No. XVI," *HR* 8 (1883-84) 458. [Gen. 49:4; 49:24; Prov. 10:12; 12:15; 10:23]

Talbot W. Chambers, "Misquoted Scriptures," *HR* 9 (1885) 42-43. [Ex. 27:21; 34:33; Hab. 2:15; Heb. 3:4]

Talbot W. Chambers, "Misquoted Scriptures. No. XIX," *HR* 10 (1885) 37-38. [Lev. 1:3; 5:3; 4:12; Prov. 17:27; Prov. 18:1; 18:8]

Talbot W. Chambers, "Misquoted Scriptures. No. XX," *HR* 10 (1885) 220-221. [Lev. 8:33; 2 Chron. 4:3; Lev. 16:31; Prov. 18:24; 37:37; 32:8; 33:10]

M. A. Altschueler, "Some Textual Remarks on the Old Testament," *AJSL* 3 (1886-87) 117-118. [Josh. 10:24; 15:12; 22:7; Judg. 1:14; 7:8; 22:38; 1 Sam. 2:27; 2 Sam. 7:23; 2 Kgs. 11:1; Jer. 31:39; Ezek. 21:31; 46:10, (11); Hab. 1:16, 17; Psa. 69:20; Prov. 30:1; Job. 27:13; 33:24, 25; Dan. 11:4; 1 Chron. 15:16; Neh. 5:2, (3)]

S. R. Driver, "Notes on Difficult Texts," *Exp, 3rd Ser.,* 5 (1887) 55-60, 259-269. [1 Sam. 1:5; 1:20; Josh. 6:18; 19:47; 2 Kgs. 15:10; Hos. 13:9; Mal. 2:7; Mic. 2:12, 13]

*T. K. Cheyne, "The Use of Mythic Phrases by the Old Testament Writers," *Exp, 3rd Ser.,*7 (1888) 20-29. [I. Psa. xxi. 3; II. Isa. xxix. 1, 2; Psa. xlvii. 2; Isa. xxxiii. 7; III. Isa. xiv. 12, 13]

T. K. Abbott, "Critical Notes on Passages in the Hebrew Text of the Old Testament," *Herm* 8 (1891-93) 61-78. [I. Lev. 20:10; II. Ex. 30:6; III. 2 Kgs. 7:13; IV. Job 24:14; V. Ps. 12:6; VI. Ps. 40:8; Ps. 59:10, 11a; Ps. 68:5, 33:34; Ps. 35:14; Ps. 49:8, 9, 10; Ps. 49:15; Ps. 14:5, 6; Ps. 53:5; Ps. 71:20, 21; Ps. 72:20; Ps. 106:48; Isa. 51:6, 7]

John P. Peters, "Notes on Some Difficult Passages in the Old Testament," *JBL* 11 (1892) 38-52. [Ez. 1:1-3, 13, 14; 1:18; 6:14; Jer. 32:11; Isa. 7:14; 8:23; 25:4-5; Psa. 118-27; 68: 12-15; Canticles 2:15]

G. H. Skipwith, "Misplaced Passages in Scripture," *JQR* 5 (1892-93) 347-348; 515-516. [Isa. 35; Jer. 10:1-16; Zech. 12:2; Amos 4:13; 5:8, 9; 9:5, 6; Isa. 11:10; Jer. 11:18-12:6; Job 13:28]

John P. Peters, "Critical Notes," *JBL* 12 (1893) 47-60. [Ez. 42:3; 41:26 & 44:3; 45:12; 45:14; 43:3; II Kgs. 3:27; 2 Sam. 1:21; Psa. 42:7]

T. K. Cheyne, "Note on 'critical notes' of Dr. J. P. Peters," *JBL* 12 (1893) 94-95. [Psa. 44 & 74; 2 Sam. 1:21; 2 Kgs. 3:27; Ez. 42:3 (LXX)]

*Duncan B. Macdonald, "Notes, Critical and Lexicographical," *JBL* 14 (1895) 57-62. [1 Sam. 2:24; 4:15; 1 Kgs. 14:4; Num. 11:4; Prov. 12:3b]

J. A. Dewald, "Exegetical Errors in the Pulpit," *LCR* 15 (1896) 274-279. [Gen. 18:19; 27:39; 44:4; Ex. 11:2; Job. 8:13; 19:25; Psal. 19:3; Prov. 14:9; Isa. 21:11; 26:19; 38:10; 40:2; Dan. 7:9; Hos. 13:9]

Samuel Sharpe, "Miscellanea Theologica. 1. On the Enigmatical Passages in the Bible," *TR* 6 (1896) 238-246. [Ezek. chaps. 34, 36 & 37; Amos 1:5 with 2 Kgs. 16:9; Jer. 25:26; Jer. 25:11-14; Jer. 51:41; Isa. 34:7; Psa. 22:16-20; The Book of Joel with 2 Kgs. chap. 16 and 2 Chron. chap. 28]

T. K. Cheyne, "On 2 Chron. XIV. 9; Job. I. 15; Prov. XXVII. 22," *ET* 8 (1896-97) 431-432.

*T. K. Cheyne, "Gleanings in Biblical Criticism and Geography," *JQR* 10 (1897-98) 565-584. [Lev. 25:34; Judg. 5:21, 22, (Deut. 7:1), (1 Chron. 6:57); Judg. 4:11; 4:2, 13, 16; I Kgs. 10:11; 18:21; 2 Kgs. 17:6, (Zeph. 1:9); 1 Chron. 4:17-19; (Ex. 31:2; Neh. 3:6); Job 38:36, Cant. 2:16, 4:6, 8; 8:14; Isa. 30:4, 5; Jer. 9:1; Hos. 6:5; Amos 3:12; 6:1-5; Mic. 1:7, (Isa. 1:31) Mic. 1:10-12, 13, 14; 5:3-5, (Psa. 55:22), (Job 41:21); Zech 9:1, 13, 15, 16; Mal. 2:11]

T. K. Cheyne, "A Few Old Testament Riddles," *ET* 10 (1898-99) 141-143. [1. Isa. 33:17; Psa. 45:23; 2. Ezek. 8:3,5; 3. Ezek. 38:2, 3; 39:1; 4. 1 Sam. 12:3]

T. K. Cheyne, "Further Contributions to Textual Criticism," *ET* 10 (1898-99) 284-286. [1.) 1 Sam. 1:6; 2.) 2 Sam. 12:26-31; 3.) 2 Kings 23:13; 4.) 2 Chron. 28:15; 5.) Ezek. 9:2; 6.) Ezek. 38:12; Judg. 9:37; 7.) Zech. 11:2 (3); 8.) Hab. 3:4; Psa. 81:8]

T. K. Cheyne, "On Job v. 5 and Other Passages," *ET* 10 (1898-99) 335-336. [Job. 5:5; Psa. 45:11; 81: 4; Amos 8:9]

T. K. Cheyne, "On I Kings x. 25; Job xli. 19; Neh. iii. 19, and Other Passages," *ET* 10 (1898-99) 330-332. [Job 20:24; 39:21; Isa. 22:8; Ezek. 39:9f.; Ps. 140ª; Neh. 3:19; 1 K. 10:25; 2 Chr. 9:24]

T. K. Cheyne, "Gleanings in Biblical Criticism, The Song of the Palanquin, &c.," *JQR* 11 (1898-99) 561-564. [Judges 5:1, 6; Cant. 1:13; 3:6-11; Hos. 3:4; 4:5]

T. K. Cheyne, "Something Better than Husks," *Exp. 5th Ser.,* 10 (1899) 32-35. [2 Kgs. 6:25; 2 Kgs. 18:17 with Isa. 36:12; Isa. 1:19, 20]

*T. K. Cheyne, "Old Testament Notes," *JBL* 18 (1899) 208-211. [3. Some Supposed Archaisms in the Old Testament: (a) 1 Sam. 17:47; (b) Jer. 9:4; (c) Ps. 28:7; (d) Ps. 45:18; (e) Ps. 116:6; (f) Job 13:9; (g) Neh. 11:17; (h) Ezek. 46:22; (i) Psa. 81:6. *pp. 210-211*]

T. K. Cheyne, "Gleanings in Biblical Criticism. (Continued)," *ET* 11 (1899-1900) 47-48. [Gen. 15:2; 35:8, 16, 19; 2 Sam. 8:1; Isa. 1:31]

T. K. Cheyne, "Gleanings in Biblical Criticism. (Continued)," *ET* 11 (1899-1900) 137-139. [1 Sam. 31:3; 2. Sam. 15:12ff.; 23:30 (end); I Kgs. 5:8, Mic. 1:13, Est. 8:10, 14; 1 Kgs. 14:10; 2 Kgs. 10:22; 10:27; 17:24, 18:34, 19:13, Isa. 37:13; 2 Kgs. 14:28; 2 Kgs. 22:14 = 2 Chron. 34:22]

*Julius A. Bewer, "Lexical Notes," *AJSL* 17 (1900-01) 168-170. [שׁמר, Amos 1:11; אתה, Deut. 33:21; אשׁר, Isa. 1:17; זָר, Isa. 1:7 (and often); רִגְמָה, Psa. 68:28; פחח, Isa. 42:22]

*T. K. Cheyne, "Biblical Difficulties," *Exp, 6th Ser.,* 3 (1901) 110-118. [1. Job 13:28; 2. Psalm 109:23; 3. Ecclesiasticus 14:15; Psalm 49:11 (E.V. 10); 4. Ecclesiasticus 43:20]

Frederick Field, "Notes on Select Passages in the Old Testament," *Exp, 6th Ser.,4* (1901) 295-298, 395-400. [Ex. 1:16; 2:3; 9:17; 10:10; 17:16; 35:22; Lev. 2:1; 16:8; 18:18; Deut. 21:14; 28:57; 33:25; Josh. 9:4; 1 Sam. 13:1; 1 Chron. 12:29; 2 Chron. 5:11; 2 Chron. 15:3-6; Neh. 5:2; 7:2; Job 9:35; 38:28; Psa. 30:5; 32:21; 50:18; 51:4; 63:1; 77:10; Prov. 11:25; 17:22; 35:11; Eccl. 2:21; 4:14; 8:11; Cant. 1:7; Isa. 7:11; 8:11; 10:4; 18:2; 26:18; 28:16]

*Julius A. Bewer, "New Lexical and Critical Suggestions," *AJSL* 18 (1901-02) 120-122. [נָבִיא "Prophet"; קוּשׁ, Isa. 29:21; קוּץ, 1 Kings 11:25; Isa 7:6; שָׁא, Psa. 35:17; זְאֵבִי ערב, Zeph. 3:3; Hab. 1:8; מוֹרֶה, Job 36:22]

*Julius A. Bewer, "Text-critical Suggestions on Hosea XII 1, IV 8; Isaiah XIV 12b; Psalm XI 1," *JBL* 21 (1902) 108-114.

T. K. Cheyne, "An Appeal for the Reconsideration of Some Testing Biblical Passages," *AJT* 9 (1905) 323-332. [Ex. 2:3; 2:10; 3:2 (Deut. 33:16); 6:12, 30; 8:5; 10:21; 12:37; 12:40 (Gen. 15:13); 12:42; 14:6f.; 14:29; (13:21 & 3:2) 16:3; 17:15, 16; 19:13; 23:19; 34:26 (Deut. 14:21b); Lev. 22:28; Deut. 22:6, 7; Deut. 16:21; 18:11; 22:9-11; Lev. 19:19; Deut. 22:11; 24:9; 2:19; 5:15; 16:8; 17:7; 25:10]

*Henry Preserved Smith, "Old Testament Notes," *JBL* 24 (1905) 27-30. [I. Nisroch and Nusku; II. Nabi'; III. Naioth; IV. 1 Chronicles 22:2; V. Genesis 35:11; VI. Judges 9:29; VII. The Emphatic ל or לֹא]

*Felix Perles, "The Fourteenth Edition of Gesenius-Bulh's Dictionary," *JQR* 18 (1905-06) 383-390. *(Review)* [II. Text Criticism: Isa. 42:3; Jer. 2:22; 10:4; 23:29; 38:11; 52:3 (= 2 Kgs. 24:20); Ezek. 32:2; Psa. 68:5; 68:19; Prov. 22:20; Job 30:14, pp. 388-390]

[Daniel S. Gregory], "The International Lessons in Their Historical and Literary Setting," *CFL, 3rd Ser.,* 14 (1911-12) 290-314. [Uzziah, King of Judah, Humbled, 2 Chron. 26; Isaiah's Vision and Call to Service, Isa. 6:1-23; Song of the Vineyard, Isa. 5:1-12; Micah's Picture of Universal Peace; Israel's Penitence and Pardon, Hosea 14:1-10; Hezekiah's Great Passover, 2 Chron. 30:1-27; The Downfall of Samaria, 2 Kings 17:1-18; Isaiah's Prophecy Concerning Sennacherib (Isa. 36:14-30; The Suffering Servant of Jehovah Isa. 52:13-53:12; Manasseh's Wickedness and Penitence, 2 Chron. 30:1-20; Josiah's Early Work of Piety in Restoring the True Religion of Israel; Josiah's Restoration of the Chosen People to their National Covenant with Jehovah, and Observance of His Law; Studies on Jeremiah]

*Felix Perles, "A Miscellany of Lexical and Textual Notes on the Bible, Chiefly in connection with the Fifteenth Edition of the Lexicon by Gesenius-Buhl," *JQR, N.S.,* 2 (1911-12) 97-132. [Zech. 6:3; Deut. 15:4-6; Isa. 24:15; Isa. 5:6; Prov. 17:22; Psa. 12:4; 46:3; Jer. 25:25; Psa. 74:6; Jer. 10:2; Prov. 31:3; 31:10; Judg. 6:2 (Job 28:11); Lam. 2; Jer. 47:5; Prov. 27:6; Jer. 10:13 (= 15:16; Psa. 135:7); Num. 21:5; Ezek. 36:3; Gen. 1:26; 22:13; 31:13;46:3; Ex. 5:12; Lev. 14:57; 19:31; Deut. 33:11; 33:16; Josh. 7:5; 17:14; 1 Sam. 1:6; 15:29 23:16; I Kgs. 10:5; 12:10; 15:30 (comp. II Chron. 15:16); Isa. 5:19; 21:2; 31:2; 44:11; 60:4; Jer. 1:15; 16:16; 30:19; 48:10; Ezek. 18:7; 22:3; 23:24; 24:4; 30:4; 37:14; 37:23; 37:26; Mic. 5:13; Zeph. 3:20; Zech. 9:2; 12:8; Ps. 10:17; 20:10; 29:3; 37:22; 45:11; 48:10; 50:19; 51:6; 78:65; 88:17; 119:43; 131:2; 146:6; 147:15; Prov. 1:18; 24:11; 25:1; 31:11; Job 21:9; 31:33; Cant. 3:6; Lam. 1:14; 1:20; 2:2; 2:4; 2:16; 2:22; 3:1; 3:49; Eccl. 1:8; 5:2; 5:5; 7:16; 7:26; Esther 1:14; Neh. 5:11 1 Chron. 29:22]

*James A. Montgomery, "Notes on the Old Testament," *JBL* 31 (1912) 140-146. [1. יגר, Gen. 31:47; 2. של שים, 1 Kgs. 20:12; 3. Sukkoth-Benoth, 2 Kgs. 17:30; 4. The barbarous Syllables in Isa. 28:10; 5. חזה, Isa. 28:15; 6. מבליג, Am. 5:9; 7. הכל, Eccles. 11:5, etc.; 8. The Interrogative particle מי or מה; 9. The Correlative use of כי and אכן]

*N. Herz, "The Exaggeration of Errors in the Massoretic," *JTS* 15 (1913-14) 258-264. [Isa. 41:21; 49:24; Hos. 7:6; Amos 4:13; Psa. 12:7; 19:5; 39:18; 1 Sam. 1:18; 1 Kgs. 6:11; II Kgs. 6:11; Isa. 2:16; 3:6; 57:9; Hos. 8:6; 11:4; 13:2; Amos. 3:12; Psa. 9:7, 8; 139:11; Job 13:14; 15:11; 21:6; Dan. 4:5; (Ecclus. 50:18)]

T. H. Weir, "Some Fresh Notes on the Text of the Old Testament," *Exp, 8th Ser.,* 7 (1914) 472-480. [1. Sam. 10:2; 11:7; 2 Sam . 1:21; 3:12; 16:5; Isa. 21:16; 28:16; 28:20; 30:17; 34:8; Jer. 46:9; Amos 4:3; Zech. 1:21; 11:3; 13:6; (Hos. 2:7); Zech. 14:3; 14:9; Mal 2:16; Psa. 6:2; 9:12; 9:20: 23:5; 49:5; 51:2; 54:1; 66:7; 78;9; 105:24; 110:4; Prov. 30:31; Psa. 76:10; 94:10, 11; Ezek. 7:14; Psa. 18:3; 21:1; 22:9]

*H. Geers, "Hebrew Textual Notes," *AJSL* 34 (1917-18) 129-134. [Neh. 12:8; Ezek. 30:9; 2 Sam. 20:14; Psa. 5:1; Job 12:21; Isa. 11:5; Ezek. 7:7; Isa. 31:8b-9a]

*E. Ben Yehuda, "Three Notes in Hebrew Lexicography," *JAOS* 37 (1917) 324-327. [1. Psalms 75:9; 2. Song of Songs 7:6; 3. Nahum 2:14]

C. F. Burney, "Notes on Some Hebrew Passages," *JTS* 21 (1919-20) 239-243. [1 Kgs. 28:21; Psa. 32:9; 45:7a; 58:9a; Job 38:14; Eccl. 4:26b; 5:10]

John Henry Burn, "Dr. Field's Old Testament Revision Notes. Transcribed from the Author's MS. by the Rev. John Henry Burn, B.D., VI.," *ET* 32 (1920-21) 139-140. [Num. 30:6-8; 35:17; 35:20; 36:3; Deut. 4:12; 4:19; 21:14; 28:57; 29:19; 33:5; Josh. 6:26; 9:4; 11:5]

E. E. Kellett, "Some Old Testament Notes and Queries," *ET* 33 (1921-22) 426. [Gen. 6:16; 49:24; 49:4, 18; Job 28; Psa. 22:3; Num. 22:5]

*G. R. Driver, "Some Hebrew Roots and Their Meanings," *JTS* 23 (1921-22) 69-73. [Postscript by C. F. Burney]

*Israel Efros, "Glosses on the Hebrew Bible," *JAOS* 42 (1922) 390. [Ex. 32:2; Deut. 32:35; Isa. 1:18 (cf. 57:2, Amos 3:10); Isa. 2:12 (cf. Hab. 2:4); Isa. 5:7; 10:13 (cf. 2 Kings 17:6; 18:11 & Ezek. 1:3); Hos. 11:4; Eccl. 1:5; 1:8; 2:1; 5:5; 9:12; 12:5]

J[ohn] H[enry] Burn, "Dr. Field's Old Testament Revision Notes," *ET* 35 (1923-24) 332-333. [1. Kgs. 4:19; 5:17; 8:50; 11:15; 17:9; 2 Kgs. 9:31; 1 Chron. 6:10; 12:29; 2 Chron. 2:10; 2:14; 2:18; 5:11; 11:23; Ezra 4:7; 10:3; 10:6; Neh. 5:2; 7:2]

*James Edward Hogg, "Exegetical Notes," *AJSL* 41 (1924-25) 267-274. [I. Exod. 1:21: "He made them houses"; II. The Tenses in Gen. 17:20; III. Gen. 16:2; IV. The Translation of יהוה]

Joseph Reider, "Some Notes to the Text of the Scriptures," *HUCA* 3 (1926) 109-116. [Isa. 44:8; Isa. 45:2; Zech. 6:6; Psa. 8:2; Psa. 68:28; Prov. 12:6; Job. 5:5; Job 5:15; Job 6:7; Job 10:8; Job 18:3; Job 20:18; Job 23:6; Job 23:10; Lam. 1:13; Eccl. 2:3; Dan. 12:7]

*H. Highfield, "Gleanings from the Septuagint," *ET* 38 (1926-27) 44-45. [1.) Gen. 37:3, 4; 2.) μεταμέλεσθαι and μετανοεῖν; 3.) Amos 6:1; 4.) Gen. chap. 5 - Ages of the Patriarchs]

*E. Power, "The shepherd's two rods in modern Palestine and in some passages of the Old Testament *(Ps. 23, 4; Zach. 11, 7 ss.; 1 Sam. 17, 43),*" *B* 9 (1928) 434-442.

Th. J. Meek, "Some Emendations in the Old Testament," *JBL* 48 (1929) 162-168. [Mic. 4:1 = Isa. 2:2; Judges 3:22; Deut. 11:2; Deut. 11:30; Num. 16:1]

*Leo Jung, "Mis-Translations a Source in Jewish and Christian Lore," *PAAJR* 5 (1933-34) 55-67. [I. Habakkuk III 2; II. The "Watchers" of Enoch; IV. Jephthah (Judges 12:7); V. Leviathan (Ps. 104:25-26); VI. Some Cases of Mis-reading as Sources of Lore; VII. Some Cases of Theological Bias. (Zech. 9:9 as quoted in Matt. 21:2-7).]

G. R. Driver, "Hebrew Notes," *ZAW* 52 (1934) 51-56. [1. Kgs. 1:9; Isa. 28:7; 30:22; 58:10; Psa. 118:10, 12; Hab. 1:8; 3:6; Psa. 39:7; 75:6]

*J. Reider, "Contributions to the Hebrew Lexicon," *ZAW* 53 (1935) 270-277. [Isa. 51:6; Psa. 74:19; Job. 24:24; 33:27; Cant. 7:6; Isa. 57:9]

*C. L. E. Hoopmann, "The Meaning of the Term, 'The Last Times'," *AusTR* 7 (1936) 7-12. [O.T. Refs. Deut. 4:30; Isa. 2:2; Micah 4:1; Joel 2:28-32]

Frank Zimmermann, "Notes on Some Difficult Old Testament Passages," *JBL* 55 (1936) 303-308. [Eccl. 3:18; Prov. 25:15; Job 34:25a; Isa. 3:9]

*E. Robertson, "The Apple of the Eye in the Masoretic Text," *JTS* 38 (1937) 56-59. [Deut. 32:10; Prov. 7:2; Psa. 27:8; Zech 2:12 (2:8 in E.V.); Lam. 2:18]

G. R. Driver, "Suggestions and Objections," *ZAW* 55 (1937) 68-72. [Isa. 58:10; Prov. 27:9; Isa. 3:20; Psa. 16:2-3]

Ioseph*[sic]* Reider, "Contributions to the Hebrew Lexicon," *RDSO* 17 (1937-38) 103-110. [Isa. 51:6; Psa. 74:19; Job 24:24; Job 33:27; Cant. 7:6]

Israel Eitan, "Biblical Studies," *HUCA* 14 (1939) 1-22. [I. Philological Studies in Hosea; Hos. 2:17; 5:7; 5:13; 9:1; 10:1; 10:5; 13:2; 13:7; II. Stray Notes to Minor Prophets; Joel 4:7; Amos 1:5, 8; Amos 5:8; III. An Unknown Element in Prov. 27:19; IV. Notes on Job—Job 2:10; 3:22; 4:10; 5:3; V. Some Philological Observations in Daniel—Daniel 2:6; 3:25; 4:33; 8:5; 8:5b; 8:22]

*Steven T. Byington, "Hebrew Marginalia I," *JBL* 60 (1941) 279-288. [Terms of Hebrew Daily Life Surviving only in Metaphor and Simile; Constructions with אל; חסד and Hushai; Two Species of Hawk; Sundry Readings in Psalms, Proverbs and Job]

*J. W. Jack, "Recent Biblical Archaeology and Biblical Text," *ET* 53 (1941-42) 368-370. [Lev. 26:30; Gen. 1:2; 2 Sam. 7:21; 1 Kgs. 10:28; 2 Kgs. 15:5; 2 Chron. 6:13; Job 28:11; Psa. 68:4; Psa. 88:4; Hos. 5:13; 10:6; Amos 1:1]

*Julius A. Bewer, "Notes on 1 Sam. 13:21; 2 Sam. 23:1; Psalm 48:8; *JBL* 61 (1942) 45-49.

Henry Englander, "A Commentary on Rashi's Grammatical Comments," *HUCA* 17 (1942-43) 427-498.

*H. L. Ginsberg, "The Ugaritic Texts and Textual Criticism," *JBL* 62 (1943) 109-115. [Isa. 51:17b, 22b; Job 28:11; 2 Sam. 1:21; Psa. 68:5; Jer. 9:20; Job 36:27-37:6]

*L. J. Liebreich, "Notes on the Greek Version of Symmachus," *JBL* 63 (1944) 397-403. [Isa. 51:23; Ez. 31:12; Job. 24:17; 29:25; 39:4]

*Steven T. Byington, "Hebrew Marginalia III," *JBL* 64 (1945) 339-355. [1.) The Sense of Certain Words; 2.) Before Noun or Pronoun; 3.) Some Hebrew Zoology: Psa. 58:5; Jer. 8:17; Isa. 59:5; Ezek. 28:12ff.; Job 39:20; 4.) Some Textual Readings (Psa. 90:5; Psa. 118:12; Psa. 139:16; Psa. 141:5; Prov. 25:27; Prov. 26:8; Prov. 26:10; Job. 34:13; Job 34:29; Job 36:17; Job 36:32; 2 Chron. 32:31; 1 Sam. 15:12); 5.) Some Interpretations (Psa. 85:9; Psa. 90: 5-6, 10, 16; Prov. 23:29, 32; Job 40:19; Cant. 4:3; 8:1; Dan. 3:16; Ezra 8:3; 10:44; Neh. 3:1; 5:15, 17]

*G. R. Driver, "Mistranslations," *PEQ* 79 (1947) 123-126. [Judg. 1:9; Isa. 15:3, (1 Sam. 9:27; Ruth 3:3, 6); Judg. 9:37, (2 Kgs. 2:2), (Judg. 19:11)]

G. R. Driver, "Hebrew Notes," *VT* 1 (1951) 241-250. [Isa. 3:16-17; 11:11; 40:3; 45:8; 46:17; Jer. 21:12; 26:6; 40:3; Hos. 6:5; Hab. 2:15; Psa. 4:7; 18:35; 41:9; 69:5; 71:16; 72:16; 75:9; Prov. 4:11; 7:10]

*Joseph Reider, "Miscellanea Hebraica," *JJS* 3 (1952) 78-86. [7. Gen. 4:7; 8. Gen. 21:16; 9. Gen. 26:14; 10. Gen. 26:14; Job 1:3; 10*[sic]*. Gen. 41:56; 11. Num. 21:17; 12. Num. 23; 13. Num. 24:3, 15; 14. Job 2:6; Nah. 2:11; 15. Jer. 20:14ff.; Job 3:3ff.; 16: Hos. 13:14b//1 Cor. 15:15]

*Joseph Reider, "Etymological Studies in Biblical Hebrew," *VT* 2 (1952) 113-130. [1. Lev. 19:28; 2. Num. 34:7f.; 3. Num. 34:8; 4. 2 Sam. 22:35; 5. Isa. 11:8; 6. Isa. 19:7; 7. Isa. 21:5; 8. Isa. 28:27, 41:15, Amos 1:3; 9. Isa. 40:20; 10. Isa. 53:9; 11. Jer. 11:15; 12. Ezek. 7:16; 13. Ezek. 21:2; 14. Ezek. 27:35; 15. Hos. 11:4; 16. Amos 6:3; 17. Ps. 17:4; 18. Isa. 58:2; 19. Psa. 90:10; 20. Prov. 3:35; 21. Prov. 11:7; 22. Prov. 14:24; 23. Job 7:15; 24. Job 8:6; 25. Job 12:6; 26. Job 15:24; 27. Job 28:27; 28. Job 30:24; 29. Job. 39:21; 30. Eccl. 2:25]

Joseph Reider, "Contributions to the Scriptural Text," *HUCA* 24 (1952-53) 85-106. [1 Sam. 14:32; 1 Kgs. 1:9; Isa. 8:22; Isa. 11:15; Isa. chap. 15; Isa. 32:19; Jer. 6:3; Jer. 48:15; Ezek. 17:21; Ezek. 21:20; 21:26; 23:24; 25:10; 27:32; Hos. 4:4; 7:9; 12:12; Amos 2:7; 5:6; 6:10; 9:9; Hab. 1:3; 3:9; Zech. 3:9; Psa. 2:11; Psa. 12:7; Psa. 17:13; Psa. 22:15; Psa. 39:6; Psa. 68:14; Psa. 68:24; Psa. 110:6; Job; 5:23; Job. 17:13 and 30:23; Job 20:19; 20:29; 23:6; 25:5; 28:4; 34:37]

Matitiahu Tsevat, "Some Biblical Notes," *HUCA* 24 (1952-53) 107-114. [Judg. 5:14; 1 Kgs. 20:5; 2 Kgs. 19:24; Isa. 65:3; Hos. 8:7b; Hos. 10:5b; Zeph. 3:17; Hag. 1:4; Psa. 2:7; Psa. 31:21; Psa. 37:35; Psa. 60:6; Prov. 10:28; Job. 28:4]

Y. Y. Rabinovitz, "On Some Biblical Passages," *EI* 3 (1954) VII. [Gen. 15:3; 31:39; 42:37; 43:9; Ex. 10:24; 1 Sam. 2:31-33; Isa. 41:8-9; 42:6; 44:2; 44:21; 44:24; Jer. 31:30-31; 32:11; Ezek. 18:7; Mal. 3:6]

Theodor H. Gaster, "Short Notes," *VT* 4 (1954) 73-79. [Gen. 49:10; 49:26; Psa. 24:6; 35:11; 41:9 48:12, 15-17; 76:11; 85:14; Prov. 8:30; Job 19:26; Hos. 7:3-6, 8, 9]

*G. R. Driver, "Problems and Solutions," *VT* 4 (1954) 223-245. ["Abbv.": Esth. 6:1; "Lost Hebrew Words" (in Eccl.) 12:9; 12:6; 1:18; 2:23; 2:2; 2:1; 8:10; 7:6; 10:9; 12:5; 2:8; Ezek. 1:24]

J[oseph] Reider, "Etymological Studies in Biblical Hebrew," *VT* 4 (1954) 276-295. [(1) Gen. 49:4; (2) Jer. 17:4; Psa. 55:23; Hos. 8:13; (3) Jer. 31:2; (4) Ez. 7:7, 10; Isa. 28:5; Judg. 7:3; (5) Ez. 28:32; (6) Am. 1:13; (7) Mic. 2:6; (8) Hab. 1:11; (9) Hab. 2:5; (10) Hab. 2:15; Job 14:19; Isa. 5:7; (11) Hab. chap. 3; (12) Psa. 104:13; (13) Prov. 26:6; (14) Prov. 29:21; (15) Prov. 31:3; Ez. 26:9; Dan. 6:19; (16) Job 6:21; (17) Job 8:14; Isa. 49:5; (18) Job 12:2; (19) Job 12:23; (20) Job 21:4; Gen. 24:27; Isa. 45:12; 49:21; (21) Job 33:17; 22:29; Ob. 6; (22) Job 37:16; (23) Job 39:27; (24) Lam. 1:12; Job 3:8]

*G. R. Driver, "Geographical Problems," *EI* 5 (1958) 16*-20*. [Num. 21:14-15; 21:17-18; 2 Sam. 2:24; 2 Sam. 8:1; 2 Kgs. 17:24]

*N. H. Tur-Sinai, "On Some Historical References in the Bible," *EI* 5 (1958) 87*-88*. [Isa. 7:8-9; Hos. 4:47; 5:1-4; 5:13 & 10:6; 10:10-14; Hos. 12:5b-9; 1 Chron. 4:22-23]

*Raphael Weiss, "Textual Notes," *Text* 6 (1958) 127-131. [I. Isa. 38:12: ספרתי for קְפַדְתִּ in 1QIs^a; II. פקד־ספר; מסעד hap. leg. 1 Kgs. 10:12; III. Psa. 14 & 53]

P. Wernberg-Møller, "Two Notes," *VT* 8 (1958) 305-308. [I. Ex. 21:35; Deut. 2:6; II. Isa. 57:9]

*Chaim Rabin, "Etymological Miscellanea," *SH* 8 (1961) 384-400. [1. אהל Qal; 2. בֶּן־אוֹנִי Gen. xxxv, 18; 3. אֹזֶן(י) Dt. xxiii.14 ≠ Aram. *zēnā;* 4. אֹחֵר(י) Gen. xxii, 13; 5. בוּך Niph. Ex. xiv, 3; 6. דִּין; 7. אֵהבוּ הֵבוּ Hos. iv. 18; 8. הָרֹן Gen. iii. 16; 9. אַפּוֹ חרה; 10. מלתחה, 2 Kings. x, 22; 11. - *ām* of *kinnām* = "lice"; 12. לחם; 13. מִין Gen. i, 21; 14. מסדרון Jud. iii, 23; 15. מהים)מֹשֶׁה (ואם ימעט הבית מהים) Ex. xii, 4; 16. "hollow measure"; 17. סֹכֵן; 18. עלוה Hos. x, 9; 19. עלז; 20. התפאר Ex. viii, 5; 21. פחז; 22. צר כחכה Pr. xxiv, 10; 23. Egyptian *q'bt* "nipple" = (?) Hebrew *qēbhāh* "Fourth stomach of a ruminant"; 23.*[sic]* קריא, קרוא "invited to a meal, etc."; 24. שֵׁאת Gen. iv, 7; 25. √שׂכח; Additional notes]

B. F. Price, "Questions and Answers," *BTr* 16 (1965) 123-127. [2. Kgs. 6:33; Job 18:20; Job 24:20; Psa. 110:3; Isa. 63:8f.; Jer. 8:20; Lam. 3:13; Ezek. 31:14-18; Dan. 5:25, 28; Hos. 4:31f.]

*Baruch A. Levine, "The Descriptive Tabernacle Texts of the Pentateuch," *JAOS* 85 (1965) 307-318. [Exodus 35-39; Leviticus 8-9 & Numbers 7]

*G. R. Driver, "Forgotten Hebrew Idioms," *ZAW* 78 (1966) 1-7. [I. 1. Ex. 10:11; 2. 1 Kgs. 20:34; II. 1. Neh. 7:3; 2. 9:5]

Daniel Sperber, "Some Tannaitic Biblical Variants," *ZAW* 79 (1967) 79-80. [Ex. 25:39; 1 Sam. 4:4; 1 Kgs. 8:7; Ex. 37:2; 1 Sam. 6:8; 1 Kgs. 8:6; 2 Chron. 35:3]

*Paul D. Hanson, "Song of Heshbon and David's *Nîr*," *HTR* 61 (1968) 297-341. [1 Kgs. 11:36, 15:4; 2 Kgs. 8:19; and 2 Chron. 21:7]

G. R. Driver, "Old Problems Re-examined," *ZAW* 80 (1968) 174-183. [1 Sam. 14:14; 20:18-20, 27; Psa. 90:4-6; Zech. 12:2-3; 14:13-14]

§577 *3.5.1 Exegetical Studies on Passages in Multiple Books of the Pentateuch - General Studies*

*Anonymous, "Sesostris, the Hornet of Exod. 23:28, Deut. 7:20, Josh. 24:12," *QCS, 3rd Ser.,* 10 (1838) 281-285.

C. Taylor, "On some passages of the Pentateuch, Judges, and 2nd Kings," *JP* 5 (1873) 54-65. [Gen. 35:18; Ex. 20:4, 5; Numb. 20:7-13]

Kemper Fullerton, "Expository Studies in the Old Testament: VII. Israel in the Wilderness," *BW* 30 (1907) 60-72. [Ex. 40:1-13, 34-38; Lev. 10:1-11; 16:5-22; Num 10:11-13, 29-36]

Frank Zimmerman*[sic]*, "An Examination of some Biblical Passages," *JBL* 65 (1946) x. [1) Ex. 2:6; 2) Lev. 19:35; 3) Num 10:31; 4) Gen. 1:1]

Frank Zimmermann, "An Examination of some Biblical Passages," *JBL* 65 (1946) 311-314. [Ex. 2:6; Lev. 19:35; Num 10:31; Gen. 1:1]

*A. Levene, "Pentateuchal Exegesis in Early Syriac and Rabbinic Sources," *StP* 1 (1957) 484-491.

Solomon Zeitlin, "Some Reflections on the Text of the Pentateuch," *JQR, N.S.,* 51 (1960-61) 321-331. [Gen. 16:5; 18:9; 19:33; 33:4; 37:(12); Num. 3:39; 9:10; 21:30; 29:15; Deut. 29:28; 28:66; Ex. 34:25; 28:40; Gen. 13:16; 26:32; 4:8; Num. 10:35-36; Lev. 27:2-3; Deut. 33:8-9; Gen. 4:1; 14:3; 49:10]

A. Ben-Shemesh, "In Arabia They Call...," *ABR* 10 (1962) 10-14. [1. Gen. 40:22; 2. Ex. 14:22, 29; 3. Exod. 15:8; 4. Gen. 49:5]

Henry R. Moeller, "Four Old Testament Problem Terms," *BTr* 13 (1962) 219-222. [1. Habitations, swords, or...? (Gen. 49:5); 2. Were beaten (Ex. 5:14); 3. To prove (Ex. 20:20); 4. The meaning of shaddai (Gen. 17:1 et passim)]

§578 *3.5.2 Studies of Manuscripts on the Pentateuch*
      [See also §236ff ← Manuscripts,
      Scrolls and Codices in General]

*John W. Barrow, "On a Hebrew MS. of the Pentateuch, from the Jewish Congregation at Kai-fung-fu in China," *JAOS* 9 (1869-71) liii.

*Schiller Szinessy, "The Prideaux Pentateuch," *SBAT* 1 (1872) 263-270.

*A. Diez Macho, "'Onqelos Manuscript with Babylonian Transliterated Vocalization in the Vatican Library (MS. Eb. 448)," *VT* 8 (1958) 113-133.

§579 *3.5.2.1 Exegetical Studies on the Book of Genesis*
      - Multiple Passages

Biblicus, "An Illustration of the Promise made to Abraham," *TRep* 4 (1784) 361-363. [12:1ff.; 17:4; 22:16ff.]

*C. Taylor, "Notes on the translation of Genesis," *JP* 3 (1871) 291-327. [4:6, 7; 6:1-4; 6:16; 9:25-27; 16:13, 14; 20:16; 27:39, 40; chap. 49]

Anonymous, "Explanation of Difficult Texts," *BS* 7 (1850) 163-172. *(by an Association of Gentlemen)* [4:7; 4:23, 24; 6:3; 9:4-6; 49:10]

Anonymous, "Exegesis of the Old Testament.—Genesis," *JSL, 3rd Ser.,* 7 (1858) 253-276.

D. E., "Emendations in the Authorized Version of the Scripture," *JSL, 3rd Ser.,* 12 (1860-61) 171-172. [1:2, 7, 16, 20, 21; 2:2, 18, 20, 23; 3:24; 4:1, 7; 6:17; 9:23, 26, 27; chap. 11; 12:6; 13:18; 14:15; 15:11, 17; 18:1, 8; 19:19; 22:14, 18; 24:53, 65; 27:3; 29:2, 17; 37:3; 39:6; 44:5, 15; 47:2, 6, 31; 49:4, 10]

Talbot W. Chambers, "Misquoted Scriptures. No. XII," *HR* 7 (1882-83) 592-593. [15:15; 24:2, 22, 30, 47; 25:30; 27:39]

Talbot W. Chambers, "Misquoted Scriptures. No. XIII," *HR* 7 (1882-83) 711-712. [12:9; 28:21; 31:19; 23:18; 37:1]

Talbot W. Chambers, "Misquoted Scriptures. No. XIV," *HR* 8 (1883-84) 105-106. [4:23; 13:18; 14:18; 15:17; 18:19]

Talbot W. Chambers, "Misquoted Scriptures. No. XV," *HR* 8 (1883-84) 279-280. [37:35; 38:14, 21, 22; 39:6; 40:16, 17; 47:15]

S. R. Driver, "The Revised Version of the Old Testament. I. The Book of Genesis," *Exp, 3rd Ser.,* 2 (1885) 1-16. [1:2, 5, 12, 21, 30, 31; 2:1, 4, 5, 14; 4:1, 7, 8, 23, 25; 6:4; 9:5, 27: 10:11; 12:6, 9; 13:10; 15:2; 16:13; 17:5; 17:16; 18:19; 22:14; 25:31; 27:39, 40; 29:32, 33, etc.; 30:11; 31:19, 21, 42, 53; 36:15; 37:35; 49:4, 5, 10, 14, 15, 19, 20, 24, 26; 50:11]

A. H. Sayce, "The Old Testament in the Light of Recent Discoveries. I," *MI* 2 (1885) 155-160. [Gen. 1; 2:2, 3; 2:8; 2:9; 2:11]

A. H. Sayce, "The Old Testament in the Light of Recent Discoveries. II," *MI* 2 (1885) 175-188. [2:14; 2:17; 2:19; 3:14; 4:1; 4:16; 4:17; 4:18; 4:26; 5:24; 6:2; 6:3; 6:4; 6:9; 6:13; 6:14; 6:15; 7:1; 7:2; 7:11; 8:4, 5; 8:7-12; 8:13; 8:21; 9:1; 9:20]

A. H. Sayce, "The Old Testament in the Light of Recent Discoveries," *MI* 3 (1885-86) 129-141. [(Part III) 10:1; 10:2; 10:3; 10:4; 10: 6; 10:7; 10:8 10:10; 10:11; 10:13; 10:14; 10:15; 10:16; 10:17; 10:22; 10:23; 10:25; 10:28; 10:30; 11:2; 11:3; 11:4]

A. H. Sayce, "The Old Testament in the Light of Recent Discoveries, No. IV," *MI* 3 (1885-86) 462-469.[11:28-31; 12:15; 14:1; 16:7; 17:5, 15; 17:23; 19:24; 19:38; 22:14; 24:29; 25:1-4; 25:13; 25:20]

Charles R. Brown, "The Revision of Genesis," *BS* 43 (1886) 507-527, 662-690. *[Text comparisons between AV and RV of 1881]*

*A. H. Sayce, "The Old Testament in the Light of Recent Discoveries. No. V.," *MI* 4 (1886) 17-23. [28:18; 31:47; 36:20; 36:32; 36:35; 36:37 37:36; chap. 39; 39:20; 40:5; 40:9-11; 40:20; 41:1; 41:8 41:16; 41:43; 41:45; 41:54: 43:32; 45:10; 46:34; 47:11]

John Fanshawe, "Jacob's Sons," *EN* 2 (1890) 180-182, 233-235, 278-279, 319-320, 378-379. [39:32, 33, 34, 35; 30:4-6; 30:7-8; 30:9-11; 30:12, 13; 30:16-18]

E[duard] König, "Notes on the Book of Genesis in Hebrew," *Exp, 5th Ser.,*7 (1898) 201-210. [1:1, 11, 21b; 4:1b; 49:25b]

*B. Jacob, "A Study in Biblical Exegesis. אֲשֶׁר־חַי," *JQR* 12 (1899-1900) 434-451

F[rederick] Field, "Notes on Select Passages in the Old Testament," *Exp, 6th Ser.,* 3 (1901) 397-400. [2:23; 4:7; 8:4(A.V.); 40:13; 40:16]

Herbert L. Willett, "Expository Studies in the Old Testament: I. The Stories of Origins," *BW* 29 (1907) 45-56. [1:1-25; 1:26-2:3; 3:1-6, 14, 15; 4:3-15; 8:1-16]

John E. McFadyen, "Expository Studies in the Old Testament: II. Abram," *BW* 29 (1907) 138-149. [12:1-8; 13:1-13; 15:1, 5-16; 18:16-33]

John E. McFadyen, "Expository Studies in the Old Testament: III: Isaac and Jacob," *BW* 29 (1907) 219-230. [26:12-25; 27:15-23, 41-45; 28:1-5, 10-24; 32:9-12, 22-30]

John E. McFadyen, "Expository Studies in the Old Testament: IV. Joseph," *BW* 29 (1907) 293-304. [37:5-28; 39:20-40:15; 41:38-49; 45:1-15; 50:15-21]

Frederick Field, "Dr. Field's Old Testament Revision Notes. Transcribed from the Author's MS. by the Rev. John Henry Burn, B.D., II.," *ET* 30 (1918-19) 181-182. [6:16; 8:4; 8:10; 20:16; 24:12; 30:27; 40:13; 40:16]

David Noel Freedman, "Notes on Genesis," *ZAW* 64 (1952-53) 190-194. [1. Grammatical Points in Genesis 1:9, 11; 2:20; 3:17; 2. The Text of Genesis 4:22; 3. The Poetic Material in Genesis 5:29; 12:1-2; 14:4, etc.]

Frank Zimmermann, "Some Textual Studies in Genesis," *JBL* 73 (1954) 97-101. [1. Gen. 22:14; 2. Gen. 24:16; 3. Gen. 35:18; 4. Gen. 41:51]

*Roderick A. F. MacKenzie, "The Divine Soliloquies in Genesis," *CBQ* 17 (1955) 277-286. [2:18; 3:22; 6:3; 6:7; 8:21s; 11:6s; 18:20s]

*T. Jansma, "Investigations into the Early Syrian Fathers on Genesis. An Approach to the Exegesis of the Nestorian Church to the Comparison of Nestorian and Jewish Exegesis," *OTS* 12 (1958) 69-181.

Genesis Chapters 1-11

Horatio B. Hackett, "The First Eleven Chapters of Genesis Attested by Their Contents," *BS* 22 (1865) 395-439.

[F. B. Procter], "Researches in Biblical Literature. The First Things (Gen. i.-xi.)," *CM, N.S.,* 1 (1887) 11-24, 94-105, 210-220, 278-291, 348-366; 2 (1887) 20-40, 105-125, 170-184, 221-231, 280-291, 370-378.

*William R. Harper, "The Pentateuchal Question. Gen. 1:1—12:5," *AJSL* 5 (1888-89) 18-73.

*A[lexander] Kohut, "The Zendavesta and the First Eleven Chapters of Genesis," *JQR* 2 (1889-90) 223-229.

*Benjamin W. Bacon, "Notes on the Analysis of Genesis I.—XXXI.," *AJSL* 7 (1890-91) 222-231.

F. H. Woods, "A Critical Examination of Genesis I to XI," *ET* 2 (1890-91) 102-104.

William R. Harper, "Some General Considerations Relating to Genesis I.-XI.," *BW* 4 (1894) 184-201.

William R. Harper, "A Theory of the Divine and Human Elements in Genesis I.-XI.," *BW* 4 (1894) 407-420.

John E. McFadyen, "Civilisation Criticized at its Source: A Study of Genesis I-XI," *HJ* 19 (1920-21) 702-711.

John M'Carthy, "Genesis I. to XI.," *MQR, 3rd Ser.,* 52 (1926) 109-111.

*Sigmund Mowinckel, "The Babylonian Matter in the Predeuteronomic Primeval History (JE) in Gen 1-11. I," *JBL* 58 (1939) 87-91.

*William F[oxwell] Albright, "The Babylonian Matter in the Predeuteronomic Primeval History (JE) in Gen 1-11. II," *JBL* 58 (1939) 91-104.

Edward F. Siegman, "Genesis 1-11 in the Seminary Scripture Course," *CBQ* 5 (1943) 318-331.

*James (Jacques) M. Voste, "A Response of the Biblical Commission," *CBQ* 10 (1948) 318-323. *[Literary form of Genesis 1-11]*

Edward P. Arbez, "Genesis I-XI and Prehistory. Part I," *AER* 123 (1950) 81-92.

Edward P. Arbez, "Genesis I-XI and Prehistory. Part II," *AER* 123 (1950) 202-213.

Edward P. Arbez, "Genesis I-XI and Prehistory. Part III," *AER* 123 (1950) 284-294.

*John A. O'Flynn, "'Humani Generis' and Sacred Scripture," *ITQ* 19 (1952) 25-32, 163-174. [Genesis chaps. 1-11, pp. 170-174]

Humphrey J. T. Johnson, "Genesis I-XI in 'A Catholic Commentary on the Holy Scripture'," *DownsR* 73 (1954-55) 13-23.

Samuel J. Schultz, "The Unity of the Race. Genesis 1-11," *JASA* 7 (1955) 50-52.

T. C. Mitchell, "The Study of Genesis I-XI," *TB* #3 (1957) 3-4.

T. C. Mitchell, "Archaeology and Genesis i-xi," *F&T* 91 (1959-60) 28-49, 128-129. (Communication by W. E. Filmer, pp. 125-128)

*John L. McKenzie, "Archaeology and Genesis 1-11," *BibT* #16 (1965) 1035-1041.

Genesis Chapters 1-9

[Nathaniel] Burwash, "Analytic study of Genesis i-ix," *CMR* 6 (1894) 64-82.

A. H. Sayce, "Archaeological Commentary on the Book of Genesis," *ET* 7 (1895-96) 206-210, 264-267, 305-308, 366-368, 461-465, 542-545. *[Chaps. 1-11]*

Genesis Chapters 1-4

E. A. Thomson, "Genesis and its First Four Chapters," *BFER* 26 (1877) 28-56.
Ernest Lussier, "'Adam in Genesis 1,1—4,24," *CBQ* 18 (1956) 137-139.

Genesis Chapters 1-3

†Anonymous, "Macdonald's Creation and the Fall," *BFER* 6 (1857) 184-216. *(Review) [Chaps. 1-3]*

Geo. H. Schodde, "The Literary Problem of Genesis I.-III.," *ONTS* 6 (1886-87) 101-105.

D. S. Gregory, "A Study in Genesis I.-III.," *HR* 42 (1901) 279-285.

A. H. Sayce, "The Archaeology of the Book of Genesis," *ET* 19 (1907-08) 137-139, 176-178, 260-263, 326-327, 423-426, 470-472. [The Creation; Genesis 1:1-3; Genesis 1:4-12; Genesis 1:14-30; Genesis 2:1-3; Paradise and the Fall (Gen 2:4-chap. 3); The Garden of Eden (Gen. 2:8-14)]

*Cuthbert Lattey, "Alleged Sources of Genesis I-III," *IER, 5th Ser.,* 10 (1917) 278-288.

E. C. Hoskyns, "Genesis I-III and St. John's Gospel," *JTS* 21 (1919-20) 210-218.

A. Zimmerman, "Genesis Chapters 1-3 and Modern Thought," *HR* 90 (1925) 92-97.

A. Zimmerman, "Four Facts for Genesis I-III," *RChR, 5th Ser.,* 4 (1925) 311-325.

P. Frank Price, "'In the Beginning'—A Study of the Early Chapters of Genesis," *USR* 52 (1940-41) 1-18. *[Chaps. 1-3]*

Arthur Geddes, "Creation, and the Blessing or the Curse upon Fruitfulness: An Anthropogeographical Interpretation of Genesis I-III," *Man* 45 (1945) #104.

Otto W. Heick, "Luther's Exposition of Genesis I-III," *LCQ* 21 (1948) 61-71.

Flemming Hvidberg, "The Canaanitic Background of Gen. I-III," *VT* 10 (1950) 285-294.

David Tobin Asselin, "The Notion of Dominion in Genesis 1-3," *CBQ* 16 (1954) 277-294.

Campion Murray, "The Origin of the World in Genesis i-iii," *ABR* 13 (1965) 1-18.

Arnold Morgan, "Aggiornamento and the Catechetics of Genesis 1-3," *AER* 156 (1967) 361-368.

Bruce Smith, "Creation, Fall and Consummation: An Interpretation of the Creation Narrative of Genesis I-III," *JCE* 8 (1965) 13-21.

Genesis Chapters 1-2

J. L., "The First of Genesis," *UQGR* 12 (1855) 277-290. *[1:1-2:3]*

Samuel Hopkins, "An Exposition of the Original Text of Genesis I. and II.," *BS* 33 (1876) 510-532, 716-739; 34 (1877) 51-69, 422-447.

A. H. Sayce, "The Old Testament in the Light of Recent Discoveries," *MI* 2 (1885) 155-160. *[chap. 1; 2:2, 3; 2:8; 2:9; 2:11]*

Dwight M. Hodge, "The First Two Chapters of Genesis," *UQGR, N.S.,* 22 (1885) 165-176.

Herbert E. Ryle, "The Early Narratives of Genesis," *ET* 2 (1890-91) 149-152. [The Creation of the Universe 1:1-2:4a (Part I)]

Theo. G. Pinches, "The Old Testament in the Light of the Literature of Assyria and Babylon," *ET* 3 (1891-92) 64-67, 165-167, 267-270, 409-411. *[1:1-2; Verse 2; 1:6-8; 1:9, 10; 1:11, 12; 1:14-18; 1:24; 1:25; 1:26, 27; 2:1; 2:2, 3]*

James Sime, "The Drama of Creation," *Exp, 5th Ser.,* 6 (1897) 309-320, 387-400, 450-459. *[1:1-2:3]*

George H. Schodde, "The Problem of Genesis I. and II.," *CFL, 3rd Ser.,* 1 (1904) 711-713.

Franklin N. Jewett, "Questions from the Pew. The Creation Narrative of Genesis I, 1—II, 4, a," *OC* 21 (1907) 481-484.

*Eduard König, "Relations of Babylonian and Old Testament Culture. III. The controvertible connection between Babylon and the Bible with regard to primitive history. (Gen. 1-2)," *HR* 57 (1909) 186-189.

*Walter Foxon, "Does the Doctrine of Evolution Destroy the Teaching of Gen. 1:1-2:3," *HR* 62 (1911) 346-353.

Francis J. Lamb, "Higher Criticism, Dr. Driver, Jural Science and Chapters i. and ii. Genesis," *CFL, 3rd Ser.,* 20 (1915) 99-103.

Francis J. Lamb, "How Driver Salted the Bible Mine," *CFL, 3rd Ser.,* 25 (1919) 461-463. [Examination of Higher Criticism in Genesis 1 & 2] (Editorial note by Jay Benson Hamilton, p. 463)

Julian Morgenstern, "The Sources of the Creation Story—Genesis 1:1-2:4," *AJSL* 36 (1919-20) 169-212.

D. E. Hart-Davies, "The First Two Chapters of Genesis Considered as a Basis of Science," *JTVI* 70 (1938) 29-66, 86-87 [(Discussion, pp. 66-79) (Communications, pp 79-86)]

Frank Lynch, "Man: His Age and Origin. Certainties from Genesis I-II," *MH* 9 (Spring, 1953) 38-44A.

William Sanford LaSor, "Notes on Genesis 1:1-2:3," *GR* 2 (1956) 26-32.

Allen A. MacRae, "The Principles of Interpreting Genesis 1 and 2," *BETS* 2 (1959) #4, 1-9.

*J. Barton Payne, "Theistic Evolution and the Hebrew of Genesis 1-2," *BETS* 8 (1965) 85-90.

Walter Wegner, "Creation and Salvation. *A Study of Genesis 1 and 2*," *CTM* 37 (1966) 520-542.

Edmund Hill, "The Truth of Genesis I-II," *Scrip* 18 (1966) 65-76.

W. F. Hambly, "Creation and Gospel. A Brief Comparison of Genesis 1,1—2,4 and John 1,1—2,12," *StEv* 5 (1968) 69-74.

Genesis Chapter 1

M. Stuart, "Critical Examination of some passages in Gen. I.; with remarks on the difficulties that attend some of the present modes of Geological reasoning," *BRCR* 7 (1836) 46-106.

T. H., "The First Chapter of Genesis," *CE* 59 (1855) 379-398. *(Review)*

Edward Biley, "The Days of Genesis I," *JSL, 4th Ser.,* 9 (1866) 435.

Thomas Hill, "The First Chapter of Genesis," *BS* 32 (1875) 303-319.

Thomas Hill, "The First Chapter of Genesis," *DTQ* 2 (1876) 511-520.

*C. M. Mead, "On Gen. ii. 5, as related to Gen i.," *SBLP* (December, 1880) 6-8.

*Charles B. Warring, "The Agreement of Science with *Genesis I*," *JCP* 3 (1883-84) 173-195.

Almoni Peloni, "The Moral Aspects of the Mosaic Narrative of the Creation. Genesis I," *Exp, 2nd Ser.,* 7 (1884) 444-454.

J. W. Dawson, "Recent Discussions of the First Chapter of Genesis," *Exp, 3rd Ser.,* 3 (1886) 284-301.

W. P. James, "Is the Account of the Creation in Genesis One of a Parallel Series?" *JTVI* 20 (1886-87) 234-246. (Discussion pp. 246-254)

*R. V. Foster, "The Word Elohim in Genesis I," *ONTS* 6 (1886-87) 241-243.

W. Gray Elmslie, "The First Chapter of Genesis," *ContR* 52 (1887) 815-830.

Charles B. Warring, "The Literal Genesis I. in the Light of Present Knowledge," *CT* 5 (1887-88) 17-29.

*Charles B. Warring, "The Babylonian Legend of Creation. Is it the Original of the Story in the First Chapter of Genesis?" *MR* 71 (1889) 809-820.

J.J. Perowne, "Notes on Genesis," *Exp, 4th Ser.* 2 (1890) 241-256, 321-336, 429-438. *[Chap. 1]*

*Charles B. Warring, "Professor Huxley versus Genesis I," *BS* 49 (1892) 638-649.

Anonymous, "Scriptural Evolution; or, The First Chapter in Genesis," *CM, 3rd Ser.,* 3 (1892) 232-242, 283-301.

Arthur T. Pierson, "Genesis," *HR* 27 (1894) 57-60. *[Gen. 1:1-31]*

*G. Frederick Wright, "The First Chapter of Genesis and Modern Science," *HR* 35 (1898) 392-399.

C[harles] B. Warring, "New Evidence for the Truth of Genesis i., or Modern Science's Contribution to Theology," *HR* 40 (1900) 161-162.

C[harles] B. Warring, "A Brief Study of Genesis I.—A New Weapon from the Divine Armory," *HR* 42 (1901) 211-215.

*Hugo Radau, "The Creation-Story of Genesis I.," *Monist* 12 (1901-02) 568-625. *[A Sumerian Theogony and Cosmogony]*

Theodore E. Schmauk, "The First Chapter of Genesis in Comparison with the Heathen Creation Myths," *LCR* 21 (1902) 10-21.

*William M. McPheeters, "Meaning of Bārā' in Genesis i," *CFL, N.S.,* 8 (1903) 10-16. *(Editorial)*

W[illiam] M. McPheeters, "Genesis I. and Astronomy," *HR* 46 (1903) 452-455.

Charles B. Warring, "On the Use of 'Good' in Genesis I," *CFL, 3rd Ser.,* 1 (1904) 171-173.

G. L. Young, "The Creation Chapter of Genesis," *CFL, 3rd Ser.,* 1 (1904) 250-253. *[Chap. 1]*

W[illiam] M. McPheeters, "'Dies Civiles' or 'Dies Ineffabiles'?" *CFL, 3rd Ser.,* 1 (1904) 633-639. *[The Word 'Day' in Genesis 1]*

Charles B. Warring, "The Days of Genesis I.—A New View," *CFL, 3rd Ser.,* 2 (1905) 156-158.

A. E. Whatham, "The Polytheism of Gen., Chap. I.," *BW* 37 (1911) 40-47.

A. E. Whatham, "The Anthropomorphism of Gen., Chap. I," *BW* 36 (1911) 120-127.

A. G. Voigt, "The Relation of Genesis I to the Following Chapters," *LQ* 41 (1911) 249-255.

*Charles Edward Smith, "The Wonders of Divine Inspiration in the First Chapter of the Bible," *CFL, 2nd Ser.,* 14 (1911-12) 12-15.

E. Walter Maunder, "The First Chapter of Genesis," *JTVI* 46 (1914) 119-142, 163-166. [(Discussion, pp. 142-150) (Communications by J. Schwartz Jr., pp. 150-151; J. Iverach Munro, pp. 151-152, 166; Heywood Smith, pp. 152-153; M. A. Alves, pp. 153-154; A. Irving, pp. 154-157; John Tuckwell, pp. 157-159; J. J. Lias, pp. 159-160; Joseph Graham, pp. 160-162; T. B. Bishop, pp. 162-163)]

W. E. Denham, "Making a World," *SWJT* 5 (1921) #4, 3-16. *[Chap. 1]*

David L. Holbrook, "The Point of View in the First Chapter of Genesis," *BS* 79 (1922) 452-466.

*Harold W. Clark, "The New Genesis," *CFL, 3rd Ser.,* 29 (1923) 40-41. *[Paraphrase of Genesis 1 based on the evolutionary theory]*

M. Lambert, "A Study of the First Chapter of Genesis," *HUCA* 1 (1924) 3-12.

*W[illiam] F[oxwell] Albright, "Contributions of Biblical Archaeology and Philology," *JBL* 43 (1924) 363-393. [1. Chaos and the Origin of Light in Genesis, pp. 363-369]

*M. D. R. Willink, "Is Genesis I. a Manifesto Against Nature Worship?" *Theo* 11 (1925) 11-15.

Josephine Rand, "The Six Days of Genesis I," *CFL, 3rd Ser.,* 34 (1928) 592-599, 658-665; 35 (1929) 24-32, 80-88, 188-197, 236-243, 294-302; 36 (1930) 409-416.

*†C. M. Mead, "On Gen. 2:5 as related to Gen. 1," *JBL* 49 (1930) xlii-xliv. *[Reprint of the Proceedings of the second meeting of the Society of Biblical Literature (may be bound separately)]*

Wilbur M. Smith, "The First Chapter of Genesis: A Notable Tribute," *CFL, 3rd Ser.,* 37 (1931) 593-594.

Ivan Panin, "The Article in Genesis One," *CFL, 3rd Ser.,* 39 (1933) 37-38.

*Robert J. Drummond, "Genesis I. and John I. 1-14," *ET* 49 (1937-38) 568.

P.*[sic]* J. Wiseman, "The Significance of the 'Six Days' of Genesis I," *JTVI* 70 (1938) 88-105. 120-125. [(Discussion pp. 105-115) (Communications by Thomas Fitzgerald, pp. 115-117; R. E. D. Clark, pp. 117-118; L. M. Davies, pp. 118-119; H. B. Clarke, p. 120)]

*John Henning, "The First Chapter of Genesis in the Liturgy," *CBQ* 10 (1948) 360-375.

R. T. Fulwood, "The Plan in the First Chapter of Genesis," *JASA* 2 (1950) #4, 1-13.

L. Johnston, "Genesis Chapter I and the Creation Myth," *Scrip* 5 (1952-53) 142-145.

A. C. Rehwaldt, "Natural Science with Reference to Genesis I," *CTM* 26 (1955) 341-359.

Nic. H. Ridderbos, "The meaning of Genesis I," *FUQ* 4 (1956-57) 221-235.

*Meredith G. Kline, "Because It had Not Rained," *WTJ* (1957-58) 146-157. [Genesis 2:5ff. and the Interpretation of Genesis 1, pp. 151-155; The Literary Genre of Genesis 1, pp. 155-167]

C. F. Whitley, "The Pattern of Creation in Genesis, Chapter 1," *JNES* 17 (1958) 32-40.

Edwin Walhout, "Sequence in the Days of Genesis One," *JASA* 11 (1959) #2, 6-8.

H. P. Hamann, "Conflicting Voices on Genesis I," *AusTR* 33 (1962) 60-62. *(Review)*

E. Bernhard Keiser, "Can the Scientists of Today Believe in Gen. 1?" *JTLC* 2 (1962) #4, 12.

Donald F. X. Connolly, "Genesis 1," *TFUQ* 37 (1962) 211-225.

*James Albertson, "Genesis 1 and the Babylonian Creation Myth," *TFUQ* 37 (1962) 226-244.

H. P. Hamann, "Again Genesis 1," *AusTR* 34 (1963) 34-40.

E. Reim, "Scientists and Theologians Discuss Gen. 1," *JTLC* 3 (1963) #5, 42-44.

J. B. Toews, "Studies in Genesis One," *JC&S* 1 (1965) #2, 3-13.

*Gene Rice, "Cosmological Ideas and Religious Truth in Genesis i," *JRT* 23 (1966-67) 15-30.

*Moshe Weinfeld, "God the Creator in Gen. I and in the Prophecy of Second Isaiah," *Tarbiz* 37 (1967-68) #2. I-II.

Genesis 1:1-13

C. F. Graebner, "Genesis 1:1-13," *AusTR* 5 (1934) 77-83, 6 (1935) 1-13.

Genesis 1:1-10

William B. Cogan, "Enuma Elish and Genesis 1-1-10," *MH* 10 (Winter, 1953-54), 25-29.

Genesis 1:1-5

Anonymous, "Origin and Propagation of Light, According to Moses," *MR* 1 (1818) 145-149. *[1:1-5]*

*Edward B. Pollard, "Two Poems of Beginnings: Genesis 1:1-5; John 1:1-18," *BW* 17 (1901) 107-110.

Genesis 1:1-3

*B. Pick, "Extracts from the Midrash Rabboth: Illustrating the Scriptures," *HR* 8 (1883-84) 893-894. *[1:1, 3]*

T. K. Cheyne, "On Genesis I., 1-3," *AJSL* 2 (1885-86) 116.

Fritz Hommel, "An Ancient Parallel to Gen. i. 1-3," *ET* 9 (1897-98) 432.

J. M. Powis Smith, "The Syntax and Meaning of Genesis 1:1-3," *AJSL* 44 (1927-28) 108-115.

*G. Douglas Young, "Biblical Chronology and Genesis 1:1-3," *JASA* 3 (1951) #4, 19-22. (Discussion, pp. 22-23)

Anton T. Pearson, "An Exegetical Study of Genesis 1:1-3," *BSQ* 2 (1953-54) #1, 14-33.

Edward J. Young, "The Relation of the First Verse of Genesis One to Verses Two and Three," *WTJ* 21 (1958-59) 133-146.

Genesis 1:1-2

J. J. Smyth, "A Criticism on Genesis 1:1, 2," *ER* 19 (1868) 424-433.

William H. Bates, "Jehovah—Jesus or Satan," *CFL, 3rd Ser.,* 31 (1925) 314. *[1:1, 2]*

Leander S. Keyser, "To Create or to Form. What is the Fundamental Difference?" *BS* 83 (1926) 47-54. *[1:1, 2]*

Edward P. Arbez and John P. Weisentoff, "Exegetical Notes on Genesis 1:1-2," *CBQ* 10 (1948) 140-150.

Genesis 1:1

W. A.-P., "The Bible's First Declaration," *ERG, 2nd Ser.,* 2 (1859-60) 31-37. *["In the Beginning God Created..."]*

*T. K. Cheyne, "Notes on Genesis I., 1, and XXIV., 14. (1) On the Rendering of Genesis I., 1, (2) On Genesis XXIV., 14 (נַעַר)," *AJSL* 2 (1885-86) 49-50.

†[J. W. Mendenhall], "בְּרֵאשִׁת (Gen. i. 1)," *MR* 70 (1888) 747. *[Untitled Editorial Remark]*

Bostwick Hawley, "'In the Beginning,' or 'In Beginning'—Which?" *MR* 71 (1889) 125-126. *[1:1]*

Henry M. Harman, "The First Word of Genesis," *MR* 71 (1889) 448. *[1:1]*

Robert W. Rogers, "The First Word of Genesis," *MR* 71 (1889) 448-449. *[1:1]*

Anonymous, "The Great Text Commentary. The Great Texts of Genesis," *ET* 10 (1898-99) 19-22. *[1:1]*

*James A. Montgomery, "Notes from the Samaritan," *JBL* 25 (1906) 49-54. [III. שלמם in the Samaritan Targum to Gen. 1[1], pp. 52-53]

Anonymous, "Exegetical Notes. Genesis i. 1," *MQR 3rd Ser.,* 45 (1919) 149.

L. Franklin Gruber, "The First Verse of Genesis," *BS* 90 (1933) 228-231.

Ivan Panin, "Genesis 1:1", *CFL, 3rd Ser.,* 39 (1933) 192-193.

P. E. Kretzmann, "'The *Heaven* and the Earth, Gen. 1, 1," *CTM* 8 (1937) 707.

Edgar J. Goodspeed, "'In the Beginning'," *RL* 17 (1948) 17-22. *[1:1]*

G. Douglas Young, "Further Light on the Translation of Genesis 1:1," *JASA* 10 (1958) #4, 2-3.

*J. C. M. Van Winden, "In the Beginning. Some Observations on the Patristic Interpretation of *Genesis* 1:1," *VC* 17 (1963) 105-121.

*William R. Lane, "The Initiation of Creation," *VT* 13 (1963) 63-73. *[1:1]*

Genesis 1:2-3

E. Abbey Tindall, "Note on Gen. I. 2, 3," *ET* 2 (1890-91) 86.

Genesis 1:2

Charles John Elliott, "Short Comments on Difficult Passages of Scripture," *CM* 3 (1876) 368-369. *[1:2]*

*A. H. Wratislaw, "Gen. I. 2 compared with I Kings XXII. 21," *ET* 2 (1890-91) 115-117.

Edward Henry Blakeney, "Note on Genesis I. 2," *ET* 2 (1890-91) 117.

C[harles] B. Warring, "Tohu: A Historical and Exegetical Study of Its Meaning in Genesis I. 2," *BS* 56 (1899) 165-168.

*John P. Peters, "The Wind of God," *JBL* 30 (1911) 44-54; 33 (1914) 81-86. *[1:2b]*

Leroy Waterman, "Cosmogonic Affinities in Genesis 1:2," *AJSL* 43 (1926-27) 177-184.

*J. P. Wilson, "Is Genesis I. 2 the Scripture Cited in James IV. 5?" *GUOST* 6 (1929-33) 8-9.

W. H. McClellan, "The meaning of ruaḥ 'Elohim in Gen. 1, 2," *B* 15 (1934) 517-527.

*J. W. Jack, "Recent Biblical Archaeology," *ET* 53 (1941-42) 367-370. [Archæology and the Biblical Text: 2 Birds Fluttering (Gen. 1:2, Deut. 32:11, Jer. 23:9), pp. 368-369]

P. W. Heward, "'And the Earth was without Form and Void.' *An enquiry into the exact meaning of Genesis I, 2,*" *JTVI* 78 (1946) 13-20, 31-34. [Communications by E. H. Betts, pp. 24-25; D. J. Wiseman, pp. 25-27; Douglas Dewar, pp. 27-28; L. M. Davies, pp. 28-29; R. B. Withers, p. 30; W. M. Powell, p. 30; W. A. Nunn, p. 30; Stanley Leathes, pp. 30-31; Edward J. G. Titterington, p. 31]

F. F. Bruce, "'And the Earth was without Form and Void.' *An enquiry into the exact meaning of Genesis I, 2,*" *JTVI* 78 (1946) 21-24, 34-37.

*Stanislaus J. Grabowski, "Spiritus Dei in Gen. 1:2 according to St. Augustine," *CBQ* 10 (1948) 13-28.

Harry M. Orlinsky, "The Plain Meaning of RU^AH in Gen. 1:2," *JQR, N.S.,* 48 (1957-58) 174-182.

Edward J. Young, "The Interpretation of Genesis 1:2," *WTJ* 23 (1960-61) 151-178.

Islwyn Blythin, "A Note on Genesis i:2," *VT* 12 (1962) 120-121.

D. F. Payne, "Approaches to Genesis i 2," *GUOST* 23 (1969-70) 61-71.

Genesis 1:3-5

H[erbert] G[ordon] May, "The Creation of Light in Genesis 1:3-5," *JBL* 58 (1939) xv.

Herbert Gordon May, "The Creation of Light in Genesis 1:3-5," *JBL* 58 (1939) 203-212.

*A. Cowper Field, "Let there be Light: A comparison of Genesis I, 3-5, and John I, with Root-Meanings of certain very Ancient Words," *JTVI* 74 (1942) 54-64, 69-71. [Communications by Charles Marston, p. 64; H. S. Curr, pp. 64-66; W. H. Molesworth, pp. 66-68; Leslie I. Moser, pp. 68-69]

Genesis 1:3

J. C. M., "Scripture Illustrated," *CongML* 21 (1838) 12-15. *[1:3]*

Anonymous, "Exegetical Notes. Genesis i. 3," *MQR, 3rd Ser.,* 45 (1919) 149-150.

Genesis 1:6-7

David Neiman, "The Supercaelian Sea," *JNES* 28 (1969) 243-249. *[1:6-7]*

Genesis 1:9

*Alphonse Mingana, "Remarks on the Hebrew of Genesis," *Exp, 8th Ser.,* 11 (1916) 303-310. *[Chap 1:9]*

D. J. Whitney, "Bible Teaching About Land and Sea," *CFL, 3rd Ser.,* 32 (1926) 528. *[1:9]*

Genesis 1:21

Almoni Peloni, "And God Created Great Whales. Genesis i.21," *Exp. 2nd Ser.,* 4 (1882) 191-209.

Genesis 1:24-27

*Alexander Heidel, "The Alleged Contradiction between Gen. 1:24-27 and 2:19," *CTM* 12 (1941) 652-657.

Genesis 1:26-31

J. Dyk, "Texts and Contexts: A Criticism on a Passage of Exposition in Dr. Brigg's 'Messianic Prophecy'," *ONTS* 9 (1889) 248-249. *[1:26-30]*

*J. J. Stewart Perowne, "Notes on Genesis," *Exp, 4th Ser.,* 3 (1891) 125-142. *[Chap 1:26ff.]*

*Arthur T. Pierson, "The Marginal Commentary. Marginal Notes on Genesis," *HR* 27 (1894) 158-162. *[1:26-31]*

Genesis 1:26-27

Anonymous, "The Great Text Commentary. The Great Texts of Genesis," *ET* 10 (1898-99) 72-75. *[1:26-27]*

G. H. Skipwith, "The Image of God," *JTS* 7 (1905-06) 624-626. *[1:26-27]*

*Herbert G. Wood, "Expository Problems. Man Created in the Image of God," *ET* 68 (1956-57) 165-168. *[1:26, 27]*

Genesis 1:26

Herbert E. Ryle, "Requests and Replies," *ET* 2 (1890-91) 138-139 *[1:26]*

Anonymous, "The Plural 'Us' in Genesis 1:26," *ONTS* 12 (1891) 374.

*Max L. Margolis, "Notes on Semitic Grammar. II," *AJSL* 12 (1895-96) 197-229. [דְּמוּת—Gen. 1:26]

I. Louis Bedford, "The Wind of God," *ET* 27 (1915-16) 384. *[1:26]*

K. G. Manz, "Image of God," *CTM* 8 (1937) 621. *[1:26LXX]*

R. McL. Wilson, "The Early History of the Exegesis of Gen 1.26," *StP* 1 (1957) 420-437.

*R. McL. Wilson, "Genesis 1:26 and the New Testament," *BTPT* 20 (1959) 117-125.

Genesis 1:27-28

Frank Allen, "The First Commandment to Man," *JASA* 12 (1960) #3, 70-74. *[1:27-28]*

Genesis 1:27

[Jay Benson Hamilton], "International Sunday School Lessons: God Created Man in His own image. Gen. 1:27," *CFL, 3rd Ser.,* 25 (1919) 254-255.

*D. J. Whitney, "In the Image of God—Genesis 1:27; John 4:24," *CFL, 3rd Ser.,* 32 (1926) 217.

*Paul Winter, "Şadoqite Fragments IV 20, 21 and the Exegesis of Genesis 1:27 in late Judaism," *ZAW* 68 (1956) 74-84.

*Paul Winter, "Genesis 1:27 and Jesus Saying on Divorce," *ZAW* 70 (1958) 260-261.

Genesis 2-11

*Walter Brueggemann, "David and His Theologian," *CBQ* 30 (1968) 156-181. *[J narrative of Gen. 2-11 and 2 Sam. 9-20; 1 Kgs. 1-2]*

Genesis 2:4-Chapter 3

*Joseph Bourke, "'Leviathan Which Yahweh Made to Laugh At'," *LofS* 13 (1958-59) 122-129. [The Second Account of Creation (Genesis ii, 4-iii), pp. 126-129]

Genesis Chapters 2-3

Crawford H. Toy, "Analysis of Gen II, III," *JBL* 10 (1891) 1-19.

*A. Van Hoonacker, "The Literary Origin of the Narrative of the Fall. Genesis II.-III.," *Exp, 8th Ser.,* 8 (1914) 481-498.

A. Van Hoonacker, "Connexion of Death with Sin according to Gen. II.-III.," *Exp, 8th Ser.,* 9 (1915) 131-143.

H. D. A. Major, "The Tree of Knowledge of Good and Evil in Genesis II and III," *Exp, 8th Ser.,* 12 (1916) 259-285.

W. E. Denham, "Lecture No. 2: The Fall of Man (Genesis 2 and 3)," *SWJT* 6 (1922) #1, 23-37.

E. Burrows, "Tilmun, Baḥrain, Paradise," *Or* #30 (1928) 3-34. [Note on the Hebrew Tradition (Gen. 2-3), pp. 21-22]

Edward Robertson, "The Paradise Narrative in Genesis 2, 3," *JMUEOS* #22 (1938) 21-35.

Louis F. Hartman, "Sin in Paradise," *CBQ* 20 (1958) 26-40. *[Chaps. 2-3]*

*J[ohn] L. McKenzie, "The Literary Characteristics of Genesis 2-3," *ThSt* 15 (1954) 541-572.

*John L. McKenzie, "The Literary Characteristics of Genesis 2-3," *TD* 6 (1958) 19-23.

Lester J. Kuyper, "Interpretation of Genesis Two—Three," *RefR* 13 (1959-60) #2, 4-14; #3, 17-29.

Norbert Lohfink, "Genesis 2-3 as 'historical etiology'," *TD* 13 (1965) 11-17.

Luis Alonso-Schokel, "Sapiential and covenant themes in Genesis 2-3," *TD* 13 (1965) 3-10.

James L. Connor, "Original Sin: Contemporary Approaches," *ThSt* 29 (1968) 215-240. [Genesis 2-3, pp. 218-219]

W. Malcolm Clark, "A Legal Background to the Yahwist's Use of 'Good and Evil' in Genesis 2-3," *JBL* 88 (1969) 266-278.

Genesis Chapter 2

William R. Harper, "The Origin of Man and His First State of Innocence. Genesis II," *BW* 3 (1894) 97-108.

*Arthur T. Pierson, "The Marginal Commentary. Marginal Notes on Genesis," *HR* 27 (1894) 158-162. *[2:2, 3, 4, 7-9, 15, 17, 18]*

J. F. McCurdy, "Light on Scriptural Texts from Recent Discoveries. Second Chapter of Genesis," *HR* 34 (1897) 309-312.

*W. Leonard, "Our First Parents," *ACR* 11 (1934) 195-212, 306-319; 12 (1935) 121-131. [Gen. 2, pp. 208-212]

Genesis 2:1-3

J. W. Natal, "On a Passage in Genesis. Does Gen. ii. 1-3 belong to the Elohistic Narrative?" *TRL* 10 (1873) 599-602. (Response by Russell Martineau, pp. 603-606)

*J. J. Stewart Perowne, "Notes on Genesis," *Exp, 4th Ser.,* 3 (1891) 125-142. *[2:1-3]*

M., "The Sabbath. Genesis 2, 1-3," *WLQ* 23 (1926) 118-135, 186-200, 267-279.

Genesis 2:2-3

R. H. Altus, "Genesis 2:2, 3," *AusTR* 15 (1944) 65-78.

Genesis 2:4-3:24

William Henry Green, "False Critical Methods Applied to Genesis II. 4—III. 24," *CFL, 3rd Ser.,* 6 (1907) 111-118.

Genesis 2:4-7

A. S. A., "Genesis II, 4-7: An Exposition," *ERG, 6th Ser.,* 3 (1876-77) 140-149.

Genesis 2:4

Paul Haupt, "The Beginning of the Judaic Account of Creation," *JAOS* 17 (1896) 158-163. *[2:4b]*

*Paul Haupt, "Etymological and Critical Notes," *AJP* 47 (1926) 305-318. [1. Bdellium and Onyx, pp. 305-307] *[2:4]*

Genesis 2:5-6

W. H. McClellan, "The Newly Proposed Translation of Genesis 2:5-6," *CBQ* 1 (1939) 106-114.

D. Kidner, "Genesis 2:5, 6:   Wet or Dry?" *TB* #17 (1966) 109-114.

Genesis 2:5

E. W. Shalders, "Biblical Notes. Genesis ii. 5," *Exp, 1st Ser.*, 7 (1878) 465-467.

*C. M. Mead, "On Gen. ii. 5, as related to Gen i.," *SBLP* (December, 1880) 6-8.

*†C. M. Mead, "On Gen. 2:5 as related to Gen. 1," *JBL* 49 (1930) xlii-xliv. *[Reprint of the Proceedings of the second meeting of the Society of Biblical Literature (may be bound separately)]*

*Meredith G. Kline, "Because It had Not Rained," *WTJ* (1957-58) 146-157. [Genesis 2:5ff., pp. 148-155; Genesis 2:5ff. and the Interpretation of Genesis 1, pp. 151-155]

Genesis 2:6

*G. R. Driver, "Notes on Notes," *B* 36 (1955) 71-73. [אֵד, Gen. 2:6, p. 71]

*E[phraim] A. Speiser, " '*ED* in the Story of Creation," *BASOR* #140 (1955) 9-11. *[2:6]*

Genesis 2:7

*Max Moll, "Light from the Post-Biblical Literature of the Jews. No. II,"*HR* 8 (1883-84) 161-162. *[2:7]*

Ernest C. Richardson, "וַיִּפַּח of Gen 2:7," *JBL* 5 (1885) 49-55.

W. H. McClellan, "Genesis 2:7 and the Evolution of the Human Body. A Study in Literal Exegesis," *AER* 72 (1925) 1-10.

Vincent M. McNally, "Genesis 2:7 and Transformism," *MH* 4 (1947-48) #4, 21-25.

Edmund F. Sutcliffe, "Questions and Answers. What is the teaching of Genesis ii, 7 about the human soul?" *Scrip* 5 (1952-53) 47-48.

Genesis 2:8-18

*William Wallace Martin, "The Creation of Woman: Genesis II. 8-18, 20b-24," *MQR, 3rd Ser.,* 52 (1926) 315-317.

Genesis 2:9

S.R.Driver,"Grammatical Notes. 1.On Genesis II., 9b,"*AJSL* 2(1885-86) 32.

C. Watt-Smyrk, "Genesis II. 9: Two Trees in Eden," *ET* 2 (1890-91) 164.

*Henry D. A. Major, "The Tree of the Knowledge of Good and Evil (Gen. II. 9, 17)," *ET* 20 (1908-09) 427-428.

Genesis 2:10-14

[J.] William Dawson, "Gold, Bedolach, and Shoham Stone. A Geographical and Mineralogical Study of Genesis II., Verses 10 to 14," *BS* 44 (1887) 377-383.

J. W[illiam] Dawson, "Gold, Bedolach, and Shoham Stone. A Geographical and Mineralogical Study of Genesis II., Verses 10 to 14," *Exp, 3rd Ser.,* 5 (1887) 201-215.

Genesis 2:11

S. Krauss, "'Euilat' in the LXX," *JQR* 11 (1898-99) 675-679. *[2:11]*

Genesis 2:12

J. Wm. Dawson, "Bdellium," *ET* 4 (1892-93) 369. *[2:12]*

Genesis 2:13

*John P. Peters, "Miscellaneous Notes," *AJSL* 1 (1884-85) 115-119. [כוּשׁ in Gen. 2:13, 10:8, p. 117]

A. H. Sayce, "Gihon," *ET* 15 (1903-04) 514-515. *[2:13]*

Genesis 2:15-25

*A. H. Sayce, "The Archaeology of the Book of Genesis," *ET* 20 (1908-09) 327-328, 505-511. *[2:15-25]*

Genesis 2:16-17

J. Gaskell, "Genesis II. 16, 17," *ET* 2 (1890-91) 118.

Genesis 2:17

*Henry D. A. Major, "The Tree of the Knowledge of Good and Evil (Gen. II. 9, 17)," *ET* 20 (1908-09) 427-428.

*Samuel Belkin, "Some Obscure Tradition Mutually Clarified in Philo and Rabbinic Literature," *JQR, 75th,* (1967) 80-103. [6. Eternal Death (Gen. 2:17) pp.93-96.]

Genesis 2:18

*P. A. Nordell, "Adam's 'Help-Meet'," *ONTS* 4 (1884-85) 368. *[2:18]*

Genesis 2:19

*Alexander Heidel, "The Alleged Contradiction between Gen. 1:24-27 and 2:19," *CTM* 12 (1941) 652-657.

Genesis 2:20-24

[W. M.] McP[heeters], "Current Criticism and Interpretation of the Old Testament," *CFL., O.S.,* 3 (1899) 432-433. *[2:20-24]*

*William Wallace Martin, "The Creation of Woman: Genesis II. 8-18, 20b-24," *MQR, 3rd Ser.,* 52 (1926) 315-317.

Genesis 2:23

*Frederick Field, "Dr. Field's Old Testament Revision Notes. Transcribed from the Author's MS. by the Rev. John Henry Burn, B.D., I.," *ET* 30 (1918-19) 85-86. *[2:23]*

Genesis 2:24

*Manfred R. Lehmann, "Gen 2:24 as the Basis for Divorce in the Halakhah and the New Testament," *ZAW* 72 (1960) 263-267.

*T. P. Considine, "Two In One Flesh. The Meaning in Sacred Scripture," *ACR* 39 (1962) 111-123. *[2:24LXX]*

Genesis 2:25

*John Edwards, "Genesis II. 25 and XLVIII. 10," *AJSL* 3 (1886-87) 263-264.

*H. W. Sydenstricker, "Exegetical Opinions and Suggestions," *CFL, O.S.,* 1 (1897) 119. *[2:25]*

Neal L. Anderson, "Exegetical Suggestions and Opinions. Gen. 2:25," *CFL, O.S.,* 1 (1897) 214-215.

Genesis Chapters 3-4

Merrill F. Unger, "Archaeology and Genesis 3-4," *BS* 110 (1953) 11-17.

Genesis Chapter 3

Anonymous, "Some Observations on the 'Nahash,' or Serpent, of the Third Chapter of Genesis," *MQR* 4 (1850) 439-448.

R. G. Jones, "The Serpent, Gen. iii," *JSL, 2nd Ser.,* 6 (1854) 238-241.

George Dana Boardman, "The Genesis of Sin: A Study in the Third Chapter of Genesis, *PR, 4th Ser.,* 6 (1880) 42-61.

Anonymous, "The Nachash of Genesis III," *MQR, 2nd Ser.,* 3 (1881) 173-178.

Anonymous, "The Serpent of Gen. III," *ONTS* 14 (1892) 122.

William R. Harper, "Paradise and the First Sin, Genesis III," *BW* 3 (1894) 176-188.

*Arthur T. Pierson, "Marginal Commentary: Notes on Genesis," *HR* 27 (1894) 260-263. *[3:1, 4, 6, 7, 8, 9, 14-19, 21, 22, 24]*

H. G. Mitchell, "The Fall and Its Consequences According to Genesis, Chapter 3," *AJT* 1 (1897) 913-926.

*H. W. Sydenstricker, "Exegetical Opinions and Suggestions," *CFL, O.S.,* 1 (1897) 119. *[3:1, 7, 10, 11]*

D. S. Gregory, "A Study in Genesis III," *HR* 42 (1901) 369-374.

Arthur E. Whatham, "The Outward Form of the Original Sin. A New Study of Genesis 3," *AJRPE* 1 (1904-05) 268-287.

Henry Hinckley, "The 'Penalty', 'Death', in Genesis iii.—A Criticism," *CFL, 3rd Ser.,* 2 (1905) 319.

A. H. M'Neile, "The Spiritual Value of Genesis, Chap. III," *ET* 17 (1905-06) 397-400.

E. Hampden-Cook, "The Serpent in Eden (Gen.III.)," *ET* 18 (1906-07) 287

Arthur E. Whatham, "Note on Genesis III. Cheyne's Traditions and beliefs on Ancient Israel," *AJRPE* 3 (1908-09) 154-159.

J. Edgar Park, "Does the Third Chapter of Genesis contain an Account of the First Sin?" *HR* 57 (1909) 391-392.

George A. Barton, "A New Babylonian Parallel to a Part of Genesis 3," *JAOS* 39 (1919) 287.

L[eander] S. Keyser, "Historicity of Genesis III," *CFL, 3rd Ser.,* 29 (1923) 198-207, 266-274.

Irwin Ross Beiler, "Genesis III in the Light of Modern Knowledge," *MR* 107 (1924) 587-600.

†R. C. Fuller, "The Serpent in Genesis, ch. iii," *Scrip* 3 (1948) 85-86.

John Trinick, "Meditation on Genesis III," *BTPT* 22 (1961) 266-271.

Ralph D. Gehrke, "Genesis Three in the Light of Key Hermeneutical Considerations," *CTM* 36 (1965) 534-560.

*W. Gunther Plaut, "Notes From a New Commentary on The Torah," *CCARJ* 14 (1967) #4. 64-69. *[Chap. 3, pp. 67-69]*

Carl Lawrenz, "Genesis III in Contemporary Interpretation," *WLQ* 66 (1969) 83-102, 185-205, 256-275.

Genesis 3:1-24

John J. Dougherty, "The Fall and its Consequences. An Exegetical Study of Gen. 3:1-24," *CBQ* 3 (1941) 220-234.

Genesis 3:1-15

Michael J. Gruenthaner, "The Serpent of *Gen.* 3:1-15," *AER* 113 (1945) 149-152.

Genesis 3:1-7

*A. H. Sayce, "The Archaeology of the Book of Genesis," *ET* 20 (1908-09) 327-328, 505-511. *[3:1-7]*

Genesis 3:1-6

W. W. Everts Jr., "Paraphrase of Genesis 3:1-6," *ONTS* 7 (1887-88) 253-255.

H. C. Ackerman, "Reconceptualization as a Principle of Exegesis (e.g., Gen. 3:1-6)," *ATR* 2 (1919-20) 71-73.

*Edward C. Meyer and Simon J. DeVries, "Preparation for Biblical Preaching. IV," *JMTSO* 6 (1967-68) #2, 22-34. *[3:1-6]*

Genesis 3:2

†Philobiblos, "Scriptures defended," *MMBR* 3 (1797) 443. *[3:2]*

Genesis 3:5

T. K. Cheyne, "On Genesis III. 5," *Exp, 3rd Ser.,* 2 (1885) 399.

T. A. Smith, "Studies in Texts. Gen. 3.5," *Theo* 58 (1955) 226-228.

Genesis 3:6

*Frederick Field, "Dr. Field's Old Testament Revision Notes. Transcribed from the Author's MS. by the Rev. John Henry Burn, B.D., I.," *ET* 30 (1918-19) 85-86. *[3:6]*

Francis J. Cosgrove, "Some Notes on Genesis iii, 6," *MH* 3 (1946-47) #4, 22-24.

Genesis 3:7

H. F. Lutz, "The *ḥagoroth* of Genesis 3[7], *JAOS* 42 (1922) 208-209.

Genesis 3:8

Anonymous, "Observations on Genesis III. 8," *MR* 1 (1818) 57-58.

Genesis 3:9

B. D. Alexander, "Genesis III. 9: Where art Thou?" *ET* 2 (1890-91) 140-141.

Genesis 3:14-19

Franklin Johnson, "The Curse upon Nature," *BQR* 6 (1884) 141-154. *[3:14-19]*

Franklin Johnson, "The Curse upon Nature," *JLTQ* 1 (1884) 406-416. *[3:14-19]*

Genesis 3:14-15

Samuel Cox, "Adam's Gospel. Genesis iii. 14, 15," *Exp, 2nd Ser.,* 7 (1884) 56-66.

B. Rigaux, "The Woman and Her Seed in Genesis 3:14-15," *TD* 6 (1958) 25-31.

Genesis 3:14

H. C. Ackerman, "Gen. 3:14," *ATR* 3 (1920-21) 328-329.

Genesis 3:15

T. J. Sawyer, "The Promise Made to the Patriarchs," *UQGR, N.S.,* 14 (1877) 5-22. *[3:15]*

Anonymous, "The Great Text Commentary. The Great Texts of Genesis," *ET* 10 (1898-99) 111-114. *[3:15]*

Anonymous, "Comparative Translation: Genesis 3:15. A Study in Modernizing the English Bible," *BW* 23 (1904) 130-131.

*Eb. Nestle, "Three Notes on Skinner's 'Genesis'," *ET* 24 (1912-13) 91-92. *[3:15]*

Francis X. Peirce, "Mary Alone is 'The Woman' of Genesis 3:15," *CBQ* 2 (1940) 245-252.

P. E. Kretzmann, "A Recent Catholic Explanation of Genesis 3:15," *CTM* 12 (1941) 948-949.

†C. Lattey, "The Protoevangelium (Gen. iii. 15)," *Scrip* 3 (1948) 21-22.

Francis X. Peirce, "The Protoevangelium," *CBQ* 13 (1951) 239-252. *[3:15]*

Antonine DeGuglielmo, "Mary in the Protoevangelium," *CBQ* 14 (1952) 104-115. *[3:15]*

R. A. Martin, "The Earliest Messianic Interpretation of Genesis 3:15," *JBL* 84 (1965) 425-427.

Genesis 3:16

*G. H. Box, "Genesis IV. and III. 16: A Suggestion," *ET* 10 (1898-99) 425-426.

*T. K. Cheyne, "Genesis IV. 7, III. 16, and IV. 1," *ET* 10 (1898-99) 476.

*Max L. Margolis, "Short Notes on the Greek Old Testament," *AJSL* 25 (1908-09) 174. *[3:16]*

Lucien Ouellette, "Woman's Doom in Gen. 3:16," *CBQ* 12 (1950) 389-399.

Genesis 3:19

W. B. Griffiths, "Genesis III. 19," *ET* 62 (1950-51) 61.

Genesis 3:21

H. W. Congdon, "Coats of Skin," *CFL, 3rd Ser.,* 28 (1922) 28-30. *[3:21]*

Genesis 3:22-23

*Edward C. Meyer and Simon J. DeVries, "Preparation for Biblical Preaching. IV," *JMTSO* 6 (1967-68) #2, 22-34. *[3:22-23]*

Genesis 3:22

Evangelus, "Illustration of Genesis III. 22," *MR* 2 (1819) 262-263.

W. Collins, "Genesis III. 22," *ET* 28 (1916-17) 94.

H. Th. Obbink, "The Explanation of Genesis III. 22," *ET* 28 (1916-17) 379.

Lester J. Kuyper, "'To know Good and Evil'," *Interp* 1 (1947) 490-492. *[3:22a]*

Genesis 3:24

*H. F. Talbot, "The Fight between Bel and the Dragon, and the Flaming Sword which turned Every Way (Gen. iii, 24) *Translated from a Chaldean Tablet,*" *SBAT* 5 (1876-77) 1-21.

Genesis Chapters 4-8

W. E. Denham, "Lectures on Genesis: Lecture III. The Destruction of the Race. Gen. 4:1-8:22," *SWJT* 6 (1922) #2, 13-24.

Genesis Chapters 4-5

*George H. Barton, "A Sumerian Source of the Fourth and Fifth Chapters of Genesis," *JBL* 34 (1915) 1-16.

*Herbert H. Gowen, "The Cainite and Sethite Genealogies of Gen. 4 and 5," *ATR* 2 (1919-20) 326-327.

Genesis Chapter 4

William R. Harper, "The Fratricide: The Cainite Civilization. Genesis IV," *BW* 3 (1894) 264-274.

*Arthur T. Pierson, "Marginal Commentary: Notes on Genesis," *HR* 27 (1894) 260-263. *[4:1-4, 7, 10, 13, 16, 23, 26]*

*W. Gunther Plaut, "Notes From a New Commentary on The Torah," *CCARJ* 14 (1967) #4, 64-69. *[Chap. 4, pp. 64-67]*

Genesis 4:1-16

G. Buchanan Gray, "Cain's Sacrifice: A New Theory," *Exp, 8th Ser.,* 21 (1921) 161-182. *[4:1-16]*

Wade P. Huie Jr., "The Mark of Cain. Genesis 4:1-16," *CTSB* 59 (1966) 4-6.

Genesis 4:1-10

A. H. Sayce, "The Archaeology of the Book of Genesis," *ET* 21 (1909-10) 519-521. *[4:1-10]*

Genesis 4:1-8

Morton S. Enslin, "Cain and Prometheus," *JBL* 86 (1967) 88-90. *[4:1-8]*

Genesis 4:1

Thomas Tyler, "The Memorial Name,—Gen. iv. 1," *JSL, 4th Ser.,* 7 (1865) 453.

*T. K. Cheyne, "Genesis IV. 7, III. 16, and IV. 1," *ET* 10 (1898-99) 476.

*Dom Adalbert Amandolini, "The Nomen Tetragrammaton in Genesis IV. 1," *DR* 132 (1903) 336-340.

Eb. Nestle, "The Septuagint Rendering of Gen. 4:1," *AJT* 9 (1905) 519.

Genesis 4:3-16

*Geza Vermes, "The Targumic Versions of Genesis iv 3-16," *ALUOS* 3 (1961-62) 81-114.

Genesis 4:3-8

Ernest W. Altvater, "Cain and Abel: Gen. 4:3-8," *BW* 32 (1908) 277-280.

Genesis 4:3-4

*Samuel Belkin, "Some Obscure Tradition Mutually Clarified in Philo and Rabbinic Literature," *JQR, 75th,* (1964-65) 80-103. [3. Bringing the First-fruits (Gen. 4:3-4), pp. 86-87]

Genesis 4:5

O. R. Sellers, "Cain's Emotions," *JBL* 70 (1951) xi. *[4:5b]*

Genesis 4:6-7

*Paul Haupt, "An Ancient Protest Against the Curse of Eve," *PAPS* 50 (1911) 505-517. *[Gen. 4:6-7, pp. 507-508]*

Genesis 4:7-8

R. C. Ford, "Cain's Envy, Genesis IV 7, 8," *ET* 2 (1890-91) 181.

Genesis 4:7

J. W. Donaldson, "On the Interpretation of Genesis Chap. iv. 7," *JSL, 1st Ser.,* 4 (1849) 124-129.

*E. Paret, "James iv. 5, in Connection with Genesis iv. 7," *AThR, N.S.,* 4 (1866) 292-298.

G. W. Samson, "New Reading of Familiar Texts in the Old Testament. No. I," *HR* 8 (1884-85) 106-107. *[Chap 4:7]*

*A. H. Sayce, "Balaam's Prophecy (Numbers XXIV. 17-24) and the God Seth," *AJSL* 4 (1887-88) 1-6. *[Gen. 4:7, p. 5]*

Alexander Stewart, "Requests and Replies," *ET* 1 (1889-90) 255-256. *[4:7]*

Anonymous, "The Great Text Commentary. The Great Texts of Genesis," *ET* 10 (1898-99) 161-163. *[4:7]*

*G. H. Box, "Genesis IV. and III. 16: A Suggestion," *ET* 10 (1898-99) 425-426.

*T. K. Cheyne, "Genesis IV. 7, III. 16, and IV. 1," *ET* 10 (1898-99) 476.

Eb. Nestle, "Genesis IV. 7," *ET* 19 (1907-08) 139.

*A. Van Hoonacker, "Expository Notes," *Exp, 8th Ser.,* 9 (1915) 452-459. [1. Gen. iv. 7: *"...And if thou doest not well..."* pp. 452-454]

*Frederick Field, "Dr. Field's Old Testament Revision Notes. Transcribed from the Author's MS. by the Rev. John Henry Burn, B.D., I.," *ET* 30 (1918-19) 85-86. *[4:7]*

Maurice A. Canney, "Ḥaṭṭā'th (Gen. IV. 7)," *ET* 36 (1924-25) 525-526.

*Israel W. Slotki, "Genesis IV. 7 and a Form of Hebrew Poetry," *ET* 38 (1926-27) 329-330.

Edward A. Mangan, "A Discussion of Gen. 4:7," *CBQ* 6 (1944) 91-93.

*G. R. Driver, "Theological and Philological Problems in the Old Testament," *JTS* 47 (1946) 156-166. [I. (ii) *Cain's Warning* (Gen. 4:7), pp. 157-160]

G. R. Castellino, "Genesis IV 7," *VT* 10 (1960) 442-445.

Genesis 4:8

Anonymous, "Morsels of Criticism," *CongML* 4 (1821) 134-135 *[Chap 4:8]*

T. J. Buckton, "Genesis IV. 8," *JSL, 4th Ser.,* 6 (1864-65) 464-465.

W. H. McClellan, "The Original Text of Genesis 4:8a," *JBL* 56 (1937) xii.

Albert Ehrman, "What Did Cain Say to Abel?" *JQR, N.S.,* 53 (1961-62) 164-167. *[Chap 4:8]*

Genesis 4:9

Anonymous, "The Great Text Commentary. The Great Texts of Genesis," *ET* 10 (1898-99) 204-207. *[4:9]*

Genesis 4:11-17

A. H. Sayce, "The Archaeology of the Book of Genesis, Chapter iv," *ET* 22 (1910-11) 426-430, 516-519. *[4:11-17]*

Genesis 4:11

Nelson Glueck, "A Note on Gen. 4:11," *JPOS* 13 (1933) 101-102.

Genesis 4:13-15

John A. Maynard, "The Mark of Cain (Gen. 4:13-15)," *ATR* 2 (1919-20) 325-326.

Genesis 4:15

Anonymous, "The Mark upon Cain," *JSL, 1st Ser.,* 5 (1850) 223-224. *[4:15]*

K. G. Manz, "Ἑπτὰ ἐκδικούμενα παραλύσει Gen. 4, 15," *CTM* 6 (1935) 775-777.

Genesis 4:17-24

*H. E. Ryle, "The Early Narratives of Genesis," *ET* 3 (1891-92) 209-214. [V. The Genealogy of the Cainites, Chap. iv. 17-24, pp. 213-214]

Genesis 4:17

*Fritz Hommel, "Assyriological Notes," *SBAP* 17 (1895) 199-207. [§12b. Gen. iv. 17, p. 207]

Genesis 4:18

*A. H. Sayce, "Miscellaneous Notes," *ZK* 2 (1885) 399-405. [10. *Irad* and *Enoch* in Genesis, p. 404] *[4:18]*

Genesis 4:19-20

Anonymous, "Lamech," *JSL, 1st Ser.,* 7 (1851) 451-453. *[Chap 4:19, 20]*

Genesis 4:20

James Kennedy, "Genesis IV. 20," *ET* 28 (1916-17) 189-190.

Genesis 4:23-24

H. P., "The Address of Lamech, Genesis IV. 23, 24," *JSL, 3rd Ser.,* 6 (1857-58) 425-427.

Henry C. Hammond, "The Song of the Sword. A Study of Genesis 4:23-24," *USR* 37 (1925-26) 58-68.

*Samuel Belkin, "Some Obscure Tradition Mutually Clarified in Philo and Rabbinic Literature," *JQR, 75th,* (1964-65) 80-103. [7. Cain to be Avenged (Gen. 4:23-24), pp. 96-98]

Patrick D. Miller Jr., "*Yeled* in the Song of Lamech," *JBL* 85 (1966) 477-478. *[Chap 4:23-24]*

Genesis 4:24

Anonymous, "The Great Text Commentary. The Great Texts of Genesis," *ET* 10 (1898-99) 260-264. *[4:24]*

*Jacob Neusner, "History and Midrash," *Jud* 9 (1960) 47-54. [Gen. 4:24, pp. 49-50]

Genesis 4:26

Edgar C. S. Gibson, "The Days of Enos, Genesis iv. 26," *Exp, 2nd Ser.,* 7 (1884) 230-237.

Anonymous, "Exegetical Suggestions and Opinions. Gen. iv. 26," *CFL, O.S.,* 1 (1897) 22-23.

J. Iverach Munro, "Genesis IV. 26," *ET* 20 (1908-09) 563.

S[amuel] Sandmel, "Interpretations of Genesis 4:26b," *JBL* 72 (1953) xviii.

Samuel Sandmel, "Genesis 4:26b," *HUCA* 32 (1961) 19-29.

Genesis Chapters 5-6

Arthur T. Pierson, "Marginal Commentary: Notes on Genesis," *HR* 27 (1894) 355-358. *[Chaps. 5-6]*

Genesis Chapter 5

†Granville Sharp, "Longevity of the Antediluvian Patriarchs as recorded in the Fifth Chapter of Genesis," *MMBR* 33 (1812) 112-114.

*Frederic Gardiner, "The Chronological Value of the Genealogy in Genesis V," *BFER* 22 (1873) 566-575.

*Frederic Gardiner, "The Chronological Value of the Genealogy in Genesis V," *BS* 30 (1873) 323-333.

*Robert Balgarnie, "'As Old as Methuselah': A Chapter in Antediluvian Chronology. Genesis V," *Exp, 1st Ser.,* 8 (1878) 449-461.

William R. Harper, "The Long-Lived Antediluvians. Genesis V," *BW* 3 (1894) 326-335.

*J[ohn] D. D[avis], "Tribes Individualized in the O.T. The Principle not Ignorable in Gen. v. and xi.," *CFL, N.S.,* 5 (1902) 191-192.

A. H. Sayce, "The Archaeology of the Book of Genesis. Chapter v," *ET* 22 (1910-11) 557-559.

*James B. Tannehill, "The Chronology of Genesis V and XI," *CFL, 3rd Ser.,* 39 (1933) 236-239, 293-296, 331-334.

Genesis 5:16

*A. H. Sayce, "Miscellaneous Notes," *ZK* 2 (1885) 399-405. [10. *Irad* and *Enoch* in Genesis, p. 404] *[5:16]*

Genesis 5:21-24

Samuel Cox, "Enoch's Gospel. Genesis v. 21-24; Hebrews xi. 5, 6; Jude 14, 15," *Exp, 2nd Ser.,* 7 (1884) 321-345.

Genesis 5:22

Alex. A. Duncan, "'After He Begat Methuselah' (Gen. v. 22)," *ET* 29 (1917-18) 523.

Genesis 5:24

Anonymous, "Exegetical Notes. Genesis v. 24," *MQR, 3rd Ser.,* 45 (1919) 150.

*John Muir, "The Significance of אִין in Genesis v. 24 and Psalm XXXIX. 13," *ET* 50 (1938-39) 476-477.

Genesis 5:29

W[illiam] R. Harper, "Genesis v. 29," *ONTS* 4 (1884-85) 279-281.

E. G. Goodenough, "The Interpretation of the Name Noah in Gen. 5:29," *JBL* 48 (1929) 138-143.

J. A. Morgenstern, "A Note on Genesis 5:29," *JBL* 49 (1930) 306-309.

Genesis 6-9

William R. Harper, "The Hebrew Stories of the Deluge. Genesis VI-IX," *BW* 4 (1894) 20-31.

Genesis 6-8

Arthur T. Pierson, "Marginal Commentary: Notes on Genesis," *HR* 27 (1894) 448-451. [Gen. 6:8-9, 13-15, 17, 18; Chap. 7; Chap. 8]

George Frederick Wright, "What the Bible Teaches Concerning the Flood: Genesis VI.-VIII.," *HR* 45 (1903) 298-304.

Genesis Chapter 6

C. H. H. Wright, "The Spirits in Prison and the Sons of God. (1 Pet. iii. 18-20, and Gen. vi.)," *BFER* 25 (1876) 51-67.

William R. Harper, "The Sons of God and the Daughters of Men. Genesis VI," *BW* 3 (1894) 440-448.

Genesis 6:1-8

Anonymous, "The Sons of God and the Daughters of Men," *ONTS* 15 (1892) 78-79. *[6:1-8]*

A. H. Sayce, "The Archaeology of the Book of Genesis. Chapter vi," *ET* 23 (1911-12) 167-170. *[6:1-8]*

Genesis 6:1-5

J. C. Knight, "The Giants and the Sons of God. A Criticism upon Genesis VI. 1-5," *JSL, 5th Ser.,* 2 (1867-68) 123-128.

Genesis 6:1-4

Anonymous, "Select passages of Scripture considered," *OQR* 3 (1847-48) 371-372. *[6:1-4]*

C. F. Keil, "The Marriages of the Sons of God with the Daughters of Men. *An exegetical investigation on Gen.* 6:1-4," *ER* 7 (1855-56) 497-526.

H. N. B., "The Exegesis of Genesis vi. 1-4," *JSL, 3rd Ser.,* 8 (1858-59) 75-89. *(Review)*

Anonymous, "The Sons of God. Genesis VI. 1-4," *MQR, 2nd Ser.,* 3 (1881) 556-561.

Emil G. Kraeling, "The Significance and Origin of Gen 6:1-4," *JNES* 6 (1947) 193-208.

N. H. Tur-Sinai, "The Riddle of Genesis VI. 1-4," *ET* 71 (1959-60) 348-350.

Meredith G. Kline, "Divine Kingship and Genesis 6:1-4," *WTJ* 24 (1961-62) 187-204.

Genesis 6:1-3

Haim Schwarzbaum, "The Overcrowded Earth," *Numen* 4 (1957) 59-74. [Part III. - Gen. 1:3, pp. 72-74]

Genesis 6:2

*Stephen H. Stackpole, "Sons of God. A Study of the Scriptural Uses of the Title," *BQR* 2 (1880) 315-333. [I. The Uses of the Title in the Old Testament, 2. Men, pp. 318-321. (Gen. 6:2)]

*Anonymous, "Genesis VI. 2, 4," *MQR, 2nd Ser.,* 4 (1882) 182.

James E. Coleran, "The Sons of God in Genesis 6, 2," *ThSt* 2 (1941) 488-509.

*John L. McKenzie, "The Divine Sonship of the Angels," *CBQ* 5 (1943) 293-300. [Gen. 6:2, pp. 294-295]

Genesis 6:3

A. [H.] Sayce, "Genesis VI. 3," *JSL, 4th Ser.,* 6 (1864-65) 467-468.

C. J. Elliott, "Short Comments on Difficult Passages in the Pentateuch," *CM* 7 (1878) 43-45. *[6:3]*

J. F. Morton, "An Exposition of Genesis VI, 3," *BQR* 1 (1879) 332-334.

*C. R. Brown, "1 Sam. 2:10 as illustrative of Gen 6:3," *JBL* 5 (1885) 91.

*G. H. Skipwith, "The Relative שׁ in Genesis," *JQR* 8 (1895-96) 706-707. *[6:3]*

G. Margoliouth, "A Fresh Explanation of Genesis VI. 3," *Exp, 5th Ser.,* 8 (1898) 33-37.

George Ricker Berry, "The Interpretation of Gen. 6:3," *AJSL* 16 (1899-1900) 47-49.

George Ricker Berry, "A Note on Gen. 6:3," *AJSL* 17 (1900-01) 128.

Alfred Guillaume, "A Note on the Meaning of Gen. 6:3," *AJSL* 56 (1939) 415-416.

C. A. Ben-Mordecai, "B'Shaggam: An Obscure Phrase in Gen. 6:3," *AJSL* 57 (1940) 306-307.

E[phraim] A. Speiser, "*YDWN,* Gen. 6:3,:" *JBL* 75 (1956) 126-129.

Virgil H. Todd, "Exegetical Note on Genesis 6:3, *CS* 6 (1958-59) #3, 3, 6.

Genesis 6:4

*Anonymous, "Genesis VI. 2, 4," *MQR, 2nd Ser.,* 4 (1882) 182.

*T. K. Cheyne, "Notes on מַבּוּל, נְפִילִיו, etc.," *AJSL* 3 (1886-87) 175-176. *[6:4]*

*Cyrus H. Gordon, "Marginal Notes on the Ancient Middle East," *JKF* 2 (1952-53) 50-61 [VI. Babyloniaca: c. קַנִים, pp. 56-57] *[6:4]*

Genesis 6:6

*Howard Crosby, "Interpretation of Some Difficult Texts," *HR* 13 (1887) 217-218. *[6:6]*

Genesis 6:9-22

A. H. Sayce, "Archaeology of the Book of Genesis. Chapter vi," *ET* 23 (1911-12) 275-278. *[6:9-22]*

Genesis 6:9

A. Hampden Lee, "The Righteousness of Noah, Genesis VI. 9," *ET* 2 (1890-91) 180-181.

H. W. Florance, "Genesis VI. 9," *ET* 4 (1892-93) 228-229.

Genesis 6:14

T. K. Cheyne, "Gen. vi. 14, Gopherwood," *ZAW* 18 (1898) 163-164.

Genesis 6:16

F[rederick] Field, "Note on Gen. vi. 16," *JP* 3 (1871) 327.

*T. K. Cheyne, "Notes on Gen. VI, 16, Isa. XVIII, 1, and Prov. XXX. 15," *SBAP* 23 (1901) 141-144. [I. *Gen.* vi, 16, pp. 141-142]

J. F. Armstrong, "A Critical Note on Genesis VI 16aα, *VT* 10 (1960) 328-333.

Genesis 6:17

Oswald T. Allis, "The Flood of Waters (Genesis vi. 17)," *PTR* 16 (1917) 103-107.

Genesis 6:26

Joseph Bruneau, "Biblical Research. IV. Textual Criticism and Exegesis 2.," *AER* 18 (1898) 282-283. *[6:26]*

Genesis 7:4-24

A. H. Sayce, "The Archaeology of the Book of Genesis. Chapter vii," *ET* 25 (1913-14) 312-314. *[7:4-24]*

Genesis 7:19-20

C. J. Elliott, "Short Comments on Difficult Passages in the Pentateuch," *CM* 7 (1878) 240-242. *[7:19, 20]*

Genesis Chapters 8-9

Arthur T. Pierson, "Marginal Commentary: Notes on Genesis," *HR* 27 (1894) 553-556. *[Chaps. 8-9]*

W. Gunther Plaut, "Commentary On Passages From *Genesis* 8 and 9," *CCARJ* 15 (1968) #1, 89-93.

Genesis 8:1-19

A. H. Sayce, "The Archaeology of the Book of Genesis. Chapter viii," *ET* 25 (1913-14) 565-568. *[8:1-19]*

Genesis 8:2-5

George F. Howe, "The Raven Speaks," *JASA* 21 (1969) 22-25.*[8:2-5]*

Genesis 8:7

Henry Heras, "'The Crow' of Noe," *CBQ* 10 (1948) 131-139. *[8:7ʊ]*

Genesis 8:8-11

W. O. E. Oesterley, "The Dove with the Olive-Leaf (Gen. VIII. 8-11)," *ET* 18 (1906-07) 377-378. *[Chap 8:8-11]*

Genesis 8:18-22

*A. H. Sayce, "The Archaeology of the Book of Genesis Chapter viii and ix.," *ET* 26 (1914-15) 421-424. *[Chap 8:18-22, pp. 421-422]*

Genesis Chapters 9-11

W. E. Denham, "Lecture on Genesis—Lecture IV. The New Start of the Race. Gen. 9-11," *SWJT* 6 (1922) #3, 39-51.

Genesis Chapter 9

*J[ohn] D. D[avis], "Tribes Individualized in the O.T. The Principle not Ignorable in Gen. v. and xi.," *CFL, N.S.,* 5 (1902) 191-192.

Genesis 9:1-17

*A. H. Sayce, "The Archaeology of the Book of Genesis Chapter viii and ix.," *ET* 26 (1914-15) 421-424. *[Chap 9:1-17, pp. 422-424]*

Genesis 9:6

*J. M. C., "Thoughts on Genesis IX. 6: in relation to capital punishment," *JSL, 4th Ser.,* 5 (1864) 314-320.

*J. M. C., "Capital Punishment and Genesis IX. 6," *JSL 4th Ser.,* 6 (1864-65) 314-319.

Genesis 9:11-17

W. E. Gladstone, "The Iris of Homer, and her Relation to Genesis ix. 11-17," *ContR* 32 (1878) 140-152.

Genesis 9:13

*A. H. Sayce, "Miscellaneous Notes," *ZA* 2 (1887) 331-340. [16. The bow of the Deluge, p. 333] *[9:13]*

Genesis 9:18-29

*H. E. Ryle, "The Early Narratives of Genesis," *ET* 3 (1891-92) 498-504. [VIII: Noah as the Vine-Dresser and His Three Sons, Genesis ix. 18-29, pp. 498-499]

Genesis 9:18-28

A. H. Sayce, "The Archaeology of the Book of Genesis. Chapter ix," *ET* 26 (1914-15) 558-560. *[9:18-28]*

Genesis 9:18-27

J. Ernest Shufelt, "Noah's Curse and Blessing. Gen. 9:18-27," *CTM* 17 (1946) 737-742.

Genesis 9:25-27

*R. D. C. Robbins, "Explanation of Some Passages in Genesis," *BS* 8 (1851) 58-64. *[9:25-27]*

Genesis 9:27

*Arthur T. Pierson, "Marginal Commentary: Notes on Genesis," *HR* 28 (1894) 63-66. *[9:27]*

Genesis Chapters 10-50

[Nathaniel] Berwash, "Analytic study of Genesis x - l," *CMR* 6 (1894) 162-170.

Genesis Chapters 10-15

A. H. Sayce, "Archaeological Commentary on Genesis," *ET* 8 (1896-97) 82-85, 180-182, 256-259, 356-359, 461-465. *[Chaps. 10-15]*

Genesis Chapters 10-11

*Arthur T. Pierson, "Marginal Commentary: Notes on Genesis," *HR* 28 (1894) 63-66. *[Chaps. 10-11]*

Genesis Chapter 10

*†Anonymous, "Allwood's Literary Antiquities of Greece," *BCQTR* 15 (1800) 539-549, 608-618; 16 (1800) 65-77. *[Chap. 10]*

*Robert Dick Wilson, "The Date of Genesis X," *PRR* 1 (1890) 252-281.

*H. E. Ryle, "The Early Narratives of Genesis," *ET* 3 (1891-92) 498-504. [VIII: The Table of the Nations, Chapter x, pp. 499-501]

Anonymous, "The Table of the Nations, Gen. 10," *ONTS* 15 (1892) 268.

J. A. Howlett, "The Ethnological Table of Moses," *IER, 3rd Ser.,* 14 (1893) 213-233. *[Chap. 10]*

A. H. Sayce, "The Mosaic Age of Genesis X.," *HR* 45 (1903) 483-486.

*Morris Jastrow Jr., "The Hamites and Semites in the Tenth Chapter of Genesis," *PAPS* 43 (1904) 173-207.

*E. Robertson, "Notes on Javan," *JQR* 20 (1907-08) 466-508. *[Chap. 10]*

*E. Robertson, "Notes on Javan. II.," *JQR* 20 (1907-08) 812-824. *[Chap. 10]*

F. C. Burkitt, "Note on the Table of Nations (Genesis X)," *JTS* 21 (1919-20) 233-238.

A. H. Sayce, "The Tenth Chapter of Genesis," *JBL* 44 (1925) 193-202.

*Basil F. C. Atkinson, "The Indo-European Peoples of Genesis X," *EQ* 1 (1929) 121-129.

*G. R. Gair, "'Syro-Mesopotamian Ethnology: As Outlined in a Biblical Document'," *EQ* 8 (1936) 225-232. *[Chap. 10]*

J. Simons, "The 'Table of Nations' (Gen. X): Its General Structure and Meaning," *OTS* 10 (1954) 155-184.

R. Laird Harris, "Racial Dispersion," *JASA* 7 (1955) #3, 52-54. *[Chap. 10]*

D. J. Wiseman, "Genesis 10: Some Archaeological Considerations," *JTVI* 87 (1955) 13-24, 116-118. [(Discussion, pp. 113-115) (Communication by F. F. Bruce, pp. 115-116)]

Michael C. Astour, "Sabtah and Sabteca: Ethiopian Pharaoh Names in Genesis 10," *JBL* 84 (1965) 422-425.

Genesis 10:1-2

A. H. Sayce, "The Archaeology of the Book of Genesis. Chapter x," *ET* 27 (1915-16) 136-138. *[10:1, 2]*

Genesis 10:2-4

*A. H. Sayce, "Geographical Notes," *JRAS* (1921) 47-55. [Javan, (Gen. 10:2, 4), pp. 53-54]

Genesis 10:3-10

A. H. Sayce, "The Archaeology of the Book of Genesis. Chapter x," *ET* 28 (1916-17) 213-216. *[10:3-10]*

Genesis 10:3

*A. Benisch, "Correspondence," *JSL, 1st Ser.,* 3 (1849) 168-170. *[10:3]*

Genesis 10:6-14

George Rawlinson, "Notices of Egypt in Genesis X. 6, 13, 14," *ONTS* 5 (1885-86) 86.

Genesis 10:8-10

George Rawlinson, "Notices of Babylon in Genesis X. 8-10," *ONTS* 5 (1885-86) 35-36.

Genesis 10:8

Henry Crossley, "Nimrod.—Genesis X. 8," *JSL, 3rd Ser.,* 12 (1860-61) 462-464.

*John P. Peters, "Miscellaneous Notes," *AJSL* 1 (1884-85) 115-119. [כּוּשׁ in Gen. 2:13, 10:8, p. 117]

Genesis 10:10-11

*Anonymous, "On the Origin of the Name Assyria.—Gen. x:10. 11," *SPR* 3 (1849-50) 630-637.

C. J. Elliott, "Short Comments on Difficult Passages in the Pentateuch," *CM* 7 (1878) 317-319. *[10:10, 11]*

Genesis 10:10

Edgar James Banks, "Warka, the Ruins of Erech (Gen. 10:10)," *BW* 25 (1905) 302-305.

*J. Dyneley Prince, "Note on Akkad," *JBL* 25 (1906) 55-57. *[10:10]*

E. G. Kraeling, "A Note on Calneh (Gen. 10:10)," *JBL* 53 (1934) xi.

E. G. Kraeling, "Calneh, Gen 10:10," *JBL* 54 (1935) 233-234.

*W[illiam] F[oxwell] Albright. "a) The End of Calneh in Shinar," *JBL* 62 (1943) v-vi. *[10:10]*

W[illiam] F[oxwell] Albright, "The End of 'Calneh in Shinar'," *JNES* 3 (1944) 254-255. *[10:10]*

*A. S. Yahuda, "Calneh in Shinar," *JBL* 65 (1946) 325-327. *[10:10]*

Genesis 10:11-15

A. H. Sayce, "The Archaeology of the Book of Genesis. Chapter x," *ET* 29 (1917-18) 71-73. *[10:11-15]*

Genesis 10:12

Eb. Nestle, "Resen.   Genesis x. 12," *ET* 15 (1903-04) 476.

Genesis 10:16-17

A. H. Sayce, "The Archaeology of the Book of Genesis. Chapter x," *ET* 29 (1917-18) 135-137. *[10:16-17]*

Genesis 10:16

*K. V. Mathew, "Ancient Religions of the Fertile Crescent—and the Sanathana Dhrama," *IJT* 8 (1959) 83-90. [Hivites (Gen. 10:16), pp. 85-86]

Genesis 10:19

*E. Power, "The site of Pentapolis," *B* 11 (1930) 23-62, 149-182. *[10:19]*

Genesis 10:21

C., "Eber and the Children of Eber," *JSL, 4th Ser.,* 6 (1864-65) 179-181. *[10:21]*

Genesis 10:22-24

*Fritz Hommel, "Arpakshad," *ET* 8 (1896-97) 283-284. *[10:22, 24]*

Genesis 10:24

*T. K. Cheyne, "Arpachshad," *ZAW* 17 (1897) 190. *[10:24]*

Genesis 10:25

Joseph Thompson, "The Division of the Earth in the Days of Peleg," *JSL, 1st Ser.*, 2 (1848) 164-166. *[10:25]*

Genesis 10:30

*Francis Brown, "Geographical," *PR* 3 (1882) 169. *[10:30]*

*C[laude] R. Conder, "Notes on Bible Geography. V. *Sephar*," *PEFQS* 37 (1905) 74. *[10:30]*

*Samuel Krauss, "Service Tree in Bible and Talmud and in Modern Palestine," *HUCA* 1 (1924) 179-217. *[10:30]*

Genesis Chapter 11

Margaret D. Gibson, "The Confusion of Tongues," *ET* 15 (1903-04) 473-474. *[Chap. 11]*

*James B. Tannehill, "The Chronology of Genesis V and XI," *CFL, 3rd Ser.*, 39 (1933) 236-239.

Genesis 11:1-9

*H. E. Ryle, "The Early Narratives of Genesis," *ET* 3 (1891-92) 498-504. [VIII: The Tower of Babel, Chapter xi. 1-9, pp. 501-502]

R. W. Dale, "The Tower of Babel. Gen. XI, 1-9," *Exp, 5th Ser.*, 3 (1896) 1-14.

*John P. Peters, "Notes on the Old Testament," *JBL* 15 (1896) 106-117. [1. The Site of the Tower of Babel (Gen 11:1-9), pp. 106-109]

J. Cheston Morris, "On Genesis xi. 1-9 as a Poetic Fragment," *PAPS* 35 (1896) 305-306.

William G. Heidt, "A Lesson by Satire—Genesis 11:1-9," *BibT* #31 (1967) 2191-2194.

*Samuel Noah Kramer, "The 'Babel of Tongues': A Sumerian Version," *JAOS* 88 (1968) 108-111. *[Ash. 1924.475//Gen. 11:1-9(?)]*

Genesis 11:1

*Samuel Noah Kramer, "Man's Golden Age: A Sumerian Parallel to Genesis XI. 1," *JAOS* 63 (1943) 191-194.

Genesis 11:2

*C. J. Ball, "The Name Shinar, Genesis xi, 2; and the meaning of זמרת in Genesis xliii, 11," *SBAP* 17 (1895) 130.

E. G. Kraeling, "The Significance of Genesis 11:2," *JBL* 66 (1947) x-xi.

Emil G. Kraeling, "Miqqedem in Gen. XI:2," *JQR, N.S.*, 38 (1947-48) 161-165.

Genesis 11:4-6

A. Clarke, "Illustration of Genesis XI. 4-6," *MR* 6 (1823) 420-423.

Genesis 11:5

*Arthur T. Pierson, "Marginal Commentary: Notes on Genesis," *HR* 28 (1894) 163-166. *[11:5]*

Genesis 11:7-9

*Arthur T. Pierson, "Marginal Commentary: Notes on Genesis," *HR* 28 (1894) 163-166. *[11:7-9]*

Genesis 11:9

*S. C. Ylvisaker, "Some Old Testament Difficulties," *WLQ* 54 (1957) 262-264. [*Bābel,*—BABEL, Gen. 11:9, pp. 262-263]

Genesis 11:10-13

*T. K. Cheyne, "Arpachshad," *ZAW* 17 (1897) 190. *[11:10-13]*

Genesis 11:12ff.

*Fritz Hommel, "Arpakshad," *ET* 8 (1896-97) 283-284. *[11:12ff.]*

Genesis 11:10-26

*H. E. Ryle, "The Early Narratives of Genesis," *ET* 3 (1891-92) 498-504. [VIII: The Genealogy of the Shemites, Chapter xi. 10-26, pp. 502-504]

Genesis 11:18

*E. G. H. Kraeling, "Geographical Notes," *AJSL* 41 (1924-25) 193-194. [II. The Names "Rachel" and "Reu" (Gen. 11:18)]

Genesis 11:26

Frederic Gardiner, "Note on Genesis XI. 26," *BS* 34 (1877) 755-761.

Genesis 11:32

C. J. Elliott, "Short Comments on Difficult Passages in the Pentateuch," *CM* 7 (1878) 351-354. *[11:32]*

Genesis Chapter 12

*Arthur T. Pierson, "Marginal Commentary: Notes on Genesis," *HR* 28 (1894) 163-166. *[Chap. 12]*

*W. Gunther Plaut, "Thou art my Sister—A commentary on Genesis, Chapters 12, 20 and 26," *CCARJ* 10 (1962-63) #1, 26-30, 51.

Genesis 12:1-3

Anonymous, "The Great Text Commentary. The Great Texts of Genesis," *ET* 10 (1898-99) 317-320. *[12:1-3]*

Genesis 12:3

J. C.-M., "Illustrations of Scripture," *CongML* 22 (1839) 26-30. *[12:3]*

*John Forbes, "The Two Promises to Abraham," *Exp, 2nd Ser.,* 8 (1884) 200-206. *[12:3]*

*Oswald T. Allis, "The Blessing of Abraham," *PTR* 25 (1927) 263-298. *[12:3]*

Paul Rotenberry, "Blessing in the Old Testament, A Study of Genesis 12:3," *RestQ* 2 (1958) 32-36.

Genesis 12:6-37:1

*William R. Harper, "The Pentateuchal Question II. Gen. 12:6—37:1," *AJSL* 5 (1888-89) 243-291; 6 (1889-90) 109-138, 161-211.

Genesis 12:6

*Eric Burrows, "Note on Moreh, Gen. XII. 6 and Moriah, Gen. XXII. 2," *JTS* 41 (1940) 161.

Genesis 12:8-21

*H[ermann] Gunkel, "The Two Accounts of Hagar. (Genesis xvi. and xii., 8-21.) Specimen of an Historico-Theological Interpretation of Genesis," *Monist* 10 (1899-1900) 321-342. *(Trans. by W. H. Carruth)*

Genesis 12:10-13:1

(   ) Luke, "Abraham and Sarah in Egypt," *IES* 4 (1965) 3-19. *[Chaps. 12:10-13:1]*

Genesis 12:10-20

*Eugene H. Maly, "Genesis 12, 10-20; 20, 1-18; 26, 7-11 and the Pentateuchal Question," *CBQ* 18 (1956) 255-262.

Genesis 12:10

*Arthur T. Pierson, "Marginal Commentary: Notes on Genesis," *HR* 28 (1894) 247-251. *[12:10]*

Anonymous, "A Case of Eisegesis," *CFL, 3rd Ser.,* 1 (1904) 442-443. *[12:10ff.]*

Genesis 12:11-20

*Ben Zion Wacholder, "How Long Did Abram Stay in Egypt? A Study in Hellenistic, Qumran and Rabbinic Chronology," *HUCA* 35 (1964) 43-56. *[12:11-20]*

Genesis 12:15

*Alphonse Mingana, "Remarks on the Hebrew of Genesis," *Exp, 8th Ser.*,
11 (1916) 303-310. *[Chap 12:15]*

Genesis 12:16

*Joseph P. Free, "Abraham's Camels," *JNES* 3 (1944) 187-193. *[12:16]*

Genesis Chapter 13

*Arthur T. Pierson, "Marginal Commentary: Notes on Genesis," *HR* 28
(1894) 247-251. *[13:1, 4, 5-7, 10, 12, 13, 14, 17, 18]*

Genesis 13:10-12

Anonymous, "The Great Text Commentary. The Great Texts of Genesis,"
ET 10 (1898-99) 354-356. *[13:10-12]*

Genesis 13:10

*[Daniel Hy.] Haigh, "Assyriaca," *ZÄS* 7 (1869) 3-5. [Gen. 13:10, p. 5]

W. W. Moore, "The Incongruous Clause in Genesis XIII. 10," *ONTS* 6
(1886-87) 237-240.

Genesis 13:11

Anonymous, "The Great Text Commentary. The Great Texts of Genesis,"
ET 25 (1913-14) 539-543. *[13:11]*

Genesis Chapter 14

Frederick Tuch, "Remarks on Genesis, Chapter XIV," *JSL, 1st Ser.,* 2 (1848)
80-100. *(Trans. by Samuel Davidson)*

Howard Crosby, "Light on Important Texts. No. XVII," *HR* 6 (1881-82)
417-418. *[Chap. 14]*

Anonymous,   "Genesis   XIV,"   *ONTS*   12   (1891)   57-58.

A. H. Sayce, "The Fourteenth Chapter of Genesis," *ET* 4 (1892-93) 14-19.

S. R. Driver, "Professor Sayce and the 'Higher Criticism'," *ET* 4 (1892-93)
95-96. *[Chap. 14]*

A. H. Sayce, "The Higher Criticism and Oriental Archaeology, A Reply to Professor Driver," *ET* 4 (1892-93) 188-189.

J. W. Southern, "Tidal King of Nations," *ET* 4 (1892-93) 192. *[Chap. 14]*

James M. McCurdy, "Light on Scriptural Texts from Recent Discoveries. The Fourteenth of Genesis.—Abraham and the Cities of the Plain; Elam and Babylonia," *HR* 31 (1896) 311-314.

*C. H. W. Johns, "Note on 'Ancient Hebrew Tradition'," *Exp, 5th Ser.,* 8 (1898) 158-160 *[Chap. 14]*

Anonymous, "The Fourteenth Chapter of Genesis," *MR* 80 (1898) 138-141.

Parke P. Flournoy, "The Discovery of the Kings," *PQ* 13 (1899) 44-54. *[Chap. 14]*

M[orris] Jastrow [Jr.], "The Fourteenth Chapter of Genesis and Recent Research," *JQR* 13 (1900-01) 42-51.

*James A. Kelso, "The Antiquity of the divine title אל עליקן in Gen. 14," *JBL* 20 (1901) 50-55.

A. H. Sayce, "The Archaeology of Genesis XIV," *ET* 17 (1905-06) 498-504.

*Andrew Craig Robinson, "The Bearing of Recent Oriental Discoveries on Old Testament History," *JTVI* 38 (1906) 154-176. (Discussion, pp. 176-181) [Genesis XIV, pp. 160-165]

Gabriel Oussani, "The XIVth Chapter of Genesis in Light of Modern Biblical Criticism and Oriental Archaeological Discoveries. I," *NYR* 2 (1906-07) 204-243. *[Part II never published]*

A. H. Sayce, "New Light on Genesis XIV. from the Cuneiform Inscriptions," *HR* 53 (1907) 91-95.

C. J. Ball, "Note on the Name Chedor-Laomer (Kudur-Lagmar), Gen. XIV.," *ET* 19 (1907-08) 41-42.

*W. T. Pilter, "Some Amorite Personal Names in Genesis XIV: Bera', Birsha', Shinab, and Shemē'ber," *SBAP* 35 (1913) 205-226.

John Howard Raven, "Genesis XIV—The Orphan Chapter," *CFL, 3rd Ser.,* 14 (1914) 215-219.

W. T. Pilter, "The Amorite Personal Names in Genesis XIV. (II.) 'The Names of the Confederates of Abraham at Hebron, and of Melchizadek'," *SBAP* 36 (1914) 125-142, 212-230.

*G. H. Richardson, "A Plea for Unprejudiced Historical Biblical Study," *BW* 45 (1915) 160-165. *[Chap. 14]*

Carl Cornill, "The Rape of Abraham's Halo. *Genesis xiv,*" *CFL, 3rd Ser.,* 22 (1916) 110.

*Theophilus G. Pinches, "Some Texts of the Relph Collection, with Notes on Babylonian Chronology and Genesis xiv," *SBAP* 39 (1917) 4-15, 55-72, 89-98.

A. H. Sayce, "The Arioch of Genesis," *SBAP* 40 (1918) 92.

Theophilus G. Pinches, "The Arioch of Genesis," *SBAP* 40 (1918) 113-114.

*Robert Dick Wilson, "Scientific Biblical Criticism," *PTR* 17 (1919) 190-240, 401-456. [A. Examples of Critical Methods, Genesis 14, pp. 191-198]

H. H. B. Ayles, "An Interesting Historical Document," *ICMM* 19 (1922-23) 219-223. *[Chap. 14]*

G. B. Michell, "New Light on Genesis XIV," *BS* 83 (1926) 190-201.

W[illiam] F[oxwell] Albright, "The Historical Background of Genesis XIV," *JSOR* 10 (1926) 231-269.

*W[illiam] F[oxwell] Albright, "New Israelite and Pre-Israelite Sites: The Spring Trip of 1929," *BASOR* #35 (1929) 1-14. [The Fourteenth Chapter of Genesis pp. 10-12]

Nahum Levison, "Cuneiform Records and Genesis XIV," *GUOST* 6 (1929-33) 62-63.

Pere Mallon, "The Five Cities of the Plain (Genesis XIV)," *PEFQS* 64 (1932) 52-56.

*Michael C. Astour, "Political and Cosmic Symbolism in Genesis 14 and in its Babylonian Sources," *LIST* 3 (1966) 65-112. [1. When and By Whom Was Genesis 14 Written? 2. The Personal and Geographical Names in Genesis 14; 3. The Characters and Historical References in the "Chedorlaomer Texts"; 4. Religious Philosophy of History and Cosmic Symbolism]

Genesis 14:1-11

*A. H. Sayce, "Miscellaneous Notes," *ZA* 4 (1889) 382-393. [32. Genesis XIV. 1-11, p. 393]

Genesis 14:1

*J. Dyneley Prince, "The name Hammurabi," *JBL* 29 (1910) 21-23. *[14:1]*

A. Reubeni, "Tid'al *(Gen. xiv.1)*, Trg-tts and Trg-nns," *PEFQS* 64 (1932) 104-106.

Genesis 14:2

*Edgar J. Banks, "Who was the Biblical Arioch of the Days of Abraham?" *OC* 28 (1914) 557-559. *[14:2]*

Genesis 14:3

Edward Sapir, "Hittite *Siyanta* and Gen. 14:3," *AJSL* 55 (1938) 86-88.

Genesis 14:4

*Arthur T. Pierson, "Marginal Commentary: Notes on Genesis," *HR* 28 (1894) 247-251. *[14:4]*

Genesis 14:5-20

Arthur T. Pierson, "Marginal Commentary: Notes on Genesis," *HR* 28 (1894) 353-357. *[14:5, 6, 18, 20]*

Genesis 14:5

W[illiam] A[ldis] W[right], "Conjectural emendation of the Samaritan Targum on Gen. XIV. 5," *JP* 6 (1875-76) 170.

*George F. Moore, "Biblical Notes," *JBL* 16 (1897) 155-165. [Ashteroth Karnaim - Gen. 14:5, pp. 155-157]

Genesis 14:9

*J. Dyneley Prince, "The name Hammurabi," *JBL* 29 (1910) 21-23. *[14:9]*

Genesis 14:14

*Eb. Nestle, "Gen. XIV. 14, in the Epistle of Barnabas," *ET* 17 (1905-06) 139-140.

*Eb. Nestle, "318 - Eliezer," *ET* 17 (1905-06) 44-45. *[14:14]*

W. R. W. Gardner, "Genesis XIV. 14 (עד־דן)," *ET* 26 (1914-15) 523-524.

*S. Gevirtz, "Abram's 318," *IEJ* 19 (1969) 110-113. *[Chap 14:14]*

Genesis 14:15

*E. G. H. Kraeling, "Geographical Notes," *AJSL* 41 (1924-25) 193-194. [I. Hobah, Gen. 14:15]

Samuel Rosenblatt, "The meaning of *wayyḥaleq 'alehem* in Genesis 14:15," *JBL* 55 (1936) vii.

Genesis 14:17-24

Loren R. Fisher, "Abraham and His Priest-King," *JBL* 81 (1962) 264-270. *[14:17-24]*

Genesis 14:17-20

T. Romeyn Beck, "Melchizedek and His Significance in the History of Redemption. An Exegetical Outline," *RChR* 32 (1885) 47-55. *[14:17-20]*

Genesis 14:18-20

James E. Coleran, "The Sacrifice of Melchisedech," *ThSt* 1 (1940) 27-36. *[14:18-20]*

G. L. Della Vida, "The God El Elyon in Genesis 14:18-20," *JBL* 62 (1943) v.

G. L. Della Vida, "El 'Elion in Genesis 14:18-20," *JBL* 63 (1944) 1-9.

T. Hanlon, "The Most High God of Genesis 14:18-20," *Scrip* 11 (1959) 110-118.

Robert Houston Smith, "Abraham and Melchizedek (Gen 14:18-20)," *ZAW* 77 (1965) 129-153.

Genesis 14:18

Charles Edo Anderson, "Who was Melchizedek?—A Suggested Emendation of Gen. 14:18," *AJSL* 19 (1902-03) 176-177.

Genesis 14:19

A. H. Sayce, "'Blessed by Abram of the Most High God'," *AJSL* 6 (1889-90) 312-314. *[14:19]*

Genesis 14:20

*W. W. Martin, "Genesis XIV. 20; XV. 1," *ONTS* 11 (1890) 45-47.

Genesis 14:24

Salomon Speier, "De Genesis Apocryphon and the Targum Jerushalmi I on Gen xiv 24," *VT* 8 (1958) 95-97.

Genesis Chapter 15

*H. H. Hawes, "The Covenants of Genesis XV. and XVII.," *USR* 4 (1892-93) 112-114.

Peter Katz, "Notes on the Septuagint, III. Coincidences between ⅅ and ℭ⁰ in Genesis XV," *JTS* 47 (1946) 166-168.

L. A. Snijders, "Genesis XV. The Covenant with Abram," *OTS* 12 (1958) 261-279.

Martin Kessler, "The 'Shield' of Abraham?" *VT* 14 (1964) 494-497. *[Chap. 15]*

Genesis 15:1-7

Arthur T. Pierson, "Marginal Commentary: Notes on Genesis," *HR* 28 (1894) 452-455. *[15:1, 2, 4-7]*

Genesis 15:1

J. C.-M., "Illustrations of Scripture," *CongML* 22 (1839) 100-104. *[15:1]*

*W. W. Martin, "Genesis XIV. 20; XV. 1," *ONTS* 11 (1890) 45-47.

Genesis 15:2-3

Merrill F. Unger, "Some Comments on the Text of Genesis 15:2-3," *JBL* 72 (1953) 49-50.

Genesis 15:2

Julius A. Bewer, "Eliezer of Damascus," *JBL* 27 (1908) 160-162. *[15:2]*

Genesis 15:6

Ira Maurice Price, "'And He Believed in Jehovah and He Reckoned It to Him for Righteousness'," *BW* 35 (1910) 267-272. *[15:6]*

Meredith G. Kline, "Abram's Amen," *WTJ* 31 (1968-69) 1-11. *[15:6]*

Genesis 15:8-18

*Arthur T. Pierson, "Marginal Commentary: Notes on Genesis," *HR* 28 (1894) 539-543. *[15:8, 9-18]*

Genesis 15:9

*Joseph Offord, "Archaeological Notes on Jewish Antiquities. XIII. *The Bird* Gozal *and Babylonian* Guzalû," *PEFQS* 48 (1916) 139-140. *[15:19]*

Genesis Chapters 16-36

A. H. Sayce, "Archaeological Commentary of Genesis," *ET* 9 (1897-98) 31-34, 177-179, 306-309, 458-461. *[Chaps. 16-36]*

Genesis Chapter 16

*H[ermann] Gunkel, "The Two Accounts of Hagar. (Genesis xvi. and xii., 8-21.) Specimen of an Historico-Theological Interpretation of Genesis," *Monist* 10 (1899-1900) 321-342. *(Trans. by W. H. Carruth)*

Genesis 16:2-12

*Arthur T. Pierson, "Marginal Commentary: Notes on Genesis," *HR* 28 (1894) 539-543. *[16:2, 4-7, 11-12]*

Genesis 16:5-14

*Edwin Cone Bissell, "Is Genesis 21:9-21 and Duplicate of Genesis 16:5-14?" *BW* 2 (1893) 407-411.

Genesis 16:11

M[itchell J.] Dahood, "The Name *yišmā''ēl* in Genesis 16, 11," *B* 49 (1968) 87-88.

Genesis 16:13

J. C.-M., "Illustrations of Scripture," *CongML* 22 (1839) 222-226. *[16:13]*

Genesis Chapter 17

*H. H. Hawes, "The Covenants of Genesis XV. and XVII.," *USR* 4 (1892-93) 112-114.

Edouard Naville, "The Seventeenth Chapter of Genesis," *ET* 33 (1921-22) 127-130.

Edouard Naville, "The Seventeenth Chapter of Genesis," *ET* 35 (1923-24) 29-30.

Genesis 17:1-25

*Arthur T. Pierson, "Marginal Commentary: Notes on Genesis," *HR* 29 (1895) 64-67. *[17:2, 5, 1-14, 17-21, 25]*

Genesis 17:1

J. C.-M., "Illustrations of Scripture," *CongML* 22 (1839) 495-499. *[17:1]*

Genesis 17:6-8

*James Scott, "Genesis XVII., 6-8 and Galatians III., 16," *ONTS* 4 (1884-85) 103-105.

Genesis 17:17

*Eb. Nestle, "'Abraham Rejoiced'," *ET* 20 (1908-09) 477. *[Gen. 17:17//John 8:56]*

*James Hope Moulton, "'Abraham Rejoiced', etc.," *ET* 20 (1908-09) 523-524. *[Gen. 17:17//John 8:56]*

Genesis 17:18

Robert G. Forrest, "The First Prayer in the Bible," *ET* 23 (1911-12) 284. *[17:18]*

Genesis Chapters 18-19

T. K. Cheyne, "On Genesis XVIII., XIX," *Exp, 3rd Ser.,* 2 (1885) 203-206.

Curtis C. Bushnell, "A Supposed Connection between Certain Passages in Ovid and Genesis, 18-19," *PAPA* 48 (1916) xv-xviii.

Genesis 18:1-19:28

J. A. Selbie, "The Destruction of Sodom," *ET* 8 (1896-97) 419-420. *[Chaps. 18:1-19:28]*

Genesis Chapter 18

*Arthur T. Pierson, "Marginal Commentary: Notes on Genesis," *HR* 29 (1895) 64-67. *[Chap. 18]*

*L. Thunberg, "Early Christian Interpretations of the Three Angels in Gen. 18," *StP* 7 (1966) 560-570.

Genesis 18:1-15

Samuel Cox, "The Conversion of Sarah. Genesis XVIII. 1-15; Hebrews XI. 11," *Exp, 1st Ser.,* 12 (1880) 345-355.

Genesis 18:17-23

*Arthur T. Pierson, "Marginal Commentary: Notes on Genesis," *HR* 29 (1895) 259-262. *[18:17, 19, 22 and 23]*

Genesis 18:18

*Samuel Belkin, "Some Obscure Tradition Mutually Clarified in Philo and Rabbinic Literature," *JQR, 75th,* (1964-65) 80-103. [Marital Abstinence (Gen. 8:18) pp. 98-100]

Genesis 18:19

Edgar I. Fripp, "Note on Genesis XVIII. 19," *ZAW* 12 (1892) 23-29.

Genesis 18:20-21

W. R. W. Gardner, "Genesis XVIII. 20, 21," *ET* 27 (1915-16) 384.

James Kennedy, "Genesis XVIII. 20. (זַעֲקַת סְדֹם וַעֲמֹרָה כִּי רָבָּה וְחַטָּאתָם כִּי כָבְדָה מְאֹד:)," *ET* 27 (1915-16) 333.

Genesis 19:1-17

*Arthur T. Pierson, "Marginal Commentary: Notes on Genesis," *HR* 29 (1895) 259-262. *[19:1, 2-, 4-10, 9-11, 12-17]*

Genesis 19:3

*G. Octavius Wray, "A Singular Custom," *PEFQS* 1 (1869) 89. *[cf. Chap. 19:3]*

Genesis 19:22

*Arthur T. Pierson, "Marginal Commentary: Notes on Genesis," *HR* 29 (1895) 256-258. *[19:22]*

Genesis 19:26

*J. Penrose Harland, "Sodom and Gomorrah: The Location of the Cities of the Plain," *BA* 5 (1942) 17-32. [The Pillar of Salt, pp. 23-26] *[19:26]*

W. Gunther Plaut, "The Pillar of Salt: a Commentary," *CCARJ* 9 (1961-62) #2, 16-21. *[19:26]*

Genesis Chapter 20

†Anonymous, "Critical Essays on Genesis, Ch. xx., and on St. Matthew Ch. ii. 17. 18., with Notes," *BCQTR, 4th Ser.,* 1 (1827) 340-348. *(Review)*

*Arthur T. Pierson, "Marginal Commentary: Notes on Genesis," *HR* 29 (1895) 256-258. *[Chap. 20]*

*W. Gunther Plaut, "Thou art my Sister—A commentary on Genesis, Chapters 12, 20 and 26," *CCARJ* 10 (1962-63) #1, 26-30, 51.

Genesis 20:1-19

Anonymous, "The Temptation of Abraham. Genesis xx. 1-19," *Exp. 1st Ser.,* 1 (1875) 314-328.

Genesis 20:1-18

*Eugene H. Maly, "Genesis 12, 10-20; 20, 1-18; 26, 7-11 and the Pentateuchal Question," *CBQ* 18 (1956) 255-262.

Genesis 20:6-21

Edgar I. Fripp, "Note on Gen. XX. 6. 8-21," *ZAW* 12 (1892) 164-166.

Genesis 20:10

*J. A. Selbie, "A Forgotten Hebrew Idiom," *ET* 11 (1899-1900) 217. *[20:10]*

Genesis 20:16

*R. D. C. Robbins, "Explanation of Some Passages in Genesis," *BS* 8 (1851) 58-64. *[20:16]*

C. R. Brown, "Genesis XX. 16," *AJSL* 1 (1884-85) 250-251.

W. R. W. Gardner, "Genesis XX. 16," *ET* 25 (1913-14) 90.

Genesis 20:17-18

Eb. Nestle, "Genesis XX. 17, 18 and Herodotus I. 105," *ET* 20 (1908-09) 476-477.

Genesis 21:1-33

*Arthur T. Pierson, "Marginal Commentary: Notes on Genesis," *HR* 29 (1895) 351-354. *[21: 1, 2, 9, 12, 21, 31, 33]*

Genesis 21:9-21

*Edwin Cone Bissell, "Is Genesis 21:9-21 and Duplicate of Genesis 16:5-14?" *BW* 2 (1893) 407-411.

Genesis Chapter 22

*Harold M. Wiener, "The Dating of Genesis XXII," *BS* 67 (1910) 351-353.

Francis J. Lamb, "Professor Kent's Historical Bible and Science," *CFL, 3rd Ser.,* 21 (1916) 8-10. *[Chap. 22]*

David Polish, "Akedat Yitzhak—The Binding of Isaac," *Jud* 6 (1957) 17-21.

J. L. McKenzie, "The Sacrifice of Isaac (Gen. 22)," *Scrip* 9 (1957) 79-84.

Genesis 22:1-19

John H. Godwin, "Abraham's Offering of Isaac, Gen. xxii, 1-19," *Exp, 2nd Ser.*, 1 (1881) 305-312.

Genesis 22:1-18

F. P. Mayser, "Abraham Offering His Son Isaac. Remarks on Genesis 22:1-18," *LCR* 20 (1901) 518-522.

Genesis 22:2-14

*Arthur T. Pierson, "Marginal Commentary: Notes on Genesis," *HR* 29 (1895) 351-354. *[22:2, 8, 14]*

Genesis 22:1-2

*Anonymous, "The Great Text Commentary. The Great Texts of Genesis," *ET* 10 (1898-99) 402-405. *[22:1-2]*

Robert H. Kennett, "Abraham and Isaac," *ICMM* 4 (1907-08) 281-289. *[22:1-2]*

Genesis 22:2

J. J. S. Worcester, "Requests and Replies," *ET* 3 (1891-92) 301-302. *[22:2]*

J. A. Paterson, "Requests and Replies," *ET* 6 (1894-95) 252. [Gen. 22:2 - The Sacrifice of Isaac]

*Eric Burrows, "Note on Moreh, Gen. XII. 6 and Moriah, Gen. XXII. 2," *JTS* 41 (1940) 161.

Genesis 22:14

Royden K. Yerkes, "The Location and Etymology of יהוה יראה Genesis XXII 14," *JBL* 31 (1912) 136-140.

A. H. Sayce, "The Temple-Mount at Jerusalem (Gen. XXII. 14)," *ET* 32 (1920-21) 506-507.

Genesis 22:17-18

*Arthur T. Pierson, "Marginal Commentary: Notes on Genesis," *HR* 29 (1895) 441-444. *[Chap 22:17-18]*

Genesis 22:18

*John Forbes, "The Two Promises to Abraham," *Exp, 2nd Ser.,* 8 (1884) 200-206. *[22:18]*

*Oswald T. Allis, "The Blessing of Abraham," *PTR* 25 (1927) 263-298. *[22:18]*

Genesis 22:20

Anonymous, "Exegetical Opinions and Suggestions. Gen. XXII., 20," *CFL, O.S.,* 2 (1898) 48.

Genesis Chapter 23

A. H. Sayce, "The Purchase of the Cave of Machpelah," *ET* 18 (1906-07) 418-422. *[Chap. 23]*

G. G. Garner, "Writing in the Ancient World: Part III. Abraham Buys a Field," *AT* 1 (1956-57) #3, 9-10. *[Chap. 23]*

*Cyrus H. Gordon, "Abraham and the Merchants of Ura," *JNES* 17 (1958) 28-31. *[Chap. 23]*

G. G. Garner, *"Genesis 23 and Biblical Criticism:* Testing a Doubt," *AT* 3 (1958-59) #4, 18-20.

Gene M. Tucker, "The Legal Background of Genesis 23," *JBL* 85 (1966) 77-84.

Clifford Wilson, "A New Discussion on Genesis 23,"*BH* 3 (1967) #3, 14-15.

*C. Rabin, *"L-* with Imperative (Gen. XXIII)," *JSS* 13 (1968) 113-124.

Genesis 23:1-20

*Arthur T. Pierson, "Marginal Commentary: Notes on Genesis," *HR* 29 (1895) 441-444. *[Chap 23:1, 2, 4, 5-20]*

Genesis 23:6

M. H. Gottstein, "נשׂיא אלהים (Gen XXIII 6)," *VT* 3 (1953) 298-299.

Cyrus H. Gordon, "Abraham the βασιλευς," *AAI* 2 (1965) 227-230. *[23:6]*

Genesis 23:10

*E[phraim] A. Speiser, "'Coming' and 'Going' at the 'City' Gate," *BASOR* #144 (1956) 20-23. *[23:10]*

*Geoffrey Evans, "'Coming' and 'Going' at the City Gate—A Discussion of Professor Speiser's Paper," *BASOR* #150 (1958) 28-33 *[23:10]*

Genesis 23:11

*J. O'Connell, "A Recent Work on the Hittites," *ITQ* 21 (1954) 68-74. *(Review) [23:11]*

Genesis 23:18

*E[phraim] A. Speiser, "'Coming' and 'Going' at the 'City' Gate," *BASOR* #144 (1956) 20-23. *[23:18]*

*Geoffrey Evans, "'Coming' and 'Going' at the City Gate—A Discussion of Professor Speiser's Paper," *BASOR* #150 (1958) 28-33 *[23:18]*

Genesis Chapter 24

*Arthur T. Pierson, "Marginal Commentary: Notes on Genesis," *HR* 29 (1895) 441-444. *[Chap 24 (misnumbered 26): 1-4, 10-67]*

Genesis 24:2

Eberhard Schrader, "'Lay Thy Hand Under My Thigh'," *ONTS* 5 (1884-85) 178. *[24:2]*

Genesis 24:14

*T. K. Cheyne, "Notes on Genesis I., 1, and XXIV., 14. (1) On the Rendering of Genesis I., 1, (2) On Genesis XXIV., 14 (נַעַר)," *AJSL* 2 (1885-86) 49-50.

Genesis 24:21

Robert Gordis, "A Note on Gen. 24:21," *AJSL* 51 (1934-35) 191-192.

Genesis 24:32

Edmund F. Sutcliffe, "Camels' Feet in the Vulgate Text of Genesis XXIV. 32?" *ET* 60 (1948-49) 193-194.

Genesis 24:56

*Salomon Speier, "The Targum Jonathan on Genesis 24:56," *JQR, N.S.,* 18 (1937-38) 301-303.

Genesis 24:63

P. Wernberg-Møller, "A note on לשוח בשדה in Gen. XXIV 63," *VT* 7 (1957) 414-416.

Genesis 25:1

†A. B. C., "Observations on Genesis XXV. 1, &c.," *TRep* 3 (1771) 244-247.

Genesis 25:5-34

Arthur T. Pierson, "Helps and Hints, Textual and Topical," *HR* 29 (1895) 537-540. *[Continuation of "Marginal Commentary: Notes on Genesis": Chap 25:5, 7-9, 19, 20, 21-34]*

Genesis 25:22

Eb. Nestle, "Genesis XXV. 22, and Luke I. 41," *ET* 8 (1896-97) 237.

Eb. Nestle, "Genesis XXV. 22," *ET* 22 (1910-11) 230.

Genesis 25:23

O[swald] T. Allis, "The Birth-Oracle to Rebekah (Gen. xxv. 23)," *EQ* 11 (1939) 97-117.

Robert A. Kraft, "A Note on the Oracle of Rebecca (Gen. XXV. 23)," *JTS, N.S.,* 13 (1962) 318-320.

Genesis 25:27-34

J. E. Yonge, "Esau and Jacob. (Genesis xxv. 27-34)," *Exp, 2nd Ser.,* 7 (1884) 345-356.

Genesis 25:28-34

*Arthur T. Pierson, "Marginal Commentary: Notes on Genesis," *HR* 30 (1895) 56-60. *[25:28-34]*

Genesis 25:29-33

F. B. Hornbrooke, "Jacob and Esau. A Sermon," *URRM* 13 (1880) 253-263. *[25:29-33]*

Genesis 25:31-34

Mary Neely, "The Transfer of a Birthright," *AT* 2 (1957-58) #1, 9-10. *[25:31-34]*

Genesis 25:34

Anonymous, "The Great Text Commentary. The Great Texts of Genesis," *ET* 10 (1898-99) 456-458. *[25:34]*

Genesis Chapter 26

*Arthur T. Pierson, "Marginal Commentary: Notes on Genesis," *HR* 30 (1895) 56-60. *[Chap. 26]*

*W. Gunther Plaut, "Thou art my Sister—A commentary on Genesis, Chapters 12, 20 and 26," *CCARJ* 10 (1962-63) #1, 26-30, 51.

Genesis 26:7-11

A. C. Graham, "A Note on Genesis XXVI. 7-11," *ET* 49 (1937-38) 236.

*Eugene H. Maly, "Genesis 12, 10-20; 20, 1-18; 26, 7-11 and the Pentateuchal Question," *CBQ* 18 (1956) 255-262.

Genesis Chapter 27

J. E. Yonge, "Esau and Jacob. Genesis xxvii," *Exp, 2nd Ser.,* 8 (1884) 67-75.

*Benjamin W. Bacon, "The Blessing of Isaac, Gen. XXVII.—A Study in Pentateuchal Analysis," *AJSL* 7 (1890-91) 143-148.

W. Gunther Plaut, "The Strange Blessing: A Modern Midrash on Genesis 27," *CCARJ* 8 (1960-61) #2, 30-34.

K. Luke, "Isaac's Blessing: Genesis 27," *Scrip* 20 (1968) 33-41.

Genesis 27:1-24

H. W. R. Lillie, "Did Jacob Tell a Lie? (Gen. xxvii. 1-24)," *ClR* 10 (1935) 97-108.

Genesis 27:2

E[phraim] A. Speiser, "'I Know Not the Day of My Death'," *JBL* 74 (1955) 252-256. *[27:2]*

Genesis 27:9-18

Arthur T. Pierson, "Marginal Commentary: Notes on Genesis," *HR* 30 (1895) 153-156. *[27:9, 16, 18]*

Genesis 27:30

George Farmer, "Genesis XXVII. 30," *ET* 28 (1916-17) 480.

Genesis 27:41

*Ralph Marcus, "A Textual-Exegetical Note on Philo's Bible," *JBL* 69 (1950) 363-365. *[27:41]*

Genesis 27:42

D. Winton Thomas, "A Note on the Meaning of מתנחם in Genesis XXVII. 42," *ET* 51 (1939-40) 252.

Genesis Chapter 28

K., "Misapprehension of Gen. xxviii," *CongML* 6 (1823) 359.

W. F., "Biblical Criticism. Reply to K. on Genesis xxviii," *CongML* 6 (1823) 519-521.

Genesis 28:10-22

Archibald Henderson, "On Jacob's Vision at Bethel, Gen. xxviii. 10-22," *ET*
4 (1892-93) 151-152.

John E. McFadyen, "Bethel," *Exp, 8th Ser.*, 26 (1923) 241-255. *[28:10-22]*

Genesis 28:10-12

*E. O. James, "The Threshold of Religion. *The Morett Lecture, 1958*," *Folk*
69 (1958) 160-174. [Gen. 28:10-12, p. 167]

Genesis 28:12

Anonymous, "Jacob's Dream; or, the Ministry of Angels. *A Discourse on
Genesis* xxviii, 12," *MR* 21 (1839) 275-284.

*J. Gwyn Griffiths, "The Celestial Ladder and the Gate of Heaven (Genesis
XXVIII. 12 and 17)," *ET* 76 (1964-65) 229-230.

*A. R. Millard, "The Celestial Ladder and the Gate of Heaven (Genesis
XXVIII. 12, 17), *ET* 78 (1966-67) 86-87.

Genesis 28:16-17

Anonymous, "The Great Text Commentary. The Great Texts of Genesis,"
ET 10 (1898-99) 517-519. *[28: 16, 17]*

Genesis 28:17

*J. Gwyn Griffiths, "The Celestial Ladder and the Gate of Heaven (Genesis
XXVIII. 12 and 17)," *ET* 76 (1964-65) 229-230.

*A. R. Millard, "The Celestial Ladder and the Gate of Heaven (Genesis
XXVIII. 12, 17), *ET* 78 (1966-67) 86-87.

Genesis 28:18

J. E. Yonge, "Jacob's Pillar. Genesis xxviii. 18," *Exp, 2nd Ser.*, 7 (1884) 66-71.

Genesis 28:19

Menahem G. Glenn, "The Word לוז in Genesis 28:19 in the LXX and in
Midrash," *JQR, N.S.*, 59 (1969-70) 73-75.

Genesis 28:20-22

Arthur T. Pierson, "Helps and Hints, Textual and Topical," *HR* 30 (1895) 251-252. *[Continuing the "Marginal Commentary: Notes on Genesis": Chap. 28:20-22]*

Genesis Chapters 29-31

Arthur T. Pierson, "Helps and Hints, Textual and Topical," *HR* 30 (1895) 345. *[Continuing the "Marginal Commentary: Notes on Genesis": Chaps. 29-31]*

Genesis 30:8

Francis I. Andersen, "Note on Genesis 30:8," *JBL* 88 (1969) 200.

Genesis 30:14

J. G. Frazer, "Jacob and the Mandrakes," *PBA* 8 (1917-18) 57-79. *[30:14]*

Genesis 30:27

Nahum M. Waldman, "A Note on Genesis 30:27b," *JQR, N.S.,* 55 (1964-65) 164-165.

William Chomsky, "The Case of Genesis 30:27b," *JQR, N.S.,* 55 (1964-65) 365-366.

Genesis 30:32

William J. Schepp, "'The Speckled and Spotted Goats and the Black Lambs Shall Be My Wages'," *JASA* 3 (1951) #2, 16-21. *[30:32ff.]*

Genesis Chapter 31

Harold M. Wiener, "The Text of Genesis XXXI," *BS* 73 (1916) 140-149.

Cyrus H. Gordon, "The Story of Jacob and Laban in the Light of the Nuzi Tablets," *BASOR* #66 (1937) 25-27. *[Chap. 31]*

Genesis 31:14-16

Millar Burrows, "The Complaint of Laban's Daughters," *JAOS* 57 (1937) 259-276. *[Chap 31:14-16]*

Genesis 31:19

Moshe Greenberg, "Another Look at Rachel's Theft of the Teraphim," *JBL* 81 (1962) 239-248. *[31:19]*

Genesis 31:34

R. A. S. Macalister, "Notes and Queries. 3. *Why did Rachel steal the Teraphim of Laban?*" *PEFQS* 37 (1905) 270-271. *[31:34]*

Genesis 31:38-39

Anonymous, "Jacob's Complaint Against Laban," *BH* 5 (1969) 7-9. *[31:38-39]*

Genesis 31:38

J. A. Montgomery, "These twenty years, etc.," *JBL* 43 (1924) 227. *[31:38]*

*J. J. Finkelstein, "An Old Babylonian Herding Contract and Genesis 31:38f.," *JAOS* 88 (1968) 30-36.

Genesis 31:42

Oswald T. Allis, "The Fear of Isaac (Genesis xxxi. 42)," *PTR* 16 (1917) 299-304.

Genesis 31:44

Francisco O. Garcia-Treto, "Genesis 31:44 and 'Gilead'," *ZAW* 79 (1969) 13-17.

Francisco O. Garcia-Treto, "Genesis 31:44 and 'Gilead'," *TUSR* 9 (1967-69) 13-18.

Genesis 31:47

*James A. Montgomery, "Notes on the Old Testament," *JBL* 31 (1912) 140-146. [1. יגר׳, Gen. 31:47, pp. 140-141]

Genesis 31:49

James Moffatt, "Opera Foris; Or, Materials for the Preacher. Second Series," *Exp, 8th Ser.,* 2 (1911) 182-192. *[31:49]*

M. J. Birks, "'Mizpah' (Gen. XXXI. 49)," *ET* 23 (1911-12) 383.

*James Moffatt, "Twisted Sayings—Mizpah," *HR* 78 (1919) 27. *[Chap. 31:49]*

[Frank M.] T[homas], "Exegetical Notes. Mizpah: An Exposition of Genesis XXXI. 49," *MQR, 3rd Ser.,* 45 (1919) 726-731.

Genesis 31:50

N. H. Snaith, "Genesis XXXI 50," *VT* 14 (1964) 373.

Genesis 31:53

Almoni Peloni, "The Fear of Father Isaac. Genesis xxxi. 53," *Exp, 2nd Ser.,* 3 (1882) 352-363.

W. R. W. Gardner, "Genesis XXXI. 53," *ET* 25 (1913-14) 426-427.

Carl Armerding, "The God of Nahor," *BS* 106 (1949) 363-366. *[31:53]*

Genesis 32-50

*Benjamin W. Bacon, "Notes on the Analysis of Gen. XXXII.—L," *AJSL* 7 (1890-91) 278-288.

Genesis Chapter 32

J. O. Skinner, "The Wrestling of Jacob at the Brook Jabbok," *UQGR, N.S.,* 12 (1875) 160-175. *[Chap. 32]*

Arthur T. Pierson, "Mahanaim and Peniel," *HR* 30 (1895) 439-441. *[Chap. 32]*

*J. Garrow Duncan, "Es-Salt," *PEFQS* 60 (1928) 28-36, 98-100. [Gen. 32 sq., pp. 99-100]

B. W. Anderson, "An Exposition of Genesis XXXII, The Traveller Unknown," *ABR* 17 (1969) 21-26.

Genesis 32:1-2

S. Prentice, "The Angels of God at Mahanaim," *JBL* 36 (1917) 151-157. *[32:1-2]*

Genesis 32:10-11

Eb. Nestle, "The First Prayer in the Bible," *ET* 23 (1911-12) 238. *[32:10, 11]*

Genesis 32:22-32

Arthur T. Pierson, "No Strength by Self-Effort," *HR* 31 (1896) 341-342. *[32: 22, 24, 25, 28-30, 32]*

Genesis 32:23-33

Nathaniel Schmidt, "The Numen of Penuel," *JBL* 45 (1926) 260-279. *[32:23-33]*

P. A. H. de Boer, "Genesis XXXII, 23-33," *NTT* 1 (1946-47) 149-163.

*Susan Lee Sherman and John Briggs Curtis, "Divine-Human Conflicts in the Old Testament," *JNES* 28 (1969) 231-242. [Gen. 32:23-33 (E.V. 32:22-23), pp. 231-232]

Genesis 32:24-32

John L. McKenzie, "Jacob at Peniel: Gn 32, 24-32," *CBQ* 25 (1963) 71-76.

Genesis 32:24-28

[Samuel Cox], "God Wrestling with Man, and Man with God. (Genesis xxxii. 24-28)," *Exp, 1st Ser.*, 10 (1879) 241-253.

Genesis 32:24-25

Wm. Taylor, "The Wrestling of Jacob," *UQGR, N.S.*, 12 (1875) 410-419. *[32:24-25]*

Anonymous, "The Great Text Commentary. The Great Texts of Genesis," *ET* 10 (1898-99) 561-563. *[32:24, 25]*

Genesis 32:25

R. Gotthiel, "The Peshiṭta Text of Gen. 32, 25," *JAOS* 33 (1913) 263-264.

Genesis 32:31

*E. J. Pilcher, "Ana-pani-Ili, illustrated from Hebrew," *SBAP* 24 (1902) 185. *[32:31]*

Genesis 33:18-20

*Eduard Nielsen, "The Burial of the Foreign Gods," *ST* 8 (1954) 103-122. *[33:18-20]*

Genesis 33:20

*Arthur T. Pierson, "Studies in Genesis," *HR* 31 (1896) 439-441. *[33:20]*

Genesis Chapter 34

Martin Kessler,"Genesis 34—An Interpretation,"*RefR* 19 (1965-66) #1, 3-8.

Genesis 34:12

*Elias J. Bickerman, "Two Legal Interpretations of the Septuagint," *RIDA, 3rd Ser.,*3 (1956) 81-104. *[34:12]*

Genesis 34:24

*E[phraim] A. Speiser, "'Coming' and 'Going' at the 'City' Gate," *BASOR* #144 (1956) 20-23. *[34:24]*

*Geoffrey Evans, "'Coming' and 'Going' at the City Gate—A Discussion of Professor Speiser's Paper," *BASOR* #150 (1958) 28-33 *[34:24]*

Genesis 35:1-22

*Arthur T. Pierson, "Studies in Genesis," *HR* 31 (1896) 439-441. *[35:1, 5, 7, 10, 11, 18, 22]*

Genesis 35:8

Anonymous, "The Oak of Weeping, "*CongML* 14 (1831) 224-226. *[Allon-bachuth (Gen. 35:8(?)]*

Genesis 35:11

*Henry Preserved Smith, "Old Testament Notes," *JBL* 24 (1905) 27-30. [V. Genesis 35:11, p. 29]

Genesis 35:1-4

*Eduard Nielsen, "The Burial of the Foreign Gods," *ST* 8 (1954) 103-122. *[35:1-4]*

Genesis 35:18

Fritz Hommel, "Ben-Ônî, Bin-Yamîn, Genesis xxxv. 18," *ET* 10 (1898-99) 92.

Genesis 35:21

Conrad Schick, "Reports by Dr. Conrad Schick. The Tower of Edar," *PEFQS* 32 (1900) 142-144. *[35:21]*

Genesis Chapter 36

Joseph Offord, "Egyptian Records Illustrative of Genesis XXXVI," *PEFQS* 49 (1917) 91-93.

Genesis 36:12

W. Bacher, "תמנע. Genesis XXXVI. 12," *JQR* 9 (1896-97) 359.

Genesis 36:31-39

*J. R. Bartlett, "The Edomite King-List of Genesis XXXVI. 31-39 and I. Chron. I. 43-50," *JTS, N.S.,* 16 (1965) 301-314.

Genesis 36:31

J. W. McGarvey, "Those Kings Who Reigned in Edom," *CFL, 3rd Ser.,* 3 (1905) 228-231. *[36:31]*

Genesis Chapters 37-50

Oxonius, "The History of Joseph and the Higher Criticism (Genesis 37-50)," *BS* 80 (1923) 186-208.

Charles T. Fritsch, "'God Was With Him'. *A Theological Study of the Joseph Narrative*," *Interp* 9 (1955) 21-34. *[Chaps. 37-50]*

Genesis 37:2-Exodus 12:51

*William R. Harper, "The Pentateuchal Question. III. Gen. 37-2—Ex. 12:51," *AJSL* 6 (1889-90) 1-48.

Genesis 37:5-Genesis Chapter 49

A. H. Sayce, "An Archaeological Commentary on Genesis," *ET* 10 (1898-99) 75-77, 171-174, 418-419, 510-511, 551-554.

Genesis Chapter 37

Smith B. Goodenow, "When Was Joseph Sold? A Critical Study of Genesis XXXVII," *BS* 44 (1887) 553-557.

Genesis 37:3-4

*C. F. Hogg, "Note on ἀγαπάω and φιλέω," *ET* 38 (1926-27) 379-380. *[37:3, 4]*

*H. Highfield, "ἀγαπάω and φιλέω: A Rejoinder," *ET* 38 (1926-27) 525. *[37:3, 4]*

Genesis 37:3

I. Abrahams, "Joseph's 'Coat of Many Colours'," *ET* 20 (1908-09) 90. *[37:3]*

Genesis 37:9

*Manfred Cassirer, "The Date of the Elohist in the Light of Genesis XXXVII. 9," *JTS* 50 (1949) 173-174.

Genesis 37:11

*A. W. Argyle, "A Parallel Between Luke II. 51 and Genesis XXXVII. 11," *ET* 65 (1953-54) 29.

Genesis 37:28

D. S. Margoliouth, "Genesis XXXVII. 28," *ET* 33 (1921-22) 39-40.

G. Ch. Aalders, "By Whom was Joseph Sold to the Ishmaelites? (Gen. xxxvii. 28)," *EQ* 9 (1937) 250-255.

Genesis Chapter 38

Luke à B., "Judah and Tamar (Gen. 38)," *Scrip* 17 (1965) 52-61.

Michael C. Astour, "Tamar and the Hierodule: An Essay in the Method of Vestigal Motifs," *JBL* 85 (1966) 185-196. *[Chap. 38]*

Genesis 38:1-5

C. A. Ben-Mordecai, "Chezib," *JBL* 58 (1939) 283-286. (Note by W. F. Albright, p. 286) *[38:1-5]*

Genesis 38:8-10

Charles F. DeVine, "The Sin of Onan, Gen. 38:8-10," *CBQ* 4 (1942) 323-340.

Genesis 38:29

Frank Zimmermann, "The Births of Perez and Zerah," *JBL* 64 (1945) 377-378. *[38:29f.]*

Genesis Chapters 39-50

William A. Ward, "Egyptian Titles in Genesis 39-50," *BS* 114 (1957) 40-59.

Genesis Chapter 39

A. M. Honeyman, "The Occasion of Joseph's Temptation," *VT* 2 (1952) 85-87. *[Chap 39]*

Genesis 39:4

*Peter Katz, "Two Kindred Corruptions in the Septuagint," *VT* 1 (1951) 261-266. [I. Gen. 39:4, pp. 261-262]

Genesis 39:7

Anonymous, "Salt's Voyage to Abyssinia," *MMBR* 39 (1815) 600-614. [Potiphar's Wife, p. 612] *[39:7ff.]*

Genesis 39:14-17

*Harry M. Orlinsky, "Critical Notes on Gen. 39:14, 17, Jud. 11:37," *JBL* 61 (1942) 87-97. [I. On the Greek-Hebrew of Gen 39 14, 17, pp. 87-92]

Genesis 40:3

Anonymous, "Exploration and Discovery," *BW* 19 (1902) 147-148. *[Gen. 40:3 variant LXX reading]*

Genesis 40:15

D. B. Redford, "The 'Land of the Hebrews' in Gen. XL 15," *VT* 15 (1965) 529-532.

Genesis 40:16-17

*Anonymous, "Illustrations of Scripture," *BRCM* 2 (1846) 413-415. [II. Gen. 40:16, 17, p. 414]

Genesis 41:5

*F. B., "On the Ears of Corn Seen in Pharaoh's Dream. XLI. 5, 22,"*BRCM* 1 (1846) 133-135.

Genesis 41:22

*F. B., "On the Ears of Corn Seen in Pharaoh's Dream. XLI. 5, 22,"*BRCM* 1 (1846) 133-135.

Genesis 41:24

Edward P. Rice, "Genesis XLI. 24," *ET* 23 (1911-12) 381-382.

Genesis 41:32

Thomas Laurie, "Genesis XLI. 32," *PR* 9 (1888) 474-476.

Genesis 41:40

Herbert Loewe, "Genesis XLI. 40," *ET* 26 (1914-15) 332.

Norman Adcock, "Genesis XLI. 40 וְעַל־פִּיךָ יִשַּׁק כָּל־עַמִּי : καὶ ἐπὶ τῷ στόματί σου ὑπακούσεται πᾶς ὁ λαός μου," *ET* 67 (1955-56) 383.

F. C. Fensham, "Genesis XLI. 40," *ET* 68 (1956-57) 284-285.

K. A. Kitchen, "The Term NŠQ in Genesis XLI. 40," *ET* 69 (1957-58) 30.

Genesis 41:43

*P. le Page Renouf, "Is אַבְרֵךְ (Gen. xli, 43) Egyptian? The Thematic Vowel in Egyptian," *SBAP* 11 (1888-89) 5-10.

Genesis 41:45

*E[douard] Naville, "The Egyptian Name of Joseph," *SBAP* 25 (1903) 157-161. *[41:45]*

*Harold M. Wiener, "The Egyptian Name of Joseph," *BS* 68 (1911) 156-159. *[41:45]*

Henry L. F. Lutz, "The Egyptian Archetype of saph^enath pa^'eneah and ψονθομφανήχ (Genesis 41:45)," *UCPSP* 10 (1931-46) 289-294.

Genesis 42:29

*Anonymous, "Remarks on Judah's Speech to His Father, as Given by Josephus," *CD* 1 (1813) 183-185. *[42:29ff.]*

Genesis 43:9

*S[heldon] H. Blank, "And All our Virtues...'," *JBL* 71 (1952) viii. *[43:9]*

*Jacob J. Rabinowitz, "Demotic Papyri of the Ptolemaic Period and Jewish Sources," *VT* 7 (1957) 398-400. [The Formula of Gen 43:9, pp. 399-400]

Genesis 43:11

*C. J. Ball, "The Name Shinar, Genesis xi, 2; and the meaning of זמרת in Genesis xliii, 11," *SBAP* 17 (1895) 130.

Genesis 43:32

*Anonymous, "Remarks on Genesis xlvi. 34, and xliii. 32," *MR* 5 (1822) 373-374.

Genesis 44:5

*A. Van Hoonacker, "Expository Notes," *Exp, 8th Ser.,* 9 (1915) 452-459. [2. Gen. xliv. 5: divination cup? pp. 454-456]

Genesis 44:12

Arvid S. Kapelrud, "Genesis XLIV 12," *VT* 4 (1954) 426-428.

Genesis 45:1-3

A. Clark, "Remarks on Genesis XLV. 1, 2, 3," *MR* 6 (1823) 23-24.

Genesis 45:9

*S. M. Drach, "Viceroy Joseph's Official Despatches. Is Bible Poetry Acrostic?" *SBAT* 6 (1878-79) 244-248. *[Chap 45:9]*

Genesis 45:23

Eb. Nestle, "Genesis XLV. 23," *ET* 22 (1910-11) 526.

Genesis Chapter 46

*Anonymous, "Notes on Bishop Colenso's New Book," *JSL, 4th Ser.,* 2 (1862-63) 385-401. [I. The Genealogy of Genesis 46, pp. 385-394.] *(Review)*

Genesis 46:29-36

*Sakae Shibayama, "Notes on *Yārad* and *'Ālāh:* Hints on Translating," *JAAR* 34 (1966) 358-362. [II. Genesis 46:29-36; pp. 360-362]

Genesis 46:34

*Anonymous, "Remarks on Genesis xlvi. 34, and xliii. 32," *MR* 5 (1822) 373-374.

Genesis 47:9

Anonymous, "The Great Text Commentary. The Great Texts of Genesis," *ET* 11 (1899-1900) 29-31. *[47:9]*

Genesis 47:12-17

*G. R. Driver, "Two Problems in the Old Testament Examined in the Light of Assyriology," *Syria* 33 (1956) 70-78. [I. The provision for Joseph's family in Egypt (Genesis xlvii, 12-17), pp. 70-73]

Genesis 47:13-27

W. Gunther Plaut, "'The Trace of Joseph'—A Commentary on Gen. 47:13-27," *CCARJ* 9 (1961-62) #3, 29-32.

Genesis 47:14-26

*L. Lund, "The Epoch of Joseph: Amenhotep IV as the Pharaoh of the Famine," *SBAP* 4 (1881-82) 96-102. [Remarks by H. Villiers Stuart, pp. 95-96; by St. Vincent Beechey, p. 102; by Samuel Birch, p. 102] *[47:14-20, 25-26]*

Genesis 47:29-31

Agide Piazzini, "Jacob's Death and Relic Worship," *BRec* 9 (1912) 291-292. *[47:29-31]*

*Franz Steiner, "Enslavement and the Early Hebrew Lineage System: An Explanation of Genesis 47:29-31; 48:1-16," *Man* 54 (1954) #102.

Genesis 47:31

James Robertson, "Requests and Replies," *ET* 3 (1891-92) 68. *[47:31 and Hebrews 11:21]*

John Newenham Hoare, "Genesis XLVII. 31 and Hebrews XI. 21," *ET* 3 (1891-92) 273.

John Rutherford, "Note on Genesis XLVII. 31," *ET* 4 (1892-93) 403-404.

Genesis 48:1-16

*Franz Steiner, "Enslavement and the Early Hebrew Lineage System: An Explanation of Genesis 47:29-31; 48:1-16," *Man* 54 (1954) #102.

Genesis 48:5

*I. Mendelsohn, "A Ugaritic Parallel to the Adoption of Ephraim and Manasseh," *IEJ* 9 (1959) 180-183. *[48:5]*

Genesis 48:9

*Jacob J. Rabinowitz, "Demotic Papyri of the Ptolemaic Period and Jewish Sources," *VT* 7 (1957) 398-400. [b. Gen. 48:9, pp. 399-400]

Genesis 48:10

*John Edwards, "Genesis II. 25 and XLVIII. 10," *AJSL* 3 (1886-87) 263-264.

Genesis 48:19

*P. S., "Dr. Maitland on Rom. xi. 25; and Genesis xlviii. 19," *JSL, 2nd Ser.,* 7 (1854-55) 299-204.

Genesis 48:20

Edwin C. Kingsbury, "He Set Ephraim Before Manasseh," *HUCA* 38 (1967) 129-136. *[48:20]*

Genesis Chapter 49

*R. Y., "The Last Blessings of Jacob. Translated from the Chaldee Targums of Jonathan ben Uziel and Jerusalem," *JSL, 2nd Ser.,* 2 (1852) 432-444. *[Chap. 49]*

*J. C. C. Clarke, "Jacob's Zodiac," *ONTS* 2 (1882-83) 155-158. *[Chap. 49]*

F. Cope Whitehouse, "The Bahr-Jūsuf and the Prophecy of Jacob," *SBAP* 8 (1885-86) 6-25 *[Chap. 49]*

†F. Cope Whitehouse, "The Prophecy of Jacob," *SBAP* 8 (1885-86) 57-58. *[Chap. 49]*

John P. Peters, "Jacob's Blessing, Genesis 49," *JBL* 6 (1886) Part 1, 99-116.

Milton S.Terry, "The Prophecy of Jacob," *MR* 68 (1886) 847-870.*[Chap. 49]*

F. C[ope] Whitehouse, "On the Canal of Joseph and other local Allusions to Middle Egypt in Genesis xlix," *JAOS* 13 (1889) xvii.

C. J. Ball, "The Testament of Jacob (Gen. xlix)," *SBAP* 17 (1895) 164-191.

T. K. Cheyne, "The Blessings of Asher, Naphtali, and Joseph," *SBAP* 21 (1899) 242-245. *[Chap. 49]*

*A. Bentzen, "Patriarchal 'benediction' and prophetic book," *HTS* 7 (1950-51) 106-109. *[Chap. 49]*

Carl Armerding, "The Last Words of Jacob: Genesis 49," *BS* 112 (1955) 320-329.

Bruce Vawter, "The Canaanite Background of Genesis 49," *CBQ* 17 (1955) 1-18.

Calum M. Carmichael, "Some Sayings in Genesis 49," *JBL* 88 (1969) 435-444.

Genesis 49:1-27

John H. Bennetch, "The Prophecy of Jacob," *BS* 95 (1938) 417-435. *[49:1-27]*

Genesis 49:5

Mitchell J. Dahood, "MKRTYHM in Genesis 49, 5," *CBQ* 23 (1961) 54-56.

Genesis 49:6

M[itchell J.] Dahood, "A New Translation of Gen 49, 6a," *B* 36 (1955) 229.

Genesis 49:7

H. W. Sheppard, "Note on the Word עֶבְרָה (Gen. XLIX 7)," *JTS* 7 (1905-06) 140-141.

Genesis 49:8-12

Engelbert Yuritch, "The Messianic Prophecy of Jacob (Genesis XLIX, 8-12)," *IER, 5th Ser.,* 20 (1922) 352-368.

Kevin Smyth, "The Prophecy Concerning Juda: Gen. 49:8-12," *CBQ* 7 (1945) 290-305.

Edwin M. Good, "The 'Blessing' of Judah, Gen 49:8-12," *JBL* 82 (1963) 427-432.

Genesis 49:10

Biblicus, "Observations on the Prophecy concerning Shilo," *TRep* 4 (1784) 473-476. *[49:10]*

H. M. G., "On the Coming of 'The Shiloh.'—Gen. xlix. 10," *JSL, 3rd Ser.,* 5 (1857) 33-42.

Clericus, "Remarks on the Recent Replies to 'Essays and Reviews'," *JSL, 4th Ser.,* 1 (1862) 204-208. *[49:10]*

H. J. Rose, "The Replies to 'Essays and Reviews'," *JSL, 4th Ser.,* 1 (1862) 448-451. *[Chap 49:10]*

*Henry M. Harman, "The Prophecy of Jacob Respecting the Messiah," *MR* 51 (1869) 411-422. *[49:10]*

T. K. Cheyne, "Miscellanea Theologica. I. A Disputed Prophecy in Genesis (xlix. 10)," *TRL* 12 (1875) 300-306.

Charles Elliott, "The Interpretation of Genesis XLIX. 10," *ONTS* 5 (1884-85) 303-308.

S. R. Driver, "*Genesis* XLIX. 10: an exegetical study," *JP* 14 (1885) 1-28.

*G. H. Skipwith, "The Relative ש in Genesis," *JQR* 8 (1895-96) 706-707. *[49:10]*

John H. Raven, "'Shiloh' in Genesis 49:10," *BM* 2 (1914) 399-416.

R. Eisler, "The Babylonian Word 'Shilu' (Ruler) in Gen. XLIX. 10," *ET* 36 (1924-25) 477.

*E. B. Pollard, "Some Traditional Misinterpretations," *CQ* 4 (1927) 92-94. *[49:10]*

W. A. Wordsworth, "'Until Shiloh Come' (Genesis XLIX. 10)," *ET* 49 (1937-38) 142-143.

Joh. Lindblom, "The political background of the Shiloh oracle," *VTS* 1 (1953) 78-87. *[49:10]*

*N. Wieder, "Notes on the New Documents of the Fourth Cave of Qumran," *JJS* 7 (1956) 71-76. [The Qumran Exposition of Gen. 49, 10, pp. 72-74]

*W. L. Moran, "Gen 49, 10 and Its Use in Ez. 21, 32," *B* 39 (1958) 405-425.

Marco Treves, "Shiloh (Gen 49:10)," *JBL* 85 (1966) 353-356.

*B. Margulis, "Gen XLIX 10/Deut XXXII 2-3," *VT* 19 (1969) 202-210.

Genesis 49:11

*Marcus Jastrow, "Light thrown on some Biblical passages by Talmudic usage," *JBL* 11 (1892) 126-130. *[49:11]*

Genesis 49:14

*James Edward Hogg, "The Meaning of הַמִּשְׁפְּתָיִם in Gen. 49:14 and Judg. 5:16," *AJSL* 43 (1926-27) 299-301.

Samuel I. Feigin, "*Ḥamôr Gārîm*, 'Castrated Ass'," *JNES* 5 (1946) 230-233. *[49:14]*

Genesis 49:20-21

W. Emery Barnes, "A Taunt-Song in Genesis XLIX 20, 21," *JTS* 33 (1931-32) 354-359.

Genesis 49:21

Fritz Hommel, "Genesis XLIX. 21," *ET* 12 (1900-01) 46.

*Max L. Margolis, "Short Notes on the Greek Old Testament," *AJSL* 25 (1908-09) 174. *[49:21]*

Genesis 49:22:26

John G. Hale, "Exegesis of Genesis XLIX, 22-26," *CongQB* 17 (1875) 506-514.

Genesis 49:22

J. M. Allegro, "A Possible Mesopotamian Background to the Joseph Blessing of Gen. xlix," *ZAW* 64 (1952-53) 249-251. *[49:22]*

Genesis 49:24-26

Edgar I. Fripp, "Note on Gen. XLIX, 24b-26," *ZAW* 11 (1891) 262-266.

E[dgar] I. Fripp, "Note on Genesis XLIX, 24b-26," *OSHTP* (1891-92) 19-21.

Genesis 49:24

*M[itchell J.] Dahood, "Is *'Eben Yiśrāēl* a Divine Title? (Gen. 49, 24)," *B* 40 (1959) 1002-1007.

Genesis 49:25-26

Isaiah Sonne, "Genesis 49:25-26," *JBL* 65 (1946) 303-306.

Genesis 49:25

*Julian Morgenstern, "The Divine Triad in Biblical Mythology," *JBL* 64 (1945) 15-37. [Gen. 49:25, p. 25f.]

Genesis 50:1-3

יוֹסֵף, "The Embalming of Jacob, Illustrated from Herodotus. Genesis L. 1-3," *CongML* 19 (1836) 152-160.

Genesis 50:22-26

*L. B. Cholmondeley, "Gn. L. 22-26, Dt. XXXIV. 4-7, Jos.XXIV. 29ff.," *ET* 46 (1934-35) 238.

Genesis 50:26

R. D. C. Robbins, "Explanation of Some Passages in Genesis," *BS* 8 (1851) 58-63. *[Chap. 50:26]*

§580 **3.5.2.2 Studies on Manuscripts of Genesis**

Albert Lowy, "On a Unique Specimen of the Lishana Shel Imrani, *The Modern Syriac of Targum Dialect of the Jews in Kurdistan and adjacent Countries; with an Account of the People by whom it is spoken,*" *SBAT* 4 (1875) 98-117. *[Genesis 1 and 2]*

*B. Pick, "Horae Samaritanae; or a Collection of Various Readings of the Samaritan Pentateuch Compared with the Hebrew and other Ancient Versions, I.—Genesis," *BS* 33 (1876) 264-288.

*John E. Gilmore and P. le Page Renouf, "Coptic Fragments (Gen. xiii and xiv, and Psalm cv)," *SBAP* 17 (1895) 251-253.

Edgar J. Goodspeed, "New Fragments of Hebrews and Genesis," *BW* 18 (1901) 223-224.

Harold R. Willoughby, "The Vienna Genesis and Rockefeller McCormick New Testament," *HR* 104 (1932) 101-102.

*O. J. Baab, "A Theory of Two Translators for the Greek Genesis," *JBL* 52 (1933) 239-243.

Henry S. Gehman, "Hebrewisms of the Old Greek Version of Genesis," *VT* 3 (1953) 141-148.

*P. Wernberg-Møller, "Some Observations on the Relationship of the Peshitta Version of the Book of Genesis to the Palestinian Targum Fragments, Published by Professor Kahle, and to Targum Onkelos," *ST* 15 (1961) 128-180.

*A. Levene, "Some Observations on the Commentaries of Isho'dad Bishop of Ḥadatta and the Manuscript Mingana 535 on Genesis," *StP* 4 (1961) 136-142.

*P. Wernberg-Møller, "Some Scribal and Linguistic Features of the Genesis Part of the Oldest Peshiṭta Manuscript (B.M. Add 14425)," *JSS* 13 (1968) 136-161.

§581 *3.5.2.3 Exegetical Studies on the Book of Exodus*

D. E., "Emendations in the Authorized Version of Scripture," *JSL, 3rd Ser.,* 13 (1861) 184-185. [2:15; 3:16, 22; 4:20, 8:9; 9:24; 11:2; 13:6, 9, 23, 35; 13:18; 14:7; 15:2; 22:2; 23:21; 33:16, 21]

B. Kurtz, "The Israelites Borrowing from the Egyptians," *ER* 16 (1865) 136-146. [3:21, 22; 11:2, 3; 12:35, 36]

S. R. Driver, "The Revised Version of the Old Testament. II. The Book of Exodus," *Exp, 3rd Ser.,* 2 (1885) 81-89. [2:10; 3:14, 15; 7:9, 13, 14; 9:31; 12:9, 36; 20:6; 20:13; 21:6; 22:8, 9; 22:20, 24:24; (34:13); 25:6; 26:6, 7 (27:21); 26:36, 37; 27:21; 29:22; 32:25; 33:7-11, 13; 24:33; chap. 35-39; 36:1; 39:33ff.; 40:17ff.]

Theodore Gerald Soares, "Expository Studies in the Old Testament: V. Israel in Egypt," *BW* 29 (1907) 376-387. [1:1-14; 2:1-15; 3:1-14; 12:21-30; 14:13-27]

Kemper Fullerton, "Expository Studies in the Old Testament: VI. The Giving of the Law and the Desert Wanderings," *BW* 29 (1907) 451-465. [16:1-15; 20:1-11; 32:1-8, 30-35]

Frederick Field, "Dr. Field's Old Testament Revision Notes. Transcribed from the Author's MS. by the Rev. John Henry Burn, B.D., III.," *ET* 30 (1918-19) 427. [1:16; 2:3; 3:14; 7:15; 8:12; 9:17; 10:10]

Frederick Field, "Dr. Field's Old Testament Revision Notes. Transcribed from the Author's MS. by the Rev. John Henry Burn, B.D., IV.," *ET* 30 (1918-19) 476-477. [17:16; 22:25; 22:29; 23:5; 35:22]

Genesis 37:2-Exodus 12:51

*William R. Harper, "The Pentateuchal Question. III. Gen. 37-2—Ex. 12:51," *AJSL* 6 (1889-90) 1-48.

Exodus Chapters 1-14

Anonymous, "Review of Some of the Principal Facts Recorded in the First Fourteen Chapters of the Book of Exodus," *MQR* 1 (1847) 272-292.

Exodus Chapters 1-7

*Benjamin W. Bacon, "JE in the Middle Books of the Pentateuch. Analysis of Ex. 1-7," *JBL* 10 (1891) 107-130.

Exodus 1:1-14

[J. Benson Hamilton], "International Sunday School Lessons: Pharaoh Oppresses Israel," *CFL, 3rd Ser.,* 25 (1919) 35. *[1:1-14]*

Exodus 1:8-11

A. H. Sayce, "The Old Testament in the Light of Recent Discoveries. No. V.," *MI* 4 (1886) 17-23. *[1:8; 1:11]*

Exodus 1:6-22

*A. Wiedemann, "On the Legends concerning the Youth of Moses," *SBAP* 11 (1888-89) 29-43, 267-282. *[1:6-22]*

Exodus 1:8-2:10

*Brevard S. Childs, "The Birth of Moses," *JBL* 84 (1965) 109-122. *[1:8-2:10]*

Exodus 1:10-22

A. H. Sayce, "Asherah; The Exodus," *ET* 7 (1895-96) 521-522. *[1:10-22]*

Exodus 1:10

William L. Holladay, "'ereṣ*— 'underworld': two more suggestions," *VT*
19 (1969) 123-124. *[1:10]*

Exodus 1:11

*L. Dickerman, "On the Site of Pithom (Exodus i.11)," *JAOS* 11 (1885) cxl-
cxlii.

D. B. Redford, "Exodus I 11," *VT* 13 (1963) 401-418.

Exodus 1:16

*W. E. Crum, "Bricks as Birth-Stool," *JEA* 28 (1942) 69. *[1:16]*

*W. E. Crum, "Corrections to Brief Communication, vol XXVIII, p. 69," *JEA*
29 (1943) 79. *[1:16]*

Exodus 1:19

James Edward Hogg, "A New Version of Exod. 1:19," *AJSL* 43 (1926-27)
297-299.

G. R. Driver, "Hebrew Mothers (Exodus i 19)," *ZAW* 67 (1955) 246-248.

Exodus 1:20-22

Anonymous, "Exodus I., 20, 21, 22," *MQR, 2nd Ser.,* 3 (1881) 167-168.

Exodus 2:1-15

*A. Wiedemann, "On the Legends concerning the Youth of Moses," *SBAP*
11 (1888-89) 29-43, 267-282. *[2:1-15]*

Exodus 2:1-10

*Donald B. Redford, "The literary motif of the exposed child (cf. Ex. ii 1-
10)," *Numen* 14 (1967) 209-228.

Exodus 2:9

Harold W. Wiener, "On Exodus II. 9," *BS* 73 (1916) 639.

Exodus 2:10

J. M. Sasson, "Bovine Symbolism in the Exodus Narrative," *VT* 18 (1968) 380-387. *[2:10]*

Exodus 2:21

*James Edward Hogg, "'A Virgin-Birth in Philo' (Exod. 2:21)," *AJSL* 44 (1927-28) 206-207.

Exodus 2:25

D. Winton Thomas, "A Note on אֱלֹהִים וַיֵּדַע in Exod. II. 25," *JTS* 49 (1948) 143-144.

Exodus Chapter 3-17:27

Anonymous, "Outline View of Exodus.—Part First—Chapters iii-xvii.27," *CFL, 3rd Ser.,* 6 (1907) 384-393.

Exodus Chapter 3-4:17

William J. O'Rouke, "Moses and the Prophetic Vocation. A Reflection on the Call of Moses in Ex. 3—4:17," *Scrip* 15 (1963) 44-55.

Exodus 3:1-15

*Julian Morgenstern, "The Elohist Narrative in Exodus 3:1-15," *AJSL* 37 (1920-21) 242-262.

Exodus 3:1-5

*Robert John Wilson, "1691-1961—A Two Hundred and Seventieth Anniversary. The Burning Bush," *ET* 73 (1961-62) 30. *[3:1-5]*

Exodus 3:1-4

*[J. Benson Hamilton], "International Sunday School Lessons: Moses the Leader of Israel," *CFL, 3rd Ser.,* 25 (1919) 36. *[3:1-4]*

Exodus 3:2-3

D[avid] N[oel] Freedman, "The Burning Bush," *B* 50 (1969) 245-246. *[3:2-3]*

Exodus 3:4-22

*Milton S. Terry, "Apocalypses of Moses," *ONTS* 8 (1888-89) 19-23. *[3:4-22]*

Exodus 3:4

James Moffatt, "Opera Foris. Materials for the Preacher," *Exp, 7th Ser.,* 5 (1908) 379-380. *[3:4]*

Exodus 3:14

H. P., "I Am that I Am, Exod. III. 14," *JSL, 3rd Ser.,* 9 (1859) 169-170.

*William Aldis Wright, "Note on two passages of Exodus," *JP* 4 (1872) 70-73. *[3:14]*

*W. R[obertson] Smith, "On the Name Jehovah (Jahve) and the Doctrine of Exodus III. 14," *BFER* 25 (1876) 153-165.

*Samuel Cox, "The Tetragrammaton. Exodus iii. 14," *Exp, 2nd Ser.,* 1 (1881) 12-24.

J. Estlin Carpenter, "Note Exodus iii. 14," *OSHTP* (1892-93) 26-27.

*William R. Arnold, "The Divine Name in Exodus iii. 14," *JBL* 24 (1905) 107-165.

W[illiam] A. Irwin, "Exod. 3:14," *AJSL* 56 (1939) 297-298.

E. Schild, "On Exodus iii 14-'I am that I am," *VT* 4 (1954) 296-302.

L. M. Pakozdy, "'I Shall be that which I shall be'," *BTr* 7 (1956) 146-149. *[3:14]*

Benedict Viviano, "A Note on Exodus 3:14," *Listen* ∅ (1965) #∅ 22-26.

Exodus 3:17

*[J. Benson Hamilton], "International Sunday School Lessons: Moses the Leader of Israel," *CFL, 3rd Ser.,* 25 (1919) 36. *[3:17]*

Exodus Chapter 4

*Hugh Rose Rae, "Had Moses a Scolding Wife?" *HR* 42 (1901) 257-260.
  [Chap. 4]

Exodus 4:11

J. C. Todd, "Note on Exodus IV. 11," *ET* 4 (1892-93) 240.

Exodus 4:14

James Moffatt, "Opera Foris. Materials for the Preacher," *Exp, 7th Ser.,* 5
  (1908) 380-382. *[4:14]*

Exodus 4:16

Harold M. Wiener, "Exodus IV. 16," *BS* 76 (1919) 234.

Exodus 4:22-23

Paul G. Bretscher, "Exodus 4:22-23 and the Voice from Heaven," *JBL* 87
  (1968) 301-311.

Exodus 4:24-26

Henry Preserved Smith, "Ethnological Parallels to Exodus iv. 24-26," *JBL*
  25 (1906) 14-24.

Joh. de Groot, "The Story of the Bloody Husband (Exodus IV 24-26)," *OTS*
  2 (1943) 10-17.

Y. Blau, "The *ḥatan damim* (Ex. IV: 24-26)," *Tarbiz* 26 (1956-57) #1, I.

H. Kosmala, "The 'Bloody Husband'," *VT* 12 (1962) 14-28. *[4:24-26]*

P. Middlekoop, "The Significance of the Story of the 'Blood Husband' (Ex.
  4:24-26)," *SEAJT* 8 (1966-67) #4, 34-38.

Julian Morgenstern, "The 'Bloody Husband' (?) (Exod. 4:24-26) Once
  Again," *HUCA* 34 (1963) 35-70.

*Susan Lee Sherman and John Briggs Curtis, "Divine-Human Conflicts in
  the Old Testament," *JNES* 28 (1969) 231-242. [Ex. 4:24-26, p. 233]

Exodus 4:24

William J. Deane, "Moses at the Inn," *BFER* 36 (1887) 433-445. *[4:24ff.]*

Exodus 4:25-26

*S. Talmon, "The 'Bloody Husband'," *ET* 3 (1954) IV. *[4:25, 26]*

Exodus Chapters 5-14

Dennis J. McCarthy, "Plagues and Sea of Reeds: Exodus 5-14," *JBL* 85 (1966) 137-158.

Exodus Chapter 5

*Charles F. Nims, "Bricks Without Straw?" *BA* 13 (1950) 22-28. *[Chap. 5]*

Exodus 5:4-5

*Samuel Daiches, "Exodus 5. 4-5, The meaning of עַם הָאָרֶץ," *JQR, N.S.,* 12 (1921-22) 33-34.

Exodus 5:22-23

Anonymous, "The Perplexity of Moses," *CongL* 7 (1878) 208-213. *[5:22-23]*

Exodus 6:1-8

*Milton S. Terry, "Apocalypses of Moses," *ONTS* 8 (1888-89) 19-23. *[6:1-8]*

Exodus 6:2-7:7

J. Wimmer, "Tradition Re-interpreted in Ex. 6, 2-7, 7," *Aug* 7 (1967) 405-418.

Exodus 6:2-3

*E. Ballantine, "Interpretation of Exodus VI. 2, 3," *BRCR* 3 (1833) 730-748.

*J. Skinner, "The Divine Names in Genesis," *Exp, 8th Ser.,* 5 (1913) 289-313, 400-420, 494-514. [I. Exodus VI. 2,3, pp. 297-313]

*W[illiam] H. B[ates], "Jehovah—Not known yet known," *CFL, 3rd Ser.,* 27 (1921) 400. *[6:2, 3]*

R[obert] D[ick] Wilson, "Critical Note on Exodus VI. 3," *PTR* 22 (1924) 108-119.

*J. Battersby Harford, "Since Wellhausen," *Exp, 9th Ser.,* 4 (1925) 83-102. [Article 2. Recent Criticism, with Special Reference to Exodus 6:2-3, pp. 84-102]

L. Aug. Heerboth, "Exodus 6, 3b. Was God Known to the Patriarchs as Jehovah?" *CTM* 4 (1933) 345-349.

John J. Davis, "The Patriarchs' Knowledge of Jehovah, A Critical Monograph on Exodus 6:3 Abridged by the Author," *GJ* 4 (1963) #1, 29-43.

Exodus 6:23

*Ed. König, "Elisabeth," *ET* 20 (1908-09) 185-186. *[6:23]*

Exodus Chapters 7-12

*Benjamin W. Bacon, "JE in the Middle Books of the Pentateuch. Analysis of Ex. 7-12," *JBL* 9 (1890) 161-200.

Exodus 7:1-5

*Milton S. Terry, "Apocalypses of Moses," *ONTS* 8 (1888-89) 19-23. *[7:1-5]*

Exodus 7:8-10:27

Dennis J. McCarthy, "Moses' Dealings with Pharaoh: Ex 7,8—10,27," *CBQ* 27 (1965) 336-347.

Exodus 7:11

*Warren R. Dawson, "The Magicians of Pharaoh: The Frazer Lecture, 1936," *Folk* 47 (1936) 234-262. *[7:11]*

Exodus 7:12

Anonymous, "The Egyptian Magicians," *CongML* 26 (1843) 114-116. *[7:12]*

Exodus 7:14

*T. K. Meek, "Some Lapses of Old Testament Translators," *JBL* 55 (1936) x. *[7:14f.]*

Exodus Chapter 9

L., "On the Apparent Discrepancies in Exodus IX and Daniel I, and II. In reply to the Queries of M. at page 369," *CongML* 2 (1819) 408-409.

Exodus 9:3

G. S. Ogden, "Notes on the Use of הויה in Exodus IX 3, *VT* 17 (1967) 483-484.

Exodus 9:13-16

B. B., "Biblianca, No. III," *QCS, N.S.,* 2 (1828) 72-75. *[9:13-16]*

Exodus 9:31-32

W. Robertson Smith, "Note on *Exodus* IX. 31, 32," *JP* 12 (1883) 299-300.

Exodus 10:10

*Joshua Bloch, "Is the Egyptian Sun God *Re* Mentioned in the Bible? (A Note on Exodus X, 10)," *JSOR* 16 (1932) 57.

*Battiscombe Gunn, "On the Supposed Mention of the Egyptian God Re' in Exodus," *EgR* 1 (1933) 33-34 *[10:10]*

*S. Rosenblatt, "A Reference to the Egyptian God Re' in the Old Testament," *JBL* 60 (1941) xi. *[10:10]*

Exodus 10:11

*Raphael Weiss, "A Note on אֹתָה in Ex 10:11," *ZAW* 76 (1964) 188.

Exodus 10:19

*A. J. Festugière, "A Note on ακριμακραγετα," *AJP* 76 (1955) 308-309. *[10:19]*

Exodus 11:1-12:36

*[J. Benson Hamilton], "International Sunday School Lessons: The Plagues and the Passover," *CFL, 3rd Ser.,* 25 (1919) 36. *[11:1-12:36]*

[J. Benson Hamilton], "International Sunday School Lessons: Plagues and the Passover ('Made in Germany')," *CFL, 3rd Ser.,* 25 (1919) 79-80. *[11:1-12:36]*

Exodus 11:7

F. Ch. Fensham, "The Dog in Ex. XI. 7," *VT* 16 (1966) 504-507.

Exodus 12:37-17:16

*Benjamin W. Bacon, "JE in the Middle Books of the Pentateuch. Analysis of Ex. 12:37-17:16," *JBL* 11 (1892) 177-200.

Exodus 12:19

*Isaac D. Gilat, "Leaven Belonging to Gentiles or to the Sanctuary," *Tarbiz* 33 (1963-64) #1, II. *[12:19]*

Exodus 12:35-36

*H. Hamann, "'Spoiling the Egyptians'," *AusTR* 11 (1940) 88-90. *[12:35-36]*

Exodus 12:37

B. H. C., "On the Number of Israelites as Given in Exodus XII. 37, etc.," *JSL, 2nd Ser.,* 2 (1852) 496-499.

Exodus 12:40

Anonymous, "Morsels of Criticism," *CongML* 4 (1821) 24. *[12:40]*

*P. E. Kretzmann, "The Chronology of the Two Covenants (Gal. 3:17 cp. with Ex. 12:40)," *CTM* 12 (1941) 606-610.

Exodus 12:42

*Martin McNamara, "Logos of the Fourth Gospel and Memra of the Palestinian Targum (Ex 12^{42})," *ET* 79 (1967-68) 115-117.

Exodus 12:46

Julian Morgenstern, "The Bones of the Paschal Lamb," *JAOS* 36 (1916) 146-153. *[12:46]*

Exodus Chapter 13—Deuteronomy Chapter 34

*William R. Harper, "The Pentateuchal Question. IV. Historical Matter of Ex. 13—Deut. 34," *AJSL* 6 (1889-90) 241-295.

Exodus 13:7-14:4

Owen C. Whitehouse, "The Route of the Exodus. Exodus xiii. 7-xiv. 4," *Exp, 2nd Ser.,* 6 (1883) 448-457.

Exodus 13:7

*A. S. Tritton, "The Casting Out of Leaven (Ex. XIII. 7; Dt. XVI. 11)," *ET* 24 (1912-13) 428.

Exodus 13:17

*G. Róheim, "The Passage of the Red Sea," *Man* 23 (1923) #96. *[13:17]*

Exodus 14:1-15:21

[J. Benson Hamilton], "International Sunday School Lessons: Crossing the Red Sea," *CFL, 3rd Ser.,* 25 (1919) 80. *[14:1-15:21]*

Exodus Chapter 14

[J. Benson Hamilton], "From the Hexateuch, the Hun Bible: 'Crossing the Red Sea' Exodus 14," *CFL, 3rd Ser.,* 25 (1919) 87-88.

*Oswald T. Allis, "Old Testament Emphases and Modern Thought. Old Testament Emphases vs. Higher Critical Theories," *PTR* 24 (1926) 252-307. [The Repetitions in Exodus XIV, pp. 259-269]

Roger Tomes, "Exodus 14: The Mighty Acts of God," *SJT* 22 (1969) 455-478.

Exodus 14:2

D. M. R., "Exegetical Studies," *BQ* 4 (1870) 481-483. *[14:2]*

Exodus 14:11

Anonymous,   "Exodus   14:11,"   *ONTS*   13   (1891)   120.

Exodus 14:15

John W. Primrose, "Exegetical Notes," *USR* 1 (1889-90) 180. *[14:15]*

Exodus 14:20

E[phraim] A. Speiser, "An Angelic 'Curse': Exodus 14:20," *JAOS* 80 (1960) 198-200.

Exodus 14:21

*John D. Davis, "The Passage of the Jordan," *CFL, N.S.,* 6 (1902) 186-189. *[14:21]*

Exodus 14:37

C[laude] R. Conder, "Notes. *Numbers of Israel,*" *PEFQS* 15 (1883) 138. *[14:37]*

Exodus Chapter 15

*Felix Perles, "On the Strophic Form of Exodus 15," *JQR, N.S.,* 17 (1926-27) 403-404.

*John D. W. Watts, "The Song of the Sea—Ex. XV," *VT* 7 (1957) 371-380.

Exodus 15:1-18

Paul Haupt, "Moses' Song of Triumph," *AJSL* 20 (1903-04) 149-172. *[15:1-18]*

Marc Rozelaar, "The Song of the Sea (Exodus XV, 1b-18)," *VT* 2 (1952) 221-228.

*Frank M. Cross, "The Song of the Sea and Canaanite Myth," *JTC* 5 (1968) 1-25. *[15:1b-18]*

George W. Coats, "The Song of the Sea," *CBQ* 31 (1969) 1-17. *[15:1b-18]*

Exodus 15:2-14

T[heodor] H. Gaster, "Notes on 'The Song of the Sea' (Exodus XV)," *ET* 48 (1936-37) 45. *[2, 13, 14]*

Exodus 15:2

C. S. S. Ellison, "Song of Moses (Exodus XV.)," *ET* 48 (1936-37) 333. *[15:2]*

D. Winton Thomas, "A Note on Exodus XV. 2," *ET* 48 (1936-37) 478.

Theodor H. Gaster, "Exodus XV. 2: עָזִּי וְזִמְרָת יָהּ," *ET* 49 (1937-38) 189.

S. E. Loewenstamm, "'The Lord is My Strength and My Glory'," *VT* 19 (1969) 464-470. *[15:2]*

Exodus 15:3

Ben Zion Bokser, "Exodus 15.3," *CJ* 16 (1961-62) #2/3, 67-68.

*P. C. Craigie, "'Yahweh is a Man of Wars'," *SJT* 22 (1969) 183-188. *[15:3]*

Exodus 15:7-21

*W. Baars, "A Targum of Exodus XV 7-21 from Cairo Geniza," *VT* 11 (1961) 340-342.

Exodus 15:8

H. H. B., "Vindication of the Translation of Exodus XV. 8," *JSL, 3rd Ser.,* 1 (1855) 347-354.

*John D. Davis, "The Passage of the Jordan," *CFL, N.S.,* 6 (1902) 186-189. *[15:8]*

Exodus Chapter 16

*W. T. Pilter, "The Manna of the Israelites," *SBAP* 39 (1917) 155-167, 187-206. [Exodus 16, pp. 189-201]

F. S. Bodenheimer, "The Manna of Sinai," *BA* 10 (1947) 2-6. *[Chap. 16]*

Exodus 16:2-12

John D. Davis, "Order of Events in Ex. XVI. 2-12," *CFL, N.S.,* 6 (1902) 9-10.

Exodus 16:15

*Paul Haupt, "Biblical Studies," *AJP* 43 (1922) 238-249. [8. The Etymology of Manna, pp. 247-249] *[16:15]*

*Samuel Belkin, "Some Obscure Tradition Mutually Clarified in Philo and Rabbinic Literature," *JQR, 75th,* (1967) 80-103. [5. Heavenly Nourishment (Ex. 16:15), pp. 90-93]

Exodus Chapter 17

*Anonymous, "The Smitten Rocks," *CongML* 19 (1836) 29-31. *[Chap. 17]*

Exodus 17:8-13

G. Margoliouth, "Moses at the Battle of Rephidim," *Exp, 5th Ser.,* 5 (1897) 119-128. *[17:8-13]*

Exodus 17:13

*A. Guillaume, "The Use of חלש in Exod. XVII. 13, Isa. XIV. 12, and Job XIV. 10," *JTS, N.S.,* 14 (1963) 91-92.

Exodus 17:15

*James A. Montgomery, "Babylonian *niš* 'oath' in West-Semitic," *JAOS* 37 (1917) 329-330. *[17:15]*

Exodus 17:16

W. F. Badè, "The 'Hand of the Throne of Jah', Exod. XVII. 16," *PAPA* 38 (1906) xl.

Exodus 18-34

*Benjamin W. Bacon, "JE in the Middle Books of the Pentateuch. Sinai-Horeb: Analysis of Ex. 18-34," *JBL* 12 (1893) 23-46.

Exodus Chapter 18

*Chr. H. W. Brekelmans, "Exodus XVIII and the Origins of Yahwism in Israel," *OTS* 10 (1954) 214-224.

Exodus 18:10

Harold M. Wiener, "The Text of Exodus XVIII. 10f.," *BS* 76 (1919) 483-484.

Exodus 18:12

A. Cody, "Exodus 18, 12: Jethro Accepts a Covenant with the Israelites," *B* 49 (1968) 153-166.

Exodus 19:1-34:35

Anonymous, "Outline View of Exodus.—Part Second—Chapters xix. 1 —xxxiv. 35," *CFL, 3rd Ser.,* 6 (1907) 462-470.

Exodus Chapter 19

Harold M. Wiener, "The 'Priests' of Exodus XIX," *BS* 47 (1910) 353.

Exodus 19:3-6

*R. Vande Walle, "An Administrative Body of Priests and a Consecrated People," *IJT* 14 (1965) 57-72. *[19:3-6]*

Exodus 19:6-9

*V. Eppstein, "Note on Exodus XIX," *JIQ* 4 (1927-28) #4, 27-28. *[19:6-9]*

Exodus 19:6

R. B. Y. Scott, "A Kingdom of Priests (Exodus xix 6)," *OTS* 8 (1950) 213-219.

Exodus 19:18-19

*V. Eppstein, "Note on Exodus XIX," *JIQ* 4 (1927-28) #4, 27-28. *[19:18, 19]*

Exodus 20:1-17

Walter Quincy Scott, "Notes on the Decalogue—Ex. 20:1-17," *BRec* 5 (1908) 76-82.

[Jay Benson Hamilton], "International Sunday School Lessons: The Ten Commandments: Exodus 20:1-17 (Made in Germany.)," *CFL, 3rd Ser.,* 25 (1919) 115-116.

Exodus 20:2-6

Benno Jacob, "The First and Second Commandments. An Excerpt from the 'Commentary on Exodus'," *Jud* 13 (1964) 3-18. *[20:2, 3-6]*

Exodus 20:2

*T. K. Meek, "Some Lapses of Old Testament Translators," *JBL* 55 (1936) x. *[20:2f.]*

Exodus 20:3-5

*J. N. M. Wijngaards, "'You shall not bow down to them or serve them'," *IJT* 18 (1969) 180-190. *[20:3-5a]*

Exodus 20:4-5

William Aldis Wright, "Notes on Exodus XX. 4, 5," *JP* 4 (1872) 156.

Exodus 20:5

*Dean A. Walker, "Note on Ex. XX 5b; Deut V 9b," *JBL* 21 (1902) 188-191.

Exodus 20:6

E. Schaller, "Exodus 20:6: Law or Gospel?" *JTLC* 5 (1965) #3, 1-14.

Exodus 20:7

Anonymous, "Comparative Translation: Exodus 20:7. A Study in Modernizing the English Bible," *BW* 21 (1903) 302-303.

Lewis B. Paton, "The Meaning of Exodus XX. 7.," *JBL* 22 (1903) 201-210.

A. Thom, "Exodus XX. 7," *ET* 23 (1911-12) 380-381.

Albert J. Wagner, "An Interpretation of Exodus 20:7," *Interp* 6 (1952) 228-229.

M. E. Andrew, "Using God. Exodus xx. 7," *ET* 74 (1962-63) 304-307.

Exodus 20:8

*John D. W. Watts, "Infinitive Absolute as Imperative and Interpretation of Exodus 20:8," *ZAW* 74 (1962) 141-145.

Exodus 20:17

*William L. Moran, "The Conclusion of the Decalogue (Ex 20,17 = Dt 5,21)," *CBQ* 29 (1967) 543-554.

Exodus 20:20

Moshe Greenberg, "נסה in Exodus 20:20 and the Purpose of the Sinaitic Theophany," *JBL* 79 (1960) 273-276.

Exodus 20:22-25

W. A. Curtis, "The Altar of Unhewn Stone," *Exp, 8th Ser.,* 6 (1913) 471-480. *[20:22 (25?)]*

Exodus 20:24-26

*C. V. Anthony, "The Order of Melchisedec," *ONTS* 3 (1883-84) 209-210. *[20:24-26]*

Edward Robertson, "The Altar of Earth (Exodus xx, 24-26)," *JJS* 1 (1948-49) 12-21.

Exodus 21:6

*Charles F. Fensham, "New Light on Exodus 21:6 and 22:7 from the Laws of Eshnunna," *JBL* 78 (1959) 160-161.

Z. W. Falk, "Exodus XXI 6," *VT* 9 (1959) 86-88.

Exodus 21:7-11

*I. Mendelsohn, "The Conditional Sale into Slavery of Free-born Daughters in Nuzi and the Law of Exodus 21:7-11," *JAOS* 55 (1935) 190-195.

Exodus 21:8

J. Hoftijzer, "Ex. XXI 8," *VT* 7 (1957) 388-391.

Exodus 21:10

R. North, "Flesh, Covering and Response, Ex. 21:10," *VT* 5 (1955) 204-206.

Shalom M. Paul, "Exod. 21:10 a Threefold Maintenance Clause," *JNES* 28 (1969) 48-53.

Exodus 21:12-17

J. G. Williams, "Concerning One of the Apodictic Formulas," *VT* 14 (1964) 484-489. *[21:12, 15-17]*

J. G. Williams, "Addenda to 'Concerning One of the Apodictic Formulas'," *VT* 15 (1965) 113-115. *[21:12, 15-17]*

Exodus 21:16

James Edward Hogg, "Exod. 21:16 ('Kidnaping')," *AJSL* 44 (1927-28) 263-264.

Exodus 21:18-19

F. Charles Fensham, "Exodus XXI 18-19 in the Light of Hittite Law §10," *VT* 10 (1960) 333-335.

Exodus 21:28

*A. Van Selms, "The Goring Ox in Babylonian and Biblical Law," *ArOr* 18 (1950) Part 4, 321-330. *[21:28ff.]*

Exodus 22:4-5

*William Aldis Wright, "Note on two passages of Exodus," *JP* 4 (1872) 70-73. *[22:4 (5)]*

Exodus 22:4

*Elias J. Bickerman, "Two Legal Interpretations of the Septuagint," *RIDA,* 3rd Ser., 3 (1956) 81-104. *[22:4]*

J. J. Rabinowitz, "Exodus XXII 4 and the Septuagint Version Thereof," *VT* 9 (1959) 40-46.

*Joseph Heinemann, "The *Targum* of Ex. XXII, 4 and the Ancient *Halakha*," *Tarbiz* 38 (1968-69) #3, v.

Exodus 22:7

*Charles F. Fensham, "New Light on Exodus 21:6 and 22:7 from the Laws of Eshnunna," *JBL* 78 (1959) 160-161.

Exodus 22:12

F. Charles Fensham, "*d* in Exodus xxii 12," *VT* 12 (1962) 337-339.

Exodus 22:15-16

*David Halivni Weiss, "A Note on ארשה לא אשר," *JBL* 81 (1962) 67-69. *[22:15 (16)]*

Exodus 22:16

*Elias J. Bickerman, "Two Legal Interpretations of the Septuagint," *RIDA, 3rd Ser.,* 3 (1956) 81-104. *[22:16]*

Exodus 22:23

James Edward Hogg, "Exod. 22:23 ('Nocturnal Thief' and 'Restitution')," *AJSL* 44 (1927-28) 58-61.

Exodus 22:28

James Moffatt, "Opera Foris. Materials for the Preacher," *Exp, 7th Ser.,* 8 (1909) 186-187. *[22:28]*

Exodus 23:18

*Norman Snaith, "Exodus 23:18 and 34:25," *JTS, N.S.,* 20 (1969) 533-534.

Exodus 23:19

*Andrew Lang, "Seething the Kid," *Man* 7 (1907) #103. *[23:19]*

*T. B. McCorkindale, "An Ancient Ritual Prohibition," *HR* 67 (1914) 227. *[23:19]*

*Max Radin, "The Kid and Its Mother's Milk," *AJSL* 40 (1923-24) 209-218. *[23:19]*

*D. Daube, "A Note on a Jewish Dietary Law," *JTS* 37 (1936) 289-291. *[23:19]*

Gustave von Grunebaum, "Exodus 23:19 in an Arabic Rhetoric," *JQR, N.S.,* 31 (1940-41) 405-406.

Exodus 23:21

Shifra and Svi Rin, "A Marginal Note on Marginal Notes," *Lĕš* 33 (1968-69) #2/3, n.p.n. [תמר in Ex. 23:21]

Exodus 23:23

Biblicus, "A conjectural Emendation of Exodus xxiii. 23," *TRep* 4 (1784) 73-74.

Exodus 23:28

*Anonymous, "Sesostris, the Hornet of Exod. 23:28, Deut. 7:20, Josh. 24:12," *QCS, 3rd Ser.,* 10 (1838) 281-285.

Exodus 24:11

Anonymous, "'They did Eat and Drink'," *BWR* 1 (1877) 363. *[24:11]*

Exodus 24:29

B., "The Horns of Moses," *CongML* 28 (1845) 23-26. *[24:29]*

Exodus 27:15-28

*W. Brryman Ridges, "On the Structure of the Tabernacle," *PEFQS* 28 (1896) 189. *[27:15, 17, 19, 23, 28]*

Exodus 28:17-20

James S. Blackwell, "Comparison of a few Versions in regard to the Precious Stones on the Jewish High-priest's Breastplate, Exodus, xxviii. 17-20," *PAPA* 13 (1881) 11-12. *[Bound with Transactions, but paged separately]*

Exodus 28:31-35

J. A. Seiss, "The Robe of the Ephod. An Exposition of Exodus 28:31-35," *ER* 6 (1854-55) 114-124.

Exodus 28:42

*Walter J. Burghardt, "Cyril of Alexandria on 'Wool and Linen'," *Tr* 2 (1944) 484-486. *[28:42 (Douay)]*

Exodus 29:32

*John P. Peters, "Miscellaneous Notes," *AJSL* 1 (1884-85) 115-199. [An Aramaean Synagogue Scroll containing Ex. 29:32ff., pp. 116-117]

Exodus 30:33

H. B. S. W., "The Holy Anointing Oil," *PEFQS* 14 (1882) 269-270 *[30:33]*

C[laude] R. Conder, "Notes. *Holy Oil*," *PEFQS* 15 (1883) 102. *[30:33]*

H. B. S. W., "The Holy Anointing Oil," *PEFQS* 15 (1883) 243. *[30:33]*

Exodus 30:34

Joseph Offord, "Archaeological Notes. *IV. Galbanum*," *PEFQS* 45 (1913) 149. *[30:34]*

Exodus Chapter 32-33:6

*M. H. Segal, "The Renewal of the Covenant at Sinai: An Essay in Exegesis," *JQR, 75th* (1967) 490-497. *[Chap. 32-33:6]*

Exodus Chapter 32

F. A. Cox, "The Golden Calf. Exodus XXXII," *JSL, 1st Ser.,* 4 (1849) 73-88.

T. H. Robinson, "The Golden Calf," *Exp, 8th Ser.,* 24 (1922) 121-135. *[Chap. 32]*

Michael Walzer, "Exodus 32 and the Theory of Holy War: The History of a Citation," *HTR* 61 (1968) 1-14.

Exodus 32:4

*G. R. Driver, "Things Old and New in the Old Testament," *MUSJ* 45 (1969) 463-478. [I. 1. ḥereṭ - Ex. 32:4, pp. 463-466]

Exodus 32:18

R. Edelmann, "Exodus 32[18]: קוֹל עֲנּוֹת אָנֹכִי שֹׁמֵעַ," *JTS, N.S.,* 1 (1950) 56.

F. L. Anderson, "A Lexicographical Note on Exodus XXXII 18," *VT* 16 (1966) 108-112.

R. Edelmann, "To עֲנּוֹת Exodus XXXII 18," *VT* 16 (1966) 355.

R. N. Whybray, "עֲנּוֹת in Exodus XXXII 18," *VT* 17 (1967) 122. *(Corr. p. 243)*

Exodus 32:20

F. C. Fensham, "The Burning of the Golden Calf and Ugarit," *IEJ* 16 (1966) 191-193. *[32:20]*

Exodus 32:22

Milton G. Evans, "Interpretation of בְרָע in Ex. xxxii. 22," *JBL* 18 (1899) 216-217.

Exodus 32:31-32

Anonymous, "Moses' Prayer to be Blotted Out of God's Book. Exodus XXXII. 31, 32," *MR* 7 (1824) 293-296.

Exodus Chapter 33

C. A. Ben-Mordecai, "Notes on Chapter 33 of Exodus," *JQR, N.S.,* 31 (1940-41) 407-410.

Exodus 33:6

I. Zolli, "The Ornament 'From Mount Horeb' (Ex. 33.6)," *JQR, N.S.,* 30 (1939-40) 71-75. *(Trans. from the Italian)*

Exodus 33:7-11

Charles M. Mead, "Examination of Ex. 33:7-11," *JBL* 1 (1881) 155-168.

C. A. Ben-Mordecai, "The Tent of Meeting," *JQR, N.S.,* 30 (1939-40) 399-401. *[33:7-11]*

Exodus 33:7

*Menahem Haran, "The Nature of the ''Ohel Mo'edh' in Pentateuchal Sources," *JSS* 5 (1960) 50-65. [The 'Ohel Mo'edh in Exodus. The Meaning of Exod. XXXIII. 7, pp. 52-54]

Exodus 33:12-34:35

*M. H. Segal, "The Renewal of the Covenant at Sinai: An Essay in Exegesis," *JQR, 75th* (1967) 490-497. *[33:12-34:35]*

Exodus 33:14

*Godfrey N. Curnock, "A Neglected Parallel (Mt. XI. 28 and Ex. XXXIII. 14)," *ET* 44 (1932-33) 141.

*E[phraim] A. Speiser, "The Biblical Idiom *Pānīm Hōlᵉkīm*," *JQR, 75th* (1967) 515-517. [פָּנֶיךָ הֹלְכִים] *[Chap. 33:14f.]*

Exodus 33:15

E. W. Shalders, "Biblical Notes. Exodus xxxiii. 15," *Exp, 1st Ser.,* 7 (1878) 467-471.

Exodus 33:19

A. D. Goode, "A Note on Exodus 33:19," *JBL* 59 (1940) xiv.

Exodus 33:22-23

William Manson, "Moses Cannot Go in Front of God," *CJRT* 2 (1925) 165. *[33:22-23]*

Exodus 33:23

*W. Peter Boyd, "The Mystery of God and Revelation," *SJT* 13 (1960) 178-182. *[33:23]*

Exodus Chapter 34

W. E. Barnes, "The Ten Words of Exodus XXXIV," *JTS* 6 (1904-05) 557-563.

Exodus 34:5

Solomon Zeitlin, "Some Reflections of the Text of the Pentateuch," *JQR,*
N.S., 52 (1961-62) 130. *[34:5]*

Exodus 34:6

*Robert C. Dentan, "The Literary Affinities of Exodus XXXIV 6f.," *VT* 13
(1963) 34-51.

Exodus 34:7

Anonymous, "Exodus xxxiv. 7," *CongML* 4 (1821) 135.

G. W., "Biblical Criticism on Exodus xxxiv. 7," *CongML* 4 (1821) 629-630.

T. K., "Biblical Criticism on Exodus xxxiv. 7," *CongML* 5 (1822) 135-136.

J. H., "Critical Examination of Exod. XXXIV. 7," *CongML* 11 (1828) 130-
131. [Editorial Reply, pp. 131-133]

B. Boothroyd, "Dr. Boothroyd on the Construction of Exodus xxxiv, 7,"
CongML 11 (1828) 244-247.

Exodus 34:21

Anonymous, "Observations on Exodus XXXIV. 21," *MR* 4 (1821) 298-299.

Exodus 34:25

*Norman Snaith, "Exodus 23:18 and 34:25," *JTS, N.S.,* 20 (1969) 533-534.

Exodus 34:26

*T. B. McCorkindale, "An Ancient Ritual Prohibition," *HR* 67 (1914) 227.
[23:19]

*Max Radin, "The Kid and Its Mother's Milk," *AJSL* 40 (1923-24) 209-218.
[23:19]

*D. Daube, "A Note on a Jewish Dietary Law," *JTS* 37 (1936) 289-291.
[23:19]

Exodus 34:28

William Wye Smith, "'The Words of the Covenant, the Ten Commandments' (Exodus xxxiv. 28)—Their Far-Reaching Nature," *HR* 37 (1899) 444-447.

Exodus 34:29-35

Charles A. Briggs, "An Exegesis of Exodus XXXIV. 29-35," *PR* 1 (1880) 565-566.

Julian Morgenstern, "Moses with the Shining Face," *HUCA* 2 (1925) 1-27. *[34:29-35]*

*James P. Wilson, "A Comparative Study of Exodus xxxiv. 29-35, and 2nd Cor. iii. 12-18, with Regard to the Veil on Moses' Face," *GUOST* 9 (1938-39) 18-21.

Exodus 35:1-40:38

Anonymous, "Outline View of Exodus.—Part Third—Chapters xxxv. 1—xl. 38," *CFL, 3rd Ser.*, 7 (1907) 57-60.

Exodus Chapters 35-39

*Baruch A. Levine, "The Descriptive Tabernacle Texts of the Pentateuch," *JAOS* 85 (1965) 307-318. [I. Exodus 35-39, pp. 307-310]

Exodus 40:17-19

F. C. Burkitt, "The Text of Exodus XL 17-19 in the Munich Palimpsest," *JTS* 29 (1927-28) 146-147.

§582 **3.5.2.4 Studies on Manuscripts of Exodus**

*B. Pick, "Horae Samaritanae; or, a Collection of Various Readings of the Samaritan Pentateuch Compared with the Hebrew and Other Ancient Versions, II.—Exodus," *BS* 33 (1876) 533-557.

Seymour de Ricci, "The Zouche Sahidic Exodus Fragment (Exodus xvi, 6—xix. 11). From the Original Manuscript," *SBAP* 28 (1906) 54-67.

P. Wernberg-Møller, "The Exodus Fragment from Massada," *VT* 10 (1960) 229-230.

§583 *3.5.2.5 Exegetical Studies on the Book of Leviticus*

*S. R. Driver, "The Revised Version of the Old Testament. III. The Books of Leviticus and Numbers," *Exp, 3rd Ser.,* 2 (1885) 211-224. [1:3; 2:1; 3:9; 5:1, 4; 5:14-6:7; 6:2-5; 6:18; 8:33marg.; 11:5, 13, 18, 29; 14:10; 16:8, 10, 26; 16:22; 17:7marg., 14; 18:18; 19:24; 21:4marg.; 23:2; 23:3, 24, 32, 39; 35:33; 26:1; 26:30, pp. 211-221]

Frederick Field, "Dr. Field's Old Testament Revision Notes. Transcribed from the Author's MS. by the Rev. John Henry Burn, B.D., V.," *ET* 30 (1918-19) 522-524. [2:1; 15:2; 16:8; 18:18; 19:20]

Leviticus Chapter 1

*John P. Peters, "The Date of Leviticus 1," *JBL* 8 (1888) 128-130.

Leviticus 3:11

Herbert Crossland, "Common Sense in Criticism," *ET* 31 (1919-20) 41-42. *[3:11]*

Leviticus 5:1

James Kennedy, "Leviticus v. 1," *ET* 29 (1917-18) 561.

Leviticus 5:2-5

Abram Spiro, "A Law on the Sharing of Information," *PAAJR* 28 (1959) 95-101. *[5:2-5]*

Leviticus 5:2-4

A[bram] Spiro, "A Law in Privity in the Pentateuch," *JBL* 58 (1939) xii. *[5:2-4]*

Leviticus 5:8

*Samuel Daiches, "The Meaning of עֹרֶף in Leviticus v. 8," *ET* 39 (1927-28) 426-427.

Leviticus Chapters 8 and 9

*Baruch A. Levine, "The Descriptive Tabernacle Texts of the Pentateuch," *JAOS* 85 (1965) 307-318. [II. Leviticus 8-9, pp. 310-314]

Leviticus Chapter 10

Samuel Cox, "The Four Nephews of Moses. Leviticus X," *Exp, 1st Ser.,* 8 (1878) 346-359.

Leviticus Chapter 11

*Royden Keith Yerkes, "The Unclean Animals of Leviticus 11 and Deuternomony 14," *JQR, N.S.,* 14 (1923-24) 1-29.

Leviticus 11:3-7

*Honeyman Gillespie and Robert Young, "Correspondence on Lev. XI. 3-7, and Deut. XIV. 6-8," *JSL, 4th Ser.,* 9 (1866) 383-400.

*W. Wright, "The Arabic Term for *Hare*," *JSL, 4th Ser.,* 10 (1866-67) 180-182. *[11:3-7]*

Leviticus 11:5

Anonymous, "The Trouble About Moses' Coney," *CFL, 3rd Ser.,* 30 (1924) 459-460. *[11:5]*

Leviticus 11:6

John Hogg, "The Hare as a Ruminant," *JSL, 4th Ser.,* 3 (1863) 430-432. *[11:6]*

Thomas John Buckton, "Rumination of the Hare," *JSL, 4th Ser.,* 3 (1863) 433-434. *[11:6]*

Leviticus 11:13-19

*William L. Moran, "The Literary Connection between Lv 11, 13-19 and Dt 14, 12-18," *CBQ* 28 (1966) 271-277.

Leviticus 12:1-5

D. I. Macht, "A Scientific Appreciation of Leviticus 12:1-5," *JBL* 52 (1933) 253-260.

Leviticus Chapters 13-14

Morris Jastrow Jr., "The So-Called Leprosy Laws, An Analysis of Leviticus, Chapters 13 and 14," *JQR, N.S.,* 4 (1913-14) 357-418.

*J. Dyneley Prince, "Note on Leprosy in the Old Testament," *JBL* 38 (1919) 30-34. *[Chaps. 13 and 14]*

Leviticus Chapter 14

Anonymous, "The Leprous House," *BWR* 1 (1877) 321-322. *[Chap. 14]*

Leviticus 14:37

Joel L. Kraemer, "*Š^eqa'^arūrōt:* A Proposed Solution for an Unexplained Hapax," *JNES* 25 (1966) 125-129. *[14:37]*

Leviticus 15:1

Z. M. Rabinowitz, "Yannay's *Qerova* to Lev. 15, 1 (Sources and Interpretation)," *Tarbiz* 28 (1958-59) #3-4, VII.

Leviticus Chapter 16

George J. Walker, "On the Typical Import of the Ordinances of the Day of Atonement. Levit. xvi," *JSL, 1st Ser.,* 3 (1849) 74-86.

David Brown, "The Day of Atonement. Leviticus xvi," *TML* 2 (1889) 1-11. *(Review)*

*David Heumark, "Crescas and Spinoza. A Memorial Paper in Honor of the Five Hundredth Anniversary of the 'Or Adonoi'," *YCCAR* 18 (1908) 277-348. [Annotation (Lev. 16), pp. 332-333]

Charles L. Feinberg, "The Scapegoat of Leviticus 16," *BS* 115 (1958) 320-333.

*Sidney B. Hoenig, "The New Qumran Pesher on Azazel," *JQR, N.S.,* 56 (1965-66) 248-253. *[Chap. 16]*

B. A. Levine, "Kippurim," *EI* 9 (1969) 136. *(English Summary) [Chap. 16]*

Leviticus 16:5-10

George Bush, "Azazel, or the Levitical Scape-Goat; *A Critical Exposition of Leviticus* 16:5-10," *BRCR, N.S.,* 8 (1842) 116-136.

Leviticus 16:5

*A. H. W., "Exegesis of Difficult Texts. Mark XV. 15, compared with Leviticus XVI. 5," *JSL, 4th Ser.,* 1 (1862) 350-358.

Leviticus 16:8-26

C. J. Ball, "Azazel (Lev. XVI. 8, 10, 26)," *AJSL* 7 (1890-91) 77-79.

Leviticus Chapters 17-26

*Lewis Bayles Paton, "The Holiness Code and Ezekiel," *PRR* 7 (1896) 98-115. *[Chaps. 17-26]*

Leviticus Chapters 17-19

*Lewis B[ayles] Paton, "The Relation of Lev. XX. to Lev. XVII-XIX," *AJSL* 10 (1893-94) 111-121.

Leviticus 17:1-9

*Franklin N. Jewett, "Questions from the Pew. The Place for Sacrificing. (Lev. xvii: 1-9; Deut. xii: 8-15.)," *OC* 21 (1907) 564-567.

Leviticus Chapter 18

A. G., "Leviticus XVIII," *TQ* 4 (1900) 319-347.

*J. H. Bernard, "The Levitical Code and the Table of Kindred and Affinity," *Exp, 8th Ser.,* 4 (1912) 20-31. *[Chap. 18]*

Leviticus 18:5

*Hans Kosmala, "Two Judaisms," *IRM* 32 (1943) 420-426. *[18:5]*

Leviticus 18:30

*W. Lock, "Philo's Interpretation of Leviticus XVIII 30," *JTS* 9 (1907-08) 300-301.

Leviticus 19:18

David Noel Freedman, "The Hebrew Old Testament and the Ministry Today. An Exegetical Study of Leviticus 19:18b," *PP* 5 (1964) #1, 9-14, 30.

Leviticus Chapter 20

*Lewis B[ayles] Paton, "The Relation of Lev. XX. to Lev. XVII-XIX," *AJSL*
10 (1893-94) 111-121.

Leviticus 20:6

*Claude R. Conder, "Notes on New Discoveries," *PEFQS* 41 (1909) 266-
275. [The Familiar Spirit (Lev. 20:6; 1 Sam. 28:3; Isa. 29:4), p. 270]

Leviticus 21:1-6

Adam C. Welch, "Note on Leviticus 21_{1-6}," *ZAW* 43 (1925) 135-137.

Leviticus 21:11

*Israel Efros, "Textual Notes on the Hebrew Bible," *JAOS* 45 (1925) 152-
154. [1. Lev. 21:11, ‏נפשת מת לא יבאעל כל‎, p. 152]

Leviticus Chapter 23

*B. D. Eerdmans, "The Hebrew Feasts in Leviticus xxiii," *Exp, 8th Ser.,* 4
(1912) 43-56.

Leviticus 23:1

*Leon J. Liebreich, "The Term Miqra'qodesh in the Synagogue Liturgy,"
JQR, 75th, (1967) 381-397.*[23:1]*

Leviticus 23:9-22

*Anonymous, "The Feasts of Jehovah," *BWR* 1 (1877) 1-48. [Lecture II.
The Wave-Sheaf and the Wave-Loaves, Lev. 23:9-22, pp. 14-29]

Leviticus 23:23-44

*Anonymous, "The Feasts of Jehovah," *BWR* 1 (1877) 1-48. [Lecture III.
The Feasts of the Future, Lev. 23:23-end: The Feast of Trumpets; The
Day of Atonement; The Feast of Tabernacles, pp. 37-48]

Leviticus 23:40

Daniel Plooij, "For the Translation of the Hebrew ‏כַּפֹּת תְּמָרִים‎ in Lev. xxiii,
40 by the Unreduplicated Plural of the Root *1b,*" *BBC* 4 (1927) 18-19.

S. Tolkowsky, "The Meaning of פְּרִי עֵץ הָדָר (Lev. XXIII, 40)," *JPOS* 8 (1928) 17-23.

Leviticus 24:10-23

H. Mittwoch, "The Story of the Blasphemer seen in a Wider Context," *VT* 15 (1965) 386-389. *[24:10-23]*

Leviticus 25:23-30

James Edward Hogg, "The Meaning of לצמתת in Lev. 25:23-30," *AJSL* 42 (1925-26) 208-210.

Leviticus 25:23

Anonymous, "The Land shall not be sold forever, Leviticus 25:23," *CMR* 5 (1893) 370-378.

Leviticus 25:30

J. J. Rabinowitz, "A Biblical Parallel to a Legal Formula from Ugarit," *VT* 8 (1958) 95. *[25:30]*

Leviticus 25:39-43

*Edwin Yamauchi, "Slaves of God," *BETS* 9 (1966) 31-50. *[25:39-43]*

Leviticus 26:30

Edmund Sinker, "'The Carcasses of Your Idols.' Leviticus xxvi. 30," *ET* 13 (1901-02) 383-384.

*J. W. Jack, "Recent Biblical Archaeology," *ET* 53 (1941-42) 367-370. [Archæology and the Biblical Text: 1. Incense Altars, (Lev. 26:30), p. 368]

Leviticus 26:31-33

W. J. Beasley, "When Prophecy Became History," *AT* 1 (1956-57) #2, 13-15. *[26:31-33]*

Leviticus 27:28

D. Sperber, "A Note on Lev. XXVII 28," *VT* 16 (1966) 515-518.

§584 *3.5.2.6 Studies on Manuscripts of the Book of Leviticus*

*B. Pick, "Horae Samaritanae; or, a Collection of Various Readings of the Samaritan Pentateuch Compared with the Hebrew and Other Ancient Versions, Leviticus," *BS* 34 (1877) 79-88.

*Adam C. Welch, "The Septuagint Version of Leviticus," *ET* 30 (1918-19) 277-278.

§585 *3.5.2.7 Exegetical Studies of Numbers*

Joseph Agar Beet, "The Holiness of God, and of the Holy," *Exp, 7th Ser.,* 2 (1906) 531-544. [11:44, 45; 19:2; 20:26; 21:8]

*S. R. Driver, "The Revised Version of the Old Testament. III. The Books of Leviticus and Numbers," *Exp, 3rd Ser.,* 2 (1885) 211-224. [4:20; 6:2; 7:89; 8:11; 11:25; 12:2, 8; 13:17, 22, 33; 18:2, 4; 21:2-3marg., 14, 30marg.; 22:5; 23:3; 24:3, 4; 24:17; 25:3; 31:10; 25:11, pp. 221-224]

Numbers Chapter 1

*George E. Mendenhall, "The Census Lists of Numbers 1 and 26" *JBL* 77 (1958) 52-66.

Numbers 3:12-13

*P. E. Kretzmann, "The Substitution of the Levites for the First-Born," *CTM* 4 (1933) 536. *[3:12-13]*

Numbers 4:15-20

James   Kennedy,   "Numbers   4:15-20,"   *JBL*   36   (1917)   48-52.

Numbers Chapter 5

Julius A. Bewer, "The Ordeal in Num., Chap. 5," *AJSL* 30 (1913-14) 36-47.

Numbers 5:11-28

A. Spiro, "The So-called Ordeal of the Suspected Wife," *JBL* 57 (1938) xi. *[5:11ff.]*

*G. R. Driver, "Two Problems in the Old Testament Examined in the Light of Assyriology," *Syria* 33 (1956) 70-78. [II. The "Waters of Bitterness" (Numbers v, 11-28), pp. 73-77]

Numbers 5:14

*Claude R. Conder, "Notes on New Discoveries," *PEFQS* 41 (1909) 266-275. [The Ordeal of Jealousy (Num. 5:14), p. 270]

Numbers 6:1-21

Morris Jastrow Jr., "The 'Nazir' Legislation," *JBL* 33 (1914) 266-285. *[6:1-21]*

Numbers 6:24-26

*Leon J. Liebreich, "The Songs of Ascents and the Priestly Blessing," *JBL* 74 (1955) 33-36. *[6:24-26]*

Numbers Chapter 7

*Baruch A. Levine, "The Descriptive Tabernacle Texts of the Pentateuch," *JAOS* 85 (1965) 307-318. [III. Numbers 7, pp. 314-318]

Numbers 7:89

W. R. W. Gardner, "Numbers VII. 89," *ET* 27 (1915-16) 521-522.

Numbers 10:29-32

John A. Irvine, "Old Texts in Modern Translations. Numbers x. 29-32 (Moffatt)," *ET* 49 (1937-38) 20-21.

Numbers 11:4

*Duncan B. Macdonald, "Notes Critical and Lexicographical," *JBL* 14 (1895) 57-62 [III. Num. 11:4, p. 58]

*W. T. Pilter, "The Manna of the Israelites," *SBAP* 39 (1917) 155-167, 187-206. [Numbers 11:4ff., pp. 201-205]

D. Beirne, "A Note on Numbers 11, 4," *B* 44 (1963) 201-203.

Numbers 11:31-32

P. E. Kretzmann, "The Number of Quails in Nu. 11:31, 32," *CTM* 11 (1940) 210-211.

Numbers Chapter 12

W. Gunther Plaut, "The Punishment of Aaron: A Commentary on Numbers 12," *CCARJ* 11 (1963-64) #2, 35-38.

Numbers 12:3

*Albert Abbott, "Was Moses the Meekest of Men?" *ET* 45 (1933-34) 524-525. *[12:3]*

Numbers 12:10

M. D., "Thoughts. I. Shame on account of God's Displeasure with us," *Exp, 3rd Ser.,* 3 (1886) 228-229. *[12:10]*

Numbers 12:14

Margaret D. Gibson, "Numbers XII. 14," *ET* 18 (1906-07) 478.

Numbers 13-14

Simon J. DeVries, "The Origin of the Murmuring Tradition," *JBL* 87 (1968) 51-58. *[Chaps. 13-14]*

Numbers 13:17-33

*Kemper Fullerton, "Expository Studies in the Old Testament: VIII. The Last Days of Moses," *BW* 30 (1907) 123-134. *[13:17-20, 23-33]*

Numbers 13:32

Morris Sigel Seale, "Numbers XIII. 32," *ET* 68 (1956-57) 28.

Numbers 14:1

James Moffatt, "Opera Foris; Or, Materials for the Preacher. Second Series. —III.," *Exp, 8th Ser.,* 2 (1911) 563-568. *[14:1]*

Numbers 14:26-38

*S. McEvenue, "A Source-Critical Problem in Num 14, 26-38," *B* 50 (1969) 453-465.

Numbers 14:44

*A. D. Singer, "Philological Notes," *JPOS* 21 (1948) 104-109. *[14:44]*

Numbers 15:32-36

J. Weingreen, "The Case of the woodgatherer (Numbers XV 32-36)," *VT* 16 (1966) 361-363.

A. Phillips, "The Case of the woodgatherer Reconsidered," *VT* 19 (1969) 125-128. *[15:32-36]*

Numbers 15:37-41

Ben Zion Bokser, "The Thread of Blue," *PAAJR* 31 (1963) 132. *[15:37-41]*

Numbers 15:38:41

*Henry Hayman, "On the Law of Fringes in Numbers and Deuteronomy," *BS* 51 (1894) 705-707. *[15:38-41]*

Numbers 16:27

*Robert H. Kennett, "Korah, Dathan, and Abiram," *ICMM* 12 (1915-16) 152-157. *[16:27]*

*Jacob Liver, "Korah, Dathan and Abiram," *SH* 8 (1961) 189-217. *[16:27]*

Numbers 16:30-34

*Greta Hort, "The Death of Qorah," *ABR* 7 (1959) 2-26. *[16:30-34]*

Numbers 16:32

*Robert H. Kennett, "Korah, Dathan, and Abiram," *ICMM* 12 (1915-16) 152-157. *[16:27]*

*Jacob Liver, "Korah, Dathan and Abiram," *SH* 8 (1961) 189-217. *[16:32]*

Numbers 17:2

Anonymous, "Writing on Rods," *CongML* 14 (1831) 613-614. *[17:2]*

Numbers 18:7

*E[phraim] A. Speiser, "Unrecognized Dedication," *IEJ* 13 (1963) 69-73. [Num. 18:7, מַתָּנָה]

Numbers 18:12

*Salomon Speier, "The Jerusalem Targum to Num. 18:12 and Deut. 34:3," *JBL* 65 (1946) 315-318.

Numbers Chapter 19

Julius A. Bewer, "The Original Significance of the Rite of the Red Cow in Numbers xix," *JBL* 24 (1905) 41-44.

Henry Preserved Smith, "Notes on the Red Heifer," *JBL* 27 (1908) 153-156. *[Chap. 19]*

Numbers Chapter 20

*Anonymous, "The Smitten Rocks," *CongML* 19 (1836) 29-31. *[Chap. 20]*

W. Gunther Plaut, "The Sin of the Brothers: A Commentary on Numbers 20," *CCARJ* 9 (1961-62) #1, 18-24.

Norman D. Hirsch, "The Sin of Moses," *CCARJ* 13 (1965-66) #3, 38-42. *[Chap. 20]*

Numbers 20:7-12

Barnard C. Taylor, "Numbers 20:7-12," *ONTS* 9 (1889) 117-118.

Numbers 21:1-9

*Kemper Fullerton, "Expository Studies in the Old Testament: VIII. The Last Days of Moses," *BW* 30 (1907) 123-134. *[21:1-9]*

Numbers 21:1-3

*B. Mazar, "The Sanctuary of Arad and the Family of Hobab the Kenite," *JNES* 24 (1965) 297-303. *[21:1-3]*

Numbers 21:1

*Menahem Naor, "The Problem of the Biblical Arad," *PAAJR* 36 (1968) 95-105. *[21:1]*

Numbers 21:4-9

Walter O. Speckhard, "Sermon Study on Numbers 21:4-9 for Judica," *CTM* 22 (1951) 119-125.

Numbers 21:6

*H. L. Parker, "'Fiery Serpents'," *PEFQS* 61 (1929) 58. *[21:6]*

Numbers 21:8

*H. H. Rowley, "Zadok and Nehushtan," *JBL* 58 (1939) 113-141. [The Brazen Serpent, Num 21:8f., pp. 132-141]

Numbers 21:9

*C. Schick, "Letters from Herr Baurath von Schick. IV. Baron Ustinoff's Collection of Antiquities at Jaffa. 10," *PEFQS* 25 (1893) 297. *[21:9]*

C. Fox, "Circle and Serpent Antiquities," *PEFQS* 26 (1894) 83-87. *[cf. Num 21:9 with part II]*

Numbers 21:14

H. Cohen, "Numbers XXI. 14," *ET* 5 (1893-94) 336.

Harold M. Wiener, "The Text of Numbers XXI. 14f.," *BS* 76 (1919) 232-234.

*N. H. Tur-Sinai, "Was There an Ancient 'Book of the Wars of the Lord'?" *BIES* 24 (1959-60) #2/3, III-IV. *[21:14]*

Numbers 21:16-18

*W. R. S[mith], "The Poetry of the Old Testament," *BQRL* 65 (1877) 26-70. [Song of the Well, p. 45] *[21:16ff.]*

Milton S. Terry, "The Song of the Well. Some Notes on Numbers XXI. 16-18," *BS* 58 (1901) 407-418.

Numbers 21:24

*G. R. Driver, "Mistranslations," *PEQ* 80 (1948) 64-65. *[21:24]*

Numbers 21:27-30

*Paul D. Hanson, "Song of Heshbon and David's *Nîr*," *HTR* 61 (1968) 297-341. *[21:27b-30]*

J. R. Bartlett, "The Historical Reference of Numbers XXI. 27-30," *PEQ* 101 (1969) 94-100.

Numbers Chapters 22-24

R. D. C. Robbins, "The Character and Prophecies of Balaam—Numbers xxii-xxiv," *BS* 3 (1846) 347-378, 699-743.

Russell Martineau, "Balaam," *TRL* 15 (1878) 327-365. *(Review) [Chaps. 22-24]*

Julius A. Bewer, "The Literary Problems of the Balaam Story in Numbers, Chapters 22-24," *AJT* 9 (1905) 238-262.

J. Hoeness, "Balaam. Numb. 22-24," *TQ* 12 (1908) 129-143, 218-243.

*Cuthbert Lattey, "Balaam: Prophet or Soothsayer? (Numbers XXII.-XXIV.)," *IER, 5th Ser.,* 22 (1923) 166-176.

*E. F. Sutcliffe, "Some Footnotes to the Fathers," *B* 6 (1925) 205-210. *[Chaps. 22-24]*

Numbers 22:2-24:25

*Samuel Cox, "Balaam: An Exposition and a Study," *Exp, 2nd Ser.,* 5 (1883) 1-10, 11-21, 120-144, 199-210, 245-258, 341-352, 401-425. [Introduction; I. The Chronicle of Balaam, 1. The Invitation, 2. The Journey, 3. First Oracle, 4. Second Oracle, 5. Third Oracle, 6. Fourth Oracle; II. The Supplementary Scriptures, 1. Adverse, 2. Favourable] *[22:2-24:25]*

*Samuel Cox, "Balaam: An Exposition and a Study. III. The Conclusion," *Exp, 2nd Ser.,* 6 (1883) 1-25. *[22:2-24:25]*

Numbers Chapter 22

E. F. Sutcliffe, "A Note on Numbers XXII," *B* 18 (1937) 439-442.

Numbers 22:5

A. S. Yahuda, "The Name of Balaam's Homeland," *JBL* 64 (1945) 547-551. *[22:5]*

Numbers 22:6

Herbert Loewe, "Numbers XXII. 6," *ET* 26 (1914-15) 378.

Numbers 22:20-22

Isaiah Parker, "The Way of God and the Way of Balaam," *ET* 27 (1904-05) 45. *[22:20-22]*

Numbers 22:21-34

T. K. Cheyne, "Arabian Parallels to Biblical Passages," *ET* 4 (1892-93) 402. *[22:21a, 22-34]*

Numbers 22:21-31

Maurice A. Canney, "Numbers XXII. 21-31," *ET* 27 (1915-16) 568.

Numbers 22:22

Anonymous, "Morsels of Criticism," *CongML* 4 (1821) 80. *[22:22]*

Numbers 22:23

W. K. Lowther Clarke, "Studies in Texts," *Theo* 10 (1925) 38-39. *[22:23]*

Numbers 22:28-30

Samuel Cox, "Balaam's Ass. Numbers xxii. 28-30," *Exp, 1st Ser.,* 8 (1878) 397-409.

Numbers 22:41-23:25

James A. Warton, "The Command to Bless. *An Exposition of Numbers 22:41-23:25,*" *Interp* 13 (1959) 37-48.

Numbers Chapters 23-24

W[illiam] F[oxwell] Albright, "The Oracles of Balaam," *JBL* 63 (1944) 207-233. *[Chaps. 23-24]*

Numbers 23:1-24:24

T. K. Cheyne, "Some Critical Difficulties in the Chapters on Balaam," *ET* 10 (1898-99) 399-402. *[23:1-24:24]*

Numbers 23:9-10

J. H. Hertz, "Numbers XXIII. 9b, 10," *ET* 45 (1933-34) 524.

Numbers 23:9

*Marcus Jastrow, "Light thrown on some Biblical passages by Talmudic usage," *JBL* 11 (1892) 126-130. *[23:9]*

Numbers 23:10

A. Thom, "Balaam's Prayer," *ET* 16 (1904-05) 334. *[23:10]*

James Moffatt, "Opera Foris; Or, Materials for the Preacher. Second Series," *Exp, 8th Ser.,* 2 (1911) 182-192. *[23:10]*

D. Winton Thomas, "The Word רֶבַע in Numbers XXIII. 10," *ET* 46 (1934-35) 285.

A. Guillaume, "A note on Numbers XXIII. 10," *VT* 12 (1962) 335-337.

Numbers 23:21

( ) Williams, "Numbers XXIII. 21. *He hath not beheld iniquity in Jacob, neither hath He seen perverseness in Israel,*" *MR* 2 (1819) 97-99.

Numbers 23:24

*Harry M. Orlinsky, "*Rāḇáṣ* for *Šāḵáḇ* in Numbers 24.9," *JQR, N.S.,* 35 (1944-45) 173-177. [II. On יְשַׁכָּב in Num. 23.24, pp. 176-177]

*Michael Wilensky, "No Emendation Needed," *JQR, N.S.,* 35 (1944-45) 435-436. *[23:24]*

Numbers 24:3-4

H. C. Ackerman, "Concerning the Nature of Balaam's Vision (Num. 24:3-4)," *ATR* 2 (1919-20) 233-234.

Numbers 24:3

*J. M. Allegro, "The Meaning of the Phrase šeṭūm hā'ayin in Num. XXIV 3, 15," *VT* 3 (1953) 78-79.

Numbers 24:4

*J. M. Allegro, "The Meaning of Nōphēl in Numbers XXIV. 4, 16," *ET* 65 (1953-54) 316-317.

Numbers 24:7

A. Bernstein, "Requests and Replies," *ET* 7 (1895-96) 158. *[24:7]*

M. D. Goldman, "Lexicographic Notes on Exegesis: A Misunderstood Passage in Numbers XXIV, 7," *ABR* 1 (1951) 60.

Numbers 24:8

Theodor H. Gaster, "Two Textual Emendations. Numbers xxiv. 8," *ET* 78 (1966-67) 267.

Numbers 24:9

*Harry M. Orlinsky, "*Rāḇáṣ* for *Šāḵáḇ* in Numbers 24.9," *JQR, N.S.,* 35 (1944-45) 173-177.

*Michael Wilensky, "No Emendation Needed," *JQR, N.S.,* 35 (1944-45) 435-436. *[24:9]*

Numbers 24:15-19

*Gilmore H. Guyot, "The Prophecy of Balaam," *CBQ* 2 (1940) 330-340.

Numbers 24:15

*J. M. Allegro, "The Meaning of the Phrase šeṭūm hā'ayin in Num. XXIV 3, 15," *VT* 3 (1953) 78-79.

Numbers 24:16

*J. M. Allegro, "The Meaning of Nōphēl in Numbers XXIV. 4, 16," *ET* 65 (1953-54) 316-317.

Numbers 24:17-24

*A. H. Sayce, "Balaam's Prophecy (Numbers XXIV. 17-24) and the God Sheth," *AJSL* 4 (1887-88) 1-6.

Numbers 24:23-25

T. K. Cheyne, "A Forgotten Kingdom in a Prophecy of Balaam," *Exp, 5th Ser.*, 3 (1896) 77-80. *[24:23, 25]*

Numbers 24:23-24

T. K. Cheyne, "Rival Restorations of Num. XXIV. 23, 24," *ET* 8 (1896-97) 520-521.

Numbers 25:9

*W. R. Coxwell Rogers, "Upon the Necessity of Cautiousness in Criticism," *JSL, 4th Ser.*, 9 (1866) 193-200. *[25:9]*

Numbers 25:18

C. Clermont-Ganneau, "Archaeological and Epigraphic Notes on Palestine. 8. *Betomarsea-Maioumas, and 'the matter of Peor'* (Numbers XXV, 18)," *PEFQS* 33 (1901) 369-374.

Numbers Chapter 26

*George E. Mendenhall, "The Census Lists of Numbers 1 and 26" *JBL* 77 (1958) 52-66.

Numbers 26:38-40

*J. Marquart, "The Genealogies of Benjamin," *JQR* 14 (1901-02) 343-351. *[Num. 26:38-40]*

Numbers 27:1-11

*N. H. Snaith, "The Daughters of Zelophehad," *VT* 16 (1966) 124-127. *[27:1-11]*

*J. Weingreen, "The Case of the Daughters of Zelophchad," *VT* 16 (1966) 518-522. *[27:1-11]*

Numbers 28:9-13

N. H. Snaith, "Numbers XXVIII 9, 11, 13 in the Ancient Versions," *VT* 19 (1969) 374.

Numbers 31:22

*Claude R. Conder, "Notes on New Discoveries," *PEFQS* 41 (1909) 266-275. [Iron (Deut. 8:9; Num. 31:22; 1 Sam. 17:7), p. 271]

Numbers 31:27

*G.R.Driver, "On תפשי המלחמה (Num. 31:27)," *JQR,N.S.,*37 (1946-47) 85.

Numbers 32:1-5

Gustav Buchdahl, "Numbers XXXII: 1-5," *CCARJ* 14 (1967) #4, 61-63.

Numbers 33:10

Samuel E. Loewenstamm, "The Death of the Upright and the World to Come," *JJS* 16 (1965) 183-186. *[33:10cd]*

Numbers 33:35

J. Braslawski, "Miscellanea. 3," *BIES* 12 (1946) XII. [Pseudo-Jonathan to Num. 33:35]

Numbers 33:40

*B. Mazar, "The Sanctuary of Arad and the Family of Hobab the Kenite," *JNES* 24 (1965) 297-303. *[33:40]*

Numbers 33:52-55

*David Heumark, "Crescas and Spinoza. A Memorial Paper in Honor of the Five Hundredth Anniversary of the 'Or Adonoi'," *YCCAR* 18 (1908) 277-348. [Num. 33:52-55, pp. 330-331]

Numbers 34:25

*W. T. Pilter, "Some Groups of Arabian Personal Names borne by the Israelites of the Mosaic Period," *SBAP* 38 (1916) 149-157, 171-180. [IV. Was the Name "Parnach" (Numb. XXXIV, 25) Persian? pp. 175-180]

Numbers 35:4-5

*Moshe Greenberg, "Idealism and Practicality in Numbers 35:4-5 and Ezekiel 45," *JAOS* 88 (1968) 59-66.

Numbers 35:9-32

R. Winterbotham, "The City of Refuge. Numbers XXXV. 9-32," *Exp, 8th Ser.*, 23 (1922) 32-40.

Numbers 35:25

*A. Spiro, "Law of Asylum in the Bible," *JBL* 59 (1940) vii-viii. *[35:25]*

Warren Driver, "The Release of Homicides from the Cities of Refuge. A Critical Monograph on Numbers 35:25, Abridged by the Author," *GJ* 1 (1960) #2, 7-22.

Numbers 36:2-3

*David Heumark, "Crescas and Spinoza. A Memorial Paper in Honor of the Five Hundredth Anniversary of the 'Or Adonoi'," *YCCAR* 18 (1908) 277-348. [Num. 36:2-3, pp. 331-332]

§586 *3.5.2.8 Studies on Manuscripts of Numbers*

A. A. Vansittart, "Old Latin palimpsest fragments at Paris," *JP* 2 (1869) 240-246. *[Numbers]*

*B. Pick, "Horae Samaritanae; or, a Collection of Various Readings of the Samaritan Pentateuch Compared with Hebrew and Other Ancient Versions, IV.—Numbers," *BS* 35 (1878) 76-92.

§587 **3.5.2.9 Exegetical Studies on the Book of Deuteronomy**

*S. R. Driver, "The Revised Version of the Old Testament. IV. The Books of Deuteronomy and Joshua," *Exp, 3rd Ser.,* 2 (1885) 289-301. [1:1, 7, 41; 2:11, 20; 3:10, 14, 17; 4:37; 5:10; 7:2; 11:21, 24; 13:13; 16:15; 18:15, 18; 19:6; 20:19; 21:4; 24:21; 29:19, 26; 31:10; 32:5, 11, 17, 24, 27, 36; 33:2, 6, 17, 21, 22, 27, 28; 34:3; 34:6, pp. 289-299]

Clyde T. Francisco, "Teaching Outline of Deuteronomy," *R&E* 61 (1964) 260-264.

Exodus Chapter 13—Deuteronomy Chapter 34

*William R. Harper, "The Pentateuchal Question. IV. Historical Matter of Ex. 13—Deut. 34," *AJSL* 6 (1889-90) 241-295.

Deuteronomy Chapters 1-4

Hinckley G. Mitchell, "Deut. I-IV," *JBL* 8 (1888) 155-159.

Henri Cazelles, "Passages in the Singular with Discourses in the Plural of Dt 1-4," *CBQ* 29 (1967) 207-219.

Deuteronomy 1:1

A. H. Sayce, "Notes and Queries. 6. *Deuteronomy i, 1,*" *PEFQS* 37 (1905) 169.

Deuteronomy 1:6-46

Allen G. Wehrli, "Panning Gold in the Old Testament," *MQ* 20 (1964) #3, 28-31. *[1:6-46]*

Deuteronomy 1:7-24

A. H. Sayce, "Ari," *ET* 15 (1903-04) 515. *[1:7, 19, 20, 24]*

Deuteronomy 1:41-43

*A. D. Singer, "Philological Notes," *JPOS* 21 (1948) 104-109. *[1:41, 43]*

Deuteronomy 2:14-16

W. L. Moran, "The End of the Unholy War and the Anti-Exodus," *B* 44 (1963) 333-342. *[2:14-16]*

Deuteronomy 3:11

Fritz Hommel, "The Bedstead (or Rather 'Couch') of Og of Bashan (Deut. III. 11)," *ET* 16 (1904-05) 472.

*Erwin Reifler, "The Evidence for the Near Eastern Origin of the Doric and the Parthenon Foot Standard," *AJA* 67 (1963) 216. *[3:11]*

Deuteronomy 3:16

*J. Simons, "Two Connected Problems Relating to the Israelite Settlement in Transjordan," *PEFQS* 79 (1947) 27-39, 87-101. [I. The Meaning of מָן + a Proper name in Deut. III, 16 and some other Geographical Texts, pp. 27-39]

*G. R. Driver, "Mistranslations," *PEQ* 80 (1948) 64-65. *[Deut. 3:16]*

Deuteronomy Chapter 4

Adam C. Welch, "The Purpose of Deuteronomy, Chapter IV," *ET* 42 (1930-31) 227-231.

Deuteronomy 4:20

*George Rust, "The Burning Bush," *ET* 73 (1961-62) 93. *[4:20]*

Deuteronomy Chapter 5

Adam C. Welch, "The Purpose of Deuteronomy, Chapter V," *ET* 41 (1929-30) 396-400.

Deuteronomy 5:3

*Fritz Hommel, "Preliminary Notice Regarding Jer. VII. 22 and Deut.V. 3," *ET* 11 (1899-1900) 429.

*Fritz Hommel, "A Rhetorical Figure in the Old Testament, Jer. VII. 22 and Deut.V. 3," *ET* 11 (1899-1900) 439-441.

*Fritz Hommel, "A Rhetorical Figure in the Old Testament, A Supplementary Note," *ET* 11 (1899-1900) 517-518. *[5:3]*

*Eb. Nestle, "A Rhetorical Figure in the Old Testament, A Supplementary Note, II.," *ET* 11 (1899-1900) 518. *[5:3]*

*James Moffatt, "A Rhetorical Figure in the Old Testament, A Supplementary Note III.," *ET* 11 (1899-1900) 518-519. *[5:3]*

*Ed. König, "A Rhetorical Figure in the Old Testament, A Supplementary Note, IV.," *ET* 11 (1899-1900) 519. *[5:3]*

Fritz Hommel, "A last Word on 'A Rhetorical Figure in the Old Testament'," *ET* 11 (1899-1900) 564. *[5:3]*

Deuteronomy 5:7-9

*J. N. M. Wijngaards, "'You shall not bow down to them or serve them'," *IJT* 18 (1969) 180-190. *[5:7-9a]*

Deuteronomy 5:9

*Dean A. Walker, "Note on Ex. XX 5b; Deut V 9b," *JBL* 21 (1902) 188-191.

Deuteronomy 5:21

*William L. Moran, "The Conclusion of the Decalogue (Ex 20,17 = Dt 5,21)," *CBQ* 29 (1967) 543-554.

Deuteronomy 5:23-6:3

W. E. Crum, "The Decalogue and Deuteronomy in Coptic," *SBAP* 25 (1903) 99-101. *[5:23-6:3]*

Deuteronomy Chapter 6

Adam C. Welch, "The Purpose of Deuteronomy, Chapter VI," *ET* 41 (1929-30) 548-551.

Deuteronomy 6:1-15

*Kemper Fullerton, "Expository Studies in the Old Testament: VIII. The Last Days of Moses," *BW* 30 (1907) 123-134. *[6:1-15]*

Deuteronomy 6:4

*F. C. Burkitt, "The Nash Papyrus, A New Photograph, with plate," *JQR* 16 (1903-04) 559-561. *[Text of the Decalogue and the Shema']*

*K. Kohler, "Shema Yisroel. *Origin and Purpose of its Daily Recital,*" *JJLP* 1 (1919) 255-264. *[6:4]*

*Lester J. Kuyper, "Deuteronomy, a Source Book for Theology," *HTS* 7 (1950-51) 181-190. *[6:4]*

Deuteronomy Chapter 7

Adam C. Welch, "The Purpose of Deuteronomy, Chapter VII," *ET* 42 (1930-31) 409-412.

Deuteronomy 7:20

*Anonymous, "Sesostris, the Hornet of Exod. 23:28, Deut. 7:20, Josh. 24:12," *QCS, 3rd Ser.,* 10 (1838) 281-285.

Deuteronomy 8:2-5

W.G.Jordan,"The Meaning of History: Deut. 8:2-5,"*BW* 31 (1908)376-381.

Deuteronomy 8:2

Anonymous, "The Great Text Commentary. The Great Texts of Deuteronomy," *ET* 19 (1907-08) 494-497. *[8:2]*

Deuteronomy 8:9

*Claude R. Conder, "Notes on New Discoveries," *PEFQS* 41 (1909) 266-275. [Iron (Deut. 8:9; Num. 31:22; 1 Sam. 17:7), p. 271]

Deuteronomy 9:11-12

*Samuel Belkin, "Some Obscure Tradition Mutually Clarified in Philo and Rabbinic Literature," *JQR, 75th,* (1967) 80-103. [9. Predestination, pp. 101-103] *[9:11-12]*

Deuteronomy 9:13

*T. K. Meek, "Some Lapses of Old Testament Translators," *JBL* 55 (1936) x. *[9:13]*

Deuteronomy 10:6-7

G. T. Manley, "A Problem in Deuteronomy," *EQ* 27 (1955) 201-204. *[10:6, 7]*

Deuteronomy 11:10

C. Langton Gurney, "Watering with the Foot," *ET* 23 (1911-12) 94. *[11:10]*

Edward J. Clifton, "Watering with the Foot," *ET* 23 (1911-12) 183. *[11:10]*

J. A. Wilson, "Watering with the Foot," *ET* 23 (1911-12) 237. *[11:10]*

W. E. Entwistle, "Wateredst it with the Foot" (Deut. XI. 10)," *ET* 23 (1911-12) 331.

Edouard Naville, "Deuteronomy XI, 10," *JRAS* (1926) 306-308.

Deuteronomy 11:16

Theophile James Meek, "Old Testament Notes," *JBL* 67 (1948) 233-239. [2. The Translation of Deut. 11:16, p. 235-236]

Deuteronomy 11:29-30

John Mills, "Reading the Cursings and Blessings to the Israelites," *JSL, 4th Ser.,* 3 (1863) 176-178. *[11:29, 30]*

Deuteronomy Chapters 12-26

Harold M. Wiener, "The arrangement of Deuteronomy 12-26," *JPOS* 6 (1926) 185-195.

Deuteronomy Chapters 12-18

Cuthbert A. Simpson, "A Study of Deuteronomy 12-18," *ATR* 34 (1952) 247-251.

Deuteronomy 12:5-6

*C. V. Anthony, "The Order of Melchisedec," *ONTS* 3 (1883-84) 209-210. *[12:5, 6]*

Deuteronomy 12:8-15

*Franklin N. Jewett, "Questions from the Pew. The Place for Sacrificing. (Lev. xvii: 1-9; Deut. xii: 8-15.)," *OC* 21 (1907) 564-567.

Deuteronomy 13:12-16

*Robert H. Kennett, "Plunder and Punishment," *ICMM* 14 (1917-18) 47-51. *[13:12-16]*

Deuteronomy Chapter 14

*Royden Keith Yerkes, "The Unclean Animals of Leviticus 11 and Deuteronomy 14," *JQR, N.S.,* 14 (1923-24) 1-29.

Deuteronomy 14:2

*Eugene Mihaly, "A Rabbinic Defense of the Election of Israel. An Analysis of Sifre Deuteronomy 32:9, Pisqa 312," *HUCA* 35 (1964) 103-143. [Appendix: "Midrash Tannaim to Deut. 14:2 (D. Hoffman), p. 73—" pp. 136-143]

Deuteronomy 14:6-8

*Honeyman Gillespie and Robert Young, "Correspondence on Lev. XI. 3-7, and Deut. XIV. 6-8," *JSL, 4th Ser.,* 9 (1866) 383-400.

*W. Wright, "The Arabic Term for *Hare*," *JSL, 4th Ser.,* 10 (1866-67) 180-182. *[14:6-8]*

Deuteronomy 14:21

S. C. Bartlett, "Novel Bible History," *BS* 54 (1897) 383-386, 572-576. *[14:21]*

*T. B. McCorkindale, "An Ancient Ritual Prohibition," *HR* 67 (1914) 227. *[14:21]*

*Max Radin, "The Kid and Its Mother's Milk," *AJSL* 40 (1923-24) 209-218. *[14:21]*

*D. Daube, "A Note on a Jewish Dietary Law," *JTS* 37 (1936) 289-291. *[14:21]*

Deuteronomy 14:22

*Ezra Fleischer, "The Reading of the Portion *'Asser Te'asser'* (Deut. XIV, 22)," *Tarbiz* 36 (1966-67) #2, II.

Deuteronomy 15:1

G. S. Goodspeed, "The Remission of Debts," *ONTS* 3 (1883-84) 153-154. *[15:1]*

Deuteronomy 16:11

*A. S. Tritton, "The Casting Out of Leaven (Ex. XIII. 7; Dt. XVI. 11)," *ET* 24 (1912-13) 428.

Deuteronomy 16:18

Deutsch, "Anxiety to Secure Just Judgment. Deut. xvi. 18," *ONTS* 1 (1882) #2, 14.

Deuteronomy 16:20

Eb. Nestle, "The Greek Rendering of Deuteronomy 16:20," *AJSL* 21 (1904-05) 131-132.

Deuteronomy 17:14-20

Harold M. Wiener, "The 'King' of Deuteronomy XVII. 14-20," *BS* 68 (1911) 491-502.

Deuteronomy Chapter 18

Edward White, "The Sin of Necromancy. *Deut. XVIII,*" *CongL* 1 (1872) 161-165.

Norman C. Habel, "Deuteronomy 18—God's Chosen Prophet," *CTM* 35 (1964) 575-582.

Deuteronomy 18:8

*G. R. Driver, "Two Problems in the Old Testament Examined in the Light of Assyriology," *Syria* 33 (1956) 70-78. [III. a prohibition to sell hereditary property (Deuteronomy XVIII, 8), pp. 77-78]

Deuteronomy 18:9-22

*P. E. Broughton, "The Call of Jeremiah; The Relation of Deut. 18:9-22 to the Call and Life of Jeremiah," *ABR* 6 (1958) 39-46.

Deuteronomy 18:10-15

G. Ernest Wright, "The Bible Versus Spiritualism, Astrology, and Magic," *McQ* 4 (1950-51) #2, 11. *[18:10-15]*

Deuteronomy 18:10

W. Robertson Smith, "On the forms of divination and magic enumerated in Deut. XVIII. 10," *JP* 13 (1884) 273-287; 14 (1885) 113-128.

Deuteronomy 18:15-19

*E. P. Barrows Jr., "The Prophet Like unto Moses," *BRCR, 3rd Ser.,* 3 (1847) 645-655. *[18:15-19]*

Deuteronomy 18:15

Anonymous, "The Great Text Commentary. The Great Texts of Deuteronomy," *ET* 24 (1912-13) 201-208. *[18:15]*

Deuteronomy 19:4

*Claude R. Conder, "Notes on New Discoveries," *PEFQS* 41 (1909) 266-275. [Landmarks (Deut. 19:4), p. 271]

Deuteronomy 20:19

G. S. Goodspeed, "The Tree of the Field: Deut. XX. 19," *ONTS* 3 (1883-84) 356-357.

Deuteronomy 21:1-9

Alexander Roifer, "The Breaking of the Heifer's Neck," *Tarbiz* 31 (1961-62) #2, I. *[21:1-9]*

Deuteronomy 21:1

*Claude R. Conder, "Notes on New Discoveries," *PEFQS* 41 (1909) 266-275. [Divorce (Deut. 21:1), p. 271-272]

Cyrus H. Gordon, "An Akkadian Parallel to Deuteronomy 21:1ff.," *RAAO* 33 (1936) 1-6.

Deuteronomy 21:3

*G. R. Driver, "Three Notes," *VT* 2 (1952) 356-357. [Deut. 21:3, pp. 356]

Deuteronomy 21:10-14

*Samuel I. Feigin, "The Captives in Cuneiform Inscriptions," *AJSL* 50 (1933-34) 217-245; 51 (1934-35) 22-29. [10. The Law concerning captive Women in Deut. 21:10-14, pp. 243-245]

Deuteronomy 21:15-17

*O. R. Sellers, "Primogeniture in Israel," *JBL* 71 (1952) vi. *[21:15-17]*

Deuteronomy 22:6

*Anonymous, "The Great Text Commentary. The Great Texts of Deuteronomy, *ET* 19 (1907-08) 547-550. *[22:6]*

Deuteronomy 22:12

*Henry Hayman, "On the Law of Fringes in Numbers and Deuteronomy," *BS* 51 (1894) 705-707. *[22:12]*

*Ben Zion Bokser, "The Thread of Blue," *PAAJR* 31 (1963) 132. *[22:12]*

Deuteronomy 22:28

*David Halivni Weiss, "A Note on אשר לא ארשה," *JBL* 81 (1962) 67-69. *[22:28]*

Deuteronomy 23:7

E. W. Heaton, "Sojourners in Egypt," *ET* 58 (1946-47) 80-82. [The word *gēr* in Deut. 23:7]

Deuteronomy 25:4

*P. le Page Renouf, "The Lay of the Threshers," *SBAP* 19 (1897) 121-122. *[cf. Deut. 25:4]*

Deuteronomy 25:11-12

Cyrus H. Gordon, "A New Akkadian Parallel to Deuteronomy 25:11-12," *JPOS* 15 (1935) 29-34.

Deuteronomy 26:5

D. D. Luckenbill, "The 'Wandering Aramaean'," *AJSL* 36 (1919-20) 244-245. *[26:5]*

W. Gunther Plaut, "The Wandering Aramean: A Commentary on Deuteronomy 26:5," *CCARJ* 9 (1961-62) #4, 18-21.

Deuteronomy 26:1-11

August J. Engelbrecht, "'We Bring Thee But Thine Own'. A Study of Deut. 26:1-11," *WSQ* 19 (1955-56) #1, 3-10.

Deuteronomy Chapter 27

Immanuel Lewy, "The puzzle of Dt. xxvii: blessing announced, but curses noted," *VT* 12 (1962) 207-211.

Deuteronomy 28:29

Anonymous, "Rabbinical Commentary," *MR* 10 (1827) 222-223. *[28:29]*

Deuteronomy 28:37

James E. Rogers, "Prophecy Fulfilled: Moses not Mistaken," *CFL, 3rd Ser.,*22 (1916) 128-129. *[28:37]*

Φ., "Biblical Illustrations," *BRCM* 3 (1847) 357-359 [III. Deut. 28:67, p. 359]

Deuteronomy 29:29

Anonymous, "The Great Text Commentary. The Great Texts of Deuteronomy," *ET* 20 (1908-09) 27-29. *[29:29]*

Deuteronomy 30:14

E. B. Cowell, "Thought, Word, and Deed," *JP* 3 (1871) 215-222. *[30:14]*

Anonymous, "The Great Text Commentary. The Great Texts of Deuteronomy," *ET* 20 (1908-09) 59-61. *[30:19]*

Deuteronomy Chapter 32

Milton S. Terry, "The Song of Moses, Deut. 32," *ONTS* 7 (1887-88) 280-283.

*Patrick W. Skehan, "A Fragment of the 'Song of Moses' (Deut. 32) from Qumran," *BASOR* #136 (1954) 12-15.

W[illiam] F[oxwell] Albright, "Some Remarks on the Song of Moses in Deuteronomy XXXII," *VT* 9 (1959) 339-346.

W. L. Moran, "Some Remarks on the Song of Moses," *B* 43 (1962) 317-327. *[Deut. 32]*

Deuteronomy 32:1-43

*James R. Boston, "The Wisdom Influence upon the Song of Moses," *JBL* 87 (1968) 198-202. *[32:1-43]*

Deuteronomy 32:2-3

*B. Margulis, "Gen XLIX 10/Deut XXXII 2-3," *VT* 19 (1969) 202-210.

Deuteronomy 32:2

H. Torczyner, "'Rains in their Time'," *BIES* 13 (1946-47) #3/4, III-IV. *[32:2]*

*M. D. Goldman, "Lexicographical Notes on Exegesis (2). Some Hebrew Words Used in Their Original Meaning," *ABR* 1 (1951) 141-142. *[32:2a, b]*

Deuteronomy 32:5

J. A. Selbie, "A Proposed Emendation of Deut. XXXII. 5," *ET* 9 (1897-98) 364.

Anonymous, "Exegetical Suggestion and Opinion. Deut. 32:5," *CFL, O.S.,* 2 (1898) 168.

Deuteronomy 32:8

*Samuel Sharpe, "Questions on Deut XXXII. 8; Psalm XLIX. 1, 2 and LXIII. 9," *JSL, 4th Ser.,* 1 (1862) 451-452.

*Q., "Explanation of Biblical Passages. Psalm xlix. 1, 2, etc.," *JSL, 4th Ser.,* 2 (1862-63) 177. *[Deut. 32:8]*

*G. R. Driver, "Three Notes,"*VT* 2 (1952) 356-357. [Deut. 32:8, pp.356-357]

Deuteronomy 32:9

*Eugene Mihaly, "A Rabbinic Defense of the Election of Israel. An Analysis of the Sifre Deuteronomy 32:9, Pisqa 312," *HUCA* 35 (1964) 103-143.

Deuteronomy 32:10

Eb. Nestle, "Deut. XXXII. 10," *ET* 18 (1906-07) 526.

Samuel A. B. Mercer, "'The Little Man of His Eye' Deut. 32:10," *ATR* 3 (1920-21) 151-152.

Deuteronomy 32:11-12

Anonymous, "The Great Text Commentary. The Great Texts of Deuteronomy," *ET* 20 (1908-09) 134-137. *[32:11-12]*

Deuteronomy 32:11

*John P. Peters, "The Wind of God," *JBL* 33 (1914) 81-86. *[32:11]*

*Joseph Offord, "Archaeological Notes on Jewish Antiquities. XIII. *The Bird* Gozal *and Babylonian* Guzalû," *PEFQS* 48 (1916) 139-140. *[32:11]*

*J. W. Jack, "Recent Biblical Archaeology," *ET* 53 (1941-42) 367-370. [Archæology and the Biblical Text: 2. Birds Fluttering (Gen. 1:2, Deut. 32:11, Jer. 23:9), pp. 368-369]

Frederic R. Howe and George F. Howe, "Moses and the Eagle," *JASA* 20 (1968) 22-24. *[32:11]*

Deuteronomy 32:25

Theodor H. Gaster, "Deuteronomy XXXII. 25," *ET* 49 (1937-38) 525.

Deuteronomy 32:26-34

Kemper Fullerton, "On Deuteronomy 32:26-34," *ZAW* 46 (1928) 138-155.

152   *Exegetical Studies on the Book of Deuteronomy*   §587 cont.

Deuteronomy 32:31

*M. D. Goldman, "The Root פלל and Its Connotation with Prayer. (Attempted Explanation of Deuteronomy XXXII, 31), *ABR* 3 (1953) 1-6.

Deuteronomy 32:32

*J. Penrose Harland, "Sodom and Gomorrah: II. The Destruction of the Cities of the Plain," *BS* 6 (1943) 41-54. [The Apple of Sodom - Deut. 32:32, pp. 49-52]

Deuteronomy 32:34-43

H. L. Ginsberg, "The Conclusion of *Ha'azinu* (Deut. 32:34-43)," *Tarbiz* 24 (1954-55) #1, I.

Deuteronomy 32:39

W. D. Macray, "A Supposed Reading of Deut. XXXII 39," *JTS* 3 (1901-02) 451.

Deuteronomy 32:42

Thomas Taylor, "Note on Deuteronomy XXXII. 42," *JQR* 10 (1897-98) 379-380.

Deuteronomy 32:43

M. H. Tur-Sinai, "Note on Deut. XXXII: 43," *Tarbiz* 24 (1954-55) #2, V.

Deuteronomy Chapter 33

R. G. Moulton, "The Last Words of Moses," *BW* 7 (1896) 339-341. *[Chap. 33 - Metered Translation]*

C. J. Ball, "The Blessing of Moses (Deut. xxxiii)," *SBAP* 18 (1896) 118-137.

Emil G. Hirsch, "Notes on Deut., Chap. 33," *AJSL* 27 (1910-11) 339-342.

W. J. Phythian-Adams, "On the Date of the 'Blessing of Moses' (Deut. XXXIII)," *JPOS* 3 (1923) 158-166.

R[obert] Gordis, "Critical Notes on the Blessing of Moses (Deut. xxxiii)," *JTS* 34 (1933) 390-392.

F[rank] M[oore] Cross and D[avid] N[oel] Freedman, "The Blessing of Moses (Deuteronomy 33)," *JBL* 67 (1948) v.

Frank M[oore] Cross Jr. and David Noel Freedman, "The Blessing of Moses," *JBL* 67 (1948) 191-210. *[Chap. 33]*

*A. Bentzen, "Patriarchal 'benediction' and prophetic book," *HTS* 7 (1950-51) 106-109. *[Chap. 33]*

Carl Armerding, "The Last Words of Moses: Deuteronomy 33," *BS* 114 (1957) 225-234.

*Patrick D. Miller Jr., "Two Critical Notes on Psalm 68 and Deuteronomy 33," *HTR* 57 (1964) 240-243.

I. L. Seeligmann, "A Psalm from Pre-Regal Times," *VT* 14 (1964) 75-92. *[Chap. 33]*

Deuteronomy 33:1

*A. F. L. Beeston, "Angels in Deuteronomy 33[1], *JTS, N.S.,* 2 (1951) 30-31.

Deuteronomy 33:2

Samuel Daiches, "Deuteronomy XXXIII. 2," *ET* 26 (1914-15) 178-179.

Deuteronomy 33:3-5

*Theodor H. Gaster, "An Ancient Eulogy of Israel: Deuteronomy 33:3-5, 26-29," *JBL* 66 (1947) 53-62.

Deuteronomy 33:4

Harold M. Wiener, "Deuteronomy XXXIII. 4: 'Moses Commanded Us a Law'," *BS* 67 (1910) 353.

Deuteronomy 33:8

Max L. Margolis, "*lĕ'iš ḥašideka,* Deut. 33:8," *JBL* 38 (1919) 35-42.

Deuteronomy 33:12

Theodor Herzl Gaster, "Deuteronomy XXXIII. 12," *ET* 46 (1934-35) 334.

Deuteronomy 33:19

*T. K. Cheyne, "Textual Criticism in the Service of Archaeology," *ET* 10 (1898-99) 238-240. [1. Dt. 33:19 (RV), pp. 238-239]

Deuteronomy 33:21

*[Friedrich] Giesebrecht, "Two Cruces Interpretum, Ps. XLV. 7 and Deut. XXXIII. 21, Removed," *AJSL* 4 (1887-88) 92-94.

Deuteronomy 33:25

Anonymous, "The Great Text Commentary. The Great Texts of Deuteronomy," *ET* 20 (1908-09) 166-169. *[33:25]*

Deuteronomy 33:26-29

*Theodor H. Gaster, "An Ancient Eulogy of Israel: Deuteronomy 33:3-5, 26-29," *JBL* 66 (1947) 53-62.

Deuteronomy 33:26

Frank M[oore] Cross Jr. and David Noel Freedman, "A Note on Deuteronomy 33:26," *BASOR* #108 (1947) 6-7.

H. L. Ginsberg, "On Bulletin 108 (Dec. 1947): 6-7," *BASOR* #110 (1948) 26. *[33:26]*

Deuteronomy 33:27

Anonymous, "The Great Text Commentary. The Great Texts of Deuteronomy," *ET* 20 (1908-09) 226-229. *[33:27]*

Robert Gordis, "The Text and Meaning of Deuteronomy 33:27," *JBL* 67 (1948) 69-72.

Deuteronomy 34:1-12

*Kemper Fullerton, "Expository Studies in the Old Testament: VIII. The Last Days of Moses," *BW* 30 (1907) 123-134. *[34:1-12]*

Deuteronomy 34:1-3

*W. F. Birch, "The Prospect from Pisgah," *PEFQS* 30 (1898) 110-120. (Remarks by C. R. Conder, pp. 120-121) *[34:1-3]*

Deuteronomy 34:1

*W. Scott Watson Jr., "Note on the Bearing of Deut. 34:1 upon the Question of the Authorship of Deuteronomy," *BW* 6 (1895) 356-357.

Deuteronomy 34:3

*Salomon Speier, "The Jerusalem Targum to Num. 18:12 and Deut. 34:3," *JBL* 65 (1946) 315-318.

Deuteronomy 34:5-6

Anonymous, "The Great Text Commentary. The Great Texts of Deuteronomy," *ET* 20 (1908-09) 253-256. *[34:5, 6]*

Deuteronomy 34:7

W[illiam] F[oxwell] Albright, "The 'Natural Force' of Moses in Light of Ugaritic," *BASOR* #94 (1944) 32-35. *[Deut. 34:7 (leḥ)]*

Deuteronomy 34:4-7

*L. B. Cholmondeley, "Gn. L. 22-26, Dt. XXXIV. 4-7, Jos.XXIV. 29ff.," *ET* 46 (1934-35) 238.

§588 *3.5.2.10 Studies on Manuscripts of Deuteronomy*

*B. Pick, "Horae Samaritanae; or, a Collection of Various Readings of the Samaritan Pentateuch Compared with Hebrew and Other Ancient Versions, V.—Deuteronomy," *BS* 35 (1878) 309-325.

Henry A. Sanders, "The Age and Ancient Home of the Biblical Manuscripts in the Freer Collection," *AJA* 13 (1909) 130-141.

Henry A. Sanders, "Some Fragments of the Oldest Beatty Papyrus in the Michigan Collection," *PAPS* 75 (1935) 313-324. [Deut. 11:17-18; 28:38-41; 28:65-66; 29:1-2; 30:10-11; 30:16; 30:19-20; 31:3-4, 31:21; 31:26; 31:29; 32:3-4; 32:10-11; 32:15 or 16; 32:22; 32:27-29]

§589 *3.5.2.11 Studies on the Decalogue*

Charles F. Schaeffer, "On the Division of the Decalogue," *ER* 7 (1855-56) 102-126.

R. Balgarnie, "Horeb: Or the Place of the Hebrew Decalogue in the Christian Church," *Exp, 2nd Ser.,* 4 (1882) 221-237.

*Anonymous, "Shapira's MSS," *ONTS* 3 (1883-84) 23-25. *[Decalogue - Text and Transmission]*

Talbot W. Chambers, "The Sanction of the Decalogue," *BS* 43 (1886) 745-762.

John P. Peters, "The Ten Words," *JBL* 6 (1886) Part 1, 140-144.

Talbot W. Chambers, "Divisions of the Decalogue," *ONTS* 6 (1886-87) 5-10.

Talbot W. Chambers, "The Perfection of the Decalogue," *ONTS* 6 (1886-87) 261-268.

R. Wittingham, "Is the Decalogue Binding on Christians?" *PER* 2 (1888-89) 169-175.

John Henry Hopkins, "Two Editions of the Decalogue," *CR* 60 (1891) 34-40.

T[albot] W. Chambers, "The Preface to the Decalogue," *PRR* 2 (1891) 122-129.

*Anthony Maas, "The Mosaic Law in the Light of Ethics," *ACQR* 17 (1892) 123-136.

Talbot W. Chambers, "The Date of the Decalogue," *HR* 23 (1892) 363-366.

Anonymous, "The Date of the Decalogue," *ONTS* 14 (1892) 308.

Talbot W. Chambers, "The Formation of the Decalogue," *HR* 25 (1893) 544-547.

Anonymous, "The Mosaic Law and the Higher Criticism," *CQR* 40 (1895) 282-321. *(Review)*

Eb. Nestle, "The Division of the Ten Commandments in the Greek and Hebrew Bible," *ET* 8 (1896-97) 426-427.

J. G. Tasker, "Decalogue," *ET* 9 (1897-98) 446.

Samuel M. Smith, "The Decalogue and the Beatitudes," *CFL, N.S.,* 1 (1900) 198-202.

D. E. Jenkins, "The Decalogue and Christian Ethics," *CFL, N.S.,* 6 (1902) 43-50.

Lewis B. Paton, "The Ten Words," *BW* 22 (1903) 22-35.

S. W. Pratt, "The Structure and Scope of the Ten Commandments," *HR* 46 (1903) 294-296.

*F. C. Burkitt, "The Nash Papyrus, A New Photograph, with plate," *JQR* 16 (1903-04) 559-561. *[Text of the Decalogue and the Shema']*

*George S. Duncan, "The Code of Moses and the Code of Hammurabi," *BW* 23 (1904) 188-193, 272-278.

George H. Schodde, "The Division of the Decalogue," *ColTM* 24 (1904) 22-27.

Rose H. Rae, "'The Finger of God'," *HR* 47 (1904) 222-223.

J. C. K. Milligan, "The Writer of the Decalogue," *CFL, 3rd Ser.,* 3 (1905) 318-320.

*Max Kellner, "The Hammurabi Code and the Code of the Covenant," *RP* 4 (1905) 99-118.

John Urquhart, "The Decalogue in the Exodus and Deuteronomy," *CFL, 3rd Ser.,* 7 (1907) 42-46.

John E. McFadyen, "The Origin of the Decalog," *HR* 54 (1907) 46-49.

William Weber, "Luther and the Decalogue," *LQ* 38 (1908) 490-510.

*B. D. Eerdmans, "The Book of the Covenant and the Decalogue," *Exp, 7th Ser.,* 8 (1909) 21-33, 158-167, 223-230.

*A. C. Knudson, "The So-Called J Decalogue," *JBL* 28 (1909) 82-99.

J. E. McFadyen, "The Mosaic Origin of the Decalogue," *Exp, 8th Ser.,* 11 (1915) 152-160, 222-231, 311-320, 384-400. [I. Ritual Decalogue; II. Egyptian Babylonian Parallels to the Ethical Decalogue; III. The Original Form of the Decalogue; IV. Can the Original Form of the Decalogue be Mosaic? *The First Commandment. The Tenth Commandment. The Fourth Commandment. The Second Commandment. The Ephod. The Teraphim. Calf Worship]*

*J. E. McFadyen, "The Mosaic Origin of the Decalogue," *Exp, 8th Ser.,* 12 (1916) 37-59, 105-117, 210-221. [The Second Commandment (continued); V. The Relation of the Decalogue to Prophecy; VI. The Decalogue and Individualism; VII. The Unique Distinction of the Decalogue]

T. H. Weir, "The Ten Words," *ICMM* 13 (1916-17) 37-40.

[John Richard Sampey], "The Ten Commandments," *CFL, 3rd Ser.,* 25 (1919) 158.

D. Meibohm, "Why Did Luther Change the Ten Commandments?" *TQ* 23 (1919) 234-241.

*William Wallace Everts, "The Laws of Moses and of Hammurabi," *R&E* 17 (1920) 37-50.

H. C. Ackerman, "The Two Tables of Stone," *ATR* 4 (1921-22) 67-69.

*H. C. Ackerman, "The Decalogue and Sacrifice," *ATR* 4 (1921-22) 241-244.

*Julius J. Price, "How the Rabbis Regarded the Commandments," *OC* 36 (1922) 564-575.

B. Jacob, "The Decalogue," *JQR, N.S.,* 14 (1923-24) 141-187.

W. Emery Barnes, "Ten Treatises on the Ten Commandments," *Exp, 9th Ser.,* 2 (1924) 7-23.

H. J. Flowers, "The Ten Commandments," *Exp, 9th Ser.,* 1 (1924) 339-356.

Anonymous, "Some Recent Work Upon the Ten Commandments," *Exp, 9th Ser.,* 1 (1924) 392-396.

Robert H. Pfeiffer, "The Oldest Decalogue," *JBL* 43 (1924) 294-310.

G. R. Berry, "The Ritual Decalogue," *JBL* 44 (1925) 39-43.

D. L. Chapin, "The Value of the Ten Commandments," *CFL, 3rd Ser.,* 35 (1929) 375-376.

L[eander] S. K[eyser], "The Ten Commandments Today," *CFL, 3rd Ser.,* 39 (1933) 71-74. *(Review)*

Harold L. Creager, "Law and Life," *LCQ* 6 (1933) 147-160. *[Decalogue]*

*Shalom Spiegel, "A Prophetic Attestation of the Decalogue: Hosea 6:5. With Some Observations on Psalms 15 and 24," *HTR* 27 (1934) 105-144.

*W[illiam] F[oxwell] Albright, "A Biblical Fragment from the Maccabaean Age: The Nash Papyrus," *JBL* 56 (1937) 145-176. *[Decalogue]*

Th. Laetsch, "What was Written on the Two Tables of the Covenant? A Study of the Methods of Modern Criticism," *CTM* 9 (1938) 746-751.

*W. R. Taylor, "A New Samaritan Inscription," *BASOR* #81 (1941) 1-5. [Postscript by W[illiam] F[oxwell] Albright, pp. 5-6]*[Decalogue]*

Albert Kleber, "The Lord's Prayer and the Decalog," *CBQ* 3 (1941) 302-320.

*Eustace J. Smith, "The Decalogue in the Preaching of Jeremias," *CBQ* 4 (1942) 197-209.

A. R. Vidler, "'The Tables of the Jewish Law'," *Theo* 46 (1943) 265-271.

Marion J. Bradshaw, "'The Greatest Commandment'," *ABBTS* 20 (1945) #4, 4-7.

Louis Hartman, "The Enumeration of the Ten Commandments," *CBQ* 7 (1945) 105-108.

Pope Pius XII, "Sermon Notes. Some Reflections of Pope Pius XII on the Ten Commandments," *ClR* 25 (1945) 26-31.

A. R. Vidler, "On Resuscitating the Decalogue," *Theo* 48 (1945) 25-30.

W. K. Lowther Clarke, "The Origin of the Decalogue," *Theo* 52 (1949) 333-336.

*J. Bowman and S. Talmon, "Samaritan Decalogue Inscriptions," *BJRL* 33 (1950-51) 211-236.

*Philip Kieval, "The Decalogue and Our Liturgy," *CJ* 7 (1950-51) #4, 20-24.

H. H. Rowley, "Moses and the Decalogue," *BJRL* 34 (1951-52) 81-118.

Kenneth J. Foreman, "The Minister and the Ten Commandments," *TT* 9 (1952-53) 175-185.

*Meredith G. Kline, "The Intrusion and the Decalogue," *WTJ* 16 (1953-54) 1-22.

Julian Morgenstern, "The Decalogue of the Holiness Code," *HUCA* 26 (1955) 1-27.

P. Prins, "The Ten Commandments in the World Today," *RefmR* 3 (1955-56) 31-39.

T. Worden, "Question and Answer. Why does the Numbering of the Ten Commandments differ from that used by Non-Catholics?" *Scrip* 7 (1955) 21.

Walther Eichrodt, "The Law and the Gospel. *The Meaning of the Ten Commandments in Israel and for Us*," *Interp* 11 (1957) 23-40.

J. J. Petuchowski, "A note on W. Kessler's 'Problemlatk des Dekalogs'," *VT* 7 (1957) 397-398.

*George W. Frey Jr., "Archaeology and Biblical Manuscripts," *UTSB* 57 (1957-58) #2, 9-13. [Translation of the 10 Commandments from the Nash Papyrus, p. 13]

Walther Eichrodt, "The Ten Commandments," *TD* 6 (1958) 177-182.

Meredith G. Kline, "The Two Tables of the Covenant," *WTJ* 22 (1959-60) 133-146.

M. J. O'Connell, "The Concept of Commandment in the Old Testament," *ThSt* 21 (1960) 351-403.

J. A. Emerton, "The problem of the Decalogue," *OSHTP* (1960-61) 28-29.

Roy L. Aldrich, "The Mosaic Ten Commandments Compared to Their Restatements in the New Testament," *BS* 118 (1961) 251-258.

H. Kosmala, "The So-Called Ritual Decalogue," *ASTI* 1 (1962) 31-61.

Franz Rosenzweig, "The Love of God, the Love of Man," *Jud* 11 (1962) 175-177.

Albert R. Jonsen, "The Decalogue: Command and Presence," *TFUQ* 38 (1963) 421-446.

Arvid S. Kapelrud, "Some recent points of view on the time and origin of the Decalogue," *ST* 18 (1964) 81-90.

David Flusser, "'Do not commit adultery.' 'Do not murder'," *Text* 4 (1964) 220-224.

*J. Philip Hyatt, "Moses and the Ethical Decalogue," *SQ/E* 26 (1965) 199-206.

Paul Tremblay, "Towards a biblical catechesis of the decalogue," *TD* 13 (1965) 112-115.

Samuel E. Karff, "The Ten Commandments: Proxy or Paradigm?" *CCARJ* 13 (1965-66) #6, 35-42.

Allen G. Wehrli, "Dusting off the Decalogue," *MQ* 21 (1965-66) #4, 3-6.

H. Hamann, "Group Responsibility and the Ten Commandments," *AusTR* 37 (1966) 97-99.

Prescott H. Williams Jr., "A Summons to obedient freedom: the ten commandments," *ASBFE* 82 (April, 1967) #7, 35-46.

*William L. Moran, "The Conclusion of the Decalogue (Ex 20,17 = Dt 5,21)," *CBQ* 29 (1967) 543-554.

Senan   Buckley,   "The   Decalogue,"   *IJT*   16   (1967)   106-120.

F. E. Vokes, "The Ten Commandments in the New Testament and in First Century Judaism," *StEv* 5 (1968) 146-154.

Raymond F. Collins, "The Ten Commandments in Current Perspective," *AER* 161 (1969) 169-182.

§590 *3.5.2.12 Studies on Individual Commandments*

I

Nathaniel Bouton, "A Practical Exposition of the First Commandment," *BJ* 1 (1842) 121-130.

Nathaniel Bouton, "Violations of the First Commandment," *BJ* 1 (1842) 166-176.

Eb. Nestle, "The First Commandment in Hebrew," *ET* 22 (1910-11) 565.

H. J. Flowers, "The First Commandment," *Exp, 9th Ser.,* 1 (1924) 416-427.

A. Maude Royden, "The First Commandment," *ET* 47 (1935-36) 296-300.

II

Nathaniel Bouton, "A Practical Exposition of the Second Commandment. Its Prohibitions," *BJ* 1 (1842) 241-251.

Nathaniel Bouton, "A Practical Exposition of the Second Commandment. Its Requirements," *BJ* 1 (1842) 264-273.

Anonymous, "The Second Commandment," *ERG, 7th Ser.,* 3 (1880-81) 110-120.

*Wilbur F. Crafts, "Social Ethics: An Outline Study of the Second Great Commandment," *HR* 46 (1903) 229-230.

C. F. Russell, "The Second Commandment," *Exp, 8th Ser.,* 8 (1914) 178-183.

H. J. Flowers, "The Second Commandment," *Exp, 9th Ser.,* 2 (1924) 325-333, 420-430.

H. Wheeler Robinson, "The Second Commandment," *ET* 47 (1935-36) 351-354.

Corwin C. Roach, "Notes and Comments," *ATR* 22 (1940) 135-136. *[The Second Commandment]*

William Young, "The Second Commandment," *CO* 5 (1947-48) 36-47.

Joseph Gutmann, "The 'Second Commandment' and the Image in Judaism," *HUCA* 32 (1961) 161-174.

*P. Middelkoop, "A Word Study. The Sense of PAQAD in the second Commandment and its general background in the O.T. in regard to the translation into the Indonesian and Timorese Languages," *SEAJT* 4 (1962-63) #3, 33-47.

*P. Middelkoop, "Paqad—A Word Study," *SEAJT* 4 (1962-63) #3, 33-47;#4, 56-65. [(i) The translation of paqad in the Second Commandment into Timorese and Indonesian, pp. 62-64]

*J. N. M. Wijngaards, "'You shall not bow down to them or serve them'," *IJT* 18 (1969) 180-190.

S. du Toit, "Aspects of the Second Commandment," *OTW* 12 (1969) 101-110.

III

Nathaniel Bouton, "Prophaneness. Exposition of the Third Commandment," *BJ* 2 (1843) 150-160.

[Johann Ernst] Gerhard, "The Third Commandment. Translated from Gerhard's Loci Theologici," *ER* 19 (1868) 548-561. *(Trans. by H.E. Jacobs)*

Robert Mackintosh, "The Third Commandment in the Old Testament," *BW* 12 (1898) 169-178.

J. Sheatsley, "Theses on the Third Commandment," *ColTM* 19 (1899) 330-345.

*F. J. Coffin, "Third commandment," *JBL* 19 (1900) 166-188.

F. P. Miller, "The True Meaning of the Third Commandment," *CFL, N.S.,* 6 (1902) 232-234.

M. Geldzaeler, "'The Third Commandment'," *OC* 19 (1905) 379-380.

W. C. Green, "On a Neglected Aspect of the Third Commandment," *Exp, 8th Ser.,* 3 (1912) 186-192.

T. H. Darlow, "What does the Third Commandment Mean?" *Exp, 8th Ser.,* 15 (1918) 351-355.

H. J. Flowers, "The Third Commandment," *Exp, 9th Ser.,* 3 (1925) 260-280, 325-339.

*A. Mackenzie, "The Law of God. With Special Reference to the Third Commandment," *AusTR* 2 (1931) 33-59.

Ivor J. Roberton, "The Third Commandment," *ET* 47 (1935-36) 405-408.

W. E. Staples, "The Third Commandment," *JBL* 48 (1939) 325-330.

IV

*William De Loss Love, "The Sabbath: Did the Early Fathers Hold that the Fourth Commandment is Abolished?" *BS* 38 (1881) 254-286.

D. D. Persse, "The Fourth Commandment," *ET* 4 (1892-93) 480.

F. M. Woods, "The Fourth Commandment the Keystone of the Ten Commandments," *USR* 7 (1895-96) 291-296.

Teunis S. Hamlin, "The Spiritual Use of the Lord's Day," *AubSRev* 3 (1899) 96-105. *[Fourth Commandment]*

S. T. Lowrie, "The Morality of the Fourth Commandment," *CFL, N.S.,* 2 (1900) 216-223.

T. Herbert Bindley, "The Relation of the Fourth Commandment to the Christian Sunday," *ICMM* 11 (1914-15) 350-357.

H. J. Flowers, "The Fourth Commandment," *Exp, 9th Ser.,* 4 (1925) 183-205.

Paul E. Kretzmann, "Propositions on the Sabbath—Sunday Question," *CTM* 4 (1933) 195-196.

James Reid, "The Fourth Commandment," *ET* 47 (1935-36) 459-462.

*E. Graebner, "Luther and the Sabbath," *AusTR* 14 (1943) 73-83; 15 (1944) 1-6.

J. W. Deenick, "The Fourth Commandment and its Fulfillment," *RTR* 28 (1969) 54-61.

V

Peter Green, "The Fifth Commandment," *ET* 47 (1935-36) 504-507.

VI

Stuart D. Morris, "The Sixth Commandment," *ET* 47 (1935-36) 538-542.

†R. C. Fuller, "The Sixth Commandment in the Old and New Testaments," *Scrip* 1 (1946) 34.

VII

Zechariah Paddock, "Excursus on the Seventh Commandment," *MR* 41 (1859) 455-464.

Anonymous, "Some Questions About the Seventh Commandment," *CQR* 119 (1934-35) 257-271.

A. Herbert Gray, "The Seventh Commandment," *ET* 48 (1936-37) 36-40.

VIII

A. E. Garvie, "The Eighth Commandment," *ET* 48 (1936-37) 84-88.

A. Troost, "Property Rights and the Eighth Commandment," *IRB* #24&25 (1966) 23-41.

IX

James Moffatt, "The Ninth Commandment," *ET* 48 (1936-37) 101-105.

X

Harrington C. Lees, "'House'," *ET* 26 (1914-15) 238. *[Tenth Commandment]*

J. R. Coats, "'Thou shalt not covet'," *ZAW* 52 (1934) 238-239.

Herbert G. Wood, "The Tenth Commandment," *ET* 48 (1936-37) 155-158.

H. H. Eckert, "A Special Application of the Tenth Commandment to Pastor and Congregation," *WLQ* 44 (1947) 192-224, 246-250.

Cyrus H. Gordon, "A Note on the Tenth Commandment," *JAAR* 31 (1963) 208-209.

(§591) **3.5.3 Exegetical Studies on Passages in Several Books of the Prophets**

(§592) **3.5.3.1 Exegetical Studies on Passages in Several Books of the Former Prophets**

§593 **3.5.3.1.1 Exegetical Studies on the Book of Joshua**

*S. R. Driver, "The Revised Version of the Old Testament. IV. The Books of Deuteronomy and Joshua," *Exp, 3rd Ser.,* 2 (1885) 289-301. [3:16; 4:24; 5:13; 6:17-7:26; 7:21 marg.; 8:32; 9:4 marg.; 11:1, 16; 12:2 marg.; 13:2; 13:3 marg.; Chaps 15-21; 19:29 marg.; 2:7 marg.; 22:11, 24, pp. 299-301]

I. G. Matthews, "Expository Studies in the Old Testament: IX. Joshua, the Successor of Moses," *BW* 30 (1907) 213-224. [1:1-11; 3:5-17; 6:8-20; 14:6-15]

*R. G. Boling, "Some Conflate Readings in Joshua-Judges," *VT* 16 (1966) 293-298.

G. R. Driver, "Notes on Joshua," *JQR, 75th* (1967) 149-165. [1:14 + 4:12; 2:15; 2:18; 3:13, 16; 5:2; 5:5; 6:1; 8:11; 8:33; 9:4; 9:5; 10:6; 12:23; 13:3; 15:6 and 18:17; 15:9, 11; 15:18; 15:36; 15:49; 17:14; 17:19; 19:26; 23:13; 24:26]

Joshua Chapter 3

S. H. Chester, "Crossing the Jordan. Joshua III," *USR* 1 (1889-90) 253-258.

C. M. Watson, "The Stoppage of the River Jordan in A.D. 1267," *PEFQS* 27 (1895) 253-261. (Notes by J. N. Dalton, p. 334; by W. E. Stevenson, pp. 334-338) *[cf. Chap. 3]*

Joseph Braslavsky, "The Earthquake and Division of the Jordan in 1546," *Zion* 3 (1937-38) #4, VI-VII. *[Chap. 3]*

Joshua 3:4

Paul P. Sayon, "The Crossing of the Jordan. Josue 3:4," *CBQ* 12 (1950) 194-227.

Joshua 3:13

Harold M. Wiener, "On Joshua III. 13," *BS* 73 (1916) 639-640.

Joshua 3:16

W. E. Stevenson, "'Adam, that is Beside Keriat,' Josh. III, 16," *PEFQS* 28 (1896) 82-83.

M[orris]   Jastrow,   "Joshua   3:16,"   *JBL*   36   (1917)   53-62.

Joshua Chapters 4-5

*Julian Morgenstern, "Kadesh-Naphtali and Ta'anach," *JQR, N.S.,* 9 (1918-19) 359-369. *[Chaps. 4-5]*

Joshua 4:1-24

E. Norfleet Gardner, "'Joshua: Sermon in Stone' (Josh. 4:1-9, 19-24)," *R&E* 33 (1936) 415-426.

Joshua 4:9

E. W. Shalders, "Biblical Note. Joshua iv. 9," *Exp, 1st Ser.,* 8 (1878) 159-160.

Joseph Hammond, "Biblical Notes. Joshua iv. 9," *Exp, 1st Ser.,* 8 (1878) 315-318. [Postscript by E. W. Shalders, p. 318]

W. H. B. Proby, "Note on the Twelve Stones from the Jordan," *PEFQS* 31 (1899) 273. (Note by C. R. Conder, p. 354) *[4:9]*

Joshua 5:9

*E. Power, "Josue 5:9 and the Institution of Circumcision," *ITQ* 18 (1951) 368-372.

Joshua Chapter 6

*Joseph Robinson, "Who Cares About Jericho?" *ET* 78 (1966-67) 83-86.

Joshua 6:26

F. W. S. O'Neill, "The Foundation of Sacrifice," *ET* 12 (1909-10) 43-44. *[6:26]*

H. J. Dunkinfield Asterly, "The Foundation of Sacrifice," *ET* 12 (1909-10) 139.

*Ian M. Blake, "Jericho (Ain Es-Sultan): Joshua's Curse and Elisha's Miracle—One Possible Explanation," *PEQ* 99 (1967) 86-97.

Joshua 7:2-5

*Joseph A. Callaway, "New Evidence on the Conquest of 'Ai," *JBL* 87 (1968) 312-320. *[7:2-5]*

Joshua 7:17

Max L. Margolis, "'Man by Man,' Joshua 7,17," *JQR, N.S.,* 3 (1912-13) 319-336.

Joshua 7:21

Hugh Macmillan, "Achan's Wedge of Gold," *ET* 9 (1897-98) 61-63. *[7:21]*

John D. Davies, "Biblical Research and Discovery. Achan's Goodly Babylonish Garment. Achan's Wedge of Gold," *CFL, O.S.,* 3 (1899) 395-396. *[7:21]*

Joshua 8:1-29

*Joseph A. Callaway, "New Evidence on the Conquest of 'Ai," *JBL* 87 (1968) 312-320. *[8:1-29]*

Joshua 8:12-16

Max L. Margolis, *"Ai* or *The City?* Joshua 8:12, 16," *JQR, N.S.,* 7 (1916-17) 491-497.

Joshua Chapter 9

Jacob Liver, "The Literary History of Joshua IX," *JSS* 8 (1963) 227-243.

Joshua Chapter 10

E. Walter Maunder, "Joshua's Long Day (Joshua, Chapter X)," *JTVI* 53 (1921) 120-135, 140-148. [Discussion, pp. 136-140]

*G. Ernest Wright, "The Literary and Historical Problem of Joshua 10 and Judges 1," *JNES* 5 (1946) 105-114.

E. Walter Maunder, "Joshua's Long Day (Joshua, Chapter X)," *JASA* 3 (1951) #3, 1-11 [Discussion and Lecturer's reply, pp. 12-20; Further Discussion, *JASA* 3 (1951) #4, pp. 16-19]

Joshua 10:6-14

John C. Young, "'The Sun Standing Still' (Joshua X. 6-14)," *ET* 36 (1924-25) 331-332.

*Michael J. Gruenthaner, "Two Sun Miracles of the Old Testament," *CBQ* 10 (1948) 271-290. [I. The Miracle of Josue, *Translation of Jos. 10:9-15, The Geographical and Historical Situation, The Authenticity of Jos. 10:12-15, The Objection of Metrical Dissonance, Schultz's Objections, Textual Variants, Analysis of vv. 12-14, Introduction: v. 12a, The Quotation from the Book of Yashar: 12b-13a, Prose Comment: vv. 13b-14;* pp. 271-283; *Ecclus. 46:4, 5, Explanation of the Miracle, Inacceptable Solutions;* pp. 284-287]

Joshua 10:11-14

Albert Kleber, "Joshue's Miracle. A Misunderstood Report of a Credible Event," *AER* 56 (1917) 477-488. *[10:11-14]*

Joshua 10:11

Judah J. Slotki, "Beth-Horon (Jos. X. 11)," *ET* 38 (1926-27) 188.

Joshua 10:12-15

[Ernst Wilhelm Hengstenberg], "On the standing still of the Sun and Moon, Josh. X. 12-15," *BRCR* 3 (1833) 720-730. *(Trans. by Edward Robinson)*

T. M. Hopkins, "An Examination of Joshua 10:12-15," *BRCR, 3rd Ser.,* 1 (1845) 97-130.

[H. M. Johnson], "Review of Rev. T. M. Hopkins's 'Examination of Joshua x, 12-15'," *MR* 27 (1845) 504-523. *(Review)*

T. M. Hopkins, "Johnson's Review of Hopkins's Examination of Josh. 10:12-15, Reviewed," *BRCR, 3rd Ser.,* 2 (1846) 268-295.

H. M. Johnson, "Postscript," *BRCR, 3rd Ser.,* 2 (1846) 763-766. *[10:12-15]*

S. Cox, "Joshua Commanding the Sun and the Moon to Stand Still. Joshua x. 12-15," *Exp, 1st Ser.,* 1 (1875) 1-15.

John Reid, "Did the Sun and Moon Stand Still? Joshua x. 12-15," *ET* 9 (1897-98) 151-154.

Joshua 10:12-14

H. T., "Joshua's Miracle," *MR* 11 (1828) 334-338. *[10:12-14]*

Howard Crosby, "Light on Important Texts. No. XXVII," *HR* 8 (1883-84) 47. *[10:12-14]*

Henry N. Russell, "The Standing Still of the Sun (Joshua x. 12-14)," *PTR* 16 (1917) 103.

Edward J. Kissane, "A New Interpretation of Josue x, 12-14," *ITQ* 14 (1919) 60-62.

John S. Holladay Jr., "The Day(s) The *Moon* Stood Still," *JBL* 87 (1968) 166-178. *[10:12-14]*

Joshua 10:12-13

E. Compton, "Joshua X. 12, 13," *EN* 2 (1890) 232.

Anonymous, "A New Explanation of Josh. 10:12, 13," *ONTS* 14 (1892) 183-184.

Godfrey N. Curnock, "Another Neglected Parallel (Joshua x. 12, 13, and Iliad ii. 410-417)," *ET* 50 (1938-39) 378.

Joshua 10:12

Albert A. Isaacs, "The Difficulties of Scripture. *Joshua x. 12,*" *EN* 2 (1890) 133-136.

R. C. Fuller, "'Sun, Stand Thou Still' (Joshua x, 12)," *Scrip* 4 (1949-51) 305-313.

Joshua 10:13

A. Van Hoonacker, "'And the Sun stood Still...' (Joshua X. 13)," *Exp, 8th Ser.,* 12 (1916) 321-339.

Joshua Chapter 11

*Julian Morgenstern, "Kadesh-Naphtali and Ta'anach," *JQR, N.S.,* 9 (1918-19) 359-369. *[Chap. 11]*

Joshua 11:1-9

*L. W. Batten, "The Conquest of Northern Canaan: Joshua xi. 1-9; Judges iv-v," *JBL* 24 (1905) 31-40.

Joshua 11:1-8

*Max L. Margolis, "ΤΕΤΡΟΠΩΜΕΝΟΥΣ. Joshua 11:6," *JBL* 33 (1914) 286-289.

N. H. Tur-Sinai, "How Far Extended the Fighting Against the Kings of Canaan Following the Battle at the Waters of Merom?" *BIES* 24 (1959-60) #1, IV-V. *[11:1-5, 7-8]*

Joshua 11:10

A. Malamat, "Hazor 'The Head of All Those Kingdoms'," *JBL* 79 (1960) 12-19.

Joshua 11:13

G. Ernest Wright, "Cities Standing on Their Tells," *BA* 2 (1939) 11-12. *[11:13]*

P. E. Kretzmann, "Joshua 11:13," *CTM* 10 (1939) 623-624.

Joshua 11:21-22

E. C. B. Maclaurin, "Anak/Ἀναξ," *VT* 15 (1965) 468-474. *[11:21, 22]*

Joshua 12:1

H[arry] M. Orlinsky, "Septuagint Variant κατέπαυσαν in Joshua 12:1," *JBL* 63 (1944) 405-406.

Joshua 12:18

George Adam Smith, "On Aphek in Sharon," *PEFQS* 27 (1895) 252-253. *[12:18]*

Joshua Chapter 15

Frank M. Cross, "A Footnote to Biblical History," *BA* 19 (1956) 12-17. *[Chap. 15]*

Joshua 15:2-5

*G. Frederick Wright, "Geological Light on the Interpretation of 'The Tongue' in Joshua 15:2, 5; 18:19," *JBL* 30 (1911) 18-28.

Joshua 15:6

Felix Perles, "A Palestinian Name of a Mountain Misunderstood," *JQR, N.S.,* 17 (1926-27) 234. *[15:6]*

Joshua 15:9

R. North, "Three Judean Hills in Jos 15, 9f.," *B* 37 (1956) 209-216.

Joshua 15:10

Hinckley G. Mitchell, "Josh. 15:10," *JBL* 8 (1888) 161, 162.

Joshua 15:48

Anonymous, "Debir (Joshua xv. 48)," *PEFQS* 10 (1878) 121-122.

Joshua 15:49

Harry M. Orlinsky, "The Supposed *qiryat-sannah* of Joshua 15:49," *JBL* 58 (1939) 255-262.

Joshua 15:52

Z. Vilnay, "Miscellanea," *BIES* 10 (1942-44) #4, III. [Arab - Jos. 15:52]

Joshua 15:59

*A. M. Honeyman, "Two Contributions to Canaanite Toponymy," *JTS* 50 (1949) 50-52. [I. Elteqe', Elteqeh, and Elteqon, pp. 50-51] *[15:59]*

Joshua 17:11

George Dahl, "The 'Three Heights' of Joshua 17:11," *JBL* 53 (1934) 381-383.

*B. D. Zaphrir (Frimorgen), "'Even Three Countries'," *BIES* 14 (1947-48) #3/4, II. *[17:11]*

Joshua 17:15-18

*Willis J. Beecher, "בראַ in Josh. 17:15, 18; and Ezek. 21:24; 23:47," *JBL* 2 (1882) 128-133.

Joshua 18:19

*G. Frederick Wright, "Geological Light on the Interpretation of 'The Tongue' in Joshua 15:2, 5; 18:19," *JBL* 30 (1911) 18-28.

Joshua 19:29

*T. K. Cheyne, "The Connection of Esau and Usöos," *ZAW* 17 (1897) 189. *[19:29]*

Joshua 19:34

C[laude] R. Conder, "Judah on Jordan. (Josh. xix, 34.)," *PEFQS* 15 (1883) 183.

Joshua 19:40-48

John Strange, "The Inheritance of Dan," *ST* 20 (1966) 120-139. *[19:40-48]*

Joshua 19:44

*A. M. Honeyman, "Two Contributions to Canaanite Toponymy," *JTS* 50 (1949) 50-52. [I. Elteqe', Elteqeh, and Elteqon, pp. 50-51] *[19:44]*

Joshua 19:46

C[laude] R. Conder, "Mejarkon," *PEFQS* 21 (1889) 24. *[19:46]*

Joshua 21:1-9

*I. G. Matthews, "Expository Studies in the Old Testament: X. Joshua, Gideon, and Samson," *BW* 30 (1907) 275-285. *[21:1-9]*

Joshua 21:23

*A. M. Honeyman, "Two Contributions to Canaanite Toponymy," *JTS* 50 (1949) 50-52. [I. Elteqe', Elteqeh, and Elteqon, pp. 50-51] *[21:23]*

Joshua 21:32

D. Winton Thomas, "The Meaning of the Name Hammoth-dor," *PEFQS* 66 (1934) 147-148. *[21:32]*

Joshua Chapter 22

W. H. Bennett, "The Transjordanic Tribes, a Study of Joshua xxii," *OSHTP* (1892-93) 8-15.

Harold M. Wiener, "The Altar of Joshua XXII," *BS* 68 (1911) 708-712.

Joshua 22:9-34

*E. C. Bissell, "Josh. 22:9-34 and the Israelitish cultus," *JBL* 7 (1887) Part 2, 61-63.

Joshua 22:10-11

W[illiam] A[ldis] Wright, "Note on Joshua XXII 10, 11," *JP* 13 (1884) 117-120.

Joshua 22:25

*Max L. Margolis, "The Aldina as a Source of the Sixtina," *JBL* 38 (1919) 51-52. *[22:25]*

Joshua 22:34

Robert Gordis, "A Note on Joshua 22:34," *AJSL* 47 (1930-31) 287-288.

Joshua Chapter 24

Harold M. Wiener, "Baal, Shechem, and the Text of Joshua XXIV," *BS* 83 (1916) 609-619.

Joshua 24:1-25

Charles H. Giblin, "Structural Patterns in Jos 24, 1-25," *CBQ* 26 (1964) 50-69.

Joshua 24:12

*Anonymous, "Sesostris, the Hornet of Exod. 23:28, Deut. 7:20, Josh. 24:12," *QCS, 3rd Ser.,* 10 (1838) 281-285.

Joshua 24:14-28

*I. G. Matthews, "Expository Studies in the Old Testament: X. Joshua, Gideon, and Samson," *BW* 30 (1907) 275-285. *[24:14-28]*

Joshua 24:29

*L. B. Cholmondeley, "Gn. L. 22-26, Dt. XXXIV. 4-7, Jos.XXIV. 29ff.," *ET* 46 (1934-35) 238.

§594 *3.5.3.1.2 Studies of Manuscripts on the Book of Joshua*

John Richard Sampey, "Some Studies in the Text of Joshua," *BQR* 12 (1890) 452-459.

Anonymous, "The Claim that the Samaritan Book of Joshua has been Found," *CFL, 3rd Ser.,* 9 (1908) 278-279.

William W. Everts, "A New Samaritan Book of Joshua," *HR* 56 (1908) 197.

M. Gaster, "On the Newly Discovered Samaritan Book of Joshua," *JRAS* (1908) 795-809.

E. N. Adler, "On the Samaritan Book of Joshua," *JRAS* (1908) 1143-1147. (Reply by M. Gaster, pp. 1148-1156)

*M. Gaster, "The Samaritan Book of Joshua and the Septuagint," *SBAP* 31 (1909) 115-127, 149-153.

E. N. Adler, "The Apocryphal Book of Joshua," *IJA* #16 (1909) 19-21.

S. Holmes, "The Relation Between the Hebrew and the LXX. Texts of the Book of Joshua," *OSHTP* (1909-10) 34-43.

M. Gaster, "The Genuine Samaritan Book of Joshua," *IJA* #20 (1910) 15-17.

Max L. Margolis, "The Washington MS. of Joshua," *JAOS* 31 (1910-11) 365-367.

*Max L. Margolis, "The Grouping of Codices in the Greek Joshua," *JQR, N.S.,* 1 (1910-11) 259-263.

Max L. Margolis, "The K Text of Joshua," *AJSL* 28 (1911-12) 1-55.

Max L. Margolis, "Additions to Field from the Lyons Codex of the Old Latin," *JAOS* 33 (1913) 254-258. *[Joshua]*

*M[ax L.] Margolis, "Corrections in the Apparatus of the Book of Joshua in the Larger Cambridge Septuagint," *JBL* 49 (1930) 234-264.

A. D. Crown, "The Date and Authenticity of the Samaritan Hebrew Book of Joshua as seen in its Territorial Allotments," *PEQ* 96 (1964) 79-100.

Harry M. Orlinsky, "The Hebrew *Vorlage* of the Septuagint of the Book of Joshua," *VTS* 17 (1969) 187-195.

§595 *3.5.3.1.3 Exegetical Studies on the Book of Judges*

*A. F. Kirkpatrick, "The Revised Version of the Old Testament:—The Books of Judges and Ruth," *Exp, 3rd Ser.,* 3 (1886) 109-124. [1:8, 9, 15, 16, 24, 30; 2:1, 2, 3, 7, 11, (13), 10, 20; 3:5, 7, 9, (15), 10, 19, (26), 25, 26; 4:11, 21; 5:2, 7, 9, 10, 11, 13, 14, 15, 16 ,17, 26, 27, 29; 6:3, 11, 13; 7:8, 23; 8:13, 16, 21, 26; 9:2, 9, 44, 52, 53; 11:37, 39, 40; 12:14; 13:12, 18, 19; 14:15; 15:13, 17, 19; 16:2, 5, 7, 18, 28; 18:7, 30; 19:1, 22, 18, 28, 48; 21:5, pp. 109-126]

S. R. Driver, "Notes on the Book of Judges," *ET* 18 (1906-07) 331-333. [1.) Divisions of the Book; 2.) Textual differences in 1:1-2:5; 3.) On the Margins of the R.V.; 4.) Improved readings and renderings suggested: 1:16; 1:36; 2:1; 5:13a; 5:29; 5:30e; 7:3; 7:6; 7:22; 7:25; 8:27; 9:15; 9:27; 9:28; 9:29; 9:31; 9:44; 11:37; 14:9; 14:15; 15:6; 16:13end, 14 (with LXX); 16:14; 18:7; 19:3; 19:12, 13, 15, etc.; 20:31; 20:33; 20:38; 20:38, 39; 20:41; 20:42; 20:43; 21:17; 21:22; 5.) Geographical locations in question]

G. R. Driver, "Problems in Judges newly Discovered," *ALUOS* 4 (1962-63) 6-25. [2:3; 3:20, 24; 3:1-2; 3:22; 5:8; 5:7 & 11; 5:9; 5:11; 5:14; 5:15; 5:22; 5:26; 6:11; 6:19; 6:25; 7:13; 7:20; 7:21; 8:4; 8:12; 8:18; 9:29; 9:31; 10:11-12; 11:35; 11:20; 11:38; 12:6; 13:23; 13:24; 15:5; 17:10; 18:1; 18:8; 19:9; 19:22; 19:28; 20:31; 20:34; 20:38; 20:43; 21:17; 21:22]

*R. G. Boling, "Some Conflate Readings in Joshua-Judges," *VT* 16 (1966) 293-298.

Judges 1:1-3:6

Eamonn O'Doherty, "The Literary Problem of Judges 1,1-3, 6," *CBQ* 18 (1956) 1-7.

Judges Chapter 1-2:5

*S. B. Gurewicz, "The Bearing of Judges i-ii. 5, on the Authorship of the Book of Judges," *ABR* 7 (1959) 37-40.

Judges Chapter 1

*G. Ernest Wright, "The Literary and Historical Problem of Joshua 10 and Judges 1," *JNES* 5 (1946) 105-114.

Judges 1:5

Augustus Poynder, "Adoni-Bezek," *ET* 7 (1895-96) 527. *[1:5]*

Judges 1:8

A. H. Sayce, "Note on Judges I. 8," *ET* 15 (1903-04) 284-285.

Eliphalet B. Terry, "Unsatisfactory Criticism: Exegesis of Judges I. 8," *CFL, 3rd Ser.,* 1 (1904) 685-687.

Judges 1:10

Augustus Poynder, "Kirjath-arba, "Judges I. 10," *ET* 10 (1898-99) 287.

Judges 1:13

George Warington, "Note on the Relation between Caleb and Othniel," *JSL, 4th Ser.,* 8 (1865-66) 338-342. *[1:13]*

Judges 1:27

*B. D. Zaphrir (Frimorgen), "'Even Three Countries'," *BIES* 14 (1947-48) #3/4, II. *[1:27]*

Judges 2:1-3:4

Nathan Stemmer, "The Introduction to Judges 2.1-3.4," *JQR, N.S.,* 57 (1966-67) 239-241.

Judges 2:6-3:6

Alexander Rofé, "The Composition of the Introduction of the Book of Judges (Judges II, 6-III,6)," *Tarbiz* 35 (1965-66) #3, I-II.

Judges 3:7-11

C. J. Ball, "Cushan-Rishathaim (Judg. III. 7-11)," *ET* 21 (1909-10) 192.

*A[braham] Malamat, "Cushan Rishathaim and the Decline of the Near East Around 1200 B.C.," *JNES* 13 (1954) 231-242. *[3:7-11]*

Judges 3:8-10

Anonymous, "Judges 3:8-10 and the Cuneiform Tablets," *ONTS* 12 (1891) 237. *[Tell-el-Amarna]*

*Millar Burrows, "Notes on Judges 3:8, 10; Neh. 2:8, 10; 3:26," *JBL* 53 (1934) xii.

Eugen Taeubler, "Cushan-Rishathaim," *HUCA* 20 (1947) 137-142. *[3:8-10]*

Judges 3:8

*J. W. Jack, "Cushan-Rishathaim (כּוּשַׁן רִשְׁעָתַיִם)," *ET* 35 (1923-24) 426-428. *[3:8]*

*J. W. Jack, "Recent Biblical Archaeology. Cush and Cushan-Rishathaim," *ET* 52 (1940-41) 114-115. *[3:8]*

Judges 3:12

E. G. Kraeling, "Difficulties in the Story of Ehud," *JBL* 54 (1935) 205-210. *[3:12f.]*

Judges 3:16

George F. Moore, "The Meaning of נמד, Jud. 3:16," *JBL* 12 (1893) 104.

Judges 3:18-19

H. B. Hackett, "Biblical Notes. 5. The 'Quarries' near Gilgal," *BS* 23 (1866) 521-522. *[3:18, 19]*

Judges 3:26

*W. F. Birch, "Seirath (Judg. iii, 26)," *PEFQS* 13 (1881) 102.

Judges 3:31

*Raphael Giveon, "A Ramesside 'Semitic' Letter," *RDSO* 37 (1962) 167-173. *[3:31]*

Judges Chapters 4-5

*L. W. Batten, "The Conquest of Northern Canaan: Joshua xi. 1-9; Judges iv-v," *JBL* 24 (1905) 31-40.

*Stanley A. Cook, "Kedesh-Naphtali and Taanach: A Theory and Some Comments," *PEFQS* 51 (1919) 188-193. *[Chaps. 4-5]*

*J. Edgar Bruns, "Judith or Jael?" *CBQ* 16 (1954) 12-14. *[Chaps. 4-5]*

Judges Chapter 4

Claude R. Conder, "Barak and Sisera. Judges iv," *PEFQS* 9 (1877) 190-192.

Judges 4:4-5

A. J. Brawer, "The estates of Debora in the Agada," *BIES* 8 (1940-41) #2, I. *[4:4-5]*

Judges 4:17-23

A. Moody Stuart, "Sisera and Jael. Judges iv. 17-23," *Exp, 3rd Ser.,* 6 (1887) 306-314.

Judges Chapter 5

Anonymous, "The Song of Deborah: Judges v," *QCS* 8 (1826) 70-73.

[Edward Robinson], "Interpretation of Judges, Chap. V. The Song of Deborah and Barak," *BRCR* 1 (1831) 568-612.

R. D. C. Robbins, "The Song of Deborah—Judges Chapter v," *BS* 12 (1855) 597-642.

D. E., "The Song of Deborah," *JSL, 3rd Ser.,* 12 (1860-61) 164-166 *[Chap. 5]*

R. G. Moulton, "Deborah's Song," *BW* 6 (1895) 260-263 *[Metered Translation of Chap. 5]*

*G. Margoliouth, "The Fifth Chapter of the Book of Judges," *Exp, 8th Ser.,* 18 (1919) 207-233.

Luke Walker, "The Song of Deborah," *NB* 1 (1920-21) 117-125, 173-185. *[Chap. 5]*

*Burton L. Goddard, "The Critic and Deborah's Song," *WTJ* 3 (1940-41) 93-112. *[Chap. 5]*

Judges 5:2

*T. Tyler, "Two Notes on the 'Song of Deborah'," *JQR* 10 (1897-98) 173-174. *[5:2]*

Abraham J. Brachman, "Judges 5:2," *JQR, N.S.,* 39 (1948-49) 413-414.

C. Rabin, "Judges V, 2 and the 'Ideology' of Deborah's War," *JJS* 6 (1955) 125-134.

P. C. Craigie, "A Note on Judges V 2," *VT* 18 (1968) 397-399.

Judges 5:3-5

Pearle S. Wood, "An Interpretation of Judges 5:3-5," *JBL* 67 (1948) vii.

Morris S. Seale, "Deborah's Ode and the Ancient Arabian Qasida," *JBL* 81 (1962) 343-347. *[5:3-5]*

Judges 5:4

*T. Tyler, "Two Notes on the 'Song of Deborah'," *JQR* 10 (1897-98) 173-174. [II. p. 174] *[5:4]*

Judges 5:8b-13

Ch. Goodwin, "The Meaning of Judges 5:8b-13," *JBL* 63 (1944) 257-262.

Judges 5:8

Geo. Bladon, "'They Chose New Gods,' Judges V. 8," *ET* 5 (1893-94) 476-477.

Norman   Snaith,   "Judges   V.   8,"   *ET*   41   (1929-30)   140.

Delbert R. Hillers, "A Note on Judges 5,8a," *CBQ* 27 (1965) 124-126.

B. Margulis, "An Exegesis of Judges V:8," *VT* 15 (1965) 66-72.

Judges 5:11

S. Speier, "On פרזנו צדקת, Judg. 5:11," *JBL* 82 (1963) 216.

Judges 5:12-24

A. D. H. Mayes, "The Historical Context of the Battle Against Sisera," *VT* 19 (1969) 353-360. *[5:12-24]*

Judges 5:14

*James A. Montgomery, "Hebraica," *JAOS* 58 (1938) 130-139. [(9) Light from the Arabic, (e) 'After thee, O Benjamin!', Jud. 5:14, p. 138]

Judges 5:15b-16

A.   D.   Crown,   "Judges   V   15b-16,"   *VT*   17   (1967)   240-242.

Judges 5:16

*James Edward Hogg, "The Meaning of המשפתים in Gen. 49:14 and Judg. 5:16," *AJSL* 43 (1926-27) 299-301.

Judges 5:17

*"The   Hebrews   and   the   Sea,"   *ONTS*   14   (1892)   307.   *[5:17]*

*Yigael Yadin, "'And Dan, why did he remain in ships?' (Judges, V, 17)," *AJBA* 1 (1968-71) #1, 9-23.

Judges 5:22

George   Farmer,   "Judges   V.   22,"   *ET*   33   (1921-22)   93.

Judges 5:23

Adelphos, "Remarks on Judges V, 23," *MR* 10 (1827) 219-221.

Judges 5:24

Agnes Smith Lewis, "Jael the Blessed. I.," *ET* 28 (1916-17) 476-477. *[5:24]*

T. L. Turner, "Jael the Blessed. II.," *ET* 28 (1916-17) 477-478. *[5:24]*

*Robert A. Aytoun, "The Ethics of the Jael Narratives," *ET* 28 (1916-17) 520-522. *[5:24]*

Judges 5:25

E. Power, "'He asked for water, milk she gave' (Iud. 5, 25)," *B* 9 (1928) 47. *[5:25]*

Judges 5:29

*Chr. A. W. Brekelmans, "Some Translation Problems," *OTS* 15 (1969) 170-176. *[5:29]*

Judges 5:30

C. Taylor, "On some passages of the Pentateuch, Judges and 2nd Kings," *JP* 5 (1873) 54-65. *[5:30]*

John P. Peters, "Judges V. 30," *AJSL* 3 (1886-87) 114-115.

Judges 6:7-10

Lewis Bayles Paton, "Outline Studies of Obscurer Prophets—The Unnamed Prophet of Judges VI. 7-10," *HR* 49 (1905) 432-433.

Judges 6:14

Owen H. Gates, "Judges 6:14," *BW* 14 (1899) 304.

Judges 6:19

D. R. Ap-Thomas, "The Ephah of Meal in Judges VI. 19," *JTS* 41 (1940) 175-177.

Judges 6:25-28

Alfred Guillaume, "A Note on הַפָּר הַשֵּׁנִי. Judges VI. 25, 26, 28," *JTS* 50 (1949) 52-53.

Judges 6:36-40

S. Tolkowsky, "Gideon's Fleece," *JPOS* 3 (1923) 197-199. *[6:36-40]*

Judges Chapters 7 and 8

S. Tolkowsky, "'Gideon's 300' (Judges vii and viii)," *JPOS* 5 (1925) 69-74.

Judges 7:2-8

D. Daube, "Gideon's Few," *JJS* 7 (1956) 155-162. *[7:2-8]*

Judges 7:3

W. E. Barnes, "Judges VII 3," *JTS* 16 (1914-15) 392-394.

Judges 7:5

Herbert L. Bishop, "'Every One that Lappeth of the Water'," *ET* 35 (1923-24) 140. *[7:5]*

Judges 7:5-6

A. Moody Stuart, "Lapping of the Water," *PEFQS* 27 (1895) 345. *[7:5-6]*

J. A. Selbie, "Lapping as a Dog," *ET* 7 (1895-96) 470-471. *[7:5-6]*

T. H. Weir, "Gideon and His Three Hundred (Judg. VII. 5, 6)," *ET* 33 (1921-22) 330; 34 (1922-23) 232.

Lucien Gautier, "Gideon and His Men," *ET* 33 (1921-22) 520. *[7:5-6]*

Victor L. Trumper, "The Choosing of Gideon's 300. Judges 7:5, 6," *JPOS* 6 (1926) 108-109.

Judges 7:7

Harry Smith, "Gideon's Three Hundred," *ET* 33 (1921-22) 93. *[7:7]*

Judges 7:9-23

*I. G. Matthews, "Expository Studies in the Old Testament: X. Joshua, Gideon, and Samson," *BW* 30 (1907) 275-285. *[7:9-23]*

Judges 7:13

*S[tephen] L[angdon], "A Babylonian Tablet on the Interpretation of Dreams," *MJ* 8 (1917) 116-122. *[7:13]*

Judges 7:25-8:25

Frank Zimmermann, "Reconstructions in Judges 7:25-8:25," *JBL* 71 (1952) 111-114.

Judges 8:4-17

Hanoch Reviv, "Two Notes to Judges VIII. 4-17," *Tarbiz* 38 (1968-69) #4, I.

Judges 8:7

*Ghosn el Howie, "Illustrations from Agricultural Life in Syria," *HR* 47 (1904) 217-218. *[8:7]*

Judges 8:14

*Jacob Leveen, "The Meaning of וַיִּכְתֹּב in Judges viii, 14," *JRAS* (1948) 61-62.

Judges 8:16

*Ghosn el Howie, "Illustrations from Agricultural Life in Syria," *HR* 47 (1904) 217-218. *[8:16]*

Judges 8:22-23

G. Henton Davies, "Judges VIII. 22-23," *VT* 13 (1963) 151-157.

Judges Chapter 9

*Eugene H. Maly, "The Jotham Fable—Anti-Monarchical?" *CBQ* 22 (1960) 299-305. *[Chap. 9]*

A. D. Crown, "A Reinterpretation of Judges IX in the Light of Its Humor," *Abr-N* 3 (1961-62) 90-98.

Judges 9:6

*C[laude] R. Conder, "City of David," *PEFQS* 15 (1883) 194-195. [אלון מצב] *[9:6]*

(Mrs.) Ghosn-el-Howie, "'The House of Millo'," *AJSL* 45 (1928-29) 64-67. *[9:6]*

Judges 9:7-20

Milton S. Terry, "Jotham's Fable," *ONTS* 3 (1883-84) 157. *[9:7-20]*

Judges 9:8-15

*W. W. Martin, "A Hebrew Parable and the Poetic Style," *MQR, 3rd Ser,.* 12 (1892) 310-319. *[9:8-15]*

Walter R. Roehrs, "Sermon Study on Judges 9:8-15. The Fable of the Bramble King," *CTM* 20 (1949) 488-495.

Uriel Simon, "The Parable of Jotham (Judges IX, 8-15): The Parable, Its Application and their Narrative Framework," *Tarbiz* 34 (1964-65) #1, I-II.

Judges 9:26-41

Harold M. Wiener, "The Criticism of the Gaal Narrative (Jud. IX. 26-41)," *BS* 76 (1919) 359-361.

Judges 9:28

G. J. Thieny, "Miscellanea Hebraica. 3. Judges ix 28," *OTS* 7 (1950) 146-148.

Robert G. Boling, "'And who is *Š-K-M*?' (Judges IX 28)," *VT* 13 (1963) 479-482.

Judges 9:29

*Henry Preserved Smith, "Old Testament Notes," *JBL* 24 (1906) 27-30. [VI. Judges 9:29, pp. 29-30]

Judges 9:31

Stanley Gevirtz, "The *Hapax Legomenon* תרמה (Judg. 9:31)," *JNES* 27 (1958) 59-60.

Judges 9:37

*Maurice A. Canney, "The Primordial Mound," *JMUEOS* #20 (1936) 25-40. *[9:37]*

John M. Wilkie, "The Peshiṭta Translation of *Ṭabbur Ha'ares* in Judges IX 37," *VT* 1 (1951) 144.

Judges 9:41

M. Naor, "'An Abimelech Dwelt in Arumah'," *BIES* 20 (1955-56) #1/2, II. *[9:41]*

Judges 9:53

Samuel Hutchings, "An Obsolete Word Examined," *PRR* 6 (1895) 332-334. ["All to"] *[9:53]*

Judges 10:6 - 1 Samuel Chapter 8

*Stanley A. Cook, "Notes on Old Testament History, III, Judges X. 6 - I Sam. VIII," *JQR* 18 (1905-06) 347-359.

Judges Chapters 11 and 12

Joseph M. Gleason, "The Sacrifice of Jephthah's Daughter," *AER* 9 (1893) 168-179. *[Chaps. 11-12]*

Judges Chapter 11

J. O. S., "Jephthah and his Daughter," *UQGR* 18 (1861) 56-67. *[Chap. 11]*

Samuel Warren, "Jephthah's Vow," *BS* 24 (1867) 238-248. *[Chap. 11]*

*A. H. van Zyl, "The Message Formula in the Book of Judges," *OTW* 2 (1959) 61-64. *[Chap. 11]*

Judges 11:1-3

*S. Feigin, "Some Cases of Adoption in Israel," *JBL* 50 (1931) 186-200. [I. The Adoption of Jephthah (Judges 11:1-3), pp. 186-196]

Judges 11:29-31

Anonymous, "Exegetical Remarks on Jephthah's Vow. Judges xi, 29-31," *CR* 4 (1851-52) 415-427.

Judges 11:30-40

Xenophon Betts, "Exposition of Jephthah's Vow, Judges 11:30-40," *BRCR, N.S.,* 9 (1843) 143-149.

W. M. Smythe, "A Brief Inquiry into the Nature of Jephthah's Vow. Judges xi: 30-40," *SPR* 2 (1848-49) 68-75.

Anonymous, "Jephthah's Vow.—Judges 11:30-40," *ER* 13 (1861-62) 28-34.

Judges 11:29-40

James A. Quarles, "Jephthah's Vow—Judges xi. 29-40," *HR* 37 (1899) 352-354.

Judges 11:30-31

H. T., "Jephthah's Daughter," *MR* 11 (1828) 30-32. *[11:30-31]*

Judges 11:31

William G. Funk, "Jephthah's Vow: A Grammatical Exposition of Judges XI. 31," *HR* 41 (1901) 351-353.

Judges 11:37

*Max L. Margolis, "A Passage in Ecclesiasticus," *ZAW* 21 (1901) 271-272. *[11:37]*

Harry M. Orlinsky, "The Corrupt Character and Origin of *wᵉyāradhtī* in Judges 11:37," *JBL* 60 (1941) x.

*Harry M. Orlinsky, "Critical Notes on Gen. 39:14, 17, Jud. 11:37," *JBL* 61 (1942) 87-97. [II. The Corrupt Character and Origin of *wᵉjāradhti* in Jud 11 37, pp. 92-97.]

*Sakae Shibayama, "Notes on *Yārad* and *'Ālāh:* Hints on Translating," *JAAR* 34 (1966) 358-362. [I. Judges 11:37, pp. 359-360]

Judges 12:1-6

Folker Willesen, "The אפרתי of the Shibboleth Incident," *VT* 8 (1958) 97-98. *[12:1-6]*

Judges 12:6

Harold Garner, "Shibboleth (Judges XII. 6)," *ET* 53 (1941-42) 242-243.

E[phraim] A. Speiser, "The Shibboleth Incident (Judges 12:6)," *BASOR* #85 (1942) 10-13.

E[phraim] A. Speiser, "The 'Shibboleth' Incident: Judges 12:6," *JBL* 61 (1942) iii.

Judges 12:7

Abd-el-Masih,   "Judges   XII.   7,"   *ET*   3   (1891-92)   479.

*Leo Jung, "Mis-Translations a Source in Jewish and Christian Lore," *PAAJR* 5 (1933-34) 55-67. [IV. Jephthah (Judges XII, 7), pp. 61-62]

Judges Chapters 13-16

*J. Blenkinsopp, "Structure and Style in Judges 13-16," *JBL* 82 (1963) 65-76.

Judges 13:22-23

Ambrose W. Vernon, "An Ancient Anticipation of Modern Unbelief. Judges 13: 22, 23," *BW* 30 (1907) 56-59.

Judges Chapters 14-15

*A. Van Selms, "The Best Man and Bride—From Sumer to St. John, with a New Interpretation of Judges, Chapters 14 and 15," *JNES* 9 (1950) 65-75.

Judges 14:14-18

J. R. Porter, "Samson's Riddle: Judges XIV. 14, 18," *JTS, N.S.*, 13 (1962) 106-109.

Judges 14:19

D. Winton Thomas, "A Note on חליצותם in Judges XIV 19," *JTS* 34 (1933) 165.

Judges 14:20

*Claude R. Conder, "Notes on New Discoveries," *PEFQS* 41 (1909) 266-275. [Samson's Friend (Judges 14:20; 15:2), p. 272]

Judges Chapter 15

Claude R. Conder, "The Rock Etam. Judges xv," *PEFQS* 8 (1876) 175-177.

Judges 15:2

*Claude R. Conder, "Notes on New Discoveries," *PEFQS* 41 (1909) 266-275. [Samson's Friend (Judges 14:20; 15:2), p. 272]

Judges 15:4-5

K. G. Manz, "Samson's Foxes," *CTM* 8 (1937) 621. *[15:4, 5]*

Judges 15:8

M. A. Canney, "Notes on Philology, etc. 'Hip and Thigh'," *JMUEOS* #3 (1913-14) 87-88. *[15:8]*

A. Mingana, "Judges XV. 8," *ET* 26 (1914-15) 332-333.

Judges 15:9-19

C[laude] R. Conder, "Ramoth Lehi. (Judg. XV, 9-19," *PEFQS* 15 (1883) 182.

Judges 15:13-15

Ambrose W. Vernon, "The Religious Value of the Figure of Samson. A Meditation on Judges 15:13-15," *BW* 32 (1908) 33-38.

Judges 15:16

Morris Jastrow Jr., "Judg. XV. 16," *AJSL* 5 (1888-89) 198.

Paul Haupt, "Samson and the Ass's Jaw," *JBL* 33 (1914) 296-298. *[15:16]*

Judges 16:1-3

*E. G. H. Kraeling, "The Early Cult of Hebron and Judges 16:1-3," *AJSL* 41 (1924-25) 174-178.

Judges 16:13ff.

G. F. Moore, "On Judges xvi. 13ff.," *JAOS* 14 (1890) clxxvi-clxxx.

Judges 16:19

F. C. Fensham, "The Shaving of Samson: A Note on Judges 16:19," *EQ* 31 (1959) 97-98.

Judges 16:20

D. Winton Thomas, "A Note on the Hebrew Text of Judges 16, 20," *AfO* 10 (1935-36) 162-163.

Judges Chapters 17 - 18

Julius Bewer, "The Composition of Judges, Chaps. 17, 18," *AJSL* 29 (1912-13) 261-283.

M. H. Segal, "The Text of Judges XVII-XVIII," *JMUEOS* #6 (1916-17) 33-48.

*H. H. Rowley, "The Danite Migration to Laish," *ET* 51 (1939-40) 466-471. *[Chaps. 17 and 18]*

Judges Chapter 17 sq.

A. Murtonen, "Some Thoughts on Judges XVII SQ," *VT* 1 (1951) 223-224.

Judges 17:6

Howard Crosby, "Light on Important Texts. No. XXIX," *HR* 8 (1883-84) 344-345. *[17:6]*

Judges 18:30

Howard Crosby, "Light on Important Texts. NO. XI," *HR* 5 (1880-81) 646-647. *[18:30]*

Judges Chapter 19

Julius A. Bewer, "The Composition of Judges, Chap. 19," *AJSL* 30 (1913-14) 81-93.

Judges 19:13

Harry M. Orlinsky, "The Import of the Kethib-Ḳere and the Masoretic Note on *L^eḳåḥ*, Judges 19:13," *JQR, N.S.,* 31 (1940-41) 59-66.

Judges Chapters 20 and 21

Julius A Bewer, "The Composition of Judges, Chaps. 20, 21," *AJSL* 30 (1913-14) 149-165.

Judges 20:16

*Samuel Daiches, "Exegetical Notes," *PEFQS* 59 (1927) 162-163. [I. Judges 20:16]

§596 *3.5.3.1.4 Studies on Manuscripts of the Book of Judges*

*A. V. Billen, "The Old Latin Version of Judges," *JTS* 43 (1942) 140-149.

*C[harles] M. Cooper, "Theodotion's Influence on the Alexandrian Text of Judges," *JBL* 66 (1947) xi.

*Charles M. Cooper, "Theodotion's Influence on the Alexandrian Text of Judges," *JBL* 67 (1948) 63-68.

*R. B. Dirksen, "Peshitta Communications IV, A sixth Century Palimpsest of Judges Reconstructed," *VT* 13 (1963) 349-355.

§597 *3.5.3.1.5 Studies on the Books of Samuel*

William W. Guth, "The Unity of the Older Saul-David Sayings," *JBL* 25 (1906) 111-135.

M. H. Segal, "Studies in the Books of Samuel I. David's Three Poems," *JQR, N.S.,* 5 (1914-15) 201-231. [1. The Elegy on the Death of Saul and Jonathan; 2. The Hymn of Triumph; 3. The Oracle of David]

M. H. Segal, "Studies in the Books of Samuel II," *JQR, N.S.,* 6 (1915-16) 267-302, 555-587. [The Composition of the Book; The Election of Saul; The Advent of David; The Story of Samuel, 1. Birth and Childhood of Samuel, 2. Samuel in his Manhood, 3. Samuel in his Old Age, a. The Election of Saul, b. the Rejection of Saul and the Adventure of Jonathan; The Story of David, a. David and Saul]

M. H. Segal, "Studies in the Books of Samuel II," *JQR, N.S.,* 8 (1917-18) 75-100. [Composition of the Book (cont.) David and Ishbosheth]

M. H. Segal, "Studies in the Books of Samuel II," *JQR, N.S.,* 9 (1918-19) 43-70. [The Composition of the Book (concluded); The First Period of David's Reign over all Israel; The Second Period of David's Reign over all Israel; Miscellaneous Pieces, Chs. 21-24]

M. H. Segal, "Studies in the Books of Samuel, Chapters III to V," *JQR, N.S.,* 10 (1919-20) 203-236, 421-444. [Some Notes on the Text; 2:1-10. The Song of Hannah; Ancient Jewish Exegesis and Modern Criticism; The Chronology of David's Reign]

Frederic Field, "Dr. Field's Old Testament Revision Notes. Transcribed from the Author's MS. by the Rev. John Henry Burn, B.D., VII.," *ET* 35 (1923-24) 45-46. [1 Sam. 13:1, 2 Sam. 10:7; 10:12; 14:20; 15:7; 17:9; 18:13; 20:8; 22:43]

§598 *3.5.3.1.5.1 Exegetical Studies on the First Book of Samuel*

A. F. Kirkpatrick, "The Revised Version of the Old Testament:—The First Book of Samuel," *Exp, 3rd Ser,* 3 (1886) 201-217. [1:1, 5, 6, 9, 15, 16, 24, 28; 2:3, 14, 22, 25, 28; 3:3, 11; 4:1, 8, 13; 5:6; 6:1, 6, 18, 19; 8:3; 9:5, 8, 16; 10:27; 12:3; 13:1; 13:21; 14:18, 19, 51; 15:12; 17:2, 6, 12, 52; 18:8, 28; 19:22; 20:19, 41; 22:6, 9; 25:6, 22; 27:8; 28:13, 16; 30:2, 20; 21:9]

T. K. Cheyne, "Critical Gleanings from I Samuel," *ET* 10 (1898-99) 520-522. [I. Sam. 6:8, 11, 15; 16:12; 17:1; 17:6; 17:52; 17:54; 30:30; 31:10]

*Stanley A. Cook, "Notes on Old Testament History, III, Judges X. 6 - I Sam. VIII," *JQR* 18 (1905-06) 347-359.

*Henry Snyder Gehman, "Exegetical Methods Employed by the Greek Translator of I Samuel," *JAOS* 70 (1950) 292-296.

1 Samuel 1:1

H. J. Flowers, "1 Samuel I. 1: אֶחָד אִישׁ," *ET* 66 (1954-55) 273.

1 Samuel 1:3

J. A. Selbie, "Requests and Replies," *ET* 13 (1901-02) 206. *[1:3]*

1 Samuel 1:5

S. R. Driver, "Grammatical Notes. 3. On 1 Samuel I., 5," *AJSL* 2 (1885-86) 37-38.

1 Samuel 1:18

J. Weingreen, "A rabbinic-type gloss in the LXX version of 1 Samuel I 18," *VT* 14 (1964) 225-228.

1 Samuel 2:1-10

C[harles] A[ugustus] Briggs, "The Song of Hannah," *PR* 6 (1885) 112-114. *[2:1-10]*

Eneas B. Goodwin, "The Old Testament 'Song of Hannah.' (I Sam. 2, 1-10)," *CUB* 5 (1899) 170-183.

Paul Haupt, "The Prototype of the Magnificant," *ZDMG* 58 (1904) 617-632. *[2:1-10]*

P. A. H. de Boer, "Confirmatum est cor meum. Remarks on the Old Latin text of the Song of Hannah 1 Samuel ii 1-10," *OTS* 13 (1963) 173-192.

1 Samuel 2:5

W. H. Bennett, "Note on the LXX of I Samuel II. 5," *ET* 13 (1901-02) 234.

1 Samuel 2:10

*C. R. Brown, "1 Sam. 2:10 as illustrative of Gen. 6:3," *JBL* 5 (1885) 91.

1 Samuel 2:13

Hugh Macmillan, "By Hook or by Crook," *ET* 8 (1896-97) 214-215. *[2:13]*

1 Samuel 2:22-25

Matitiahu Tsevat, "The Death of the Sons of Eli," *JAAR* 32 (1964) 355-358. *[2:22-25]*

1 Samuel 2:24

*Duncan B. Macdonald, "Notes, Critical and Lexicographical," *JBL* 14 (1895) 57-62. [I. 1 Sam 2:24, p. 57]

1 Samuel 2:33

Harold M. Wiener, "The Text of I Samuel II 33," *JPOS* 8 (1928) 63.

1 Samuel 2:27-36

*Matitiahu Tsevat, "Studies in the Book of Samuel," *HUCA* 32 (1961) 191-216. [I Interpretation of I Samuel 2:27-36; the Narrative of *Kareth*, pp. 191-209]

1 Samuel 2:35

S. B. Randall, "1 Samuel II., 35," *ONTS* 4 (1884-85) 316-317.

1 Samuel 3:1-21

*I. G. Matthews, "Expository Studies in the Old Testament: XI. Ruth and Samuel," *BW* 30 (1907) 361-368. *[3:1-21]*

1 Samuel 3:2f.

*L. W. Batten, "The Sanctuary at Shiloh, and Samuel's sleeping therein," *JBL* 19 (1900) 29-33. *[3:2f.]*

1 Samuel 4:13

*Max Krenkel, "Some Emendations to the Text of Samuel," *ONTS* 2 (1882-83) 170-171. *[4:13]*

1 Samuel 4:15

*Duncan B. Macdonald, "Notes, Critical and Lexicographical," *JBL* 14 (1895) 57-62. [II. 1 Sam 4:15, pp. 57-58]

1 Samuel Chapters 5 and 6

*J. Campbell Gibson, "Was it Bubonic Plague?" *ET* 12 (1900-01) 378-380. *[Chaps. 5 and 6]*

Alexander S. Crichton, "The Plague in the Land of the Philistines," *Exp, 8th Ser.,* 10 (1915) 558-565. *[Chaps. 5 and 6]*

*R. Havelock Charles, "Emerods," *ET* 20 (1908-09) 332-333. *[Chap. 5]*

*Joseph Offord, "Archaeological Notes on Jewish Antiquities . XV. *Propagation of Plague by Insects and Rodents in the Old Testament and Monumental Records,*" *PEFQS* 48 (1916) 141-143. *[Chap. 5]*

1 Samuel 5:4

*Claude R. Conder, "Notes on New Discoveries," *PEFQS* 41 (1909) 266-275. [Dagon (1 Chron. 10:10; see 1 Sam. 5:4), p. 274]

1 Samuel 5:6-6:16

G. R. Driver, "The Plague of the Philistines (1 Samuel v, 6-vi, 16)," *JRAS* (1950) 50-52.

1 Samuel 5:6

*Geo. J. Dann, "'Mice' and 'Emerods'," *ET* 15 (1903-04) 476-478. *[5:6]*

1 Samuel 5:17-19

John Urquhart, "'Difficulties' in the Account of the Restoration of the Captured Ark: I Sam. v. 17-19," *CFL, 3rd Ser.,* 9 (1908) 157-159.

1 Samuel Chapter 6

*Elihu Grant, "The Excavations at Old Beth Shemesh, Palestine, See I Samuel VI," *JAAR* 1 (1933) #1, 22.

*N. H. Tur-Sinai, "The Ark of God at Beit Shemesh (1 Sam. VI) and Peres 'Uzza (2 Sam VI; 1 Chron. XIII)," *VT* 1 (1951) 275-286.

1 Samuel 6:1-18

*R. Havelock Charles, "Emerods," *ET* 20 (1908-09) 332-333. *[6:1-18]*

1 Samuel 6:3

D. Winton Thomas, "A Note on וְנוֹדַע לָכֶם in I Samuel VI. 3," *JTS, N.S.*, 11 (1960) 52-53.

1 Samuel 6:4-11

*C[onrad] Schick, "Letters from Herr Baurath von Schick. IV. Baron Ustinoff's Collection of Antiquities at Jaffa. 8," *PEFQS* 25 (1893) 296-297. *[6:4-11]*

*Oldfield Thomas, "Remarks on Facsimile of Metal Mouse in the Collection of Baron Ustinoff at Jaffa," *PEFQS* 26 (1894) 189-190. *[6:4-11]*

1 Samuel 6:4-5

*Geo. J. Dann, "'Mice' and 'Emerods'," *ET* 15 (1903-04) 476-478. *[6:4-5]*

1 Samuel 6:8-15

*E. Sapir, "Hebrew *'argáz*, A Philistine Word," *JAOS* 56 (1936) 272-281. *[6:8, 11, 15]*

1 Samuel 6:8

W. H. Bennett, "The Coffer ('Argāz). Note on the Text of I Samuel vi. 8," *ET* 13 (1901-02) 234.

1 Samuel 6:19

Julius A. Bewer, "The Original Reading of 1 Sam. 6:19a," *JBL* 57 (1938) 89-91.

O[swald] T. Allis, "The Punishment of the Men of Bethshemesh," *EQ* 15 (1943) 298-307. *[6:19]*

1 Samuel 7:1-13

*I. G. Matthews, "Expository Studies in the Old Testament: XI. Ruth and Samuel," *BW* 30 (1907) 361-368. *[7:1-13]*

1 Samuel 7:2

Joseph Blenkinsopp, "Kiriath-Jearim and the Ark," *JBL* 88 (1969) 143-156. *[7:2]*

1 Samuel 7:5

W. J. Phythian-Adams, "The Mizpah of 1 Samuel 7:5&c.," *JPOS* 3 (1923) 13-20.

1 Samuel 8:4-17

*I. Mendelsohn, "Samuel's Denunciation of Kingship in the Light of the Akkadian Documents from Ugarit," *BASOR* #143 (1956) 17-22. *[8:4-17]*

1 Samuel Chapters 9-14

*Stanley A. Cook, "Notes on Old Testament History, II, Saul," *JQR* 18 (1905-06) 121-134. *[Chaps. 9-14]*

1 Samuel 9:1-11:15

Christian E Hauer Jr., "Does 1 Samuel 9:1-11:15 Reflect the Extension of Saul's Dominions?" *JBL* 86 (1967) 306-310.

1 Samuel Chapters 9-10

Claude R. Conder, "Saul's Journey to Zuph. 1 Sam. ix and x," *PEFQS* 9 (1877) 37-40.

W. F. Birch, "The Nameless City. 1 Sam. ix., x," *PEFQS* 11 (1879) 130-131.

Claude R. Conder, "The Nameless City," *PEFQS* 11 (1879) 171-172. *[Chaps. 9 and 10]*

1 Samuel Chapter 9

W. F. Birch, "The Nameless City," *PEFQS* 12 (1880) 104-106, 240. *[Chap. 9]*

W. F. Birch, "The Nameless City," *PEFQS* 15 (1883) 48-52. *[Chap. 9]*

C[onrad] Schick, "Saul's Journey. (1 Sam. ix.)," *PEFQS* 15 (1883) 110-112.

H. B. S. W., "The Nameless City, and Saul's Journey to and from it," *PEFQS* 15 (1883) 156-157. (Note by W. F. Birch, pp. 157-159) *[Chap. 9]*

C[laude] R. Conder, "Saul's Journey," *PEFQS* 15 (1883) 183-184. *[Chap. 9]*

1 Samuel 9:6-13

*Archibald Henderson, "Kirjath Jearim," *PEFQS* 14 (1882) 63-64. *[9:6, 11, 13]*

1 Samuel 9:7

H. F. B. Compston, "The Prophet's Profit (1 Sam. IX. 7)," *ET* 21 (1909-10) 138.

1 Samuel 9:16-17

William J. Deane, "Saul's Three Signs," *BFER* 37 (1888) 405-421. *[9:16-17 etc.]*

1 Samuel 9:24

Macy M. Skinner, "העליה, 1 Sam 9:24," *JBL* 15 (1896) 82-86.

1 Samuel 10:2

Matitiahu Tsevat, "Studies in the Book of Samuel," *HUCA* 33 (1962) 107-118. [II. Interpretation of I Sam. 10:2; Saul at Rachel's Tomb]

1 Samuel 10:5-13

*Hugh Duncan, "The Sons of the Prophets," *GUOST* 2 (1901-07) 24-27. *[10:5-13]*

1 Samuel 10:5-12

*Victor Eppstein, "Was Saul also among the prophets?" *ZAW* 81 (1969) 287-304. *[10:5-6, 10-12]*

1 Samuel 10:5

*B. Maisler, "Topographical Studies III," *BIES* 10 (1942-44) #2/3, III. [3. Give 'at ha-Elohim (1 Sam. 10:5)]

1 Samuel 10:12

*A. Van Hoonacker, "Expository Notes," *Exp, 8th Ser.*, 9 (1915) 452-459. [3. 1 Samuel 10:12: *And who is their father?* or: *his father?* pp. 456-459]

Lucien Gautier, "'And Who is Their Father?' (I Sam. X. 12)," *ET* 29 (1917-18) 379-380.

J. G. Walker, "Who is their father?" *Theo* 31 (1935) 348. *[10:12]*

1 Samuel 10:13-16

D. R. Ap-Thomas, "Saul's 'Uncle'," *VT* 11 (1961) 241-245. *[10:13-16]*

1 Samuel 10:27

Harold M. Wiener, "The Text of I Samuel X 27," *JPOS* 8 (1928) 125.

1 Samuel 12:3

*E[phraim] A. Speiser, "Of Shoes and Shekels (I Samuel 12:3; 13:21)," *BASOR* #77 (1940) 15-20.

1 Samuel 12:11

*J. Willcock, "1 Samuel XII. 11; Hebrews XI. 32," *ET* 28 (1916-17) 41-42.

1 Samuel 12:12

Daniel Lys, "Who is Our President? *From Text to Sermon on I Samuel 12:12," Interp* 21 (1967) 401-420.

1 Samuel 12:20-25

Charles Vince, "The Farewell Counsel of Samuel," *CongL* 1 (1872) 519-530. *[12:20, 24, 25]*

1 Samuel 13:1

F. J. Briggs, "I Samuel XIII. 1," *ET* 50 (1938-39) 94.

1 Samuel 13:3-4

*W. F. Birch, "Varieties. *The Garrison," PEFQS* 14 (1882) 266.[I Sam. 13:3, 4]

C[laude] R. Conder, "Notes. *The Garrison," PEFQS* 15 (1883) 101. *[13:3, 4]*

H. B. S. W., "Pillar or Garrison?" *PEFQS* 15 (1883) 243-244. *[13:3, 4]*

1 Samuel 13:19-22

*E. J. Pilcher, "Hebrew Weights in the Book of Samuel," *PEFQS* 48 (1916) 77-85. *[13:19-22]*

1 Samuel 13:19-21

G. Ernest Wright, "I Samuel 13:19-21," *BA* 6 (1943) 33-36.

1 Samuel 13:21

S[teven] T. Byington, "1 Sam. 13:21," *JBL* 39 (1920) 77-80.

(   ) Raffaeli, "I Sam. 13:21," *JBL* 40 (1921) 184.

Herbert L. Bishop, "The interpretation of 1 Sam. xiii, 21," *PEFQS* 56 (1924) 47-48.

*E[phraim] A. Speiser, "Of Shoes and Shekels (I Samuel 12:3; 13:21)," *BASOR* #77 (1940) 15-20.

*Julius A. Bewer, "Notes on 1 Sam 13 21; 2 Sam 23 1; Psalm 48 8," *JBL* 61 (1942) 45-49. [1 Sam 13:21, pp. 45-46]

Robert Gordis, "A Note of 1 Sam. 13:21," *JBL* 61 (1942) 209-211.

G. R. Driver, "In aller Kürze. (2) On the Heb. פְּצִירָה (I Samuel XIII 21)," *AfO* 15 (1945-51) 68.

1 Samuel Chapter 14

J. A. Stokes Little, "Was Saul a Hachish-Eater?" *ET* 15 (1903-04) 239. *[Chap. 14]*

*George Henslow, "Did Jonathan taste Hachish?" *ET* 15 (1903-04) 336. *[Chap. 14]*

*Benj. W. Bacon, "Was Saul a Hachish-Eater?" *ET* 15 (1903-04) 380. *[Chap. 14]*

1 Samuel 14:1-46

Joseph Blenkinsopp, "Jonathan's Sacrilege. 1 Sm 14, 1-46: A Study in Literary History," *CBQ* 26 (1964) 423-429.

1 Samuel 14:3

*Matitiahu Tsevat, "Studies in the Book of Samuel," *HUCA* 32 (1961) 191-216. [Excursus I; I Samuel 14:3a, pp. 209-214]

1 Samuel 14:11

*W. F. B[irch], "Varieties. 2. *The Garrison*," *PEFQS* 15 (1883) 150. [1 Sam. 14:11 - pillar]

1 Samuel 14:14

*W. F. Birch, "Varieties. *The Garrison*," *PEFQS* 14 (1882) 266. [I Sam. 14:14]

1 Samuel 14:15

Harold M. Wiener, "The Text of I Samuel XIV 15a," *JPOS* 8 (1928) 125.

1 Samuel 14:23-35

*J. M. Grintz, "'Ye Shall not Eat *on* the Blood'," *Zion* 31 (1966) #1/2, I-II. *[14:23-35]*

1 Samuel 14:41

A. Toeg, "A Textual Note on 1 Samuel XIV 41," *VT* 19 (1969) 493-498.

1 Samuel Chapter 15

Walter G. White, "I Samuel XV," *ET* 30 (1918-19) 88.

W. McKane, "A Note on Esther IX and 1 Samuel XV," *JTS, N.S.,* 12 (1961) 260-261.

1 Samuel 15:7

*T. K. Cheyne, "Textual Criticism in the Service of Archaeology," *ET* 10 (1898-99) 238-240. [2. I. Sam. 15:7; 27:8 (RV), p. 239]

1 Samuel 15:22-23

*Sh. Yeivin, "Philological Notes 10," *Lĕš* 32 (1967-68) #1/2, I-II. [2. I Sam. 15:22-23]

1 Samuel 15:22

H. H. Rowley, "A note on the Septuagint Text of 1 Sam. XV 22A," *VT* 1 (1951) 67-68.

1 Samuel 15:32

S. Talmon, "1 Sam. XV 32b—a case of conflated readings?" *VT* 11 (1961) 456-457.

1 Samuel Chapter 16

*W. A. Lambert, "Alleged Discrepancies in I. Samuel XVI. and XVII.," *CFL*, *N.S.*, 8 (1903) 47-50.

Graham Gilmer, "Did the Lord Instruct Samuel to Lie?" *BS* 96 (1939) 341-343. *[Chap. 16]*

1 Samuel 16:12

*Max Krenkel, "Some Emendations to the Text of Samuel," *ONTS* 2 (1882-83) 170-171. *[16:12]*

1 Samuel 16:20

Henry S. Morais, "The Emendation of 1 Sam. XVI. 20," *AJSL* 2 (1885-86) 249.

1 Samuel Chapter 17

*W. A. Lambert, "Alleged Discrepancies in I. Samuel XVI. and XVII.," *CFL*, *N.S.*, 8 (1903) 47-50.

*W. E. Staples, "Cultic Motifs in Hebrew Thought," *AJSL* 55 (1938) 44-55. [1 Sam. 17, pp. 50-51]

P. A. H. de Boer, "1 Samuel XVII. Notes on the Text and the Ancient Versions," *OTS* 1 (1942) 79-104.

1 Samuel 17:1-3

*Claude R. Conder, "David and Goliath," *PEFQS* 7 (1875) 191-195. *[17:1-3]*

1 Samuel 17:7

*Claude R. Conder, "Notes on New Discoveries," *PEFQS* 41 (1909) 266-275. [Iron (Deut. 8:9; Num. 31:22; 1 Sam. 17:7), p. 271]

1 Samuel 17:52

*Claude R. Conder, "David and Goliath," *PEFQS* 7 (1875) 191-195. *[17:52]*

1 Samuel 17:55

J. W. McGarvey, "'Abner, Whose Son is This Youth?'—Alleged Contradiction in the History of David's Youth," *CFL, 3rd Ser.,* 12 (1910) 6-8. *[17:55]*

1 Samuel 17:58

Albert A. Isaacs, "The difficulties of Scripture. *1 Samuel xvii. 58.*," *EN* 1 (1889) 176-178.

1 Samuel Chapters 18-31

P. A. H. de Boer, "Research into the Text of 1 Samuel xviii-xxxi," *OTS* 6 (1949) 1-100.

1 Samuel 19:13

H. L. Simpson, "Putting a God to Bed," *Exp, 8th Ser.,* 26 (1923) 174-184. *[19:13]*

1 Samuel 19:18-24

*Hugh Duncan, "The Sons of the Prophets," *GUOST* 2 (1901-07) 24-27. *[19:18-24]*

1 Samuel 19:20-24

*Victor Eppstein, "Was Saul also among the prophets?" *ZAW* 81 (1969) 287-304. *[19:20b-24]*

1 Samuel 19:22-23

*Henry Preserved Smith, "Old Testament Notes," *JBL* 24 (1905) 27-30. [III. Naioth. 1 Sam. 19:22, 23, p. 29]

1 Samuel 20:3

*John Wesley Rice, "On the Septuagint Text of I Samuel 20.3 and Epistle of Jeremiah 26," *AJP* 21 (1900) 445-447.

1 Samuel 20:19

*A. Guillaume, "מֵאוֹד in I Samuel XX, 19," *PEQ* 86 (1954) 83-86.

1 Samuel 20:23

*Emunah Finkelstein, "An Ignored Haplography in Samuel," *JSS* 4 (1959) 356-357. *[20:23]*

1 Samuel 20:30

Joshua Finkel, "An Overlooked Motif in the Aḥiqar Romance," *JBL* 55 (1936) xix. *[20:30]*

Joshua Finkel, "Filial Loyalty as a Testimony of Legitimacy," *JBL* 55 (1936) 133-143. *[20:30]*

*T. Grahame Bailey, "Contributions and Comments. Note on Two Passages in Dr. Moffat's 'Old Testament'," *ET* 36 (1924-25) 380-381. [*Ref.* *JRAS* (1925) 334-338] *[20:30]*

1 Samuel 20:42

*Emunah Finkelstein, "An Ignored Haplography in Samuel," *JSS* 4 (1959) 356-357. *[20:42]*

1 Samuel 21:1-14

Henri Cazelles, "David's Monarchy and the Gibeonite Claim (II Sam. xxi, 1-14)," *PEQ* 87 (1955) 165-175.

1 Samuel 21:8

S. T. Byington, "1 Sam. 21:8," *JBL* 39 (1920) 82.

1 Samuel 21:13 (14)

Henry S. Gehman, "A Note on 1 Samuel 21:13 (14)," *JBL* 67 (1948) 241-243.

1 Samuel 21:14

H[enry] S. Gehman, "Note on I Samuel 21:14," *JBL* 67 (1948) vi.

1 Samuel 22:4

David Stiven, "The Hold (1 Samuel XXII. 4, etc.)," *GUOST* 5 (1923-28) 30-32.

1 Samuel 25:1

*Anonymous, "Biblical Illustrations. From Jowett's Christian Researches," *SP* 3 (1830) 106-108. [House of the Dead, p. 106.] *[25:1]*

1 Samuel 25:6

G. R. Driver, "A Lost Colloquialism in the Old Testament (I Samuel XXV. 6)," *JTS, N.S.,* 8 (1957) 272-273.

1 Samuel 25:18

*A. Malamat, "Scales of Rationing in Pap. Anastasi I and the Bible," *BIES* 19 (1955) #3/4, ii. *[25:18]*

1 Samuel 25:29

Tayler Lewis, "A Glimpse of Old Testament Eschatology. 1 Samuel XXV, 29," *MR* 65 (1883) 231-244.

M. A. Canney, "The Bundle of Life," *OOR* 1 (1926) #1, 22-23. *[25:29]*

*M. A. Murray, "The Bundle of Life," *AEE* 15 (1930) 65-73. *[25:29]*

1 Samuel 26:4

R. Thornhill, "A Note on אל־נכון. 1 Sam. XXVI 4," *VT* 14 (1964) 462-466.

1 Samuel 26:8

*Max Krenkel, "Some Emendations to the Text of Samuel," *ONTS* 2 (1882-83) 170-171. *[26:8]*

1 Samuel 26:20

*W. E. Barnes, "Two Interesting Passages. The Septuagint and the Massoretic Text," *ET* 6 (1894-95) 223-225. [(A) I Sam. 26:20, pp. 223-224]

1 Samuel 26:23

*Max Krenkel, "Some Emendations to the Text of Samuel," *ONTS* 2 (1882-83) 170-171. *[26:23]*

1 Samuel 27:6

*Max Krenkel, "Some Emendations to the Text of Samuel," *ONTS* 2 (1882-83) 170-171. *[27:6]*

1 Samuel 27:8

*T. K. Cheyne, "Textual Criticism in the Service of Archaeology," *ET* 10 (1898-99) 238-240. [2. I. Sam. 15:7; 27:8 (RV), p. 239]

1 Samuel 28:3-20

Milton S. Terry, "Saul's Interview with the Witch of Endor. I Samuel XXVIII, 3-20," *MR* 51 (1869) 528-544.

1 Samuel 28:3-7

D. H. Gordon, "The Mistress of the Bottle: A Query," *Man* 31 (1931) #244. *[28:3, 7]*

H. J. Rose, "Ba'alathobh," *Man* 32 (1932) #69 *[28:3, 7]*

1 Samuel 28:3

*Claude R. Conder, "Notes on New Discoveries," *PEFQS* 41 (1909) 266-275. [The Familiar Spirit (Lev. 20:6; 1 Sam. 28:3; Isa. 29:4), p. 270]

1 Samuel 28:7-25

Anonymous, "Critical Remarks on the Story of the Witch of Endor. I Sam. chap. xxviii. 7-25," *CongML* 1 (1818) 641-648.

1 Samuel 28:8ff.

*J. A Montgomery, "Soul Gods," *HTR* 34 (1941) 321-322. *[28:8ff.]*

1 Samuel 29:1

M. Naor and Z. Kallai, "Varia," *BIES* 25 (1961) #4, II. *[29:1]*

§599 *3.5.3.1.5.2 Exegetical Studies on the Second Book of Samuel*

A. F. Kirkpatrick, "The Revised Version of the Old Testament:—The Second Book of Samuel," *Exp, 3rd Ser.,* 3 (1886) 354-370. [1:18, 14, 21, 8; 3:8; 4:2, 6marg.; 5:6, 8, 21; 6:5, 17, 19; 7:19, 23, 27; 8:1, 3, 4, 13, 18; 10:6; 12:30, 31marg.; 13:18; 14:14; 15:7, 12, 17, 28, 12, 14; 17:3, 17, 25; 18:13, 21, 29; 19:25, 43; 20:24; 21:4, 8, 10, 16, 19; 22:6, 9, 12, 33, 34, 46, 51; 23:3, 4, 5, 8, 9, 20; 24:23]

2 Samuel Chapter 1

M. D. Goldman, "Lexicographical Notes on Exegesis (4): An Instance of Metonymy in II Samuel I," *ABR* 3 (1953) 48.

2 Samuel 1:17-19

A. Guillaume, "David's Lament over Saul and Jonathan," *JTS* 16 (1914-15) 491-494. *[1:17-19]*

2 Samuel 1:18

V. E. Reichert, "A Note on 'Qesheth' (II Sam. 1:18)," *JBL* 70 (1951) xiv.

2 Samuel 1:19-27

[Edward Robinson], "The LameNt of David over Saul and Jonathan, II Sam. I. 19-27. Translation and Commentary," *BRCR* 4 (1834) 594-605.

C. T. B., "David's Lamentation Over Saul and Jonathan," *CE* 37 (1844) 233-234. *[1:19-27 - paraphrase]*

W. P., "The Lament of David over Saul and Jonathan. 2 Samuel i. 19-27," *CE* 38 (1845) 351-352. *[paraphrase]*

James Kennedy, "David's Lament over Saul and Jonathan: II Sam. 1:19-27," *AJSL* 32 (1915-16) 118-125.

2 Samuel 1:19-21

W. E[mery] Barnes, "Two Passages in David's Lament," *JTS* 16 (1915-16) 394-396. *[1:19, 21]*

2 Samuel 1:21

H. L. Ginsberg, *"WŠDY TRWMWT* (BH³ *TRWMT*), II Sam. 1 21," *JBL* 57 (1938) xi.

H. L. Ginsberg, "A Ugaritic Parallel to 2 Sam. 1:21," *JBL* 57 (1938) 209-214.

*Robert Gordis, "The Biblical Root *ŠDY-ŠD:* Notes on 2 Sam. i. 21; Jer. xviii. 14; Ps. xci. 6; Job v. 21," *JTS* 41 (1940) 34-43.

*E[phraim] A. Speiser, "An Analogue to 2 Sam. 1:21, *'AQHT* 1 44-45," *JBL* 69 (1950) 377-378.

*T. L. Fenton, "Ugaritica—Biblica," *UF* 1 (1969) 65-70. *[1:21]*

2 Samuel 2:12-16

L. W. Batten, "Helkath Hazzurim, 2 Samuel 2, 12-16," *ZAW* 26(1906) 90-94.

2 Samuel 2:14

(Yadin) Yigael Sukenik, "'Let the young men, I pray thee, arise and play before us' (2 Sam. II, 14ff.)," *JPOS* 21 (1948) 110-116.

2 Samuel 2:22

*Dunlop Moore, "Have We in I Sam. II. 22 a Valid Witness to the Existence of the Mosaic Tabernacle in the Days of Eli?" *ET* 8 (1896-97) 139-141.

2 Samuel 3:8-11

G. Margoliouth, "Abner's Answer to Ishbosheth (2 Sam iii. 8-11)," *Exp, 8th Ser.,* 10 (1915) 155-162.

2 Samuel 3:26

Anonymous, "The Spring of Sirah (2 Sam. iii. 26)," *PEFQS* 10 (1878) 121.

2 Samuel Chapter 4

*(Lady) Ramsey, "'Her that kept the Door'," *ET* 27 (1915-16) 314-316. *[Chap. 4]*

2 Samuel Chapter 5

Anonymous, "Interesting Finds in Tumuli Near Jerusalem," *BASOR* #10 (1923) 2-3. *[Chap. 5]*

2 Samuel 5:6-25

*J. F. Springer and A. Yohannan, "A New Branch of Textual Criticism," *AQ* 2 (1923) 11-24. [II. Sam. 5:6-25, pp. 13-16]

2 Samuel 5:6-9

W. Emery Barnes, "David's 'Capture' of the Jebusite' 'Citadel' of Zion (2 Sam. v. 6-9)," *Exp, 8th Ser.,* 7 (1914) 29-39.

William F[oxwell] Albright, "The Ṣinnôr in the Story of David's Capture of Jerusalem," *JPOS* 2 (1922) 286-290 *[5:6-9]*

2 Samuel 5:6-8

W. F. Birch, "Zion, the City of David," *PEFQS* 17 (1885) 61-65. *[5:6-8]*

E. L. Sukenik, "The Account of David's Capture of Jerusalem," *JPOS* 8 (1928) 12-16. *[5:6-8]*

J. J. Glück, "The conquest of Jerusalem in the account of II Sam. 5:6-8a," *OTW* 9 (1966) 98-105.

2 Samuel 5:8

W.F. Birch, "Defence of the Gutter (Tzinnor)," *PEFQS* 22 (1890) 200-204. *[5:8]*

Paul E. Kretzmann, "What Was the 'Tsinnor' of 2 Sam 5, 8?" *CTM* 3 (1932) 621.

Eric F. F. Bishop, "The Lame and the Blind," *ET* 60 (1948-49) 355. *[5:8]*

2 Samuel 5:23-24

*David Yellin, "Emek ha-bakha: Bekhaim," *JPOS* 3 (1923) 191-192. *[5:23-24]*

2 Samuel Chapter 6

*N. H. Tur-Sinai, "The Ark of God at Beit Shemesh (1 Sam. VI) and Peres 'Uzza (2 Sam VI; 1 Chron. XIII)," *VT* 1 (1951) 275-286.

*J. R. Porter, "The Interpretation of 2 Samuel VI and Psalm CXXXII," *JTS, N.S.,* 5 (1954) 161-173.

*Paul H. Levenson, "Daniel and Michal: A Tragic Marriage," *CCARJ* 16 (1969) #4, 79-82. *[Chap. 6]*

2 Samuel 6:3-11

David Connor, "Did Uzzah Die by Lightning? (2 Sam. VI. 3-11)," *ET* 27 (1915-16) 285-286.

2 Samuel 6:6

A. W. Marget, "נכון גורן in 2 Sam. 6:6," *JBL* 39 (1920) 70-76.

2 Samuel 6:11

Alex. Maclaren, "The Ark in the House of Obed-Edom," *HR* 18 (1889) 325-330. *[6:11]*

2 Samuel 6:12

A. Phillips, "David's Linen Ephod," *VT* 19 (1969) 485-487. *[6:12ff.]*

2 Samuel 6:20

Harry M. Orlinsky, "*HĀ-RŌQDĪM* for *HĀ-RĒQĪM* in 2 Sam. 6:20," *JBL* 45 (1946) 25-35.

2 Samuel Chapter 7

John L. McKenzie, "The Dynastic Oracle: II Samuel 7," *ThSt* 8 (1947) 187-218.

C. J. Labuschagne, "Some remarks on the prayer of David in II Sam. 7," *OTW* 3 (1960) 28-35.

E. S. Mulder, "The Prophecy of Nathan in II Sam. 7," *OTW* 3 (1960) 36-42.

*Dennis J. McCarthy, "II Samuel 7 and the Structure of Deuteronomic History," *JBL* 84 (1965) 131-138.

*Dale Goldsmith, "Acts 13:33-37: A *Pesher* on II Samuel 7," *JBL* 87 (1968) 321-234.

2 Samuel 7:2

Howard Crosby, "A Thought on 2 Samuel VII: 2," *HR* 18 (1889) 166-167.

Howard Crosby, "The Ark at Kirjath-jearim," *HR* 18 (1889) 260-262. *[7:2]*

Oswald Loretz, "The *Perfectum Copulativum* in 2 Sm 7, 9-11," *CBQ* 23 (1961) 294-296. *(Trans. by Roland E. Murphy)*

2 Samuel 7:11-16

Matitiahu Tsevat, "Studies in the Book of Samuel," *HUCA* 34 (1963) 71-82. [III The Steadfast House: What was David Promised in II Sam. 7:11b-16?]

2 Samuel 7:13-16

M[atitiahu] Tsevat, "The House of David in Nathan's Prophecy," *B* 46 (1965) 353-356. *[7:13-16]*

2 Samuel 7:19

*Willis J. Beecher, "Three Notes," *JBL* 8 (1888) 137-142. [I. 2 Sam. 7:19, pp. 137-139]

2 Samuel 7:21

*J. W. Jack, "Recent Biblical Archaeology," *ET* 53 (1941-42) 367-370. [Archæology and the Biblical Text: 3. Thy Servant a Dog (2 Sam 7:21), p. 369]

2 Samuel 7:22

*John Wesley Rice, "Notes. Notes on the Septuagint Text of II Sam. 7:22 and Isa. 42:21," *AJP* 22 (1901) 318-320.

2 Samuel 8:1

S. Tolkowsky, "Metheg ah-ammah," *JPOS* 1 (1920-21) 195-201. *[8:1]*

2 Samuel 8:2

H. Highfield, "The Interpretation of 2 Sam VIII. 2," *ET* 23 (1911-12) 40.

S. Tolkowsky, "The Measuring of the Moabites with the Line (2 Samuel 8:2)," *JPOS* 4 (1924) 118-121.

2 Samuel 8:4

L. W. Batten, "David's Destruction of the Syrian Chariots," *ZAW* 28 (1908) 188-192. *[8:4]*

2 Samuel 8:11

*M. L. Whately, "Chariots, Runners, & Torches," *ERG, 3rd Ser.*, 2 (1863-64) 289. *[8:11]*

2 Samuel Chapter 10

*John D. Davis, "Medeba or the Waters of Rabbah," *PTR* 20 (1922) 305-310. *[Chap. 10]*

Charles B. Chavel, "David's War Against the Ammonites," *JQR, N.S.*, 30 (1939-40) 257-261. *[Chap. 10]*

2 Samuel 10:12

Raphael Giveon, "'The Cities of Our God' (II Sam 10:12)," *JBL* 83 (1964) 415-416.

2 Samuel 11:1-5

H. Hirsch Cohen, "David and Bathsheba," *JAAR* 33 (1965) 142-148. *[11:1-5]*

2 Samuel 11:2-1 Kings 2:11

J. W. Wevers, "Exegetical Principles Underlying the Greek Text of II Samuel 11:2-I Kings 2:11," *JBL* 72 (1953) xv.

2 Samuel 11:2

J. Blenkinsopp, "Theme and motif in the succession history (2 Sam. xi. 2ff) and the Yarwist corpus," *VTS* 15 (1965) 44-57.

2 Samuel 12:

*S. L. Bowman, "Does the Bible Sanction Polygamy? 2 Sam. xii., 1-10," *CFL, 3rd Ser.,* 1 (1904) 221-223.

2 Samuel 12:1-6

*S. P. T. Prideaux, "The Wisaga," *ET* 55 (1943-44) 278 *[12:1-6]*

2 Samuel 12:5-6

A. Phillips, "The Interpretation of 2 Samuel XII 5-6," *VT* 16 (1966) 242-244.

2 Samuel 12:14

Reuven Yaron, "The Coptos Decree and 2 Sam. XII 14," *VT* 9 (1959) 89-91.

2 Samuel 12:26-27

T. K. Cheyne, "2 Samuel XII. 26, 27," *ET* 9 (1897-98) 143-144.

Lucien Gautier, "2 Samuel XII. 26, 27," *ET* 9 (1897-98) 290.

2 Samuel 12:27

T. K. Cheyne, "Prince Adrammelech: King Jareb: and the City of Waters," *ET* 9 (1897-98) 428-429. *[12:27]*

George A. Barton, "On the Reading עיר המים 2 Sam. 12:27," *JBL* 27 (1908) 147-152.

2 Samuel 12:31

G. C. O'Ceallaigh, "'And so David Did to *all the Cities* of Ammon'," *VT* 12 (1962) 179-189. *[12:31]*

2 Samuel 13:5-8

H. Highfield, "What Kind of Food was it that Tamar Made for Amnon? (2 Sam. XIII 5-8)," *ET* 23 (1911-12) 39.

2 Samuel 13:23

H. Seebass, "Ephraim in 2 Sam. XIII 23," *VT* 14 (1964) 497-500.

2 Samuel 14:25

Samuel Cox, "Absalom. 2 Samuel xiv. 25," *Exp, 2nd Ser.,* 8 (1884) 176-187.

2 Samuel 14:26

Anonymous, "Morsels of Criticism," *CongML* 4 (1821) 80. *[14:26]*

2 Samuel 14:27

T. W. Rosmarin, "Note on 2 Sam 14:27," *JBL* 52 (1933) 261-262.

2 Samuel Chapters 15-18

J. Weingreen, "The Rebellion of Absalom," *VT* 19 (1969) 263-266. *[Chaps. 15-18]*

2 Samuel 15:1-30

F. Hecht, "II Samuel 15:1-30: The historical and theological view of the revolt of Absalom," *Min* 4 (1963-64) 168-171.

2 Samuel 15:22-23

*Sh. Yeivin, "Philological Notes 10," *Lěš* 32 (1967-68) #1/2, I-II. [2. Sam. 15:22-23]

2 Samuel 17:11

*E[phraim] A. Speiser, "The Biblical Idiom *Pānīm Hōlᵉkīm*," *JQR, 75th* (1967) 515-517. [פָּנֶיךָ הֹלְכִים] *[Chap. 17:11.]*

2 Samuel 18:5

P. Haupt, "Deal Gently with the Young Man," *JBL* 45 (1926) 357. *[18:5]*

2 Samuel 18:19-32

J. R. Schumaker, "Joab and Ahimaaz—2 Samuel xviii. 19-32," *CFL, 3rd Ser.,* 9 (1908) 401-402.

2 Samuel 18:23

J. E. M'Ouat, "2 Sam XVIII. 23: דֶּרֶךְ הַכִּכָּר," *ET* 15 (1903-04) 426.

2 Samuel 20:3

J. M. Allegro, "The Meaning of Ḥayyûṭ in 2 Samuel 20, 3," *JTS, N.S.,* 3 (1952) 40-41.

2 Samuel 20:14-22

J. Sherman Potter, "The Unknown Heroine of 'Maacah's Meadows'. A *Study of 2 Samuel 20:14-22," HR* 107 (1934) 56-59.

2 Samuel 20:19

E. J. Pilcher, "A Mother in Israel," *PEFQS* 54 (1922) 38-41. *[20:19]*

2 Samuel 20:24

W. D. Morris, "Taskwork. אשר על המס (2 S. 20²⁴)—Minister of Public Works *(corvee)," ET* 17 (1905-06) 524.

2 Samuel 21:1-14

W. G. Jordan, "Homiletics and Criticism: II Samuel 21:1-14," *BW* 33 (1909) 32-37.

J. E. McFadyen, "History and Homiletics: A Study in 2 Samuel XXI. 1-14," *Exp, 8th Ser.,* 20 (1920) 241-261.

*J. F. Springer and A. Yohannan, "A New Branch of Textual Criticism," *AQ* 2 (1923) 11-24. [II. Sam. 21:1-14, pp. 13-16]

Arvid S. Kapelrud, "King and Fertility: A Discussion of II Sam 21:1-14," *NTTO* 56 (1955) 113-122.

2 Samuel 21:8

J. J. Gluck, "Merab or Michal," *ZAW* 77 (1965) 72-81. *[21:8]*

2 Samuel 21:10

H. L. Simpson, "Rizpah's Watch," *Exp, 8th Ser.,* 26 (1923) 100-108. *[21:10]*

2 Samuel 21:15-22

*F. Willesen, "The Philistine Corps of the Scimitar from Gath," *JSS* 3 (1958) 327-335. *[21:15-22]*

2 Samuel 21:15-16

Harold M. Wiener, "The Text of II Samuel XXI 15-16," *JPOS* 8 (1928) 63-64.

2 Samuel Chapter 22

*William Henry Bennett, "Notes on a Comparison of the Texts of Psalm XVIII. and 2 Samuel XXII," *AJSL* 3 (1886-87) 65-86.

*F[rank] M[oore] Cross Jr., "Notes on II Samuel 22 = Psalm 18," *JBL* 68 (1949) xi.

Frank Moore Cross Jr. and David Noel Freedman, "A Royal Song of Thanksgiving—II Samuel 22 = Psalm 18," *JBL* 72 (1953) 15-34.

2 Samuel 22:5-6

*John A. Maynard, "Sheol and Belial," *ATR* 1 (1918-19) 92-93. *[22:5-6]*

2 Samuel 22:12-13

Samuel I. Feigin, "The Heavenly Sieve," *JNES* 9 (1950) 40-43. *[22:12-13]*

2 Samuel 22:35

*Claude R. Conder, "Notes on New Discoveries," *PEFQS* 41 (1909) 266-275. [Bow of Steel (2 Sam. 22:35), p. 274]

2 Samuel 22:36

*P[aul] Peters, "Luther's Rendition of II Samuel 22:36 and Psalm 18:36: und wenn du mich demuetigest, machst du mich gross," *WLQ* 52 (1955) 137-143.

2 Samuel 23:1-7

Anonymous, "The Last Words of David. 2 Samuel xxiii. 1-7," *CongL* 1 (1872) 88-98.

2 Samuel 23:1

*Julius A. Bewer, "Notes on 1 Sam 13 21; 2 Sam 23 1; Psalm 48: 8," *JBL* 61 (1942) 45-49. [2 Samuel 23:1, pp. 47-48]

2 Samuel 23:3-5

G. W. D., "The Last Words of David," *ERG, 5th Ser.*, 1 (1870-71) 189-195. *[23:3-5]*

G. W. D., "The Last Words of David. 2 Sam. XXIII. 3-5," *ERG, 5th Ser.*, 1 (1870-71) 247-256.

2 Samuel 23:6-7

J. Morgenstern, "II Samuel 23:6-7," *JBL* 38 (1919) 43-45.

2 Samuel 23:7

G. H. Handler, "2 Sam. XXIII. 7," *ET* 8 (1896-97) 565-566.

J. A. Selbie, "2 Sam. XXIII 7," *ET* 9 (1897-98) 47.

2 Samuel 23:8

Paul Peters, "Luther's Text-Critical Study of 2 Samuel 23:8," *CTM* 18 (1947) 641-652.

2 Samuel 23:20

W. D. Morris, "Arels of Moab," *ET* 17 (1905-06) 141-142. *[23:20]*

2 Samuel Chapter 24

Oscar T. Morgan, "The Numbering of Israel," *HR* 52 (1906) 132. *[Chap. 24]*

A. H. Sayce, "The Hittite Name Araunah," *JTS* 22 (1920-21) 267-268. *[Chap 24]*

*Luke Walker, "The Threshing Floor of Araunah," *NB* 9 (1928) 87-95. *[Chap. 24]*

2 Samuel 24:1

Albert A. Isaacs, "The difficulties of Scripture. '2 *Samuel xxiv. 1.'," EN* 3 (1891) 212-213.

2 Samuel 24:6

Selah Merrill, "Tahtim Hodshi and Dan Jaan," *PR* 4 (1883) 414-417. *[24:6]*

Patrick W. Skehan, "Joab's Census: How Far North (2 Sm 24,6)?" *CBQ* 31 (1969) 42-49.

§600　*3.5.3.1.6 Studies on the Manuscripts of the Books of Samuel*

*H. St. J. Thackeray, "The Greek Translators of the Four Books of the Kings," *JTS* 8 (1906-07) 262-278.

H. W. Sheppard, "Variants in the Consonantal Text of G. I in the Books of Samuel and Kings," *JTS* 22 (1920-21) 36-60.

H. S. Gehman, "The Greek Translator at Work on the Text of I Samuel," *JBL* 66 (1947) xi.

D. M. C. Englert, "The Peshitto of II Samuel," *JBL* 67 (1948) xi.

J. B[arton] Payne, "Revision in the Coptic (Sahidic) text of I Samuel," *JBL* 68 (1949) xi.

*J. W. Wevers, "Exegetical Principles Underlying the Greek Text of II Samuel 11:2 - I Kings 2:11," *JBL* 72 (1953) xv.

*J. Barton Payne, "The Sahidic Coptic Text of 1 Samuel," *JBL* 72 (1953) 51-61.

*Lawrence Feinberg, "A Papyrus Text of I Kingdoms (I Samuel)," *HTR* 62 (1969) 349-374. [23:28-24:2; 24:6-8; 24:12-13; 24:18-20]

W. Baars, "A Forgotten Fragment of the Greek Text of the Books of Samuel," *OTS* 14 (1965) 201-205.

§601 *3.5.3.1.7 Exegetical Studies on the Books of Kings*

*H. St. J. Thackeray, "The Greek Translators of the Four Books of the Kings," *JTS* 8 (1906-07) 262-278.

*Henry S. Gehman, "The Armenian Version of I. and II. Kings and its Affinities," *JAOS* 54 (1934) 52-59.

John Wm. Wevers, "A Study in the Hebrew Variants in the Books of Kings," *ZAW* 61 (1945-48) 43-76.

John W. Wevers, "Double Readings in the Books of Kings," *JBL* 65 (1946) 307-310.

*John W. Wevers, "Principles of Interpretation Guiding the Fourth Translator of the Book of the Kingdoms. (3 K. 22,1 - 4 K. 25,30)," *CBQ* 14 (1952) 40-52.

J[ohn] W. Wevers, "Exegetical Tendencies on the Part of the Fourth Translator of the Books of the Kingdoms (3K. 22:1-4:K. 25:30)," *JBL* 71 (1952) vi.

§602 *3.5.3.1.7.1 Exegetical Studies on the First Book of Kings*

A. F. Kirkpatrick, "The Revised Version of the Old Testament:—The First Book of Kings," *Exp, 3rd Ser.,* 4 (1886) 60-67. [1:18, 20, 39; 2:19; 4:5, 12, 16; 4:19, 24; 5:18; 6:ff., 6:4, 8; 7:2, 18, 24; 8:8, 31, 65; 9:8, 13, 18; 10:5, 15, 28; 12:31, 33; 13:12; 19:3marg, 18; 20:38, 41; 21:23; 22:38]

*J. A. Montgomery, "Notes on I Kings," *JBL* 55 (1936) xi. [4:3; 4:19; 9:18; 9:13; 9:26; 10:15; 10:19]

J. W. Wevers, "The Hebrew Variants of I Kings," *JBL* 64 (1945) viii.

1 Kings Chapters 1-2

*Stanley A. Cook, "Notes on Old Testament History, I, The Life of David," *JQR* 17 (1904-05) 782-799. *[Chaps. 1 and 2]*

Leroy Waterman, "Some Historical and Literary Consequences of Probable Displacement in I Kings 1-2," *JAOS* 60 (1940) 383-390.

*Walter Brueggemann, "David and His Theologian," *CBQ* 30 (1968) 156-181. *[Chaps. 1 and 2]*

1 Kings Chapter 1

*Moncure D. Conway, "The Judgment of Solomon," *OC* 12 (1898) 72-79. *[Chap. 1]*

1 Kings 1:33

*Claude R. Conder, "Notes on New Discoveries," *PEFQS* 41 (1909) 266-275. [Mules (1 Kgs. 1:33), p. 274]

1 Kings 1:41

Edmund F. Sutcliffe, "Simultaneity in Hebrew: A Note on I Kings i. 41," *JSS* 3 (1958) 80-81.

1 Kings 2:12-21:43

J. W. Wevers, "Exegetical Principles underlying the Septuagint Text of 1 Kings ii 12-xxi 43," *OTS* 8 (1950) 300-322.

*D. W. Gooding, "Pedantic Timetabling in 3rd Book of Reigns," *VT* 15 (1965) 153-166. *[2:12-21:43, especially 6:1-7:51]*

1 Kings Chapter 2

J. A. Montgomery, "The Supplement at End of 3 Kingdoms 2 [I Reg 2]," *ZAW* 50 (1932) 124-129.

1 Kings 2:8-9

*D. W. Gooding, "The Shimei Duplicate and its Satellite Miscellanies in 3 Reigns II," *JSS* 13 (1968) 76-92. *[2:8-9 MT; 2:8-9 LXX and 2:36-46 MT; 2:36-46 LXX]*

1 Kings 2:33-45

Reuven Yaron, "A Ramessid Parallel to 1 K II 33, 44-45," *VT* 8 (1958) 432-433.

1 Kings 2:36-46

*D. W. Gooding, "The Shimei Duplicate and its Satellite Miscellanies in 3 Reigns II," *JSS* 13 (1968) 76-92. *[2:8-9 MT; 2:8-9 LXX and 2:36-46 MT; 2:36-46 LXX]*

*James A. Montgomery, "Hebraica," *JAOS* 58 (1938) 130-139. [(9) Light from the Arabic, (c) I Kings 2:46a(LXX), p. 137]

1 Kings Chapters 3-11

Bazalel Porten, "The Structure and Theme of the Solomon Narrative (I Kings 3-11)," *HUCA* 39 (1968) 93-128.

1 Kings 3:1

T. K. Cheyne, "The N. Arabian Land of Muṣri in Early Hebrew Tradition," *JQR* 11 (1898-99) 551-560 [III. Solomon's "Egyptian" Marriage (I Kgs. 3:1), pp. 559-560]

1 Kings 4:2-6

*A. van Selms, "The Origin of the Title 'The King's Friend'," *JNES* 16 (1957) 118-122. *[4:2-6]*

1 Kings 4:7-19

*G. Ernest Wright, "The Provinces of Solomon (I Kings 4:7-19)," *EI* 8 (1967) 58*-68*.

1 Kings 4:7

*I. Shifman, "Royal Service Obligations in Palestine in the First Half of the First Millennium B.C., according to Biblical Tradition," *VDI* (1967) #1, 48. *[4:7]*

1 Kings 4:31

H. A. A. Kennedy, "I Kings IV. 31," *ET* 23 (1911-12) 95-96.

1 Kings 5:7-8

*I. Shifman, "Royal Service Obligations in Palestine in the First Half of the First Millennium B.C., according to Biblical Tradition," *VDI* (1967) #1, 48. *[5:7-8]*

1 Kings 5:18

†C. Lucas, "The Rev. C. Lucas on New Translations of the Bible," *MMBR* 43 (1817) 13-14. *[5:18]*

1 Kings 5:27-30

*James A. Montgomery, "Hebraica," *JAOS* 58 (1938) 130-139. [(6) A case of arithmetical proportion (I Kings 5:27, 30 // II Chron. 2:2, 17), p. 135]

1 Kings 6:1-7:51

*D. W. Gooding, "Pedantic Timetabling in 3rd Book of Reigns," *VT* 15 (1965) 153-166. *[6:1-7:51]*

1 Kings 6:7

*Cyrus Alder, "The Cotton Grotto, an Ancient Quarry in Jerusalem," *JQR* 8 (1895-96) 384-391. *[6:7]*

1 Kings 6:36

*H. C. Thomson, "A Row of Cedar Beams," *PEQ* 92 (1960) 57-63. *[6:36]*

1 Kings Chapter 7

*J. L. Myres, "King Solomon's Temple and Other Buildings and Works of Art," *PEQ* 80 (1948) 14-41. *[1 Kings Chapter 7]*

1 Kings 7:12

*H. C. Thomson, "A Row of Cedar Beams," *PEQ* 92 (1960) 57-63. *[7:12]*

1 Kings 7:20

William A. Irwin, "I Kings 7:20," *JNES* 4 (1945) 53-54.

1 Kings 7:46

George F. Moore, "1 Kings 7:46," *JBL* 13 (1894) 77-79.

1 Kings 8:12-13

Oliver Shaw Rankin and W. W. D. Gardiner, "An Utterance of Solomon," *Exp, 9th Ser.,* 4 (1925) 430-436. *[8:12-13]*

1 Kings 8:21

Anonymous, "Comparative Translation: 1 Kings 8:21. A study in Modernizing the English Bible," *BW* 21 (1903) 139.

1 Kings 8:53

F. C. Burkitt, "The Lucianic Text of I Kings VIII 53b," *JTS* 10 (1908-09) 439-446.

*H. St. J. Thackeray, "New Light on the Books of Jashar (A Study of 3 Regn. VIII 53^b LXX)," *JTS* 11 (1909-10) 518-532.

1 Kings 9:10-10:33

D. W. Gooding, "Text-Sequence and Translation-Revision in 3 Reigns IX 10 - X 33," *VT* 19 (1969) 448-463.

1 Kings 9:10-18

*T. K. Cheyne, "The Land of Cabul," *SBAP* 21 (1899) 177-179. *[9:10-18]*

1 Kings 9:10-14

*F. Charles Fensham, "The Treaty between Solomon and Hiram and the Alalakh Tablets," *JBL* 79 (1960) 59-60. *[9:10-14]*

1 Kings 9:13

*James A. Montgomery, "Hebraica," *JAOS* 58 (1938) 130-139. [(3) The land of Cabul (I Kings 9:13), p. 133]

Allan Johnson, "1 Kings IX. 13," *ET* 66 (1954-55) 32.

1 Kings 9:15-25

*D. W. Gooding, "Pedantic Timetabling in 3rd Book of Reigns," *VT* 15 (1965) 153-166. *[9:15-25]*

1 Kings 9:16

J. Goldwasser, "Siamon's Campaign in Palestine," *BIES* 14 (1947-48) #3/4, I. *[9:16]*

1 Kings 9:26-10:29

*Harold M. Parker Jr., "Solomon and the Queen of Sheba," *IR* 24 (1967) #3, 17-24. *[9:26-10:29]*

1 Kings 10:1-13

*Stewart Perowne, "Note on I Kings, Chapter X, 1-13 (II Chronicles, Chapter IX, 1-12)," *PEQ* 71 (1939) 199-202.

1 Kings 10:11

*T. K. Cheyne, "Textual Criticism in the Service of Archaeology," *ET* 10 (1898-99) 238-240. [3. I Kgs. 10:11 (RV), pp. 239-240]

1 Kings 10:15

H. A. Williamson, "Text of I Kings X. 15," *ET* 42 (1930-31) 479.

1 Kings 10:22

T. K. Cheyne, "1 Kings X. 22," *Exp, 4th Ser.,* 3 (1891) 469-470.

*Sidney Smith, "The Threshing Floor at the City Gate," *PEQ* 78 (1946) 5-14. *[22:10]*

1 Kings 10:25

*Stanley A. Cook, "Notes on I Kings X. 25; Neh. III. 19," *ET* 10 (1898-99) 279-281.

*James A. Montgomery, "Hebraica," *JAOS* 58 (1938) 130-139. [(9) Light from the Arabic, (b) I Kings 10:25 (= II Ch. 9:24) p.137]

1 Kings 10:28

*J. W. Jack, "Recent Biblical Archaeology," *ET* 53 (1941-42) 367-370. [Archæology and the Biblical Text: 4. The Land of Ḳuë (1 Kings 10:28), p. 369]

1 Kings Chapter 11

*Moncure D. Conway, "Solomonic Literature," *OC* 12 (1898) 321-335. [Solomon and Satans. (1 Kings 11) 321-325]

1 Kings 11:14

*T. K. Cheyne, "The N. Arabian Land of Muṣri in Early Hebrew Tradition," *JQR* 11 (1898-99) 551-560. [I. The History of Hadad the Edomite (I Kgs. 11:14ff), pp. 551-556]

1 Kings 11:26-40

*T. K. Cheyne, "The N. Arabian Land of Muṣri in Early Hebrew Tradition," *JQR* 11 (1898-99) 551-560. [II. The History of Jeroboam (I. Kings 11:26-40), pp. 556-559]

1 Kings Chapter 12

*Abraham Malamat, "Organs of Statecraft in the Israelite Monarchy," *BA* 28 (1965) 34-65. *[Chap. 12]*

1 Kings 12:28-29

*S. B. Gurewicz, "When Did the Cult Associated with the 'Golden Calves' Fully Develop in the Northern Kingdom?" *ABR* 3 (1953) 41-44. *[12:28-29]*

1 Kings 12:29-30

F. W. Farrar, "Was There a Golden Calf at Dan? A Note on 1 Kings XII. 29, 30 and Other Passages," *Exp, 4th Ser.,* 8 (1893) 254-265.

1 Kings 12:31-33

Julian Morgenstern, "The Festival of Jeroboam I," *JBL* 83 (1964) 109-118. *[12:31-33]*

1 Kings Chapter 13

Anonymous, "Remarks on Scripture Characters, and on the Case of the Old Prophet, Mentioned in 1 Kings: Ch. XIII," *MR* 7 (1824) 338-339.

W. R. Worthington, "The Old Prophet Who Dwelt in Samaria: I Kings XIII," *HR* 39 (1900) 449-450.

1 Kings 13:1-11

Harry Smith, "The Disobedient Prophet," *ET* 24 (1912-13) 135-136. *[13:1, 11]*

226 **Exegetical Studies on the First Book of Kings** §602 cont.

1 Kings 13:29-30

*F. W. Farrar, "Was There a Golden Calf at Dan? A Note on 1 Kings XIII, 29, 30 and Other Passages," *Exp, 4th Ser.,* 8 (1893) 254-265.

1 Kings 14:1-20

*Joseph Reider, "Prolegomena to a Greek-Hebrew and Hebrew-Greek Index to Aquila," *JQR, N.S.,* 7 (1916-17) 287-366. [Chapter IV, The Hebrew Text Underlying Aquila's Version, (and Appendices), Appendix IV - 3 Kings 14:1-20, pp. 362-364]

1 Kings 14:10

*A. Ăhuvya, "עצור ועזוב בישראל," *Lĕš* 30 (1965-66) #3, n.p.n.*[Curse formula in 1 Kings 14:10; 21:21; 2 Kings 9:8]*

1 Kings 14:24

*Edward Carpenter, "On the Connection Between Homo-sexuality and Divination and the Importance of the Intermediate Sexes in Early Civilizations," *AJRPE* 4 (1910-11) 219-243. *[14:24]*

1 Kings 15:12

*Edward Carpenter, "On the Connection Between Homo-sexuality and Divination and the Importance of the Intermediate Sexes in Early Civilizations," *AJRPE* 4 (1910-11) 219-243. *[15:12]*

1 Kings 16:9

*Joseph Offord, "Arza and Aziza, and other Archæological Notes," *SBAP* 23 (1901) 244-247. [1 Kings 16:9, pp. 244-245]

1 Kings 16:22

J. Max Miller, "So Tibni Died (1 Kings XVI 22)," *VT* 18 (1968) 392-394.

1 Kings 16:24

Paul E. Kretzmann, "Interesting Archaeological News," *CTM* 3 (1932) 537. *[16:24]*

1 Kings 16:34

Anonymous, "Traditionary Interpretation. The punishment of Hiel, the re-builder of Jericho," *JSL, 3rd Ser.,* 3 (1856) 364-371. *[16:34]*

Theodore F. Wright, "How Was the Curse of Jericho Fulfilled? (I Kings 16:34.)," *BW* 23 (1904) 263-266.

*N. Wieder, "Notes on the New Documents from the Fourth Cave of Qumran," *JJS* 7 (1956) 71-76. [The Messianic Testimonia and the Re-building of Jericho, (1 Kg. 16:34), pp. 75-76]

*Ian M. Blake, "Jericho (Ain Es-Sultan): Joshua's Curse and Elisha's Miracle—One Possible Explanation," *PEQ* 99 (1967) 86-97. *[16:34]*

1 Kings Chapter 17

James Strachan, "Requests and Replies," *ET* 11 (1899-1900) 61. *[Chap. 17]*

1 Kings 17:4-6

Archd. R. S. Kennedy, "Requests and Replies," *ET* 5 (1893-94) 60. *[17:4, 6]*

Alex. Gregory, "Ravens and Arabians," *ET* 5 (1893-94) 130. *[17:4, 6]*

1 Kings 17:6

Morris Sigel Seale, "The Black Arabs of the Jordan Valley," *ET* 68 (1956-57) 28. *[17:6]*

J. W. Wenham, "The Black Arabs of the Jordan Valley," *ET* 68 (1956-57) 121. *[17:6]*

1 Kings 17:17-24

John E. M'Fadyen, "Did Elijah Cut Himself for the Dead?" *ET* 14 (1902-03) 143-144. *[17:17-24]*

1 Kings 17:21

*Eb. Nestle, "The Reading of the Septuagint in 1 Kings XVII. 21 and 2 Kings IV. 34," *ET* 14 (1902-03) 185-186.

1 Kings Chapter 18

Sydney   Archbell,   "I   Kings   XVIII,"   *ET*   40   (1928-29)   563.

*Raphael Patai, "The 'Control of Rain' in Ancient Palestine. A Study in Comparative Religion," *HUCA* 14 (1939) 251-286. [1 Kings 18, pp. 254-258]

*Mary Neely, "*The Canaanites:* The God that Answered by Fire," *AT* 4 (1959-60) #2, 6-8. *[Chap. 18]*

*Julian Morgenstern, "The King-God Among the Western Semites and the Meaning of Epiphanes," *VT* 10 (1960) 138-197. [1 Kings 18, pp. 171-174]

1 Kings 18:1-8

*E. W. Todd, "The Reforms of Hezekiah and Josiah," *SJT* 9 (1956) 288-293. *[18:1-8]*

1 Kings 18:5

Harry M. Orlinsky, "On the Commonly Proposed *lēk wᵉnaʿᵃḇôr* of I Kings 18 5," *JBL* 59 (1940) 515-517.

1 Kings 18:21

Morris Jastrow Jr., "הסעפים 1 Kings 18:21," *JBL* 17 (1898) 108-110.

*Joseph Offord, "Dancing Worship," *SBAP* 21 (1899) 253. *[18:21]*

1 Kings 18:27

*I. Aharoni, "Note on 1 Kings 18:27 and 2 Kings 18:27," *JPOS* 6 (1926) 109.

Leo Hayman, "A Note on I Kings 18:27," *JNES* 10 (1951) 57-58.

1 Kings 18:30-39

*C. M. Mead, "El Mohrakah, or the Place of Elijah's Sacrifice," *BS* 30 (1873) 672-696.

1 Kings 18:31-38

A. Lucas, "The Miracle on Mount Carmel," *PEQ* 77 (1945) 49-50. *[18:31-38]*

1 Kings 18:36-39

O. H. E. Burmester, "The Bohairic Pericope of III Kingdoms XVIII 36-39," *JTS* 36 (1935) 156-160.

1 Kings 18:40ff.

C. M. Botley, "Folk-Memory in Palestine," *Folk* 71 (1960) 255-256. *[18:40ff.]*

1 Kings 18:42

*James A. Montgomery, "Hebraica," *JAOS* 58 (1938) 130-139. [(9) Light from the Arabic, (a) I Kings 18:42, p. 136]

1 Kings 18:43

*Charles Druitt, "The *'Via Maris'*," *PEFQS* 20 (1888) 166-167. *[18:43]*

G. Schumacher, "The *'Via Maris'*. A Reply," *PEFQS* 21 (1889) 78-79. *[18:43]*

G. Schumacher, "The *'Via Maris'*," *PEFQS* 21 (1889) 152-153. *[18:43]*

1 Kings Chapter 19

G. Margoliouth, "Elijah on Mount Horeb," *Exp, 8th Ser.,* 15 (1918) 139-157. *[Chap. 19]*

E. L. Allen, "The Theophany at Horeb. (1 Kings 19)," *ET* 33 (1921-22) 230-231.

Malcom McQueen, "The Theophany at Horeb (1 Kings 19)," *ET* 34 (1922-23) 331-332.

1 Kings 19:3

Clifton P. Brown, "What Frightened Elijah?" *ET* 44 (1932-33) 236-237. *[19:3]*

1 Kings 19:9ff.

W. P. Paterson, "Elijah on Horeb," *ET* 4 (1892-93) 321-322. *[19:9ff.]*

1 Kings 19:10-14

Richard M. Frank, "A Note on 3 Kings 19, 10.14," *CBQ* 25 (1963) 410-414.

1 Kings 19:19-21

*Hugh J. Blair, "Putting One's Hand to the Plough. Luke ix. 62 in the light of 1 Kings xix. 19-21," *ET* 79 (1967-68) 342-343.

1 Kings Chapter 20

*Y. Yadin, "Some Aspects of the Strategy of Ahab and David (1 K 20; 2 Sam 11)," *B* 36 (1955) 332-351.

*J. Maxwell Miller, "The Rest of the Acts of Jehoahaz (1 Kings 20; 22:1-38)," *ZAW* 80 (1968) 337-342.

1 Kings 20:1-10

Theophile J. Meek, "I Kings 20:1-10," *JBL* 78 (1959) 73-75.

1 Kings 20:1

*Anonymous, "Benhadad," *ET* 29 (1917-18) 156-160. *[20:1]*

1 Kings 20:12

*James A. Montgomery, "Notes on the Old Testament," *JBL* 31 (1912) 140-146. [2. שׂים עַל, 1 Kings 20:12, p. 141]

1 Kings 20:28f.

*William R. Arnold, "Solomon's Horse-trade," *JAOS* 26 (1905) 104. *[20:28f.]*

1 Kings 20:31

H. T. C. Weatherhead, "Rope on the Head," *ET* 25 (1913-14) 232. *[20:31]*

J. Steele, "Rope on the Head," *ET* 25 (1913-14) 332. *[20:31]*

1 Kings 20:35-43

*Hugh Duncan, "The Sons of the Prophets," *GUOST* 2 (1901-07) 24-27. *[20:35-43]*

1 Kings Chapter 21

*B. D. Napier, "The Omrides of Jezreel," *VT* 9 (1959) 366-378. *[Chap. 21]*

*Anonymous, "Jezebel and the Goddess of Love. Canaanite myths referring to the goddess Anat provide an interesting background to the story of Naboth's vineyard, 1 Kings 21," *BH* 2 (1965) #3, 4-9.

Francis I. Andersen, "The Socio-Juridical Background of the Naboth Incident," *JBL* 85 (1966) 46-57 *[Chap. 21]*

1 Kings 21:19

*B. D. Napier, "The Omrides of Jezreel," *VT* 9 (1959) 366-378. *[21:19]*

1 Kings Chapter 22

Dean A. Walker, "True and False Prophets in I Kings, Chap. 22," *BW* 20 (1902) 272-277.

P. S. P. Handcock, "Identification of an Unnamed Old Testament King," *ET* 22 (1910-11) 370-372. *[Chap. 22]*

1 Kings 22:1-38

*J. Maxwell Miller, "The Rest of the Acts of Jehoahaz (1 Kings 20; 22:1-38)," *ZAW* 80 (1968) 337-342.

1 Kings 22:1-2

*Julian Morgenstern, "Chronological Data on the Dynasty of Omri," *JBL* 59 (1940) 385-396. *[22:1, 2]*

1 Kings 22:19-23

Anonymous, "Expository Items. 1 Kings XXII. 19-23," *MQR, 2nd Ser.,* 2 (1880) 565.

1 Kings 22:21

*A. H. Wratislaw, "Gen. I. 2 compared with I Kings XXII. 21," *ET* 2 (1890-91) 115-117.

1 Kings 22:46

*Edward Carpenter, "On the Connection Between Homo-sexuality and Divination and the Importance of the Intermediate Sexes in Early Civilizations," *AJRPE* 4 (1910-11) 219-243. *[22:46]*

§603 *3.5.3.1.7.2 Exegetical Studies on the Second Book of Kings*

A. F. Kirkpatrick, "The Revised Version of the Old Testament:—The Second Book of Kings," *Exp, 3rd Ser.,* 4 (1886) 107-112. [4:10; 5:26; 8:10, 13; 9:1; 10:12; 11:2, 4, 8, 12, 14, 16; 12:4; 16:6; 18:4; 19:7, 23, 24, 31marg.; 20:4, 9; 22:14]

2 Kings 2:1-18

*Hugh Duncan, "The Sons of the Prophets," *GUOST* 2 (1901-07) 24-27. *[2:1-18]*

Hermann Gunkel, "Elisha—The Successor of Elijah (2 Kings II. 1-18)," *ET* 41 (1929-30) 182-186.

2 Kings 2:3

Anonymous, "The Sons of the Prophets. 2 Kings II. 3," *MQR, 2nd Ser.,* 3 (1881) 561-564.

Henry Lansdell, "The Departure of Elijah," *CM* 18 (1884) 129-137. *(Sermon) [2:3]*

2 Kings 2:8

H. Hamann, "The Book of the Law found by Hilkiah," *AusTR* 9 (1938) 60-61. *[2:8]*

2 Kings 2:19-22

*Ian M. Blake, "Jericho (Ain Es-Sultan): Joshua's Curse and Elisha's Miracle—One Possible Explanation," *PEQ* 99 (1967) 86-97. *[2:19-22]*

2 Kings 2:19

Herbert Booth Smith, "Elisha and the City Fathers," *HR* 78 (1919) 152-157.
  (Sermon) [2:19]

2 Kings 2:23-25

Richard G. Messner, "Elisha and the Bears, A Critical Monograph on 2
  Kings 2:23-25 Abridged by the Author," *GJ* 3 (1962) #2, 12-24.

2 Kings 2:23-24

Anonymous, "'Go up, thou Bald-head'," *CongML* 14 (1831) 549-551.
  [2:23, 24]

S. Cox, "The Doom of the Children of Bethel. 2 Kings ii. 23, 24," *Exp, 1st
  Ser.,* 3 (1876) 414-427.

W[illiam] H. B[ates], "Elisha—The Little Children (Young Men) and the
  Bears," *CFL, 3rd Ser.,* 29 (1923) 124-126. *[2:23, 24]*

2 Kings 2:23

†R. C. Fuller, "The Boys and the Bears (IV Kings ii, 23)," *Scrip* 4 (1949-51)
  26-27.

2 Kings 4:1-7

*Hugh Duncan, "The Sons of the Prophets," *GUOST* 2 (1901-07) 24-27.
  [4:1-7]

2 Kings 4:6

*(Lady) Ramsey, "'Her that kept the Door'," *ET* 27 (1915-16) 314-316.
  [4:6LXX]

2 Kings 4:7-28

*Leo Adler, "The Natural Boundaries of the Administrative Division of Isra-
  el under Solomon," *BIES* 16 (1951) #1/2, II. *[4:7-28]*

2 Kings 4:26

Henry Holloway, "2 Kings IV. 26. A Side-Light from East Africa," *ET* 34
  (1922-23) 526.

2 Kings 4:34-35

*James A. Montgomery, "Hebraica," *JAOS* 58 (1938) 130-139. [(9) Light from the Arabic, (a) II Kings 4:34, 35, p. 137]

2 Kings 4:34

*Eb. Nestle, "The Reading of the Septuagint in 1 Kings XVII. 21 and 2 Kings IV. 34," *ET* 14 (1902-03) 185-186.

2 Kings 4:38-41

*Hugh Duncan, "The Sons of the Prophets," *GUOST* 2 (1901-07) 24-27. [4:38-41]

2 Kings Chapter 5

C[laude] R. Conder, "Notes on Biblical Antiquities. 1. *Naaman and Elisha* (2 Kings V)," *PEFQS* 37 (1905) 155.

2 Kings 5:12

*Ernest W. Gurney Masterman, "The Rivers of Damascus," *ET* 13 (1901-02) 215-220. [5:12]

2 Kings 5:13

C. Taylor, "On some passages of the Pentateuch, Judges, and 2nd Kings," *JP* 5 (1873) 54-65. [5:13]

2 Kings 5:15-18

A. T. Rich, "A Suggested Exegesis of 2 Kings V. 15-18," *ET* 59 (1947-48) 278.

2 Kings 5:17-19

George M. Rae, "A Note on Naaman. 2 Kings V. 17-19," *ET* 12 (1900-01) 142-143.

2 Kings 5:22

*Hugh Duncan, "The Sons of the Prophets," *GUOST* 2 (1901-07) 24-27. [5:22]

2 Kings 6:1-7

*Hugh Duncan, "The Sons of the Prophets," *GUOST* 2 (1901-07) 24-27. *[6:1-7]*

2 Kings 6:1-4

G. Henton Davies, "The Balance of Freedom. A Sermon on II Kings 6:1-4," *Interp* 6 (1952) 415-419.

2 Kings 6:8-17

Alexander B. Grosart, "Lost or Latent Powers of the Five Senses, with Relation to 2 Kings VI. 8-17 and St. Luke XXIV. 13-35," *Exp, 4th Ser.,* 4 (1891) 108-119.

2 Kings 6:15-19

*Patrick D. Miller Jr., "The Divine Council and the Prophetic Call to War," *VT* 18 (1968) 100-107. [2 Kgs. 6:15-19, pp. 106-107]

2 Kings 6:16-22

D. W. Gooding, "An Impossible Shrine," *VT* 15 (1965) 405-420. *[6:16-22(MT); 6:17-21(LXX)]*

2 Kings 6:23

J. Kaplan, "'And He Prepared Great Provision for Them'," *BIES* 17 (1952-53) #1/2, III. *[6:23]*

2 Kings 6:25

Anonymous, "2 Kings vi 25," *CongML* 4 (1821) 135.

2 Kings 7:6

*Patrick D. Miller Jr., "The Divine Council and the Prophetic Call to War," *VT* 18 (1968) 100-107. [2 Kgs. 7:6, p. 107]

2 Kings 8:7-15

*Stephen H. Langdon, "Pir-idri (Ben-Hadad) King of Syria," *ET* 23 (1911-12) 68-69. *[8:7-15]*

2 Kings 8:10-11

H. A. Williamson, "Interpretation of 2 Kings VIII. 10, 11," *ET* 38 (1926-27) 379.

2 Kings 8:10

C. J. Labuschagne, "Did Elisha Deliberately Lie?—A Note on II Kings 8:10," *ZAW* 77 (1965) 327-328.

2 Kings 9:25

Paul Haupt, "The Phrase רככים צמדים in 2 Kings IX 25," *JBL* 21 (1902) 74-77.

2 Kings 10:21

R. M. Spence, "On the Meaning of the Phrase פֶּה לָפֶה in 2 Kings X. 21," *ET* 9 (1897-98) 237-238.

2 Kings 11:12

Samuel A. B. Mercer, "The Testimony of II Kings 11:12," *ATR* 6 (1923-24) 44-45.

2 Kings 11:20

*H. G. Tomkins, "The Name Genubath," *SBAP* 10 (1887-88) 372. (Remarks by P. le Page Renouf, pp. 373-376) *[11:20]*

2 Kings 12:10

William McKane, "A Note on 2 Kings 12:10 (Evv 12:9)," *ZAW* 71 (1959) 260-265.

2 Kings 12:15

*Z. W. Falk, "Craftsmen and Faith," *Tarbiz* 28 (1958-59) #3/4, I. *[12:15]*

2 Kings Chapter 13

Howell M. Haydn, "A Suggestion as to the First Form of II Kings 13," *AJSL* 26 (1909-10) 73-80.

2 Kings 13:6-10

*Leo M. Kaiser, "A New Greek Word and 2 Kings 13:6, 9, 10," *CBQ* 10 (1948) 406-407.

2 Kings 13:14-19

G. Margoliouth, "A Test of Strength and its Sequels," *Exp, 8th Ser.,* 10 (1915) 546-557. *[13:14-19]*

2 Kings 14:8-9

Walter R. Roehrs, "Sermon Study on 2 Kings 14:8-9. The Thistle of Pride," *CTM* 20 (1949) 652-659. *(Sermon)*

2 Kings 14:23-29

*Menahem Haran, "The Rise and Decline of the Empire of Jeroboam ben Joash," *VT* 17 (1967) 266-297.

2 Kings 14:28

C[yrus] H. Gordon, "'Her Restored Damascus and Hamath from "Judah" into Israel' (II Kings 14:28)," *JBL* 70 (1951) xiv.

2 Kings 15:5

*J. W. Jack, "Recent Biblical Archaeology," *ET* 53 (1941-42) 367-370. [Archæology and the Biblical Text: 5. Azariah's Leprosy (2 Kgs 15:5), p. 369]

*S. B. Gurewicz, "Some Examples of Modern Hebrew Exegeses of the OT," *ABR* 11 (1963) 15-23. [3. "BETH HAḤOPHSHITH", II Kings, xv: 5, p. 22]

2 Kings 15:13-23

W. J. Chapman, "The Problem of Inconsequent Post-Dating in II Kings XV. 13, 17 and 23," *HUCA* 2 (1925) 57-61.

2 Kings 15:29

*J. F. McCurdy, "Light on Scriptural Texts from Recent Discoveries. Assyrian Politics and Israel's First Captivity.—2 Kings xv. 29," *HR* 32 (1896) 119-121.

2 Kings 15:30

W. E[mery] Barnes, "Not a Gloss (2 Kings XV 30b)," *JTS* 8 (1906-07) 294-296.

2 Kings Chapter 16

*B. Oded, "The Historical Background of the War between Rezin and Pekah against Ahaz," *Tarbiz* 38 (1968-69) #3, I-II. *[Chap. 16]*

*Peter R. Ackroyd, "Historians and Prophets," *SEÅ* 33 (1968) 18-37 (54). [2 Kgs. 16, pp. 23-26]

2 Kings 16:2

*J. A. Selbie, "Requests and Replies," *ET* 10 (1898-99) 60. *[Ahaz's age at Hezekiah's birth - 16:2]*

2 Kings 16:5

*K. Budde, "Isaiah vii. 1 and 2 Kings xvi. 5," *ET* 11 (1899-1900) 327-330.

2 Kings 16:20

*J. A. Selbie, "Requests and Replies," *ET* 10 (1898-99) 60. *[Ahaz's age at Hezekiah's birth - 16:20]*

2 Kings Chapter 17

*James A. Montgomery, "Brief Communications," *JBL* 33 (1914) 78-80. [1. Tartak, 2 Kings 17, p. 78]

John MacDonald, "The Structure of II Kings xvii," *GUOST* 23 (1969-70) 29-41.

2 Kings 17:1

Edmund A. Parker, "A Note on the Chronology of 2 Kings 17:1," *AUSS* 6 (1968) 129-133.

2 Kings 17:24

*T. K. Cheyne, "Gleanings in the Books of Kings," *ET* 10 (1898-99) 429. *[17:24]*

2 Kings 17:27

M. Paul Shalom, "Sargon's Administrative Diction in II Kings 17:27," *JBL* 88 (1969) 73-74.

2 Kings 17:29

*T. K. Cheyne, "Gleanings in the Books of Kings," *ET* 10 (1898-99) 429. *[17:29]*

2 Kings 17:30

*Fritz Hommel, "The God Ashima of Hamath," *ET* 23 (1911-12) 93. *[17:30]*

*James A Montgomery, "Notes on the Old Testament," *JBL* 31 (1912) 140-146. [3. Sukkoth-Benoth, 2 Kings 17:30, p. 141]

2 Kings Chapters 18 and 19

G. G. Garner, "*Assyria and the Bible:* Part 3. Sennacherib and Hezekiah. Assyrian Records Confirm a Biblical Narrative," *AT* 5 (1960-61) #4, 3-7. *[Chaps. 18 and 19]*

2 Kings Chapter 18

*William Hayes Ward, "Light on Scriptural Texts from Recent Discoveries. The Siege of Lachish," *HR* 30 (1895) 27-29. *[Chap. 18]*

2 Kings 18:1-2

*J. A. Selbie, "Requests and Replies," *ET* 10 (1898-99) 60. *[Ahaz's age at Hezekiah's birth - 18:1, 2]*

2 Kings 18:13-19:36

*Siegfried H. Horn, "Did Sennacherib Campaign Once or Twice Against Hezekiah?" *AUSS* 4 (1966) 1-28. *[18:13-19:36]*

2 Kings 18:13-17

*R.D.Barnett,"The Siege of Lachish," *IEJ* 8 (1958) 161-164.*[18:13, 14, 17]*

2 Kings 18:13-14

Anonymous, "Side-Lights. Hezekiah and Sennacherib," *DTQ* 1 (1875) 144. *[18:13-14]*

2 Kings 18:13

J. F. McCurdy, "Light on Scriptural Texts from Recent Discoveries. Old Testament Emphasis on Secular History," *HR* 32 (1896) 411-413. *[18:13]*

2 Kings 18:17

*Millar Burrows, "The Conduit of the Upper Pool," *ZAW* 70 (1958) 221-227. *[18:17]*

2 Kings 18:26

*C. F. Burney, "Old Testament Notes. I. 'The Jews' Language': 2 Kings XVIII 26 = Isa. XXXVI 11," *JTS* 13 (1911-12) 417-20.

2 Kings 18:27

*I. Aharoni, "Note on 1 Kings 18:27 and 2 Kings 18:27," *JPOS* 6 (1926) 109.

2 Kings 18:34

*Fritz Hommel, "Hena' and 'Awwâ," *ET* 9 (1897-98) 330-331. *[18:34]*

*T. K. Cheyne, "Gleanings in the Books of Kings," *ET* 10 (1898-99) 429. *[18:34]*

2 Kings 19:9

Anonymous ,"'The King of Ethiopia'—2 Kings xix 9," *HR* 40 (1900) 542-543.

2 Kings 19:13

*Fritz Hommel, "Hena' and 'Awwâ," *ET* 9 (1897-98) 330-331. *[19:13]*

2 Kings 19:17

*S. Talmon, "A Case of Faulty Harmonization," *VT* 5 (1955) 206-208. *[Isa. 37:18 X 2 Kings 19:17]*

2 Kings 19:20-28

*Theophile J. Meek, "The Metrical Structure of II Kings 19:20-28," *CQ* 18 (1941) 126-131.

2 Kings 19:21-28

*K. Budde, "The Poem in 2 Kings XIX 21-28 (Isaiah XXXVII 22-29)," *JTS* 35 (1934) 307-313.

2 Kings 19:21

*H. F. B. Compston, "The Parsing of *Bāzāh* in 2 Kings XIX 21 = Isaiah XXXVII 22," *JTS* 1909-10) 545-546.

2 Kings 19:25

*H. S. Gehman, "Note on II Kings 19:25 and Isaiah 37:27," *JBL* 64 (1945) iv-v.

2 Kings 19:26-27

F. C. Burkitt, "The so-called *Quinta* of 4 Kings," *SBAP* 24 (1902) 216-219. *[19:26-27]*

[F. C. Burkitt], "On 2 Kings XIX 26, 27," *JTS* 34 (1933) 369-372.

2 Kings 19:26

E. Nestle, "The Septuagint Rendering of 2 Kings XIX 26," *SBAP* 25 (1903) 63.

2 Kings 19:27

W. St. C[had] Boscawen, "The Murderer of Sennacherib," *BOR* 8 (1895-1900) 259-261. *[19:27]*

2 Kings 19:35

*W. Arthur Cornaby, "2 Kings xix. 35 (Is. xxxvii. 36) and Herodotus, ii. 141," *ET* 25 (1913-14) 379-380.

2 Kings 19:36-37

*C.H.W.Johns,"Sennacherib's Murder,"*ET* 7(1895-96) 238-239.*[19:36, 37]*

2 Kings 19:35-37

*C. H. W. Johns, "The Biblical Account of Sennacherib's Murder," *SBAP* 21 (1899) 174-175. *[19:35-37]*

2 Kings 19:37

J. P. Lettinga, "A note on 2 Kings xix 37," *VT* 7 (1957) 105-106.

2 Kings Chapter 20

*†G. B., "P.S.," *JSL, 3rd Ser.,* 4 (1856-57) 161-164. *[The Dial of Ahaz - 2 Kgs. 20]*

2 Kings 20:1-11

*Michael J. Gruenthaner, "Two Sun Miracles of the Old Testament," *CBQ* 10 (1948) 271-290. [II. The Regression of the Shadow, *Textual Criticism, a) Kings, b) Isaias, Nature of the Miracle, Explanation of the Miracle,* pp. 287-290] *[20:1-11]*

2 Kings 20:7-11

*K. Fullerton, "The Original Text of 2 Kings 20:7-11 = Isaiah 38:7, 8, 21f.," *JBL* 44 (1925) 44-62.

2 Kings 20:8-11

*Y. Yadin, "'The Dial of Ahaz'," *EI* 5 (1958) 88*-89*. *[20:8-11]*

2 Kings Chapters 22 and 23

*Alexander Freed, "The Code Spoken of in II Kings 22-23," *JBL* 40 (1921) 76-80.

2 Kings Chapter 22

*E. W. Todd, "The Reforms of Hezekiah and Josiah," *SJT* 9 (1956) 288-293. *[Chap. 22]*

2 Kings 22:5-7

*Z. W. Falk, "Craftsmen and Faith," *Tarbiz* 28 (1958-59) #3/4, I. *[22:5-7]*

2 Kings 23:4

*Edward Carpenter, "On the Connection Between Homo-sexuality and Divination and the Importance of the Intermediate Sexes Generally in Early Civilizations," *AJRPE* 4 (1910-11) 219-243. *[23:4]*

2 Kings 23:8

*B. Maisler, "Topographical Studies: 1. 'From Geba to Beersheba'," *BIES* 8 (1940-41) #1, II. *[23:8]*

2 Kings 23:10-13

John Skinner, "Requests and Replies," *ET* 1 (1889-90) 232. *[Passing through the fire of Moloch - 23:10, 13]*

2 Kings 23:10

Alexander Lang, "'Passing Through the Fire'," *ContR* 70 (1896) 232-246. *[23:10]*

2 Kings 23:29

*C. E. Goddard, "A Tradition Current in the Third Century B.C.," *JBL* 46 (1927) 106-110.

Anonymous, "A Pharaoh Slays the King of Judah. The Biblical narrative makes occasional references to later, that is 1st millennium B.C., Egyptian history. Investigation of these contacts often assists in the interpretation of the texts concerned," *BH* 2 (1965) #2, 16-21. *[23:29]*

Anonymous, "A Comment on the Pharaoh Necho who is referred to at 2 Kings 23:29," *BH* 5 (1969) 24-25. [Erratum, p. 43]

2 Kings 24:18ff.

*Peter R. Ackroyd, "Historians and Prophets," *SEÅ* 33 (1968) 18-54. [2 Kgs. 24:18ff., pp. 41-42]

2 Kings Chapter 25

*E. J. Smit, "The relation between the texts of II Kings 25 and Jeremiah," *OTW* 11 (1968) 77-81.

2 Kings 25:18

James Oscar Boyd, "'The Second Priest'," *CFL, N.S.,* 6 (1902) 298. *[25:18]*

§604 *3.5.3.1.8 Studies on the Manuscripts of the Books of Kings*

W. Emery Barnes, "The Peshitta Version of 2 Kings," *JTS* 6 (1904-05) 220-232.

W. E[mery] Barnes, "The Peshitta Version of 2 Kings. (A Continuation)," *JTS* 11 (1909-10) 533-542.

H[enry] S. Gehman, "The Old Ethiopic Version of 1 Kings and Its Affinities," *JBL* 50 (1931) 81-114.

*Henry S. Gehman, "The Armenian Version of I. and II. Kings and its Affinities," *JAOS* 54 (1934) 52-59.

J. W. Wevers, "On the Textual History of Codex B in the Book of Kings," *JBL* 70 (1951) xv.

John Wm. Wevers, "A Study in the Textual History of the Codex Vaticanus in the Books of Kings," *ZAW* 64 (1952-53) 178-189.

§605 *3.5.3.2 Exegetical Studies on Passages in Several Books of the Latter Prophets*

*William Selwyn, "Hebrew Notes," *JCSP* 3 (1857) 137-140. [I. Isa. 8:21, 22; II. Isa. 9:2; III. Isa. 36:15; IV. Isa. 63:8, 9; V. Hosea. 6:5; VI. Joel 2:20; VII. Nahum 2:3; VIII. Job 10:15]

*E. B. Pollard, "Other Traditional Misinterpretations," *CQ* 4 (1927) 204-206. [Hos. 8:7; 4:17; 4:9; 24:2, 1-3; 3:3; Hab. 2:2; Isa. 35:8]

*G. R. Driver, "Hebrew Notes on Prophets and Proverbs," *JTS* 41 (1940) 162-175. [Isa. 8:20; 9:8; 10:33; 15:3; 17:5; 22:3; 27:11; 31:4; 33:6; 34:15; 38:13; 43:14; 44:8; 45:1; 49:15; 49:18; 50:4; 51:8; 53:12; 60:16; 61:7; 65:4; Jer. 2:19; 2:31; 8:5; 9:6; 9:7; 18:20; 23:39; 27:8; 27:10; 48:45; 50:24; Ezek. 1:24; 6:6; 21:25; 24:17, 22; 27:6; 27:32; 28:14; 32:20; 34:12; 47:7; 48:35; Hos. 7:12; 7:14; Joel 1:7; Amos 4:13; 6:2; 7:4; Jonah 4:2; Mic. 4:10; 6:2; Nahum 2:2; 3:6; Hab. 1:8; Zeph. 2:9; Zech. 1:15; 2:4; 3:9; 13:8]

(§606) *3.5.3.2.1 Exegetical Studies of Passages on Several Books of the Major Prophets*

§607   *3.5.3.2.1.1 Exegetical Studies on the Book of Isaiah - Chapters 1-39*

Talbot W. Chambers, "Misquoted Scriptures. No. IX," *HR* 7 (1882-83) 223-224. [Isa. 1:31; 8:19; 10:18; 44:8; 24:15]

Talbot W. Chambers, "Misquoted Scriptures. No. X," *HR* 7 (1882-83) 293-294. [Isa. 26:19; 27:5; 27:8; 28:10, 11]

K.Kohler, "Emendations of the Hebrew Text of Isaiah," *AJSL* 2 (1885-86) 39-48. [Isa. 1:4, 6, 7, 9, 11, 12-13, 17, 23, 25, 28, 29, 31; 2:2-4, 5, 9, 10, 11, 12, 17, 20, 21-22; 3:1, 3, 4, 6, 8, 10-11, 12, 14-15, 15, 16, 18, 24, 26; 4:2, 5; 5:1, 9, 12, 13, 17, 23, 25, 26, 28, 29, 30; 8:21, 22, 23; 9:1-6, 7, 8, 10, 12, 14, 16, 17; 10:1, 3, 4; 6:1, 2, 5, 11, 13; 7:1, 2, 3, 4, 6, 8-9b, 10, 11, 13-16; 8:1, 4, 6, 7, 8, 10, 11, 12, 13, 14, 15, 16, 18, 19, 21, 22, 24-26, 27, 33, 34]

T. K. Cheyne, "The Revised Version of the Old Testament—The Book of Isaiah I," *Exp, 3rd Ser.,* 6 (1887) 442-461.

T. K. Cheyne, "The Book of Isaiah in the Revised Version II," *Exp, 3rd Ser.,* 7 (1888) 279-292.

*Gray Herbert Skipwith, "Gleanings from Isaiah," *JQR* 7 (1894-95) 470-480.

*R. M. Moffat, "The Servant of the Lord," *ET* 13 (1901-02) 7-10, 67-69, 174-178. [Isa. 42:1-7; 49:1-9a; 50:4-9; 52:13; chap. 53]

F. R. Montgomery Hitchcock, "Notes on Isaiah," *ET* 19 (1907-08) 473-474. [Isa. 28:16; 52:13; 53:5; 53:7; 53:11]

Theophilus J. Gaehr, "Shear-Jashub; or the Remnant Sections in Isaiah," *BS* 79 (1922) 363-371. [Isa. 1:8-9; 4:2-3; 6:13; 7:3; 10:14; 8:1-3, 18; 9:6-7; 10:20-22; 11:11-12, 16; 28:5; 30:15-17; 35:8-10; (51:11); (40:31; 37:31, 32); 46:3; 49:6; 52:8; 56:8; 59:20; 63:16-17; 65:8-9; 66:19, 22]

Edward Robertson, "Some Obscure Passages in Isaiah," *AJSL* 49 (1932-33) 313-324. [1. Isa. 6:13; 2: Isa. 8:19-22; 3. Isa. 10:15; 4. Isa. 10:18; 5. Isa. 10:34]

Israel Eitan, "A Contribution to Isaiah Exegesis (Notes and Short Studies in Biblical Philology)," *HUCA* 12&13 (1937-38) 55-88. [1:27; 3:17; 3:20; 5:14; 7:6; 7:16; 8:10; 10:13; 10:32; 11:1; 11:13; 11:14; 13:3; 13:12; 13:22; 14:10; 14:12; 14:19; 15:4; 15:5; 15:9; 17:6; 17:11; 17:13; 18:4; 19:10; 21:2; 21:5; 21:17; 22:17-18; 22:21; 22:23; 22:24; 23:1; 23:6-7; 23:10; 23:11; 24:11; 25:1; 28:3; 28:7; 28:16; 29:5; 29:8; 30:13; 30:16; 30:18; 30:22; 31:4; 32:6; 32:14; 34:17; 37:25; 41:2-3; 41:9; 41:10, 23; 41:17; 41:20; 41:21; 41:25; 41:29; 44:8; 44:9; 44:11; 44:12; 44:13; 44:14; 44:20; 44:21b; 44:23a; 44:28; 45:1; 45:8; 45:12; 45:16; 46:11; 47:12; 49:15; 49:16; 50:7-9; 53:12; 54:3; 54:5; 57:6; 57:10; 58:13; 59:6; 60:4; 60:12; 60:13; 60:14; 61:3; 61:4; 61:6; 61:7; 63:3; 63:4; 66:14a; 66:14b]

H. L. Ginsberg, "Exegetical Sidelights on Isaiah's Hopes for the Future," *JBL* 66 (1947) iv. [(1) 4:2-6; (2) 9:1-6; (3) 10:33-34; (4) 22:1-14; (5) 31:4]

H. L. Ginsberg, "Some Emendations in Isaiah," *JBL* 49 (1950) 51-60. [3:9b; 5:11-12, 14-17, 23; 10:1-2; 22:17-18a; 28:2a; 30:4; 33:4; 41:24, 25, 28b; 49:7; 56:11; 57:6-11; 61:3; 66:12a]

*Theophile J. Meek, "Some Passages Bearing on the Date of Second Isaiah," *HUCA* 23 (1950-51) Part 1, 173-184. [1. Isa. 41:2a; 2. Isa. 43:14b; 3. Isa. 44:28; 4. Isa. 45:1a; 5. Isa. 48:14; 6. Isa. 48:20]

*Julian Morgenstern, "The Loss of Words at the Ends of Lines in Manuscripts of Hebrew Poetry," *HUCA* 25 (1954) 41-83. [Isa; 40:22, 25, 27: 42:16; 24a, 25a; 43:19-20; 44:6a; 58:10b; 50:2bβ; 60:11b; 61:1c; 63:7c; 49:18b; 60:2a; 46:13b; 45:3a; 46:6b; 45:14c; 44:18; 54:16; 34:1-35:8]

Mitchell Dahood, "Some Ambiguous Texts in Isaias (30, 15; 52, 2; 33, 2; 40, 5; 45, 1)," *CBQ* 20 (1958) 41-49.

Patrick W. Skehan, "Some Textual Problems in Isaia," *CBQ* 22 (1960) 47-55. [5:30; 8:16-20; 8:21-22, (14:24-27); 8:23-9:1; 14:19; 43:17; 45:11; 49:21; 57:13]

Mitchell J. Dahood, "Textual Problems in Isaia," *CBQ* 22 (1960) 400-409. [Is 23,2; Metaphor in Is 49,26a; Is 53,10a(MT); Is 65,3b; Is 65,4a]

*S. Talmon, "DSIa as a Witness to Ancient Exegesis of the Book of Isaiah," *ASTI* 1 (1962) 62-72. [Isa. 19:10; 26:9; 19:9; 39:22; 9:6; 14:11; 26:16]

*M. H. Goshen-Gottstein, "Theory and Practice of Textual Criticism. *The Text-critical Use of the Septuagint,*" *Text* 3 (1963) 130-158. [Isa. 5:18; 4:5; 46:1; 5:29; 43:12; 9:2; 44:25; 45:8-9; 45:23]

*Yehuda Komlos, "Etymological Elucidations in the Aramaic Targum of Isaiah," *Tarbiz* 37 (1967-68) #1, II-III. [Isa. 3:24; 48:19; 20:5; 60:16; 5:13; 30:8; 10:6; 26:2]

Clyde T. Francisco, "Isaiah in the Christian Proclamation," *R&E* 65 (1968) 471-482. [1:1-20; 2:2-4; 3:1-15; 5:1-7; 6:1-13; 10:15-19; 11:6-9; Chaps. 13-23; Chaps. 24-27; Chaps. 28-33; 28:16; 29:2-14; 30:15; 31:1-9; 32:4; 33:20; 37:1, 14; 40:1-2; 40:3-5;40:8; 40:28-31; 41:21-29; 42:1-9; 43:11; 45:22; 46:1-4; 47:1-10; 49:14-16; 49:4-11; 51:9, 17; 52:1; 53:4-6; 53:11; 54:2; 55:1-13; 56:10-11; Chaps. 57-59; 58:4ff.; 60:1-22; 61:1ff.; 63:15-64:12; 65:13-15; 66:1-2; 66:23-24]

Isaiah Chapters 1-39

George A. Smith, "The Messiah in Isaiah i.-xxxix.," *TRFCCQ* 1 (1886-87) 322-338.

Louise Pettibone Smith, "The Use of the Word הורה in Isaiah, Chapters 1-39," *AJSL* 46 (1929-30) 1-21.

G. R. Driver, "Linguistic and Textual Problems: Isaiah I-XXXIX," *JTS* 38 (1937) 36-50. [1:4; 1:17; 1:18; 3:12; 3:17; 5:6; 5:17; 10:25; 10:29; 11:5; 15:7; 16:4; 16:8; 19:11; 21:2; 22:6; 22:13; 14:1; 14:11; 15:11; 26:9; 26:10; 26:16; 27:6; 27:8; 28:15; 30:18; 30:28; 30:32; 31:9; 34:11-12; 38:10; 38:14; 38:16; 38:17; 39:1]

R. B. Y. Scott, "Biblical Research and the Work of the Pastor. *Recent Study in Isaiah 1-39*," *Interp* 11 (1957) 259-268.

Georg Fohrer, "The Origin, Composition and Tradition of Isaiah i-xxxix," *ALUOS* 3 (1961-62) 3-38.

G. R. Driver, "Isaiah I-XXXIX: Textual and Linguistic Problems," *JSS* 13 (1968) 36-57. [1:5; 2:9; 3:22; 5:13; 5:18; 6:13; 7:6; 7:15; 7:16; 7:25; 8:9; 9:6; 10:16-18; 10:22; 10:33; 10:34; 13:7-8; 14:10; 14:11; 14:20; 14:31; 15:1; 15:5; 16:2; 16:3; 17:11; 18:1; 18:2, 7; 19:17; 21:1; 21:2; 22:3; 22:5; 22:9; 22:17; 22:24; 23:9; 23:11; 24:16; 26:9; 27:6; 29:3; 29:4; 30:15; 30:32; 31:9; 32:14; 32:19; 33:9; 33:18; 33:21; 33:23; 34:4; 34:5; 34:8; 35:7; 38:8; 38:10; 38:13; 38:12, 13; 38:15]

Isaiah Chapters 1-35

*William Popper, "Parallelism in Isaiah. Chapters 1-35 and 37.22-35. A Reconstructed Text (Hebrew)," *UCPSP* 1 (1907-23) #5, 1-116.

*Marshall S. Hurwitz, "The Septuagint of Isaiah 36-39 in Relation to That of 1-35, 40-66," *HUCA* 28 (1957) 75-83.

Isaiah Chapters 1-23

W. B. Stevenson, "A Neglected Literary Usage," *GUOST* 6 (1929-33) 14-21. [Interjected speed in Isaiah i-xxiii, pp. 18-21]

Isaiah Chapters 1-12

Eugene C. Caldwell, "Through Judgment to Glory—A Book Study of Isaiah," *USR* 28 (1916-17) 331-343. [Part I. Chapters 1-12]

N. H. Tur-Sinai, "A Contribution to the Understanding of Isaiah I-XII," *SH* 8 (1961) 145-188.

Robert J. Marshall, "The Structure of Isaiah 1-12," *BRes* 7 (1962) 19-32.

*Robert J. Marshall, "The Unity of Isaiah 1-12," *LQ, N.S.,* 14 (1962) 21-38.

Mary Cecily, "The Concept of Sin and Holiness in the Book of Emmanuel (Is. 1-12)," *Scrip* 18 (1966) 112-116.

Isaiah Chapters 1-10

William Popper, "Studies in Biblical Parallelism. Part II. Parallelism in Isaiah, Chapters 1-10," *UCPSP* 1 (1907-23) 267-444.

Isaiah Chapter 1

[David N. Lord], "A Designation and Classification of the Figures of Isaiah, Chap. I.," *TLJ* 1 (1848-49) 604-631.

Lloyd Robinson, "Isaiah I," *ET* 3 (1891-92) 174.

R. Kelly, "Isaiah I," *ET* 3 (1891-92) 508-509.

E. Robertson, "Isaiah Chapter I," *ZAW* 52 (1934) 231-236.

L. G. Rignell, "Isaiah Chapter I," *ST* 11 (1957) 140-158.

S. Abramski, "'Slag' and 'Tin' in the First Chapter of Isaiah," *EI* 5 (1958) 89*.

*Judah Stampfer, "On Translating Biblical Poetry. *Isaiah,* Chapters 1 and 2:1-4," *Jud* 14 (1965) 501-510.

Isaiah 1:1-20

Kyle M. Yates, "Isaiah 1:1-20," *R&E* 34 (1937) 44-47.

Isaiah 1:1-9

Douglas R. Jones, "Exposition of Isaiah Chapter One Verses One to Nine," *SJT* 17 (1964) 463-477.

Isaiah 1:1-8

John Moncure, "The Meaning of KL in Isaiah 1:1-8," *R&E* 22 (1925) 450-452.

Isaiah 1:3

J. Robertson, "Isaiah I. 3," *ET* 4 (1892-93) 432.

Anonymous, "In the Study. The Unnatural Children," *ET* 20 (1908-09) 552-554. [Suggestions for the Study of Isaiah i. 3]

Isaiah 1:4

T. B. M'Corkindale, "Isaiah I. 4," *ET* 3 (1891-92) 174-175.

*A. Guillaume, "Hebrew Notes," *PEQ* 79 (1947) 40-44. *[1:4, p. 40]*

Isaiah 1:5-6

Thomas Franklin Day, "Isaiah 1:5, 6," *BW* 13 (1899) 340.

Isaiah 1:8

F. Jarratt, "The Cottage in the Vineyard. Isaiah i. 8," *ET* 3 (1891-92) 464.

Isaiah 1:10-20

K. Fullerton, "The Rhythmical Analysis of Isaiah 1:10-20," *JBL* 38 (1919) 53-63.

Isaiah 1:10-17

Douglas Jones, "Exposition of Isaiah Chapter One Verses Ten to Seventeen," *SJT* 18 (1965) 457-471.

Isaiah 1:13

Hugh H. Currie, "Isaiah I. 13," *ET* 3 (1891-92) 110-111.

Isaiah 1:16

A. M. Honeyman, "Isaiah 1:16 הִזַּכּוּ," *VT* 1 (1951) 63-65.

Isaiah 1:18-20

Walter R. Betteridge, "'Obedience and not Sacrifice.' An Exposition of Isaiah I:18-20," *BW* 38 (1911) 41-49.

Douglas R. Jones, "Exposition of Isaiah Chapter One Verses Eighteen to Twenty," *SJT* 19 (1966) 319-327.

Isaiah 1:18

Marshall B. Lang, "A Comparison. Isaiah I. 18 and Ephesians IV. 25-29," *ET* 8 (1896-97) 405-406.

*Owen H. Gates, "Notes on Isaiah 1:18b and 7:14b-16," *AJSL* 17 (1900-01) 16-21.

C. F. Burney, "Old Testament Notes. I. The Interpretation of Isaiah I. 18," *JTS* 11 (1909-10) 433-438.

W. A. Maier, "Vagaries of Tendential Exegesis as Illustrated by the Interpretation of Is. 1, 18," *CTM* 3 (1932) 175-180.

Robert Duncan Culver, "Isaiah 1:18—Declaration, Exclamation or Interrogation," *BETS* 12 (1969) 133-142.

Isaiah 1:25

Leo Hyman, "A Note on Isa. 1:25," *JNES* 9 (1950) 217.

Isaiah 1:27

James Kennedy, "Isaiah I. 27," *ET* 27 (1915-16) 523.

Isaiah 1:31

M. Tsevat, "Isaiah I 31," *VT* 19 (1969) 261-263.

Isaiah Chapters 2-4

Hugh H. Currie, "Isaiah II-IV. A Discourse by an Old Testament Prophet from a Popular Text," *ET* 3 (1891-92) 321-322.

Isaiah Chapter 2

[David N. Lord], "A Designation of the Figures of Isaiah Chap. II.," *TLJ* 2 (1849-50) 1-14.

*W. W. Cannon, "The Disarmament Passage in Isaiah ii. and Micah iv," *Theo* 24 (1932) 2-8.

Isaiah 2:1-5

*Israel Friedlaender, "The Present Position and the Original Form of the Prophecy of Eternal Peace in Isaiah 2:1-5 and Micah 4:1-5," *JQR, N.S.,* 6 (1915-16) 405-413.

Isaiah 2:1-4

*Judah Stampfer, "On Translating Biblical Poetry. *Isaiah,* Chapters 1 and 2:1-4," *Jud* 14 (1965) 501-510.

Isaiah 2:1

Peter R. Ackroyd, "A Note on Isaiah 2:1," *ZAW* 75 (1963) 320-321.

Isaiah 2:2-4

Anonymous, "Expository: Isaiah II. 2-4," *ERG, 1st Ser.,* 3 (1856-57) 161-166.

Alfred Huddle, "Isaiah II. 2-4," *ET* 3 (1891-92) 272-273.

Isaiah 2:4

†R. C. Fuller, "'Swords and Ploughshares' (Is. ii, 4)," *Scrip* 4 (1949-51) 150.

Isaiah 2:5

F. Flint, "Thoughts Suggestive for a Sermon on Isaiah II. 5," *ET* 3 (1891-92) 111.

*G. W. Skipwith, "On the Structure of the Book of Micah, and On Isaiah ii. 2-5," *JQR* 6 (1893-94) 583-586.

*Kemper Fullerton, "Studies in Isaiah," *JBL* 35 (1916) 134-142. [I. On Is. 2:5 and Mi 4:5, pp. 134-139]

Isaiah 2:6-22

Edward R. Hamme, "A Study of Isaiah 2:6-22," *CTSQ* 7 (1929-30) #2, 7-10.

Isaiah 2:6-21

Kemper Fullerton, "The Original Form of the Refrains in Isa. 2:6-21," *JBL* 38 (1919) 64-76.

Isaiah 2:6

*J. A. Bewer, "Textual Suggestions on Isa. 2:6; 66:3; Zeph. 2:2-5," *JBL* 27 (1908) 163-166.

D. Winton Thomas, "A Lost Hebrew Word in Isaiah II. 6," *JTS, N.S.,* 13 (1962) 323-324.

D. Winton Thomas, "The Text of Jesaia II 6 and the Word שׂפק," *ZAW* 75 (1963) 88-90.

R. Davidson, "The Interpretation of Isaiah II 6ff.," *VT* 16 (1966) 1-7.

Isaiah 2:9-21

Alfred C. G. Rendell, "The Lord Grafted in Righteousness. Note on Isaiah ii. 9-21," *ET* 3 (1891-92) 223-224.

Isaiah 2:16

*W. Emery Barnes, "Requests and Replies," *ET* 11 (1899-1900) 108. *[2:16]*

Isaiah 2:20

*Theophile James Meek, "Old Testament Notes," *JBL* 67 (1948) 233-239. [5. Compounds with Suffixes (Isa. 2:20; Lam. 1:7, 5:15, p. 239)]

Isaiah Chapters 3 and 4

[David N. Lord], "A Designation of the Figures of Isaiah, Chap. III. and IV.," *TLJ* 2 (1849-50) 222-240.

Isaiah Chapter 3

*H. F. B. Compston, "Ladies' Finery in Isaiah iii," *CQR* 103 (1926-27) 316-330.

Isaiah 3:1-15

*Louise P. Smith, "The Date of Isaiah 3:1-15," *JBL* 61 (1942) iv.

Isaiah 3:10-11

W. L. Holladay, "Isa. III 10-11: An Archaic Wisdom Passage," *VT* 18 (1968) 481-487.

Isaiah 3:12

*M[orris] Jastrow, "Notes on the Targum as a Commentary," *ONTS* 3 (1883-84) 52-53. *[3:12]*

Isaiah 3:16-24

*H. J. D. Astley, "Ladies' Fashions in Jerusalem. Circ. 735 B.C.—Isa. III. 16-24," *ICMM* 16 (1919-20) 127-134.

Isaiah Chapter 4

N. Rounds, "Spiritual Interpretation of Isaiah IV," *MR* 33 (1851) 262-270.

*"Philo.", "Notes on Scripture, Excerpts, Short Comments," *TLJ* 8 (1855-56) 200-220. [Chap. 4, pp. 200-201]

Isaiah 4:2

*R. P. Stebbins, "Criticism of Some Passages in Isaiah interpreted by J. B. Alexander, as predicting the Messiah," *JBL* 5 (1885) 79-82. [Isa. 4:2, pp. 79-80]

*J. G. Baldwin, "*Ṣemaḥ* as a technical term in the prophets," *VT* 14 (1964) 93-97. [1. Isa. IV 2, pp. 93-94]

Isaiah Chapters 5 and 6

[David N. Lord], "A Designation of the Figures of Isaiah Chap V. and VI.," *TLJ* 2 (1849-50) 402-420.

Isaiah 5:1-14

William Creighton Graham, "Notes on the Interpretation of Isaiah 5:1-14," *AJSL* 45 (1928-29) 167-178.

Isaiah 5:1-7

Anonymous, "Remarks on Isaiah v. 1-7," *JSL, 2nd Ser.,* 5 (1853-54) 163-173.

T. K. Cheyne, "Short Exegetical Notes II. Isa. v. 1-7," *MI* 3 (1885-86) 472-473.

J. A. Selbie, "The Parable of the Vineyard in Isa. V. 1-7," *ET* 10 (1898-99) 325.

Isaiah 5:1-6

A. Marmorstein, "A Greek Lyric and a Hebrew Prophet," *JQR, N.S.,* 37 (1946-47) 169-173. *[5:1-6]*

Isaiah 5:1-2

John P. Peters, "A Hebrew Folksong," *JBL* 33 (1914) 158-159. *[5:1-2]*

Isaiah 5:2-4

*Steven T. Byington, "Hebrew Marginalia," *JBL* 64 (1945) 339-355. [1.) The Sense of Certain Words: באשים (Isa. 5:2, 4), pp. 341-343]

Isaiah 5:9-10

E. W. Shalders, "Biblical Notes. Isaiah v. 9, 10," *Exp, 1st Ser.,* 7 (1878) 471-474.

Isaiah 5:14-18

R. R. Ottley, "On the LXX of Isaiah V 14, 17, 18," *JTS* 4 (1902-03) 269-270.

Isaiah 5:14

J. A. Emerton, "The Textual Problems of Isaiah V 14," *VT* 17 (1967) 135-142.

Isaiah 5:16

Aaron Mirsky, "The Third Benediction of the *'Amida* and the Passage 'The Lord of Hosts is Exalted' (Is. V, 16)," *Tarbiz* 38 (1968-69) #3, V-VI.

Isaiah 5:18

*Robert H. Kennett, "Ropes of Love or Cords of Vanity?" *ICMM* 13 (1916-17) 122-127. *[5:18]*

*Mitchell J. Dahood, "Ugaritic *ṭat* and Isaia 5, 18," *CBQ* 22 (1960) 73-75.

Isaiah 5:28

*G. R. Driver, "Uncertain Hebrew Words," *JTS* 45 (1944) 13-14. *[5:28]*

Isaiah Chapter 6

E. H., "Critical, Philological, and Exegetical Notes on the Sixth Chapter of Isaiah," *CongML* 20 (1837) 684-691.

P. Thomson, "The Call and Commission of Isaiah. Isaiah VI," *Exp, 1st Ser.,* 11 (1880) 119-137.

Walter M. Patton, "Isaiah VI.—An essay in interpretation," *CMR* 7 (1895) 239-244.

*Ivan Engnell, "The Call of Isaiah. An exegetical and comparative study," *UAÅ* (1949) Band 1, #4, 1-68. *[Chap. 6]*

Leon J. Liebereich, "The Position of Chapter Six in the Book of Isaiah," *HUCA* 25 (1954) 37-40.

Julian Price Love, "The Call of Isaiah. *An Exposition of Isaiah 6,"* *Interp* 11 (1957) 282-296.

John Killinger, "Remembering the Shape of the Holy. Isaiah 6," *VDR* 10 (1966) #2, 8-12.

*E. Lacheman, "The Seraphim of Isaiah 6," *JQR, N.S.,*59 (1968-69) 71-72.

Isaiah 6:1-12

*Daniel S. Gregory, "Introductory View to the Subsequent Lessons," *CFL, 3rd Ser.,* 14 (1911-12) 283-289. [III. The Study of the Historic Aim of the Prophet-Scribes, ii. "Isaiah's Vision and Call to Service", pp. 292-293]*[6:1-12]*

Isaiah 6:1-11

M. M. Kaplan, "Isaiah 6:1-11," *JBL* 45 (1926) 251-259.

Isaiah 6:1-8

Samuel Cox, *"The Vision of Isaiah.* Isaiah vi. 1-8, I. Historical Introduction," *Exp, 2nd Ser.,* 2 (1881) 18-27.

Samuel Cox, *"The Vision of Isaiah.* Isaiah vi. 1-8, II. The Vision," *Exp, 2nd Ser.,* 2 (1881) 81-91.

*W. Emery Barnes, "The Task of the Prophets," *ICMM* 16 (1919-20) 187-199. *[6:1-8]*

Fred. Kramer, "Sermon Study on Isaiah 6:1-8 for Trinity," *CTM* 22 (1951) 265-274.

Isaiah 6:3

Norman Walker, "The Origin of the 'Thrice-Holy'," *NTS* 5 (1958-59) 132-133. *[6:3LXX]*

Burton M. Leiser, "The Trisagion of Isaiah's Vision," *NTS* 6 (1959-60) 261-263. *[6:3]*

Norman Walker, "Disagion versus Trisagion," *NTS* 7 (1960-61) 170-171. *[6:3]*

Isaiah 6:5-8

J. E. Swallow, "The Terror of Holiness. Isaiah vi. 5-8," *ET* 3 (1891-92) 417.

Isaiah 6:8-13

Samuel Cox, *"The Vision of Isaiah.* Isaiah vi. 8-13, III. The Summons," *Exp, 2nd Ser.,* 2 (1881) 217-230.

Isaiah 6:9-13

*W. Emery Barnes, "The Task of the Prophets," *ICMM* 16 (1919-20) 187-199. *[6:9-13a, 13b]*

Andrew F. Key, "The Magical Background of Isaiah 6:9-13," *JBL* 86 (1967) 198-204.

Isaiah 6:9-11

R. E. Wolfe, "Earliest Phase of Isaiah's Prophetic Thought," *JBL* 60 (1941) v. *[6:9-11]*

Isaiah 6:9-10

Anonymous, "Philological Examination of Isaiah VI. 9, 10," *PQR* 9 (1860-61) 588-595.

Isaiah 6:10

†C. Lattey, "Did God 'Harden' the Heart of Israel (Isaias vi, 10)?" *Scrip* 3 (1948) 48-49.

Isaiah 6:12-13

Flemming Hvidberg, "The Messeba and the Holy Seed," *NTTO* 56 (1955) 97-99. *[6:12, 13]*

Isaiah 6:13

*A. Guillaume, "Hebrew Notes," *PEQ* 79 (1947) 40-44. [pp. 41-42] *[6:13]*

*Wm. H. Brownlee, "The Text of Isaiah VI 13 in the Light of DSIa," *VT* 1 (1951) 296-298.

*J. Sawyer, "The Qumran Reading of Isaiah 6, 13," *ASTI* 3 (1964) 111-113.

Isaiah Chapters 7-12

John Forbes, "Isaiah VII.-XII. The Prophecy of Immanuel or of the Virgin and Child," *PR* 7 (1886) 690-713.

Isaiah Chapters 7-9

Philalethes, "New Translation and Exposition of Part of the Book of Isaiah," *CongML* 23 (1840) 433-443. *[Chaps. 7-9]*

Isaiah 7:1-9:7

George W. Davis, "The Child Prophecies of Isaiah. Isaiah 7:1-9:7," *BW* 4 (1894) 259-265.

Isaiah Chapters 7 and 8

*Peter R. Ackroyd, "Historians and Prophets," *SEÅ* 33 (1968) 18-54. [Isa. 7-8, pp. 26-33]

Isaiah Chapter 7

[David N. Lord], "A Designation and Exposition of the Figures of Isaiah, Chap. VII.," *TLJ* 2 (1849-50) 633-653.

Samuel N. Deinard, "Notes on Isaiah, Chap. 7," *AJSL* 15 (1898-99) 165-167.

Reidar B. Bjornard, "Isaiah VII Once More," *Found* 3 (1960) 70-73.

*B. Oded, "The Historical Background of the War between Rezin and Pekah against Ahaz," *Tarbiz* 38 (1968-69) #3, I-II. *[Chap. 7]*

Isaiah 7:1-17

Emil G. Kraeling, "The Immanuel Prophecy," *JBL* 50 (1831) 277-297 *[7:1-17]*

Frank Zimmerman, "The Immanuel Prophecy," *JQR, N.S.,* 52 (1961-62) 154-159. *[7:1-17]*

Isaiah 7:1-16

Sheldon H. Blank, "Immanuel and Which Isaiah?" *JNES* 13 (1954) 83-85. *[7:1-16]*

Isaiah 7:1

*K. Budde, "Isaiah vii. 1 and 2 Kings xvi. 5," *ET* 11 (1899-1900) 327-330.

Isaiah 7:3

George St. Clair, "The Fuller's Field," *PEFQS* 23 (1891) 189-190. *[7:3]*

*Millar Burrows, "The Conduit of the Upper Pool," *ZAW* 70 (1958) 221-227. *[7:3]*

Isaiah 7:4

Norman E. Wagner, "A note on Isaiah VII 4," *VT* 8 (1958) 438.

Isaiah 7:6

Adolph Brux, "נַקִיצֶנָּה וְנַבְקִעֶנָּה אֵלֵינוּ" in Isaiah 7:6," *AJSL* 39 (1922-23) 68-71.

S. Speier, "Uneqiṣennah, Isaiah 7:6a," *JBL* 72 (1953) xiv.

William F[oxwell] Albright, "The Son of Tabeel (Isaiah 7:6)," *BASOR* #140 (1955) 34-35.

Isaiah 7:7-9

*Kemper Fullerton, "Studies in Isaiah," *JBL* 35 (1916) 134-142. [II. On Is. 7:7-9, pp. 140-142]

Isaiah 7:8-9

†C. Lattey, "How did the Prophecy of Isaias vii, 8-9 affect King Achaz?" *Scrip* 3 (1948) 50.

Isaiah 7:8

Anonymous, "Critical Remarks on an alleged interpolation in Isaiah 7:8," *PRev* 9 (1837) 558-575.

Melville Scott, "Isaiah VII. 8," *ET* 38 (1926-27) 525-526.

James Barr, "Did Isaiah Know About Hebrew 'Root Meanings'?" *ET* 75 (1963-64) 242. *[7:8]*

Isaiah 7:9

Denis Wortman, "A Kaleidoscopic Text—Isa vii. 9," *HR* 37 (1899) 540-544.

Isaiah 7:10-23

*Ereunetes, "Observations on Isaiah vii. 10-23. viii. 5-19," *TRep* 5 (1786) 38-56.

Isaiah 7:10-17

C. R. Brown, "Exegesis of Isa. 7:10-17," *JBL* 9 (1890) 118-127.

A. A. Bevan, "The Sign Given to King Ahaz," *JQR* 6 (1893-94) 220-222. *[7:10-17]*

John J. Scullion, "An Approach to the Understanding of Isaiah 7:10-17," *JBL* 87 (1968) 288-300.

Isaiah 7:10-16

H.*, "The Prediction concerning Immanuel. Isaiah vii. 10-16," *CongML* 10 (1827) 22-26.

J. C. Knight, "Butter and Honey a 'Sign' to Ahaz, of Evil; a Criticism upon Isaiah VII. 10-16," *JSL, 5th Ser.,* 2 (1867-68) 337-348.

W. K. Lowther Clarke, "The Virgin Birth in Recent Discussion," *Theo* 13 (1926) 78-92. [O.T. refs.: II. Isa. 7:10-16, pp. 82-84]

Isaiah 7:10-14

Edward Meyer, "Interpreting the Scriptures for Advent and Christmas. Fourth Sunday in Advent. Isaiah 7:10-14," *JMTSO* 4 (1965-66) #1, 17-20.

Isaiah 7:12

Lewis B. Paton, "Isaiah 7:12," *BW* 13 (1899) 197.

Isaiah 7:13-17

Edward L. Curtis, "The Prophecy Concerning Immanuel: Isaiah VII. 13-17," *ONTS* 11 (1890) 276-280.

Anonymous, "The Sign of Emmanuel (Is. 7, 13-17)," *CBQ* 19 (1957) 15.

Isaiah 7:14-25

W. McKane, "The Interpretation of Isaiah VII 14-25," *VT* 17 (1967) 208-219.

Isaiah 7:14-17

A. G. Mitchell, "Immanuel. Prophecy and Fulfillment," *AR* 15 (1891) 439-447. *[7:14-17]*

Isaiah 7:14-16

N. A. Folsom, "Interpretation of Isaiah 7:14-16," *LTR* 4 (1837) 167-181.

D. H. W., "On the True Messianic Import of Isaiah vii., 14-16," *JSL, 3rd Ser.,* 2 (1855-56) 317-325.

*R. P. Stebbins, "Criticism of Some Passages in Isaiah interpreted by J. B. Alexander, as predicting the Messiah," *JBL* 5 (1885) 79-82. [Isa. 7:14-16, pp. 80-82]

*Owen H. Gates, "Notes on Isaiah 1:18b and 7:14b-16," *AJSL* 17 (1900-01) 16-21.

*A. M. Haggard, "A Difficult Messianic Prophecy," *BS* 72 (1915) 154-158. *[7:14-16]*

E. Power, "The Emmanuel Prophecy of Isaias," *IER, 5th Ser.,* 70 (1948) 289-304. *[7:14-16]*

Edward J. Young, "The Immanuel Prophecy—Isaiah 7:14-16," *WTJ* 15 (1952-53) 97-124.

Edward J. Young, "The Immanuel Prophecy—Isaiah 7:14-16—II.," *WTJ* 16 (1953-54) 23-50.

P. Peters, "Isaiah 7:14-16," *WSQ* 58 (1961) 101-122, 170-195.

Isaiah 7:14-15

W. W. Martin, "Immanuel—Prediction, Content, Fulfillment," *MR* 73 (1891) 699-708. *[7:14, 15]*

Isaiah 7:14

Iota, "Remarks on Isaiah VII. 14," *SP* 3 (1830) 404-414.

James Sullivan and Samuel West, "Original Correspondence between the Late Gov. Sullivan and Dr. Samuel West, on Isaiah VII. 14, and Matt. I. 22, 23," *SP* 3 (1830) 458-467.

Henry Ferguson, "Is ΠΑΡΘΕΝΟΣ the Correct Rendering of עלמה in Isaiah VII. 14?" *BS* 34 (1877) 762-766.

Niger, "Immanuel. Isaiah VII. 14," *Exp, 1st Ser.,* 10 (1879) 331-341.

*John P. Peters, "Miscellaneous Notes," *AJSL* 1 (1884-85) 242-243. *[7:14]*

John P. Peters, "Isaiah VII. 14," *AJSL* 2 (1885-86) 175.

Willis J. Beecher, "The Prophecy of the Virgin Mother. Isa. vii:14," *HR* 17 (1889) 354-358.

David M. Sweets, "Isaiah vii. 14," *HR* 28 (1894) 552-555.

S. L. Bowman, "Isaiah's Prediction of the Mother of the Messiah," *MR* 84 (1902) 939-952. *[7:14]*

*C. F. Burney, "Old Testament Notes. I. The 'Sign of Immanuel'," *JTS* 10 (1908-09) 580-584. *[7:14]*

*G. Buchanan Gray, "The Virgin Birth in Relation to the Interpretation of Isaiah 7:14," *Exp, 8th Ser.,* 1 (1911) 289-308.

P. Boylan, "The Sign of Isaias VII. 14," *ITQ* 7 (1912) 203-215.

Allen H. Godbey, "The Word 'Virgin' in Isaiah VII. 14," *MQR, 3rd Ser.,* 50 (1924) 513-522.

R[obert] D[ick]Wilson, "The Meaning of 'Alma (A.V. 'Virgin') in Isaiah VII. 14," *PTR* 24 (1926) 308-316.

Cuthbert Lattey, "The Emmanuel Prophecy: Isaias 7:14," *CBQ* 8 (1946) 369-376.

Cuthbert Lattey, "The Term 'Almah in Is. 7:14," *CBQ* 9 (1947) 89-95.

Cuthbert Lattey, "Various Interpretations of Is. 7:14," *CBQ* 9 (1947) 147-154.

Carl Gaenssle, "Another Look at 'Almah,' in Is. 7:14," *CTM* 24 (1953) 443-445.

Alfred von Rohr Sauer, "The Almah Translation in Is. 7:14," *CTM* 24 (1953) 551-559.

Cyrus H. Gordon, "'Almah in Isaiah 7:14," *JAAR* 21 (1953) 106.

Dale Moody, "Isaiah 7:14 in the Revised Standard Version," *R&E* 50 (1953) 61-68.

G. A. F. Knight, "The Virgin and the Old Testament," *RTR* 12 (1953) 1-12. *[7:14]*

Eric Kahn, "Virgin-Birth: Isaias 7:14," *Scotist* [9] (1953) 25-41.

P. Peters, "Luther's Translation of Almah in Isaiah 7:14," *WLQ* 50 (1953) 64-66.

Dewey M. Beegle, "Virgin or Young Woman? An Exegetical Study of Isaiah 7:14," *ASW* 8 (1954) #1, 20-34.

Ernest R. Lacheman, "Apropos of Isaiah 7:14," *JAAR* 22 (1954) 43.

James N. Bulman, "The Virgin Birth in Recent Discussion," *R&E* 51 (1954) 470-494. *[7:14]*

*Wallace I. Wolverton, "Judgment in Advent. Notes on Isaiah 8:5-15 and 7:14," *ATR* 37 (1955) 284-291.

*Harold L. Creager, "The Immanuel Passage as Messianic Prophecy," *LQ, N.S.,* 7 (1955) 339-343. *[7:14]*

Kurt Carl Hartmann, "More about the RSV and Isaiah 7:14," *LQ, N.S.,*7 (1955) 344-347.

Robert G. Bratcher, "A Study of Isaiah 7:14, Its Meaning and Use in the Masoretic Text, the Septuagint and the Gospel of Matthew," *BTr* 9 (1958) 97-126.

Stefan Porubcan, "The Word *'ôt* in Isaia 7, 14," *CBQ* 22 (1960) 144-159.

Walter Mueller, "A Virgin Shall Conceive," *EQ* 32 (1960) 203-207. *[7:14]*

Edward J. Young, "The Promise of a Saviour-King. Isaiah 7:14," *SR* 8 (1961-62) 26-49.

Charles L. Feinberg, "The Virgin Birth in the Old Testament and Isaiah 7:14," *BS* 119 (1962) 251-258.

M. McNamara, "The Emmanuel Prophecy and its Context," *Scrip* 14 (1962) 118-125. *[7:14]*

M. McNamara, "The Emmanuel Prophecy and its Context *(concluded)[sic],*" *Scrip* 15 (1963) 19-23. *[7:14]*

M. McNamara, "The Emmanuel Prophecy and its Context—III," *Scrip* 15 (1963) 80-88. *[7:14]*

Joseph P. Breenan, "Virgin and Child in Isaiah 7:14," *BibT* #15 (1964) 968-974.

*John McHugh, "The Date of Hezekiah's Birth," *VT* 14 (1964) 446-453. *[7:14]*

R. E. Honsey, "'Alma in Isaiah 7:14," *LSQ* 6 (1965-66) #3, 16-18.

[Clifford A. Wilson], "Your Questions Answered. What am I to believe about the word 'virgin' as applied to Isaiah 7:14?" *BH* 4 (1968) 13-15.

Edward E. Hindson, "Development of the Interpretation of Isaiah 7:14, A Tribute to Dr. Edward J. Young," *GJ* 10 (1969) #2, 19-25.

Isaiah 7:15

J. M. Powis Smith, "Butter and Honey," *AJSL* 40 (1923-24) 292-294. *[7:15]*

†D. Leahy, "The Child in Isaias vii, 15," *Scrip* 2 (1947) 80-82.

Isaiah 7:16

Thomas E. Bird, "Who was the Boy in Isaias 7:16?" *CBQ* 6 (1944) 435-443.

Isaiah 7:25

James Kennedy, "Isaiah VII. 25 וְשָׁיִת: שָׁמִיר יִרְאַת שָׁמָּה לֹא־תָבוֹא," *ET* 8 (1896-97) 477-478.

Isaiah Chapters 8-10

C. Taylor, "Note on Isaiah VIII.-X.," *JP* 6 (1875-76) 149-159.

Isaiah Chapter 8

[David N. Lord], "A Designation and Exposition of the Figures of Isaiah, Chap. VIII.," *TLJ* 3 (1850-51) 60-70.

Isaiah 8:1

*Peter Katz, "Notes on the Septuagint, I. Isaiah VIII. 1a," *JTS* 47 (1946) 30-31.

Frank Talmage, "חרט אנקש in Isaiah 8:1," *HTR* 60 (1967) 465-468.

Isaiah 8:5-19

*Ereunetes, "Observations on Isaiah vii. 10-23. viii. 5-19," *TRep* 5 (1786) 38-56.

Isaiah 8:5-15

*Wallace I. Wolverton, "Judgment in Advent. Notes on Isaiah 8:5-15 and 7:14," *ATR* 37 (1955) 284-291.

Isaiah 8:5-10

K. Fullerton, "The Interpretation of Isaiah 8:5-10," *JBL* 43 (1924) 253-289.

Isaiah 8:6-8

Thomas Franklin Day, "Isaiah 8:6-8," *BW* 13 (1899) 340.

Isaiah 8:6

Samuel Cox, "The Waters of Shiloah. Isaiah viii. 6," *Exp, 1st Ser.,* 6 (1877) 353-367.

W. F. Birch, "The Waters of Shiloah that Go Softly. (Isaiah viii, 6.)," *PEFQS* 21 (1889) 35-38.

Alfred Gill, "Note on Isaiah VIII. 6," *ET* 3 (1891-92) 372.

S. N. Deinard, "A Note on Isaiah 8:6," *AJSL* 16 (1899-1900) 51-52.

F. C. Burkitt, "The Waters of Shiloah that Go Softly: A Note on Isaiah VIII 6," *JTS* 12 (1910-11) 294-295.

H. W. Sheppard, "ΤΟΥ ΣΙΛΩΑΜ : הַשִּׁלֹחַ Isa. VIII 6," *JTS* 16 (1914-15) 414-416.

A. M. Honeyman, "Traces of an Early Diacritic Sign in Isaiah 8:6b," *JBL* 63 (1944) 45-50.

Isaiah 8:8

R. C. Faithfull, "Immanuel," *ET* 32 (1920-21) 45. *[8:8]*

Isaiah 8:11-14

*G. R. Driver, "Two Misunderstood Passages in the Old Testament," *JTS,* *N.S.,*6 (1955) 82-87. [Isaiah viii. 11-14, pp. 82-84]

Isaiah 8:14-16

Kleinere Beitrage, "The Jewel of Discernment (A study of stone symbolism)," *BZ* 11 (1967) 109-116 *[8:14-16]*

Isaiah 8:14

Anonymous, "Jehovah-Jesus a Sanctuary," *ERG, 2nd Ser.,* 1 (1858-59) 87-91. *[8:14]*

Isaiah 8:16

*"Philo.", "Notes on Scripture, Excerpts, Short Comments," *TLJ* 8 (1855-56) 200-220. *[8:16]*

Isaiah 8:18-22

*Hugh H. Currie, "From Light to Darkness: From Darkness to Light, Isaiah viii, 18-22; ix. 2," *ET* 4 (1892-93) 229.

Isaiah 8:20

Hinckley G. Mitchell, "Two Papers. Isa. 8:20, a new translation," *JBL* 7 (1887) Part 1, 65-68.

Isaiah 8:23

*H. L. Ginsberg, "An Unrecognized Allusion to Kings Pekah and Hoshea of Israel (Isa. 8:23)," *EI* 5 (1958) 61*-65*.

J. A. Emerton, "Some Linguistic and Historical Problems in Isaiah VIII. 23," *JSS* 14 (1969) 151-175.

Isaiah 8:30

*H. L. Ginsberg, "An Unrecognized Allusion to Kings Pekah and Hoshea of Israel (Isa. 8:23)," *EI* 5 (1958) 61*-65*.[Addendum: A Note on Isa. 8:30, p. 65*]

Isaiah Chapter 9

Philalethes, "A new Interpretation of Isaiah, ix. &c.," *TRep* 6 (1788) 344-347.

[David N. Lord], "A Designation and Exposition of the Figures of Isaiah, Chapter IX.," *TLJ* 3 (1850-51) 287-302.

Carl Umhau Wolf, "Luther on the Christmas Prophecy, Isaiah 9," *LQ, N.S.,* 5 (1953) 388-390.

Isaiah 9:1-7

*Daniel S. Gregory, "The International Lessons in Their Literary and Historical Setting," *CFL, 3rd Ser.,* 1 (1904) 725-733. [The Prince of Peace, Isa. 9:1-7, pp. 732-733]

R. H. Kennett, "The Prophecy in Isaiah IX 1-7," *JTS* 7 (1905-06) 321-342.

R. H. Kennett, "The Prophecy of Isaiah IX. 1-7. (*A Reply to Dr Burney*)," *JTS* 12 (1910-11) 114-118.

M. Treves, "Little Prince Pele-Joez," *VT* 17 (1967) 464-477. *[9:1-7]*

Isaiah 9:1-2

Samuel A. B. Mercer, "Isaiah 9:1-2," *ATR* 2 (1919-20) 152-153.

Isaiah 9:1

*Charles Druitt, "The *'Via Maris',*" *PEFQS* 20 (1888) 166-167. *[9:1]*

Albert A. Isaacs, "The Difficulties of Scripture," *EN* 4 (1892) 166-169. [Isaiah ix. 1.]

Isaiah 9:2-7

*M[argaret] B. Crook, "A Suggested Occasion for Isaiah 9:2-7 and 11:1-9," *JBL* 68 (1949) x-xi.

*Margaret B. Crook, "A Suggested Occasion for Isaiah 9:2-7 and 11:1-9," *JBL* 68 (1949) 213-224.

*M[argaret] B. Crook, "Did Amos & Micah Know Isaiah 9:2-7 & 11:1-9?" *JBL* 70 (1951) xiii.

*M[argaret] B. Crook, "Did Amos & Micah Know Isaiah 9:2-7 & 11:1-9?" *JBL* 73 (1954) 144-151.

Lars G. Rignell, "A Study of Isaiah 9:2-7," *LQ, N.S.,* 7 (1955) 31-35.

Isaiah 9:2

*Hugh H. Currie, "From Light to Darkness: From Darkness to Light, Isaiah viii, 18-22; ix. 2," *ET* 4 (1892-93) 229.

E[dward] Robertson, "A Note on Isaiah ix:2," *JMUEOS* #23 (1942) 18-20.

Isaiah 9:4

C. F. Burney, "Old Testament Notes. II. The 'Boot' of Isaiah IX 4," *JTS* 11 (1909-10) 438-443.

Isaiah 9:5-6

*G. R. Driver, "Three Notes," *VT* 2 (1952) 356-357. [Isaiah ix 5-6, p. 357]

Isaiah 9:5

Samuel J. Bertie, "'Everlasting Father' (אֲבִי־עַד), Isaiah ix. 5," *ET* 3 (1891-92) 509.

George Jeshurun, "A Note on Isaiah 9:5," *JBL* 53 (1934) 384.

Norman H. Snaith, "The Interpretation of El Gibbor in Isaiah IX. 5 (EVV, 6)," *ET* 52 (1940-41) 36-37.

Isaiah 9:6-7

T. W. Chambers, "'The Everlasting Father'," *JBL* 1 (1881) 169-171. *[9:6, 7]*

T. W. Chambers, "The Everlasting Father," *DTQ, N.S.,* 2 (1883) 411-413. *[9:6, 7]*

Edward L. Curtis, "The Prophecy Concerning the Child of the Four Names: Isaiah IX, 6, 7," *ONTS* 11 (1890) 336-341.

Isaiah 9:6

Anglo-Scotus, "An Attempt to explain Isaiah ix. 6," *TRep* 5 (1786) 182-184.

T. K., "Morsels of Criticism on Isaiah IX. 6," *CongML* 5 (1822) 305.

Anonymous, "Comparative Translation: Isaiah 9:6. A Study in Modernizing the English Bible," *BW* 22 (1903) 449-450.

William H. Marquess, "El Gibbor. Isaiah 9:6," *BR* 3 (1918) 616-620.

William H. McClellan, "'El Gibbor'," *CBQ* 6 (1944) 276-288. *[9:6]*

†J. M. T. Barton, "The Meaning of Isaias ix, 6," *Scrip* 1 (1946) 31.

Isaiah 9:8-10:4

*Anonymous, "Transpositions in the Prophetical Books of the Old Testament," *BRCM* 1 (1846) 153-157. *[9:8-10:4]*

Richard G. Moulton, "Doom of the North," *BW* 7 (1896) 20-21. *[Paraphrase]*

Isaiah 9:8

*D. Winton Thomas, "A Note on the Meaning of ידע in Hosea ix.7 and Isaiah ix. 8," *JTS* 42 (1941) 43-44.

Isaiah 9:18

*W. Robertson Smith, "Old Testament notes," *JP* 13 (1884) 61-66. [I. נעתם Isaiah 9:18 (19), pp. 61-62]

William L. Moran, "The Putative Root *'tm* in Is. 9:18," *CBQ* 12 (1950) 153-154.

Isaiah 9:19-20

A. M. Honeyman, "An Unnoticed Euphemism in Isaiah IX 19-20?" *VT* 1 (1951) 221-223

Meir Wallenstein, "An Unnoticed Euphemism in Isaiah IX 19-20?" *VT* 2 (1952) 179-180.

Isaiah 9:19

*T. K. Cheyne, "Notes on Obscure Passages in the Prophets," *Exp, 5th Ser.,* 5 (1897) 41-51. *[9:19 (Heb 18), pp. 49-50]*

Isaiah Chapter 10

[David N. Lord], "A Designation and Exposition of the Figures of Isaiah, Chapter X.," *TLJ* 3 (1850-51) 384-395.

Kemper Fullerton, "The Problem of Isaiah, Chapter 10," *AJSL* 34 (1917-18) 170-184.

Isaiah 10:1-19

G. A. F. Knight, "Studies in Texts. A Paraphrase of Isaiah x. 1-19," *Theo* 59 (1956) 418-419.

Isaiah 10:3

S. N. Deinard, "Isaiah, Chap. 10:3b," *AJSL* 15 (1898-99) 114-115.

Isaiah 10:4

*T. K. Cheyne, "Notes on Obscure Passages in the Prophets," *Exp, 5th Ser.,* 5 (1897) 41-51. *[10:4, pp. 50-51]*

*C. J. Labuschagne, "Ugaritic *blt* and *biltî* in Is. X 4," *VT* 14 (1963) 97-99.

Isaiah 10:8

*John P. Peters, "Miscellaneous Notes," *AJSL* 1 (1884-85) 242-243. *[10:8]*

Isaiah 10:11-12

Patrick W. Skehan, "A Note on Is 10, 11b-12a," *CBQ* 14 (1952) 236.

Isaiah 10:27-28

*W. Robertson Smith, "Old Testament notes," *JP* 13 (1884) 61-66. [Isa. x. 27, 28, pp. 62-65]

Isaiah 10:28-34

W. F. Birch, "Sennacherib's Catastrophe at Nob. Isaiah X, 28-34," *PEFQS* 23 (1891) 314-318.

Isaiah 10:28-32

W. F. Birch, "Sennacherib's Catastrophe at Nob. (Isaiah X, 28-32)," *PEFQS* 34 (1902) 197-198.

Henry H. Walker, "Where are Madmenah and the Gebim?" *JPOS* 13 (1933) 90-93. *[10:28-32]*

Isaiah 10:31

J. Press, "Miscellanea 1," *BIES* 12 (1946) XI. *[10:31]*

Isaiah Chapters 11-35

William Popper, "Studies in Biblical Parallelism. Part III. Parallelism in Isaiah, Chapters 11-35," *UCPSP* 1 (1907-23) 445-551.

Isaiah Chapters 11 and 12

[David N. Lord], "A Designation and Exposition of the Figures of Isaiah, Chapters XI. and XII.," *TLJ* 3 (1850-51) 595-612.

Isaiah Chapter 11

Edward L. Curtis, "Isaiah's Prophecy Concerning the Shoot of Jesse and His Kingdom: Isaiah XI," *ONTS* 12 (1891) 13-19.

Isaiah 11:1-10

Everett Tilson, "Interpreting the Scriptures for Advent and Christmas. Second Sunday in Advent. Isaiah 11:1-10," *JTMSO* 4 (1965-66) #1, 6-12.

Isaiah 11:1-9

H. Rood, "The Branch and his Kingdom. Interpretation of Isaiah 11:1-9," *BJ* (1842) 85-94.

*M[argaret] B. Crook, "A Suggested Occasion for Isaiah 9:2-7 and 11:1-9," *JBL* 68 (1949) x-xi.

*Margaret B. Crook, "A Suggested Occasion for Isaiah 9:2-7 and 11:1-9," *JBL* 68 (1949) 213-224.

*M[argaret] B. Crook, "Did Amos & Micah Know Isaiah 9:2-7 & 11:1-9?" *JBL* 70 (1951) xiii.

*M[argaret] B. Crook, "Did Amos & Micah Know Isaiah 9:2-7 & 11:1-9?" *JBL* 73 (1954) 144-151.

Isaiah 11:1-8

*G. Buchanan Gray, "The strophic division of Isaiah 21:1-10 and Isaiah 11:1-8," *ZAW* 32 (1912) 190-198.

Isaiah 11:4

*"Philo.", "Notes on Scripture, Excerpts, Short Comments," *TLJ* 8 (1855-56) 200-220. *[11:4, pp. 201-202]*

Isaiah 11:15

*John P. Peters, "Miscellaneous Notes," *AJSL* 1 (1884-85) 242-243. *[11:15]*

Isaiah Chapter 12

William Henry Cobb, "Examination of Isa. 12," *JBL* 10 (1891) 131-143.

Frederick A. Baepler, "Sermon Study on Isaiah 12 for Third Sunday After Trinity," *CTM* 22 (1951) 343-351.

Isaiah 12:2

*Frederic Gardiner, "On the Duplication of the Tetragrammaton in Isaiah 12:2; 26:4," *ONTS* 9 (1889) 219-223.

*T. K. Cheyne, "Requests and Replies," *ET* 10 (1898-99) 444. *[12:2]*

Isaiah Chapters 13-66

Eugene C. Caldwell, "Through Judgment to Glory—A Book Study of Isaiah," *USR* 29 (1917-18) 52-64. [Article II—Chapters 13-66]

Isaiah Chapters 13 and 14

H. B. H., "Distinctness of Scripture Prophecy. with an examination of Isaiah, chapters XIII, XIV, 23," *CRB* 9 (1844) 173-198.

B. B. Edwards, "Translation of the Thirteenth and Fourteenth Chapters of Isaiah, with Explanatory Notes," *BS* 6 (1849) 765-785. [Translation; Subject; Outline of the Representation; Explanatory Notes; Author of the Passage; Rule of Interpretation; Note on Babylon]

[David N. Lord], "A Designation and Exposition of the Figures of Isaiah, Chapters XIII. and XIV.," *TLJ* 4 (1851-52) 62-82.

*W. M. McPheeters, "Dr. Driver on the Authorship of Isaiah XIII. and XIV.," *PQ* 8 (1894) 187-208, 489-511.

J. P. Peters, "Notes on Isaiah," *JBL* 38 (1919) 77-93. *[Chaps. 13 and 14]*

*S[tephen] H. Langdon, "The Star Hêlēl, Jupiter?" *ET* 42 (1930-31) 172-174. *[Chaps. 13 and 14]*

Isaiah Chapter 13

William Henry Cobb, "An Examination of Isaiah XIII," *BS* 49 (1892) 471-495.

Isaiah 13:1ff.

*Patrick D. Miller Jr., "The Divine Council and the Prophetic Call to War," *VT* 18 (1968) 100-107. [Isa. 13:1ff., pp. 102-103]

Isaiah 13:2-14:23

*R. C. Ford, "Isaiah XIII. 2-XIV. 23, and Zephaniah," *ET* 4 (1892-93) 224-225.

Isaiah 13:4-13

*"Philo.", "Notes on Scripture, Excerpts, Short Comments," *TLJ* 8 (1855-56) 200-220. *[13:4-13, p. 202]*

Isaiah 13:6

*Robert Gordis, "The Biblical Root ŠDY-ŠD: Notes on 2 Sam. i. 21; Jer. xviii. 14; Ps. xci. 6; Job v. 21," *JTS* 41 (1940) 34-43 [V. Isa. 13:6, pp. 42-43]

Isaiah 13:19-20

Harry Goehring, "The Fall of Babylon—Historical or Future? A Critical Monograph on Isaiah 13:19-20 Abridged by the Author," *GJ* 2 (1961) #1, 23-34.

Isaiah Chapter 14

William Henry Cobb, "Ode in Isa. 14," *JBL* 15 (1896) 18-35.

Isaiah 14:4-21

Frederick A. Vanderburgh, "The Ode of the King of Babylon, Isaiah XIV 4b-21," *AJSL* 29 (1912-13) 111-121.

Isaiah 14:4

H[arry] M. Orlinsky, "*Madhebah* in Isaiah XIV 4," *VT* 7 (1957) 202-203.

Isaiah 14:12

*N. A. Koenig, "Lucifer," *ET* 18 (1906-07) 479. *[14:12]*

*S. A. Hirsch, "Isaiah 14:12. שחר בן הילל," *JQR, N.S.,* 11 (1920-21) 197-199.

*A. Guillaume, "The Use of חלש in Exod. XVII. 13, Isa. XIV. 12, and Job XIV. 10," *JTS, N.S.,* 14 (1963) 91-92.

Isaiah 14:13

*M[itchell] Dahood, "Punic *hkkbm 'l* and Isaiah 14:13," *Or, N.S.,* 34 (1965) 170-172.

Isaiah 14:19

James T. Hudson, "Isaiah XIV. 19. וְאַתָּה הָשְׁלַכְתָּ מִקִּבְרְךָ כְּנֵצֶר נִתְעָב לְבוּשׁ הֲרֻגִים," *ET* 40 (1928-29) 93.

Ludwig Köhler, "Isaiah XIV. 19," *ET* 40 (1928-29) 236-237; 41 (1929-30) 142.

Isaiah 14:24-27

Wm. H. Cobb, "A Question of Space," *ONTS* 13 (1891) 338-343. *[14:24-27]*

Isaiah 14:28-32

*[David N. Lord], "A Designation and Exposition of the Figures of Isaiah, Chapters XIV., 28-32, XV., XVI., and XVII.," *TLJ* 4 (1851-52) 218-233.

Kemper Fullerton, "Isaiah 14:28-32," *AJSL* 42 (1925-26) 86-109.

W. A. Irwin, "The Exposition of Isaiah 14:28-32," *AJSL* 44 (1927-28) 73-87.

C. C. Torrey, "The Original Position of Isa 14:28-32," *JBL* 57 (1938) xii.

Isaiah 14:28

Julius A. Bewer, "The Date in Isa. 14:28," *AJSL* 54 (1937) 62.

Isaiah 14:31

B. Kedar-Kopfstein, "A Note on Isaiah XVI, 31," *Text* 2 (1962) 143-145.

Isaiah Chapters 15-17

*[David N. Lord], "A Designation and Exposition of the Figures of Isaiah, Chapters XIV., 28-32, XV., XVI., and XVII.," *TLJ* 4 (1851-52) 218-233.

Isaiah Chapters 15-16

W[ilhelm] Gesenius, "Exegesis of Isaiah XV. XVI.," *BRCR* 7 (1836) 107-161. *(Trans. by W. S. Tyler)*

Isaiah 15:1-16:5

E. Power, "The prophecy of Isaias against Moab (Is. 15, 1-16, 5)," *B* 13 (1932) 435-451.

Isaiah 16:6ff.

*Burke O. Long, "The Divine Funeral Lament," *JBL* 85 (1966) 85-86. *[16:6ff.]*

Isaiah 17:1

A. B. C., "The Burden of Damascus," *JSL, 3rd Ser.,* 14 (1861-62) 431. *[17:1]*

M. R. E., "The Prophecy Against Damascus," *JSL, 4th Ser.,* 1 (1862) 168-169. *[17:1]*

Isaiah 17:12-18:7

Anonymous, "Translation of Isaiah XVII. 12 to XVIII. 7; with a Brief Explanation of the Meaning of the Prophecy," *QCS* 8 (1826) 565-567.

[Wilhelm] Gesenius, "Commentary on Isaiah 17:12-14. 18:1-7," *BRCR* 8 (1836) 195-220. *(Trans. by Wm. S. Tyler)*

Anonymous, "Translation of Isaiah 17:12—18:7, with a Brief Commentary," *CRB* 2 (1837) 372-375.

Isaiah Chapters 18-20

[David N. Lord], "A Designation and Exposition of the Figures of Isaiah. Chapters XVIII., XIX., and XX.," *TLJ* 4 (1851-52) 426-446.

Isaiah Chapter 18

†Anonymous, "Critical Disquisitions, by the Bishop of Rochester," *BCQTR* 14 (1799) 130-135. *(Review) [Chap. 18]*

John Thomas, "New Translation of Isaiah, Chap. XVIII.," *ATG* 2 (1835-36) 111-114.

W. H. C., "Isaiah XVIII., Translation and Notes," *JSL, 4th Ser.,* 3 (1863) 273-296.

Alfred   Huddle,   "Isaiah   XVIII,"   *ET*   4   (1892-93)   178-179.

Hugh H. Currie, "Isaiah's Message to Ethiopia, Isaiah xviii," *ET* 4 (1892-93) 384.

Clarence True Wilson, "The United States in Prophecy: Isaiah's Vision of Our Country," *CFL, 3rd Ser.,* 40 (1934) 270-278. *[Chap. 18]*

A. Lincoln Shute, "'The United States in Prophecy:' 'Isaiah's Vision of Our Country' Isaiah 18," *CFL, 3rd Ser.,* 41 (1935) 137-146.

G. L. Young, "Prophecy and the United States," *CFL, 3rd Ser.,* 41 (1935) 146-148. *[Chap. 18]*

Isaiah 18:1-2

J. McG., "Critical Remarks on Isaiah XVIII. 1, 2," *JSL, 3rd Ser.,* 14 (1861-62) 310-324.

Isaiah 18:1

*T. K. Cheyne, "Notes on Gen. VI, Isa. XVIII, 1, and Prov. XXX. 15," *SBAP* 23 (1901) 141-144. [II.—*Isa.* xviii, 1, pp. 142-143]

Isaiah 18:4

Anonymous, "Jehovah Resting: Isaiah 18:4," *ONTS* 10 (1890) 244.

Isaiah 18:7

Anonymous, "The Land Shadowing with Wings," *BWR* 1 (1877) 326-329. *[18:7]*

Isaiah Chapter 19

T. K. Cheyne, "The Nineteenth Chapter of Isaiah," *ZAW* 13 (1893) 125-128.

*Israel Eitan, "An Egyptian Loan Word in Is. 19," *JQR, N.S.,* 15 (1924-25) 419-420. [שתתיה]

Isaiah 19:5-15

Anonymous, "The Burden of Egypt," *SPR* 11 (1858-59) 91-99. *[19:5-11, 15]*

Isaiah 19:7

T. W. Thacker, "A Note on ערות (Isa. XIX 7)," *JTS* 34 (1933) 163-165.

A. Guillaume, "A Note on Isaiah XIX. ₇, ערות על־יאור על־פי יאור וכל מזרל יאור ייבש ונדש ונדף ואיננו," *JTS, N.S.,* 14 (1963) 382-383.

Isaiah 19:10

Anonymous, "Ægyptian Breweries," *MMBR* 20 (1805) 538. *[19:10]*

M. D. Goldman, "Lexicographical Notes on Exegesis (3): A Proposed Translation of Isaiah XIX, 10," *ABR* 2 (1952) 50.

Isaiah 19:18-20

*F. Blaess, "'The Altar to the Lord' and the Great Pyramid. Isaiah 19:18-20," *AusTR* 8 (1937) 70-84, 97-103.

Isaiah 19:18

T. K. Cheyne, "Isaiah XIX. 18," *Exp, 4th Ser.,* 3 (1891) 470.

*F. C. Burkitt, "On Isaiah XIX 18: On St. Ephriam's Quotation of Matt. XXI 3," *JTS* 1 (1899-1900) 568-571.

Isaiah 19:23-25

Iain Wilson, "In That Day. *From Text to Sermon on Isaiah 19:23-25,*" *Interp* 21 (1967) 66-86.

Isaiah Chapter 20

R. E. Wolfe, "Identity of the Prophet in Isaiah 20," *JBL* 70 (1951) xiii.

Isaiah 20:6

C. F. Burney, "Old Testament Notes. II. The Interpretation of Isa. XX 6," *JTS* 13 (1911-12) 420-423.

Isaiah Chapter 21

[David N. Lord], "A Designation and Exposition of the Figures of Isaiah, Chapter XXI.," *TLJ* 5 (1852-53) 74-79.

C. Boutflower, "Isaiah XXI in the Light of Assyrian History. I.," *JTS* 14 (1912-13) 501-515.

C. Boutflower, "Isaiah XXI in the Light of Assyrian History. II.," *JTS* 15 (1913-14) 1-13.

Isaiah 21:1-10

H.*, "The Fall of Babylon predicted. Isaiah xxi. 1-10," *CongML* 10 (1827) 247-250.

Anonymous, "Translation of Isaiah XXI. 1-10, with Explanatory Remarks. *The Oracle concerning the Desert of the Sea,*" *QCS, N.S.,* 1 (1827) 623-625.

William Henry Cobb, "Isaiah 21:1-10 reexamined," *JBL* 17 (1898) 40-61.

W. Emery Barnes, "A Fresh Interpretation of Isaiah XXI 1-10," *JTS* 1 (1899-1900) 583-592.

*G. Buchanan Gray, "The strophic division of Isaiah 21:1-10 and Isaiah 11:1-8," *ZAW* 32 (1912) 190-198.

Julian [J.] Obermann, "Yahweh's Victory Over the Babylonian Pantheon. The Archetype of Is. 21 1-10," *JBL* 48 (1929) 307-328.

Julian J. Obermann, "Yahweh's Victory over The Babylonian Pantheon: The Archetype of Is. 21 1-10," *JIQ* 6 (1929-30) #2, 1-14.

R. B. Y. Scott, "Isaiah 21:1-10: The Inside of a Prophet's Mind," *JBL* 71 (1952) x-xi.

R. B. Y. Scott, "Isaiah XXI 1-10; The Inside of a Prophet's Mind," *VT* 2 (1952) 278-282.

Isaiah 21:11-12

Anonymous, "The Oracle of Dumah," *CongL* 1 (1872) 337-344 *[21:11-12]*

Armstrong Black, "'The Burden of Dumah', Isaiah XXI. 11, 12," *Exp, 5th Ser.,* 9 (1899) 48-56.

Isaiah Chapter 22

[David N. Lord], "A Designation and Exposition of the Figures of Isaiah, Chapter XXII.," *TLJ* 5 (1852-53) 233-241.

Isaiah 22:5

A. Guillaume, "A Note on the Meaning of Isaiah XXII. 5," *JTS, N.S.,* 14 (1963) 383-385.

*G. H. Box, "Some Textual Suggestions on Two Passages in Isaiah," *ET* 19 (1907-08) 563-564. *[22:5b]*

Isaiah 22:15-25

Kemper Fullerton, "A New Chapter Out of the Life of Isaiah," *AJT* 9 (1905) 621-642. *[22:15-25]*

Isaiah 22:15-20

*Eduard König, "Shebna and Eliakim," *AJT* 10 (1906) 675-686. *[22:15-18, 20ff.]*

Isaiah 22:24

Albert A. Isaacs, "The Difficulties of Scripture," *EN* 4 (1892) 362-365. *[22:24]*

Isaiah Chapter 23

[David N. Lord], "A Designation and Exposition of the Figures of Isaiah, Chapter XXIII.," *TLJ* 5 (1852-53) 461-469.

Isaiah 23:16

W. B. Stevenson, "Isaiah xxiii, 16," *GUOST* 11 (1942-44) 47.

Isaiah 23:17-18

*G. A. Simcox, "Tyre," *SBAP* 12 (1889-90) 457-459. *[23:17-18]*

Isaiah Chapters 24-27

William M. McPheeters, "The Authenticity of Isaiah XXIV.—XXVII.," *PQ* 10 (1896) 31-45.

A. F. Almer, "Studies in Isaiah, Chapters 24-27," *AQ* 10 (1931) 363-373.

*A. H. van Zyl, "Isaiah 24-27: Their Date of Origin," *OTW* 5 (1962) 44-57.

G. W. Anderson, "Isaiah xxiv-xxvii reconsidered," *VTS* 9 (1963) 118-126.

Isaiah Chapter 24

[David N. Lord], "A Designation and Exposition of the Figures of Isaiah, Chapter XXIV.," *TLJ* 6 (1853-54) 321-329.

Isaiah 24:9

*G. R. Driver, "Hebrew Notes," *JBL* 68 (1949) 57-59. *[24:9]*

Isaiah Chapters 25 and 26

[David N. Lord], "A Designation and Exposition of the Figures of Isaiah, Chapters XXV. and XXVI.," *TLJ* 6 (1853-54) 479-493.

Isaiah 25:1-5

*G. Buchanan Gray, "Critical Discussions. Isaiah 26; 25:1-5; 34:12-14," *ZAW* 31 (1911) 111-117.

*G. H. Box, "Some Textual Suggestions on Two Passages in Isaiah," *ET* 19 (1907-08) 563-564. *[25:1-5]*

Isaiah 25:7-8

Samuel Cox, "The Veil and Web of Death Destroyed by Christ. Isaiah xxv. 7, 8," *Exp, 2nd Ser.*, 4 (1882) 331-342.

Isaiah Chapter 26

*G. Buchanan Gray, "Critical Discussions. Isaiah 26; 25:1-5; 34:12-14," *ZAW* 31 (1911) 111-117.

Leona G. Running, "Syriac Variants in Isaiah 26," *AUSS* 5 (1967) 46-58.

Isaiah 26:3

Anonymous, "Comparative Translation: Isaiah 26:3. A Study in Modernizing the English Bible," *BW* 24 (1904) 283-284.

Isaiah 26:4

*Frederic Gardiner, "On the Duplication of the Tetragrammaton in Isaiah 12:2; 26:4," *ONTS* 9 (1889) 219-223.

*T. K. Cheyne, "Requests and Replies," *ET* 10 (1898-99) 444. *[26:4]*

Isaiah 26:19

Theo Laetsch, "Sermonic Study of Isaiah 26:19," *CTM* 20 (1949) 175-180.

Isaiah Chapter 27

[David N. Lord], "A Designation and Exposition of the Figures of Isaiah, Chapter XXVII.," *TLJ* 7 (1854-55) 145-151.

Isaiah 27:1

C. F. Burney, "Old Testament Notes. III. The Three Serpents of Isaiah XXVII 1," *JTS* 11 (1909-10) 443-447.

Isaiah 27:2-6

Edward Robertson, "Isaiah XXVII 2-6," *ZAW* 47 (1929) 197-206. [1. Isa. XXVII 2-6 an Arabic Poem? 2. The Hebrew Text underlying the divergent LXX of Isaiah XXVII 2-6]

Isaiah 27:8

Samuel Daiches, "An Explanation of Isaiah 27:8," *JQR, N.S.*, 6 (1915-16) 399-404.

Isaiah 27:13

F. C. Fensham, "The Preposition *B* in Isaiah 27:13," *EQ* 29 (1957) 157-158.

Isaiah Chapter 28

[David N. Lord], "A Designation and Exposition of the Figures of Isaiah, Chapter XXVIII.," *TLJ* 7 (1854-55) 306-314.

Isaiah 28:1-13

*Daniel S. Gregory, "International Lessons in Their Literary and Historical Setting," *CFL, 3rd Ser.,* 1 (1904) 665-674. *[Fourth Lesson on Isaiah 28:1-13, pp. 673-674]*

Isaiah 28:7-13

S. Cox., "Precept upon Precept. Isaiah xxviii. 7-13," *Exp, 1st Ser.,* 1 (1875) 98-104.

Isaiah 28:9-13

*William W. Hallo, "Isaiah 28:9-13 and the Ugaritic Abecedaries," *JBL* 77 (1958) 324-338.

Isaiah 28:10

*James A. Montgomery, "Notes on the Old Testament," *JBL* 31 (1912) 140-146. [4. The Barbarous Syllables in Isa. 28:10, pp. 141-142]

Isaiah 28:15

*James A. Montgomery, "Notes on the Old Testament," *JBL* 31 (1912) 140-146. [הזה, Isa. 28:15, p. 142]

Isaiah 28:16

Anonymous, "The Great Text Commentary. The Great Texts of Isaiah," *ET* 23 (1911-12) 203-208. *[28:16]*

Kemper Fullerton, "The Stone of the Foundation," *AJSL* 37 (1920-21) 1-50. *[28:16]*

*Kleinere Beitrage, "The Jewel of Discernment (A study of stone symbolism)," *BZ* 11 (1967) 109-116. *[28:16]*

Isaiah 28:23-29

S. Cox, "The Parable of the Ploughman and the Thresher. Isaiah xxviii. 23-29," *Exp, 1st Ser.,* 1 (1875) 89-98.

P. Peters, "The Parable of the Plowman. An Exegetical and Homiletical Study of Isaiah 28, 23-29," *WLQ* 45 (1948) 38-52.

Walter R. Roehrs, "Sermon Study on Isaiah 28:23-29. A Parable of God's Husbandry," *CTM* 20 (1949) 352-358.

L. J. Liebreich, "The Parable Taken from the Farmer's Labors in Isaiah XXVIII, 23-29," *Tarbiz* 24 (1954-55) #2, I-II.

Isaiah 28:25

*S. C. Thexton, "A Note on Isaiah XXVIII 25 and 28," *VT* 2 (1952) 81-83.

Isaiah 28:28

*S. C. Thexton, "A Note on Isaiah XXVIII 25 and 28," *VT* 2 (1952) 81-83.

Isaiah Chapter 29

[David N. Lord], "A Designation and Exposition of the Figures of Isaiah, Chapter XXIX.," *TLJ* 7 (1854-55) 433-446.

Isaiah 29:4

*Claude R. Conder, "Notes on New Discoveries," *PEFQS* 41 (1909) 266-275. [The Familiar Spirit (Lev. 20:6; 1 Sam. 28:3; Isa. 29:4), p. 270]

Isaiah 29:16

Theodore H. Robinson, "Note on the Text of Isaiah 29:16," *ZAW* 49 (1931) 322-323.

Isaiah Chapters 30 and 31

[David N. Lord], "A Designation and Exposition of the Figures of Isaiah, Chapters XXX. and XXXI.," *TLJ* 7 (1854-55) 625-638.

Isaiah 30:1-8

W. B. Stevenson, "Isaiah 30. 1-8," *GUOST* 6 (1929-33) 68-69.

Isaiah 30:1

M[itchell] Dahood, "Accusative *'ēṣāh,* 'Wood,' in Isaiah 30, 1b," *B* 50 (1969) 57-58.

Isaiah 30:7

Ross G. Murison, "Rahab. רַהַב הֵם שָׁבֶת," *ET* 16 (1904-05) 190. *[30:7]*

Isaiah 30:15

Anonymous, "The Great Text Commentary. The Great Texts of Isaiah," *ET* 23 (1911-12) 300-305. *[30:15]*

Isaiah 30:26

*R. Gordis, "Midrash in the Prophets," *JBL* 49 (1930) 417-422. *[30:26]*

Isaiah 30:27-33

Alfred Guillaume, "Isaiah's Oracle Against Assyria (Isaiah 30, 27-33), in the Light of Archæology," *BSOAS* 17 (1955) 413-415.

Isaiah Chapters 32 and 33

[David N. Lord], "A Designation and Exposition of the Figures of Isaiah, Chapters XXXII. and XXXIII.," *TLJ* 8 (1855-56) 149-162.

Isaiah Chapter 32

*E. C. Selwyn, "An Oracle of the Lord in Isaiah xxxii," *Exp, 8th Ser.,* 5 (1913) 167-177.

Isaiah 32:5

*"Philo.", "Notes on Scripture, Excerpts, Short Comments," *TLJ* 8 (1855-56) 200-220. *[32:5, p. 204]*

Isaiah 32:11

Cyrus H. Gordon, "Methods of Biblical Archaeology: An Illustration," *CQ* 27 (1950) 309-312. *[32:11]*

Isaiah 32:20

T. S. Williams, "'Blessed Are Ye That Sow Beside All Waters,' Isa. XXXII. 20," *ET* 4 (1892-93) 568.

Isaiah 33:2

Augustus Poynder, "'Be Thou Their Arm Every Morning,' Isa. xxxiii. 2," *ET* 13 (1901-02) 94.

Isaiah 33:7

Siegfried J. Schwantes, "A Historical Approach to the *'r'lm* of Is 33:7," *AUSS* 3 (1965) 158-166.

Isaiah 33:17

Howard Crosby, "Exposition of xxxiii: 17," *HR* 15 (1888) 257-258.

Isaiah Chapters 34 and 35

*H. Graetz, "Isaiah XXXIV and XXXV, *JQR* 4 (1891-92) 1-8.

T. K. Cheyne, "Note on Prof. Grätz's Article on Isaiah XXXIV., XXXV," *JQR* 4 (1891-92) 332.

Isaiah Chapter 34

[David N. Lord], "A Designation and Exposition of the Figures of Isaiah, Chapter XXXIV.," *TLJ* 8 (1855-56) 512-520.

Anonymous, "Answers to Correspondents. II. The Desolation of Edom," *TLJ* 12 (1859-60) 685-691. *[Chap. 34]*

*James Muilenburg, "Literary Character of Isaiah 34," *JBL* 59 (1940) vii, 339-365.

*Marvin Pope, "Isaiah 34 in Relation to Isaiah 35, 40-66," *JBL* 70 (1951) xiii.

*Marvin Pope, "Isaiah 34 in Relation to Isaiah 35, 40-66," *JBL* 71 (1952) 235-243.

Edward J. Young, "Isaiah 34 and Its Position in the Prophecy," *WTJ* 27 (1964-65) 93-114.

*Julian Morgenstern, "Further Light from the Book of Isaiah upon the Catastrophe of 485 B.C.," *HUCA* 37 (1966) 1-28. [Isa. 34, pp. 4-12]

Isaiah 34:5

Lootfy Levonian, "Isaiah XXXIV. 5," *ET* 24 (1912-13) 45-46.

Isaiah 34:12-14

*G. Buchanan Gray, "Critical Discussions. Isaiah 26; 25:1-5; 34:12-14," *ZAW* 31 (1911) 111-127.

Isaiah 34:14

*G. R. Driver, "Lilith. *Heb.* לילית *'goat-sucker, night-jar'* (Is. xxxiv, 14)," *PEQ* 91 (1959) 55-58.

Isaiah 34:15

Fritz Hommel, "Isaiah XXXIV. 15," *ET* 12 (1900-01) 336.

Isaiah Chapter 35

[David N. Lord], "A Designation and Exposition of the Figures of Isaiah, Chapter XXXV.," *TLJ* 9 (1856-57) 333-340.

*R. B. Y. Scott, "The Relation of Isaiah, Chapter 35, to Deutero-Isaiah," *AJSL* 52 (1935-36) 178-191.

*A. T. Olmstead, "II Isaiah and Isaiah, Chapter 35," *AJSL* 53 (1936-37) 251-253.

*Marvin Pope, "Isaiah 34 in Relation to Isaiah 35, 40-66," *JBL* 70 (1951) xiii.

*Marvin Pope, "Isaiah 34 in Relation to Isaiah 35, 40-66," *JBL* 71 (1952) 235-243.

Isaiah 35:3-6

*C. P. Coffin, "An Old Testament Prophecy and Some New Testament Miracle Stories," *JAAR* 11 (1943) 162-166. *[35:3-6]*

Isaiah 35:4

*P. Wernberg-Møller, "Two Difficult Passages in the Old Testament," *ZAW* 69 (1957) 69-73. [(b) ISA. 35:4, pp. 71-73]

Isaiah 35:7

Melville Scott, "Isaiah XXXV. 7," *ET* 37 (1925-26) 236.

Isaiah 35:8

*( ) Ozer, "Remarks on Isaiah xxxv. 8, and Habakkuk ii. 2," *CongML* 14 (1831) 479-481.

*E. B. Pollard, "Other Traditional Misinterpretations," *CQ* 4 (1927) 204-206. *[35:8]*

Isaiah Chapters 36-39

A. H. Sayce, "Critical Examination of Isaiah xxxvi.—xxxix. on the Basis of Recent Assyrian Discoveries," *TRL* 10 (1873) 15-31.

*Marshall S. Hurwitz, "The Septuagint of Isaiah 36-39 in Relation to That of 1-35, 40-66," *HUCA* 28 (1957) 75-83.

Isaiah 36:1-37:7

*Siegfried H. Horn, "Did Sennacherib Campaign Once or Twice Against Hezekiah?" *AUSS* 4 (1966) 1-28. *[36:1-37:7]*

Isaiah 36:3

*Eduard König, "Shebna and Eliakim," *AJT* 10 (1906) 675-686. *[36:3]*

Isaiah 36:11

*C. F. Burney, "Old Testament Notes. I. 'The Jews' Language': 2 Kings XVIII 26 = Isa. XXXVI 11," *JTS* 13 (1911-12) 417-20.

Isaiah 36:19

*Fritz Hommel, "Hena' and 'Awwâ," *ET* 9 (1897-98) 330-331. *[36:19]*

Isaiah Chapter 37

*Frank E. Allen, "The Destruction of Sennacherib's Army: Was it a Miracle?" *CFL, 3rd Ser.,* 40 (1934) 205-208. *[Chap. 37]*

Isaiah 37:18

*S. Talmon, "A Case of Faulty Harmonization," *VT* 5 (1955) 206-208. *[Isa. 37:18 ✗ 2 Kings 19:17]*

Isaiah 37:22-35

*William Popper, "Parallelism in Isaiah. Chapters 1-35 and 37.22-35. A Reconstructed Text (Hebrew)," *UCPSP* 1 (1907-23) #5, 1-116.

Isaiah 37:22-29

*K. Budde, "The Poem in 2 Kings XIX 21-28 (Isaiah XXXVII 22-29)," *JTS* 35 (1934) 307-313.

Isaiah 37:22

*H. F. B. Compston, "The Parsing of *Bāzāh* in 2 Kings XIX 21 = Isaiah XXXVII 22," *JTS* 1909-10) 545-546.

Isaiah 37:25

P. J. Calderone, "The Rivers of 'Maṣor'," *B* 42 (1961) 423-432. *[37:25]*

Isaiah 37:27

*H.S.Gehman,"Note on II Kings19:25 and Isaiah 37:27,"*JBL* 64(1945) iv-v.

Isaiah 37:31

James Moffatt, "Opera Foris. Materials for the Preacher," *Exp, 7th Ser.,* 5 (1908) 383-384. *[37:31]*

*S. Iwry, "והנמצא—A Striking Variant Reading in 1QIs^a," *Text* 5 (1966) 34-43. *[37:31]*

Isaiah 37:36-38

*C. H. W. Johns, "The Biblical Account of Sennacherib's Murder," *SBAP* 21 (1899) 174-175. *[37:36-38]*

Isaiah 37:36

*W. Arthur Cornaby, "2 Kings xix. 35 (Is. xxxvii. 36) and Herodotus, ii. 141," *ET* 25 (1913-14) 379-380.

Isaiah 37:13

*Fritz Hommel, "Hena' and 'Awwâ," *ET* 9 (1897-98) 330-331. *[36:19]*

Isaiah Chapter 38

*†G. B., "P.S.," *JSL, 3rd Ser.,* 4 (1856-57) 161-164. *[The Dial of Ahaz - Isa. 38]*

Isaiah 38:1-8

*Michael J. Gruenthaner, "Two Sun Miracles of the Old Testament," *CBQ* 10 (1948) 217-290. [II. The Regression of the Shadow, *Textual Criticism, a) Kings, b) Isaias, Nature of the Miracle, Explanation of the Miracle,* pp. 287-290] *[38:1-8]*

Isaiah 38:7-8

*K. Fullerton, "The Original Text of 2 Kings 20:7-11 = Isaiah 38:7, 8, 21f.," *JBL* 44 (1925) 44-62.

*Y. Yadin, "'The Dial of Ahaz'," *EI* 5 (1958) 88*-89*. *[38:7-8]*

Isaiah 38:8

R. Balgarnie, "The Shadow Reversed on the Sun-Dial of Ahaz," *HR* 29 (1895) 170-173. *[38:8]*

John Binney, "The Colophon at Isa. 38:8 in Peshitta Version," *JBL* 14 (1895) 92-94.

Anonymous, "The Sun Dial of Ahaz," *AT* 2 (1957-58) #1, 14-15.

Isaiah 38:9-22

J. R., "Critical Remarks on the Prayer of Hezekiah. Isaiah, chap. XXXVIII. 9-22," *JSL, 2nd Ser.,* 5 (1853-54) 424-429.

Isaiah 38:9-20

P. A. H. de Boer, "Notes on Text and Meaning of Isaiah XXXVIII 9-20," *OTS* 9 (1951) 170-186.

Isaiah 38:15-16

Samuel Daiches, "Isaiah, XXXVIII. 15, 16," *ET* 25 (1913-14) 364.

Isaiah 38:21-22

*Michael J. Gruenthaner, "Two Sun Miracles of the Old Testament," *CBQ* 10 (1948) 271-290. [II. The Regression of the Shadow, *Textual Criticism, a) Kings, b) Isaias, Nature of the Miracle, Explanation of the Miracle,* pp. 287-290] *[38:21. 22]*

Isaiah 38:21ff.

*K. Fullerton, "The Original Text of 2 Kings 20:7-11 = Isaiah 38:7, 8, 21f.," *JBL* 44 (1925) 44-62.

§608   *3.5.3.2.1.2 Exegetical Studies on Deutero-Isaiah*

A. A. Bevan, "Notes on certain passages in Deutero-Isaiah," *JP* 17 (1888) 125-127. [40:19; 44:11; 45:14; 52:2]

David Yellin, "The Use of Ellipsis in 'Second Isaiah'," *JPOS* 1 (1920-21) 132-137. [40:26; 44:7; 43:13; 42:10; 49:17; 49:19; 41:2; 51:13; 65:15; 65:5; 41:4; 44:12; 40:15]

G. R. Driver, "Linguistic and Textual Problems: Isaiah XL—LXVI," *JTS* 36 (1935) 396-406. [40:20; 41:11; 41:14; 45:9; 46:1; 46:6; 46:8; 47:11; 47:15; 48:10; 49:7; 51:4-5; 51:6; 51:14; 52:5; 53:8; 53:10; 55:1; 55:4; 58:12; 63:18; 65:20]

G. R. Driver, "Linguistic and Textual Problems: Isaiah XL—LXVI," *JTS* 38 (1937) 48-50.[42:20; 53:2; 53:3; 58:7; 64:6] *[This is an untitled article]*

*Marvin Pope, "Isaiah 34 in Relation to Isaiah 35, 40-66," *JBL* 70 (1951) xiii.

*Marvin Pope, "Isaiah 34 in Relation to Isaiah 35, 40-66," *JBL* 71 (1952) 235-243.

C. F. Whitley, "Textual Notes on Deutero-Isaiah," *VT* 11 (1961) 457-461. [43:28; 45:9; 45:11b; 46:1; 53:8-9a]

Isaiah Chapters 40-66

Wm. Henry Cobb, "The Language of Isaiah XL.—LXVI.," *BS* 38 (1881) 658-686; 39 (1882) 104-132.

A. B. Davidson, "The Book of Isaiah: Chapters xl.-lxvi," *Exp, 2nd Ser.,* 6 (1883) 81-98.

A. B. Davidson, *"The Book of Isaiah:* Chapters XL. - LXVI. II. The Prologue," *Exp, 2nd Ser.,* 6 (1883) 186-203.

A. B. Davidson, *"The Book of Isaiah:* Chapters XL. - LXVI," *Exp, 2nd Ser.,* 7 (1884) 81-103, 251-267. [3. Jehovah, God of Israel, the Incomparable; 4. Jehovah, the First and the Last]

A. B. Davidson, *"The Book of Isaiah:* Chapters XL. - LXVI," *Exp, 2nd Ser.,* 8 (1884) 250-269, 350-369, 430-451. [5. Israel the Servant of the Lord; 6. The Servant of the Lord; 7. The Work of the Servant of the Lord]

William Henry Cobb, "The Revised Version of Isaiah XL.—LXVI.," *BS* 43 (1886) 303-317.

A. C. Courtice, "'The servant of Jehovah' (Isaiah XL- LXVI)," *CMR* 2 (1890) 7-23, 147-154.

L. W. Batten, "The Historical Movement Traceable in Isaiah XL- LXVI," *AR* 16 (1891) 178-188.

T. K. Cheyne, "Brevia. Mr. G. A. Smith's *Exposition of Isaiah xl.-lxvi,*" *Exp, 4th Ser.,* 3 (1891) 150-160. *(Review)*

W. H. Marquess, "Outline Study of Isaiah XL-LXVI," *CFL, N.S.,* 1 (1900) 107-112.

*Alois Barta, "Syntax of the Sentences in Isaiah 40-66," *AJSL* 17 (1900-01) 22-46.

A. Van Hoonacker, "The Servant of the Lord in Isaiah XLff.," *Exp, 8th Ser.,* 11 (1916) 183-210.

Theodore H. Robinson, "Isaiah XL.—LXVI.: A Fresh Discussion," *ET* 45 (1933-34) 425-426. *(Review)*

*Ethan Mengers, "The Creation Doctrine of Isaiah 40-66," *WSQ* 20 (1956-57) #3, 2-14.

*Marshall S. Hurwitz, "The Septuagint of Isaiah 36-39 in Relation to That of 1-35, 40-66," *HUCA* 28 (1957) 75-83.

B. O. Banwell, "A Suggested Analysis of Isaiah XL. - LXVI.," *ET* 76 (1964-65) 166.

Norman H. Snaith, "Isaiah 40-66. A study of the teaching of the Second Isaiah and its consequences," *VTS* 14 (1967) 135-264. *[Reprinted with Additions and Corrections, 1977]*

*Clyde J. Hurst, "Guidelines for Interpreting Old Testament Prophecy Applied to Isaiah 40-66," *SWJT, N.S.,* 11 (1968-69) #1, 29-44.

F. B. Huey Jr., "Great Themes in Isaiah 40-66," *SWJT, N.S.,* 11 (1968-69) #1, 45-58.

Isaiah Chapters 40-60

*A. Schoors, "The Rîb-Pattern in Isaiah XL-LX," *BTPT* 30 (1969) 25-38.

Isaiah Chapters 40-55

Karl Budde, "The So-called 'Ebed-Yahweh Songs' and the Meaning of the Term 'Servant of Yahweh' in Isaiah Chaps. 40-55," *AJT* 3 (1899) 499-540.

T. H. Weir, "A New Theory of 'the Servant of Jehovah' in Isaiah 40-55," *WR* 169 (1908) 309-314.

*W. B. Stevenson, "The Second Person Singular and Second Person Plural of Address in Isaiah 40-55, *Preface,*" *GUOST* 3 (1907-12) 31-32.

*S. F. Hunter, "The Second Person Singular and Second Person Plural of Address in Isaiah 40-55," *GUOST* 3 (1907-12) 32-36.

H. G. Mitchell, "The Servant of Yahweh in Isa. 40-55," *JBL* 38 (1919) 113-128.

*Robert H. Pfeiffer, "The Dual Origin of Hebrew Monotheism," *JBL* 46 (1927) 193-206. [Critical Note: The priority of Job over Is. 40-55," pp. 202-205]

Otto Eissfeldt, "The Ebed-Jahwe in Isaiah XL. - LV. in the Light of the Israelite Conceptions of the Community and the Individual, the Ideal and the Real," *ET* 44 (1932-33) 261-268.

L. G. Rignell, "A study of Isaiah ch. 40-55," *AULLUÅ, N.S.,* 52 (1956) #5, 1-93.

George A. F. Knight, "The Word Becoming Flesh (The Relevance of Isaiah 40-55)," *McQ* 15 (1961-62) #4, 3-9, 29.

Robert Sumner Jackson, "The Prophetic Vision. *The Nature of the Utterance in Isaiah 40-55,*" *Interp* 16 (1962) 65-75.

*B. J. van der Merwe, "Echoes from the teaching of Hosea in Isaiah 40-55," *OTW* 7&8 (1964-65) 90-99.

Jean McGowan, "Reflections on Isaiah 40—55: The Prophetic Minority within the Unreformed Community," *BibT* #30 (1967) 2121-2126.

*B. J. van der Merwe, "'Actualizing Eschatology' in Isaiah 40-55," *TEP* 1 (1968) 16-18.

Prescott Williams, "The Poems About Incomparable Yahweh's Servant in Isaiah 40-55," *SWJT, N.S.,* 11 (1968-69) #1, 73-88.

Prescott H. Williams Jr., "The future tense of God is Yahweh: A study of Isaiah 40-55," *ASBFE* 84 (April, 1969) #7, 17-28.

D. E. Hollenberg, "Nationalism and 'The Nations' in Isaiah XL-LV," *VT* 19 (1969) 23-36.

Isaiah Chapters 40-48

Owen H. Gates, "Fulfilment of Prediction in Isaiah Chaps. 40-48," *AJT* 3 (1899) 67-83.

Isaiah 40:15

Alfred Huddle, "'The Isles' Isaiah xl. 15," *ET* 5 (1893-94) 523.

Isaiah 40:18-20

Paul Haupt, "*Měsukkân,* Acacia Nilotica," *JBL* 36 (1917) 145. *[40:18-20]*

Paul Trudinger, "'To whom then will you liken God?' (A Note on the Interpretation of Isaiah XL 18-20)," *VT* 17 (1967) 220-225.

Isaiah 40:20

A. R. Millard and I. R. Snook, "Isaiah 40:20, Towards a Solution," *TB* #14 (1964) 12-13.

Isaiah 40:25

Aug. Pieper, "The Holy One," *JTLC* 3 (1963) #2, 18-20 *[40:25]*

Isaiah 40:26

*Patrick D. Miller Jr., "The Divine Council and the Prophetic Call to War," *VT* 18 (1968) 100-107. [Isa. 40:26 and 45:12, pp. 105-106]

Isaiah 40:27-31

Andrew R. Osborn, "Isaiah 40:27-31," *BR* 16 (1931) 411-414.

Isaiah 40:31

Abel H. Huizinga, "A Practical Exegesis of Isaiah XL. 31," *PRR* 5 (1894) 89-94.

Isaiah 40:66

*D. A. Murray, "The Authorship of Isaiah xl. 66," *HR* 27 (1894) 168-176.

Isaiah Chapter 41

[David N. Lord], "A Designation and Exposition of the Figures of Isaiah, Chap. XLI.," *TLJ* 9 (1856-57) 687-698.

Wm. H. Cobb, "A New Translation of Isaiah XLI," *ONTS* 4 (1884-85) 133-134.

Charles C. Torrey, "Isaiah 41," *HTR* 44 (1951) 121-136.

Isaiah 41:2-3

*Bruce Malina, "Matthew 2 and Is 41, 2-3: a possible relationship?" *SBFLA* 17 (1967) 290-302.

Isaiah 41:5-7

W. E[mery] Barnes, "A Misunderstood Passage (Isaiah XLI 5-7)," *JTS* 4 (1902-03) 266-269.

S. R. Driver, "Note on Isaiah XLI 5-7," *JTS* 4 (1902-03) 434-435.

A. F. Kirkpatrick, "Note on Isaiah XLI 5-7," *JTS* 4 (1902-03) 435.

Isaiah 41:8-20

*W. B. Stevenson, "The Interpretation of Isaiah xli. 8-20 and li. 1-8," *Exp, 8th Ser.,* 6 (1913) 209-221.

Isaiah 41:14-16

E. John Hamlin, "The Meaning of 'Mountains and Hills' in Isa. 41:14-16," *JNES* 13 (1954) 185-190.

Isaiah 41:14

F. Jarratt, "'Thou Worm Jacob,' Isaiah xli. 14," *ET* 5 (1893-94) 478-479.

Isaiah 41:18-19

S. A. Hirsch, "Isaiah XLI 18, 19," *JQR* 14 (1901-02) 134-135.

Isaiah 41:18

Owen C. Whitehouse, "On Isaiah XLI. 18," *Exp, 3rd Ser.,* 4 (1886) 479-480.

Isaiah 41:27

Neil J. McEleney, "The Translation of Isaias 41, 27," *CBQ* 19 (1957) 441-443.

C. F. Whitley, "A Note on Isa. XLI. 27," *JSS* 2 (1957) 327-328.

D. Winton Thomas, "A Note on the Hebrew Text of Isaiah XLI. 27," *JTS, N.S.,* 18 (1967) 127-128.

Isaiah Chapter 42

[David N. Lord], "A Designation and Exposition of the Figures of Isaiah, Chap. XLII.," *TLJ* 10 (1857-58) 501-514.

Isaiah 42:1-9

Morgan Phillips, "Interpreting the Scriptures for Advent and Christmas. First Sunday after Christmas Day. Isaiah 42:1-9," *JMTSO* 4 (1965-66) #1, 26-28.

Isaiah 42:1-7

W. E[mery] Barnes, "Cyrus the 'Servant of Jehovah,' Isa. xlii 1-4(7)," *JTS* 32 (1930-31) 32-39.

Isaiah 42:1-4

Ralph Marcus, "The 'Plain Meaning' of Isaiah 42:1-4," *HTR* 30 (1937) 249-259.

Isaiah 42:2-4

Ralph Marcus, "The 'Plain Meaning' of Isaiah 42 2-4," *JBL* 56 (1937) x.

Isaiah 42:1

T. K., "Hebrew Idiom," *CongML* 5 (1822) 694. *[42:1]*

R. B. Y. Scott, "My Servant, my Chosen (Isaiah 42:1)," *JBL* 53 (1934) iii.

Isaiah 42:2

Eb. Nestle, "Matthew XII. 19—Isaiah XLII. 2," *ET* 20 (1908-09) 92-93, 189.

W. C. Allen, "Matthew XII. 19—Isaiah XLII. 2," *ET* 20 (1908-09) 140-141.

Isaiah 42:3-4

*J. C. K., "The Smoking Flax," *JSL, 3rd Ser.,* 6 (1857-58) 438-441. *[42:3, 4]*

Isaiah 42:10-17

*H. L. Ginsberg, "A Strand in the Cord of Hebraic Hymnody," *EI* 9 (1969) 45-50. [2nd Isaiah, (42-:10-17), pp. 47-48] *[Non-Hebrew Section]*

Isaiah 42:13

David Noel Freedman, "Isaiah 42, 13," *CBQ* 30 (1968) 225-226.

Isaiah 42:21

*John Wesley Rice, "Notes. Notes on the Septuagint Text of II Sam. 7:22 and Isa. 42:21," *AJP* 22 (1901) 318-320.

Isaiah Chapter 43

[David N. Lord], "A Designation and Exposition of the Figures of Isaiah, Chap. XLIII.," *TLJ* 10 (1857-58) 661-670.

Isaiah 43:13

*Robert A. Aytoun, "'No One Shall Snatch Them Out of My Hand'," *ET* 31 (1919-20) 475-476. *[Isaiah 43:13 //John 10:28-30]*

Isaiah 43:14

W. E[mery] Barnes, "The Masoretic Reading of Isaiah XLIII 14," *JTS* 29 (1927-28) 252-255.

Alfred Guillaume, "Isaiah XLIII. 14, לְמַעַנְכֶם שִׁלַּחְתִּי בָבֶלָה וְהוֹרַדְתִּי כֻלָּם וְכַשְׂדִּים בָּאֳנִיּוֹת רִנָּתָם,בְּרִיחִים" *JTS* 49 (1948) 54-55.

Isaiah 43:19

*John C. Trever, "Isaiah 43:19 according to the First Isaiah Scroll (DSIa)," *BASOR* #121 (1951) 13-16.

*John C. Trever, "Some Corrections Regarding Isaiah 43:19 in the Isaiah Scroll," *BASOR* #126 (1952) 26-27.

Isaiah 43:22-28

*A. Schoors, "The Rîb-Pattern in Isaiah XL-LX," *BTPT* 30 (1969) 25-38. [1. Is. XLIII, 22-28, pp. 26-29]

Isaiah 43:22-25

Melville Scott, "Isaiah xliii. 22-25," *ET* 37 (1925-26) 270-271.

Isaiah Chapters 44 and 45

[David N. Lord], "A Designation and Exposition of the Figures of Isaiah, Chapters XLIV. and XLV.," *TLJ* 12 (1859-60) 153-176.

Isaiah 44:4

J. M. Allegro, "The Meaning of בין in Isaiah XLIV, 4," *ZAW* 61 (1949) 154-156.

Isaiah 44:5

*Alfred Guillaume, "Isaiah XLIV. 5, in the Light of the Elephantine Papyri," *ET* 32 (1920-21) 377-378.

Isaiah 44:12-14

Joseph Strauss, "Isaiah XLIV. 12, 13, 14, etc.," *ET* 9 (1897-98) 425-426.

Isaiah 44:12-13

Ed. König, "Isaiah XLIV. 12, 13," *ET* 9 (1897-98) 563-566.

Isaiah 44:14

*J. Dyneley Prince, "Notes on Psa. 2:11, 12, and on ארזֶ, Isa. 44:14," *JBL* 19 (1900) 1-4.

Isaiah 44:28-45:1-13

Howard Crosby, "Dr. Cheyne on Isaiah," *ONTS* 7 (1887-88) 186. *[44:28-45:1-13]*

Isaiah 45:7

*L[awrence H.] Mills, "The Dualism of Isaiah lxv. 7: Was it Zoroastrian?" *IAQR, 3rd Ser.,* 20 (1906) 286-294.

Isaiah 45:9

Charles L. Carhart, "The Potsherd in Isaiah 45:9," *BW* 13 (1899) 252-254.

Alger F. Johns, "A Note on Isaiah 45:9," *AUSS* 1 (1963) 62-64.

Isaiah 45:11

*"Philo.", "Notes on Scripture, Excerpts, Short Comments," *TLJ* 8 (1855-56) 200-220. *[45:11, pp. 205-208]*

W. F. Lofthouse, "Old Texts in Modern Translations. Isaiah lxv. 11 (Moffatt)," *ET* 69 (1937-38) 102-105.

Isaiah 45:12

C. H. W. Johns, "Isaiah XLV. 12, Meni, 'That Number'," *ET* 10 (1898-99) 423.

*Patrick D. Miller Jr., "The Divine Council and the Prophetic Call to War," *VT* 18 (1968) 100-107. [Isa. 40:26 and 45:12, pp. 105-106]

Isaiah 45:15

Theodor Herzl Gaster, "The Hidden God," *AEE* 17 (1932) 68. *[45:15]*

Isaiah 45:18

*"Philo.", "Notes on Scripture, Excerpts, Short Comments," *TLJ* 8 (1855-56) 200-220. *[45:18, pp. 204-205]*

Isaiah Chapters 46-48

[David N. Lord], "A Designation and Exposition of the Figures of Isaiah, Chapters XLVI., XLVII., and XLVIII.," *TLJ* 12 (1859-60) 318-352.

Isaiah 46:4

Jacob Rabinowitz, "A Note on Isaiah 46:4," *JBL* 73 (1954) 237.

Isaiah Chapter 47

*D. H. Muller, "Strophic Forms in Isaiah XLVII," *JQR* 12 (1899-1900) 377-379.

Isaiah 47:13

Fritz Hommel, "The Word הברו in Isaiah XLVII. 13," *ET* 12 (1900-01) 239.

Isaiah 48:7

*J. van Zijl, "Is. XLVIII 7 according to the Targum Br. Mus. Or. Ms 2211," *VT* 18 (1968) 560-561.

Isaiah 48:8

W. H. Cobb, "On the Textual Crux in Isa. 48:8," *JBL* 39 (1920) 168-170.

Isaiah Chapters 49-55

Julian Morgenstern, "Isaiah 49-55," *HUCA* 35 (1964) 1-35.

Isaiah Chapters 49-51

[David N. Lord], "A Designation and Exposition of the Figures of Isaiah, Chapters XLIX., L., and LI.," *TLJ* 12 (1859-60) 438-463.

Isaiah 49:1-6

J. A. Bewer, "Two Notes on Isaiah 49:1-6," *JBL* 54 (1935) iii.

*Charles H. Giblin, "A Note on the Composition of Isaias 49,1-6(9a)," *CBQ* 21 (1959) 207-212.

Isaiah 49:3

Anonymous, "Isaiah 49:3," *R&E* 9 (1912) 400.

Harry M. Orlinsky, "'Israel' in Isa. XLIX, 3: A Problem in the Methodology of Textual Criticism," *EI* 8 (1967) 42*-45*.

Isaiah 49:6

*Harry M. Orlinsky, "'A Light of the Nations': A Problem in Biblical Theology," *JQR, 75th* (1967) 409-428. *[49:6]*

Isaiah 49:8-13

Edward C. Meyer and Simon J. De Vries, "Preparation for Biblical Preaching. II," *JMTSO* 6 (1967-68) #1, 30-40, *[49:8-13]*

Isaiah 49:9

*Charles H. Giblin, "A Note on the Composition of Isaias 49,1-6(9a)," *CBQ* 21 (1959) 207-212.

D. Winton Thomas, "A Note on דְּרָכִים in Isaiah XLIX. 9b," *JTS, N.S.,* 19 (1968) 203-204.

Isaiah 49:12

*T[errien] de Lacouperie, "The Sinim of Isaiah, not the Chinese," *BOR* 1 (1886-87) 45-48. *[49:12]*

*C[laude] R. Conder, "Notes on Biblical Geography. IV. *Sinim,*" *PEFQS* 37 (1905) 74. *[49:12]*

Edward J. Kissane, "'The Land of Sinim' (Is. 49:12)," *ITQ* 21 (1954) 63-64.

Isaiah 49:16-17

I. Blythin, "A Note on Isaiah XLIX 16-17," *VT* 17 (1966) 229-230.

Isaiah 49:16

Hayyim Rosenrauch, "Note on Is. 49:16," *JQR, N.S.,*36 (1945-46) 81.

Isaiah 49:17

*D. Flusser, "The Text of Isa. xlix, 17 in the DSS," *Text* 2 (1962) 140-142.

Isaiah 49:19

*C. J. Ball, "Note on the Wood called *Ukarina,*" *SBAP* 11 (1888-89) 143-144. *[49:19]*

Isaiah Chapters 50-66

S. Lawrence Brown, "Introduction to the Study of Isaiah 50-66," *ICMM* 7 (1910-11) 396-403.

Isaiah Chapter 50

Kyle   M.   Yates,   "Isaiah   50,"   *CRP*   2   (1933)   291-297.

Kyle M. Yates, "An Exposition of Isaiah L," *R&E* 31 (1934) 372-378.

Isaiah 50:4-10

Theo. Laetsch, "Sermonic Study on Is. 50:4-10," *CTM* 20 (1949) 100-108.

Isaiah 50:4

H. Yalon, "לדעת לעות את יעף דבר" (Is. 50, 4)," *Lěš,* 30 (1965-66)#4, n.p.n.

Isaiah Chapters 51-63

*H. L. Ginsberg, "The Arm of YHWH in Isaiah 51-63 and the Text of Isa. 53:10-11," *JBL* 77 (1958) 152-156.

Isaiah Chapters 51-53

*J. L. Helberg, "Nahum—Jonah—Lamentations—Isaiah 51-53 (A Possibility for Establishing a Connection)," *OTW* 12 (1969) 46-55.

Isaiah 51:1-11

F. Holmgren, "Chiastsic structure in Isaiah LI 1-11," *VT* 19 (1969) 196-201.

Isaiah 51:1-8

*W. B. Stevenson, "The Interpretation of Isaiah xli. 8-20 and li. 1-8," *Exp, 8th Ser.,* 6 (1913) 209-221.

Isaiah 51:2

*Ed. König, "'A Fateful Dogma'," *ET* 16 (1904-05) 332-334. *[51:2]*

Isaiah 51:6

*Joseph Reider, "Contributions to the Hebrew lexicon," *RDSO* 17 (1937-38) 103-110. [1. Isa. 51:6, pp. 103-104]

Isaiah 51:6

*Peter Katz, "Two Kindred Corruptions in the Septuagint," *VT* 1 (1951) 261-266. [II. Isa. 51:6, pp. 262-265]

Isaiah 51:9-11

William C. Martin, "An Exegesis of Isaiah 51:9-11," *RestQ* 9 (1966) 151-159.

Isaiah 51:13

Julian Morgenstern, "'The Oppressor' of Isa. 51:13—Who Was He?" *JBL* 81 (1962) 25-34.

Isaiah 51:18

C[lifford] A. W[ilson], "Your Questions Answered. Jerusalem as a Drunken Parent?" *BH* 3 (1967) #4, 20-21. *[51:18]*

Isaiah Chapters 52-53

*E. C. Wines, "The Doctrine of Atonement as taught in Isaiah LII. LIII.," *TLJ* 6 (1853-54) 404-417.

Wolcott Calkins, "The Great Messianic Prophecy," *PQPR* 6 (1877) 421-438. *[Chaps. 52 and 53]*

[David N. Lord], "A Designation and Exposition of the Figures of Isaiah, Chapters LII. and LIII.," *TLJ* 12 (1859-60) 663-677.

C. H. H. Wright, "The Pre-Christian Jewish Interpretation of Isaiah LII., LIII," *Exp, 3rd Ser.,* 7 (1888) 364-377, 401-420.

W. Emery Barnes, "The Servant of Jehovah (Isaiah lii-liii)," *ICMM* 13 (1916-17) 115-127.

Isaiah 52:13-Chapter 53

[Ernst Wilhelm] Hengstenberg, "Interpretation of Isaiah LII. 13—LIII.," *BRCR* 2 (1832) 310-367, 499-540. *(Trans. by James F. Warner)*

Samuel H. Turner, "Jewish Commentaries on Isaiah chap. LII. 13 - LIII," *JSL, 1st Ser.,* 6 (1850) 346-377. [Introduction; Commentary of Rabbi Solomon Jarchi; Commentary of Rabbi David Kimchi; Commentary of Rabbi Aben Ezra; Translation of the Targum; Targum of Jonathan ben Uzziel]

J. W. Lindsay, "Exposition of Isaiah LII, 13-LIII," *MR* 42 (1860) 92-105.

Hermann Schultz, "Vicarious Suffering," *JSL, 5th Ser.,* 2 (1867-68) 81-96. *[52:13-Chap. 53]*

R. P. Stebbins, "Servant of Jehovah, Isa. lii:13-liii," *JBL* 4 (1884) 65-79.

Samuel Ives Curtiss, "Is the Modern Critical Theory of the Servant in Isaiah 52: 13-53 Subversive of Its New Testament Application to Christ?" *BW* 8 (1896) 354-363.

Isaiah 52:2

Anonymous, "Biblical Illustrations. From Jowett's Christian Researches," *SP* 3 (1830) 106-108. [Isa. 52:2, p. 107]

Isaiah 52:5

Sheldon H. Blank, "Isaiah 52:5 and the Profanation of the Name," *HUCA* 25 (1954) 1-8.

Isaiah 52:12-53:13

*Paul Haupt, "Philological and Archaeological Studies," *AJP* 45 (1924) 238-259. [5. Salvation and Redemption, Isa. 52:12-53:13, pp. 247-249]

Isaiah 52:13 - 53:12

Milton S. Terry, "Isaiah's Vision of the Cross," *MR* 62 (1880) 45-72. *[52:13-53:12]*

[Nathaniel] Burwash, "Isaiah lii. 13: liii. 12," *CMR* 4 (1892) 145-151.

W. H. Turton, "The Passion Prophecy of Isaiah," *BS* 79 (1922) 72-84. *[52:13-53:12]*

John R. Mackay, "Isaiah lii. 13-liii.12: An Analysis," *EQ* 3 (1931) 307-336.

Merwin A. Stone, "'The Golden Passional of the Old Testament. A Study of Isaiah 52:13-53:12," *BS* 91 (1934) 211-232, 337-353.

L. G. Rignell, "Isa. LII 13 - LIII 12," *VT* 3 (1953) 87-92.

Norman Snaith, "The Suffering Servant: Isaiah 52^{13} - 53^{12}, *PQL* 2 (1956) 209-214.

W. J. Dalton, "The Fourth Song of the Servant of Yahweh: Is. 52:13-53:12," *Scrip* 10 (1958) 1-10.

H. G. Murcott, "Isaiah 52:13—53:12: The suffering Servant," *Min* 3 (1962-63) 64-70.

R. E. O'Donnell, "A Possible Source for the Suffering of the Servant in Isaiah 52:13-53:12," *DunR* 4 (1964) 29-42.

Isaiah 52:13-53:6

R. H. Altus, "Isaiah 52:13-53:6," *AusTR* 25 (1954) 1-8.

Isaiah 52:13

Anonymous, "Concerning a Hebrew Elegy," *MMBR* 6 (1798) 98-99. *[52:13]*

Isaiah 52:14

*A. Rubinstein, "Isaiah LII 14 מִשְׁחַת and the DSIa Variant," *B* 35 (1954) 475-479.

Isaiah 52:15

Tayler Lewis, "The Purifying Messiah.—Interpretation of Isaiah LII. 15," *BS* 30 (1873) 166-177.

*C. Taylor, "An interpretation of יזה גוים," *JP* 8 (1879) 62-66. *[52:15]*

George F. Moore, "On יזה in Isa. 52:15," *JBL* 9 (1890) 216-222.

T. K. Cheyne, "Isaiah LII. 15," *Exp, 4th Ser.,* 3 (1891) 400.

Edward J. Young, "The Interpretation of יזה in Isaiah 52:15," *WTJ* 3 (1940-41) 125-132.

Jacob Leveen, "יזה" in Isaiah LII. 15," *JJS* 7 (1956) 93-94, 220.

Isaiah Chapter 53

[Jas. Cohen], "A Vindication of the Scriptural Messianic Interpretation of the LIII. of Isaiah," *SPR* 10 (1857-58) 201-232, 377-410.

S. D. F. S., "The Climax of Messianic Prophecy in Isaiah LIII," *BFER* 19 (1870) 305-334.

*Wolcott Calkins, "The Great Messianic Prophecy," *DTQ* 4 (1878) 19-30. *[Chap. 53]*

[Paton James] Gloag, "The Non-Messianic Interpretations of Isaiah LIII," *ONTS* 4 (1884-85) 129-131.

W. W. Martin, "The Suffering Servant, as Recorded in Isaiah LIII," *BS* 51 (1894) 143-157.

Anonymous, "The 53rd Chapter of Isaiah," *BW* 9 (1897) 32-33. *[A strophic structural arrangement]*

T. G., "The Servant of the Lord," *TQ* 2 (1898) 300-320. *[Chap. 53]*

J. A. Selbie, "Bertholet on Isaiah LIII," *ET* 10 (1898-99) 266.

*Meade C. Williams, "Reference of Isaiah liii. and Acts viii. to Jesus Christ, the Crucified," *CFL, 3rd Ser.,* 3 (1905) 135-138.

D. S. Margoliouth, "Recent Exposition of Isaiah liii," *Exp, 7th Ser.,* 6 (1908) 59-68.

E. V. Haserodt, "Treatise on Isaiah 53," *TQ* 21 (1917) 89-110.

Philip Shiteside, "The Servant of Yahweh (Isaiah LIII.)," *IER, 5th Ser.,* 18 (1921) 610-617.

J. M. Powis Smith, "The Ethical Significance of Isaiah, Chapter 53," *JR* 3 (1923) 132-140.

Anonymous, "Isaiah 53," *TTM* 7 (1924) 133-140.

John Monteith, "A New View of Isaiah LIII," *ET* 36 (1924-25) 498-502.

*Leroy Waterman, "The Martyred Servant Motif of Isaiah 53," *JBL* 56 (1937) 27-34.

Frederick A. Aston, "The Servant of the Lord in Isaiah LIII," *EQ* 11 (1939) 193-206.

C. R. North, "Who was the Servant of the Lord in Isaiah 53?" *OSHTP* (1939-40) 19-22.

*Christopher R. North, "Who was the Servant of the Lord in Isaiah LIII?" *ET* 52 (1940-41) 181-184, 219-221.

Hans. Sidon, "The Suffering Servant (Isaiah 53)," *CCQ* 5 (1947-48) #1, 10-16.

Ottomar Krueger, "Outlines on Isaiah 53," *CTM* 20 (1949) 30-36.

*Edward J. Young, "The Origin of the Suffering Servant Idea," *WTJ* 13 (1950-51) 19-34. *[Chap. 53]*

*John Hoad, "Some New Testament References to Isaiah 53," *ET* 68 (1956-57) 254-255.

Aug. Pieper, "Is. 53 and the New Testament Gospel," *JTLC* 5 (1965) #2, 22-28.

Isaiah 53:2

Anonymous, "The Great Text Commentary. The Great Texts of Isaiah," *ET* 23 (1911-12) 400-402. *[Chap. 53:2]*

A. R. Millard, "Notes II., Isaiah 53:2," *TB* #20 (1969) 127.

Isaiah 53:3

*T. H. Robinson, "Note on the Text and Interpretation of Isaiah liii. 3. 11," *ET* 71 (1959-60) 383.

Isaiah 53:5-6

*G. R. Driver, "Mistranslations," *ET* 57 (1945-46), 249. *[53:5, 6]*

Isaiah 53:7-12

R. H. Altus, "Isaiah 53:7-12," *AusTR* 22 (1951) 1-10.

Isaiah 53:7

W. L. Wardle, "Isaiah LIII. 7. I.," *JMUEOS* #3 (1913-14) 91-92.

M. A. Canney, "Isaiah LIII. 7. II.," *JMUEOS* #3 (1913-14) 93.

Isaiah 53:8

Howard Crosby, "Light on Important Texts. No. XXVIII," *HR* 8 (1883-84) 165-166. *[53:8]*

G. W. Ashstrom, "Notes to Isaiah 53:8f.," *BZ, N.S.,* 13 (1969) 95-98.

Isaiah 53:9

*George Farmer, "Isaiah LIII. 9, 11," *ET* 5 (1893-94) 381.

N. Herz, "Isaiah LIII. 9," *ET* 7 (1895-96) 526-527.

A. Bernstein, "Isaiah LIII. 9," *ET* 7 (1895-96) 567.

Isaiah 53:10-12

Isaiah Sonne, "Isaiah 53:10-12," *JBL* 78 (1959) 335-342.

Isaiah 53:11-12

Benjamin Douglass, "An Exposition of Isaiah LIII. 11, 12," *ONTS* 6 (1886-87) 173-175

Isaiah 53:11

*George Farmer, "Isaiah LIII. 9, 11," *ET* 5 (1893-94) 381.

*J.-M. P. Bauchet, "Notes on the Recently-Found Hebrew Manuscripts," *Scrip* 4 (1949-51) 115-117. [A New Reading of Isaiah liii 11]

I. L. Seeligmann, "Δεῖξαι αὐτῷ φῶς," *Tarbiz* 27 (1957-58) #2/3, II.

*T. H. Robinson, "Note on the Text and Interpretation of Isaiah liii. 3, 11," *ET* 71 (1959-60) 383.

*L. C. Allen, "Isaiah LIII. 11 and its Echoes," *VE* 1 (1962) 24-28.

Islwyn Blythin, "A Consideration of Difficulties in the Hebrew Text of Isaiah 53:11," *BTr* 17 (1966) 27-31.

Isaiah Chapters 54-57

[David N. Lord], "Designation and Exposition of the Figures of Isaiah, Chapters LIV., LV., LVI., and LVII.," *TLJ* 13 (1860-61) 149-173.

Isaiah 54:17

D. S. Margoliouth, "Note on Isaiah LIV. 17," *JQR* 9 (1896-97) 376.

Anonymous, "Exegetical Suggestion and Opinion. Isaiah 54:17," *CFL, O.S.,* 2 (1898) 168.

Isaiah Chapter 55

Walter Brueggemann, "Isaiah 55 and Deuteronomic Theology," *ZAW* 80 (1968) 191-203.

Isaiah 55:1-5

*Julian Morgenstern, "Two Prophecies from 520-516 B.C.," *HUCA* 22 (1949) 365-431. *[55:1-5]*

Isaiah 55:3

William Glynne, "'The Sure Mercies of David'," *ET* 29 (1917-18) 425-427. *[55:3]*

Duncan Cameron, "'The Sure Mercies of David'," *ET* 29 (1917-18) 562. *[55:3]*

Isaiah 55:6-13

*Julian Morgenstern, "Two Prophecies of the Fourth Century B.C. and the Evolution of Yom Kippur," *HUCA* 24 (1952-53) 1-74. *[55:6-13]*

Isaiah 55:6-11

J. Henry Gienapp, "Sermon Study on Isaiah 55:6-11 for Rogate," *CTM* 22 (1951) 192-203.

Isaiah 55:6

Alexander Warrack, "The Lost Lord. Isa. lv. 6," *ET* 5 (1893-94) 564-565.

Isaiah 55:10-11

Alex. Warrack, "Isaiah lv. 10, 11," *ET* 5 (1893-94) 220-222.

J. Robertson, "Isaiah lv. 10, 11," *ET* 5 (1893-94) 309-310.

§609 *3.5.3.2.1.3 Exegetical Studies on Trito-Isaiah*

W. S. McCullough, "A Re-examination of Isaiah 56-66," *JBL* 67 (1948) 27-36.

Isaiah 57:6

W. H. Irwin, "'The Smooth Stones of the Wady'? Isaiah 57, 6," *CBQ* 29 (1967) 31-40.

Isaiah 57:14-21

*W. W. Cannon, "Isaiah c. 57₁₄₋₂₁. c.c. 60-62," *ZAW* 52 (1934) 75-77.

Isaiah 57:17

Arie Rubinstein, "Isaiah LVII 17, הַסְתֵּר וְאֶקְצֹף and the DSIa Variant," *VT* 4 (1954) 200-201.

Isaiah Chapters 58-60

[David N. Lord], "Designation and Exposition of the Figures of Isaiah, Chapters LVIII., LIX., and LX.," *TLJ* 13 (1860-61) 310-343.

Isaiah Chapter 58

*Julian Morgenstern, "Two Prophecies of the Fourth Century B.C. and the Evolution of Yom Kippur," *HUCA* 24 (1952-53) 1-74. *[Chap. 58]*

H. Kosmala, "Form and Structure of Isaiah 58," *ASTI* 5 (1966-67) 69-81.

Isaiah 58:13-14

*Howard Crosby, "The Sabbath," *HR* 19 (1890) 261-262. *[58:13, 14]*

Isaiah 59:10

T. K. Cheyne, "A dark passage in Isaiah," *ZAW* 25 (1905) 172. *[59:10]*

Isaiah 59:16-17

*Frederick C. Harding, "The Oracle Against Edom (Isa. 63:1-6 and 59:16-17)," *JBL* 33 (1914) 213-227.

*Anonymous, "The Oracle Against Edom, Isa. 63:1-6; 59:16-17," *HR* 71 (1916) 57.

Isaiah 59:16

*Arie Rubinstein, "Word-Substitution in Isaiah LXIII. 5 and LIX. 16," *JSS* 8 (1963) 52-55.

Isaiah Chapters 60-62

*W. W. Cannon, "Isaiah c. 57_{14-21}. c.c. 60-62," *ZAW* 52 (1934) 75-77.

Isaiah Chapter 60

(   ) M., "60th Chapter of Isaiah Paraphrased," *ATG* 5 (1838-39) 383-385.

*"Philo.", "Notes on Scripture, Excerpts, Short Comments," *TLJ* 8 (1855-56) 200-220. *[Chap. 60, pp. 208-212]*

Isaiah 60:1-3

*Julian Morgenstern, "Two Prophecies from 520-516 B.C.," *HUCA* 22 (1949) 365-431. *[60:1-3]*

Isaiah 60:1-2

*Theodor H. Gaster, "'Ba'al is Risen...': An Ancient Hebrew Passion Play from Ras Shamra-Ugarit," *Iraq* 6 (1939) 109-143. [Isa. 60:1-2, p. 116]

Isaiah 60:5-7

*Julian Morgenstern, "Two Prophecies from 520-516 B.C.," *HUCA* 22 (1949) 365-431. *[60:5-7]*

Isaiah 60:8-22

*Julian Morgenstern, "Further Light from the Book of Isaiah upon the Catastrophe of 485 B.C.," *HUCA* 37 (1966) 1-28. [Isa. 60:8-22, pp. 17-24]

Isaiah 60:13

*C. J. Ball, "Note on the Wood called *Ukarina*," *SBAP* 11 (1888-89) 143-144. *[60:13]*

Isaiah 60:19

A. B. Bruce, "Israel's God Her Glory. Isaiah LX. 19," *Exp, 1st Ser.,* 10 (1879) 433-443.

Isaiah 60:21

I. F. M. Brayley, "'Yahweh Is the Guardian of His Plantation' [Is 60, 21]," *B* 41 (1960) 275-286.

Isaiah Chapters 61-63

[David N. Lord], "Designation and Exposition of the Figures of Isaiah, Chapters LXI., LXII., and LXIII.," *TLJ* 13 (1860-61) 511-526.

Isaiah Chapter 61

Julian Morgenstern, "Isaiah 61," *HUCA* 40 (1969) 109-121.

Isaiah 61:1-2

*Merrill P. Miller, "The Function of Isa. 61:1-2 in 11Q Melchizadek," *JBL* 88 (1969) 467-469.

Isaiah 61:1

Anonymous, "From a Preacher's Preparation Book, Isaiah lxi, 1," *ET* 9 (1897-98) 492-493.

Isaiah 61:2

*"Philo.", "Notes on Scripture, Excerpts, Short Comments," *TLJ* 8 (1855-56) 200-220. [The acceptable year of the Lord, (Isa. 61:2), pp. 212-217]

Isaiah 62:10-12

*Arndt L. Halverson, "The Second Sunday in Advent. I. Old Testament and Epistle," *LTSR* (Nov., 1966) 20-23. *[62:10-12]*

Isaiah Chapter 63

*Ivor Buse, "The Markan Account of the Baptism of Jesus and Isaiah LXIII," *JTS, N.S.,* 7 (1956) 74-75.

Isaiah 63:1-6

*Frederick C. Harding, "The Oracle Against Edom (Isa. 63:1-6 and 59:16-17)," *JBL* 33 (1914) 213-227.

*Anonymous, "The Oracle Against Edom, Isa. 63:1-6; 59:16-17," *HR* 71 (1916) 57.

*Julian Morgenstern, "Further Light from the Book of Isaiah upon the Catastrophe of 485 B.C.," *HUCA* 37 (1966) 1-28. [Isa. 63:1-6, pp. 14-17]

Isaiah 63:3

Cyrus H. Gordon and Edward J. Young, "אגאלתי (Isaiah 63:3)," *WTJ* 14 (1951-52) 54.

Isaiah 63:5

*Arie Rubinstein, "Word-Substitution in Isaiah LXIII. 5 and LIX. 16," *JSS* 8 (1963) 52-55.

Isaiah 63:7-14

Julian Morgenstern, "Isaiah 63:7-14," *HUCA* 23 (1950-51) Part 1, 185-203.

Isaiah 63:9

John Kellas, "Note on Isaiah LXIII. 9," *ET* 28 (1906-07) 384.

P. Winter, "ΟΥ ΔΙΑ ΧΕΙΡ ΠΡΕΣΒΕΩΣ ΟΥΔΕ ΔΙΑ ΧΕΙΡ ΣΕΡΑΦ ΟΥΔΕ ΔΙΑ ΧΕΙΡ ΑΓΓΕΛΟΥ. Isa. LXIII 9 (GK) and the Passover Haggadah," *VT* 4 (1954) 439-441.

*Stuart D. Currie, "Isaiah 63, 9 and the transfiguration in Mark," *ASBFE* 82 (Nov., 1966) #3, 7-34.

Isaiah Chapters 64-66

[David N. Lord], "Designation and Exposition of the Figures of Isaiah, Chapters LXIV., LXV., and LXVI.," *TLJ* 13 (1860-61) 558-583.

Isaiah Chapter 64

C. H. Spurgeon, "The Exposition of Isaiah LXIV," *BofT* #5 (1967) 33-35.

Isaiah 64:4-5

Sheldon H. Blank, "'And All Our Virtues'—An Interpretation of Isaiah 64:4b-5a," *JBL* 71 (1952) 149-154.

Isaiah 64:5

Albert A. Isaacs, "The difficulties of Scripture," *EN* 4 (1892) 19-22. *[Isa. lxiv. 5]*

James Kennedy, "Isaiah lxiv. 5, הֵן אַתָּה קָצַפְתָּ וַנֶּחֱטָא בָּהֶם עוֹלָם וְנִוָּשֵׁעַ:," *ET* 8 (1896-97) 44-46.

Isaiah 64:6

Anonymous, "On Isaiah LXIV. 6," *CD, N.S.,* 3 (1821) 426-429.

*S[heldon] H. Blank, "And All our Virtues…'," *JBL* 71 (1952) viii. *[64:6]*

Isaiah Chapter 65

Aug. L. Heerboth, "The 'New Creation' According to Is. 65," *CTM* 5 (1934) 29-37.

Isaiah 65:11

Eb. Nestle, "Isaiah lxv. 11," *ET* 10 (1898-99) 475.

Isaiah 65:15

T. K. Cheyne, "Isaiah LXV. 15," *Exp, 4th Ser.,* 4 (1891) 158-160.

H. St. J. Thackeray, "'A New Name' (Not 'Another Name'): Isaiah LXV 15," *JTS* 12 (1910-11) 112-114.

Isaiah 65:17-23

*"Philo.", "Notes on Scripture, Excerpts, Short Comments," *TLJ* 8 (1855-56) 200-220. *[65:17-23, pp. 217-220]*

Isaiah 65:20

John Skinner, "Requests and Replies," *ET* 11 (1899-1900) 61-62. *[65:20d]*

Isaiah 65:24

Anonymous, "Exegetical Notes. Isaiah lxv. 24," *MQR, 3rd Ser.,* 45 (1919) 151-152.

Isaiah 66:1-6

James D. Smart, "A New Interpretation of Isaiah LXVI. 1-6," *ET* 46 (1934-35) 420-424.

Isaiah 66:3

*James. A. Bewer, "Textual Suggestions on Isaiah 2:6, 66:3, Zeph. 2:2-5," *JBL* 27 (1908) 163-166.

Isaiah 66:5

Samuel Cox, "The Bigotry of Illumination. Isaiah lxvi. 5," *Exp, 1st Ser.,* 9 (1879) 53-67.

Isaiah 66:8

*James Moffatt, "Opera Foris. Materials for the Preacher," *Exp, 7th Ser.,* 5 (1908) 82-83. *[66:8]*

Isaiah 66:11

Stephen   Langdon,   "Isaiah   66:11,"   *AJSL*   20   (1903-04)   259.

Isaiah 66:12-24

*S. Burnham, "The Conditional Element in Prophecy Illustrated by Isaiah 66:12-24 and other passages," *ONTS* 10 (1890) 73-77.

Isaiah 66:12

*James Moffatt, "Opera Foris. Materials for the Preacher," *Exp, 7th Ser.,* 5 (1908) 82-83. *[66:12]*

Isaiah 66:17

*G. H. Skipwith, "Leaves from the 'Golden Bough'," *JQR* 8 (1895-96) 704-706. *[66:17]*

Isaiah 66:18-24

J. Darsow, "Isaiah 66:18-24," *AusTR* 11 (1940) 97-110.

Isaiah 66:24

John Thomas, "Isaiah, chapt. lxvi: ver. 24," *ATG* 5 (1838-39) 423.

§610 *3.5.3.2.1.4 Studies on Manuscripts of the Book of Isaiah*
[See also: Qumran Texts→]

*John Taylor, "Job and Isaiah in the 'Zeitschrift f. A.T. Wissenschaft'," *ET* 17 (1905-06) 277-278. *[Peshiṭta Text of Isaiah]*

G. B. Gray, "The Greek Version of Isaiah: Is it the Work of a Single Translator," *JTS* 12 (1910-11) 286-293.

*J. M. Paul Bauchet, "The Newly Discovered Scrolls of the Judean Desert," *CBQ* 11 (1949) 308-315. [I. Text of the Newly Found Is. 42-44 Compared with the Masoretic, pp. 310-312]

E. R. Rowlands, "The Targum and the Peshiṭta Version of the Book of Isaiah," *VT* 9 (1959) 178-191.

A. Diez-Macho, "A New Fragment of Isaiah with Babylonian Pointing," *Text* 1 (1960) 132-143.

*Robert A. Kraft, "Barnabas' Isaiah Text and Melito's *Paschal Homily*," *JBL* 80 (1961) 371-373.

Leona G. Running, "An Investigation of the Syriac Version of Isaiah," *AUSS* 3 (1965) 138-157; 4 (1966) 37-64, 135-148.

*Bruce E. Donovan, "Notes and Observations. An Isaiah Fragment in the Library of Congress," *HTR* 61 (1968) 625-628. *[23:4-7 and 23:10-13]*

§611 *3.5.3.2.1.5 Exegetical Studies on the Book of Jeremiah*

†Anonymous, "The Text of Jeremiah," *BFER* 9 (1860) 396-413. *(Review)*

Henry Preserved Smith, "The Text of Jeremiah," *AJSL* 3 (1886-87) 193-200.

G. R. Driver, "Linguistic and Textual Problems: Jeremiah," *JQR, N.S.,* 28 (1937-38) 97-129. [1:13; Ib. 14; 2:6; Ib. 24; 3:23; 4:5; Ib. 16; Ib. 20; 5:2; Ib. 3; Ib. 26; Ib. 28-29; 6:6; Ib.; 15; Ib. 16; Ib. 26-30; 7:9; Ib. 28; 8:6; Ib. 13; Ib. 18; 9:6; 10:2; Ib. 13; 13:16; Ib. 27; 15:8; Ib. 15-16; 17:4; Ib. 13; 19:13; 20:9; 22:30; 23:19; Ib. 38; 34:9; Ib. 18; 36:14; 41:9; 43:9; 45:4; 48:5; 48:12; Ib. 18; Ib. 35; 49:3; Ib. 4; Ib. 16; Ib. 21; Ib. 23; Ib. 25; 50:6; 51:11; Ib. 39; Ib. 56]

Joseph Reider, "Remarks on Driver's Textual Problems. (*JQR* XXVIII, 97ff.)," *JQR, N.S.,* 28 (1937-38) 293.

*H. F. D. Sparks, "St. Matthew's References to Jeremiah," *JTS, N.S.,* 1 (1950) 155-156.

John Joseph Owens, "Word Studies in Jeremiah," *R&E* 58 (1961) 474-488. [1:5, 10; 1:6-7; 1:11, 13; 2:2; 2:5; 2:6, 8; 2:9; 2:15; 2:19; 2:21; 2:24; 3:23; 4:3; 4:23-28; 4:2; 23:1-8; 23:9-40; 7:6; 25:12; 27:2]

J. Wash Watts, "Outline of Jeremiah," *R&E* 58 (1961) 489-491.

Walter C. Klein, "Commentary on Jeremiah," *ATR* 45 (1963) 121-158, 284-309. [Introduction, The Age, The Book, The Prophet; The Word; Bibliography; Commentary, I. Prophecies of Jeremiah: Chapters 1-25; II. Episodes in the Life of Jeremiah: Chapters 26-45; III. Fixing the Destinies of the Nations: Chapters 46-51; IV. How Jeremiah's Predictions Came True: Chapter 52]

B. Kedar-Kopfstein, "Textual Gleanings from the Vulgate to Jeremiah," *Text* 7 (1969) 36-58.

Jeremiah Chapters 1-25:13

George F. Hall, "The Septuagint Text of Jeremiah 1 to 25.13," *AQ* 18 (1939) 144-150.

Jeremiah Chapters 1-10

Charles C. Torrey, "The Background of Jeremiah 1-10," *JBL* 56 (1937) 193-216.

Jeremiah 1:4-19

Julius A. Bewer, "Historical Criticism of Jer. 1:4-19," *AJT* 6 (1902) 510-518.

*E. Norfleet Gardner, "'Jeremiah: Prophet of Doom' (Jer. 1:4-10; 4:18-28)," *R&E* 35 (1938) 159-169.

Jeremiah 1:4-10

Frank North, "Jeremiah's Call; A Critical Analysis of Jeremiah 1:4-10," *JBL* 67 (1948) xi.

Wilhelm Vischer, "The Vocation of the Prophet to the Nations. *An Exegesis of Jeremiah 1:4-10*," *Interp* 9 (1955) 310-317. *(Trans. by Suzanne de Dietrich)*

Jeremiah 1:4-5

M. Gulula, "An Egyptian Parallel to Jeremia I 4-5," *VT* 17 (1967) 114.

Jeremiah 1:11-12

Pearl Stone Wood, "Jeremiah's Figure of the Almond Rod," *JBL* 61 (1942) 99-110. *[1:11-12]*

Jeremiah 1:13

W. A. Irwin, "The Face of the Pot, Jeremiah 1:13b," *AJSL* 47 (1930-31) 288-289.

John R. Gray, "Jeremiah I. 13," *ET* 63 (1951-52) 126.

Edward L. Bode, "The Seething Cauldron—Jer. 1:13," *BibT* #42 (1969) 2898-2903.

Jeremiah 2:1-4:2

S. R. Driver, "Specimen of a New Translation of the Prophets," *Exp, 6th Ser.,* 6 (1902) 321-334. *[2:1-4:2]*

Jeremiah Chapter 2

*Jacob Milgrom, "The Date of Jeremiah, Chapter 2," *JNES* 14 (1955) 65-69.

Jeremiah 2:1-9

Frank North, "A Method for Recovering the Deuteronomistic Book of Jeremiah and His Oracles," *JBL* 69 (1950) xiii. *[2:1-9]*

Jeremiah 2:4-13

Prescott H. Williams, "The Fatal and foolish exchange: Living water for 'Nothings': A study of Jeremiah 2:4-13," *ASBFE* 81 (Sept., 1965) #1, 3-59.

Jeremiah 2:10-13

D. David Garland, "Exegesis of Jeremiah 2:10-13," *SWJT, N.S.,* 2 (1959-60) #2, 27-32.

Jeremiah 2:13

Anonymous, "The Great Text Commentary. The Great Texts of Jeremiah," *ET* 16 (1904-05) 400-402. *[2:13]*

Jeremiah 2:20

*William Holladay, "On Every High Hill and under Every Green Tree," *VT* 11 (1961) 170-176. *[2:20]*

Jeremiah 2:23-25

K. E. Bailey and W. L. Holladay, "The 'Young Camel' and 'Wild Ass' in Jer. II 23-25," *VT* 18 (1968) 256-260.

Jeremiah 2:24

Paul. Haupt, "*aṵṵát näfš,* Rut, Heat," *JBL* 35 (1916) 319-320. *[2:24]*

Jeremiah 3:1

Patrick Cummins, "Jerome Against Jerome. A Study of Jeremias 3:1," *CBQ* 6 (1944) 85-90.

J. D. Martin, "The Forensic Background to Jeremiah III 1," *VT* 19 (1969) 82-92.

Jeremiah 4:3-6:30

*S. R. Driver, "Translations from the Prophets. Jeremiah iv.3-vi.30," *Exp, 6th Ser.*, 7 (1903) 37-48.

Jeremiah 4:5-31

*Patrick Cummins, "Jeremias, Orator," *CBQ* 11 (1949) 191-201. *[4:5-31]*

Jeremiah 4:5-6

*James H. Gailey Jr., "The Sword and the Heart. *An Exposition of Jeremiah 4:5-6, 30*," *Interp* 9 (1955) 294-309.

Jeremiah 4:5

D. Winton Thomas, "מלאו in Jeremiah IV. 5: A Military Term," *JJS* 3 (1952) 47-52.

Jeremiah 4:11

T. H. Robinson, "Note on the Text of Jer. IV 11," *JTS* 23 (1921-22) 68.

Jeremiah 4:16-17

C. Rabin, "Noṣerim," *Text* 5 (1966) 44-52. *[4:16-17]*

Jeremiah 4:18-28

*E. Norfleet Gardner, "'Jeremiah: Prophet of Doom' (Jer. 1:4-10; 4:18-28)," *R&E* 35 (1938) 159-169.

Jeremiah 4:23-28

*Victor Eppstein, "The Day of Yahweh in Jeremiah 4:23-28," *JBL* 87 (1968) 93-97.

Jeremiah 4:29

Israel Efros, "An Emendation to Jer. 4. 29," *JAOS* 41 (1921) 75.

Isidor S. Levitan, "Dr. Efros' Emendation of Jer. 4. 29," *JAOS* 41 (1921) 316.

Jeremiah 4:30

*James H. Gailey Jr., "The Sword and the Heart. *An Exposition of Jeremiah 4:5-6, 30,*" *Interp* 9 (1955) 294-309.

Jeremiah 5:3

E. F. Sutcliffe, "A Note on Jeremiah V. 3," *JSS* 5 (1960) 348-349.

Jeremiah 5:8

M[arcus] Jastrow Sr., "Jeremiah 5:8," *AJSL* 13 (1896-97) 216-217.

Jeremiah 5:12

E. F. Sutcliffe, "A Note on לֹא הוּא Jer 5, 12," *B* 41 (1960) 287-290.

Jeremiah 5:28

Theodor H. Gaster, "Jeremiah V. 28.   דִּין יָתוֹם וְיַצְלִיחוּ וּמִשְׁפַּט אֶבְיוֹנִים
לֹא שָׁפָטוּ:," *ET* 56 (1944-45) 54.

C. T. Gilwhite, "Jeremiah V. 28," *ET* 56 (1944-45) 138.

D. Winton Thomas, "Jeremiah V. 28," *ET* 57 (1945-46) 54-55.

Jeremiah 5:31

W. L. Holladay, "'The Priests scrape out on their hands,' Jeremiah V:31," *VT* 15 (1965) 111-113.

Jeremiah 6:16

Anonymous, "The Great Text Commentary. The Great Texts of Jeremiah," *ET* 16 (1904-05) 455-458. *[6:16]*

Achilles Taylor, "The Old Paths (Jer. VI. 16)," *ET* 33 (1921-22) 522-523.

Jeremiah 6:27-30

*T. H. Robinson, "The Text of Jeremiah VI 27-30 in the Light of Ezekiel XXII 17-22," *JTS* 16 (1914-15) 482-490.

*G. R. Driver, "Two Misunderstood Passages in the Old Testament," *JTS, N.S.,* 6 (1955) 82-87. [Jeremiah vi. 27-30, pp. 84-87]

Jeremiah 7:1-9:22

*S. R. Driver, "Translations from the Prophets. Jeremiah vii.1-ix.22," *Exp, 6th Ser.,* 7 (1903) 147-160.

Jeremiah Chapter 7

Everett Tilson, "The Segregation of God," *JMTSO* 3 (1964-65) #2, 18-27. *[Chap. 7]*

Jeremiah 7:1-15

*Adam C. Welch, "Jeremiah's Temple Address," *Exp, 8th Ser.,* 22 (1921) 46-59. *[7:1-15]*

Walther Eichrodt, "The Right Interpretation of the Old Testament: A Study of Jeremiah 7:1-15," *TT* 7 (1950-51) 15-25.

Jeremiah 7:4

C. F. Whitley, "A Note on Jeremiah 7⁴," *JTS, N.S.,* 5 (1954) 57-59.

E. F. Sutcliffe, "A Gloss in Jeremiah VII 4," *VT* 5 (1955) 313-314.

Jeremiah 7:18

*R. A. S. Macalister, "Notes and Queries. (1.) *Sacrificial Cakes*," *PEFQS* 40 (1908) 75. *[7:18]*

*A. Carr, "Notes and Queries. 6. *Sacrificial Cakes*," *PEFQS* 40 (1908) 168. *[7:18]*

Jeremiah 7:21-29

*Adam C. Welch, "Jeremiah's Temple Address," *Exp, 8th Ser.,* 22 (1921) 46-59. *[7:21-29]*

Jeremiah 7:21-23

Preston A. Laury, "Jeremiah VII, 21, 22, 23," *LCR* 32 (1913) 552-555.

Jeremiah 7:22-23

J[ohn] D. D[avis], "Editorial Notes," *CFL, N.S.,* 3 (1901) 186-188. *[7:22, 23]*

Ed. König, "On the Meaning and Scope of Jeremiah vii. 22, 23," *Exp, 6th Ser.,* 6 (1902) 135-154, 208-218, 366-377.

*William L. Baxter, "Smooth Stone Out of the Brook," *PTR* 19 (1921) 177-224. [The Pseudo-Jeremiah (Jer. 7:22-23), pp. 211-216]

Jeremiah 7:22

*Fritz Hommel, "Preliminary Notice Regarding Jer. VII. 22 and Deut.V. 3," *ET* 11 (1899-1900) 429.

*Fritz Hommel, "A Rhetorical Figure in the Old Testament, Jer. VII. 22 and Deut.V. 3," *ET* 11 (1899-1900) 439-441.

Lucien Gautier, "Jeremiah VII. 22," *ET* 11 (1899-1900) 478.

*Fritz Hommel, "A Rhetorical Figure in the Old Testament, A Supplementary Note," *ET* 11 (1899-1900) 517-518. *[7:22]*

*Eb. Nestle, "A Rhetorical Figure in the Old Testament, A Supplementary Note, II.," *ET* 11 (1899-1900) 518. *[7:22]*

*James Moffatt, "A Rhetorical Figure in the Old Testament, A Supplementary Note III.," *ET* 11 (1899-1900) 518-519. *[7:22]*

*Ed. König, "A Rhetorical Figure in the Old Testament, A Supplementary Note, IV.," *ET* 11 (1899-1900) 519. *[7:22]*

Fritz Hommel, "A last Word on 'A Rhetorical Figure in the Old Testament'," *ET* 11 (1899-1900) 564. *[7:22]*

*Frederick LaRue King, "A Destructive Critic's Perverse Interpretation of the Scriptures," *CFL, 3rd Ser.,* 5 (1906) 17-23. *[7:22]*

J. A. Motyer, "Jeremiah VII, 22," *TB* #1 (1956) 4-5.

Jeremiah 7:32

Alfred Cave, "Requests and Replies," *ET* 1 (1889-90) 231. *[7:32]*

Jeremiah 8:19

W. L. Holladay, "The so-called 'Deuteronomic Gloss' in Jer. viii 19b," *VT* 12 (1962) 494-498.

Jeremiah 8:20

*A. G. Laurie, "Some Misconstrued Texts," *UQGR, N.S.*, 11 (1874) 424-438. *[8:20, pp. 425-426]*

Anonymous, "The Great Text Commentary. The Great Texts of Jeremiah," *ET* 16 (1904-05) 493-496. *[8:20]*

Jeremiah 8:22

F[rederick] Field, "Note on Jeremiah VIII. 22," *JP 13* (1884-85) 114-116.

*W. Robertson Nicoll, "Old Testament Notes," *Exp, 3rd Ser.*, 1 (1885) 160. *[8:22]*

Jeremiah 8:23

Stanley Gevirtz, "The Ugaritic Parallel to Jeremiah 8:23," *JNES* 20 (1961) 41-46.

Jeremiah 9:17

*M. D. Goldman, "Lexicographical Notes on Exegesis (2). Some Hebrew Words Used in Their Original Meaning," *ABR* 1 (1951) 141-142. *[9:17b, c]*

Jeremiah 9:20

*Endre A. D. Singer, "Ugaritic Gleanings," *BIES* 11 (1944-45) #1/2, I-II. [2. Jer. 9:20 // II AB v-vii]

S. E. Loewenstamm, "'Arubotenu/'Armenotenu," *BIES* 13 (1946-47) #1/2, II. *[9:20]*

S. M. Paul, "Cuneiform Light on Jer 9, 20," *B* 49 (1968) 373-376.

Jeremiah 9:23-11:17

*S. R. Driver, "Translations from the Prophets. Jeremiah ix. 23-xi. 17," *Exp, 6th Ser.*, 7 (1903) 229-235.

Jeremiah 10:1-16

P. R. Ackroyd, "Jeremiah X. 1-16," *JTS, N.S.*, 14 (1963) 385-390.

Thomas W. Overholt, "The Falsehood of Idolatry: An Interpretation of Jer. X. 1-16," *JTS, N.S.,* 16 (1965) 1-12.

Jeremiah 10:6-8

S. R. Driver, "Grammatical Notes. 2. On כָּמוֹךָ מֵאֵין (Jer. X. 6, 8)," *AJSL* 2 (1885-86) 34-37.

Jeremiah 10:13

*Edward J. Kissane, "'Who Maketh Lightnings for the Rain'," *JTS, N.S.,* 3 (1952) 214-216. *[10:13]*

Jeremiah 11:9-12:6

*S. R. Driver, "Translations from the Prophets. Jeremiah xi. 9- xii. 6," *Exp, 6th Ser.,* 7 (1903) 316-320.

Jeremiah 11:15-16

J. Philip Hyatt, "The Original Text of Jeremiah 11:15-16," *JBL* 60 (1941) 57-60.

Jeremiah 11:18-12:6

H. H. Rowley, "The Text and Interpretation of Jer. 11:18-12:6," *AJSL* 42 (1925-26) 217-227.

Jeremiah 11:19

*Benjamin W. Bacon, "Was Saul a Hachish-Eater?" *ET* 15 (1903-04) 380. *[11:19]*

*F. C. Burkitt, "Justin Martyr and Jeremiah XI 19," *JTS* 33 (1931-32) 371-373.

Jeremiah 12:1-5

William McKane, "The Interpretation of Jeremiah XII. 1-5," *GUOST* 20 (1963-64) 38-48.

Jeremiah 12:5

Anonymous, "The Great Text Commentary. The Great Texts of Jeremiah," *ET* 16 (1904-05) 556-558. *[12:5]*

Albert Ehrman, "A Note on בוטח in Jer. XII. 5," *JSS* 5 (1960) 153.

Jeremiah 12:6

G. R. Driver, "Jeremiah, XII, 6," *JJS* 5 (1954) 177-178.

Jeremiah 12:7-16:9

*S. R. Driver, "Translations from the Prophets. Jeremiah xii. 7- xvi. 9," *Exp, 6th Ser.,* 7 (1903) 353-369.

Jeremiah 12:9

*J. A. Emerton, "Notes on Jeremiah 12:9 and on some suggestions of J. D. Michaelis about the Hebrew words *naḥā, 'æbrā,* and *jadǎ'*," *ZAW* 81 (1969) 182-191.

Jeremiah 13:1-11

W. F. Birch, "Hiding Places in Canaan. I. Jeremiah's Girdle and Farah," *PEFQS* 12 (1880) 235-236. *[13:1-11]*

Jeremiah 13:18

*Mitchell J. Dahood, "Two Textual Notes on Jeremia," *CBQ* 23 (1961) 462-464. *[13:18b]*

Jeremiah 13:21

H. A. Williamson, "Jeremiah XIII. 21," *ET* 37 (1924-25) 45.

Jeremiah 13:22-23

J. A. B., "The Ethiopian's Skin, and the Leopard's Spots," *ERG, 3rd Ser.,* 3 (1864-65) 82-88. *[13:22, 23]*

Jeremiah 13:23

Anonymous, "The Great Text Commentary. The Great Texts of Jeremiah," *ET* 17 (1905-06) 34-37. *[13:23]*

Jeremiah 14:3

*Samuel E. Loewenstamm, "The Nouns צַעַר, צעור (Kethīb) צָעִיר (Qeré)," *Tarbiẓ* 36 (1966-67) #2, I-II. *[14:3]*

Jeremiah 14:4

S. Marenof, "A Note on Jer. 14:4," *AJSL* 55 (1938) 198-200.

Jeremiah 14:18

D. W[inton] Thomas, "A Note on ולא ידעו in Jeremiah XIV 18," *JTS* 39 (1938) 273-274.

Jeremiah 15:10-21

Erhard Gerstenberger, "Jeremiah's Complaints: Observations on Jer. 15:10-21," *JBL* 82 (1963) 393-408.

Jeremiah 15:10-12

*James Muilenburg, "A Confession of Jeremiah," *USQR* 4 (1948-49) #2, 15-18. *[15:10-12]*

Jeremiah 15:15-21

*James Muilenburg, "A Confession of Jeremiah," *USQR* 4 (1948-49) #2, 15-18. *[15:15-21]*

Jeremiah 15:19

P. Peters, "Opening Address Delivered at the Lutheran Theological Seminary in Thiensville, Wisconsin, June 20, 1944," *WLQ* 41 (1944) 209-217. *[15:19]*

Jeremiah 16:10-20:18

*S. R. Driver, "Translation from the Prophets," *Exp, 6th Ser.,* 9 (1904) 104-120. *[16:10-20:18]*

Jeremiah 16:16

G. Ch. Aalders, "The Fishers and the Hunters," *EQ* 30 (1958) 133-139. *[16:16]*

Jeremiah 17:1-2

C. Lattey, "The Text of Jeremiah XVII. 1-2," *ET* 60 (1948-49) 52-53.

Jeremiah 17:5-8

Anonymous, "The Great Text Commentary. The Great Texts of Jeremiah," *ET* 17 (1905-06) 59-63. *[17:5-8]*

R. Davidson, "The Interpretation of Jeremiah XVII 5-8," *VT* 9 (1959) 202-205.

Jeremiah 17:9

N. H., "On Jeremiah xvii. 9," *CD, N.S.,* 3 (1821) 262-263.

Jeremiah 17:11

F. H. Woods, "Note on Jeremiah XVII. 11," *ET* 20 (1908-09) 375-376.

Jeremiah 17:31

M[itchell J.] Dahood, "The Metaphor in Jeremiah 17, 31," *B* 48 (1967) 109-110.

Jeremiah Chapter 18

George C. M. Douglas, "Jeremiah's Use of the Figure of the Potter," *ET* 3 (1891-92) 14. *[Chap. 18]*

Jeremiah 18:1-17

R. Waddy Moss, "A Study of Jeremiah's Use (XVIII. 1-17) of the Figure of the Potter," *ET* 2 (1890-91) 274-275.

Jeremiah 18:1-10

*E. H. Plumptre, "The Potter and the Clay. Jer. XVIII. 1-10; Rom. IX. 19-24," *Exp, 1st Ser.,* 4 (1876) 369-480.

Jeremiah 18:4

Anonymous, "The Great Text Commentary. The Great Texts of Jeremiah," *ET* 17 (1905-06) 116-119. *[18:4]*

Jeremiah 18:13-17

Frank North, "Astray in Paths of Old; Critical Analysis of Jeremiah 18:13-17," *JBL* 66 (1947) vii.

Jeremiah 18:14-15

Mitchell Dahood, "Philological Notes on Jer 18:14-15," *ZAW* 74 (1962) 207-209.

Jeremiah 18:14

*Robert Gordis, "The Biblical Root *ŠDY-ŠD:* Notes on 2 Sam. i. 21; Jer. xviii. 14; Ps. xci. 6; Job v. 21," *JTS* 41 (1940) 34-43.

Jeremiah 19:14-20:6

*Frank North, "The True Rationale for Critical Analysis," *JBL* 68 (1949) x. *[19:14-20:6]*

Jeremiah 20:4

H. Tattam, "A Coptic Version of Jeremiah XX. 4," *JSL, 4th Ser.,* 2 (1862-63) 466-467.

Jeremiah 20:6

Eb. Nestle, "Pashhur = Magor-Missabib," *ET* 18 (1906-07) 382. *[20:6]*

A. M. Honeyman, "*māgôr mis-sabîb* and Jeremiah's Pun," *VT* 4 (1954) 424-426. *[20:6]*

P. Wernberg-Møller, "The Pronoun אתמה and Jeremiah's Pun," *VT* 6 (1956) 315-316. *[20:6]*

N. Walker, "The Massoretic Pointing of Jeremiah's Pun," *VT* 7 (1957) 413. *[20:6]*

Jeremiah 20:7

M. D. Goldman, "Lexicographical Notes on Exegesis; (2) Supposed Jester's Figure Based on a Meaning Given to a Biblical Verb," *ABR* 1 (1951) 140-141. *[20:7a, b]*

Jeremiah 21:9

*S. P. T. Prideaux, "'My Life Shall be to Thee for a Prey'," *ET* 43 (1931-32) 288. *[21:9]*

Jeremiah 21:11-22:30(-23)

Adam C. Welch, "A Problem in Jeremiah," *ET* 26 (1914-15) 429-430. *[21:11-22:30(-23)]*

Jeremiah Chapter 22

*S. R. Driver, "Translations from the Prophets: Jeremiah xxii., xxiii.," *Exp, 6th Ser.,* 8 (1903) 12-23.

Jeremiah 22:10-12

Corwin C. Roach, "Notes and Comments," *ATR* 23 (1941) 347-348. *[22:10-12]*

Jeremiah 22:18

*Mitchell J. Dahood, "Two Textual Notes on Jeremia," *CBQ* 23 (1961) 462-464. *[22:18]*

Jeremiah 22:23

*Samuel Daiches, "Exegetical Notes," *PEFQS* 59 (1927) 162-163. [II. Jer. 22:23, p. 163]

Jeremiah 22:28

John Franklin Genung, "'This Man Coniah'," *BW* 36 (1911) 89-99.

Jeremiah Chapter 23

*S. R. Driver, "Translations from the Prophets: Jeremiah xxii., xxiii.," *Exp, 6th Ser.,* 8 (1903) 12-23.

*J. T. E. Renner, "False and True Prophecy, *A Study of a Problem on the Basis of Jeremiah 23 and 28,*" *RTR* 25 (1966) 95-104.

Jeremiah 23:1-8

Jeremy Rutland, "The Kingdom of God," *Them* 4 (1967) #2, 2-10. *[23:1-8]*

Jeremiah 23:3-5

*J. G. Baldwin, "Ṣemaḥ as a technical term in the Prophets," *VT* 14 (1964) 93-97. [2. Jer. XXIII 3-5 and XXXIII 14-26, pp. 94-97]

Jeremiah 23:5-6

*S. A. Worcester, "Comparison of Jeremiah 23:5, 6 and 33:14-16," *BS* 15 (1858) 128-131.

Anonymous, "The Great Text Commentary. The Great Texts of Jeremiah," *ET* 17 (1905-06) 172-175. *[23:5, 6]*

*Daniel Leibel, "צדקנו יהוה'," *Tarbiz* 34 (1964-65) #3, v. *[23:5-6]*

Jeremiah 23:5

J. Swetnam, "Some Observations on the Background of צדיק in Jeremias 23, 5a," *B* 46 (1965) 29-40.

Jeremiah 23:6

James Hope Moulton, "Requests and Replies," *ET* 10 (1898-99) 14. [Jer. 23:6 - The Lord Our Righteousness]

*Hugo McCord, "The Meaning of YHWH *Tsidhkēnu* ('The Lord Our Righteousness') in Jeremiah 23:6 and 33:16," *RestQ* 6 (1962) 114-121.

Jeremiah 23:9

*J. W. Jack, "Recent Biblical Archaeology," *ET* 53 (1941-42) 367-370. [Archæology and the Biblical Text: 2. Birds Fluttering (Gen. 1:2, Deut. 32:11; Jer. 23:9), pp. 368-369]

Jeremiah 23:25-26

Isaiah Sonne, "Curious Misreadings of Abbreviation Signs in Jer 23:25-26," *JBL* 70 (1951) v.

Jeremiah 23:30

R. J. Zwi Werblowsky, "Stealing the Word," *VT* 6 (1956) 105-106. *[23:30]*

Jeremiah Chapter 24

Frank North, "Two Baskets of Figs: a Critical Analysis of Jer 24," *JBL* 65 (1946) v.

Jeremiah 24:1

D. Winton Thomas, "A Note on מוּעָדִים in Jeremiah 24, 1," *JTS, N.S.,* 3 (1952) 55.

Jeremiah Chapter 25

*W. H. Kent, "Rabbinical Studies. I," *AER* 26 (1902) 297-308. [VII. The Biblical Cryptogram, pp. 304-305] *[Chap. 25]*

*S. R. Driver, "Translation from the Prophets," *Exp, 6th Ser.,* 9 (1904) 399-400. *[Chap. 25]*

Jeremiah 25:9

*Werner E. Lemke, "'Nebuchadrezzar, My Servant'," *CBQ* 28 (1966) 45-50. *[25:9; 25:9LXX]*

Jeremiah 25:10

Nathan Morris, "Jeremiah 25, 10," *GUOST* 6 (1929-33) 68.

Jeremiah Chapters 26-45

Martin Kessler, "Jeremiah Chapters 26-45 Reconsidered," *JNES* 27 (1968) 81-88.

Jeremiah Chapter 26

David W. Amram, "The Trial of Jeremiah," *BW* 16 (1900) 431-437. *[Chap. 26]*

*Adam C. Welch, "Jeremiah's Temple Address," *Exp, 8th Ser.,* 22 (1921) 46-59. *[Chap. 26]*

Jeremiah 26:1-15

Alex Wm. C. Guebert, "Sermon Study on Jeremiah 26:1-15 for Oculi," *CTM* 22 (1951) 46-53.

Jeremiah 26:20

*A. Malamat, "'Elnathan ben 'Akhbor and the Prophet 'Uriahu of Qiryat-Hayearim," *BIES* 14 (1947-48) #1/2, II. *[Jer. 26:20//Lachish Letters III, 11. 14-18]*

Jeremiah Chapters 27-29

Thomas W. Overholt, "Jeremiah 27-29: The Question of False Prophecy," *JAAR* 35 (1967) 241-249.

Jeremiah 27:6

J. F. McCurdy, "Light on Scriptural Text from Recent Discoveries. Jer. xxvii. 6: 'Nebuchadnezzar King of Babylon, my Servant'," *HR* 36 (1898) 504-507.

*Werner E. Lemke, "'Nebuchadrezzar, My Servant'," *CBQ* 28 (1966) 45-50. *[27:6]*

Jeremiah 27:12-13

James Moffatt, "Opera Foris. Materials for the Preacher," *Exp, 7th Ser.,* 8 (1909) 378. *[27:12-13]*

Jeremiah Chapter 28

*J. T. E. Renner, "False and True Prophecy, *A Study of a Problem on the Basis of Jeremiah 23 and 28*," *RTR* 25 (1966) 95-104.

Jeremiah 29:22

*John P. Peters, "Notes on the Old Testament," *JBL* 15 (1896) 106-117. [2. The Three Children in the Fiery Furnace (Dan. 3; Jer 29:22), pp. 109-111]

Jeremiah Chapters 30-31

*S. R. Driver, "Translations from the Prophets. Jeremiah xxx.-xxxi.," *Exp, 6th Ser.,* 9 (1904) 174-185. *[Chaps. 30-31]*

Jeremiah Chapter 31

Wilber B. Wallis, "Irony in Jeremiah's Prophecy of a New Covenant," *BETS* 12 (1969) 107-110. *[Chap. 31]*

Jeremiah 31:1-10

*G. A. Smith, "Jeremiah in the Siege," *Exp, 8th Ser.,* 8 (1923) 1-14. *[31:1-10]*

Jeremiah 31:1

M. D. Goldman, "Lexicographical Notes on Exegesis (3) A Root and its Causative," *ABR* 2 (1952) 49. *[31:1(2)]*

Jeremiah 31:3

Anonymous, "The Great Text Commentary. The Great Texts of Jeremiah," *ET* 17 (1905-06) 216-219. *[31:3]*

Geerhardus Vos, "Jeremiah's Plaint and its Answer," *PTR* 26 (1928) 481-495. *[31:3]*

Jeremiah 31:15

*†Anonymous, "The Authorized Translation of the Bible," *BCQTR, N.S.,* 6 (1829) 232-240. [Jer. 31:15, pp. 235, 238f.]

*Eric Burrows, "Cuneiform and Old Testament: Three Notes," *JTS* 28 (1926-27) 184-185. [III. *Bakītu mušēniḳtu* (C.T. 16, 10, 26) (Jer. 31:15), p. 185]

Jeremiah 31:18

M. D. Goldman, "Lexicographical Notes on Exegesis (2) An Instance of Dittography(?)," *ABR* 1 (1951) 139. *[31:18]*

Jeremiah 31:22

W. W. Davies, "Exegetical Notes on Jer. xxxi. 22," *HR* 24 (1892) 71-74.

Anonymous, "The Meaning of Jer. 31:22," *ONTS* 15 (1892) 165-166.

J. Edgar Bruns, "Mary in Jeremias 31:22," *AER* 136 (1957) 28-31.

*Johannes B. Bauer, "τὰ θηλυκὰ ἀπανδρωθέντα [Clem. Alex., Excerpta ex Theodoto 21,3]—A Quotation from Jeremiah XXXI. 22?" *NTS* 8 (1961-62) 56-58.

Charles L. Feinberg, "Jeremiah 31:22: Proverb, Promise, or Prophecy?" *BS* 123 (1966) 315-324; 124 (1967) 16-21.

W. L. Holladay, "Jer. XXXI 22b reconsidered: 'The Woman Encompasses the Man'," *VT* 16 (1966) 236-239.

Jeremiah 31:31-34

A. B. Bruce, "Jeremiah's Prophecy of the New Covenant. Jeremiah XXXI. 31-34," *Exp, 1st Ser.,* 11 (1880) 65-78.

Anonymous, "The Great Text Commentary. The Great Texts of Jeremiah," *ET* 17 (1905-06) 271-274. *[31:31-34]*

W. J. Moulton, "The New Covenant in Jeremiah," *Exp, 7th Ser.,* 1 (1906) 370-382. *[31:31-34]*

Henry S. Gehman, "An Insight and a Realization. *A Study of the New Covenant,*" *Interp* 9 (1955) 279-293. *[31:31-34]*

John Bright, "An Exercise in Hermeneutics. *Jeremiah 31:31-34,*" *Interp* 20 (1966) 188-210.

Jeremiah 31:33-34

Anonymous, "Comparative Translation: Jeremiah 31:33, 34. A Study in Modernizing the English Bible," *BW* 23 (1904) 443-444.

Jeremiah 31:35-37

*"Philo.", "Notes on Scripture, Excerpts, Short Comments," *TLJ* 8 (1855-56) 200-220. *[31:35-37, pp. 203-204]*

Jeremiah 31:38-40

W. F. Birch, "Note on Jeremiah XXXI, 38-40," *PEFQS* 14 (1882) 58-59.

Jeremiah 33:1ff.

*Hermas, "An Attempt to prove the perpetual Obligation of the Jewish Ritual," *TRep* 5 (1786) 403-430. [Jer. 33:1ff., pp. 417-424]

Jeremiah 33:14-26

*Patrick Cummins, "A Test Case in Text Transmission. Jeremias 33:14-26," *CBQ* 2 (1940) 15-27.

*J. G. Baldwin, "Ṣemaḥ as a technical term in the Prophets," *VT* 14 (1964) 93-97. [2. Jer. XXIII 3-5 and XXXIII 14-26, pp. 94-97]

Jeremiah 33:14-16

*S. A. Worcester, "Comparison of Jeremiah 23:5, 6 and 33:14-16," *BS* 15 (1858) 128-131.

*Daniel Leibel, "'צדקנו יהוה'," *Tarbiz* 34 (1964-65) #3, V. *[33:14-16]*

Jeremiah 33:16

*Hugo McCord, "The Meaning of YHWH *Tsidhkēnu* ('The Lord Our Righteousness') in Jeremiah 23:6 and 33:16," *RestQ* 6 (1962) 114-121.

Jeremiah 34:1-7

*G. A. Smith, "Jeremiah in the Siege," *Exp, 8th Ser.,* 8 (1923) 1-14. *[34:1-7]*

Jeremiah 34:5

*Werner E. Lemke, "'Nebuchadrezzar, My Servant'," *CBQ* 28 (1966) 45-50. *[34:5]*

Jeremiah Chapter 35

*S. R. Driver, "Translations from the Prophets. Jeremiah xxxv.," *Exp, 6th Ser.,* 9 (1904) 394-400.

Jeremiah 35:30

*Meir Weiss, "In the Footsteps of one Biblical Metaphor (Methodological Remarks and Exegetical, and Historical Notices)," *Tarbiz* 34 (1964-65) #2, I-II; #3, I-II; #4, I-II. [3. Jer. 35:30] *[Title varies]*

Jeremiah Chapter 36

Martin Kessler, "The Significance of Jer 36," *ZAW* 81 (1969) 381-383.

Jeremiah 36:22-24

Anonymous, "The Great Text Commentary. The Great Texts of Jeremiah," *ET* 17 (1905-06) 307-309. *[36:22-24]*

Jeremiah 36:25

*A. Malamat, "'Elnathan ben 'Akhbor and the Prophet 'Uriahu of Qiryat-Hayearim," *BIES* 14 (1947-48) #1/2, II. *[36:25]*

Jeremiah Chapters 37-44

*Peter R. Ackroyd, "Historians and Prophets," *SEÅ* 33 (1968) 18-54. [Jer. 37-44, pp. 43-50]

Jeremiah 37:1-10

*G. A. Smith, "Jeremiah in the Siege," *Exp, 8th Ser.,* 26 (1923) 1-14. *[37:1-10]*

Jeremiah 38:2

*S. P. T. Prideaux, "'My Life Shall be to Thee for a Prey'," *ET* 43 (1931-32) 288. *[38:2]*

Jeremiah Chapter 39

Adam C. Welch, "Jeremiah's Letter to the Exiles in Babylon," *Exp, 8th Ser.,* 22 (1921) 358-372. *[Chap. 39]*

*E. J. Smit, "The relation between the texts of II Kings 25 and Jeremiah," *OTW* 11 (1968) 77-81. *[Chap. 39]*

Jeremiah 39:3

*Claude R. Conder, "Notes on New Discoveries," *PEFQS* 41 (1909) 266-275. [Sarsechim (Jer. 39:3), p. 275]

Julius A. Bewer, "Nergalsharezer Shamgar in Jer. 39:3," *AJSL* 42 (1925-26) 130.

*S. Feigin, "The Babylonian Officials in Jeremiah 39:3, 13," *JBL* 45 (1926) 149-155.

J. P. Hyatt, "The Babylonian Officials in Jeremiah 39:3," *JBL* 72 (1953) xxii.

Jeremiah 39:13

*S. Feigin, "The Babylonian Officials in Jeremiah 39:3, 13," *JBL* 45 (1926) 149-155.

Jeremiah 39:14

*S. Spiegel, "The Seal of Gedaliah (Lachish) and Jeremiah," *JBL* 60 (1941) vi. *[39:14]*

Jeremiah 39:18

*S. P. T. Prideaux, "'My Life Shall be to Thee for a Prey'," *ET* 43 (1931-32) 288. *[39:18]*

Jeremiah 43:5-7

Frederic Gardiner, "Various Topics III. The Jew and the Greek," *JBL* 8 (1888) 150-151. *[43:5-7]*

Jeremiah 43:10-11

*John Skinner, "Requests and Replies," *ET* 3 (1891-92) 68. [The Second Temple and the Visions of Ezekiel (43:10, 11)]

Jeremiah 43:10

*Werner E. Lemke, "'Nebuchadrezzar, My Servant'," *CBQ* 28 (1966) 45-50. *[43:10]*

Jeremiah 43:12

J. van Doorslaer, "'Sicut Amicitur Pastor Pallio Suo...'," *CBQ* 13 (1951) 314-325. *[43:12]*

Jeremiah 44:17-19

Paul E. Kretzmann, "Late Archaeological News from Palestine," *CTM* 4 (1933) 49. *[44:17-19]*

Jeremiah 44:19

*R. A. S. Macalister, "Notes and Queries. (1.) *Sacrificial Cakes*," *PEFQS* 40 (1908) 75. *[44:19]*

*A. Carr, "Notes and Queries. 6. *Sacrificial Cakes*," *PEFQS* 40 (1908) 168. *[44:19]*

Jeremiah 45:4-5

H. Wheeler Robinson, "Old Texts in Modern Translations. Jeremiah xlv. 4, 5 (McFadyen)," *ET* 49 (1937-38) 204-206.

Jeremiah 45:5

*S. P. T. Prideaux, "'My Life Shall be to Thee for a Prey'," *ET* 43 (1931-32) 288. *[45:5]*

Jeremiah Chapter 46-47:28

*S. R. Driver, "Translations from the Prophets. Jeremiah xlvi. xlvii. 28," *Exp, 6th Ser.,* 10 (1904) 61-73.

Jeremiah Chapter 46

C. L. Carhart, "A War-Song of Long Ago," *BW* 26 (1905) 224-227. *[Chap. 46]*

Jeremiah Chapter 47

*A. Malamat, "The Historical Setting of Two Biblical Prophecies of the Nations," *IEJ* 1 (1950-51) 149-159. *[Chap. 47]*

Jeremiah 47:29-Chapter 49

*S. R. Driver, "Translations from the Prophets. Jeremiah xlvii. 29-xlix," *Exp, 6th Ser.,* 10 (1904) 138-148.

Jeremiah 48:1-6

*Menahem Dyman, "An Archaic Remnant in Prophetic Literature," *BIES* 13 (1946-47) #1/2, II. *[48:1-6]*

Jeremiah 48:4

*Samuel E. Loewenstamm, "The Nouns צַעַר, צָעוּר (Kethīb) צָעִיר (Qeré)," *Tarbiz* 36 (1966-67) #2, I-II. *[48:4]*

Jeremiah 48:11

Anonymous, "The Great Text Commentary. The Great Texts of Jeremiah," *ET* 17 (1905-06) 379-381. *[48:11]*

*W. A. Irwin, "An Ancient Biblical Text," *AJSL* 48 (1931-32) 184-193. *[48:11]*

Jeremiah 48:16-24

*Menahem Dyman, "An Archaic Remnant in Prophetic Literature," *BIES* 13 (1946-47) #1/2, II. *[48:16-24]*

Jeremiah 48:29ff.

*Burke O. Long, "The Divine Funeral Lament," *JBL* 85 (1966) 85-86. *[48:29ff.]*

Jeremiah 48:29-38

*Menahem Dyman, "An Archaic Remnant in Prophetic Literature," *BIES* 13 (1946-47) #1/2, II. *[48:29-38]*

Jeremiah 48:34

*Cyrus H. Gordon, "Marginal Notes on the Ancient Middle East," *JKF* 2 (1952-53) 50-61. [Jer. 48:34, p. 54f.]

Jeremiah 48:37

*T. L. Fenton, "Ugaritica—Biblica," *UF* 1 (1969) 65-70. *[48:37]*

Jeremiah 49:1-6

F[rank] North, "An Analysis of Jeremiah's Prophecy against Ammon," *JBL* 64 (1945) iii-iv. *[49:1-6]*

Frank North, "The Oracle Against the Ammonites in Jeremiah 49:1-6," *JBL* 65 (1946) 37-49.

Jeremiah 49:20

*Samuel E. Loewenstamm, "The Nouns צֹעַר, צָעוּר (Kethīb) צָעִיר (Qeré)," *Tarbiz* 36 (1966-67) #2, I-II. *[49:20]*

Jeremiah Chapters 50-51

Theodore H. Robinson, "The Structure of Jeremiah L, LI," *JTS* 19 (1917-18) 251-265.

Jeremiah 50:10

*Werner E. Lemke, "'Nebuchadrezzar, My Servant'," *CBQ* 28 (1966) 45-50. *[50:10]*

Jeremiah 51:16

*Edward J. Kissane, "'Who Maketh Lightnings for the Rain'," *JTS, N.S.,* 3 (1952) 214-216. *[51:16]*

Jeremiah 51:27-28

*Patrick D. Miller Jr., "The Divine Council and the Prophetic Call to War," *VT* 18 (1968) 100-107. [Jer. 51:27-28, pp. 104-105]

Jeremiah 51:27

Judah M. Rosenthal, "Minni—Allemania?" *JQR, N.S.,* 48 (1957-58) 204-207. *[51:27]*

Jeremiah Chapter 52

*E. J. Smit, "The relation between the texts of II Kings 25 and Jeremiah," *OTW* 11 (1968) 77-81. *[Chap. 52]*

*Peter R. Ackroyd, "Historians and Prophets," *SEÅ* 33 (1968) 18-54. [Jer. 52, pp. 42-43]

Jeremiah 52:28-30

E. J. Smit, "Jer. 52:28-30: A Chronological Crux?" *OTW* 12 (1969) 111-121.

§612 *3.5.3.2.1.6 Studies on Manuscripts of the Book of Jeremiah*

Henry Preserved Smith, "Professor Workman on the Variations Between the Hebrew and Greek Text of Jeremiah," *JBL* 9 (1890) 107-117.

*Bernhard Pick, "The Text of Jeremiah in the Polychrome Edition of the Old Testament," *HR* 33 (1897) 354-356.

*R. K. Yerkes, "The Lucian Version of the Old Testament as Illustrated from Jeremiah 1-3," *JBL* 37 (1918) 163-192.

Robert P. Blake, "Khanmeti Palimpsest Fragments of the Old Georgian Version of Jeremiah," *HTR* 25 (1932) 225-272.

*P. L. Hedley, "The Georgian Fragments of Jeremiah," *JTS* 34 (1933) 392-395.

M. Wallenstein, "A Dated Tenth Century Hebrew Parchment Fragment from the Cairo Genīzah in the Gaster Collection in the John Rylands Library," *BJRL* 40 (1957-58) 551-558.

Richard M. Frank, "The Jeremias of Pethion Ibn Ayyûb Al-Sahhâr," *CBQ* 21 (1959) 136-170.

J. Gerald Janzen, "Double Readings in the Text of Jeremiah," *HTR* 60 (1967) 433-447.

§613 *3.5.3.2.1.7 Exegetical Studies on the Book of Ezekiel*

G. F. Moore, "The Text of Ezekiel," *AR* 7 (1887) 93-104.

Crawford H. Toy, "Text-Critical notes on Ezekiel," *JBL* 15 (1896) 54-58. [**1**.-5:11; **2**.-19:2; **3**.-19:7; **4**.-23:5, 12; **5**.-24:17; **6**.-25:6; **7**.-30:5; **8**.-36:5]

Hans H. Spoer, "Emendations in the Text of Ezekiel," *AJSL* 19 (1902-03) 174-176. [24:21; 36:10-12; 37:19; 37:22; 37:22αβ]

Julius A. Bewer, "Textual and Exegetical Notes on the Book of Ezekiel," *JBL* 72 (1953) 158-168. [10:22; 19:5; 19:10; 20:25-27; 21:15; 21:32; 21:33-37; 25:9; 27:23; 31:3; 31:18b; 39:11; 39:14-15; 40:38-43; 42:2-4; 42:14]

G. R. Driver, "Ezekiel: Linguistic and Textual Problems," *B* 35 (1954) 145-159, 299-312. [1:4; 1:7; 1:14; 1:16; 1:18; 1:24; 2:10; 2:13; 4:2; 5:11; 7:6; 7:21; 7:23; 8:3; 8:7-9; 10:22; 12:3; 12:5; 13:3; 13:6; 13:11, 13; 15:2; 16:3; 16:15; 16:16; 16:30; 16:32; 16:47; 17:3; 17:5; 17:7; 17:17; 19:3; 19:5; 19:9; 21:21; 23:24; 23:40; 23:43; 24:17; 25:13; 25:15; 26:13; 27:16; 27:18; 27:21; 27:22; 27:28; 27:30; 27:34; 28:7; 28:12; 28:14; 29:5; 29:7; 29:16; 30:9; 31:3; 31:12; 32:22-26; 32:27; 33:31; 34:2; 34:12; 34:26; 34:30; 35:11; 36:13; 37:7; 37:11; 38:7; 38:18; 39:9; 40:5; 40:16; 41:6; 41:7; 41:9-10; 41:16; 41:17-18; 41:21; 41:23-24; 42:18; 43:7; 43:11; 43:14, 17; 43:17; 44:3; 44:7; 44:9; 44:18; 44:24; 44:25; 44:30; 46:22; 46:23; 47:7; 48:35]

*Gareth Lloyd Jones, "Jewish Exegesis and the English Bible," *ASTI* 7 (1968-69) 53-63. [7:7a; 7:7b; 7:11; 16:4; 16:30; 16:36; 16:43; 44:18]

Ezekiel Chapters 1-30

Allan A. MacRae, "The Key to Ezekiel's First Thirty Chapters," *BS* 122 (1965) 227-233.

Ezekiel Chapters 1-3

*[Daniel S.Gregory], "The International Lessons in Their Historical and Literary Setting," *CFL, 3rd Ser.,* 14 (1911-12) 357-371. [Ezekiel Chaps. 1-3 and 40-48, pp. 359-360]

Paul Auvray, "Ezekiel 1-3: a literary analysis," *TD* 12 (1964) 159-164.

Ezekiel 1:1-28

(   ) Luke, "Ezekiel's Vision of Jahweh's Glory (Ez 1, 1-28)," *IES* 1 (1962) 144-160.

(   ) Luke, "Ezekiel's Vision of Jahweh's Glory (Ez 1, 1-28), II," *IES* 1 (1962) 196-204.

Ezekiel Chapter 1

Edward White, "The Chariot of the Cherubim. Notes on the Prophet Ezekiel, Chap. I.," *CongL* 4 (1875) 604-615.

*E. J. Pilcher, "Notes and Queries. (3.) *Bronze Objects from Nablus,*" *PEFQS* 41 (1909) 73-74. *[Chap. 1]*

Norman Snaith, "The Chariot," *PQL* 3 (1957) 110-114. *[Chap. 1]*

Ezekiel 1:1-4

K. Budde, "Dr. Ed. Konig on Ezekiel I. 1-4," *ET* 13 (1901-02) 41-43.

Ezekiel 1:1-3

K. Budde, "The Opening Verses of the Book of Ezekiel," *ET* 12 (1900-01) 39-43, 525-527.

Ed. König, "The Opening Verses of the Book of Ezekiel," *ET* 12 (1900-01) 375-376. *[1:1-3]*

G. R. Berry, "The Title of Ezekiel (1:1-3)," *JBL* 51 (1932) 54-57.

Julius A. Bewer, "The Text of Ezek. 1:1-3," *AJSL* 50 (1933-34) 96-101.

N. H. Tur-Sinai, "The Double Dating of Ezekiel i, 1-3," *BIES* 23 (1959) #1/2, I.

Ezekiel 1:1

Ed. König, "The Opening Verses of Ezekiel," *ET* 13 (1901-02) 95. *[1:1]*

C. F. Whitley, "The 'Thirtieth' Year in Ezekiel I 1," *VT* 9 (1959) 326-330.

S. G. Taylor, "A Reconsideration of the 'Thirtieth Year' in Ezekiel 1:1," *TB* #17 (1966) 119-120.

Ezekiel 1:7

John Moncure, "The Soles of Calves' Feet," *R&E* 23 (1926) 319-320. *[1:7]*

Ezekiel 1:8

James Moffatt, "Opera Foris. Materials for the Preacher," *Exp, 7th Ser.,* 6 (1908) 94-95. *[1:8]*

*Charles C. Torrey, "Notes on Ezekiel," *JBL* 58 (1939) 69-86. [1. The 'Four Quarters' in Ezekiel's Descriptions, pp. 69-71] *[1:8]*

Ezekiel 1:13

*W. E. Barnes, "Two Interesting Passages. The Septuagint and the Massoretic Text," *ET* 6 (1894-95) 223-225. [(B) Ezekiel 1:13, pp. 224-225]

A. B. Davidson, "The Septuagint and the Massoretic Text, Ezekiel 1:13," *ET* 6 (1894-95) 283-284.

Ezekiel 1:15-21

*Anonymous, "In the Study. Wheels by the Chebar," *ET* 20 (1908-09) 307-308. *[1:15-21]*

Ezekiel 1:15-18

*Charles C. Torrey, "Notes on Ezekiel," *JBL* 58 (1939) 69-86. [2. The Eyes in the Wheels, pp. 71-73] *[1:15-18]*

Ezekiel 1:21

*I. W. Slotki, "The Metre and Text of Ps. XXIX. 3, 4, 9, and Ezekiel I. 21," *JTS* 31 (1929-30) 186-189.

Ezekiel 1:28

*Anonymous, "In the Study. Wheels by the Chebar," *ET* 20 (1908-09) 307-308. *[1:28]*

John Merle Rife, "Ezekiel's Vision by the River Chebar (Ezekiel 1:28)," *BS* 88 (1931) 105-109.

Ezekiel 2:4

W. E. Barnes, "On Ezekiel II 4," *JTS* 34 (1933) 373-374.

Ezekiel 2:6

G. R. Driver, "Ezekiel II 6: 'Sitting Upon Scorpions'," *JTS* 35 (1934) 54-55.

Ezekiel Chapter 4

F. H. Woods, "Ezekiel, Chapter iv.; a Psychological and Pathological Problem," *Exp, 7th Ser.,* 8 (1909) 48-55.

Ezekiel 4:5-6

*B. Thiering, "The Qumran Interpretation of Ezekiel 4:5-6," *AJBA* 1 (1968-71) #2, 30-34.

Ezekiel 7:5-14

J. A. Bewer, "On the Text of Ezekiel 7:5-14," *JBL* 45 (1926) 223-231.

Ezekiel 7:5

*Israel W. Slotki, "Faded Letters in Ancient Texts," *JMUEOS* #13 (1927) 60-64. *[7:5]*

Ezekiel Chapter 8

Herbert H. Gowen, "Did Jahweh Forsake the Temple? (Ezekiel 8)," *ATR* 2 (1919-20) 327-328.

*Theodor H. Gaster, "Ezekiel and the Mysteries," *JBL* 60 (1941) 289-310. [I. Ezekiel, Chapter VIII, pp. 289-290]

Ezekiel 8:7-8

Ernest W. Gurney Masterman, "Notes from Damascus. *Superstitious Custom Connected with the Building up of a Door,*" *PEFQS* 29 (1897) 148. (Note by C. R. Conder, p. 212) *[cf. Ezekiel 8:7-8]*

Ezekiel 8:17

Robert Gordis, "'The Branch to the Nose' A Note on Ezekiel VIII 17," *JTS* 37 (1936) 284-288.

H. W. F. Saggs, "The Branch to the Nose," *JTS, N.S.*, 11 (1960) 318-329. *[8:17]*

Nahum M. Sarna, "Ezekiel 8:17. A Fresh Examination," *HTR* 57 (1964) 347-352.

Ezekiel 9:8

Edward J. Young, "אני ונאשאר ('And I Was Left'), Ezekiel 9:8," *JQR, N.S.*, 42 (1951-52) 319-320.

Ezekiel 10:6-22

*Anonymous, "In the Study. Wheels by the Chebar," *ET* 20 (1908-09) 307-308. *[10:6-22(?)]*

Ezekiel 10:11-12

*Charles C. Torrey, "Notes on Ezekiel," *JBL* 58 (1939) 69-86. [2. The Eyes in the Wheels, pp. 71-73] *[10:11, 12]*

Ezekiel 10:22

*G. R. Driver, "Notes on Notes," *B* 36 (1955) 71-73. [ואתם איש אל־עבר, פניו ילכי Ezek 10:22 p. 73.]

Ezekiel 11:5-12

*Charles C. Torrey, "Notes on Ezekiel," *JBL* 58 (1939) 69-86. [5. A Serious Misunderstanding, pp. 83-86] *[11:5-12]*

Ezekiel 11:14-21

*Charles C. Torrey, "Notes on Ezekiel," *JBL* 58 (1939) 69-86. [5. A Serious Misunderstanding, pp. 83-86] *[11:14-21]*

Ezekiel 11:21

Hinckley G. Mitchell, "Ezek. 11:21," *JBL* 8 (1888) 162.

Ezekiel 13:17-23

G. Lansing, "Biblical Notes. 1. Pillows and Kerchiefs (Ezekiel xiii. 17-23)," *BFER* 27 (1878) 610-616.

W. H. Brownlee, "Exorcising the Souls from Ezekiel 13:17-23," *JBL* 69 (1950) 367-373.

Ezekiel 13:17-21

J. G. Frazer, "Hunting for Souls," *ET* 20 (1908-09) 554-555. *[13:17-21]*

Ezekiel 13:18-21

J. A. Selbie, "Ezekiel XIII. 18-21," *ET* 15 (1903-04) 75.

Ezekiel 14:1-8

J. Schoneveld, "Ezekiel XIV 1-8," *OTS* 15 (1969) 193-204.

Ezekiel 14:12-20

*Samuel Daiches, "Ezekiel and the Babylonian Account of the Deluge. Notes on Ezek. XIV. 12-20," *JQR* 17 (1904-05) 441-455.

Ezekiel 16:4

I. W. Slotki, "Ezekiel XVI 4," *JTS* 27 (1925-26) 271-272.

*Israel W. Slotki, "Faded Letters in Ancient Texts," *JMUEOS* #13 (1927) 60-64. *[16:4]*

Ezekiel 16:30

Joseph A. Fitzmyer, "A Note on Ez 16, 30," *CBQ* 23 (1961) 460-462.

Ezekiel 16:36

*L. E. Elliott-Binns, "James I. 21 and Ezekiel XVI. 36: An Odd Coincidence," *ET* 66 (1954-55) 273.

Ezekiel Chapter 17

Louise P[ettibone] Smith, "Ezekiel 17 and Some Related Passages," *JBL* 57 (1938) xvii.

Louise Pettibone Smith, "The Eagle(s) of Ezekiel 17," *JBL* 58 (1939) 43-50.

Moshe Greenberg, "Ezekiel 17 and the Policy of Psammetichus II," *JBL* 76 (1957) 304-309.

Ezekiel 17:1-10

*R. S. Foster, "A Note on Ezekiel XVII 1-10 and 22-24," *VT* 8 (1958) 374-379.

Ezekiel 17:22-24

*R. S. Foster, "A Note on Ezekiel XVII 1-10 and and 22-24," *VT* 8 (1958) 374-379.

Ezekiel 18:10

Israel W. Slotki, "Ezek. 18:10," *AJSL* 43 (1926-27) 63-66.

*Israel W. Slotki, "Faded Letters in Ancient Texts," *JMUEOS* #13 (1927) 60-64. *[18:10]*

Ezekiel 19:7

H. A. Williamson, "The Text of Ezekiel XIX. 7," *ET* 34 (1922-23) 378.

*G. R. Driver, "Hebrew Notes," *JBL* 68 (1949) 57-59. *[19:7]*

Ezekiel 20:3

*André [A.] Neher, "A Reflection on the Silence of God. 'I Will Not Be Inquired of by You' (*Ezekiel* 20:3)," *Jud* 16 (1967) 434-442. *(Trans. by Minnette Grunmann)*

Ezekiel 20:31

*I. Yeivin, "Notes and Communications. 1. A Unique Combination of Accents," *Text* 1 (1960) 209-210. *[20:31]*

Ezekiel 20:37-38

Paul Haupt, "Dolly and Buck-Tub in Ezekiel," *JBL* 36 (1917) 142-145. *[20:37-38]*

Ezekiel 20:39

*J. M. Powis Smith, "Some Textual Suggestions," *AJSL* 37 (1920-21) 238-240. [III. Ezek. 20:39, pp. 239-240]

Ezekiel 21:1

Harvey H. Guthrie Jr., "Ezekiel 21[1]," *ZAW* 74 (1962) 268-281.

Ezekiel 21:14-22

*Paul Haupt, "Etymological and Critical Notes," *AJP* 47 (1926) 305-318. [6. Ezekiel's Song of the Sword, pp. 315-318] *[21:14-22]*

Ezekiel 21:15

*Israel W. Slotki, "Faded Letters in Ancient Texts," *JMUEOS* #13 (1927) 60-64. *[E.V. 21:15]*

Ezekiel 21:20

*Israel W. Slotki, "Faded Letters in Ancient Texts," *JMUEOS* #13 (1927) 60-64. *[21:20]*

Ezekiel 21:21

*Israel W. Slotki, "Faded Letters in Ancient Texts," *JMUEOS* #13 (1927) 60-64. *[21:21]*

Ezekiel 21:24

*Willis J. Beecher, "ברא in Josh. 17:15, 18; and Ezek. 21:24, 23:47," *JBL* 2 (1882) 128-133.

Ezekiel 21:27

†Virgilus, "A Criticism of Ezekiel xxi. 27," *TRep* 3 (1771) 253-255.

Ezekiel 21:32

*W. L. Moran, "Gen 49,10 and Its Use in Ez 21,32," *B* 39 (1958) 405-425.

Ezekiel 22:17-22

*T. H. Robinson, "The Text of Jeremiah VI 27-30 in the Light of Ezekiel XXII 17-22," *JTS* 16 (1914-15) 482-490.

Ezekiel Chapter 23

Judah J. Slotki, "Ezekiel XXIII. 4," *ET* 40 (1928-29) 46.

Ezekiel 23:47

*Willis J. Beecher, "ברא in Josh. 17:15, 18; and Ezek. 21:24, 23:47," *JBL* 2 (1882) 128-133.

Ezekiel 24:1-14

J. L. Kelso, "Ezekiel's Parable of the Corroded Copper Cauldron," *JBL* 64 (1945) 391-393. *[24:1-14]*

Ezekiel 24:7-8

*James Niel, "The Natives of Palestine," *PEFQS* 13 (1881) 325-327. *[24:7, 8]*

Ezekiel 24:10

William Duff McHardy, "Ezekiel XXIV, 10," *JJS* 2 (1950-51) 155.

Ezekiel Chapters 26-28

W. E. Barnes, "Ezekiel's Denunciation of Tyre. (Ezek. xxvi-xxviii.)," *JTS* 35 (1934) 50-54.

Ezekiel Chapter 26

W. Arndt, "The Interpretation of Difficult Bible Passages," *CTM* 17 (1946) 181-197. [O.T. Refs., pp. 194ff.] *[Chap. 26]*

Ezekiel 26:1

*Charles C. Torrey, "Notes on Ezekiel," *JBL* 58 (1939) 69-86. [3. The Dates in 26 1 and 29 1, pp. 73-76]

Ezekiel 26:12

W. Emery Barnes, "Requests and Replies," *ET* 11 (1899-1900) 108. *[26:12]*

Ezekiel Chapter 27

*Sidney Smith, "The Ship Tyre," *PEQ* 85 (1953) 97-100. *[Chap. 27]*

Frederick L. Moriarty, "The Lament over Tyre (Ez. 27)," *Greg* 46 (1965) 83-88.

Ezekiel 27:1ff.

Burke O. Long, "The Divine Funeral Lament," *JBL* 85 (1966) 85-86. *[27:1ff.]*

Ezekiel 27:6

*C. J. Ball, "Note on the Wood called *Ukarina*," *SBAP* 11 (1888-89) 143-144. *[27:6(?)]*

Ezekiel 27:19

*Alan Millard, "Ezekiel XXVII. 19: The Wine Trade of Damascus," *JSS* 7 (1962) 201-203.

Ezekiel 27:32

A. Guillaume, "The Meaning of כדמה in Ezek. XXVII. 32," *JTS, N.S.,* 13 (1962) 324-325.

M[itchell] Dahood, "Accadian-Ugaritic *dmt* in Ezekiel 27, 32," *B* 45 (1964) 83-84.

Ezekiel Chapter 28

A. Bevan, "The King of Tyre in Ezekiel XXVIII," *JTS* 4 (1902-03) 500-505.

*A. Van Hoonacker, "The Literary Origin of the Narrative of the Fall. Genesis II.-III.," *Exp, 8th Ser.,* 8 (1914) 481-498. [Ezek. 28, pp. 491-494]

*Norman C. Habel, "Ezekiel 28 and the Fall of the First Man," *CTM* 38 (1967) 516-524.

*D. Neiman, "Eden, the Garden of God," *AAASH* 17 (1969) 109-124. *[Chap. 28]*

Ezekiel 28:1-19

K. Yaron, "The Dirge of the King of Tyre," *ASTI* 3 (1964) 28-57. *[28:1-19]*

Ezekiel 28:3

Chas. E. Scrimgeour, "Ezekiel and the Phoenician Script," *ET* 20 (1908-09) 526-527. *[28:3]*

Ezekiel 28:12-18

John L. McKenzie, "Mythological Allusions in Ezek 28:12-18," *JBL* 75 (1956) 322-327.

Ezekiel 28:12

Theodor H. Gaster, "Ezekiel XXVIII. 12: אַתָּה חוֹתֵם תָּכְנִית מָלֵא חָכְמָה וּכְלִיל יֹפִי,"*ET* 51 (1939-40) 156.

Ezekiel 28:13

*G. R. Driver, "Uncertain Hebrew Words," *JTS* 45 (1944) 13-14. *[28:13]*

Ezekiel 28:17

Theodor H. Gaster, "Ezekiel XXVIII. 17: גָּבַהּ לִבְּךָ בְּיָפְיֶךָ שִׁחַתָּ חָכְמָתְךָ עַל־יִפְעָתֶךָ," *ET* 62 (1950-51) 124.

Ezekiel 29:1

*Charles C. Torrey, "Notes on Ezekiel," *JBL* 58 (1939) 69-86. [3. The Dates in 26 1 and 29 1, pp. 73-76]

Ezekiel 29:8-16

H. H. B., "The Forty Years of Egypt's Desolation," *JSL, 3rd Ser.,* 3 (1856) 420-421. *[29:8-16]*

Ezekiel 29:19

A. H. Sayce, "Notes on Ezekiel XXIX 19, and Baal-Khamman," *SBAP* 34 (1912) 26, 27.

Ezekiel Chapter 31

*D. Neiman, "Eden, the Garden of God," *AAASH* 17 (1969) 109-124. *[Chap. 31]*

Ezekiel 31:14

Hinckley G. Mitchell, "Ezek. 31:14," *JBL* 8 (1888) 162.

Ezekiel 32:17-32

F. H. Woods, "A Note on Ezekiel xxxii 17-32," *ET* 22 (1910-11) 21-24.

Ezekiel 32:18-32

G. A. Frank Knight, "Ezekiel XXXII. 18-32," *ET* 5 (1893-94) 475-476.

Ezekiel 33:7-16

Edward C. Meyer and Simon J. De Vries, "Preparation for Biblical Preaching. VI," *JMTSO* 7 (1969) 59-69. *[33:7-16]*

Ezekiel 33:32

M[itchell] Dahood, "An Allusion to Koshar in Ezekiel 33, 32," *B* 44 (1963) 531-532.

Ezekiel Chapter 34

W. J. Ferrar, "The Failure of Government. (Ezekiel XXXIV)," *Exp, 8th Ser.,* 24 (1922) 316-320.

W[illiam] H. Brownlee, "Ezekiel's Poetic Indictment of the Shepherds (chap. 34)," *JBL* 70 (1951) vi.

Ezekiel 34:1-10

William H. Brownlee, "Ezekiel's Poetic Indictment of the Shepherds," *HTR* 51 (1958) 191-204. *[Chap. 34, especially vv. 1-10]*

Ezekiel Chapters 37-39

R. H. Altus, "Ezekiel 37-39," *AusTR* 17 (1946) 1-18, 37-41.

Ezekiel Chapter 37

*Harald Riesenfeld, "The Resurrection in Ezekiel XXXVII and in the Dura-Europos Paintings," *UUÅ* (1948) #11, 1-40.

William R. Farmer, "The Geography of Ezekiel's River of Life," *BA* 19 (1956) 17-22. *[Chap. 37]*

Joseph A. Grassi, "The Resurrection and the Ezechiel[sic]* Panel of the Dura-Europa Synagogue," *BibT* #11 (1964) 721-726.

Ezekiel 37:1-14

W. Emery Barnes, "Ezekiel's Vision of a Resurrection (Ezekiel XXXVII. 1-14)," *Exp, 8th Ser.,* 14 (1917) 290-297.

*J. Grassi, "Ezekiel xxxvii. 1-14 and the New Testament," *NTS* 11 (1964-65) 162-164.

Richard A. Hasler, "'Come, Creator Spirit'," *HQ* 6 (1965-66) #1, 69-71. *[37:1-14]*

Ezekiel 37:1-4

F. F. G., "The Valley of Dry Bones. (Ezekiel xxxvii. 1-4)," *ERG, 4th Ser.,* 2 (1867-68) 261-267.

Ezekiel 37:4-14

Lewis Way, "Revival of the Hope of Israel. *A Paraphrase of Ezekiel xxxvii. 4-14,*" *EN* 1 (1889) 240.

Ezekiel 37:15-28

*William Rosenau, "Ezekiel 37:15-28. What Happened to the Ten Tribes," *HUCA, Jubilee Volume,* (1925) 79-88.

Ezekiel 37:16-17

W. E[mery] Barnes, "Two Trees Become One: Ezek. xxxvii 16-17," *JTS* 39 (1938) 391-393.

Ezekiel Chapters 38 and 39

Eduard König, "Ezekiel 38-39 and the War," *HR* 71 (1916) 7-10.

E. L. Langston, "The Times of the Gentiles in Relation to the End of the Age," *JTVI* 54 (1922) 160-173, 177. (Discussion, pp. 173-177) [Ezek. chaps. 38 and 39, pp. 170-172]

J. Dwight Pentecost, "Where Do the Events of Ezekiel 38-39 Fit into the Prophetic Picture?" *BS* 114 (1957) 334-346.

Ezekiel Chapter 48

C[ameron] M. Mackay, "The City and the Sanctuary (Ezekiel XLVIII)," *PTR* 20 (1922) 399-417.

§614 *3.5.3.2.1.8 Studies on Manuscripts of the Book of Ezekiel*

H[enry] S[nyder] Gehman, "The Scheide Text of Ezekiel," *JBL* 56 (1937) xii-xiii.

Henry Snyder Gehman, "The Relations between the Hebrew Text of Ezekiel and that of the John H. Scheide Papyri," *JAOS* 58 (1938) 92-102.

Henry Snyder Gehman, "The Relations between the Text of the John H. Scheide Papyri and that of Other Greek MSS. of Ezekiel," *JBL* 57 (1938) 281-288.

F[loyd] V. Filson, "Omission of Ezekiel 12:26-28 and 36:23b-38 in Greek Papyrus Codex 967," *JBL* 62 (1943) iii.

Floyd V. Filson, "The Omission of Ezek. 12:26-28 and 36:23b-38 in Codex 967," *JBL* 62 (1943) 27-32.

J. B[arton] Payne, "The Relationship of the Chester Beatty Biblical Papyri of Ezekiel to Codex Vaticanus," *JBL* 67 (1948) x.

J[ohn] W. Wevers, "Evidence of the Scheide Papyri for the Translation of the Status Constructus in Ezekiel," *JBL* 68 (1949) xi.

*J. Barton Payne, "The Relationship of the Chester Beatty Papyri of Ezekiel to Codex Vaticanus," *JBL* 68 (1949) 251-265.

John Wm. Wevers, "Evidence of the Text of the John H. Scheide Papyri for the Translation of the Status Constructus in Ezekiel," *JBL* 70 (1951) 211-216.

§615 *3.5.3.2.2 Exegetical Studies on Passages in Several Books of the Minor Prophets*

G. R. Driver, "Linguistic and Textual Problems: Minor Prophets. II," *JTS* 39 (1938) 260-273. [Amos 1:1; 1:5; 1:13; 2:8; 3:4; 3:5; 3:12; 4:10; 5:9; 6:10; 7:8; 8:3; 8:3-4; 8:4; 8:12; 9:10; 9:13; Micah 1:6; 1:10-11; 1:12; 1:16; 2:3; 2:7; 2:8; 2:11; 4:7; 4:11; 6:5; 6:9; 6:10; 6:14; 7:2-3; 7:3-4; 7:11; Nahum 1:8-10; 1:12; 1:14; 2:6; 2:12; 2:14; 3:11; 3:16; 3:18; 4:19; 6:3; 8:13; 14:3]

G. R. Driver, "Linguistic and Textual Problems: Minor Prophets. III," *JTS* 39 (1938) 393-405. [Zephaniah 1:17; 1:18; 2:2; 2:4; 2:5; 3:5; Habakkuk 1:3; 1:7; 1:8; 1:11;2:4; 2:5; 2:10; 2:18; 3:2; 3:4; 3:10-11; 3:12; 3:13; 3:14; 3:17; Obadiah v. 5; v. 13; Haggai 2:17; Malachi 1:3; 2:4; 2:5; 2:6; 2:15; Joel 1:18; 2:17; 2:20; 2:23; 4:9-11; 4:21; Zechariah 2:2; 2:4; 2:12; 6:7; 7:2; 10:2; 10:7; 13:5; 14:14; (Hos. 6:9; 10:9-10; Nahum 1:10)]

Solomon B. Freehof, "Some Text Rearrangements in the Minor Prophets," *JQR, N.S.*, 32 (1941-42) 303-308.

§616 *3.5.3.2.3 Studies on Manuscripts of the Books of the Minor Prophets*

Christian D. Ginsburg, "The Babylonian Codex of Hosea and Joel, also the Book of Jonah, dated A.D. 916 *(now at St. Petersburg),* compared with the received Massoretic Texts," *SBAT* 5 (1876-77) 129-176, 475-549.

*W. O. E. Oesterley, "The Old Latin Texts of the Minor Prophets. I.," *JTS* 5 (1903-04) 76-88.

*W. O. E. Oesterley, "The Old Latin Texts of the Minor Prophets. II.," *JTS* 5 (1903-04) 242-253.

*W. O. E. Oesterley, "The Old Latin Texts of the Minor Prophets. III.," *JTS* 5 (1903-04) 378-386.

*W. O. E. Oesterley, "The Old Latin Texts of the Minor Prophets. IV.," *JTS* 5 (1903-04) 570-579.

*W. O. E. Oesterley, "The Old Latin Texts of the Minor Prophets. V.," *JTS* 6 (1904-05) 67-70.

*W. O. E. Oesterley, "The Old Latin Texts of the Minor Prophets. Appendix," *JTS* 6 (1904-05) 217-220.

*H[enry] A. Sanders, "A Papyrus Manuscript of the Minor Prophets," *HTR* 14 (1921) 181-187.

Anonymous, "A New Biblical Papyrus Manuscript," *HR* 83 (1922) 49. *[Greek MS - Amos 7:9 to Malachi 2:9]*

Henry A. Sanders, "A Subscription of the Freer Papyrus of the Minor Prophets," *AJA* 28 (1924) 75.

H. I[dris] Bell and H. Thompson, "A Greek-Coptic Glossary to Hosea and Amos," *JEA* 11 (1925) 241-246.

*H. St. J. Thackeray, "The Minor Prophets in the Freer Collection and the Berlin Fragment of Genesis," *JTS* 30 (1928-29) 218-219. *(Review)*

*P. Katz, "Justin's Old Testament quotations and the Greek Dodekapropheton Scroll," *StP* 1 (1957) 343-353.

§617 *3.5.3.2.3.1 Exegetical Studies on the Book of Hosea*

*A. B. Davidson, "The Prophet Hosea," *Exp, 1st Ser.,* 9 (1879) 241-264.

Marcus E. W. Johnson, "A Paraphrastic Analysis of Hosea," *TML* 6 (1891) 95-107.

W. R. W. Gardner, "Notes on Certain Passages in Hosea," *AJSL* 18 (1901-02) 177-183. [2:8; 3:4; 4:5, 6; 4:8; 4:10, 11; 4:13; 4:14; 4:18; 6:7; 6:9; 6:9, 10; 7:5; 7:8; 7:12; 7:14; 7:15; 8:1; 8:6, 7; 8:7; 9:4; 9:6; 9:10; 9:15; 10:1; 10:9; 11:6; 12:10; 13:15; 14:3; 14:9]

*Paul Haupt, "Masora," *JBL* 37 (1918) 219-228. [11:1, 4; 12:1, 2, 9; 12:4, 5a, 13, pp. 225-226]

W. W. Cannon, "The Text of Hosea," *Exp, 9th Ser.,* 1 (1924) 24-30, 87-93, 176-185, 251-266.

*E. B. Pollard, "Other Traditional Misinterpretations," *CQ* 4 (1927) 204-206. *[8:7; 4:17; 4:9]*

Fleming James, "Thoughts on Hosea," *ATR* 12 (1929-30) 213-224.

G. R. Driver, "Linguistic and Textual Problems: Minor Prophets. I," *JTS* 39 (1938) 154-166. [2:7; 2:17; 4:4-5; 4:12; 6:3; 6:4; 6:5; 6:9; 6:10; 7:3-6; 7:16; 8:7; 8:10; 8:13; 9:1; 9:4; 9:7-8; 9:10; 9:13; 9:14; 9:16; 10:10; 10:11; 10:12; 11:3-5; 12:10; 12:12; 13:1; 13:2; 13:3; 13:7; 13:8; 13:13; 13:15; 14:1; 14:3; 14:6-7]

John Joseph Owens, "Exegetical Study of Hosea," *R&E* 54 (1957) 522-543.

Frances Sparling North, "Hosea's Introduction to His Book," *VT* 8 (1958) 429-433.

Hans Walter Wolff, "Guilt and Salvation. *A Study of the Prophecy of Hosea,*" *Interp* 15 (1961) 274-285. *(Trans. by Lloyd Gaston)*

Robert G. Boling, "Prodigal Sons on Trial: A Study in the Prophecy of Hosea," *McQ* 19 (1965-66) 13-27, 38.

Hosea Chapters 1-3

*Grey Hubert Skipwith, "Gleanings from Isaiah," *JQR* 7 (1894-95) 470-480. [*Note on the order of the text in Hosea* i-iii, p. 480]

C[rawford] H. Toy, "Note on Hosea 1-3," *JBL* 32 (1913) 75-79.

Th. Laetsch, "Studies in Hos. 1-3," *CTM* 2 (1931) 909-920; 3 (1932) 33-45, 120-127, 187-196, 262-268.

E. R. Lacheman, "A Review of Hosea, Chaps. 1-3," *JBL* 70 (1951) v.

A. Douglas Tushingham, "A Reconsideration of Hosea, Chapters 1-3," *JNES* 12 (1953) 150-159.

Leroy Waterman, "Hosea, Chapters 1-3, in Retrospect and Prospect," *JNES* 14 (1955) 100-109.

John Carmody, "Lessons of Hosea 1-3," *BibT* #40 (1969) 2773-2780.

Hosea Chapters 1 and 2

Francis B. Denio, "What is the Nature of the Discourse in Hosea 1, 2?" *ONTS* 7 (1887-88) 249-253.

Jas. G. Murphy, "Another View of Hosea 1 and 2," *ONTS* 7 (1887-88) 319-320.

Hosea 2:2

W. L. Holladay, "'ERES*— 'Underworld': Two More Suggestions," *VT* 19 (1969) 123-124. *[2:2]*

Hosea 2:4-5

Cyrus H. Gordon, "Hos 2:4-5 in the Light of New Semitic Inscriptions," *ZAW* 54 (1936) 277-280.

Cyrus H. Gordon, "Mitteilungen 2. Zu ZAW 1936, 277ff.," *ZAW* 55 (1937) 176. *[2:4-5]*

Hosea 2:7

David N. Freedman, "פשתי in Hosea 2:7," *JBL* 74 (1955) 275.

Hosea 2:23-24

A. Guillaume, "A Note on Hosea II. 23, 24 (21, 22)," *JTS, N.S.,* 15 (1964) 57-58.

Hosea 2:22

*John L. McKenzie, "Knowledge of God in Hosea," *JBL* 74 (1955) 22-27. *[2:22]*

Hosea 2:23

Samuel Cox, "Hosea's Children. Hosea II. 23," *Exp, 1st Ser.,* 10 (1879) 422-432.

Hosea Chapters 3:1-5

*J. F. Springer and A. Yohannan, "A New Branch of Textual Criticism," *AQ* 2 (1923) 11-24. [Hos. 3:1-5, pp. 13-16]

Hosea 3:2

*Cyrus H. Gordon, "*TRḤ, ṮN* and *NKR* in the Ras Shamra Tablets," *JBL* 67 (1958) 407-410. [Hos. 3:2, p. 409]

Hosea 3:4-5

Cornelius Walker, "Israel's Exile and Restoration: An Exposition," *HR* 38 (1899) 254-259. *[3:4, 5]*

Hosea Chapters 4-14

W. H. Cobb, "On the Text of Hosea 4-14," *JBL* 36 (1917) 63-74.

Earle Bennett Cross, "Love Strives with Justice. A Translation of Hosea 4-14 in Rhythm to Match that of the Hebrew," *CRDSB* 7 (1934-35) 151-166.

Hosea Chapter 4

Jared J. Jackson, "Yahweh v. Cohen et al. God's Lawsuit with Priest and People—Hosea 4," *PP* 7 (1966) #4, 28-32.

Hosea 4:2

J. M. Powis Smith, "A Note on Hos. 4:2," *AJT* 19 (1915) 275-276.

Hosea 4:4

Samuel Feigin, "וְעַמְּךָ כִּמְרִיבֵי כֹהֵן Hos. 4:4b," *AJSL* 42 (1925-26) 64-68.

Hosea 4:17

J. R. Johnson, "Exposition of Hosea IV: 17," *OQR* 3 (1847-48) 450-455.

J. G. G., "Ephraim is Joined to Idols: Let Him Alone. (Hosea iv. 17.)," *ERG, 4th Ser.,* 2 (1867-68) 239-249.

Hosea 5:4

*John L. McKenzie, "Knowledge of God in Hosea," *JBL* 74 (1955) 22-27. *[5:4]*

Hosea 5:8-6:6

Edwin M. Good, "Hosea 5:8-6:6: An Alternative to Alt," *JBL* 85 (1966) 273-286.

Hosea 5:11

*Fritz Hommel, "A New Divine Name in the Old Testament," *ET* 10 (1898-99) 329-330. *[5:11]*

T. K. Cheyne, "Professor Hommel on Hos. V. 11, with a Suggestion on Baasha," *ET* 10 (1898-99) 375.

Ed. König, "Hos V. 11b and the Moon's Light," *ET* 10 (1898-99) 376-378.

Hosea 5:13

*Anonymous, "Exegetical Suggestion and Opinion.   Hosea 5:13, 10:6," *CFL, O.S.,* 2 (1898) 168.

*T. K. Cheyne, "Note on King Jareb," *Exp, 5th Ser.,* 7 (1898) 320. *[5:13]*

*J. W. Jack, "Recent Biblical Archaeology," *ET* 53 (1941-42) 367-370. [Archæology and the Biblical Text: 10. Great King (Hos 5:13 & 10:6), p. 370]

Hosea Chapter 6

Adam C. Welch, "Revival After Three Days," *ET* 30 (1918-19) 234-235. *[Chap. 6]*

Hosea 6:1-3

P. Lilly, "Note on Hosea VI. 1-3," *Exp, 2nd Ser.,* 7 (1884) 472.

R. H. Altus, "Hosea 6:1-3," *AusTR* 7 (1936) 116-120.

Hosea 6:2

C. Taylor, "Note on Hosea VI. 2," *ET* 14 (1902-03) 213.

J. Wijngaards, "Death and Resurrection in Covenant Context (Hos. VI 2)," *VT* 17 (1967) 226-239.

Hosea 6:3

James Moffatt, "Opera Foris; Or, Materials for the Preacher. Second Series," *Exp, 8th Ser.,* 2 (1911) 182-192. *[6:3]*

*John L. McKenzie, "Knowledge of God in Hosea," *JBL* 74 (1955) 22-27. *[6:3]*

Hosea 6:4-9

N. H. Torczyner, "'Gilead, a city of them that work iniquity'," *BIES* 11 (1944-45) #1/2, I. *[6:4-9]*

Hosea 6:5

*Shalom Spiegel, "A Prophetic Attestation of the Decalogue: Hosea 6:5. With Some Observations on Psalms 15 and 24," *HTR* 27 (1934) 105-144.

I. Zolli, "Note on Hosea 6:5," *JQR, N.S.,* 31 (1940-41) 79-82.

Hosea 6:7

B[enjamin] B. Warfield, "Hosea vi. 7: Adam or Man?" *CFL, N.S.,* 8 (1903) 1-10. *(Editorial)*

Hosea 7:4-10

S. M. Paul, "The Image of the Oven and the Cake in Hosea VII 4-10," *VT* 18 (1968) 114-120.

Hosea 8:1

*Theodor H. Gaster, "Notes on the Minor Prophets," *JTS* 38 (1937) 163-165. *[8:1]*

Hosea 8:4

Henri Cazelles, "The Problem of the Kings in Osee 8:4," *CBQ* 11 (1949) 14-25.

Hosea 8:12

*William Henry Green, "Hosea viii. 12 and Its Testimony to the Pentateuch," *PR* 7 (1886) 585-608.

Geo. Jeshurun, "A Note on Hosea VIII, 12," *JSOR* 11 (1927) 222-224.

Hosea 8:13

E. W. Nicholson, "Problems in Hosea VIII 13," *VT* 16 (1966) 355-358.

Hosea 9:7

*D. Winton Thomas, "A Note on the Meaning of ידע in Hosea ix. 7 and Isaiah ix. 8," *JTS* 42 (1941) 43-44.

Hosea 9:8

R. Dobbie, "The Text of Hosea IX 8," *VT* 5 (1955) 199-203.

Hosea 9:10-17

*Paul Haupt, "Shalman and Beth-arbel," *BAVSS* 10 (1927) Heft 2 121-126. *[9:10-17]*

Hosea 9:15

Norbert Lohfink, "Hate and Love in Osee 9,15," *CBQ* 25 (1963) 417.

Hosea 10:1-8

*Paul Haupt, "Shalman and Beth-arbel," *BAVSS* 10 (1927) Heft 2 121-126. *[10:1-8]*

Hosea 10:4

James Moffatt, "Opera Foris. Materials for the Preacher," *Exp, 7th Ser.,* 8 (1909) 378-380. *[10:4]*

Hosea 10:6

*Anonymous, "Exegetical Suggestion and Opinion. Hosea 5:13, 10:6," *CFL, O.S.,* 2 (1898) 168.

*T. K. Cheyne, "Note on King Jareb," *Exp, 5th Ser.,* 7 (1898) 320. *[10:6]*

*J. W. Jack, "Recent Biblical Archaeology," *ET* 53 (1941-42) 367-370. [Archæology and the Biblical Text: 10. Great King (Hos 5:13 & 10:6), p. 370]

Hosea 10:7

*H. L. Ginsberg, "Notes on the Minor Prophets," *ET* 3 (1954) IV. *[10:7]*

Chayim Cohen, "'Foam' in Hosea 10:7," *JANES* 2 (1969-70) 25-29.

Hosea 10:11

*M. H. Goshen-Gottstein, "'Ephraim is a well-trained heifer' and Ugaritic *mdl*," *B* 41 (1960) 64-66. *[10:11]*

Edward Robertson, "Textual Criticism of Hosea X, 11," *GUOST* 8 (1936-37) 16-17.

Hosea 10:12

*Cecil Roth, "The Teacher of Righteousness and the Prophecy of Joel," *VT* 13 (1963) 91-95. [Note by D. Flusser, on Hos. 10:12, p. 95]

Hosea 10:14

J. J. Dillon, "Excursus on Hosea X. 14," *CM, 3rd Ser.,* 13 (1897) 186-189.

N. Harz, "Hosea 10:14," *AJSL* 14 (1897-98) 207-208.

Hosea 10:15

*H. L. Ginsberg, "Notes on the Minor Prophets," *ET* 3 (1954) IV. *[10:15b]*

Hosea Chapter 11

Dietrich Ritschl, "God's Conversion. *An Exposition of Hosea 11*," *Interp* 15 (1961) 286-303.

Hosea 11:1-11

*Emery Barnes, "The Prophet of the Love of God," *Exp, 8th Ser.,* 9 (1915) 97-108. *[11:1-11]*

Hosea 11:1

Albert A. Isaacs, "The Difficulties of Scripture. *Hosea xi. 1.*," *EN* 3 (1891) 117-119.

*P. Haupt, "Masora," *JBL* 37 (1918) 219-228. *[11:1]*

Hosea 11:3

M. D. Goldman, "Lexicographical Notes on Exegesis (5): The Real Interpretation of Hosea XI. 3," *ABR* 4 (1954-55) 91-92.

Hosea 11:4

*Robert H. Kennett, "Ropes of Love or Cords of Vanity," *ICMM* 13 (1916-17) 122-127. *[11:4]*

*P. Haupt, "Masora," *JBL* 37 (1918) 219-228. *[11:4]*

I. J. Peritz, "The Text of Hosea 11:4b," *JBL* 53 (1934) xii.

Hosea 11:7

W. H. Griffith Thomas, "Hosea XI. 7," *ET* 18 (1906-07) 378.

James Gilroy, "Hosea XI. 7," *ET* 18 (1906-07) 378-379.

E[praim] A. Speiser, "תלואים למשובתי, Hosea 11:7," *JBL* 44 (1925) 189-191.

Hosea 11:8-9

*George S. Glanzman, "Two Notes: Am 3,15 and Os 11,8-9," *CBQ* 23 (1961) 227-233.

Hosea 12

M. Gertner, "An Attempt at an Interpretation of Hosea XII," *VT* 10 (1960) 272-284.

Hosea 12:1-15

*C. V. Pilcher, "Hosea's Interpretation of the Story of Jacob," *CJRT* 6 (1929) 259-264. *[12:1-15]*

Hosea 12:1-14

H. L. Ginsberg, "Hosea's Ephraim, More Fool Than Knave: A New Interpretation of Hosea 12:1-14," *JBL* 80 (1961) 339-347.

Hosea 12:1-2

*P. Haupt, "Masora," *JBL* 37 (1918) 219-228. *[12:1a, 2a]*

Hosea 12:1

Ch. W. Reines, "Hosea XII, 1," *JJS* 2 (1950-51) 156-157.

*Theodor H. Gaster, "Notes on the Minor Prophets," *JTS* 38 (1937) 163-165. *[12:1]*

Hosea 12:2

D. J. McCarthy, "Hosea XII 2: Covenant by Oil," *VT* 14 (1964) 215-221.

K. Deller, "*šmn bll* (Hosea 12, 2). Additional Evidence," *B* 46 (1965) 349-352.

Hosea 12:3-6

W. L. Holladay, "Chiasmus, the Key to Hosea XII 3-6," *VT* 16 (1966) 53-64.

Hosea 12:4-5

*R. Gordis, "Midrash in the Prophets," *JBL* 49 (1930) 417-422. *[12:4, 5]*

Hosea 12:5

Aage Bentzen, "The Weeping of Jacob, Hos XII 5a," *VT* 1 (1951) 58-59.

Hosea 12:9

*P. Haupt, "Masora," *JBL* 37 (1918) 219-228. *[12:9]*

Hosea 12:15

*C. V. Pilcher, "Hosea's Interpretation of the Story of Jacob," *CJRT* 6 (1929) 259-264. *[12:15b]*

Hosea 13:1

*C. V. Pilcher, "Hosea's Interpretation of the Story of Jacob," *CJRT* 6 (1929) 259-264. *[13:1]*

Hosea 14:3

Robert Gordis, "The Text and Meaning of Hosea XIV 3," *VT* 5 (1955) 88-90.

Hosea 14:8

L. M. Simmons, "Notes and Discussion. Hosea XIV 8," *JQR* 2 (1889-90) 533.

Buchanan Blake, "The Divine Sufficiency, A Note on Hos. xiv. 8," *ET* 7 (1895-96) 288.

James Spence, "Anath and Asherah, Hos. xiv. 8," *ET* 7 (1895-96) 426-427.

T. K. Cheyne, "On Hos. XIV. 8 (9)," *ET* 9 (1897-98) 331.

§618 *3.5.3.2.3.2 Studies on Manuscripts of the Book of Hosea*

Gaylard H. Patterson, "The Septuagint Text of Hosea Compared with the Massoretic Text," *AJSL* 7 (1890-91) 190-221.

Julius A. Bewer, "Some Ancient Variants in Hosea with Scribe's or Corrector's Mark," *JBL* 30 (1911) 61-65.

§619 *3.5.3.2.3.3 Exegetical Studies on the Book of Joel*

J. Bodensieck, "The Book of Joel," *WSQ* 7 (1943-44) #4, 7-18.

Joel Chapter 1

*E. Norfleet Gardner, "'Joel: God's Place in the World' (Joel 1; 2:2-18a; 21-32)," *R&E* 36 (1939) 177-186.

Joel 1:17

M. Sprengling, "Joel 1:17a," *JBL* 38 (1919) 129-141.

Joel 2:12-19

Roger L. Buhr, "A Call to Repentance. Joel 2:12-19," *Amb* 9 (1960-61) 121-124.

Joel 2:2-18

*E. Norfleet Gardner, "'Joel: God's Place in the World' (Joel 1; 2:2-18a; 21-32)," *R&E* 36 (1939) 177-186.

Joel 2:21-32

*E. Norfleet Gardner, "'Joel: God's Place in the World' (Joel 1; 2:2-18a; 21-32)," *R&E* 36 (1939) 177-186.

Joel 2:23

G. W. Ahlström, "Hammōreh liṣdāqāh in Joel ii 23," *VTS* 17 (1969) 25-36.

P. Peters, "Luther's 'Lehrer zur Gerechtigkeit,' in Joel 2:23," *WLQ* 55 (1958) 50-61, 206-216.

*O. R. Sellers, "A Possible Old Testament Reference to the Teacher of Righteousness," *IEJ* 5 (1955) 93-95. *[2:23]*

Joel 3:4

James Moffatt, "Opera Foris. Materials for the Preacher," *Exp, 7th Ser.,* 6 (1908) 95-96. *[3:4]*

Joel 3:16 (4:16)

*William J. Beecher, "Some Instances of Quotations," *HR* 51 (1906) 49-51. *[Amos 1:2 // Joel 3:16 (4:16)]*

Joel 3:18 (4:18)

*William J. Beecher, "Some Instances of Quotations," *HR* 51 (1906) 49-51. *[Amos 9:13 // Joel 3:18 (4:18)]*

Joel 4:9ff.

*Patrick D. Miller Jr., "The Divine Council and the Prophetic Call to War," *VT* 18 (1968) 100-107. [Joel 4:9ff., pp. 103-104]

Joel 4:15-17

*Meir Weiss, "In the Footsteps of one Biblical Metaphor (Methodological Remarks and Exegetical, and Historical Notices)," *Tarbiz̧* 34 (1964-65) #2, I-II; #3, I-II; #4,I-II. [2. Joel 4:15-17]*[Title Varies]*

Joel 4:17-21

A[dam] C. Welch, "Joel IV 17-21," *JTS* 22 (1920-21) 266-267.

§620 *3.5.3.2.3.4 Studies on Manuscripts of the Book of Joel*

§621 *3.5.3.2.3.5 Exegetical Studies on the Book of Amos*

Anonymous, "The Book of Amos," *HR* 22 (1891) 73. *[Outline]*

Charles C. Torrey, "On the text of Amos 5:26; 6:1, 2; 7:2," *JBL* 113 (1894) 61-63.

Charles C. Torrey, "Notes on Amos 2:7; 6:10; 8:3; 9:8-10," *JBL* 15 (1896) 151-154.

William R. Harper, "The Utterances of Amos Arranged Strophically. I. Judgments upon the Nations, 1:3-2:5," *BW* 12 (1898) 86-89.

William R. Harper, "The Utterances of Amos Arranged Strophically. II. Judgment against Israel, 2:6-16. III. The Roar of the Lion: Destruction is Coming, 3:1-8. IV. The Doom of Samaria, 3:9-4:3," *BW* 12 (1898) 179-182.

William R. Harper, "The Utterances of Amos Arranged Strophically. V. Israel's Failure to Understand Divine Judgment, 4:4-13. VI. A Dirge Announcing Israel's Coming Destruction, 5:1-6; 8:9. VII. Transgressors shall Come to Grief, 5:7-10, 17. VIII. The Doom of Captivity, 5:18-6:14," *BW* 12 (1898) 251-256.

William R. Harper, "The Utterances of Amos Arranged Strophically. VIII.*[sic]* Three Visions of Destructions, 7:1-9. IX. An Accusation and a Reply, 7:10-17. X. A Fourth Vision of Destruction with an Explanatory Discourse, 8:1-14. XI. A Fifth Vision of Destruction with a Description of the Ruin, 9:1-8a. XII. A Later Voice of Promise, 9:8b-15," *BW* 12 (1898) 333-338.

Max L. Margolis, "Notes on Some Passages in Amos," *AJSL* 17 (1900-01) 170-171. *[3:12; 4:3; 4:5; 5:6]*

James A. Montgomery, "Notes on Amos," *JBL* 23 (1904) 94-96. *[1:1; 7:2, 5; 7:4]*

John D. W. Watts, "An Old Hymn Preserved in the Book of Amos," *JNES* 15 (1956) 33-39. *[4:13; 5:8; 9:5-6]*

Clyde T. Francisco, "Expository Outline of the Book of Amos," *R&E* 63 (1966) 427-428.

John Joseph Owens, "Exegetical Studies in the Book of Amos," *R&E* 63 (1966) 429-440.

Roy L. Honeycutt Jr., "The Lion Has Roared! An Expository Outline of the Book of Amos," *SWJT, N.S.*, 9 (1966-67) #1, 27-36.

Walter Brueggemann, "Amos' Intercessory Formulas," *VT* 19 (1969) 385-399.

Amos Chapters 1-2

John Smith, "The Burden of Amos," *ET* 11 (1899-1900) 83-88. *[Chaps. 1 and 2]*

Meir Weiss, "'Because Three...and Because Four' (Amos. I-II)," *Tarbiz* 36 (1966-67) #4, I.

Meir Weiss, "The Pattern of Numerical Sequence in Amos 1-2," *JBL* 86 (1967) 416-423.

Amos 1:2-2:6

A. Bentzen, "The Ritual Background of Amos i 2-ii 6," *OTS* 8 (1950) 85-99.

*Menahem Haran, "The Rise and Decline of the Empire of Jeroboam ben Joash," *VT* 17 (1967) 266-297. [II. The Historical Background of Am. i 2 - ii 6, pp. 272-278]

M. Haran, "Observations on the Historical Background of Amos 1:2-2:6," *IEJ* 18 (1968) 201-212.

Amos 1:1-15

Michel Bernard, "Amos 1:1-15," *Min* 5 (1964-65) 66-69. [A. General Introduction; B. First Part - Chapters 1 and 2]

Amos 1:1

*John Taylor, "A New Hebrew Lexicon," *ET* 3 (1891-92) 479-480. *[1:1]*

Theophile J. Meek, "The Accusative of Time in Amos 1:1," *JAOS* 61 (1941)
63-64.

Theophile J. Meek, "Again the Accusative of Time in Amos 1:1," *JAOS* 61
(1941) 190-191.

*J. W. Jack, "Recent Biblical Archaeology," *ET* 53 (1941-42) 367-370.
[Archæology and the Biblical Text: 11. The 'Herdsman' Amos (Amos
1:1), p. 370]

Amos 1:2

*William J. Beecher, "Some Instances of Quotations," *HR* 51 (1906) 49-51.
[Amos 1:2 // Joel 3:16 (4:16)]

Amos 1:3-2:5

William R. Harper, "Suggestions Concerning the Original Text and Structure of Amos 1:3-2:5," *AJT* 1 (1897) 140-145.

Amos 1:3-2:3

Crawford H. Toy, "The Judgment of Foreign Peoples in Amos i. 3 - ii. 3,"
JBL 25 (1906) 25-28.

Amos 1:3

B. Kingston Soper, "For Three Transgressions and for Four. A New Interpretation of Amos i. 3, etc.," *ET* 71 (1959-60) 86-87.

Amos 1:5

A[braham] Malamat, "'The Sceptre-Holder from Beth Eden' and the
Inscriptions from Til-Barsib," *BIES* 16 (1951) #1/2 III. *[1:5]*

*Abraham Malamat, "Amos 1:5 in the Light of the Til Barsip Inscriptions," *BASOR* #129 (1953) 25-26.

Amos 1:6-12

Paul Haupt, "Heb. *galûṭ šôĕlmâ*, A Peaceful Colony," *JBL* 35 (1916) 288-292. *[1:6-12]*

Amos 1:6

*John P. Peters, "Miscellaneous Notes," *AJSL* 1 (1884-85) 242-243. *[1:6]*

Amos 1:9

John Priest, "The Covenant of Brothers," *JBL* 84 (1965) 400-406. *[1:9]*

Amos 1:11

Max L. Margolis, "Another Haggadic Element in the Septuagint," *AJSL* 12 (1895-96) 267. *[1:11LXX]*

Amos 1:13

*R. Burn, "Conjectures on Some Minor Prophets," *ET* 38 (1926-27) 377-378. *[1:13]*

Amos 1:15

*John Taylor, "Notes on Siegfried and Stade's New Hebrew Lexicon, II," *ET* 3 (1891-92) 520-521. *[1:15]*

Amos 2:1-16

Michel Bernard, "Amos 2:1-16," *Min* 5 (1964-65) 118-120.

Amos 2:6-16

Samuel Cox, "*The Harvest Cart:* or, the Oracle of Amos Against Israel. Amos II. 6-16," *Exp, 2nd Ser.,* 8 (1884) 321-338.

Amos 2:6-8

M. A. Beek, "The Religious Background of Amos II 6-8," *OTS* 5 (1948) 132-141.

Amos 2:6

*G. H. Box, "Amos II. 6 and VIII. 6," *ET* 12 (1900-01) 377-378.

W. O. E. Oesterley, "The Symbolism of the 'Pair of Shoes' in Amos ii, 6," *SBAP* 23 (1901) 36-38.

Amos 2:7

*John Taylor, "Notes on Siegfried and Stade's New Hebrew Lexicon, II," *ET* 3 (1891-92) 520-521. *[2:7]*

*Julius A. Bewer, "Critical Notes on Amos 2:7 and 8:4," *AJSL* 19 (1902-03) 116-117.

J[ulius] A. Bewer, "Note on Amos 2:7," *JBL* 28 (1909) 200-202.

*H. L. Ginsberg, "Notes on the Minor Prophets," *EI* 3 (1954) IV. *[2:7]*

*M[itchell] Dahood, "'To pawn one's cloak'," *B* 42 (1961) 359-366. *[2:7]*

Amos 2:8

W. O. E. Oesterley, "Amos II. 8: 'Pledged Clothes'," *ET* 13 (1901-02) 40-41.

Amos 2:9

*John Taylor, "Notes on Siegfried and Stade's New Hebrew Lexicon, II," *ET* 3 (1891-92) 520-521. *[2:9]*

Amos 2:10

*T. R. Hobbs, "Amos 3:1b and 2:10," *ZAW* 81 (1969) 384-387.

Amos 2:13

George Farmer, "Notes and Queries. 2. *Note on the Emendation of Amos* ii, 13 *(A. V.) proposed in Q.S.,* 1912, *p.* 102," *PEFQS* 44 (1912) 159.

*R. Burn, "Conjectures on Some Minor Prophets," *ET* 38 (1926-27) 377-378. *[2:13]*

*Julian Morgenstern, "The Loss of Words at the Ends of Lines in Manuscripts of Hebrew Poetry," *HUCA* 25 (1954) 41-83. *[2:13]*

Amos 3:1-15

Michel Bernard, "Amos 3:1-15," *Min* 6 (1965-66) 21-23. [C. Part II - Chapters 3 to 6]

Amos 3:1-2

*Lawrence A. Sinclair, "The Courtroom Motif in the Book of Amos," *JBL* 85 (1966) 351-353. *[3:1-2]*

Amos 3:1b

*T. R. Hobbs, "Amos 3:1b and 2:10," *ZAW* 81 (1969) 384-387.

Amos 3:3-8

Samuel Daiches, "Amos III. 3-8," *ET* 26 (1914-15) 237.

Amos 3:3

J. F. McCurdy, "Light on Scriptural Texts from Recent Discoveries," *HR* 32 (1896) 24-27. *[3:3]*

*E. B. Pollard, "Other Traditional Misinterpretations," *CQ* 4 (1927) 204-206. *[3:3]*

D. Winton Thomas, "Note on נוֹעָדוּ in Amos III. 3," *JTS, N.S.,* 7 (1956) 69-70.

Amos 3:5

*H. S. Gehman, "Philological Notes on Two Hebrew Words," *JBL* 58 (1939) vi. [Amos 3:5 - *môqēsh*]

Amos 3:9-12

*Lawrence A. Sinclair, "The Courtroom Motif in the Book of Amos," *JBL* 85 (1966) 351-353. *[3:9-12]*

Amos 3:11

John Taylor, "Notes on Siegfried and Stade's New Hebrew Lexicon, III," *ET* 4 (1892-93) 48. *[3:11]*

H. S. Pelser, "Amos 3:11—a communication," *OTW* 7&8 (1964-65) 153-156.

Amos 3:12

*John Taylor, "Notes on Siegfried and Stade's New Hebrew Lexicon, IV," *ET* 4 (1892-93) 130-132. *[3:12]*

A. Guillaume, "Hebrew Notes," *PEQ* 79 (1947) 40-44. *[3:12, pp. 42-44]*

Joseph Reider, "The Meaning of *dmeshek* in Amos 3:12," *JBL* 67 (1948) vi.

Joseph Reider, "דמשק" in Amos 3:12," *JBL* 67 (1948) 245-248.

I. Rabinowitz, "The Crux at Amos iii 12," *VT* 11 (1961) 228-231.

Henry R. Moeller, "Ambiguity at Amos 3:12," *BTr* 15 (1964) 31-34.

Amos 3:15

*George S. Glanzman, "Two Notes: Am 3,15 and Os 11,8-9," *CBQ* 23 (1961) 227-233.

Amos 4:1-5:17

Michel Bernard, "Amos 4:1-5:17," *Min* 6 (1965-66) 98-105. [C. Part II - Chapters 3 to 5:17]

Amos 4:2

Siegfried J. Schwantes, "A Note on Amos 4:2b," *ZAW* 79 (1967) 82-83.

Amos 4:4-13

W. Brueggemann, "Amos IV:4-13 and Israel's covenant worship," *VT* 15 (1965) 1-15.

Amos 4:6-11

*Willis J. Beecher, "The Jehovah Hymn in Amos," *HR* 18 (1889) 62-65. *[4:6-11]*

Amos 4:10

S. Speier, "Had Rashi Another *Vorlage* on Amos 4, 10 than is Found in the Usual Editions?" *Lĕš* 33 (1968-69) #1, n.p.n.

Amos 4:12

*A. G. Laurie, "Some Misconstrued Texts," *UQGR, N.S.,* 11 (1874) 424-438. *[4:12, pp. 424-425]*

Amos 4:13

*Willis J. Beecher, "The Jehovah Hymn in Amos," *HR* 18 (1889) 62-65. *[4:13]*

*H. R. Smythe, "The Interpretation of Amos 4^{13} in St. Athanasius and Diymus," *JTS, N.S.,* 1 (1950) 158-168.

Amos Chapter 5

H. Neil Richardson, "Apart From Justice And Righteousness There Is No Life: An Exegetical Study Of Amos 5," *WSR* 62 (1969-70) 5-11.

Amos 5:6

John P. Peters, "Amos V. 6," *AJSL* 2 (1885-86) 175.

Amos 5:7

John D. W. Watts, "Note on the Text of Amos V 7," *VT* 4 (1954) 215-216.

Amos 5:8 and 9

*G. R. Driver, "Two Astronomical Passages in the Old Testament," *JTS, N.S.,* 4 (1953) 208-212.

Amos 5:8

F. C. Burkitt, "An Additional Note to Amos v. 8," *Exp, 6th Ser.,* 1 (1900) 460-461.

Amos 5:9

*James A. Montgomery, "Notes on the Old Testament," *JBL* 31 (1912) 140-146. [6. מבלינ, Amos 5:9, p. 143]

*R. Burn, "Conjectures on Some Minor Prophets," *ET* 38 (1926-27) 377-378. *[5:9]*

Amos 5:9a

*J. J. Glück, "Three notes on the book of Amos," *OTW* 7&8 (1964-65) 115-121. [Amos 5:9a—*hammablîg;* 5:16b—*'ikkār;* 7:14—*bôlēs*]

Amos 5:11

*T. L. Fenton, "Ugaritica—Biblica," *UF* 1 (1969) 65-70. *[5:11]*

Amos 5:14

Lewis B. Paton, "Amos 5:14," *BW* 12 (1899) 196-197.

Amos 5:16b

*J. J. Glück, "Three notes on the book of Amos," *OTW* 7&8 (1964-65) 115-121. [Amos 5:9a—*hammablîg;* 5:16b—*'ikkār;* 7:14—*bôlēs*]

Amos 5:18-6:14

T. G. Soares, "Social Sins and National Doom. An Exposition of Amos 5:18-6:14," *BW* 31 (1908) 62-67.

Amos 5:18-27

Michel Bernard, "Amos 5:18-27," *Min* 6 (1965-66) 158-162. [C. Part II - Chapters 3 to 6]

Amos 5:21-27

*W. Muss-Arnolt, "Amos v. 26 (21-27)," *Exp, 6th Ser.,* 2 (1900) 414-428.

Amos 5:21

Thomas Franklin Day, "Amos 5:21," *BW* 12 (1899) 340-341.

Amos 5:23-24

J. Philip Hyatt, "The Translation and Meaning of Amos 5:23-24," *ZAW* 68 (1956) 17-24.

Amos 5:25-27

*John P. Peters, "Miscellaneous Notes," *AJSL* 1 (1884-85) 242-243. *[5:25-27]*

Nathaniel Schmidt, "On the Text and Interpretation of Amos 5:25-27," *JBL* 13 (1894) 1-15.

Amos 5:25-26

F. B. Denio, "The Interpretation of Amos v., 25, 26," *ONTS* 5 (1884-85) 335-337.

H. A. Williamson, "Rendering of Amos v. 25, 26," *ET* 36 (1924-25) 430-431.

Amos 5:25

*Duncan B. Macdonald, "Old Testament Notes," *JBL* 18 (1899) 212-215. [2. Amos 5:25, pp. 214-215]

*Frederick LaRue King, "A Destructive Critic's Perverse Interpretation of the Scriptures," *CFL, 3rd Ser.,* 5 (1906) 17-23. *[5:25]*

Robert   Dobbie,   "Amos   5:25,"   *GUOST*   17   (1957-58)   62-64.

Amos 5:26

*John Taylor, "Notes on Siegfried and Stade's New Hebrew Lexicon, IV," *ET* 4 (1892-93) 130-132. *[5:26]*

*W. Muss-Arnolt, "Amos v. 26 (21-27)," *Exp, 6th Ser.,* 2 (1900) 414-428.

*Eric Burrows, "Cuneiform and Old Testament: Three Notes," *JTS* 28 (1926-27) 184-185. [I. *Sakkūt in Amos* (Amos 5:26), pp. 184-185]

E[phraim] A. Speiser, "Note on Amos 5:26," *BASOR* #108 (1947) 5-6.

Amos 6:1-14

Michel Bernard, "Amos 6:1-14," *Min* 7 (1966-67) 178-183. [C. Part II - Chapters 3 to 6]

Amos 6:2

John   P.   Peters,   "Amos   VI.   2,"   *AJSL*   2   (1885-86)   175.

Samuel   Daiches,   "Amos   VI.   2,"   *ET*   26   (1914-15)   562-563.

Amos 6:5

*T. K. Cheyne, "The Witness of Amos to David as a Psalmist (Amos vi. 5)," *ET* 9 (1897-98) 334.

*James A. Montgomery, "Notes from the Samaritan," *JBL* 25 (1906) 49-54. [II. The Root פרש, Amos 6:5, pp. 51-52]

Samuel Daiches, "Amos VI. 5," *ET* 26 (1914-15) 521-522.

Amos 6:9-10

G. H. Box and W. O. E. Oesterley, "Amos VI. 9 and 10," *ET* 12 (1900-01) 235-236.

Amos 6:10

*G. R. Driver, "A Hebrew Burial Custom," *ZAW* 66 (1954) 314-315. *[6:10]*

Amos 6:12

*R. Burn, "Conjectures on Some Minor Prophets," *ET* 38 (1926-27) 377-378. *[6:12]*

Amos 7:1-8:3

Michel Bernard, "Amos 7:1-8:3," *Min* 8 (1968) 77-82. [Part III - Chapters 6 to 9]

Amos 7:4

Delbert R. Hillers, "Amos 7,4 and Ancient Parallels," *CBQ* 26 (1964) 221-225.

Amos 7:10-17

Paul Haupt, "Was Amos a Sheepman?" *JBL* 35 (1916) 280-287. *[7:10-17]*

Amos 7:14

*John Taylor, "A New Hebrew Lexicon," *ET* 3 (1891-92) 479-480. *[7:14]*

G. R. Driver, "Amos vii. 14 'I was [am] no prophet, neither was [am] I a prophet's son,' (R.V.)," *ET* 67 (1955-56) 91-92.

J. MacCormack, "Amos vii. 14 'I was [am] no prophet, neither was [am] I a prophet's son,' (R.V.)," *ET* 67 (1955-56) 318.

Peter R. Ackroyd, "Amos VII. 14," *ET* 68 (1956-57) 94.

G. R. Driver, "Was Explicative in Amos VII. 14," *ET* 68 (1956-57) 301-302.

*J. J. Glück, "Three notes on the book of Amos," *OTW* 7&8 (1964-65) 115-121. [Amos 5:9a—*hammablîg;* 5:16b—*'ikkār;* 7:14—*bôlēs*]

Jimmy J. Roberts, "A Note on Amos 7:14 and Its Context," *RestQ* 8 (1965) 174-177.

H. Neil Richardson, "A Critical Note on Amos 7:14," *JBL* 85 (1966) 89.

Amos 8:1-3

Samuel E. Loewenstamm, "A Remark on the Typology of the Prophetic Vision (Amos VIII, 1-3)," *Tarbiz* 34 (1964-65) #4, III.

Amos 8:1-2

Bruce D. Rahtjen, "A Critical Note on Amos 8:1-2," *JBL* 83 (1964) 416-417.

Amos 8:4-9:7

Michel Bernard, "Amos 8:4 - 9:7," *Min* 8 (1968) 185-190. [Part III - Chapters 6-9]

Amos 8:4

*Julius A. Bewer, "Critical Notes on Amos 2:7 and 8:4," *AJSL* 19 (1902-03) 116-117.

*H. L. Ginsberg, "Notes on the Minor Prophets," *EI* 3 (1954) IV. *[8:4]*

Amos 8:6

*G. H Box, "Amos II. 6 and VIII. 6," *ET* 12 (1900-01) 377-378.

Amos 8:13

*Julian Morgenstern, "The Loss of Words at the Ends of Lines in Manuscripts of Hebrew Poetry," *HUCA* 25 (1954) 41-83. *[8:13]*

Amos 8:14

Fritz Hommel, "The God Ashima of Hamath," *ET* 23 (1911-12) 93. *[8:14]*

Amos 9:1-3

*William J. Beecher, "Some Instances of Quotations," *HR* 51 (1906) 49-51. *[Amos 9:1-3 // Joel 3:18 (4:18)]*

Amos 9:1

*Max L. Margolis, "Notes on Semitic Grammar. III," *AJSL* 19 (1902-03) 45-48. [An Abnormal Hebrew Form in Amos 9:1 - וּבְצַעַם‎ / וּבְצָעַם‎]

Amos 9:7-15

*T. K. Cheyne, "Notes on Obscure Passages in the Prophets," *Exp, 5th Ser.,* 5 (1897) 41-51. *[9:7-15, pp. 44-48]*

Amos 9:8-15

Michel Bernard, "Amos 9:8-15," *Min* 9 (1969) 22-26. [Part III - Chapters 6 to 9]

Amos 9:11-12

Albert A. Isaacs, "The Difficulties of Scripture. *Amos ix, 11, 12,*" *EN* 2 (1890) 459-461.

Amos 9:13-15

*William J. Beecher, "Some Instances of Quotations," *HR* 51 (1906) 49-51. *[Amos 9:13-15]*

Amos 9:13

P. J. Maclagan, "Amos IX. 13," *ET* 26 (1914-15) 237.

§622 *3.5.3.2.3.6 Studies on Manuscripts of the Book of Amos*

Everett Bosshard, "Septuagint Codices V, 62 and 147 in the Book of Amos," *JBL* 58 (1939) 331-348.

§623 *3.5.3.2.3.7 Exegetical Studies on the Book of Obadiah*

*J. Dyneley Prince, "Old Testament Notes," *JBL* 16 (1897) 175-177. [The Word מזור in Obadiah 7, pp. 176-177]

A. H. Sayce, "The Land of Sepharad," *ET* 13 (1901-02) 308-309. *[v. 20]*

Anonymous, "Sardis and Obadiah 20," *HR* 75 (1918) 142.

V. D. Siddons, "Obadiah 5," *ET* 38 (1926-27) 331.

*R. Burn, "Conjectures on Some Minor Prophets," *ET* 38 (1926-27) 377-378. *[v.13a]*

Maurice A. Canney, "Obadiah 7," *ET* 40 (1928-29) 526-527.

John Gray, "The Diaspora of Israel and Judah in Obadiah v. 20," *ZAW* 65 (1953-54) 53-59.

(§624) *3.5.3.2.3.8 Studies on Manuscripts of the Book of Obadiah*

§625 *3.5.3.2.3.9 Exegetical Studies on the Book of Jonah*

E. B. Pusey, "Pusey's Commentary on Jonah," *ThE* 3 (1866) 121-181.

Jonah 1:4

David Noel Freedman, "Jonah 1:4b," *JBL* 77 (1958) 161-162.

Jonah 1:17

*Anonymous, "Defence of Jonah's History. Jon. i. 17, ii. 1-10. *Abridged from King's 'Morsels of Criticism',*" *SP* 3 (1830) 161-163.

Anonymous, "'Prepared a Great Fish' Jonah i. 17," *CFL, 3rd Ser.,* 21 (1916) 21-22.

Jonah 2:1-4:11

*Daniel S. Gregory, "The International Lessons in Their Historical and Literary Setting," *CFL, 3rd Ser.,* 14 (1911-12) 179-193. [Jonah 2:1-4:11, pp. 191-193]

Jonah 2:1-10

*Anonymous, "Defence of Jonah's History. Jon. i. 17, ii. 1-10. *Abridged from King's 'Morsels of Criticism',*" *SP* 3 (1830) 161-163.

Jonah 2:1

George M. Landes, "The 'Three Days and Three Nights' Motif in Jonah 2:1," *JBL* 86 (1967) 446-450.

Jonah 3:3

Albert A. Isaacs, "The Difficulties of Scripture. *Jonah iii. 3,*" *EN* 2 (1890) 25-27.

Jonah 3:5

John Taylor, "Requests and Replies," *ET* 11 (1899-1900) 25. *[3:5]*

Jonah 3:10

*Howard Crosby, "Interpretation of Some Difficult Texts," *HR* 13 (1887) 217-218. *[3:10]*

Jonah 4:4

*Chr. A. W. Brekelmans, "Some Translation Problems," *OTS* 15 (1969) 170-176. *[4:4]*

Jonah 4:6

*Henry Lobdell, "Correspondence," *BS* 12 (1855) 396-398. [Remarks by C. E. Stowe, pp. 398-401] *[Jonah's Gourd - Jonah 4:6, 10]*

Jonah 4:8

J. Davies Bryan, "A Silent East Wind," *ET* 39 (1927-28) 332. *[4:8]*

Jonah 4:9

*Chr. A. W. Brekelmans, "Some Translation Problems," *OTS* 15 (1969) 170-176. *[4:9]*

Jonah 4:10

*Henry Lobdell, "Correspondence," *BS* 12 (1855) 396-398. [Remarks by C. E. Stowe, pp. 398-401] *[Jonah's Gourd - Jonah 4:6, 10]*

§626 *3.5.3.2.3.10 Studies on Manuscripts of the Book of Jonah*

Herbert C. Youtie, "A Codex of Jonah: Berl. Sept. 18 + P.S.I. X, 1164," *HTR* 38 (1945) 195-197.

§627 *3.5.3.2.3.11 Exegetical Studies on the Book of Micah*

Paul Haupt, "Critical Notes on Micah," *AJSL* 26 (1909-10) 201-252.

Paul Haupt, "Notes on Micah," *AJSL* 27 (1910-11) 1-63.

Micah Chapter 1

D. K. Innes, "Some Notes on Micah, Chapter I," *EQ* 39 (1967) 225-227.

Micah 1:2

G. G. V. Stonehouse, "A Note on Micah I. 2b," *ET* 21 (1909-10) 377-379.

J[ohn] T. Willis, "Some Suggestions on the Interpretation of Micah I 2," *VT* 18 (1968) 372-379.

Micah 1:5

A. Kuenen, "Micah I. 5," *AJSL* 2 (1885-86) 234-236.

Micah 1:10-16

T. K. Cheyne, "Geographical Gains from Textual Criticism," *Exp, 5th Ser.,*10 (1899) 228-232. *[1:10-16]*

William Creighton Graham, "Some Suggestions Toward the Interpretation of Micah 1:10-16," *AJSL* 47 (1930-31) 237-258.

S. J. Schwantes, "Critical Notes on Micah I 10-16," *VT* 14 (1964) 454-461.

Micah 1:10

C[laude] R. Conder, "Notes on Disputed Points. *House of Aphrah*," *PEFQS* 13 (1881) 85. *[1:10]*

Micah 1:12

B. J. van der Merwe, "Micah 1:12 and its possible parallels in pre-exilic prophetism," *OTW* 11 (1968) 45-53.

Micah 1:14

A. Demsky, "The House of Achzib. A Critical Note on Micah 1:14b," *IEJ* 16 (1966) 211-215.

Micah Chapter 2

D. K. Innes, "Some Notes on Micah, Chapter II," *EQ* 41 (1969) 10-13.

Micah 2:1

James Moffatt, "Opera Foris. Materials for the Preacher," *Exp, 7th Ser.,* 8 (1909) 188-189. *[2:1]*

J[ohn] T. Willis, "On the Text of Micah 2,1aαβ," *B* 48 (1967) 534-541.

Micah 2:2

*J. M. Powis Smith, "Some Textual Suggestions," *AJSL* 37 (1920-21) 238-240. [I. Mic. 2:2, pp. 238-239]

Micah 2:6-11

*A. H. Edelkoot, "Prophet and Prophet," *OTS* 5 (1948) 179-189. *[2:6-11]*

Micah Chapters 3-5

*John T. Willis, "The Structure of Micah 3-5 and the Function of Micah 5: 9-14 in the Book" *ZAW* 81 (1969) 191-214.

Micah Chapters 3 and 4

D. K. Innes, "Some Notes on Micah, Chapters III and IV," *EQ* 41 (1969) 109-112.

Micah 3:1

John T. Willis, "A Note on ואמר in Micah 3:1," *ZAW* 80 (1968) 50-54.

Micah 3:5-8

Anonymous,"True Prophet versus False Prophet,"*R&E* 9 (1912) 557.*[3:5-8]*

*A. H. Edelkoot, "Prophet and Prophet," *OTS* 5 (1948) 179-189. *[3:5-8]*

Micah Chapters 4-7

T. K. Cheyne, "Professor G. A. Smith on the Criticism of Micah iv-vii," *ET* 7 (1895-96) 527-528.

George Adam Smith, "Professor Cheyne on my Criticism of Micah iv.-vii," *ET* 8 (1896-97) 48.

Micah Chapter 4

*W. W. Cannon, "The Disarmament Passage in Isaiah ii. and Micah iv," *Theo* 24 (1932) 2-8.

Micah 4:1-5

Israel Friedlaender, "The Present Position and the Original Form of the Prophecy of Eternal Peace in Isaiah 2:1-5 and Micah 4:1-5," *JQR, N.S.,* 6 (1915-16) 405-413.

Micah 4:5

Anonymous, "Micah 4:5," *ONTS* 10 (1890) 243.

*Kemper Fullerton, "Studies in Isaiah," *JBL* 35 (1916) 134-142. [I. On Is. 2:5 and Mi. 4:5," pp. 134-139]

Micah 4:8-5:6

W. E. Barnes, "A Messianic Prophecy (Micah iv. 8-v. 6 [Heb. v. 5])," *Exp, 6th Ser.,* 10 (1904) 376-388.

Micah 4:10

T. K. Cheyne, "Micah's Prophecy of the Babylonian Captivity. Micah iv. 10," *Exp, 2nd Ser.,* 2 (1881) 154-158.

Micah 4:14-5:5

J[ohn] T. Willis, "Micah IV 14 - V 5—A Unit," *VT* 18 (1968) 529-547.

Micah Chapter 5

Margaret B. Crook, "The Promise of Micah 5," *JBL* 70 (1951) 313-320.

D. K. Innes, "Some Notes on Micah, Chapter V," *EQ* 41 (1969) 169-171.

Micah 5:1-3

Adam C. Welch, "Micah V. 1-3 (Eng. 2-4)," *ET* 13 (1901-02) 234-236.

Micah 5:1-2

H. S. Pelzer, "Some remarks regarding the contrast in Micah 5:1 and 2," *OTW* 11 (1968) 35-44.

Micah 5:1

Anonymous, "Micah's Prophecy of Christ," *PRev* 35 (1863) 610-622. *[5:1]*

*Anonymous, "Micah's Prophecy of Christ," *BFER* 13 (1864) 195-204. *[5:1]*

Joseph A. Fitzmyer, "*l^e* as a Preposition and a Particle in Micah 5, 1 (5,2)," *CBQ* 18 (1956) 10-13.

S. J. Schwantes, "A Note on Micah 5:1 (Hebrew 4:14)," *AUSS* 1 (1963) 105-107.

John T. Willis, "Micah 5:1," *JQR, N.S.,* 58 (1967-68) 317-323.

Micah 5:2-8

Th. Laetsch, "Sermonic Study on Micah 5:2-8," *CTM* 19 (1948) 889-903.

Micah 5:2

Franklin Jewett, "Questions from the Pew. The Bethlehem Prophecy (Micah, v. 2)," *OC* 21 (1907) 238-240.

J. W. Wevers, "A Note on Micah 5:2," *JBL* 67 (1948) vii.

Micah 5:4-5

K. J. Cathcart, "Notes on Micah 5, 4-5," *B* 49 (1968) 511-514.

Micah 5:9-14

*John T. Willis, "The Structure of Micah 3-5 and the Function of Micah 5: 9-14 in the Book" *ZAW* 81 (1969) 191-214.

John T. Willis, "The Authenticity and Meaning of Micah 5:9-14," *ZAW* 81 (1969) 353-368.

Micah 5:13

*Theodor H. Gaster, "Notes on the Minor Prophets," *JTS* 38 (1937) 163-165. *[5:13]*

P. J. van Zijl, "A possible explanation of Micah 5:13 in the light of comparative semitic languages," *OTW* 11 (1968) 73-76.

Micah Chapters 6 and 7

F. C. Burkitt, "Micah 6 and 7 a Northern Prophecy," *JBL* 45 (1926) 159-161.

D. K. Innes, "Some Notes on Micah, Chapters VI and VII," *EQ* 41 (1969) 216-220.

Micah 6:1-8

G. W. Anderson, "A Study of Micah 6:1-8," *SJT* 4 (1951) 191-197.

*Paul Watson, "Form Criticism and an Exegesis of Micah 6:1-8," *RestQ* 7 (1963) 61-72.

John T. Willis, "Micah 6:6-8. *Studien zu Sprache, Form und Auslegung* by Theodor Lescow," *VT* 18 (1968) 273-278. *(Review)*

Micah 6:8-9

*H. L. Ginsberg, "Notes on the Minor Prophets," *EI* 3 (1954) IV. *[6:8, 9]*

Micah 6:8

J. H. Hertz, "Micah VI. 8," *ET* 46 (1934-35) 188.

*J. Philip Hyatt, "On the Meaning and Origin of Micah 6:8," *ATR* 34 (1952) 232-239.

T. Torrance, "The Prophet Micah and his Famous Saying," *EQ* 24 (1952) 206-214. *[6:8]*

Micah 6:10

*Theodor H. Gaster, "Notes on the Minor Prophets," *JTS* 38 (1937) 163-165. *[6:10]*

Micah 6:13-16

*H. L. Ginsberg, "Notes on the Minor Prophets," *EI* 3 (1954) IV. *[6:13-16]*

Micah 6:14

Albert Ehrman, "A Note on עָשָׁה in Mic. 6:14," *JNES* 18 (1959) 156.

Micah Chapter 7

Bo Reicke, "Liturgical Traditions in Micah 7," *HTR* 60 (1967) 349-367.

Micah 7:14-20

Theo. Laetsch, "Sermon Study on Micah 7:14-20," *CTM* 18 (1947) 348-359.

Micah 7:18

*T[heophile] J. Meek, "Hebrew Poetic Structure as a Translation Guide," *JBL* 57 (1938) viii. *[7:18]*

§628 *3.5.3.2.3.12 Studies on Manuscripts of the Book of Micah*

Henry Preserved Smith, "The Text of Micah," *AJSL* 4 (1887-88) 75-81.

R. E. Wolfe, "Variant Micah Manuscripts," *JBL* 61 (1942) iv.

§629 *3.5.3.2.3.13 Exegetical Studies on the Book of Nahum*

*B. B. Edwards, "Translation of the Prophecy of Nahum with Notes," *BS* 5 (1848) 551-576. [Introductory Remarks; Nineveh and the Assyrian Empire; Time in which the Prophecy was delivered; Native Place of Nahum; Style and Manner of Nahum; General Outline of the Argument; Translation; Notes]

*Anonymous, "The Hebrew Text of the Prophecy of Nahum," *ONTS* 2 (1882-83) 42-54. *[Interwoven with the following article]*

*Anonymous, "A Translation of the Prophecy of Nahum in Parallel Columns with the Authorized Version," *ONTS* 2 (1882-83) 43-55.

Paul Haupt, "The Book of Nahum," *JBL* 26 (1907) 1-53.

S. J. de Vries, "The Acrostic of Nahum in the Jerusalem Liturgy," *VT* 16 (1966) 476-481.

Nahum Chapter 1-2:3

William R. Arnold, "The Composition of Nahum 1-2:3," *ZAW* 21 (1901) 225-265.

W. W. Cannon, "Some Notes on Nahum I.-II. 3," *Exp, 9th Ser.,* 3 (1925) 280-286.

W. W. Cannon, "Some Notes on Nahum I.-II. 3. (c) The Acrostic Poem," *Exp, 9th Ser.,* 4 (1925) 102-110.

Nahum Chapter 1

M. Berlin, "Nahum I and the Age of the Alphabetical Acrostics," *JQR* 13 (1900-01) 681-682.

A. van Selms, "The alphabetic Hymn in Nahum 1," *OTW* 12 (1969) 33-45.

Nahum 1:4

*R. Burn, "Conjectures on Some Minor Prophets," *ET* 38 (1926-27) 377-378. *[1:4]*

Nahum 1:5

J. P. van der Westhuyzen, "A Proposed new rendering of Nah. 1:5b," *OTW* 12 (1969) 27-32.

Nahum 1:9-2:3

William C. Graham, "The Interpretation of Nahum 1:9-2:3," *AJSL* 44 (1927-28) 37-48.

Nahum 1:12-2:14

Paul Ruben, "An Oracle of Nahum," *SBAP* 20 (1898) 173-185. *[1:12-2:14]*

Nahum 1:12

*J[oseph] Reider, "An Acrostic on Ashur in the Bible," *JBL* 56 (1937) x. *[1:12]*

Joseph Reider, "The Name Ashur in the Initials of a Difficult Phrase in the Bible," *JAOS* 58 (1938) 153-155. *[1:12]*

*T[heodor] H. Gaster, "Two Notes on Nahum," *JBL* 63 (1944) 51-52. *[1:12]*

Nahum 2:3-4

*M. L. Whately, "Chariots, Runners, & Torches," *ERG, 3rd Ser.,* 2 (1863-64) 289. *[2:3, 4]*

Nahum 2:4

*T. K. Cheyne, "Influence of Assyrian in unexpected places," *JBL* 17 (1898) 103-107. [4. Nah. 2:4, pp. 106-107]

*T[heodor] H. Gaster, "Two Notes on Nahum," *JBL* 63 (1944) 51-52. *[2:4]*

Nahum 2:6

*R. Burn, "Conjectures on Some Minor Prophets," *ET* 38 (1926-27) 377-378. *[2:6]*

Nahum 2:7

A. B. Davidson, "Nahum II. 7," *ET* 7 (1895-96) 568.

T. K. Cheyne, "Nahum ii. 7: Athaliah; Janoah: A Correction," *ET* 8 (1896-97) 48.

*T. K. Cheyne, "Notes on Obscure Passages in the Prophets," *Exp, 5th Ser.,* 5 (1897) 41-51. *[2:7, pp. 48-49]*

Nahum 2:8

*T. K. Cheyne, "Notes on Psa. 22:25 and Nah. 2:8," *JBL* 15 (1896) 198.

M. A. Canney, "Nahum II. 8," *JMUEOS* #3 (1913-14) 89.

*R. Burn, "Conjectures on Some Minor Prophets," *ET* 38 (1926-27) 377-378. *[2:8]*

Julius L .Siegel, "וְהֻצַּב גֻּלְתָה הֹעֲלָתָה, Nah. 2:8," *AJSL* 46 (1929-30) 139-140.

Joseph Reider, "A Solution to *haṣṣab* in Nahum 2:8," *JBL* 55 (1936) vi.

Joseph Reider, "A new Ishtar Epithet in the Bible," *JNES* 8 (1949) 104-107. *[2:8]*

G. R. Driver, "Farewell to Queen Huzzab!" *JTS, N.S.,* 15 (1964)296-298. *[2:8]*

Nahum 2:11

*J. J. Glück, *"pārûr — pā'rûr —* a Case of Biblical Paronomasia," *OTW* 12 (1969) 21-26. *[2:11b (A.V. v. 10)]*

Nahum 2:13

*N. Wieder, "Notes on the New Documents from the Fourth Cave of Qumran," *JJS* 7 (1956) 71-76. [The Title "Great Ones", (Nah. 2:13) p. 72]

Nahum 3:1-11

*R. Weiss, "A Comparison Between the Massoretic and the Qumran Texts of Nahum III, 1-11," *RdQ* 4 (1962-63) 433-439.

Nahum 3:4

*Sidney B. Hoenig, "The Pesher Nahum 'Talmud'," *JBL* 86 (1967) 441-445. *[Nah. 3:4 and 4QpNah]*

Nahum 3:8

James Moffatt, "Opera Foris. Materials for the Preacher," *Exp, 7th Ser.,* 6 (1908) 282-283. *[3:8]*

J. Van Doorslaer, "No Amon," *CBQ* 11 (1949) 280-295. *[3:8]*

Nahum 3:11

*Theodor H. Gaster, "Notes on the Minor Prophets," *JTS* 38 (1937) 163-165. *[3:11]*

§630 *3.5.3.2.3.14 Studies on Manuscripts of the Book of Nahum*

*Anonymous, "The Hebrew Text of the Prophecy of Nahum," *ONTS* 2 (1882-83) 42-54. *[Interwoven with the following article]*

*Anonymous, "A Translation of the Prophecy of Nahum in Parallel Columns with the Authorized Version," *ONTS* 2 (1882-83) 43-55.

W. H. Marquess, J. W. Payne, W. W. Lovejoy, and W. H. Carmichael, "A Translation of the Septuagint of the Prophecy of Nahum," *ONTS* 2 (1882-83) 56-58.

*F. J. Gurney, C. E. Crandall, and O. O. Fletcher, "A Translation of the Targum (Jonathan) of the Prophecy of Nahum," *ONTS* 2 (1882-83) 58-61.

C. L. Logan, A. C. Chute, J. E. Hamilton, J. F. Baker, and J. W. Weddell, "A Translation of the Vulgate of the Prophecy of Nahum," *ONTS* 2 (1882-83) 61-63.

*Michael Adler, "A Specimen of a Commentary and Collated Text of the Targum to the Prophets (Nahum)," *JQR* 7 (1894-95) 630-657.

*R. Weiss, "A Comparison Between the Massoretic and the Qumran Texts of Nahum III, 1-11," *RdQ* 4 (1962-63) 433-439.

§631 *3.5.3.2.3.15 Exegetical Studies on the Book of Habakkuk*

Habakkuk Chapters 1 and 2

W. B. Stevenson, "The Interpretation of Habakkuk I., II.," *Exp, 6th Ser.,* 5 (1902) 388-400.

W. W. Cannon, "The Integrity of Habakkuk cc. 1. 2.," *ZAW* 43 (1925) 62-90.

Habakkuk 2:1

Lewis B. Paton, "Habakkuk 2:1," *BW* 13 (1899) 197.

Habakkuk 2:2-4

Anonymous, "Comparative Translation: Habakkuk 2:2-4. A Study in Modernizing the English Bible," *BW* 23 (1904) 287-288.

Habakkuk 2:2

*(   ) Ozer, "Remarks on Isaiah xxxv. 8, and Habakkuk ii. 2," *CongML* 14 (1831) 479-481.

Buchanan Blake, R. M. Spence, W. P. Paterson, J. Rose, and A. B. Davidson, "Notes on Habakkuk II. 2," *ET* 3 (1891-92) 167-168.

Anonymous, "Habakkuk 2:2 'That He May Run That Readeth It'," *OTS* 14 (1892) 183.

P. Haupt, "He Who Runs May Read," *JBL* 40 (1921) 181-182. *[2:2b]*

*E. B. Pollard, "Other Traditional Misinterpretations," *CQ* 4 (1927) 204-206. *[2:2]*

John Marshall Holt, "'So He May Run Who Reads It'," *JBL* 83 (1964) 298-302. *[2:2]*

Habakkuk 2:4-5

William Creighton Graham, "A Note on Habakkuk 2:4-5," *AJSL* 42 (1925-26) 128-129.

*H. L. Ginsberg, "Notes on the Minor Prophets," *EI* 3 (1954) IV. *[2:4-5]*

William H. Brownlee, "The Placarded Revelation of Habakkuk," *JBL* 82 (1963) 319-325. *[2:4-5]*

Habakkuk 2:4

George B. Stevens, "The Just Shall Live by Faith," *BW* 23 (1904) 267-271. *[2:4]*

Ira Maurice Price, "The Just Shall Live by Faith: Habakkuk 2:4," *BW* 35 (1910) 39-45.

William M. McPheeters, *"Emunah* in Habakkuk 2:4," *BR* 3 (1918) 290-296.

R. B. Y. Scott, "The Text of Habakkuk II. 4," *ET* 35 (1923-24) 187.

P. J. M. Southwell, "A Note on Habakkuk II. 4," *JTS, N.S.,* 19 (1968) 614-617.

Habakkuk 2:13-14

*H. L. Ginsberg, "Notes on the Minor Prophets," *EI* 3 (1954) IV. *[2:13a, 14]*

Habakkuk 2:17

*J. M. Powis Smith, "Some Textual Suggestions," *AJSL* 37 (1920-21) 238-240. [II. Hab. 2:17, p. 239]

Habakkuk Chapter 3

J. R., "Critical Remarks on the Third Chapter of Habakkuk, with Suggested Improvements of the Authorized Version," *JSL, 2nd Ser.,* 6 (1854) 384-392.

James Strong, "The Prayer of Habakkuk. (Chap. III.)," *MR* 43 (1861) 73-89.

Max L. Margolis, "The Character of the Anonymous Greek Version of Habakkuk, Chapter 3," *AJSL* 24 (1907-08) 76-85.

H. St. J. Thackeray, "Primitive Lectionary Notes in the Psalm of Habakkuk," *JTS* 12 (1910-11) 191-213. *[Chap. 3]*

F. J. Stephens, "The Babylonian Dragon Myth in Habakkuk 3," *JBL* 43 (1924) 290-293.

William A. Irwin, "The Psalm of Habakkuk," *JNES* 1 (1942) 10-40. *[Chap 3]*

William A. Irwin, "The Mythological Background of Habakkuk, Chapter 3," *JNES* 15 (1956) 47-50.

E. M. Good, "The Barberini Greek Version of Habakkuk III," *VT* 9 (1959) 11-30.

J. H. Eaton, "The Origin and Meaning of Habakkuk 3," *ZAW* 76 (1964) 144-171.

W. Baars, "A new witness to the text of the Barberini Greek version of Habakkuk III," *VT* 15 (1965) 381-382.

L. M. Muntingh, "Tēman and Paran in the prayer of Habakkuk," *OTW* 12 (1969) 64-70. *[Chap. 3]*

Habakkuk 3:2-19

H. Northcote, "The Song of Habakkuk," *ET* 25 (1913-14) 522-524. *[3:2-19]*

Habakkuk 3:2

*Leo Jung, "Mis-Translations a Source in Jewish and Christian Lore," *PAAJR* 5 (1933-34) 55-67. [I *Habakkuk III 2*, pp. 56-58]

Habakkuk 3:4

William R. Arnold, "The Interpretation of לו מידו קרנים Hab. 3:4," *AJSL* 21 (1904-05) 167-172.

Theodor H. Gaster, "On Habakkuk 3:4," *JBL* 62 (1943) 345-346.

Habakkuk 3:7

*W[illiam] F[oxwell] Albright, "Two Letters from Ugarit (Ras Shamra)," *BASOR* #82 (1941) 43-49. [A Canaanite Letter from Ugarit and Habakkuk 3:7, pp. 46-47]

G. R. Driver, "On Habakkuk 3:7," *JBL* 62 (1943) 121.

Habakkuk 3:10-15

William Hayes Ward, "Habakkuk 3:10, 11, 15," *AJT* 1 (1897) 137-140.

Habakkuk 3:13-15

*Herbert G. May, "Some Cosmic Connotations of *mayim rabbîm*, 'Many Waters'," *JBL* 74 (1955) 9-21. *[3:13-15]*

Habakkuk 3:17-19

W. W. Ketchum, "A Study of Habakkuk 3:17-19," *BRec* 4 (1907) 15-20.

(§632) *3.5.3.2.3.16 Studies on Manuscripts of the Book of Habakkuk*

§633 *3.5.3.2.3.17 Exegetical Studies on the Book of Zephaniah*

*R. C. Ford, "Isaiah XIII. 2 - XIV. 23, and Zephaniah," *ET* 4 (1892-93) 224-225.

B. A. Copass, "Zephaniah—The Princely Young Preacher in Jerusalem," *SWJT* 5 (1921) #3, 67-74.

*Israel Efros, "Brief Notes. *Textual Notes on the Hebrew Bible,*" *JAOS* 45 (1925) 152-154. [**3**. Zeph. 2:8; **4**. Zeph. 2:14; **5**. Zeph 3:3; **6**. Zeph. 3:6]

Zephaniah 1:9

W. H. Bennett, "Sir J. G. Frazer on 'Those That Leap Over (*or* On) the Threshold' (Zeph. I. 9)," *ET* 30 (1918-19) 379-380.

Zephaniah 1:14-18

P[aul] Haupt, "The Prototype of the Dies Irae," *JBL* 38 (1919) 142-151. *[1:14-18]*

Zephaniah 2:1

John Gray, "A metaphor from the building in Zephaniah II 1," *VT* 3 (1953) 404-407.

Zephaniah 2:2-5

*J. A. Bewer, "Textual Suggestions on Isa 2:6; 66:3; Zeph. 2:2-5," *JBL* 27 (1908) 163-166.

Zephaniah 2:4

D. Winton Thomas, "A Pun on the Name Ashdod in Zephaniah II. 4," *ET* 74 (1962-63) 63.

Zephaniah 3:10

Fritz Hommel, "בַּהּ־פוּצַי in Zeph III. 10," *ET* 11 (1899-1900) 92-93.

Zephaniah 3:17

*Theodor H. Gaster, "Two Textual Emendations. Zephaniah iii. 17," *ET* 78
(1966-67) 267.

(§634) *3.5.3.2.3.18 Studies on Manuscripts of the Book of Zephaniah*

§635 *3.5.3.2.3.19 Exegetical Studies on the Book of Haggai*

T. V. Moore, "Haggai. A New Translation with Expository Notes," *MQR* 9
(1855) 202-228.

*P. R. Ackroyd, "Some Interpretive Glosses in the Book of Haggai," *JJS* 7
(1956) 163-168. [2:5a; 2:9LXX; 2:14LXX; 2:17]

Francis Sparling North, "Critical Analysis of the Book of Haggai," *ZAW* 68
(1956) 25-46.

Haggai 1:1-13

*Arthur Pollok Sym, "A Textual Study in Zechariah and Haggai," *ET* 7
(1895-96) 257-260, 317-321. *[1:2, 1-5, 13]*

Haggai 2:7

Milton S. Terry, "'The Desire of All Nations'," *MR* 75 (1893) 268-272.*[2:7]*

*E. B. Pollard, "Some Traditional Misinterpretations," *CQ* 4 (1927) 92-94.
[2:7]

Haggai 2:10-19

J. Morgenstern, "The Fast in Jerusalem on the Twenty-fourth of the Ninth
Month," *JBL* 66 (1947) vii. *[2:10-19]*

T. N. Townsend, "Additional Comments on Haggai II 10-19," *VT* 18 (1968)
559-560.

Haggai 2:10-14

H. G. May, "'This People' and 'This Nation' in Haggai," *VT* 18 (1968) 190-
197. *[2:10-14]*

Haggai 2:11-14

George L. Robinson, "Haggai 2:11-14," *BW* 13 (1899) 341.

Haggai 2:14

Paul Haupt, "The Septuagintal Addition to Haggai 2:14," *JBL* 36 (1917) 148-150.

W. M. McPheeters, "The Time of the Verbs in Haggai 2:14," *ONTS* 12 (1891) 304-305.

(§636) *3.5.3.2.3.20 Studies on Manuscripts of the Book of Haggai*

§637 *3.5.3.2.3.21 Exegetical Studies on the Book of Zechariah*

T. V. Moore, "Zechariah," *MQR* 7 (1853) 121-136, 211-232, 321-339; 8 (1854) 9-29, 194-213, 321-339.

James Stalker, "The Parables of Zechariah. Introductory" *ET* 5 (1893-94) 153-156.

Alfred Huddle, "'The Angel That Talked with Me'," *ET* 6 (1894-95) 334-335. *[1:7-6:8; 1:17(LXX); 6:5(LXX)]*

Paul Haupt, "The Visions of Zechariah," *JBL* 32 (1913) 101-122.

B. A. Copass, "Zechariah—The Great Preacher after the Return of the Jews from the Babylonish Captivity," *SWJT* 5 (1921) #4, 70-79.

Charles Lee Feinberg, "Exegetical Studies in Zechariah," *BS* 97 (1940) 189-199. [I. The Prophet Zechariah; II. The Historical Background; III. The Style of the Book; IV. The Interpretation of the Prophecy; V. The Importance of the Book; VI. The Critical Question; VII. The Plan of the Prophecy]

Zechariah Chapters 1-8

Eiji Asada, "The Hebrew Text of Zechariah 1-8, compared with the Different Ancient Versions," *AJSL* 12 (1895-96) 173-196.

T. M'William, "The Prophecies of Zechariah. (I-VIII)," *ET* 13 (1901-02) 549-554.

Peter R. Ackroyd, "The Book of Haggai and Zechariah I-VIII," *JJS* 3 (1952) 151-156. [I. The Contents of Zechariah I-VIII; II. The Dates in Zechariah I-VIII; III. The Compilation of Zechariah I-VIII; IV. Conclusion]

Zechariah Chapters 1-6

E. C. Gordon, "The Prophecies of Zechariah, Chaps. I-VI. A Biblical Study," *CFL, O.S.,* 3 (1899) 373-379.

Zechariah 1:1-6

Charles Lee Feinberg, "Exegetical Studies in Zechariah," *BS* 97 (1940) 318-324. [I. An Exhortation to Repentance, 1:1-6]

Zechariah 1:1

*Lewis B. Paton, "Notes on Zechariah," *JBL* 18 (1899) 177-183. [1:1sq., p. 180f.]

Zechariah 1:7-6:15

Charles Lee Feinberg, "Exegetical Studies in Zechariah," *BS* 97 (1940) 435-447; 98 (1941) 56-68, 169-182, 447-458; 99 (1942) 56-66. [II. The Prophet's Night-Visions, 1:7-6:15]

Zechariah 1:8

*A. Van Hoonacker, "Zech. i 8, 10 s.; vi 1 ss. and the *Dul-Azag* of the Babylonians," *JTS* 16 (1914-15) 250-252.

Zechariah 1:10

*A. Van Hoonacker, "Zech. i 8, 10 s.; vi 1 ss. and the *Dul-Azag* of the Babylonians," *JTS* 16 (1914-15) 250-252.

Zechariah 1:7-17

James Stalker, "The Parables of Zechariah. The Parable of the Horsemen (Chap 1:7-17)," *ET* 5 (1893-94) 198-201.

Zechariah 1:18-21

James Stalker, "The Parables of Zechariah. The Parable of the Carpenters (Chap 1:18-21)," *ET* 5 (1893-94) 311-314.

H. H. Currie, "The Victory That Overcometh the World, Zech. i. 18-21," *ET* 6 (1894-95) 331-332.

Zechariah Chapter 2

†Anonymous, "Wintle on Zechariah, Chapter II," *BCQTR* 13 (1799) 655-656. *(Review)*

James Stalker, "The Parables of Zechariah. The Parable of the Wall of Fire (Chap. 2)," *ET* 5 (1893-94) 405-409.

Zechariah 2:1-5

Lukas Vischer, "The Temple of God. First Bible Lecture (Monday) Zechariah 2:1-5," *MidS* 5 (1965-66) #3, 90-97.

Zechariah 2:12

*Th. C. Vriezen, "Two Old Cruces," *OTS* 5 (1948) 80-91. *[2:12]*

Zechariah Chapter 3

James Stalker, "The Parables of Zechariah. The Parable of the High Priest (Chap. 3)," *ET* 5 (1893-94) 500-503.

*Lewis B. Paton, "Notes on Zechariah," *JBL* 18 (1899) 177-183. [Chap. 3, pp. 181-183]

*John D. Davis, "The Reclothing and Coronation of Joshua, Zechariah iii and vi," *PTR* 18 (1920) 256-268.

Zechariah 3:4

D. W[inton] Thomas, "A Note on מחלצות, in Zech. III 4," *JTS* 33 (1931-32) 279-280.

Zechariah Chapter 4

James Stalker, "The Parables of Zechariah. The Parable of the Golden Candlestick (Chap 4)," *ET* 6 (1894-95) 26-30.

Zechariah 4:8-10

E. E. Le Bas, "Zechariah's Climax to the Career of the Corner-Stone," *PEQ* 83 (1951) 139-155. *[4:8-10]*

Zechariah Chapter 5

George Bladon, "The Parable of the Ephah," *ET* 6 (1894-95) 525-526.
[*Chap. 5*]

*F. Jarratt, "Rabbinic Interpretation of the Vision of the Ephah in Zechariah
V," *ET* 6 (1894-95) 566-567.

Zechariah 5:1-4

James Stalker, "The Parables of Zechariah. The Parable of the Flying Roll
(Chap. 5:1-4)," *ET* 6 (1894-95) 110-113.

Zechariah 5:5-11

James Stalker, "The Parables of Zechariah. The Parable of the Ephah (Chap.
5:5-11)," *ET* 6 (1894-95) 232-235.

*G. H. Skipwith, "Leaves from the 'Golden Bough'," *JQR* 8 (1895-96) 704-
706. [Zech. 5:5-11, p. 706]

Shlomo Marenof, "Note Concerning the Meaning of the Word 'Ephah,'
Zechariah 5:5-11," *AJSL* 48 (1931-32) 264-267.

*Susan Lee Sherman and John Briggs Curtis, "Divine-Human Conflicts in
the Old Testament," *JNES* 28 (1969) 231-242. [Zech 5:5-11, pp. 235
and 241]

Zechariah 5:5f.

Anonymous, "Zechariah V 5f.," *Exp, 9th Ser.,* 1 (1924) 140.

Zechariah Chapter 6

*John D. Davis, "The Reclothing and Coronation of Joshua, Zechariah iii
and vi," *PTR* 18 (1920) 256-268.

Zechariah 6:1-8

James Stalker, "The Parables of Zechariah. The Parable of the Chariots
(Chap. 6:1-8)," *ET* 6 (1894-95) 297-300.

Zechariah 6:1-7

E. C. Bissell, "On Zech. 6:1-7," *JBL* 6 (1886) Part 1, 117-118.

Zechariah 6:1ss.

*A. Van Hoonacker, "Zech. i 8, 10 s.; vi 1 ss. and the *Dul-Azag* of the Babylonians," *JTS* 16 (1914-15) 250-252.

Zechariah 6:9-15

Anonymous, "Joshua, the High Priest, as a Symbol of the Branch," *TLJ* 4 (1851-52) 159-162. *[6:9-15]*

George Wisely, "Symbolical and Verbal Prophecy," *ERG, 9th Ser.,* 2 (1887) 267-271. *[6:9-15] (Second Article Not Published)*

Zechariah 7:1-8:23

Charles Lee Feinberg, "Exegetical Studies in Zechariah," *BS* 99 (1942) 56-66, 166-179, 332-343, 428-439; 100 (1943) 256-262. [III. The Question and the Answer concerning Fasting, 7:1-8:23, pp. 332-343]

Zechariah 7:2

J. Philip Hyatt, "A Neo-Babylonian Parallel to *Bethel-Sar-Eṣer,* Zech 7 2," *JBL* 56 (1937) 387-394.

Zechariah 7:4-10

W. F. Beck, "Sermon Study on Zech. 7:4-10 for the Thirteenth Sunday After Trinity," *CTM* 22 (1951) 500-512.

Zechariah 7:8sq.

*Lewis B. Paton, "Notes on Zechariah," *JBL* 18 (1899) 177-183. [Zech 7:8sq., p. 180]

Zechariah 8:12

John C. Gibson, "'The Seed of Peace,' Zech viii. 12," *ET* 6 (1894-95) 567.

Zechariah 8:16-19

W. B. Stevenson, "Zechariah 8. 16-19," *GUOST* 6 (1929-33) 68.

Zechariah 8:20-23

Julian Morgenstern, "The First Proselyte Movement to Judaism," *JBL* 68 (1949) ix. *[8:20-23]*

Zechariah Chapters 9-14

J. A. Selbie, "Van Hoonacker on Zec. IX.—XIV.," *ET* 14 (1902-03) 162-163.

Charles Lee Feinberg, "Exegetical Studies in Zechariah," *BS* 100 (1943) 390-396, 513-523; 101 (1944) 76-82, 187-192, 434-445; 102 (1945) 55-73, 417-432; 103 (1946) 28-38, 161-175. [IV. The Future of the World Powers, Israel, and the Kingdom of Messiah, 9-14, pp. 390-396]

T. Jansma, "Inquiry into the Hebrew Text and Ancient Versions of Zechariah ix-xiv," *OTS* 7 (1950) 1-142.

Leroy Waterman, "The Camouflaged Purge of Three Messianic Conspirators," *JNES* 13 (1954) 73-78. *Chaps. 9-14]*

Zechariah Chapters 9-11

D. R. Jones, "A Fresh Interpretation of Zechariah IX-XI," *VT* 12 (1962) 241-259.

Zechariah 9:1-10

E. G. H. Kraeling, "The Historical Situation in Zech. 9:1-10," *AJSL* 41 (1924-25) 24-33.

Zechariah 9:1-6

*A[braham] Malamat, "The Historical Setting of Two Biblical Prophecies on the Nations," *IEJ* 1 (1950-51) 149-159. *[9:1-6]*

Zechariah 9:1

Mitchell J. Dahood, "Zacharia 9,1 *'ēn 'ādām*," *CBQ* 25 (1963) 123-124.

Zechariah 9:9-10

Charles W. F. Smith, "The Horse and the Ass in the Bible, An Essay on Zechariah 9:9, 10," *ATR* 27 (1945) 86-96.

Zechariah 9:9

*Leo Jung, "Mis-Translations a Source in Jewish and Christian Lore," *PAAJR* 5 (1933-34) 55-67. [VII. Some Cases of Theological Bias. (Zech. 9:9 as quoted in Matt. 21:2-7)]

*L. Fuerbringer, "Brief Studies in the Prophets," *CTM* 19 (1948) 499-515. [Zech. 9:9, pp. 499-501] *(Trans. by G. V. Schick)*

Zechariah 9:16

*Julius A. Bewer, "Two Suggestions on Prov 30:31 and Zech 9:16," *JBL* 67 (1948) 61-62.

Zechariah 10:4

Albert A. Isaacs, "The Difficulties of Scripture," *EN* 4 (1892) 411-414. *[10:4]*

Zechariah 10:11

A. A. Bevan, "Notes on Zechariah X. 11," *JP* 18 (1889-90) 88.

F. J. Botha, "Zechariah X. 11a וְעָבַר בַּיָּם צָרָה," *ET* 66 (1954-55) 177.

D. Winton Thomas, "Zechariah X. 11a," *ET* 66 (1954-55) 272-273.

Zechariah Chapters 11 and 12

G. A. Cooke, "The Unknown Martyr: A Study of Zech. 11 and 12," *ATR* 6 (1923-24) 97-105.

Zechariah Chapter 11

R. Winterbotham, "The Good Shepherd of Zechariah XI," *Exp, 5th Ser.,* 6 (1897) 127-139.

*Paul Haupt, "Etymological and Critical Notes," *AJP* 47 (1926) 305-318. [5. Onias and Alcimus, pp. 312-315] *[Chap. 11]*

Zechariah 11:4-17

S. Feigin, "Some Notes on Zechariah 11:4-17," *JBL* 44 (1925) 203-213.

*William Walter Cannon, "Some Notes on Zechariah c. 11," *AfO* 4 (1927) 139-146. [2. The oracle 11, 4-17+13, 7-9, pp. 143-146]

Zechariah 11:8

D. Sperber, "Kāra-bān," *L* 34 (1969-70) #1/2, 4. *[English Supplement]* *[11:8]* [קרבן]

Zechariah 11:12-13

*L. Fuerbringer, "Brief Studies in the Prophets," *CTM* 19 (1948) 499-515. [Zech. 11:12-13, pp. 501-509] *(Trans. by G. V. Schick)*

Zechariah 11:13

*W. R. B., "Zechariah XI. 13; Matthew XXVII. 9," *JSL, 3rd Ser.,* 12 (1860-61) 459-460.

*Charles C. Torrey, "The Foundry of the Second Temple," *JBL* 55 (1936) 247-260. *[11:13]*

Zechariah Chapters 12-13:1

R. H. Kennett, "Zechariah XII-XIII 1," *JTS* 28 (1926-27) 1-9.

Zechariah Chapter 12

Anonymous, "Zechariah XII," *BWR* 1 (1877) 299-301.

Matitiahu Tsevat, "Sociological and Historical Observations on Zechariah XII," *Tarbiz* 25 (1956-57) #2, I.

Zechariah 12:2

*R. Giveon, "'In the Valley of Megiddon' (Zech. xii: ii) (Notes on the Historical Geography of the Region East of Megiddo)," *JJS* 8 (1957) 155-164.

Zechariah 12:10

*James Strong, "*Quotation of the Prophecy of Christ's Transfixion.—* Zech. xii, 10; John xix, 37," *MR* 32 (1850) 338-339.

*L. Fuerbringer, "Brief Studies in the Prophets," *CTM* 19 (1948) 499-515. [Zech.12:10, pp. 512-515] *(Trans. by G. V. Schick)*

Zechariah 12:11

Geo. Bladon, "Zechariah XII. 11," *ET* 6 (1894-95) 188.

*James A. Montgomery, "Brief Communications," *JBL* 33 (1914) 78-80. [2. The Wailing of Hadad-Rimmon (Zech. 12:11, pp. 78-80]

Zechariah 13:7-9

*Anonymous, "Transpositions in the Prophetical Books of the Old Testament," *BRCM* 1 (1846) 153-157. *[13:7-9]*

*William Walter Cannon, "Some Notes on Zechariah c. 11," *AfO* 4 (1927) 139-146. [2. The oracle 11, 4-17+13, 7-9, pp. 143-146]

Zechariah 13:7

*L. Fuerbringer, "Brief Studies in the Prophets," *CTM* 19 (1948) 499-515. [Zech. 13:7, pp. 509-511] *(Trans. by G. V. Schick)*

*Samuel E. Loewenstamm, "The Nouns צֵעַר, צֵעוּר (Kethīb) צָעִיר (Qeré)," *Tarbiẕ* 36 (1966-67) #2, I-II. *[13:7]*

Zechariah Chapter 14

John J. Owen, "Exposition of Zechariah XIV," *BS* 18 (1861) 358-383.

H. Graetz, "Biblical Studies I—The Last Chapter of Zechariah," *JQR* 3 (1890-91) 208-219.

*Albert Hiorth, "Concerning Irrigation in Ancient and Modern Times, the Cultivation and Electrification of Palestine with the Mediterranean as the Source of Power," *JTVI* 55 (1923) 133-144, 154-157. (Discussion, pp. 145-154) *[Chap. 14]*

Zechariah 14:4-8

*A. Hiorth, "From the River of Egypt unto the Great River, the River of Euphrates. *A Suggested Solution of the Arab-Israel Problem in the Promised Land,*" *JTVI* 70 (1938) 126-145, 150-152. (Discussion, pp. 146-149). *[14:4-8]*

Zechariah 14:5

Anonymous, "The Mount of Olive Cleft," *BWR* 1 (1877) 279-281. *[14:5]*

Herbert Loewe, "Zechariah XIV. 5," *ET* 52 (1940-41) 277-279.

Zechariah 14:10

*B. Maisler, "Topographical Studies: 1. 'From Geba to Beersheba'," *BIES* 8 (1940-41) #1, II. *[14:10]*

Zechariah 14:21

Anonymous, "Zechariah xiv. 21," *CongML* 4 (1821) 135-136.

*Cecil Roth, "The Cleansing of the Temple and Zechariah xiv 21," *NT* 4 (1960) 174-181.

§638 *3.5.3.2.3.22 Studies on Manuscripts of the Book of Zechariah*

*F. P. Ramsay, "Textual Emendation and Higher Criticism," *USR* 13 (1901-02) 13-18. *[Particular reference to Zechariah]*

§639 *3.5.3.2.3.23 Exegetical Studies on the Book of Malachi*

T. V. Moore, "A New Translation and Exposition of Malachi," *MR* 37 (1855) 9-26, 169-187.

Anonymous, "Jewish Exposition of Malachi," *PRev* 27 (1855) 308-327.

H. J. Weber, "Notes on Malachi," *AJSL* 3 (1886-87) 43-44. [Mal. 1:3; 1:9; 2:3; 2:12; 2:15; (3:24)]

Anonymous, "Where is the God of Heaven," *CCBQ* 6 (1963) #3, 3-40. [I. Rebuke of the People who doubt the love of the Lord, Malachi 1:2-5; II. Rebuke of the priests who despise the temple of the Lord, Malachi 1:6-14; 2:1-19; III. Rebuke of the people who defile the laws of the Lord, Malachi 2:10-12, 13-16; IV. Rebuke of the people who deny the Judgment of the Lord, Malachi 2:17-3:6; V. Rebuke of the people who defraud the work of the Lord; Malachi 3:7-12, 13-18; VI. Rebuke of the people through declaration of the day of the Lord, Malachi 4:1-6]

Joseph D., Herzog, "Malachi - A New Translation," *CCARJ* 13 (1965-66) #3, 34-37

Malachi 1:2-3

Robert H. Kennett, "'Was not Esau Jacob's brother? saith the Lord: Yet I loved Jacob, and hated Esau'," *ICMM* 4 (1907-08) 33-40. *[1:2, 3]*

Malachi 1:3

A. Lincoln Shute, "'Esau I Hated'," *R&E* 33 (1936) 260-265. *[1:3]*

Malachi 1:11

Talbot Chambers, "The World-Wide Pure Offering," *PR* 4 (1883) 160-164. *[1:11]*

T. K. Cheyne, "On Malachi i. 11. The Invisible Church in Hebrew Prophecy," *MI* 2 (1885) 77-79.

George Farmer, "Malachi I. 11," *ET* 7 (1895-96) 191-192, 287.

J. T. Marshall, "Malachi I, 11," *ET* 7 (1895-96) 192, 287-288. *[Untitled Article]*

P. A. Verhoef, "Some notes on Malachi 1:11," *OTW* 9 (1966) 163-172.

James Swetnam, "Malachi 1,11: An Interpretation," *CBQ* 31 (1969) 200-209.

Malachi 2:3

*Matitiahu Tsevat, "Studies in the Book of Samuel," *HUCA* 32 (1961) 191-216. [Mal. 2:3LXX, pp. 214-216]

Malachi 2:10-16

*J. G. Matthews, "Tammuz Worship in the Book of Malachi," *JPOS* 11 (1931) 42-50. *[2:10-16]*

Malachi 2:11

*H. Isaacs, "Malachi II. 11; Psalm LXIX. 5," *JQR* 11 (1898-99) 526.

Malachi 2:12

Charles C. Torrey, "עֵד וְעֹנֶה in Malachi ii 12," *JBL* 24 (1905) 176-178.

Malachi 2:15

John Merlin Powis Smith, "A Note on Malachi 2:15a," *AJSL* 28 (1911-12) 204-206.

Malachi Chapter 3

*[Daniel S. Gregory], "The International Lessons in Their Historical and Literary Setting," *CFL, 3rd Ser.,* 14 (1911-12) 357-371. [Mal. chap. 3, pp. 369-370]

Malachi 3:1-7

Fred D. Grealy, "Interpreting the Scriptures for Advent and Christmas. First Sunday in Advent. Malachi 3:1-7b," *JMTSO* 4 (1965-66) #1, 1-6.

Malachi 3:1-3

*Charles Rufus Brown, "The Interpretation of Malachi 3:1-3; 4:1-6 [in Hebrew 3:1-3, 19-24.]," *BW* 14 (1899) 417-420.

Malachi 3:1

*Anonymous, "'Elias who was to come'," *JSL, 4th Ser.,* 10 (1866-67) 371-376. *[3:1]*

*Henry A. Sanders, "The New Testament Quotation of a Twice-Repeated Prophecy," *BS* 71 (1914) 275-282. *[3:1]*

Malachi 3:10

William H. Marquess, "Malachi 3:10, Last Clause," *BR* 3 (1918) 454-458.

Malachi 3:13-4:3

Duncan Cameron, "A Study of Malachi," *GUOST* 8 (1936-37) 9-12. *[3:13-4:3]*

Malachi 3:14

*D. Winton Thomas, "The Root צנע in Hebrew and the Meaning of קדרנית in Malachi III, 14," *JJS* 1 (1948-49) 182-188.

Malachi 3:16-17

*Duncan Cameron, "A Message from Malachi," *ET* 32 (1920-21) 408-410. *[3:16-17]*

Malachi 3:17

R. B. Woodworth, "'A Peculiar Treasure.'—Mal. III. 17," *PQ* 11 (1897) 240-242.

Malachi 4:1-6

*Charles Rufus Brown, "The Interpretation of Malachi 3:1-3; 4:1-6 [in Hebrew 3:1-3, 19-24.]," *BW* 14 (1899) 417-420.

Malachi 4:2

Maurice A. Canney, "The Sun of Righteousness. Malachi iii. 20 (iv. 2)," *JMUEOS* #6 (1916-17) 67-70.

Malachi 4:5-6

*G., "The Burial of Moses: With Remarks on Mal. IV. 5, 6, and the Reappearance of Enoch and Elijah as the Apocalyptic Witnesses," *JSL, 2nd Ser.,* 6 (1854) 135-165.

*G. "The Burial of Moses: with Remarks on Mal. IV. 5, 6, and the Reappearance of Enoch and Elijah as the Apocalyptic Witnesses," *MQR* 8 (1854) 394-427.

Albert A. Isaacs, "The Difficulties of Scripture. Malachi iv 5,6," *EN* 3 (1891) 73-75.

Malachi 4:5

John Richards, "The Coming of Elijah," *TLJ* 9 (1856-57) 587-609. *[4:5]*

Malachi 4:6

*Anonymous, "'Elias who was to come'," *JSL, 4th Ser.,* 10 (1866-67) 371-376. *[4:6]*

§640 *3.5.3.2.3.24 Studies on Manuscripts of the Book of Malachi*

Lars Kruse-Blinkenberg, "The Pesitta of the Book of Malachi," *ST* 20 (1966) 95-199.

Lars Kruse-Blinkenberg, "The Book of Malachi, according to Codes Syro-Hexaplaris Ambrosianus," *ST* 21 (1967) 62-82.

§641 *3.5.4 Exegetical Studies on Passages in Several Books of the Hagiographa*

T. Donald, "The Semitic Field of 'Folly' in Proverbs, Job, Psalms, and Ecclesiastes," *VT* 13 (1963) 285-292.

§642 *3.5.4.1 Exegetical Studies on Passages in Several Poetical Books*

*T. K. Cheyne, "On Some Suspected Passages in the Poetical Books of the Old Testament," *JQR* 10 (1897-98) 13-17. [Ecclesiasticus 11:19; Psa. 22:9; 37:5; 58:7; Job 16:18-17:5; 19:25-29; Prov. 2:7; Job 6:13; Prov. 8:21; Ecclesiasticus 42:3; Prov. 8:24, 26, 31; Job 37:12; Prov. 31:1]

G. R. Driver, "Problems in Job and Psalms Reconsidered," *JTS* 40 (1939) 391-394.

*Steven T. Byington, "Hebrew Marginalia I," *JBL* 60 (1941) 279-288. [Sundry Readings in Psalms, Proverbs, and Job: Psa. 27:8; Prov. 8:16; Psa. 64:7-9; Job 19:26; pp. 284-288]

G. R. Driver, "Mistranslations," *ET* 57 (1945-46) 192-193, 249. [Psa. 106:43; Job 18:17; Psa. 13:3; 22:18; Job 7:15; Psa. 14:4-6= Isa. 53:5, 6]

*Jacob Milgrom, "The Cultic שגגה and Its Influence in Psalms and Job," *JQR, N.S.,* 58 (1967-68) 115-125.

§643 *3.5.4.1.1 Exegetical Studies on the Book of Job*

J. L. B., "Exegesis of the Book of Job," *JSL, 3rd Ser.,* 8 (1858-59) 325-344. *(Review)*

R. Y., "New Translation of the Book of Job," *JSL, 3rd Ser.,* 13 (1861) 361-411.

H.D.,"Difficult Passages in Job,"*JSL 4th Ser.,* 8 (1865-66)374-379. [2:4; 3:8, 14; 4:19, 20; 5:7; 6:18; 7:12, 20; 8:17; 11:7, 12; 12:5; 13:14; 15:12, 33]

H. D., "Difficult Passages in Job," *JSL, 4th Ser.,* 9 (1866) 304-314. [16:21; 17:6; 18:13, 14, 20; 19:20, 25-27, 29; 20:11, 21; 22:20, 24, 30; 23:17; 24:1, 11, 16; 26:5, 12, 13; 27:19; 28:3, 4, 5; 29:4, 18; 30:2, 24; 31:31, 35]

H. D., "Difficult Passages in Job.—Chap. xxxii.–xlii," *JSL, 4th Ser.,* 10 (1866-67) 377-387. [33:19, 23, 27; 34:23, 31, 33; 35:15; 36:17, 18, 19, 32, 33; 37:4, 7, 11, 17, 20-22, 23; 38:8, 14, 30, 31; 39:4, 9, 13, 19, 24; 40:15, 21; 41:1, 6, 8, 13, 18, 22, 25, 30]

J. M. Rodwell, "The Book of Job.—A Revised Translation," *JSL, 5th Ser.,* 1 (1867) 208-224, 399-422; 2 (1867-68) 129-151, 352-367.

S. Cox, *"The Book of Job.* Introduction," *Exp, 1st Ser.,* 4 (1876) 1-29.

Talbot W. Chambers, "Misquoted Scriptures. No. VI," *HR* 7 (1882-83) 55-56. [4:6; 5:6, 7, 24; 8:13; 11:12]

A. B. Davidson, "The Revised Version of the Old Testament:—The Book of Job," *Exp, 3rd Ser.,* 4 (1886) 274-293, 424-439.

T. K. Cheyne, "The Text of Job," *JQR* 9 (1896-97) 573-580.

T. K. Cheyne, "More Critical Gleanings in Job," *ET* 10 (1898-99) 380-382. [3:4, 5; 5:3; 7:15-16; 11:17; 13:12b; 13:15; 18:18; 30:18]

N. Herz, "Some Difficult Passages in Job," *ZAW* 20 (1900) 160-163. [4:19b, 4:20b; 5:26a; 12:2-6; 15:29; 15:30c; 15:31-32a; 29:18; 29:24]

N. Herz, "Dr. Kautzsch on 'The So-called Popular Book of Job'," *ET* 12 (1900-01) 109-110. *(Review)* [Job 3:19a; 11:6; 21:30; 31:26]

Hans H. Spoer, "Emendations in the Text of the Book of Job," *AJSL* 19 (1902-03) 52-53. [8:8, 9; 8:14; 13:28-14:1; 14:10; 14:22; 19:20; 19:29; 21:16; 21:17]

E. G. King, "Some Notes on the Text of Job," *JTS* 15 (1913-14) 74-81. [16:7, 8; 17:7; 19:27; 20:7; 31:21; 33:21; 36:4; 37:19-21]

G. Buchanan Gray, "Critical Notes of the Text of Job," *AJSL* 36 (1919-20) 95-102. [7:4; 17:1, 11; 17:14; 18:2; 19:14, 15; 24:20a; 32:14]

A. F. Almer, "The Book of Job," *AQ* 4 (1925) 365-371.

*E. B. Pollard, "Further Misinterpretation of Familiar Passages," *CQ* 4 (1927) 323-330. *[The Book of Job]*

Harry M. Orlinsky, "Some Corruptions in the Greek Text of Job," *JQR, N.S.,* 26 (1935-36) 133-145. [8:16; 15:2; 15:5; 15:33; 21:24; 27:12; 32:7]

G. R. Driver, "Problems in Job," *AJSL* 52 (1935-36) 160-170. [12:17; 23:7; 23:10; 23:17; 25:5; 27:8; 28:4; 29:17; 30:13; 30:14; 30:24-25; 31:23; 31:35; 38:24; 38:36; 38:41; 39:10; 39:14; 41:4; 41:22]

Steven T. Byington, "Some Bits of Hebrew. IV. Texts in Job," *ET* 57 (1945-46) 110-111. [22:11; 23:10; 23:11-12; 24:10a, 11a; 24:17; (28:18) 29:14; 32:9; (32:6; 33:1; 32:15); 33:22; 27:8; 26:13]

Peter Katz, "Notes on the Septuagint, VI. Some Further Passages in Job," *JTS* 68 (1947) 195-196. [15:2; 33:16; 4:16; 10:2; 27:18; 23:2; 24:7; 24:5; 40:18; 14:5]

E. F. Sutcliffe, "Notes on Job, Textual and Exegetical. 6, 18; 11, 12; 31, 35; 34, 17. 20; 36, 27-33; 37, 1," *B* 30 (1949) 66-90.

E. F. Sutcliffe, "Further Notes on Job, Textual and Exegetical. 6, 2-3. 13; 8, 16-17; 19, 20. 26," *B* 31 (1950) 365-378.

Nahum M. Sarna, "Some Instances of the Enclitic *-m* in Job," *JJS* 6 (1955) 108-110. [5:15; 7:15; 8:8; 8:18; 15:8; 17:7]

G. R. Driver, "Problems in the Hebrew text of Job," *VTS* 3 (1955) 72-93. [3:8; 4:14; 6:4; 7:5; 9:27; 10:22; 14:12; 15:4; 15:22; 16:12; 17:2; 18:2; 18:15; 19:20; 20:23-25; 21:21; 22:26; 26:9; 29:17-20; 31:12; 35:14; 38:24; 38:37; 39:3]

Job Chapters 1 and 2

S. Cox, "*The Book of Job.* I. The Prologue (*Chaps.* i *and* ii)," *Exp, 1st Ser.,* 4 (1876) 81-112, 161-179.

Job 1:15

*T. K. Cheyne, "On 2 Ch. xiv. 9; Job i. 15; Prov. xxviii. 22," *ET* 8 (1896-97) 431-432.

Job 1:17

Fritz Hommel, "Havilah in Job I. 17?" *ET* 8 (1896-97) 431.

Eb. Nestle, "Job I. 17," *ET* 8 (1896-97) 432.

Job 1:21

*Samuel A. B. Mercer, "Passages in Job," *ATR* 1 (1918-19) 333-334. *[1:21]*

Job 2:9

H.   T.   Potten,   "Job   II.   9,"   *ET*   19   (1907-08)   143.

R.   F.   Bevan,   "Job   II.   9,"   *ET*   19   (1907-08)   190-191.

Albert   Bonus,   "Job   II.   9,"   *ET*   19   (1907-08)   283-284.

H.   T.   Potten,   "Job   II.   9,"   *ET*   19   (1907-08)   143.

Job Chapter 3

*Marcus, "Paraphrase of Job," *MR* 17 (1835) 230-235. *[Chap. 3]*

S. Cox, *"The Book of Job.* II. The Curse (*Chapter* iii.)," *Exp, 1st Ser.,* 4 (1876) 241-256.

D. N. Freedman, "The Structure of Job 3," *B* 49 (1968) 503-508.

Job 3:3

Sheldon H. Blank, "'Perish the Day!' A Misdirected Curse (Job III, 3)," *BIES* 19 (1954-55) III.

Job 3:8

E.   Ullendorff,   "Job   III   8,"   *VT*   11   (1961)   350-351.

Job 3:14

T. K. Cheyne, "On Job III. 14, הַבֹּנִים הָרְבוֹה לָמוֹ," *AJSL* 4 (1887-88) 123.

Job 3:25

Robert L. Katz, "A Psychoanalytic Comment on Job 3.25," *HUCA* 29 (1958) 377-383.

Job Chapters 4-5

S. Cox, *"The Book of Job.* III. The First Colloquy. (Chapters IV.—XIV.) (1) Eliphaz to Job. (Chapters IV. and V.)," *Exp, 1st Ser.,* 4 (1876) 321-341.

Job 4:12

Hugh T. Henry, "Mediaeval Comment on Job iv., 12," *ACQR* 42 (1917) 371-396.

Job 4:15

M[itchell] Dahood, "Ś'RT 'Storm' in Job 4, 15," *B* 48 (1967) 544-545.

Job 4:18

*T. Spicer, "Remarks on the Vision of Eliphaz," *MR* 7 (1824) 453-455. *[4:18]*

Job 5:3

*A. A. Bevan, "Notes on Job V. 3, 5," *JP* 26 (1898-99) 303-305.

Judah J. Slotki, "The Re-emergence of an Akko," *ET* 43 (1931-32) 288. *[5:3]*

J. H. Johnson, "Notes and Comments," *ATR* 22 (1940) 47-48. *[5:3f.]*

Job 5:5

*A. A. Bevan, "Notes on Job V. 3, 5," *JP* 26 (1898-99) 303-305.

Fritz Hommel, "Job V. 5," *ET* 10 (1898-99) 283-284.

Job 5:6-8

J. E. Compton, "The Punctuation of Job V. 6-8," *ET* 24 (1912-13) 476.

Job 5:7

T. K. Cheyne, "Job V. 7," *ZAW* 11 (1891) 184.

Job 5:8

Harry M. Orlinsky, "Job 5.8, a Problem in Greek-Hebrew Methodology," *JQR, N.S.,* 25 (1934-35) 271-278.

Job 5:21

T. K. Cheyne, "Job V. 21," *Exp, 4th Ser.,* 3 (1891) 400.

*Robert Gordis, "The Biblical Root *ŠDY-ŠD:* Notes on 2 Sam. i. 21; Jer. xviii. 14; Ps. xci. 6; Job v. 21," *JTS* 41 (1940) 34-43.

Job 5:23

Arthur S. Peake, "'In League with the Stones of the Field'," *ET* 34 (1922-23) 42-43. *[5:23]*

Job 5:24

*F. D. Coggan, "The Meaning of חשא in Job V. 24," *JMUEOS* #17 (1932) 53-56.

Job Chapters 6 and 7

S. Cox, "*The Book of Job*. III. The First Colloquy. (Chapters IV.—XIV.) (2.) Job to Eliphaz. (Chapters VI. and VII.)," *Exp, 1st Ser.,* 4 (1876) 401-430.

Job Chapter 6

J. Challis, "Translation of Job (Chap. VI) from the Septuagint," *JSL, 3rd Ser.,* 11 (1860) 203-204.

Job 6:4

D. Castelli, "Job VI 4," *JQR* 1 (1888-89) 286.

Job 6:6

A. R. Millard, "What has no taste? (Job 6:6)," *UF* 1 (1969) 210.

Job 6:15-19

*Stewart Perowne, "Two Notes on the Book of Job," *PEQ* 71 (1939) 202-203. *[6:15-19]*

Job 6:16

*Patrick W. Skehan, "Second Thoughts on Job 6,16 and 6,25," *CBQ* 31 (1969) 210-212.

Job 6:25

T. K. Cheyne, "On Job VI. 25," *Exp, 3rd Ser.,* 4 (1886) 79-80.

N. S. Doniach, "Job VI. 25. מרץ√," *JTS* 31 (1929-30) 291.

W. Emery Barnes, "Job VI. 25. √מרץ," *JTS* 31 (1929-30) 291-292.

*Patrick W. Skehan, "Second Thoughts on Job 6,16 and 6,25," *CBQ* 31 (1969) 210-212.

Job 7:4

J. Reider, "מַדֻּד in Job 7:4," *JBL* 39 (1920) 60-65.

Job 7:12

Mitchell Dahood, "Mišmār 'Muzzle' in Job 7 12," *JBL* 80 (1961) 270-271.

Job 7:15

Archibald R. S. Kennedy, "Requests and Replies," *ET* 2 (1890-91) 85. *[7:15]*

Job Chapters 8-11

George A. Barton, "Some Text-Critical Notes on Job," *JBL* 42 (1923) 29-32. *[Chaps. 8-11]*

Job Chapter 8

S. Cox, "*The Book of Job.* III. The First Colloquy. (Chapters IV.—XIV.) (3.) Bildad to Job. (Chapter VIII.)," *Exp, 1st Ser.,* 5 (1877) 26-36.

W. A. Irwin, "The first speech of Bildad," *ZAW* 51 (1933) 205-216. *[Chap. 8]*

Job 8:11

*Samuel A. B. Mercer, "Passages in Job," *ATR* 1 (1918-19) 333-334. *[8:11]*

Job Chapters 9 and 10

S. Cox, "*The Book of Job.* III. The First Colloquy. (Chapters IV.—XIV.) (4.) Job to Bildad. (Chapters IX. and X.)," *Exp, 1st Ser.,* 5 (1877) 36-56, 113-123.

Kemper Fullerton, "On Job 9 and 10," *JBL* 53 (1934) 321-349.

Kemper Fullerton, "Job, Chapters 9 and 10," *AJSL* 55 (1938) 225-269.

Job 9:3

E. E. Kellett, "A Suggestion," *ET* 44 (1932-33) 283-284. *[9:3]*

Job 9:9

Theodore Cooper, "The Chambers of the South—Job, IX, 9," *OC* 24 (1910) 500-504.

*N. Herz, "The Astral Terms in Job IX 9, XXXVIII 31-32," *JTS* 14 (1912-13) 575-577.

*G. R. Driver, "Two Astronomical Passages in the O.T.," *JTS, N.S.,* 7 (1956) 1-11. *[9:9 (R.V.)]*

Job 9:22

A. B. Davidson, "Request and Replies," *ET* 7 (1895-96) 219. *[9:22]*

Job 9:23

Frank Zimmermann, "Note on Job 9^{23}," *JTS, N.S.,* 2 (1951) 165-66.

Job 9:31

Marvin H. Pope, "The Word שַׁחַת in Job 9 31," *JBL* 83 (1964) 269-278.

Job 10:15

*William Selwyn, "Hebrew Notes," *JCSP* 3 (1857) 137-140. [VIII. Job 10:15, p. 140]

Job Chapter 11

S. Cox, "*The Book of Job.* III. The First Colloquy. (Chapters IV.—XIV.) (5.) Zophar to Job (Chapter XI.)," *Exp, 1st Ser.,* 5 (1877) 123-134.

Job 11:6

*John Thomas, "'Double for All Her Sins'. A Critical Exposition," *Exp, 5th Ser.,* 4 (1896) 370-380. *[11:6]*

Thomas Tyler, "Some Observations on Job XI. 6," *JQR* 11 (1898-99) 529-532.

Job 11:12

*Hayyim Rosenrauch, "Critical Notes: II. The Hebrew Equivalent to Accadic lip(p)u," *JQR, N.S.,* 36 (1945-46) 81. *[11:12]*

Job Chapters 12-14

S. Cox, *"The Book of Job.* III. The First Colloquy. (Chapters IV.—XIV.) (6.) Job to Zophar. (Chapters XII.—XIV.)," *Exp, 1st Ser.,* 8 (1877) 172-196, 273-289.

Job 12:7-9

Antonine DeGuglielmo, "Job 12:7-9 and the Knowability of God," *CBQ* 6 (1944) 476-482.

Job 12:10

*M[itchell] Dahood, "Ugaritic *ušn,* Job 12,10 and 11QPs^{a}Plea 3-4," *B* 47 (1966) 207-208.

Job 12:19

Nahum M. Sarna, "איתנים, Job 12:19," *JBL* 74 (1955) 272-273. *(Footnote 13 cont. on p. 274)*

Job 13:9-11

William B. Stevenson, "Job XIII. 9-11: A New Interpretation," *ET* 62 (1950-51) 93.

Job 13:15

*Talbot W. Chambers, "Misquoted Scriptures. No. I," *HR* 6 (1881-82) 471-472. *[13:15]*

Job 13:28

*C. Taylor, "Studies in Ben Sira," *JQR* 10 (1897-98) 470-488. [I. Job xiii. 28 and Ecclesiasticus xliii. 20, pp. 471-472]

Job Chapter 14

Tayler Lewis, "Spirituality of the Book of Job as Exhibited in a Commentary on Chapter XIV, Examined in Connection with Other Passages," *BS* 6 (1849) 205-229, 486-507.

[Tayler Lewis], "The Spirituality of the Book of Job, as exhibited in a Commentary on Chapter XIV., examined in connection with other Passages," *BFER* 3 (1854) 775-817.

Job 14:4

*Joseph Parker, "Notes on Scripture Passages," *ERG, 9th Ser.,* 3 (1887-88) 33-37. [I. Job 14:4, pp. 33-35]

*J. K. Zink, "Uncleanness and Sin. A Study of Job XIV 4 and Psalm LI 7," *VT* 17 (1967) 354-361.

Job 14:10

*A.Guillaume, "The Use of חלֹשׁ in Exod. XVII. 13, Isa. XIV. 12, and Job XIV. 10," *JTS, N.S.,* 14 (1963) 91-92.

Job 14:12

Harry M. Orlinsky, "The Hebrew and Greek Texts of Job 14:12," *JQR, N.S.,* 18 (1937-38) 57-68.

Job Chapter 15

S. Cox, *"The Book of Job.* IV. The Second Colloquy. (Chapters XV. —XXI.)," *Exp, 1st Ser.,* 7 (1878) 1-22 [1. Eliphaz to Job (Chapter XV.)]

Job 15:2

Peter Katz, "Notes on the Septuagint, V. Job XV. 2," *JTS* 48 (1947) 194.

Job 15:15

*T. Spicer, "Remarks on the Vision of Eliphaz," *MR* 7 (1824) 453-455. *[15:15]*

Job Chapter 16

S. Cox, *"The Book of Job.* IV. The Second Colloquy. (Chapters XV. —XXI.) 2. Job to Eliphaz (Chaps. XVI., XVII.)," *Exp, 1st Ser.,* 7 (1878) 100-123.

Job 16:4

Oswald Loretz, "ḤBR in Jb 16,4," *CBQ* 23 (1961) 293-294. *(Trans. by Louis F. Hartman)*

Job 17:11

B. B. Lieberman*[sic]*, "A Note on Job XVII. 11. יָמַי עָבְרוּ זִמֹּתַי נִתְּקוּ מוֹרָשֵׁי לְבָבִי," *ET* 34 (1922-23) 330-331.

Job Chapter 18

S. Cox, *"The Book of Job.* IV. The Second Colloquy. (Chapters XV. —XXI.) 3.—Bildad to Job (Chapter XVIII.)," *Exp, 1st Ser.,* 7 (1878) 176-194.

Nahum M. Sarna, "The Mythological Background of Job 18," *JBL* 82 (1963) 315-318.

Job Chapter 19

H. T., "Remarks on Job XIX," *MR* 10 (1827) 25-26.

S. Cox, *"The Book of Job.* IV. The Second Colloquy. (Chapters XV. —XXI.) 4.—Job to Bildad (Chapter XIX.)," *Exp, 1st Ser.,* 7 (1878) 264-278.

David R. Blumenthal, "A Play on Words in the Nineteenth Chapter of Job," *VT* 16 (1966) 497-501.

Job 19:19

*T. Penar, "Job 19, 19 in the Light of Ben Sira 6, 11," *B* 48 (1967) 293-295.

Job 19:23-29

*Samuel Cox, *"The Book of Job.* The Inscription (Chapter XIX. Verses 23-29.)," *Exp, 1st Ser.,* 7 (1878) 321-347.

Job 19:23-27

Isaac Robinson, "An Exegesis of Job 19:23-27," *BJ* 2 (1843) 21-28, 80-89.

George T. Walker, "Job's Testimony to the Resurrection," *JSL* 1st Ser., 1 (1848) 374-377. *[19:23-27]*

W. B. Hutton, "The Book of Job: With Reference to Chap. XIX. 23-27," *Exp, 3rd Ser.,* 8 (1888) 127-151.

W. Taylor Smith, "New Rendering of Job XIX. 23-27," *ET* 3 (1891-92) 60.

R. H. Altus, "Job 19:23-27," *AusTR* 9 (1938) 78-84.

Leroy Waterman, "Note on Job 19:23-27: Job's Triumph of Faith," *JBL* 69 (1950) 379-380.

Job 19:23-24

*C[laude] R. Conder, "Notes on Biblical Antiquities. 3. *Writing with Lead,*" *PEFQS* 37 (1905) 156. *[19:23, 24]*

*F. C. Burkitt, "On *Celtis* 'A Chisel': A Study in Textual Tradition," *JTS* 17 (1915-16) 389-397. *[19:23, 24]*

Job 19:24

*F. C. Burkitt, "On *Celtis* 'A Chisel': A Further Note," *JTS* 22 (1920-21) 380-381. *[19:24]*

*Aelred Baker, "The Strange Case of Job's Chisel," *CBQ* 31 (1969) 370-379. *[19:24]*

Job 19:25-29

A. B. Davidson, "Job XIX. 25-29," *ET* 9 (1897-98) 192.

Job 19:25-27

[George Henry Augustus Ewald], "Professor Ewald on Job XIX. 25-27," *BRCM* 1 (1846) 23-25.

C. Taylor, "A theory of *Job* XIX. 25-27," *JP* 3 (1871) 128-152.

J. I. Mombert, "On Job 19:25-27," *JBL* 2 (1882) 27-39; 3 (1883) 154-155.

Alexander Stewart, "Does Job Refer to the Resurrection in Chapter XIX. 25-27?" *ERG, 9th Ser.,* 1 (1886-87) 108-115.

W. W. Davis, "Exegesis of Job XIX: 25-27," *HR* 16 (1888) 358-362.

*J. B. Remensnyder, "Job xix. 25-27 and the Immortality and Resurrection in the Old Testament," *HR* 28 (1894) 463-465.

N. Herz, "Job XIX. 25-27," *ET* 10 (1898-99) 47-48.

R. M. Spence, "Job XIX. 25-27," *ET* 10 (1898-99) 91.

Anonymous, "Comparative Translation: Job 19:25-27. A Study in Modernizing the English Bible," *BW* 22 (1903) 301-303.

*John Taylor, "Job and Isaiah in the 'Zeitschrift f. A.T. Wissenschaft'," *ET* 17 (1905-06) 277-278. [Job 19:25-27, p. 277]

A. Mackenzie, "Job xix. 25-27a," *AusTR* 1 (1930) 36-39.

Alexander Carson Hanna, "The Word 'Aphar and as a Determinative for the Study of Job XIX: 25-27," *R&E* 28 (1931) 387-397.

W. N. Donovan, "2) Note on the LXX of Job 19:25-27," *JBL* 54 (1935) xii.

S. C. Ylvisker, "Job 19:25-27," *WLQ* 52 (1955) 36-42.

Th. J. Meek, "Job XIX 25-27," *VT* 6 (1956) 100-103.

Job 19:25-26

Geo. P. Gould, "Requests and Replies," *ET* 4 (1892-93) 127. *[19:25, 26]*

Job 19:26

J. A. Selbie, "A 'Crux Interpretum,' (Job XIX. 26)," *ET* 11 (1899-1900) 183-184.

Job 19:29

L. R. Fisher, "ŠDYN in Job XIX 29," *VT* 11 (1961) 342-343.

Job Chapters 20-21

Balmer H. Kelly, "Truth in Contradiction. *A Study of Job 20 and 21,*" *Interp* 15 (1961) 147-156.

Job Chapter 20

S. Cox, "*The Book of Job.* IV. The Second Colloquy. (Chapters XV.
—XXI.) 5.—Zophar to Job. (Chapter XX.)," *Exp, 1st Ser.,* 7 (1878) 437-
453.

Job Chapter 21

S. Cox, "*The Book of Job.* IV. The Second Colloquy. (Chapters XV.
—XXI.)," *Exp, 1st Ser.,* 8 (1878) 1-22. [6. Job to Zophar (Chap. xxi)]

Job 21:14-15

[Wilbert W. White], "Job XXI. 14, 15," *BM* 1 (1913) 885-886. *(Editorial)*

Job 21:27

B. Liebermann, "Note on Job XXI. 27. הֵן יָדַעְתִּי מַחְשְׁבוֹתֵיכֶם וּמְזִמּוֹת
עָלַי תַּחְמֹסוּ," *ET* 35 (1923-24) 286.

Job Chapter 22

S. Cox, "*The Book of Job.* V. The Third Colloquy. (Chapters XXII.
—XXVI.)," *Exp, 1st Ser.,* 8 (1878) 81-97. [1.—Eliphaz to Job (Chapter
XXII)]

Job 22:21

Wilson B. Bishai, "Notes on HSKN in Job 22:21," *JNES* 20 (1961) 258-259.

Job 22:22

M[itchell] Dahood, "The Metaphor in Job 22,22," *B* 47 (1966) 108-109.

Job 22:24-25

T. K. Cheyne, "Two Disputed Hebrew Words in Familiar Passages," *ET* 10
(1898-99) 94-95. [1. בצר Job 22:24, 25; 2. תּוֹעָפוֹת Job 22:25]

Job 22:29-30

Robert Gordis, "Corporate Personality in Job: A Note on 22:29—30," *JNES*
4 (1945) 54-55.

Job 22:30

Nahum N. Sarna, "A Crux Interpretum in Job 22:30 יִמַלֵּט אִי־נָקִי," *JNES* 15 (1956) 118-119.

Clive Thexton, "A Note on Job XXII. 30," *ET* 88 (1966-67) 342-343.

Job Chapters 23 and 24

S. Cox, "*The Book of Job.* V. The Third Colloquy. (Chapters XXII. —XXVI.), 2.—Job to Eliphaz. (Chapters XXIII., XXIV.)," *Exp, 1st Ser.,* 8 (1878) 161-182.

Job Chapters 24-30

*George A. Barton, "A Composition of Job 24-30," *JBL* 30 (1911) 66-77.

Job 24:10-11

Edmund F. Sutcliffe, "A Note on Job XXIV. 10, 11," *JTS* 50 (1949) 174-176.

Job 24:24

*Joseph Reider, "Contributions to the Hebrew lexicon," *RDSO* 17 (1937-38) 103-110. [3. Job. 24:24, pp. 106-108]

Job Chapters 25 and 26

S. Cox, "*The Book of Job.* V. The Third Colloquy. (Chapters XXII. —XXVI.), 3.—Bildad to Job. (Chapter XXV.)," *Exp, 1st Ser.,* 8 (1878) 270-287. [4.—Job to Bildad (Chapter XXVI.), p. 276ff.]

Job 26:7

E. J. Pilcher, "Notes and Queries. 1," *PEFQS* 48 (1916) 153. *[26:7]*

Harold H. Hartzler, "The Hole in the North," *JASA* 2 (1950) #1, 16-19. *[26:7]*

Job 26:12-13

D. G. Lyon, "On the text of Job 26:12, 13," *JBL* 14 (1894) 131-135.

*Samuel Daiches, "Job XXVI 12-13 and the Babylonian Story of Creation," *ZA* 25 (1911) 1-8.

Job Chapters 27-31

Samuel Cox, *"The Book of Job.* VI. The Soliloquy of Job (Chapters xxvii.—xxxi.)," *Exp, 1st Ser.,* 9 (1879) 284-307.

Job Chapter 28

E. P. Barrows, "Interpretation of the Twenty-Eighth Chapter of Job," *BS* 10 (1853) 264-284.

Samuel Cox, "The Soliloquy of Job. First Monologue. (Chapter xxviii)," *Exp, 1st Ser.,* 9 (1879) 329-345.

R. G. Moulton, "Two Sonnets from Job," *BW* 7 (1896) 252-254. *[Chap. 28]*

Steven T. Byington, "Hebrew Marginalia II: Job 28," *JBL* 61 (1942) 205-207.

*P. A. H. de Boer, "The counsellor," *VTS* 3 (1955) 42-71. [Job chap. 28, pp. 68-69]

Job 28:4

Anonymous, "Observations on Job XXVIII. 4," *MR* 5 (1822) 171-172.

LeRoy*[sic]* Waterman, "Note on Job 28:4," *JBL* 69 (1950) ix.

Leroy Waterman, "Note on Job 28:4," *JBL* 71 (1952) 167-170.

Job 28:11

*J. W. Jack, "Recent Biblical Archaeology," *ET* 53 (1941-42) 367-370. [Archæology and the Biblical Text: 7. Binding the Springs (Job 28:11), p. 369]

Job Chapters 29-31

Samuel Cox, "The Soliloquy of Job. Second Monologue. (Chapters xxix.—xxxi.)," *Exp, 1st Ser.,* 9 (1879) 430-459.

*P. W. Skehan, "Job's Final Plea (Job 29 - 31) and the Lord's Reply (Job 38 - 41)," *B* 45 (1964) 51-62.

Job 29:4

D. Winton Thomas, "The Interpretation of בְּסוֹד in Job 29:4," *JBL* 65 (1946) 63-66.

Job 29:18

Henry Heras, "The Standard of Job's Immortality," *CBQ* 11 (1949) 263-279. *[29:18]*

M[itchell] Dahood, "Nest and Phoenix in Job 29, 18," *B* 48 (1967) 542-544.

Job 29:26

*David Yellin, "A Hitherto Unnoticed Meaning of נפל‎," *JPOS* 6 (1926) 164-166. *[29:26]*

Job 30:1

George Jeshurun, "A Note on Job XXX: 1," *JSOR* 12 (1928) 153-154.

Job Chapter 31

Samuel Cox, "The Soliloquy of Job. Second Monologue (Chapter XXXI)," *Exp, 2nd Ser.,* 10 (1879) 27-48.

Robert A. Aytoun, "A Critical Study of Job's 'Oath of Clearance'," *ICMM* 16 (1919-20) 291-298. *[Chap. 31]*

Sheldon H. Blank, "An Effective Literary Device in Job 31," *JBL* 69 (1950) ix.

Sheldon H. Blank, "An Effective Literary Device in Job XXXI," *JJS* 2 (1950-51) 105-107.

Job 31:26-27

James Moffatt, "Opera Foris; Or, Materials for the Preacher. Second Series. —III.," *Exp, 8th Ser.,* 2 (1911) 563-568. *[31:26-27]*

Job Chapters 32-37

*Henry Ferguson, "The Authenticity of Job XXXII-XXXVII," *CR* 29 (1877) 420-434.

*Henry Ferguson, "The Authenticity of Elihu's Speech: Job XXXII-XXXVII," *DTQ* 3 (1877) 613-621.

Samuel Cox, *"The Book of Job.* VII.—The Intervention of Elihu: (Chapters XXXII.—XXXVII.)," *Exp, 1st Ser.,* 10 (1879) 99-116.

George A. Barton, "Some Text-Critical Notes on the Elihu-Speeches, Job 32-37," *JBL* 43 (1924) 228. *[34:6; 34:16; 34:2; 35:3; 36:24; 36:33; 37:7]*

Job Chapters 32 and 33

*Robert Gordis, "Elihu the Intruder: A Study of the Authenticity of Job (Chapters 32-33)," *LIST* 1 (1963) 60-78.

Job Chapter 32

Patrick W. Skehan, "'I Will Speak Up!' (Job 32)," *CBQ* 31 (1969) 380-382.

Job 32:6-33:33

*Samuel Cox, *"The Book of Job.* VII.—The Intervention of Elihu. First Discourse (Chapters XXXII. 6-XXXIII. 33)," *Exp, 1st Ser.,* 10 (1879) 173-195.

Job 32:19

A. Guillaume, "An Archaeological and Philological Note on Job XXXII, 19," *PEQ* 93 (1961) 147-150.

Job Chapter 33

Patrick W. Skehan, "The Pit (Job 33)," *CBQ* 31 (1969) 382.

Job 33:18

*Daniel Leibel, "עבר בשלח," *Tarbiẓ* 33 (1963-64) #3, I. *[33:18]*

Job 33:27

*Joseph Reider, "Contributions to the Hebrew lexicon," *RDSO* 17 (1937-38) 103-110. [4. Job 33:27, pp. 108-109]

Job Chapter 34

Samuel Cox, *"The Book of Job.* VII.—The Intervention of Elihu. Second Discourse. (Chapter XXXIV.)," *Exp, 1st Ser.,* 10 (1879) 341-364.

Job 34:13

*Joseph Offord, "Arza and Aziza, and other Archæological Notes," *SBAP* 23 (1901) 244-247. [Job 34:13 and 37:12, p. 244]

Job 34:20

Dom Connolly, "On Job XXXIV 20," *JTS* 2 (1900-01) 300-301.

Job Chapter 35

Samuel Cox, *"The Book of Job.* VII.—The Intervention of Elihu. Third Discourse. (Chapter XXXV.)," *Exp, 1st Ser.,* 11 (1880) 33-43.

Job Chapters 36 and 37

Samuel Cox, *"The Book of Job.* VII.—The Intervention of Elihu. Fourth Discourse. (Chapters XXXVI. and XXXVII.)," *Exp, 1st Ser.,* 11 (1880) 264-296.

Job 36:5

Shaul Esh, "Job xxxvi 5a in Tannaitic Tradition," *VT* 7 (1957) 190-191.

Job 36:12

*Daniel Leibel, "עבר בשלח," *Tarbiz* 33 (1963-64) #3, I. *[36:12]*

Job 36:14

U., "An Attempt to restore the original Text in Job xxxvi. 14," *TRep* 1 (1769) 448-450.

Job 36:16

Patrick W. Skehan, "Job 36, 16 Vulgate," *CBQ* 16 (1954) 295-301.

Job 36:27-28

*Paul Haupt, "Philological Studies. 2. Wine and Blood," *AJP* 45 (1924) 48-50. *[36:27-28]*

Job 37:7

D. Winton Thomas, "Note on לְדַעַת in Job 37[7]," *JTS, N.S.,* 5 (1954) 56-57.

Job 37:9-10

Anonymous, "The Phenomena of Freezing Water in the Book of Job," *SPR* 6 (1852-53) 254-259. *[37:9, 10]*

*T. K. Cheyne, "Influence of Assyrian in unexpected places," *JBL* 18 (1898) 103-107. [2. Job 37:9, 10, pp. 105-106]

Job 37:12

*Joseph Offord, "Arza and Aziza, and other Archæological Notes," *SBAP* 23 (1901) 244-247. [Job 34:13 and 37:12, p. 244]

Job 37:22

D. Winton Thomas, "Job XXXVII 22," *JJS* 1 (1948-49) 116-117.

Job Chapters 38-42

Carpus, "Jehovah's Answer to Job's Doubts. Job xxxviii.-xlii," *Exp, 1st Ser.,* 2 (1875) 147-164.

Millar Burrows, "The Voice from the Whirlwind," *JBL* 47 (1928) 117-132. *[Chaps. 38-42]*

Job 38:1-42:6

Samuel Cox, "*The Book of Job.* VIII. The Theophany. (Chapters XXXVIII. —XLII. 6)," *Exp, 1st Ser.,* 12 (1880) 1-23.

Job Chapters 38-41

*P. W. Skehan, "Job's Final Plea (Job 29 - 31) and the Lord's Reply (Job 38 - 41)," *B* 45 (1964) 51-62.

Job 38:11-40:5

Samuel Cox, "*The Book of Job.* VIII. The Theophany. 1. First Divine Remonstrance (Ch. XXXVIII. 11—XL. 5)," *Exp, 1st Ser.,* 12 (1880) 143-170.

Job 38:1

*Stewart Perowne, "Two Notes on the Book of Job," *PEQ* 71 (1939) 202-203. *[38:1]*

Job 38:12-15

*G. R. Driver, "Two Astronomical Passages in the Old Testament," *JTS, N.S.,* 4 (1953) 208-212. *[38:12-15]*

Job 38:31-38

*T. K. Cheyne, "Influence of Assyrian in unexpected places," *JBL* 17 (1898) 103-107. [1. Job 38:31-38, pp. 103-105]

Job 38:31-32

John G. Lansing, "Pleiades, Orion and Mazzaroth. Job XXXVIII., 31, 32," *AJSL* 1 (1884-85) 236-241.

*N. Herz, "The Astral Terms in Job IX 9, XXXVIII 31-32," *JTS* 14 (1912-13) 575-577.

*G. R. Driver, "Two Astronomical Passages in the O.T.," *JTS, N.S.,* 7 (1956) 1-11. *[38:31-32 (R.V.)]*

Job 38:32

H. F. Talbot, "On the *Mazzoroth* of Job xxxviii, 32," *SBAT* 1 (1872) 339-342.

Job Chapter 39

†U., "An Illustration, by Transposition, of Part of the 39th Chapter of Job," *TRep* 1 (1769) 219-220.

Job 39:13-18

George F. Howe, "Job and the Ostrich: A Case Study in Biblical Accuracy," *JASA* 15 (1963) 107-110. *[39:13-18]*

Job 39:19-25

L. P. Olds, "Job's War-Horse. Observations on the Celebrated Description of the War-Horse in Job XXXIX. 19-25," *MQR* 14 (1860) 581-587.

Job 40:2

Kemper Fullerton, "On the Text and Significance of Job 40:2," *AJSL* 49 (1932-33) 197-211.

Frank Zimmermann, "Supplementary Observations on Job 40:2," *AJSL* 51 (1934-35) 46-47.

Job 40:4

*F. J. Stephens, "The Gesture of Attentive Humility in the Old Testament and in Babylonian Art," *JBL* 53 (1934) xi. *[40:4]*

Job 40:6-42:6

Samuel Cox, *"The Book of Job.* VIII. The Theophany. Second Divine Remonstrance (Ch. XL. 6—XLII. 6)," *Exp, 1st Ser.,* 12 (1880) 199-216.

Job 40:12

M[itchell] Dahood, *"HDK* in Job 40, 12," *B* 49 (1968) 509-510.

Job 40:15

*Samuel A. B. Mercer, "Passages in Job," *ATR* 1 (1918-19) 333-334. *[40:15]*

Job 40:23-24

L. H. C. Shuttleworth, "Job XL. 23 and 24," *ET* 16 (1904-05) 238-239.

Job 40:29

D. Winton Thomas, "Job XL 29b: Text and Translation," *VT* 14 (1964) 114-116.

R[obert] Gordis, "Job XL 29 - An Additional Note," *VT* 14 (1964) 491-494.

Job 42:7-17

Samuel Cox, *"The Book of Job.* IX.-The Epilogue (Chapter XLII. 7-17)," *Exp, 1st Ser.,* 12 (1880) 245-258.

L. W. Batten, "The Epilogue to the Book of Job," *ATR* 15 (1933) 125-128. *[42:7-17]*

Job 42:14

A. M. Honeyman, "The Septuagint and Amalthea's Horn," *GUOST* 11 (1942-44) 51-52. *[42:14]*

Job 42:17

*Eb. Nestle, "Job the Fifth, and Moses the Seventh, from Abraham," *ET* 19 (1907-08) 474-475. *[42:17b-17e LXX]*

§644 *3.5.4.1.2 Studies on Manuscripts of the Book of Job*

E. Amelineau, "The Sahidic Translation of the Book of Job," *SBAT* 9 (1886-93) 405-475. *(French and Sahidic Text)*

T. K. Cheyne, "A Sahidic Version of the Book of Job," *SBAP* 9 (1886-87) 374.

T. K. Cheyne, "Dillman on the Text of Job," *Exp, 4th Ser.,* 4 (1891) 142-145. *(Review)*

William Aldis Wright, "French glosses in the Leipsic MS. No. 102 (13th Cent.) from the commentary on Job," *JP* 31 (1908-10) 299-317.

*James Jeffrey, "The Massoretic Text and the Septuagint Compared, with special reference to the Book of Job," *ET* 36 (1924-25) 70-73.

Edward Ulback, "An Arabic Version of the Book of Job," *OC* 46 (1932) 782-786.

Leander Zimmerman, "The Septuagint Appendix to Job," *Scotist* 16 (1960) 48-59.

§645 *3.5.4.1.3 Exegetical Studies on the Book of Psalms - General Studies*

*†Anonymous, "Burder on Oriental Customs," *BCQTR* 23 (1804) 166-169. [Psa. 16 - Title; 20:5; 42:3; 44:20; 45:3; 56:8; 58:6; 59:14; 69:9; 72:10; 75:4, 5]

Q., "Observations on Some Portions of the Psalms," *MR* 3 (1820) 294-297. [5:10; 18:26; 55:15; 69:22-25, 26, 28]

Anonymous, "Observations on Some Portions of the Psalms," *MR* 3 (1820) 294-297. [28:26; 55:15; 29:22, 25, 27, 28]

D. F., "Noyes's Translation of the Psalms," *CE* 43 (1847) 204-216. *(Review)*

*†Anonymous, "Translation of the Hebrew Psalter," *ERL* 7 (1847) 71-87. *(Review)* [4:5; 16:10; 19:11; 16:2; 15:10; 58:8; 110:3]

[A. Tholuck], "Introduction to the Translation and Exposition of the Psalms by A. Tholuck," *BRCM* 4 (1847-48) 344-359. *(Trans. by M.N.)*

J. F. Thrupp, "Emendations on the Psalms," *JCSP* 4 (1857-60) 254-262. [I. Psa. 22:22; II. 71:6; III. 76:11; IV. 140:9, 10, 11]

Anonymous, "New Readings in the Psalms," *CE* 73 (1862) 227-242. *(Review)* [Psa. 151; 45; 49; 80]

T[aylor] L[ewis], "Exegetical Notes," *PR* 1 (1880) 164-166. [93:3; 5:4; 12:3; 90:3]

Talbot W. Chambers, "Misquoted Scriptures. No. V," *HR* 6 (1881-82) 714-715. [8:5; 9:17; 16:2; 17:15]

E[dward] G. King, "Notes on the Revised Version of the Psalter," *MI* 4 (1886) 24-44. [4:7, 8; 9:6; 9:17; 10:3, 4; 19:3; 28:4, 5; *103:20;* 41:3; 1:1; 29:9, 10; 37:8; 45:8; 45:13; 42:4; 102:16, 17; 119:106; *108:10; 38:13, 14; 67:6;* 58:9; 68:11; 68:16; 78:71; 90:12; 48:8, 9; 47:3, 5; 17:13, 14; 21:6; 41:8; 48:14; 48:17; 95:7; 119:50; *16:10;* 4:4; 8:5; 16:10; 22:8; 68:18; 116:10; 13:1; 18:4, 5; 116:3; 30:4 & 97:13; 85:13; 78:43; 36:7, 8; 36:8, 9; 42:1; 51:2, 7; 5:3; 116:11; 25:6, 7, 10; *89:1, 2, 14, 24, 28, 33, 49;* 143:8, 12; 31:7, 16, 21; *33:4, 8, 11, 17; 107:1, 8, 15, 21, 31, 43;* 3:4; 22:29; 22:8 *(References in italics are not actually quoted in text of article)*]

T. K. Cheyne, "The Book of Psalms in the Revised Version," *Exp, 3rd Ser.,* 5 (1887) 304-313. [2:1, 2:12; 3:4; 4:8; 7:7; 8:5; 10:14; 10:18; 16:3; 16:10; 17:14; 18:29; 22:1; 22:8; 22:29; 24:6; 29:1; 32:9; 35:15, 16, 21; 36:1; 40:9; 42:4; 42:5; 45:3; 45:6; 45:13; 49:5, 14; 58:1]

T. K. Cheyne, "The Revised Version of the Old Testament:—The Book of Psalms II," *Exp, 3rd Ser.,* 6 (1887) 38-53. *[No Subdivisions]*

Samuel Davidson, "Notes on the Psalms," *AJSL* 4 (1887-88) 158-166. [2:12; 4:3; 6:11; 8:2; 12:7; 16:3; Psalm 18; Psalm 19; 22:17; 25:11; 29:2; 32:9; 36:3; 37:38; 39:3; 42:5; Psalm 45; 48:3; Psalm 51; Psalm 53; Psalm 55; Psalm 56; 57:4, 5; 58:2, 10; 60:6, (5); 64:7-9; 65:6; Psalm 67; Psalm 68; Psalm 69; Psalm 70; Psalm 72; 73:4, 24; 74:19; 76:5; 77:11, 17-20]

Samuel Davidson, "Notes on the Psalms," *AJSL* 5 (1888-89) 97-109. [78:63, (66); 80:14, 17, 19; Psalm 81; 82:6, 7; 84:4; 87:1, 3; Psalm 88: (8, 16); 89:51; 90:4, 5, 9; Psalm 91; 94:17, 21; 95:4, 7, 8; Psalm 96: 99:3; Psalm 101; 104:1, 4, 24; 105:18, 37; 106:48; 107:3, 4, 17-22, 39, 40; 108:11, 12; Psalm 109; Psalm 110; 112:4, (10); 113:10; Psalm 115; 116:10, 11; Psalm 117: (1); 118:27; 119:83, 91, 147, 126; Psalms 120-134; 120:(2); 121:1, 3; 122:(2), 4, (5), 6; 124:3; 127:2; 128:2; 129:2, 6; Psalm 130:(8-10); Psalm 134; Psalm 135; 138:1, 2b; 139:9, 11, 12, 14, 16-18, 20, 24; Psalms 140-142; 141:5, 6, 7, 9; 142:4, 8; 143:3, 6, 9, 10; 144:2, 4, 14; 144:12, 15; Psalm 145; Psalm 146; 147:1, (12-20); 148:5, 6, 14; 149:9; 150:1]

John Taylor, "A Critical Edition of the Psalter, I.," *ET* 5 (1893-94) 39-40. [2:11; 4:4; 4:5; 7:8 & 9]

John Taylor, "Kautzsch's New Edition of the Psalter, II.," *ET* 5 (1893-94) 130-131. [8:2b; 9:7]

John Taylor, "Kautzsch's New Edition of the Psalter, III," *ET* 5 (1893-94) 181-182. [9:10; 10:1; 9:15; 9:17; 10:15]

John Taylor, "Kautzsch's New Edition of the Psalter, IV," *ET* 5 (1893-94) 335-336. [12:6, 8, 9; 13:9; 16:2]

A[ugustus] S. Carrier, "Studies in the Psalms—Psalms XVI, XVII, LXIX, LXXIII," *CFL, N.S.,* 1 (1900) 163-168.

Augustus S. Carrier, "Notes on the Psalms," *AJSL* 17 (1900-01) 54-59. [42:8; 8:1; 23:1; 16:11; 46:10; 2:4; (91:1, 2); 24:2; 2:1; 2:2; 24:2; 49:8-10]

D.H. Weir, "Notes on the Text of the Psalms," *Exp, 6th Ser.*, 5 (1902) 156-160. [15:4c; 16:2-3; 16:3; 17:15; 20:15; 20:10; chap. 21; 22:17; 22:18 (17), 23; 22:26 (25); 24:6; 25:22; 26:2; 26:9; 27:4c; 27:8; 28:5; 29:2; 29:3; 30:13; 31:13; 31:3; 32:8, 9; 33:15; 33:16; 34:4; 34:18; 35:14; 35:17; 36:2; 36:3 (2); 37:20; 37:23; 37:37; 37:40; 40:5; 40:8; 42:7; 42:8; 42:10; 43:1; chap. 44; 44:5; 44:6; 45:5; 46:6; 47:3; 48:3; 48:4; 48:10; 49:6; 49:12; 49:14; 49:15; 55:3; 55:13; 56:6; 57:2; 57:12; 58:8; 60:8 (6); 61:3; chap. 62; 62:3; 64:6; 65:2; 66:2; 66:9; 66:12; 68:11; 68:14; 68:15; 69:4; 69:6; 69:9]

D. H. Weir, "Notes on the Text of the Psalms," *Exp, 6th Ser.*, 6 (1902) 236-240. [69:11; 69:21; 69:33; 71:7; 71:20; 71:21; 71:22; 72:3; 72:6; 72:8; 73:1; 73:8; 74:5; 77:11; 78:12; 78:31; 78:48; 78:63; 78:65; 78:69; 79:2; 80:7; 80:16; 80;19; 81:6; 81:11; 81:17; 82:1; 82:7; 83:6; 83:19; 84:3; 84:4; 84:6; 84:12; 85:9; 85:14; 86:2; 86:14; 87:1; 87:5; 88:6; chap 89; 89:20; 89:51; 90:6; 90:9; 91:3; 94:10; 94:21; 95:4; 101:1; 102:4; 102:8; 102:18; 103:5; 103:11; 104:8; 106:7; 106:37; 106:38; 106:39]

E. H. Askwith, "Psalms in Times of Sickness," *Exp, 8th Ser.*, 23 (1922) 278-285. [Psa. 30; 38: 39; 41; 88]

*E. H. Askwith, "The Hope of Immortality in the Psalter," *Exp, 8th Ser.*, 25 (1923) 74-80. [Psa. 16; 17; 49; 73]

*Herbert H. Gowen, "The Nature Poems of the Psalter," *ATR* 6 (1923-24) 14-28. [19:2, 7; Psa. 29; Psa. 28; Psa. 65; Psa. 104]

Ed. König, "Recent Misinterpretations of the Psalter," *MR* 109 (1926) 737-743. [74:9a; 118:16; 110:2; 19:4b; 74:12-17; 93:1; 47:1; 144:1-8, 9-15]

Anonymous, "The Advent Psalm," *MR* 111 (1928) 934-935. [Psalms 93; 96; 97; 98; 99; and 100]

A. H. Finn, "Conjectural Emendations in the Psalms," *JTVI* 61 (1929) 167-184, 190. (Discussion, pp. 184-189) [Psa. 2:12; 22:17; 68:15; 73:10; 77:7, 12; 118:27]

Samuel Daiches, "Some New Exegetical Points in the Psalms," *ET* 43 (1931-32) 346-348. [1.) Psa. 10:3; 2.) 11:5; 3.) 11:7b (37:3); 4.) 35:15 (31:21)]

W. A. Irwin, "Critical Notes on Five Psalms," *AJSL* 49 (1932-33) 9-20. [Psalm 5; Psalm 6; Psalm 7; Psalm 15; Psalm 24]

G.R. Driver, "Notes on the Psalms," *JTS* 36 (1935) 147-156. [6:7; 12:7; 12:8; 20:8; 30:8; 38:8; 52:11; 58:3; 60:5; 64:6-7; 64:9; 137:3]

Henry M. Smyth, "Comments on the New Psalter," *ACM* 40 (1936) 206-211. [16:10; 68:11; 72:6; 87:5; 119:165; 139:4; 150:1]

G. R. Driver, "Textual and Linguistic Problems of the Book of the Psalms," *HTR* 29 (1936) 171-195. [12:8; 13:5; 17:1; 17:4-5; 18:27; 18:35; 18:43; 18:46; 20:6; 21:10; 22:16-17; 22:25; 22:30; 25:18-19; 27:8-9; 35:12; 35:15-17; 38:13; 45:4-5; 45:9; 52:9; 55:15-16; 55:19-20; 58:8; 60:6; 68:5; 69:15; 71:6, 15; 72:16; 77:7; 80:5; 81:16; 84:6; 85:11; 90:4-6; 90:10; 102:24-25; 118:12; 119:30; 119:117; 119:118; 119:130; 123:4; 140:6; 141:4; 141:5; 144:12; 144:13; 144:13-14]

W[illiam]. H. McClellan, "Obscurities in the Latin Psalter," *CBQ* 1 (1939) 69-72, 150-153, 243-248, 353-357. [4:7-8; 5:5; 7:7b-8; 9:7c; 11:7b; 13:3d; 15:3-4a; 16:9b-10a; 16:11; 16:13b-14a; 16:14b; 17:46; 20:12; 21:2; 30:13a; 31:4b; 34:20; 35:3; 39:6b]

William H. McClellan, "Obscurities in the Latin Psalter," *CBQ* 2 (1940) 64-69, 173-178, 253-258, 341-345; 3 (1941) 55-60, 167-173, 259-265, 356-361; 4 (1942) 58-62, 152-158, 252-257, 349-354; 5 (1943) 80-84, 207-213, 345-349, 466-471; 6 (1944) 99-103, 353-356. [39:7b; 39:13b; 40:4b; 40:7c-8a; 40:9b; 41:7c; 43:19b; 44:5d; 44:14a; 46:10b; 48:8a; 48:9b-11a; 48:14b; 49:23b; 54:20c; 54:22a-b; 55:7c-8a; 55:9-10a; 56:5b; 57:10; 57:12a; 59:10a-b; 61:4c-d; 61:5a-b; 61:10c; 62:11b; 63:4b; 63:7b-c; 63:8-9a; 64:4b; 64:14a; 65:3b; 67:5b; 67:7; 67:10a; 67:12; 67:13; 67:14; 67:15; 67:16-17a; 67:19; 67:21; 67:23; 67:24b; 67:27b; 67:28a; 67:31; 70:15c; 71:6a; 71:7b; 71:16a; 73:5a; 73:14b; 74:3a; 74:7; 74:9b; 76:11; 77:69a; 79:14b; 83:6-8; 86:4-7; 87:6a; 87:11b; 88:34b; 88:36b; 88:45a; 89:9c; 89:10d; 89:12; 90:3b; 90:6b-c; 91:11a; 91:12b; 91:15b; 93:15b; 93:20b; 98:4b; 99:3b; 100:7c; 100:8a; 101:11b; 103:17b; 103:25a; 103:26b; 104:28b; 105:7c; 107:10a; 108:6b; 108:23b; 109:3; 109:7; 110:2b; 113 (ii):14a; 117:27b; 118:70a; 118:83a; 118:138; 121:3; 126:2; 126:4b; 126:5b; 128:3; 128:6a; 130:2; 138:6; 138:11; 138:16c-d; 138:18b; 138:20; 139:10; 140:5c-7a; 140:10b; 143:13b; 149:5b]

G. R. Driver, "Notes on the Psalms. I. 1-72," *JTS* 43 (1942) 149-160. (Corr. *JTS* 44 (1943), p. 23). [2:2; 4:5; 5:4; 5:5; 6:8; 7:5; 9:17; 10:3-5; 10:8; 12:9; 15:4; 17:9; 17:11; 17:12; 17:4; 27:3; 31:14; 32:9; 35:14; 36:3; 37:8; 37:35; 38:10; 38:12; 39:3; 41:4; 41:9; 42:4; 44:9; 45:5; 45:14; 45:16; 48:14; 49:9-10; 49:14; 50:20; 51:8; 51:12; 55:4; 56:9; 56:11; 57:7; 58:2; 59:5; 59:12; 59:13; 60:7; 62:8; 64:4; 64:7; 65:13; 66:11; 68:20; 68:24; 68:25; 68:28; 68:35; 69:11; 69:13; 71:10; 72:3; 72:16]

*B. D. Eerdmans, "On the Road to Monotheism," *OTS* 1 (1942) 105-125. [Ps. 87: 139; 22:82; 58; 71:6-12; 85; 42:7-12]

*B. D. Eerdmans, "Thoda-Songs and Temple-Singers in the Pre-Exilic Period," *OTS* 1 (1942) 162-175. [118:2-4; 115:9-12; 124:1; 129:1]

*B. D. Eerdmans, "The Chasidim," *OTS* 1 (1942) 176-257. [Ps. 4; 2-9; 32:1-11; 50:1-23; 16:1-11; 79:1-3; 116-:1-19; 149:1-9; 44:2-27; 60:3-13; 141:1-10; 31:2-25; 69:2-37; 94:1-23; 145-:1-21; 86:9-11; 97:6-10; 93:1-5; 95:1-11; 96:1-13; 97:1-12; 98:1-9; 99:1-9; 46:2-12; 47:2-10; 48:2-15; 49:1-11; 74:1-23; 73:1-12; 3:2-9; 7:2-18; 26:1-12; 37:1-40]

*G. R. Driver, "Notes on the Psalms. II. 73-150," *JTS* 44 (1943) 12-23. [73:7; 73:20; 73:24; 74:1; 74:3; 74:6; 74:20; 75:7; 75:10; 76:5-6; 76:12; 77:5; 78:49; 78:67; 80:6; 80:16; 83:17; 84:7; 84:11; 85:4; 85:5; 85:9; 87:5; 88:6; 88:8; 88:10; 88:16; 88:17; 89:9; 89:10; 89:34; 89:44; 90:2; 90:7; 90:10; 93:1; 98:2; 99:1; 101:5; 102:8; 102:27; 104:11; 105:22; 105:28; 105:35; 106:7; 106:43; 108:7; 109:24; 110:2; 113:3; 116:10; 116:14, 18; 120:7; 124:7; 131:2; 132:15; 139:11; 139:16: 139:16-17; 139:20; 140:9-10; 141:4; 144:12]

A. Guillaume, "Notes on the Psalms. II. 73-150," *JTS* 45 (1944) 14-15. [74:1; 83:17; 88:6; 102:27; 113:3] *(Reply to Driver - above)*

*S. D. Goitein, "The City of Adam in the Book of Psalms?" *BIES* 13 (1946-47) #3/4, II-III. [Psalms 78; 60; and 68:18]

*B. D. Eerdmans, "The Hebrew Book of Psalms," *OTS* 4 (1947) 1-610. [Pss. I-CL, 91-610]

James A. Kleist, "Suggestions for a More Rhythmical English Version of the Psalms," *CBQ* 10 (1948) 310-314. [Psalm 3; 4; 28; 42:121; 125; 126; 129; 130]

T. E. Bird, "Some Queries on the New Psalter," *CBQ* 11 (1949) 76-82, 179-187, 296-308. [The New Latin Psalter: Psa. 1:1, 3e, 6a; 2:4a, 11, 12; 5:4b, 5; 7:5b; Psa. 8; 9:2(Heb); 9:22-39 (Heb 10), vv. 26(5), 38(17); 10:4c; 12:3; 13:5a; 14:4c; 15:2b; 16:3b, 4ab, 7b, 11, 13, 14; 17:5, 9, 12, 27b, 35b, 36c; 18:8b, 12b, 14; 19:6; 20:10a, 13; 21:2b, 3, 11, 12, 16a, 18a, 18b, 30a; Psa. 22; 24:1; 25:8; 26:6bc, 12; 27:3b; 28:9a; 29:7a, 8a; 30:3c-4a, 12, 18b; 31:4b, 6ab, 7; 33:22; 34:14, 17b, 20b; 35:3, 6a, 8a, 11a; 36:1a, 7c, 8b, 3b, 7cd, 14c, 20bc, 23, 34d, 35; 37:8, 13a, 18, 20; 38:3a, 4b; 39:2, 5b, 7b; 40:4b, 7b, 8a, 13a; 41:5b; 42:4b; 43:5; 44:6, 14, 15; 45:4cd, 5b, 47:3c, 5, 6, 48:13, 21, 14, 15cd; 49:10b; 50:3, 8]

T. E. Bird, "Some Queries on the New Psalter (*Continued*)," *CBQ* 12 (1950) 34-47, 213-220, 301-310. [51:3bc, 7ab, 9cd; 54:4b, 9, 10a, 10b-12, 15b; 55:5a, 8a, 9ab; 56:5abc; 57:2a, 8b, 10; 58:8a, 10a, 11-12; 60:3; 63:7; 64:2, 8; 65:6; 67:9b, 12, 14a, 16, 18, 19c, 23, 28b, 29, 30, 31c, 35, 36a; 68:5cd, 13, 14cd, 23, 33; 69:4, 70:3, 6c, 14b, 15c, 21a; 71:9, 12; 72:1, 4, 14, 21; 73:3a, 4, 5, 6, 8b, 14, 19, 20b; 75:6, 8b, 11-13; 76:5a, 11a; 77:25a, 63b; 78:8a, 9; 79:16-18; 80:6b, 6c, 7a, 17; 81:7; 82:4b, 10b, 12a; 83:6, 7; 84:14b; 85:2b, 3, 11b; 86:7; 87:2, 6b; 88:20b, 48b, 51b; 89:5, 6b, 10, 17bc; 90:4c; 91:11; 92:4; 96:10a; 97:3ab; 98:4a; 100:4; 101:2, 3, 8a, 9b; 103:4, 10, 17b, 35c; 104:18; 105:4, 5, 7d, 15b, 19b; 109:3; 111:3, 5b; Psa. 114-115; 115:11a; 117:10b, 11b, 12b; 118:38a, 66a, 69a, 82, 83b, 89b, 119a, 128, 138; 126:2b, 2d; 129:4, 5de; 133:1; 136:3; 137:2de, 8; 138:5a, 14c, 16a, 17a, 18b, 20; 139:9cd; 140:3, 5, 7; 142:8a; 143:12cd, 13; 147:17]

H. L. Ginsberg, "Some Emendations in Psalms," *HUCA* 23 (1950-51) Part 1, 97-104. [2:11-12; 4:7; 8:2-3; 8:4; 9:6, 16, 18, 20, 21; 10:16; 22:17, 21; 23:3b; 68:22; 72:16; 92:16; 104:3; 104:13; 114:7; 116:12; 118:10-12, v.12]

Patrick W. Skehan, "Some Short Psalms," *AER* 124 (1951) 104-109. [Ps. 86(87); 129(130); 120(121); 130(131)]

Parochus, "The 'Vengeful' Psalms," *Scrip* 6 (1953-54) 144-147. [Pss. 17; 34; 51; 58; 68:23-9; 108:6-20; 136 etc.]

Leon J. Liebreich, "The Hymns of the Levites for the Days of the Weeks," *EI* 3 (1954) X-XI. [Ps. 24; 48; 82; 94; 81; 93; and 92]

Sigmund Mowinckel, "Notes on the Psalms," *ST* 13 (1959) 134-165. [5:4; 8:2b-3; 9:8; 10:3-4, 6-7, 8, 10, 14, 15; 11:6a; Ps. 14 = Ps. 53; 12:6-8; 16:2-4a; 17:14; 18:12-13; 18:44, 49; 27:12; 32:8b; 35:13, 18; 37:26; 39:4; 41:4b; 42:4b, 9; 43:2; 46:5; 51:6b-7; 51:8; 51:16; 52:7; 58:3; 58:8; 58:10; 59:13a; 60:8; 62:4; 64:7, 9; 74:19; 76:5; 76:11; 79:8; 80:15; 81:8c; 86:7; 88:19; 89:3, 50; 92:16; 95:7; 97:9; 98:2; 99:2, 8a; 102:5-6, 14, 24-25, 28; 104:8; 105:11f.; 106:3, 43a, b; 109:39a; 113:6; 115:12; 130:5-6; 135:13-14; 146:8; (18:2-3; 27:8; 35:14a; 35:20c; 36:8a; 39:3-4; 44:3; 48:12a; 55:11-12; 56:4-5; 56:9; 59:8; 78:6-7; 78:49-50; 80:3a; 83:19; 88:10a; 92:9; 139:14-15; 140:5-6; 146:6-7); (22:24; 91:15)]

Anonymous, "Questions and Answers. Psalms 1-50," *BTr* 12 (1961) 80-84. [2:12; 4:2; 5:3; 7:5; 8:5; 10:5; 12:2; 13:2; 15:2; 17:10; 18:9; 18:26; 19:3; 22:20; 22:26; 25:13; 26:6; 29:1; 29:2; 29:11; 31:7; 31:10; 31:22; 32:6; 32:9; 35:10; 35:13; 35:15; 37:3; 37:37-38; 41:7; 44:19; 49:5; 50:7-9; 50:22]

Anonymous, "Questions and Answers. Psalms 51-100," *BTr* 12 (1961) 134-139. [51:8 (10); 51:10 (12); 51:12 (14); 58:1 (2); 58:2 (3); 60:4 (6); 63:1 (2); 63:7 (8); 64:8 (9); 65:2-3 (3-4); 65:5 (6); 65:6 (7); 65:8 (9); 65:10 (11) 65:12 (13) 66:12; 68:13 (14); 68:26 (27); 68:35 (35); 69:13 (14); 69:21 (22) 72:10; 73:13; 73:24; 75:3 (4); 75:4 (5); 76:5 (6); 78:46; 80:4 (5); 80:5 (6) 80:10 (11) 81:5 (6); 81:6 (7); 81:15; 83:13 (14); 84:6 (7); 85:1 (2); 85:8 (9); 86:2; 87:4; 88:18 (19); 89:19; 89:44; 90:9; 91:16; 92:3 (4); 94:20; 95:10; 96:8; 96:13; 97:10]

Anonymous, "Questions and Answers, Psalms 101-150," *BTr* 13 (1962) 44-47. [102:12 (13); 103:5; 104:3a; 104:3b; 104:26; 105:4; 105:28; 106:28; 109:10; 109:21; 110:5; 112:4; 118:12; 118:27; 119; 119:49; 119:56; 119:109; 119:119; 119:130; 119:139; 119:140; 119:147-8; 120 title; 120:4; 124:8; 129:6; 135:3; 136:10; 137:2; 137:7; 139:6; 139:14; 145:2; 146:10; 148:7]

Peter F. Ellis, "'Come, let us go up to the mountain of the Lord!'," *BibT* #7 (1963) 433-438. [Psalms 122, 129, 130, 132]

*Arthur Candeland, "Psalms and the Preacher," *PQL* 10 (1964) 256-263. [I. The Psalms in Worship: 96:4-6; 145:1-7; Ps. 139; 104:6-9; 33:14-15, 21, 24; 145:15-16; 10:2-4; 34:1-6]

Arthur Candeland, "Psalms and the Preacher," *PQL* 10 (1964) 346-352. [II. The Psalms and Personal Experience: 44:17-22; 22:22; Ps. 40; 107:17ff.; 59:1-4; 32:5; Ps. 63; Ps. 73]

C. Berkelmans, "Some Considerations on the Translation of the Psalms by M. Dahood. I. The Preposition *b* = *from* in the Psalms According to M. Dahood," *UF* 1 (1969) 5-14. [2:4; 3:3; 19:15; 10:1; 10:14; 11:2; 64:5; 15:2; 60:8; 99:7; 15:4; 17:4; 17:5; 21:8; 16:8; 18:9; 18:14; 27:5; 31:22; 33:19; 36:6; 38:15; 45:3; 46:3; 55:16; 58:7; 58:11; 59:8; 59:12; 59:14; 66:7; 68:6; 68:19; 68:22; 78:26; 81:8; 83:11; 91:15]

(Book I)

Psalms 1 and 2

Anonymous, "The British Museum, Consisting of Copies of Original Papers in that National Depository," *MMBR* 45 (1818) 523-525. [A Jesuit's Exposition upon the First and Second Psalm, p. 525]

Josiah W. Gibbs, "Notes on the Septuagint Version of Psalms I. II.," *BRCR, N.S.,* 11 (1844) 441-446.

Ernest Lussier, "The New Latin Psalter: an Exegetical Commentary," *CBQ* 9 (1947) 226-234. *[Psa. 1 and 2]*

Psalm 1

Anonymous, "The First Psalm," *ERG, 2nd Ser.,* 3 (1860-61) 76-80.

*Samuel Cox, "The First Psalm," *Exp, 2nd Ser.,* 1 (1881) 81-103. [1. The Author of the Psalm; 2. The Theme of the Psalm]

Anonymous, "The Tenses of the First Psalm," *ONTS* 3 (1883-84) 261-263.

James Frame, "The Holy and Happy Divinely Described. An Exposition of the First Psalm," *ERG, 8th Ser.,* 3 (1884-85) 41-51.

C. B. Hulbert, "A Homiletic Inspection of the First Psalm," *HR* 38 (1899) 259-260.

Hermann Gunkel, "Psalm 1: An Interpretation,"*BW* 21 (1903) 120-123.

J. Dinnen Gilmore, "Studies in the Psalms. The Song of the Two Ways—Psalm i," *HR* 53 (1907) 53. *[Outline]*

W. R. W. Gardner, "Professor Briggs on Psalm I.—A Suggestion," *ET* 20 (1908-09) 565-566.

Anonymous, "The Psalm 'Beatus Vir' in the Breviary," *AER* 46 (1912) 587-592. *[Psa. 1]*

*James Kennedy, "Plea for a Fuller Criticism of the Massoretic Text, with Illustrations from the First Psalm," *Exp, 8th Ser.,* 5 (1913) 378-384.

Charles Edward Smith, "The Two Schools of the First Psalm," *CFL, 3rd Ser.,* 22 (1916) 124-126.

[Frank M.] T[homas], "Exegetical Notes. The Values of a Godward Life. Psalm i," *MQR, 3rd Ser.,* 46 (1920) 159-161.

Edward P. Arbez, "A Study of Psalm 1," *CBQ* 7 (1945) 398-404.

J. Leo Green, "Word Studies in the First Psalm," *R&E* 42 (1945) 407-412.

Theodore F. Nickel, "Sermon Study on Psalm One for Sixth Sunday After Trinity," *CTM* 22 (1951) 430-438.

M.-L. Martin, "Psalm 1: The blessedness of the righteous," *Min* 4 (1963-64) 18-21.

*S. Bullough, "The Question of Metre in Psalm I," *VT* 17 (1967) 42-49

Bruce C. Stark, "Aspects of Psalm 1," *ATB* 1 (1968) #1, 19-24.

Psalm 1:2

H. T., "Observations on Psalm I, 1, 2," *MR* 10 (1827) 253-255.

James Robson, "Psalm i. 2," *ET* 39 (1927-28) 90.

Psalm 1:3

I. J. Peritz, "Note on the Translation of Psalm 1:3d," *JBL* 55 (1936) vii.

Psalm 1:6

James Moffatt, "Opera Foris. Materials for the Preacher," *Exp, 7th Ser.,* 5 (1908) 382-383. *[1:6]*

F[rank] M. T[homas], "Exegetical Notes. Psalm i. 6," *MQR, 3rd Ser.,* 44 (1918) 700.

Psalm 2

G. B., "Exercitation on the Second Psalm," *QCS, 3rd Ser.,* 1 (1829) 100-111.

C. E. Stowe, "Translation and Exposition of the Second Psalm," *BS* 7 (1850) 352-359. [I. Messianic Application of the Psalm; II. Structure of the Psalm; III. Translation; IV. Notes on the Translation; V. Fulfillment of the Prophecy; VI. Practical Uses of this Prophecy]

Stephen M. Vail, "Exposition of the Second Psalm," *MR* 41 (1859) 118-129.

Anonymous, "The Second Psalm," *ERG, 2nd Ser.,* 3 (1860-61) 80-87.

Samuel Cox, "The Second Psalm," *Exp, 2nd Ser.,* 3 (1882) 13-35.

R., "The Tenses of the Second Psalm," *ONTS* 3 (1883-84) 357-358.

Thomas H. Rich, "Psalm 2," *JBL* 5 (1885) 83.

Phillips Brooks, "The Second Psalm," *CongL* 15 (1886) 348-355.

Talbot W. Chambers, "Studies in the Psalter. No. I.—The Second Psalm," *HR* 17 (1889) 78-82.

W. E. Barnes, "The Interpretation of the Second Psalm," *Exp, 5th Ser.,* 6 (1897) 304-308.

*A. S. Carrier, "A Study of Psalms II, CX, LXV, and LXXII," *CFL, O.S.,* 3 (1899) 136-140.

J. Dinnen Gilmore, "Studies in the Psalms. *The Kingdom of Christ Revealed.*—Psalm ii," *HR* 53 (1907) 213. *[Outline]*

*S. R. Driver, "The Method of Studying the Psalter. With Special Application to some of the Messianic Psalms," *Exp, 7th Ser.,* 9 (1910) 20-41. *[Psa. 2]*

H. H. Rowley, "The Text and Structure of Psalm II," *JTS* 42 (1941) 143-154.

Isaiah Sonne, "The Second Psalm," *HUCA* 19 (1945-46) 43-55.

P. P. Saydon, "The Divine Sonship of Christ in Psalm II," *Scrip* 3 (1948) 32-35.

*M. Treves, "Two Acrostic Psalms," *VT* 15 (1965) 81-90. *[Psa. 2]*

B. Lindars, "Is Psalm II an Acrostic Poem?" *VT* 17 (1967) 60-67.

Psalm 2:1

W. K. Lowther Clarke, "Notes. 1. The Psalms," *Theo* 12 (1926) 217-218. *[Psa.2:1]*

Psalm 2:3-5

*Cyrus Adler, "Notes on the Johns Hopkins and Abbott collections of Egyptian antiquities, with the translation of two Coptic inscriptions by Mr. W. Max Müller," *JAOS* 15 (1893) xxxi-xxxiv. *[Psa. 2:3-5]*

Psalm 2:3

†R. C. Fuller, "The Meaning of Psalm II, Verse 3," *Scrip* 4 (1949-51) 249-250.

Psalm 2:7

O. S. Stearns, "Exegesis of Psalm II., 7," *ONTS* 2 (1882-83) 107-111.

John H. C. Fritz, "Does Psalm 2, 7 Teach the Eternal Generation of the Son?" *TM* 9 (1929) 69-80.

G. H. Jones, "'The Decree of Yahweh' Ps. II:7," *VT* 15 (1965) 336-344.

Psalm 2:9

*J. Gwyn Griffiths, "P. Oslo 1, 105-9 and Metternich Stela, 85-6," *JEA* 25 (1939) 101. *[2:9]*

Albert Kelber, "Ps. 2:9 in the Light of an Ancient Ceremony," *CBQ* 5 (1943) 63-67.

Psalm 2:11-12

*J. Dyneley Prince, "Notes on Psa, 2:11, 12, and on אֲרָז, Isa. 44:14," *JBL* 19 (1900) 1-4.

*R. H. Charles, "Two Passages in the Psalms," *ET* 32 (1920-21) 539-541. *[2:11, 12]*

R. S. T. Haslehurst, "Studies in Texts. (*b*) Ps. ii. 11, 12," *Theo* 15 (1927) 220.

Psalm 2:12

A. Benisch, "Bible Translation," *JSL, 4th Ser.,* 2 (1862-63) 451-452. *[2:12]*

W. E. Barnes, "The Text of Psalm II 12, ('Kiss the Son' E.V., נַשְּׁקוּ בַר)," *JTS* 18 (1916-17) 24-29.

Samuel A. B. Mercer, "'Kiss the Son'—Ps. 2:12," *ATR* 2 (1919-20) 324-325.

J. A. F. Maynard, "'Kiss the Chosen One' (Ps 2:12)," *JBL* 57 (1938) xi.

Julian Morgenstern, "נַשְּׁקוּ בַר," *JQR, N.S.,* 32 (1941-42) 371-385. *[2:12]*

*S. C. Ylvisaker, "Some Old Testament Difficulties," *WLQ* 54 (1957) 262-264. [*Bar* in the expression *nashsh qu'bar,* Ps. 2:12, pp. 263-264]

Psalms 3 and 4

Ernest Lussier, "The New Latin Psalter: An Exegetical Commentary, II. Psalms 3 and 4," *CBQ* 9 (1947) 324-328.

Psalm 3

Anonymous, "The Third Psalm. A Psalm of David, on Occasion of his Fleeing from before Absalom his Son," *ERG, 2nd Ser.,* 4 (1861-62) 166-170.

Samuel Cox, "The Third Psalm," *Exp, 2nd Ser.,* 3 (1882) 94-106.

Psalm 3:5

*John DeWitt, "Exegetical Notes on the Psalms," *PRR* 1 (1890) 106-110, 287-288, 476-479. [5. Psalm 3:5, pp. 476-477]

Psalm 4

Samuel Cox, "The Fourth Psalm," *Exp, 2nd Ser.,* 3 (1882) 178-190.

T. K. Cheyne, "Studies in Practical Exegesis. II. Psalm IV," *Exp, 3rd Ser.,* 8 (1888) 428-438.

J. Dinnen Gilmore, "Studies in the Psalms. The Believer's Evening Psalm. Ps. iv," *HR* 53 (1907) 292. *[Outline]*

*W. E. Barnes, "Bible Translation—Official and Unofficial: A Study of Psalm IV in English," *JTS* 28 (1926-27) 39-48.

Psalm 4:4

*John Taylor, "Requests and Replies. Psalms iv. 4; viii. 2," *ET* 5 (1893-94) 315.

Psalm 4:6-9

*E. H. Askwith, "Some Obscure Passages in the Psalms," *Exp, 8th Ser.,* 19 (1920) 313-320. [Psa. 4:6-9, pp. 314-315]

Psalm 4:6-8

*John DeWitt, "Exegetical Notes on the Psalms," *PRR* 1 (1890) 106-110, 287-288, 476-479. [Psalm 4:6-8, pp. 477-478]

Psalm 4:6

W. Bradfield, "'Summum Bonum'," *ET* 3 (1891-92) 104. *[4:6]*

Anonymous, "The Great Text Commentary. Psalm IV. 6," *ET* 22 (1910-11) 15-21.

Psalm 4:7

*Mitchell Dahood, "Philological Notes on the Psalms," *ThSt* 14 (1953) 85-88. *[4:7, pp. 85-86]*

Psalms 5 and 6

Ernest Lussier, "The New Latin Psalter: An Exegetical Commentary, III. Psalms 5 and 6," *CBQ* 9 (1947) 465-470.

Psalm 5

J. Dinnen Gilmore, "Studies in the Psalms. The Believer's Morning Prayer. Ps. v," *HR* 54 (1907) 50. *[Outline]*

Psalm 5:1

Jacob Leveen, "The Meaning of אֶל־הַנְּחִילוֹת (Ps. v. 1)," *JTS* 39 (1938) 66-67.

Psalm 5:10

*W. C., "On the Imprecations of David. In what matter shall the imprecations of David in Ps. v. 10, and in other places, be reconciled with the spirit of piety, and the inspiration of the Psalms?" *QCS* 1 (1819) 613-616.

Psalm 6

J. Dinnen Gilmore, "Studies in the Psalms. Pleas for a Suffering Saint in Ps. vi," *HR* 54 (1907) 130. *[Outline]*

J. Dinnen Gilmore, "Studies in the Psalms. Song of Eight Steps—Psalm vi," *HR* 54 (1907) 130. *[Outline]*

Psalms 7 and 8

Ernest Lussier, "The New Latin Psalter: An Exegetical Commentary IV—Psalms 7; 8," *CBQ* 10 (1948) 81-86.

Psalm 7

J. Dinnen Gilmore, "Studies in the Psalms. The Erring of the Wicked —Psalm vii," *HR* 54 (1907) 130. *[Outline]*

J. Leveen, "The Textual Problems of Psalm VII," *VT* 16 (1966) 439-445.

Psalm 7:1-2

*J. Dinnen Gilmore, "Studies in the Psalms. The Beginning and the End: A Contrast. Psalm vii, 1, 2, and 17," *HR* 54 (1907) 290. *[Outline]*

Psalm 7:12-13

J[acob] Leveen, "Psalm VII, 12-13," *JRAS* (1946) 81-83.

Psalm 7:15

*G. J. Thierry, "Remarks on Various Passages of the Psalms," *OTS* 13 (1963) 77-97. *[7:15]*

Psalm 7:17

*J. Dinnen Gilmore, "Studies in the Psalms. The Beginning and the End: A Contrast. Psalm vii, 1, 2, and 17," *HR* 54 (1907) 290. *[Outline]*

Psalm 8

Anonymous, "Psalm VIII," *ATG* 5 (1838-39) 107-108. *[Paraphrase]*

Stephen M. Vail, "Exposition of the Eighth Psalm," *MR* 42 (1860) 640-648.

John De Witt, "Studies in the Psalms. No. I," *HR* 10 (1885) 31-35. *[Psalm 8]*

John Forbes, "Psalm VIII," *MI* 3 (1885-86) 228-240.

E. C. Bissell, "The 'Protoevangelium' and the Eighth Psa.," *JBL* 6 (1886) Part 2, 64-68.

T. K. Cheyne, "Studies in Practical Exegesis. Psalm VIII," *Exp, 3rd Ser.,* 10 (1889) 81-89.

Talbot W. Chambers, "Studies in the Psalter. No. XXXV.—The 8th Psalm," *HR* 22 (1891) 456-459.

Hermann Gunkel, "Psalm 8: An Interpretation," *BW* 21 (1903) 206-209.

Hans H. Spoer, "The Reconstruction of Psalm viii," *JBL* 22 (1903) 75-84.

George A. Barton, "The Eighth Psalm: An Interpretation," *BW* 24 (1904) 343-346.

J. Dinnen Gilmore, "Studies in the Psalms. The Song of the Wine-press. Psalm viii," *HR* 54 (1907) 290. *[Outline]*

P. A. H. de Boer, "Jahu's Ordination of Heaven and Earth. An Essay on Psalm VIII," *OTS* 2 (1943) 171-193.

*Julian Morgenstern, "Psalms 8 and 19A," *HUCA* 19 (1945-46) 491-523.

John H. Hicks, "Psalm VIII. A Translation and Interpretation," *PSTJ* 1 (1947-48) #2, 6-8.

*D. Paech, "Is Psalm 8 Messianic?" *AusTR* 27 (1956) 109-128.

John H. Scammon, "Psalm 8 in the RSV," *Found* 1 (1958) #2, 78.

*H. W. Huppenbauer, "God and Nature in the Psalms," *GBT* 3 (1966-71) #6, 19-32. *[Psalm 8]*

*Brevard Childs, "Psalm 8 in the Context of the Christian Canon," *Interp* 23 (1969) 20-31.

Psalm 8:1

*D. Muir, "Three Obscure O.T. Passages," *ET* 41 (1929-30) 44-45. *[8:1]*

Psalm 8:2-3

H. M. Haydn, "'Out of the Mouth of Babes and Sucklings.' A Suggestion for Psalm viii. 2, 3," *Exp, 8th Ser.,* 13 (1917) 232-240.

Psalm 8:2

*M. Stuart, "Hebrew Criticisms," *BS* 9 (1852) 51-77. [No. II. Suggestions respecting the much controverted of Psalm VIII. 2, pp. 73-77]

*John DeWitt, "Exegetical Notes on the Psalms," *PRR* 1 (1890) 106-110, 287-288, 476-479. [3. Psalm 8:2, pp. 287-288]

*John Taylor, "Requests and Replies. Psalms iv. 4; viii. 2," *ET* 5 (1893-94) 315.

Psalm 8:4

Anonymous, "The Great Text Commentary.   The Great Texts of the Psalms," *ET* 22 (1910-11) 61-70. *[8:4]*

Psalm 8:5

*John DeWitt, "Exegetical Notes on the Psalms," *PRR* 1 (1890) 106-110, 287-288, 476-479. [4. Psalm 8:5, p. 288]

Psalms 9 and 10

T. K. Abbott, "On the Alphabetical Arrangement of the Ninth and Tenth Psalms," *Herm* 7 (1889-90) 21-28.

T. K. Abbott, "On the Alphabetical Arrangement of Ps. IX and X with some other emendations," *ZAW* 16 (1896) 292-294.

M. Berlin, "Psalms IX and X," *JQR* 13 (1900-01) 669-681.

G. Buchanan Gray, "The Alphabetic Structure of Psalms ix. and x.," *Exp,* *7th Ser.,* 2 (1906) 233-253.

Ernest Lussier, "The New Latin Psalter: An Exegetical Commentary V— Psalms 9; 10," *CBQ* 10 (1948) 196-202.

Robert Gordis, "Psalm 9-10—A Textual and Exegetical Study," *JQR* 48 (1957-58) 104-122.

Psalm 9

J. Dinnen Gilmore, "Studies in the Psalms. A Joyous Song of Praise. Psalm ix," *HR* 54 (1907) 453. *[Outline]*

J. Dinnen Gilmore, "Studies in the Psalms. The Lord a Hiding-Place. Psalm ix," *HR* 55 (1908) 50. *[Outline]*

Donald A. Fraser, "A Rimed Version of Psalm IX," *HR* 65 (1913) 395.

Patrick W. Skehan, "A Broken Acrostic and Psalm 9," *CBQ* 27 (1965) 1-5.

Psalm 10

J. Dinnen Gilmore, "Studies in the Psalms. The Song of the Oppressed. Psalm x," *HR* 55 (1908) 50. *[Alternative Edition, p. 132][Outline]*

J. Leveen, "Psalm X: A Reconstruction," *JTS* 45 (1944) 16-21.

W. G. Simpson, "Some Egyptian light on a translation Problem in Psalm X," *VT* 19 (1969) 128-131.

Psalm 10:3

*G. J. Thierry, "Remarks on Various Passages of the Psalms," *OTS* 13 (1963) 77-97. *[10:3]*

Psalm 10:4

*Talbot W. Chambers, "Misquoted Scriptures. No. I," *HR* 6 (1881-82) 471-472. *[10:4]*

Psalm 10:17-18

Jacob Leveen, "A Note on Psalm 10:17-18," *JBL* 67 (1948) 249-250.

Psalm 10:17

J. Dinnen Gilmore, "Studies in the Psalms. The Boast of Faith. Psalm x. 17," *HR* 55 (1908) 212. *[Outline]*

Psalms 11-13

*Ernest Lussier, "The New Latin Psalter: An Exegetical Commentary VI—Psalms 11, 12, 13, and 52," *CBQ* 10 (1948) 291-295.

Psalm 11

*÷Anonymous, "Travell on the Psalms," *BCQTR* 6 (1795) 625-628. *(Review) [Psalm 11]*

J. Dinnen Gilmore, "Studies in the Psalms. A Debate Between Fear and Faith. Psalm xi," *HR* 55 (1908) 130. *[Outline]*

Isaiah Sonne, "Psalm Eleven," *JBL* 68 (1949) 241-245.

Julian Morgenstern, "Psalm 11," *JBL* 69 (1950) 221-231.

Psalm 11:3

George L. Robinson, "Psalm 11:3," *BW* 14 (1899) 304-305.

Psalm 12

J. Dinnen Gilmore, "Studies in the Psalms. An Appeal for Help in Evil Days. Psalm xii," *HR* 55 (1908) 212. *[Outline]*

Psalm 12:6

*G. M. Mackie, "The Pestle and the Mortar," *ET* 8 (1896-97) 521-522. *[12:6]*

Psalm 12:7-9

*K. Budde, "Psalm Problems. I.," *ET* 12 (1900-01) 139-142. *[12:7, 8, 9]*

Psalm 12:7

J. A. Selbie, "A Crux Interpretum," *ET* 8 (1896-97) 170. *[12:7]*

T. K. Cheyne, "Textual Criticism of the Psalms," *ET* 8 (1896-97) 236-237. *[12:7]*

*T. K. Cheyne, "On Proverbs XXVII. 21, 22; Psalm XII. 7 (6)," *ET* 8 (1896-97) 335-336.

*Eb. Nestle, "Ps. XII. 7 and Prov. XXVII. 21, 22," *ET* 8 (1896-97) 379.

T. K. Cheyne, "The Text of Ps. 12, 7," *ZAW* 17 (1897) 188-189.

Psalm 12:9

Eugene Zolli, "*Kerum* in Ps. 12:9: a Hapax Legomenon," *CBQ* 12 (1950) 7-9.

*P. Wernberg-Møller, "Two Difficult Passages in the Old Testament," *ZAW* 69 (1957) 69-73. [Psa. 12:9, pp. 69-71]

Psalm 13

J. Dinnen Gilmore, "Studies in the Psalms. Experience of One Who Feels Forgotten and Forsaken of God. Psalm xiii," *HR* 55 (1908) 295. *[Outline]*

Psalms 14 and 15

Ernest Lussier, "The New Latin Psalter: An Exegetical Commentary VI—
Psalms 14 and 15," *CBQ* 10 (1948) 408-412.

Psalm 14

*Edward G. King, "On the Text of Psalms XIV. and LIII," *AJSL* 2 (1885-86)
237-239.

*K. Budde, "Psalm Problems. II," *ET* 12 (1900-01) 285-288. *[Psalm 14]*

J. Dinnen Gilmore, "Studies in the Psalms. The Corruption of the Natural
Man. Psalm xiv," *HR* 55 (1908) 295. *[Outline]*

*John A. Hutton, "From Jahweh to Elohim: From the Particular to the Uni-
versal," *Exp, 8th Ser.,* 13 (1917) 454-460. *[Psalm 14]*

*C. C. Torrey, "The Archetype of Psalms 14 and 53," *JBL* 46 (1927) 186-
192.

*B. D. Eerdmans, "Psalm XIV, LIII and the Elohim-Psalms," *OTS* 1 (1942)
258-267.

Psalm 14:1

T. K.*[sic]*, "Morsels of Criticism. Reply to T. K.," *CongML* 5 (1822) 358-
359. *[14:1]*

Anonymous, "The Great Text Commentary, Psalm XIV. 1," *ET* 22 (1910-11)
201-207.

W. D. Niven, "Psalm XIV. 1," *ET* 22 (1910-11) 565-566.

Psalm 15

J. Dinnen Gilmore, "Studies in the Psalms. A Citizen of Zion Described.
Psalm xv," *HR* 55 (1908) 380. *[Outline]*

*Shalom Spiegel, "A Prophetic Attestation of the Decalogue: Hosea 6:5.
With Some Observations on Psalm 15 and 24," *HTR* 27 (1934) 105-144.

Psalm 15:3

A. Clarke, "Illustration of Psalm XV. 3," *MR* 7 (1824) 55-56.

Psalm 15:4

Mitchell J. Dahood, "A Note on Psalm 15,4 (14,4)," *CBQ* 16 (1954) 302.

Psalm 16 and 17

*A. S. Carrier, "Studies in the Psalms—Psalms XVI, XVII, XLIX, LXXIII," *CFL, N.S.,* 1 (1900) 163-168.

Ernest Lussier, "The New Latin Psalter: An Exegetical Commentary, VIII —Ps. 16; 17," *CBQ* 11 (1949) 82-88.

Psalm 16

M. Stuart, "Interpretation of Psalm XVI," *BRCR* 1 (1831) 51-110.

E. W. D.*[sic]*, "Remarks on the Sixteenth Psalm," *CRB* 11 (1846) 155-168.

S. M. Vail, "The Sixteenth Psalm," *MR* 44 (1862) 615-627.

W. Robertson Smith, "The Sixteenth Psalm," *Exp, 1st Ser.,* 4 (1876) 341-372.

T. K. Cheyne, "Studies in Practical Exegesis: Psalm XVI," *Exp, 3rd Ser.,* 10 (1889) 210-224.

Talbot W. Chambers, "Studies in the Psalter.   No. II.—The Sixteenth Psalm," *HR* 17 (1889) 172-176.

R. Balgarnie, "David's Golden Psalm," *TML* 2 (1889) 268-273. *[Psalm 16]*

Willis J. Beecher, "The Sixteenth Psalm," *HR* 32 (1896) 444-447.

J. Dinnen Gilmore, "Studies in the Psalms. Confidence in God. Psalm xvi," *HR* 55 (1908) 380. *[Outline]*

S. R. Driver, "The Method of Studying the Psalter. Psalm XVI," *Exp, 7th Ser.,* 10 (1910) 26-37.

W. Leonard, "The Psalm of the Resurrection," *ACR* 11 (1934) 105-117. [Ps. 16 (15), pp. 107-117]

H. W. Boers, "Psalm 16 and the historical origin of the Christian faith," *ZNW* 60 (1969) 105-110.

Psalm 16:1-4

*John DeWitt, "Exegetical Notes on the Psalms," *PRR* 1 (1890) 106-110, 287-288, 476-479. [1. Psalm 16:1-4, pp. 106-109]

T. K. Cheyne, "Psalm XVI. 1-4," *ET* 3 (1891-92) 164.

T. K. Cheyne, "Old Testament Notes, A New View of Psalm xvi. 1-4," *Exp, 4th Ser.,* 5 (1892) 77-78.

S. C. Ylvisaker, "Difficulties in the Hebrew Text of the Old Testament. Psalm XVI, 1-4," *WLQ* 54 (1957) 139-144.

Psalm 16:2-3

Anonymous, "The Dependent One," *BWR* 1 (1877) 303. *[16:2, 3]*

Psalm 16:3

John Taylor, "Kautzsch's New Edition of the Psalter, V," *ET* 5 (1893-94) 384. *[16:3]*

Psalm 16:9-11

Anonymous, "Comparative Translation: Psalm 16:9-11. A Study in Modernizing the English Bible," *BW* 24 (1904) 126-127.

Psalm 16:8-11

Edward L. Curtis, "An Interpretation: Psalm 16:8-11," *BW* 24 (1904) 112-116.

Psalm 16:10

*Talbot W. Chambers, "Misquoted Scriptures. No. I," *HR* 6 (1881-82) 471-472. *[16:10]*

Sara F. Hoyt, "The Holy One in Psalm 16, 10," *JAOS* 32 (1912) 120-125.

J. J. Huckle, "Psalm 16:10B: A Consideration," *DunR* 4 (1964) 43-55.

Psalm 16:11

Anonymous, "The Great Text Commentary. The Great Texts of the Psalms," *ET* 22 (1910-11) 254-260. *[16:11]*

*W. H. Bass, "Acts II. 28 and Psalm XVI. 11," *ET* 29 (1917-18) 522.

Psalm 17

Talbot W. Chambers, "Studies in the Psalter. No. XIV. The Seventeenth Psalm," *HR* 19 (1890) 257-261.

T. K. Cheyne, "The Seventeenth Psalm," *Exp, 6th Ser.,* 4 (1901) 241-252.

J. Dinnen Gilmore, "Studies in the Psalms. Confidence in Jehovah's Righteousness. Psalm xvii," *HR* 55 (1908) 380. *[Outline]*

E. J. Kissane, "Some critical notes on Psalm 17," *B* 9 (1928) 89-96.

J. Leveen, "Textual Problems of Psalm XVII," *VT* 11 (1961) 48-54.

Frederick Newmann, "Hate in the Bible," *HQ* 8 (1968) #2, 64-68. *[Psalm 17]*

Psalm 17:3-14

John Taylor, "Kautzsch's New Edition of the Psalter, VI," *ET* 5 (1893-94) 430-432. *[17:3, 11, 14]*

Psalm 17:10-12

*A. S. Carrier, "Psalm 17:10-12, 15," *BW* 13 (1899) 341-342.

Psalm 17:15

*A. S. Carrier, "Psalm 17:10-12, 15," *BW* 13 (1899) 341-342.

Samuel Daiches, "Psalm XVII. 15," *ET* 20 (1908-09) 472-473.

Psalms 18-20

Ernest Lussier, "The New Latin Psalter: An Exegetical Commentary. IX: Psalms 18, 19, and 20," *CBQ* 11 (1949) 207-212.

Psalm 18

†Anonymous, "Translation of Psalm xviii," *MMBR* 6 (1798) 199. *[Psalm xviii. translated into Verse from the Hebrew]*

*William Henry Bennett, "Notes on a Comparison of the Texts of Psalm XVIII. and 2 Samuel XXII," *AJSL* 3 (1886-87) 65-86.

J. Dinnen Gilmore, "Studies in the Psalms. Praise for Manifold Mercies. Psalm xviii," *HR* 56 (1908) 222. *[Outline]*

Donald A. Fraser, "A Rimed*[sic]* Version of Psalm XVIII," *HR* 70 (1915) 226-227.

*John P. Peters, "Another Folk Song," *JBL* 40 (1921) 81-85. [Psalm 18, pp. 83-85]

*F[rank] M[oore] Cross Jr., "Notes on II Samuel 22 = Psalm 18," *JBL* 68 (1949) xi.

Psalm 18:4-5

*John A. Maynard, "Sheol and Belial," *ATR* 1 (1918-19) 92-93. *[2 Sam. 22:5-6; Psa. 18:4-5]*

Psalm 18:6-16

*Anonymous, "The Theophany Celebrated Psalm XVIII. 6-16. Real, not Figurative," *TLJ* 4 (1851-52) 91-116.

Psalm 18:30

W. Fletcher Flett, "Psalm XVIII. 30," *ET* 42 (1930-31) 526.

Psalm 18:36

George R. Macphail, "A Gaelic Gloss from Bobbio," *ET* 21 (1909-10) 280-281. *[18:36]*

*P. Peters, "Luther's Rendition of II Samuel 22:36 and Psalm 18:36: und wenn du mich demuetigest, machst du mich gross," *WLQ* 52 (1955) 137-143.

Psalm 18:45

*J. H. Eaton, "Some Questions of Philology and Exegesis in the Psalms," *JTS, N.S.,*19 (1968) 603-609. *[Psalm xviii. 45* יכחש לי, pp. 603-604]

Psalm 19

Anonymous, "Psalm XIX. The Works and Words of God," *ERG, 2nd Ser.,* 4 (1861-62) 233-239.

Oswald Dykes, "The Nineteenth Psalm Read in the Light of Ancient Nature-Worship," *Exp, 1st Ser.,* 9 (1879) 42-53.

O. S. Stearns, "A Paraphrase of the Nineteenth Psalm," *ONTS* 3 (1883-84) 150-152.

Talbot W. Chambers, "The Unity of the Nineteenth Psalm," *ONTS* 4 (1884-85) 320-321.

Talbot W. Chambers, "Studies in the Psalter. No. III.—The Nineteenth Psalm," *HR* 17 (1889) 253-257.

John D. Davis, "The Nineteenth Psalm in the Criticism of the Nineteenth Century," *PTR* 3 (1905) 353-375.

J. [Dinnen] Gilmore, "Studies in the Psalms. The Song of the Two Books. Psalm XIX," *HR* 56 (1908) 305. *[Outline]*

Anonymous, "The Glory Psalm," *HR* 57 (1909) 391. *[Psalm 19]*

R. B. Woodworth, "Psalm 19 and Christopher Columbus," *USR* 46 (1934-35) 39-44.

*Julian Morgenstern, "Psalms 8 and 19A," *HUCA* 19 (1945-46) 491-523.

H. Leo Eddleman, "Word Pictures in the Word. An Exposition of Psalm 19," *R&E* 49 (1952) 413-424.

J. van der Ploeg, "Psalm XIX and some of its problems," *JEOL* #17 (1963) 193-201.

A. H. van Zyl, "Psalm 19," *OTW* 9 (1966) 142-158.

*H. W. Huppenbauer, "God and Nature in the Psalms," *GBT* 3 (1966-71) #6, 19-32. *[Psalm 19]*

Psalm 19:1-6

Hermann Gunkel, "Psalm 19:1-6: An Interpretation," *BW* 21 (1903) 281-283.

Psalm 19:4-5

*K. Budde, "Psalm Problems. I.," *ET* 12 (1900-01) 139-142. *[19:4, 5]*

Psalm 19:4

R. Laird Harris, "The Testimony of the Skies. The Hebrew Text of Psalm 19:4," *CTM* 14 (1943) 214-218.

Psalm 19:5

R. Kraetzschmar, "Psalm XIX. 5," *ET* 12 (1900-01) 567-568.

Psalm 19:7-9

George Matheson, "The Outer and the Inner Glory. Psalm XIX. 7-9," *Exp, 1st Ser.,* 12 (1880) 89-104.

Psalm 19:10

*J. H. Eaton, "Some Questions of Philology and Exegesis in the Psalms," *JTS, N.S.,*19 (1968) 603-609. [*Psalm xix.. 10* טהורה, pp. 604-605]

Psalm 19:12-13

Anonymous, "Comparative Translation: Psalm 19:12, 13. A Study in Modernizing the English Bible," *BW* 21 (1903) 447-448.

Psalm 19:12

*M. D. Goldman, "Lexicographical Notes on Exegesis (5)," *ABR* 4 (1954-55) 85-92. [b. Psalm XIX. 12, pp. 88-89]

Psalm 19:14

*M. D. Goldman, "Lexicographical Notes on Exegesis (5)," *ABR* 4 (1954-55) 85-92. [a. Psalm XIX. 14, pp. 87-88]

Psalm 20

J. Dinnen Gilmore, "Studies in the Psalms. The Soldier's Battle-Song. Psalm 20," *HR* 60 (1910) 393. *[Outline]*

Adam C. Welch, "Some Misunderstood Psalms. III. Psalm XX," *ET* 37 (1925-26) 408-410.

Psalm 20:2

*Paul Haupt, "Assyr. *dagâlu,* to look for, in the OT," *JBL* 37 (1918) 229-232. *[20:2]*

Psalm 20:3

H. F. B. Compston, "Psalm XX. 3," *ET* 24 (1912-13) 427.

Psalm 20:4-10

*Paul Haupt, "Assyr. *dagâlu,* to look for, in the OT," *JBL* 37 (1918) 229-232. *[20:4-6, 7-10]*

Psalm 20:7

J. R. Birtle, "Psalm XX. 7: An Exegetical Note," *ET* 38 (1926-27) 234.

Psalms 21 and 22

Ernest Lussier, "The New Latin Psalter: An Exegetical Commentary. X: Psalms 21 and 22," *CBQ* 11 (1949) 316-322.

Psalm 21

J. Dinnen Gilmore, "Studies in the Psalms. A Song of Triumphs and Victory. Psalm 21," *HR* 60 (1910) 393. *[Outline]*

F. Charles Fensham, "Ps 21—A Covenant-Song?" *ZAW* 77 (1965) 193-202.

Psalm 21:6

*Eb. Nestle, "Ps. XXI. 6 and Prov. XXVII. 21, 22," *ET* 8 (1896-97) 287-288.

Psalm 21:10

*G. R. Driver, "*ana utûnim nadû,*" *AfO* 18 (1957-58) 129. *[21:10]*

*F. J. Morrow Jr., "Psalm XXI 10—An example of Haplography," *VT* 18 (1968) 558-559.

Psalm 22

Franz Delitzsch, "The Subject of the Twenty-Second Psalm," *ThE* 2 (1865) 193-194.

F. G. Hibbard, "The Twenty-Second Psalm, as Illustrating the Subjective Method of Prophetic Christological Revelation," *MR* 52 (1870) 98-110, 366-378.

Talbot W. Chambers, "Studies in the Psalter. No. XXXVI.—The 22d Psalm," *HR* 22 (1891) 554-557.

C. H. Mockridge, "The Twenty-second Psalm—Messianic Missionary," *HR* 31 (1896) 256-259.

Alvah Hovey, "The Twenty-Second Psalm," *BW* 22 (1903) 107-115.

S. R. Driver, "The Method of Studying the Psalter. Psalm XXII," *Exp, 7th Ser.,* 9 (1910) 507-524.

E. F. Sutcliffe, "The Messianic Character of the Twenty-First Psalm," *IER, 5th Ser.,* 18 (1921) 348-363. *[Psalm 22]*

*John Torrance, "Ps. XXII.—As Used by Christ and St. Paul," *ET* 44 (1932-33) 382.

R. H. Altus, "Sermon Study on Psalm 22," *AusTR* 14 (1943) 1-14.

W. Leonard, "Eli Eli, Lamma Sabarthani: the great Passion Psalm," *ACR* 23 (1946) 7-16. *[Psalm 21 (22)]*

Stanley B. Frost, "Psalm 22: An Exposition," *CJT* 8 (1962) 102-115.

Loren R. Fisher, "Betrayed by Friends. *An Expository Study of Psalm 22,*" *Interp* 18 (1964) 20-38.

Psalm 22:1

John Quasten, "'The Waters of Refreshment'," *CBQ* 1 (1939) 325-332. *[Psalm 22: (Heb. 23) 1]*

Psalm 22:10

*G. J. Thierry, "Remarks on Various Passages of the Psalms," *OTS* 13 (1963) 77-97. *[22:10]*

Psalm 22:13 (12)

S. R. Driver, "A Correction," *ET* 11 (1899-1900) 233. *[22:13(12)]*

*T. K. Cheyne, "The Septuagint in 'The Encyclopedia Biblica'," *ET* 11 (1899-1900) 285. *[22:13(12)]*

Psalm 22:16

J. W. Southern, "'They pierced my hands and my feet,' Psalm xxii. 16," *ET* 4 (1892-93) 46-47.

Wm. Kean, "'They pierced my hands and my feet'," *ET* 4 (1892-93) 191-192. *[22:16]*

R. C. W. Raban, "'They pierced my hands and my feet'," *ET* 4 (1892-93) 528. *[22:16]*

*W. E. Barnes, "Two Psalm Notes," *JTS* 37 (1936) 385-387. *[22:16 (Heb. 17)]*

Psalm 22:17

Robert W. Landis, "The True Import of כָּאֲרִי יָדַי וְרַגְלָי in Psalm 22:17, commonly translated, 'They pierced my hands and my feet'," *BS* 8 (1851) 802-822.

*M. Stuart, "Hebrew Criticisms," *BS* 9 (1852) 51-77. [I. A word more on Psalm xxii. 17, pp. 71-73]

Frederick Kramer, "Psalms XXII. 17—כאֲרי ידי ורגלי," *AJSL* 8 (1891-92) 98-100.

H. G. Ross, "Psalm xxii. 17," *ET* 16 (1904-05) 523-524.

Ed. König, "Psalm xxii. 17b," *ET* 17 (1905-06) 140.

*Samuel Daiches, "The Meaning of כארי in Psalm 22, v. 17," *JRAS* (1933) 401-403.

Psalm 22:25

*T. K. Cheyne, "Notes on Psa. 22:25 and Nah. 2:8," *JBL* 15 (1896) 198.

Psalm 22:28-32

C. Krahmalkov, "Psalm 22, 28-32," *B* 50 (1969) 389-392.

Psalm 22:29-31

Albert A. Isaacs, "The difficulties of Scripture, *Psalm xxii, 29-31,*" *EN* 4 (1892) 218-221.

Psalm 22:29

*Robert A. Aytoun, "'Himself He Cannot Save,' (Ps. xxii 29 and Mark xv 31)," *JTS* 21 (1919-20) 245-248.

Psalms 23 and 24

Ernest Lussier, "The New Latin Psalter: An Exegetical Commentary XI: Psalms 23 and 24," *CBQ* 11 (1949) 447-452.

Psalm 23

Anonymous, "Specimen of a New Translation," *CongML* 3 (1820) 595-596. *[Psalm 23]*

Onesimus, "Remarks on the 23rd Psalm," *CongML* 8 (1825) 172-176.

Joel Parker, "Practical Exposition of Psalm 23," *BJ* 1 (1842) 177-184.

J. S. B., "Professor Tholuck on the Twenty-third Psalm," *CongML* 25 (1842) 145-152.

R. Balgarnie, "Hengstenbergs's Theory of the Twenty-third Psalm," *BFER* 28 (1879) 327-336.

B. F. Simpson, "An Exegesis of the Twenty-third Psalm," *ONTS* 3 (1883-84) 240-249.

Talbot W. Chambers, "Studies in the Psalter. No. XIV. The Twenty-third Psalm," *HR* 19 (1890) 153-157.

F. P. Ramsay, "The XXIII Psalm," *JAOS* 16 (1894-96) cxciii-cxciv.

George Adam Smith, "The Twenty-third Psalm," *Exp, 5th Ser.,* 1 (1895) 33-44.

*Marshall B. Lang, "The Beatitudes in the Twenty-third Psalm," *ET* 10 (1898-99) 46-47.

Armstrong Black, "The Twenty-third Psalm," *Exp, 5th Ser.,* 10 (1899) 35-54.

George Francis Greene, "The Twenty-Third Psalm," *CFL, N.S.,* 8 (1903) 329-335.

John E. McFadyen, "The Messages of the Psalms: Psalm 23," *BW* 26 (1905) 15-19.

G. F Hamilton, "Psalm xxiii," *ET* 17 (1905-06) 431.

V. Gelesnoff, "The Twenty-third Psalm," *CFL, 3rd Ser.,* 5 (1906) 221-223.

Anonymous, "A Psalm of Over-running Joy (Ps. xxiii)," *HR* 56 (1908) 372.

Andrew C. Zenos, "The Shepherd Psalm," *HR* 56 (1908) 387-388. *[Psalm 23]*

*Ellen Adelaide Copp, "Is the Radical Higher Criticism Scientific?—Tested by Briggs on the Psalms," *CFL, 3rd Ser.,* 13 (1910) 17-21. *[Psalm 23]*

W. M. McPheeters, "Psalm 23: A Translation and Some Notes," *HR* 63 (1912) 479-480.

*A. T. Burnbridge, "The Date and Interpretation of the XXIII. Psalm," *ICMM* 9 (1912-13) 71-78.

J. Simon, "The Good Shepherd Psalm," *AER* 55 (1916) 1-10. *[Psalm 23]*

G. W. Gasque, "The Twenty-third Psalm," *CFL, 3rd Ser.,* 26 (1920) 470-473.

D[avid] S. K[ennedy], "The Shepherd Psalm: A Review of Life," *CFL, 3rd Ser.,* 31 (1925) 117-118.

Edward Tallmadge Root, "A Twenty-Third Psalm for the Twentieth Century," *HR* 105 (1932) 387-388. *[Paraphrase]*

Julian Morgenstern, "Psalm 23," *JBL* 65 (1946) 13-24.

J. J. Owens, "The Jahweh Psalm," *R&E* 44 (1947) 186-193.

*Theophile James Meek, "Old Testament Notes," *JBL* 67 (1948) 233-239. [1. The Metrical Structure of Psalm 23, pp. 233-235]

*G. J. Thierry, "Notes on Hebrew Grammar and Etymology," *OTS* 9 (1951) 1-17. [Psa. 23, pp. 13-14]

E. Vogt, "The 'Place in Life' of Ps 23," *B* 34 (1953) 195-211.

Norman   Snaith,   "Psalm   23,"   *PQL*   2   (1956)   17-22.

*Constance Naish and Gillian Story, "'The Lord is My Goat Hunter'," *BTr* 14 (1963) 91-92.

*G. J. Thierry, "Remarks on Various Passages of the Psalms," *OTS* 13 (1963) 77-97. *[Psalm 23]*

A.   H.   van   Zyl,   "Psalm   23,"   *OTW*   6   (1963)   64-83.

Peter Steese, "Herbert and Crashaw: Two Paraphrases of the Twenty-Third Psalm," *JAAR* 33 (1965) 137-141.

A. L. Merrill, "Psalm XXIII and the Jerusalem Tradition," *VT* 15 (1965) 354-360.

Psalm 23:1-3

Dean W. Walker, "Realism in Psalm 23:1-3," *BW* 2 (1893) 430-433.

Psalm 23:1

Anonymous, "The Great Text Commentary. The Great Texts of the Psalms," *ET* 22 (1910-11) 302-306. *[23:1]*

Psalm 23:3f.

*John Eaton, "Problems of Translation in Psalm 23:3f.," *BTr* 16 (1965) 171-175.

Psalm 23:4

T. K. Cheyne, "Short Exegetical Notes. I. Ps. xxiii. 4.," *MI* 3 (1885-86) 470-472.

John S. Clemens, "On the Expression 'The Valley of the Shadow of Death' in Psalm XXIII. 4," *ET* 5 (1893-94) 288.

Psalm 23:5

T. H. Weir, "Ps. XXIII. 5," *ET* 27 (1915-16) 428-429.

F[rank] M. T[homas], " Exegetical Notes. Psalm xxiii. 5," *MQR, 3rd Ser.,*44 (1918) 702.

Psalm 23:6

J. A. Selbie, "Requests and Replies," *ET* 8 (1896-97) 205. [וְשַׁבְתִּי in Psa. 23:6]

Robert A. Aytoun, "Psalm XXIII. 6 and the 'Hound of Heaven'," *ET* 28 (1916-17) 281-282.

Psalm 24

*H. H. Kitchener, "Note on Gaza," *PEFQS* 10 (1878) 199-200. *[Psalm 24 LXX]*

Talbot W. Chambers, "Studies in the Psalter. No. IV.—The Twenty-fourth Psalm," *HR* 17 (1889) 350-354.

Howard Crosby, "Light on Important Texts. No. XIX," *HR* 6 (1881-82) 533-534. *[Psalm 24]*

John Forbes, "The Twenty-fourth Psalm," *BFER* 36 (1887) 67-75.

T. K. Cheyne, "Studies in Practical Exegesis: Psalm XXIV," *Exp, 3rd Ser.,* 10 (1889) 438-449.

George S. Goodspeed, "The Twenty-fourth Psalm: An Expository Sketch," *ONTS* 9 (1889) 329-335.

Herman Gunkel, "Psalm 24: An Interpretation," *BW* 21 (1903) 366-370.

J. Dinnen Gilmore, "Studies in the Psalms. The Song of Ascension, Psalm 24," *HR* 64 (1912) 309.

*I. W. Slotki, "The Text and the Ancient Form of Recital of Psalm 24 and Psalm 124," *JBL* 51 (1932) 214-226.

J. D. Smart, "The Eschatological Interpretation of Psalm 24," *JBL* 52 (1933) 175-180.

*Shalom Spiegel, "A Prophetic Attestation of the Decalogue: Hosea 6:5. With Some Observations on Psalm 15 and 24," *HTR* 27 (1934) 105-144.

Psalm 24:7ff.

Anonymous, "Coming of the King," *MR* 111 (1928) 460. *[24:7ff.]*

Psalms 25 - 27

Ernest Lussier, "The New Latin Psalter: An Exegetical Commentary XII: Psalms 25; 26; 27," *CBQ* 12 (1950) 69-74.

Psalm 25

*Emil G. Hirsch, "Note on Psalms 34 and 25," *AJSL* 18 (1901-02) 167-173.

J. Dinnen Gilmore, "Studies in the Psalms. Confidence in Prayer, Psalm 25," *HR* 24 (1912) 309.

Psalm 26

*T. K. Cheyne, "The Twenty-sixth and Twenty-eighth Psalms," *Exp, 4th Ser.,* 1 (1890) 37-49.

J. Dinnen Gilmore, "Studies in the Psalms. Resorting unto God, Psalm 26," *HR* 64 (1912) 393. *[Outline]*

Psalm 27

J. Dinnen Gilmore, "Studies in the Psalms. How Faith is Maintained, Psalm 27," *HR* 64 (1912) 393. *[Outline]*

I. W. Slotki, "The Metre and Text of Psalm XXVII," *JTS* 31 (1929-30) 387-395.

T. Torrance, "The Twenty-seventh Psalm," *EQ* 22 (1950) 40-44.

Psalm 27:1-5

Gerald J. Blidstein, "T'hillim 27," *YR* 4 (1965) 21-23. *[27:1, 4, 5]*

Psalm 27:13

M. Berlin, "Note on לולא, Ps. XXVII. 13, &c.," *JQR* 12 (1899-1900) 732.

Psalms 28 and 29

*Ernest Lussier, "The New Latin Psalter: An Exegetical Commentary XIII: Psalms 28 and 29," *CBQ* 12 (1950) 208-212.

Psalm 28

*T. K. Cheyne, "The Twenty-sixth and Twenty-eighth Psalms," *Exp, 4th Ser.*, 1 (1890) 37-49.

J. Dinnen Gilmore, "Studies in the Psalms. Suffering, Supplication, and Song, Psalm 28," *HR* 64 (1912) 393. *[Outline]*

Psalm 29

R. Balgarnie, "David's Thunder-Psalm. Psalm xxix," *TML* 5 (1891) 418-424.

J. Dinnen Gilmore, "Studies in the Psalms. Gloria in Excelsis: Pax in Terris, Psalm 29," *HR* 64 (1912) 393. *[Outline]*

*H. L. Ginsberg, "Canaanite Vestiges in the Psalter," *JBL* 56 (1937) iv. *[Psalm 29]*

Theodor H. Gaster, "Psalm 29," *JQR, N.S.,* 37 (1946-47) 55-65.

Frank M. Cross Jr., "Notes on a Canaanite Psalm in the Old Testament," *BASOR* #117 (1950) 19-21. *[Psalm 29]*

F. C. Fensham, "Psalm 29 And Ugarit," *OTW* 6 (1963) 84-99.

*H. W. Huppenbauer, "God and Nature in the Psalms," *GBT* 3 (1966-71) #6, 19-32. *[Psalm 29]*

Psalm 29:2

*P. R. Ackroyd, "Some Notes on the Psalms," *JTS, N.S.,* 17 (1966) 392-399. [3. The interpretation of קֹדֶשׁ הַדְרַת *(Ps. xxix. 2, xcvi. 9; 1 Chron. xvi. 29; 2 Chron. xx. 21)*, pp. 393-396]

Psalm 29:6

J. Smith, "Requests and Replies," *ET* 2 (1890-91) 139. *[29:6 LXX]*

Maurice H. Farbridge, "Psalm XXIX. 6," *ET* 29 (1917-18) 137-138.

*H. L. Ginsberg, "A Strand in the Cord of Hebraic Hymnody," *EI* 9 (1969) 45-50. *[Psalm 29, pp. 45-46] (Non-Hebrew Section)*

Psalm 29:8

W. Ewing, "Requests and Replies," *ET* 6 (1894-95) 25-26. *[29:8]*

*H. L. Ginsberg, "An Ancient Name of the Syrian Desert," *BIES* 6 (1938-39) #2, III. *[29:8]*

H. L. Ginsberg, "The Wilderness of Kadesh (Ps 29:8)," *JBL* 58 (1939) xi.

Psalm 29:10

*T. K. Cheyne, "Notes on מַבּוּל, נְפִילִים,etc.," *AJSL* 3 (1886-87) 175-176. [1. Ps. 29:10, מַבּוּל, p. 175]

Psalms 30 and 31

*Ernest Lussier, "The New Latin Psalter: An Exegetical Commentary XIV: Psalms 30 and 31," *CBQ* 12 (1950) 321-326.

Psalm 30

A. Steward, "The Thirtieth Psalm," *ERG, 7th Ser.,* 2 (1879-80) 186-191.

J. Dinnen Gilmore, "Studies in the Psalms. Guest for Every Home, Psalm 30," *HR* 66 (1913) 58. *[Outline]*

Psalm 31

J. Dinnen Gilmore, "Studies in the Psalms. From Darkness to Light, Psalm 31," *HR* 66 (1913) 58. *[Outline]*

W.Leonard,"In Manus Tuas: Psalm 30,"*ACR* 23 (1946) 186-195.*[Psalm 31]*

Psalm 31:15

Anonymous, "The Great Text Commentary. The Great Texts of the Psalms," *ET* 24 (1912-13) 491-495. *[31:15]*

J. Dinnen Gilmore, "Studies in the Psalms. Treasures in Reserve, Psalm 31:19," *HR* 66 (1913) 58. *[Outline]*

Psalm 31:20

Eb. Nestle, "Psalm XXXI. 20," *ET* 23 (1911-12) 184.

T. K. Cheyne, "Psalm XXXI. 20," *ET* 23 (1911-12) 281.

A. D. Martin, "Psalm XXXI. 20," *ET* 23 (1911-12) 332.

Psalms 32 and 33

Ernest Lussier, "The New Latin Psalter: An Exegetical Commentary XV: Psalms 32 and 33," *CBQ* 12 (1950) 450-457.

Psalm 32

T. K. Cheyne, "Studies in Practical Exegesis. I. Psalm XXXII," *Exp, 3rd Ser.,* 8 (1888) 379-388.

Talbot W. Chambers, "Studies in the Psalter. No. IX.—The Thirty-second Psalm," *HR* 18 (1889) 257-260.

E. C. Gordon, "Psalm XXXII," *CFL, N.S.,* 8 (1903) 220-226.

Andrew C. Zenos, "The Thirty-Second Psalm," *HR* 56 (1908) 304.

J. Dinnen Gilmore, "Studies in the Psalms. Blessedness and its Attainment, Psalm 32," *HR* 66 (1913) 231. *[Outline]*

*A. Guilding, "Some Obscured Rubrics and Lectionary Allusions in the Psalter," *JTS, N.S.,* 3 (1952) 41-55. [Psalm 32. A Psalm for the day of atonement, pp. 47-48]

Psalm 32:1-2

*Albert G. Mackinnon, "An Impressionist Sketch of Sin," *ET* 15 (1903-04) 380-381. *[32:1-2]*

Psalm 32:3

J. Kennedy, "Psalm XXXII 3," *JTS* 22 (1920-21) 381-382.

Psalm 32:7

J. R. Hudson, "'Thou Wilt Compass Me About with Songs of Deliverance' (Ps. XXXII. 7)," *ET* 27 (1915-16) 334.

Psalm 32:8

*James Moffatt, "Opera Foris; Or, Materials for the Preacher. Second Series," *Exp, 8th Ser.,* 2 (1911) 182-192. *[32:8]*

Psalm 32:9

James Kennedy, "Psalm XXXII 9," *JTS* 21 (1919-20) 328-329.

P[hilip] M[auro], "The Horse and the Mule (Psalm 32:9)," *CFL, 3rd Ser.,* 31 (1925) 172-173.

George Castellino, "Psalm XXXII 9," *VT* 2 (1952) 37-42.

Psalm 32:11

J. Dinnen Gilmore, "Studies in the Psalms. A Believer's Gladness. Psalm 32:11," *HR* 66 (1913) 231. *[Outline]*

Psalm 33

Talbot W. Chambers, "Studies in the Psalter. No. XXIII.—The Thirty-Third Psalm," *HR* 20 (1890) 447-451.

J. Dinnen Gilmore, "Studies in the Psalms. A Song of Praise, Psalm 33," *HR* 67 (1914) 143. *[Outline]*

William Wallace Martin, "The Thirty-Third Psalm as an Alphabetical Psalm: A Reconstruction," *AJSL* 41 (1924-25) 248-252.

D[avid] S. K[ennedy], "Psalm Thirty-three," *CFL, 3rd Ser.,* 32 (1926) 558.

Augustine, "St. Augustine's Sermon on Psalm XXXIII: I," *LofS* 12 (1957-58) 124-133. *(Trans. by Edmund Hill)*

Augustine, "St. Augustine's Sermon on Psalm XXXIII: II," *LofS* 12 (1957-58) 176-181. *(Trans. by Edmund Hill)*

Augustine, "St. Augustine's Sermon on Psalm XXXIII: III," *LofS* 12 (1957-58) 223-227. *(Trans. by Edmund Hill)*

Psalm 34

Talbot W. Chambers, "Studies in the Psalter. No. XIX—The Thirty-fourth Psalm," *HR* 20 (1890) 60-64.

*Emil G. Hirsch, "Note on Psalms 34 and 25," *AJSL* 18 (1901-02) 167-173.

J. Dinnen Gilmore, "Studies in the Psalms. A Song of Complete Deliverance, Psalm 34," *HR* 67 (1914) 143. *[Outline Study]*

J. Dinnen Gilmore, "Studies in the Psalms. Seven Things the Lord Does for Me, Psalm 34," *HR* 67 (1914) 143. *[Outline Study]*

*Leon J. Liebreich, "Psalms 34 and 145 in the Light of Their Key Words," *HUCA* 27 (1956) 181-192.

Psalm 34:1

Patrick W. Skehan, "Note on Psalm 34, 1," *CBQ* 14 (1952) 226.

Psalm 34:3

J. Dinnen Gilmore, "Studies in the Psalms. An Invitation to United Praise, Psalm 34:3," *HR* 67 (1914) 143. *[Outline Study]*

Psalm 34:8

Samuel Cox, "David's Testimony to the Divine Goodness. Psalm xxxiv. 8," *Exp, 2nd Ser.,* 4 (1882) 411-420.

Psalm 34:10

Augustus Poynder, "'The Young Lions,' Psalm xxxiv. 10," *ET* 17 (1905-06) 46.

Psalm 34:11

*Paul Haupt, "Mistranslated Lines in Proverbs," *JBL* 45 (1926) 354-356. [Psa. 34:11, p. 356]

Psalm 34:21

Theodore H. Robinson, "Note on Psalm xxxiv. 21," *ET* 52 (1940-41) 117.

Psalm 35

J. Dinnen Gilmore, "Studies in the Psalms. The Prayer of the Persecuted One, Psalm 35," *HR* 67 (1914) 143. *[Outline Study]*

Psalm 35:3

*T. K. Cheyne, "Influence of Assyrian in unexpected places," *JBL* 17 (1898) 103-107. [3. Psa. 35:3, p. 106]

Psalm 35:13

A. S. Aglen, "Note on Psalm XXXV. 13," *Exp, 2nd Ser.*, 8 (1884) 237-238.

Psalm 35:15

D. Winton Thomas, "Psalm XXXV. 15f," *JTS, N.S.*, 12 (1961) 50-51.

Psalm 35:16

*Samuel Daiches, "Psalm XXXV, 16. The Meaning of מָעוֹג," *JRAS* (1935) 355-358.

Psalm 36

Talbot W. Chambers, "Studies in the Psalter. No. XXXIII.—The 36th Psalm," *HR* 22 (1891) 263-266.

J. Dinnen Gilmore, "Studies in the Psalms. The Grievous Estate of the Wicked, Psalm 36," *HR* 67 (1914) 401.

Psalm 37

*James Oscar Boyd, "Psalms xxxvii., xlix., lxxxiii., as Theodicies," *CFL, N.S.*, 3 (1901) 115-119.

J. Dinnen Gilmore, "Studies in the Psalms. Do Not Worry, Psalm 37," *HR* 67 (1914) 401.

Psalm 37:7

Anonymous, "The Great Text Commentary. The Great Texts of the Psalms," *ET* 22 (1910-11) 352-358. *[37:7]*

Psalm 37:37

*D. Muir, "Three Obscure O.T. Passages," *ET* 41 (1929-30) 44-45. *[37:37]*

Psalm 38

J. D[innen] Gilmore, "Studies in the Psalms. The Remembrance of Sin, Psalm 38," *HR* 68 (1914) 487.

Psalm 38:11

D. W. Thomas, "A Note on לִבִּי סְחַרְחַר in Psalm XXXVIII 11," *JTS* 40 (1939) 390-391.

Psalm 39

T. K. Cheyne, "Studies in the Criticism of the Psalms," *Exp, 5th Ser.,* 9 (1899) 252-263, 334-344. *[Psalm 39]*

Psalm 39:13

*John Muir, "The Significance of אַיִן in Genesis V. 24 and Psalm XXXIX. 13," ET 50 (1938-39) 476-477.

Psalms 40-72

Henry S. Morais, "An Examination of Psalms XL.—LXXII.," *AJSL* 3 (1886-87) 46-48.

Psalm 40

S. R. Driver, "The Method of Studying the Psalter. Psalm XL," *Exp, 7th Ser.,* 9 (1910) 348-357.

J. D[innen] Gilmore, "Studies in the Psalms. Messiah—Risen, Rejoicing, Expecting. Psalm 40," *HR* 69 (1915) 57. *[Outline Study]*

B. D. Eerdmans, "Psalm XL," *OTS* 1 (1942) 268-273.

Nic. H. Ridderbos, "The Structure of Psalm XL," *OTS* 14 (1965) 296-304.

Psalm 40:3

*Paul Haupt, "Heb. *ḥayén,* misery," *BAVSS* 10 (1927) 210-212. *[40:3]*

Psalm 40:6

W. R. B., "On the True Reading and Correct Interpretation of Psalm xl. 6," *JSL, 3rd Ser.,* 10 (1859-60) 249-266.

*Frederick LaRue King, "A Destructive Critic's Perverse Interpretation of the Scriptures," *CFL, 3rd Ser.,* 5 (1906) 17-23. *[40:6]*

Psalm 40:7-8

P. Haupt, "Mine Ears Hast Thou Opened," *JBL* 38 (1919) 183-185. *[40:7-8]*

Psalm 40:8

*W. Bacher, "Contributions to Biblical Exegesis by Rudolph von Ihering," *JQR* 8 (1895-96) 185-188. [Ps. 40:8, p. 188]

Psalm 40:14

M. D. Goldman, "Lexicographic Notes on Exegesis: Proposed Emendation in Psalms," *ABR* 1 (1951) 59. *[40:14]*

Psalms 41 and 42

Romanus Rios, "Thirst for God (Psalm 41 and 42)," *Scrip* 2 (1947) 34-38.

Psalm 41

J. Dinnen Gilmore, "Studies in the Psalms. Consider Him, Psalm 41," *HR* 69 (1915) 312. *[Outline Study]*

Samuel Daiches, "Interpretation of Psalm XLI," *JRAS* (1936) 284-287.

B. D. Eerdmans, "Psalm XLI," *OTS* 1 (1942) 274-278.

Richard Rolle, "Psalm 41," *LofS* 6 (1951-52) 394-396.

Psalm 41:2

*J. H. Eaton, "Some Questions of Philology and Exegesis in the Psalms," *JTS, N.S.,*19 (1968) 603-609. [*Psalm xli. 2* משכיל, pp. 605-607]

Psalm 41:3

James Kennedy, "Psalm XLI. 3," *ET* 29 (1917-18) 287-288.

Psalm 41:6-10

Jacob Leveen, "A Displaced Verse in Psalm xli," *VT* 1 (1951) 65-66. *[41:6-10]*

(Book II)

Psalms 42-72

Sidney I. Esterson, "The Commentary of Rabbi David Ḳimḥi on Psalms 42-72. Edited on the Basis of Manuscripts and Early Editions," *HUCA* 10 (1935) 309-443.

Leon Nemoy, "Salmon ben Jeroham's Commentary on Psalms 42-72," *JQR, N.S.,* 48 (1957-58) 58-65.

Psalm 42 and 43

Willis J. Beecher, "Psalms XLII. and XLIII," *HR* 20 (1890) 166-170.

Hermann Gunkel, "Psalms 42 and 43: An Interpretation," *BW* 21 (1903) 433-439.

*R. W. Stewart, "'Tears Shall Take Comfort.' A Study of Psalms XLII., XLIII," *ET* 39 (1927-28) 140-141.

C. V. Pilcher, "Hermann Gunkel on Psalms 42, 43," *CJRT* 7 (1930) 314-319.

H. H. Rowley, "The Structure of Ps. XLII-XLIII," *B* 21 (1940) 45-50.

Psalm 42

J. D[innen] Gilmore, "Studies in the Psalms. Looking Backward, Psalm 42," *HR* 70 (1915) 59. *[Outline Study]*

W. S. McKenzie, "Psalm Forty-Second. A Study and Metrical Version," *BQR* 13 (1891) 658-668.

Psalm 42:1

George R. Macphail, "'As the heart panteth after the water brooks' (Ps. XLII. 1)," *ET* 21 (1909-10) 137.

Psalm 42:3

*R. W. Stewart, "'Tears Shall Take Comfort.' A Study of Psalms XLII., XLIII," *ET* 39 (1927-28) 140-141. *[42:3]*

Psalm 42:4-6

James Moffatt, "Opera Foris; Or, Materials for the Preacher. Second Series. —II.," *Exp, 8th Ser.,* 2 (1911) 380-384. *[42:4, 6]*

Psalm 42:7

X., "'In the Spirit'. Dominus Illuminato. Psalm xlii. 7," *Theo* 1 (1920) 235.

Psalm 42:8

Theodor H. Gaster, "Psalm 42:8," *JBL* 73 (1954) 237-238.

Psalm 43

J. D[innen] Gilmore, "Studies in the Psalms. Looking Forward, Psalm 43," *HR* 70 (1915) 59. *[Outline Study]*

Psalm 43:4

X., "'In the Spirit'. Dominus Illuminato. Psalm xliii. 4," *Theo* 1 (1920) 93.

Psalm 43:20-23 LXX

G. D. Kilpatrick, "A Fragment of Psalm XLIII (LXX). 20-3," *JTS* 50 (1949) 176-177.

Psalm 44

Augustine, "Christ as King from a sermon of St Augustine on Psalm 44," *LofS* 14 (1959-60) 172-175.

Psalm 45

John Thomas, "An Ode to the King Messiah, and His Queen. *Psalm XLV. —Long Metre,*" *ATG* 5 (1838-39) 265-270.

*†Anonymous, "Translation of the Hebrew Psalter," *ERL* 7 (1847) 71-87. *(Review) [Psalm 45]*

Talbot W. Chambers, "Studies in the Psalter. No. V. The Forty-fifth Psalm," *HR* 17 (1889) 422-446.

Thos. Hill Rich, "Psalm XLV," *ONTS* 11 (1890) 349-354.

*A. S. Carrier, "A Study of Psalms II, CX, LXV, and LXXII," *CFL, O.S.,* 3 (1899) 136-140.

Waldo S. Pratt, "Comparative Study of Psalm 45," *JBL* 19 (1900) 189-218.

W.W. Martin, "A Psalmist's Epithalamion," *AJSL* 19 (1902-03) 49-51 *[Psalm 45]*

S. R. Driver, "The Method of Studying the Psalter. Psalm XLV. An Ode Celebrating a Royal Marriage," *Exp, 7th Ser.,* 9 (1910) 114-131.

J. de Zwaan, "Psalm XLV," *Exp, 7th Ser.,* 10 (1910) 526-543.

Theodor H. Gaster, "Psalm 45," *JBL* 74 (1955) 239-251.

Brendan McGrath, "Reflections on Psalm 45," *BibT* #26 (1966) 1837-1842.

Psalm 45:6

Oswald T. Allis, "'Thy Throne, O God, is forever and ever,' A Study in Higher Critical Method," *PTR* 21 (1923) 236-266. *[45:6 (M.T. 7)]*

*S. Rosenblatt, "Notes on the Psalter," *JBL* 50 (1931) 308-310. *[45:6]*

Psalm 45:7

*[Friedrich] Giesebrecht, "Two Cruces Interpretum, Ps. XLV. 7 and Deut. XXXIII. 21, Removed," *AJSL* 4 (1887-88) 92-94.

*Willis J. Beecher, "Three Notes," *JBL* 8 (1888) 137-142. [II. Psa. 45:7, pp. 139-140]

W. G. Elmslie, "Brevia: Psalm xlv, 7," *Exp, 4th Ser.,* 1 (1890) 240.

J. R. Porter, "Psalm XLV. 7," *JTS, N.S.,* 12 (1961) 51-53.

J. A. Emerton, "The Syntactical Problem of Psalm XLV. 7," *JSS* 13 (1968) 58-63.

Psalm 45:8

Fred L. Moriarty, "A Note on Syntax," *MH* 1 (1944-45) #4, 2-3. *[45:8]*

Psalm 45:9

John G. Lansing, "קְצִיעוֹת אֲהָלוֹת—Psalm XLV. 9(8)," *PR* 6 (1885) 534-536.

*Claude R. Conder, "Notes on New Discoveries," *PEFQS* 41 (1909) 266-275. [Shegal (Psalm 45:9; Dan. 5:2, 3, 23), p. 275]

Psalm 45:16

G. Margoliouth, "Note on Psalm XLV. 16," *ET* 3 (1891-92) 478-479.

Psalm 46

John De Witt, "Studies in the Psalms. No. II," *HR* 10 (1885) 471-474. *[Psalm 46]*

Talbot W. Chambers, "Studies in the Psalter. No. XXV. The Forty-sixth Psalm," *HR* 21 (1891) 72-76.

Hermann Gunkel, "Psalm 46: An Interpretation," *BW* 21 (1903) 28-37.

John E. McFadyen, "The Messages of the Psalms: Psalm 46," *BW* 27 (1906) 99-103.

G. Viehweg, "Sermon Study on Psalm 46 for Reformation," *CTM* 22 (1951) 665-673.

E. Reim, "Luther and the 46th Ps.," *JTLC* 7 (1967) #3, 1-7.

Psalm 46:1

James Kennedy, "Psalm XLVI. 1," *ET* 31 (1919-20) 523-524.

Psalm 46:3

Theodor H. Gaster, "Psalm XLVI. 3 עַל־כֵּן לֹא־נִירָא בְּהָמִיר אֶרֶץ וּבְמוֹט הָרִים בְּלֵב יַמִּים," *ET* 71 (1959-60) 287.

Psalm 46:4

*W. E. Barnes, "Three Notes on Psalm XLVI," *JTS* 20 (1918-19) 178-182. *[46:5a(4a E.V.)]*

Psalm 46:7-11

*W. E. Barnes, "Three Notes on Psalm XLVI," *JTS* 20 (1918-19) 178-182. *[46:8, 12(7, 11 E.V.)]*

Psalm 46:9

*W. E. Barnes, "Three Notes on Psalm XLVI," *JTS* 20 (1918-19) 178-182. *[46:10a(9a E.V.)]*

Psalm 47

J. Muilenburg, "Psalm 47," *JBL* 63 (1944) 235-256.

Psalm 47:3-10

Millar Burrows, "Mitteilungen 1. כִּי in Ps. 47:3. 8a. and 10c," *ZAW* 55 (1937) 176.

Psalm 48

Julian Morgenstern, "Psalm 48," *HUCA* 16 (1941) 1-95.

Mitchell Dahood, "The Language and Date of Psalm 48 (47)," *CBQ* 16 (1954) 15-19.

M. Palmer, "The Cardinal Points in Psalm 48," *B* 46 (1965) 357-358.

Psalm 48:8

*Julius A. Bewer, "Notes on 1 Sam 13 21; 2 Sam 23 1; Psalm 48: 8," *JBL* 61 (1942) 45-49. [Psa. 48:8, pp. 48-49]

Psalm 48:9

*Q., "Explanation of Biblical Passages. Psalm xlix. 1, 2, etc.," *JSL, 4th Ser.,* 2 (1862-63) 177. *[48:9]*

Psalm 49

B. H. C., "An Exposition and Translation of Psalm xlix," *JSL, 2nd Ser.,* 6 (1854) 369-384.

Niger, "The Sheep of Death. Psalm XLIX," *Exp, 1st Ser.,* 10 (1879) 466-475.

Talbot W. Chambers, "Studies in the Psalter. No. VI.—The Forty-ninth Psalm," *HR* 17 (1889) 540-544.

*James Oscar Boyd, "Psalms xxxvii., xlix., lxxxiii., as Theodicies," *CFL, N.S.,* 3 (1901) 115-119.

*A. Guilding, "Some Obscure Rubrics and Lectionary Allusions in the Psalter," *JTS, N.S.,* 3 (1952) 41-55. [Psalm 49. A Psalm for the 7th Shebat, pp. 42-44]

Psalm 49:1-2

*Samuel Sharpe, "Questions on Deut XXXII. 8; Psalm XLIX. 1, 2 and LXIII. 9," *JSL, 4th Ser.,* 1 (1862) 451-452.

*Q., "Explanation of Biblical Passages. Psalm xlix. 1, 2, etc.," *JSL, 4th Ser.,* 2 (1862-63) 177. *[48:9]*

J. H., "Psalm XLIX. 1, 2," *JSL, 4th Ser.,* 2 (1862-63) 177-178.

Psalm 49:3

J. H., "Biblical Difficulties;—Psalm XLIX.3," *JSL, 4th Ser.,* 3 (1863) 443-444.

Psalm 49:7

T. K. Cheyne, "On Psalm XLIX. 7," *Exp, 3rd Ser.,* 2 (1885) 400.

Psalm 49:12

*John DeWitt, "Exegetical Notes on the Psalms," *PRR* 1 (1890) 106-110, 287-288, 476-479. [2. Psalm 49:12, pp. 109-110]

Psalm 49:15-16

C. Lattey, "A Note on Psalm XLIX. 15-16," *ET* 63 (1951-52) 288.

Psalm 49:15

*A. A. Bevan, "Psalm XLIX. 15; L. 20; LXXX. 7; LXXXV. 14," *JP* 18 (1889-90) 143-144.

Psalm 50

*Crawford H. Toy, "On the Asaph Psalms," *JBL* 6 (1886) Part 1, 73-85. *[Psalm 50]*

Talbot W. Chambers, "Studies in the Psalter. No. VII. The Fiftieth Psalm," *HR* 18 (1889) 58-62.

John E. M'Intyre, "The Fiftieth Psalm: A Blast Against Animal Sacrifice. (A Suggested Textual Emendation)," *ET* 43 (1931-32) 429-430.

*A. Capell, "God is the Plaintiff," *Coll* 2 (1966-68) 195-203. *[Psalm 50]*

Psalm 50:20

*A. A. Bevan, "Psalm XLIX. 15; L. 20; LXXX. 7; LXXXV. 14," *JP* 18 (1889-90) 143-144.

Psalm 50:21

Arthur T. Pierson, "Man's Misconstruction of God. Psalm l. 21," *HR* 32 (1896) 54-55.

Psalm 51

†John Thomas, "Metrical Version of Psalm LI," *ATG* 2 (1835-36) 255-259.

F. W. Newman, "Some Considerations concerning Psalm 51," *ModR* 1 (1880) 439-442.

Talbot W. Chambers, "Studies in the Psalter. No. VIII. The Fifty-first Psalm," *HR* 18 (1889) 162-166.

H. H. Almond, "Professor Driver on Psalm LI," *ET* 3 (1891-92) 425-426.

John Fanshawe, "A few Remarks on Psalm LI.," *EN* 4 (1892) 324-325.

Everett Falconer Harrison, "A Study of Psalm 51," *BS* 92 (1935) 26-38.

Gurdon Corning Oxtoby, "Conscience and Confession. A Study of the Fifty-First Psalm," *Interp* 3 (1949) 415-426.

P. P. Saydon, "The Psalm 'Miserere'," *Scrip* 6 (1953-54) 37-41. *[Psalm 50 (Vulgate / 51 Hebrew]*

Psalm 51:4

Anonymous, "Against Thee, *Thee Only,* Have I Sinned. (Ps. li. 4.)," *ERG, 3rd Ser.,* 2 (1863-64) 233-238.

Anonymous, "The Great Text Commentary. The Great Texts of the Psalms," *ET* 26 (1914-15) 124-128. *[51:4]*

Psalm 51:5

George Cron, "A Popular Exposition of Psalm LI, 5," *ERG, 8th Ser.,* 2 (1883-84) 273-278.

T. K. Cheyne, "Psalm LI. 5," *Exp, 4th Ser.,* 4 (1891) 398.

Psalm 51:7

*J. K. Zink, "Uncleanness and Sin. A Study of Job XIV 4 and Psalm LI 7," *VT* 17 (1967) 354-361.

Psalm 51:12-13

G. W. A., "Exegetical Studies," *BQ* 3 (1869) 486. *[51:12, 13]*

Psalm 51:12

John Theodore Mueller, "Notes on Ps. 51:12," *CTM* 18 (1947) 294-295.

Psalm 51:17

Anonymous, "The Great Text Commentary. The Great Texts of the Psalms," *ET* 22 (1910-11) 396-402. *[51:17]*

Psalm 52

*Ernest Lussier, "The New Latin Psalter: An Exegetical Commentary VI— Psalms 11, 12, 13, and 52," *CBQ* 10 (1948) 291-295.

Psalm 53

*Edward G. King, "On the Text of Psalms XIV. and LIII," *AJSL* 2 (1885-86) 237-239.

*K. Budde, "Psalm Problems. II," *ET* 12 (1900-01) 285-288. *[Psalm 53]*

*John A. Hutton, "From Jahweh to Elohim: From the Particular to the Universal," *Exp, 8th Ser.,* 13 (1917) 454-460. *[Psalm 53]*

*C. C. Torrey, "The Archetype of Psalms 14 and 53," *JBL* 46 (1927) 186-192.

*B. D. Eerdmans, "Psalm XIV, LIII and the Elohim-Psalms," *OTS* 1 (1942) 258-267.

Psalm 54:1-4

*†Anonymous, "New Translations of the Book of Psalms," *BCQTR, 4th Ser.,* 9 (1831) 404-440. *(Review)* [Psalm 54:1-4, pp. 436-438]

Psalm 55

Talbot W. Chambers, "Studies in the Psalter. No. XXII. The Fifty-fifth Psalm," *HR* 20 (1890) 355-358.

Allan Hoben, "Psalm 55, Partly Modernized, for a Defeated Chicago Merchant," *BW* 23 (1904) 122.

B. D. Eerdmans, "Psalm LV," *OTS* 1 (1942) 279-286.

Psalm 55:4

*T. L. Fenton, "Ugaritica—Biblica," *UF* 1 (1969) 65-70. *[55:4]*

Psalm 55:14(13)

C. Lattey, "A Note on Psalm LV. 14 (13) (כְּעֶרְכִּי)," *ET* 64 (1952-53) 221-222.

Psalm 56

John Thomas, "Psalm LVI, L. M., A Song of the Suffering Messiah," *ATG* 5 (1838-39) 379-383.

Psalm 56:6

*Mitchell Dahood, "Philological Notes on the Psalms," *ThSt* 14 (1953) 85-88. *[56:6, pp. 87-88]*

Psalm 56:8

T. K. Cheyne, "Psalm LVI. 8," *ET* 9 (1897-98) 519-520.

Psalm 57

William Y. Turner, "Psalm LVII," *ET* 61 (1949-50) 160.

Psalm 57:4-5

*G. Buchanan Gray, "Critical Remarks on Pss. LVII 4, 5, and LIX 12," *JQR* 10 (1897-98) 182-184.

Israel W. Slotki, "The Meaning and Metre of Psalm LVII. 4-5," *JMUEOS* #18 (1932) 61-65.

Psalm 58:7

Mitchell J. Dahood, "The Etymology of *Malṭāʿôt* (Ps. 58,7)," *CBQ* 17 (1955) 300-303.

Psalm 58:9

David I. Macht, "A Pharmacological Note in Psalm 58^9," *JAOS* 42 (1922) 280-285.

Psalm 58:10(9)

A. Nairne, "Psalm LVIII 10 (9)," *JTS* 16 (1914-15) 252-254.

Psalm 59:12

*G. Buchanan Gray, "Critical Remarks on Pss. LVII 4, 5, and LIX 12," *JQR* 10 (1897-98) 182-184.

Psalm 60:7

P., "Explanation of Psalm, lx—7," *QCS* 1 (1819) 20.

Psalm 60:8

*Ch. R. North, "Psalm LX 8 // CVIII 8," *VT* 17 (1967) 242-243.

Psalm 60:10

*Anonymous, "Illustrations of Scripture," *BRCM* 2 (1846) 413-415. [I. Psa. 60:10, pp. 413-414]

Psalm 61

Hugh Rae, "'Weary of the Solitude': Exposition of Psalm lxi," *HR* 38 (1899) 67-72, 166-170.

Psalm 62

W. Emery Barnes, "Psalm LXII," *Exp, 8th Ser.,* 21 (1921) 120-125.

Psalm 62:12

A. M. Honeyman, "ʾ̣ID, ḌŪ and Psalm LXII 12," *VT* 11 (1961) 348-350.

Psalm 63

T. K. Cheyne, "The Sixty-Third Psalm," *Exp, 4th Ser.,* 2 (1890) 50-60.

Talbot W. Chambers, "Studies in the Psalter. No. XXXIV.—The 63d Psalm," *HR* 22 (1891) 358-361.

Psalm 63:6(7)

William H. Marquess, "Psalm 63:6 (Hebrew, v. 7)," *BR* 3 (1918) 127-132.

Psalm 63:9-10

Henry Crossley, "The Hands of the Sword," *JSL, 4th Ser.,* 2 (1862-63) 434-440. *[63:9-10]*

Psalm 65:3:

*T. K. Cheyne, "Old Testament Notes," *JBL* 18 (1899) 208-211. [2. On Psalm 65:3, pp. 209-210]

*R. F. Bevan, "A Great Text Mistranslated," *ET* 48 (1936-37) 476-478. *[65:3 A.V.]*

Psalm 65:14

*S. R. Driver, "Requests and Replies," *ET* 11 (1899-1900) 230-231. *[65:14]*

Psalm 67

Duncan Cameron, "Psalm LXVII," *ET* 24 (1912-13) 284-285.

Psalm 68

Wm. W. Turner, "Interpretation of Psalm LXVIII," *BS* 5 (1848) 312-341.

T. K. Cheyne, "Psalm LXVIII," *Exp, 4th Ser.,* 2 (1890) 181-193.

Talbot W. Chambers, "Studies in the Psalter. No. XXI. The Sixty-Eighth Psalm," *HR* 20 (1890) 254-259.

Peyton H. Hoge, "The Origin of Psalm LXVIII," *PQ* 4 (1890) 98-110.

C. J. Ball, "Psalm LXVIII *Exurgat Deus,*" *JTS* 11 (1909-10) 415-432.

J. Arendzen, "Paraphrase of Psalm 67: 'Exurgat Deus'," *AER* 49 (1913) 286-293. *[Psalm 68]*

B. D. Eerdmans, "Psalm LXVIII," *ET* 46 (1934-35) 169-172.

B. D. Eerdmans, "Psalm LXVIII," *OTS* 1 (1942) 287-296.

W[illiam] F[oxwell] Albright, "A Catalogue of Early Hebrew Lyric Poems (Psalm 68)," *HUCA* 23 (1950-51) Part 1, 1-39.

Samuel Iwry, "Notes on Psalm 68," *JBL* 71 (1952) 161-165.

*W[illiam] F[oxwell] Albright, "Notes on Psalms 68 and 134," *NTTO* 56 (1955) 1-12.

J. H. Darby, "A Whitsuntide Psalm," *ClR* 42 (1957) 264-269. *[Psalm 68 (Vulgate 67)]*

*Patrick D. Miller Jr., "Two Critical Notes on Psalm 68 and Deuteronomy 33," *HTR* 57 (1964) 240-243.

Psalm 68:4

*J. W. Jack, "Recent Biblical Archaeology," *ET* 53 (1941-42) 367-370. [Archæology and the Biblical Text: 8. Riding the Clouds (Ps 68:4), pp. 369-370]

Psalm 68:5

A. Guillaume, "A Note on Psalm LXVIII. 5, ביה שמו ועלזו לפניו," *JTS, N.S.,* 13 (1962) 322-323.

Psalm 68:10

D. W. Goodwin, "A rare spelling, or a rare root in Psalm LXVIII 10?" *VT* 14 (1964) 490-491.

Psalm 68:11-14

*E. H. Askwith, "Some Obscure Passages in the Psalms," *Exp, 8th Ser.,* 19 (1920) 313-320. [Psa. 68:11-14, pp. 316-317]

Psalm 68:13

M. L. Whately, "Ye Shall be as the Wings of a Dove," *ERG, 3rd Ser.,* 2 (1863-64) 288-289. *[68:13]*

Crayden Edmunds, "Psalm LXVIII. 13," *ET* 16 (1904-05) 187.

Psalm 68:14

A. P. Cox, "'Snow in Salmon,' Psalm lxviii. 14," *ET* 17 (1905-06) 94-95.

Psalm 68:15

Sidney Jellicoe, "A Note on עַל־מוּת (Psalm LXVIII. 15)," *JTS* 49 (1948) 52-53.

Psalm 68:18

Eb. Nestle, "Psalm LXVIII. 18 (19) in the Syriac Bible," *ET* 14 (1902-03) 142-143.

Anonymous, "The Great Text Commentary. The Great Texts of the Psalms," *ET* 17 (1910-11) 439-444. *[68:18]*

Psalm 68:23

F. Charles Fensham, "Ps. 68:23 in the Light of Recently Discovered Ugaritic Tablets," *JNES* 19 (1960) 292-293.

Psalm 68:28-32

T. K. Cheyne, "Pathros in the Psalter," *ET* 3 (1891-92) 568. *[68:28, 31, 32]*

T.K. Cheyne, "Pathros in the Psalter," *JBL* 11 (1892) 125-126. *[68:28, 31, 32]*

Psalm 68:28-31

T. K. Cheyne, "On Ps. 68, 28. 31," *ZAW* 19 (1899) 156-157.

Psalm 69

W. Emery Barnes, "Psalm lxix," *Exp, 6th Ser.,* 9 (1904) 332-338.

W. Leonard, "Venom and Vinegar. The 'Sitio' Psalm," *ACR* 23 (1946) 103-118. *[Psalm 69 (Vulgate 68)]*

Psalm 69:3

*Paul Haupt, "Heb. *jayén,* misery," *BAVSS* 10 (1927) 210-212. *[69:3]*

Psalm 69:5

*H. Isaacs, "Malachi II. 11; Psalm LXIX. 5," *JQR* 11(1898-99) 526.

*M. D. Goldman, "Lexicographical Notes on Exegesis (5)," *ABR* 4 (1954-55) 85-92. [c. Psalm LXIX. 5, pp. 89-90]

Psalm 71

Frederick R. Swallow, "The Keys of God's Household," *Scrip* 11 (1959) 118-123. *[Psalm 71]*

*E. Reim, "The Problem of Translation—Ps 71 and 73," *JTLC* 6 (1966) #3, 1-7.

Psalm 71:18

H. G. Enelow, "A Note on Psalm LXXI. 18," *ET* 24 (1912-13) 429-430.

Psalm 72

John Thomas, "Hymn to Jehovah. Economistic of the Reign of the Messiah over Israel and the World. *Psalm LXXII.—Peculiar Metre,*" *ATG* 5 (1838-39) 243-246.

Henry C. Graves, "The Seventy-Second Psalm," *ONTS* 3 (1883-84) 399-401. *[Paraphrase and Criticism]*

Talbot W. Chambers, "Studies in the Psalter. No. XIII. The Seventy-second Psalm," *HR* 19 (1890) 64-68.

Thos. Hill Rich, "Psalm LXXII," *ONTS* 13 (1891) 35-40.

*A. S. Carrier, "A Study of Psalms II, CX, LXV, and LXXII," *CFL, O.S.,* 3 (1899) 136-140.

William G. Seiple, "The Seventy-Second Psalm," *JBL* 33 (1914) 170-197.

P. W. Skehan, "Strophic Structure in Ps 72 (71)," *B* 40 (1959) 302-308.

P. W. Skehan, "Strophic Structure in Ps 72 (71)," *SBO* 1 (1959) 168-174.

Psalm 72:1

Anonymous,"Expository: Psalm LXXII. 1,"*ERG, 1st Ser.,* 3 (1856-57) 207-221.

Psalm 72:9

*Willis J. Beecher, "Three Notes," *JBL* 8 (1888) 137-142. [III. Psa. 72, especially verses 9 and 17, pp. 140-142]

*G. R. Driver, "Notes on Notes," *B* 36 (1955) 71-73. [צִיִּים, Psa. 72:9, p. 71]

Psalm 72:15

Anonymous, "Psalm LXXII. 15," *MQR, 2nd Ser.,* 2 (1880) 187-188.

Psalm 72:16

G. S. G., "The Word 'Handful' in Psalm 72:16," *ONTS* 1 (1882) #1, 15.

Psalm 72:17

Biblicus, "A Supplement to the Illustration of the Promise made to Abraham," *TRep* 5 (1786) 108-110. *[72:17]*

*Willis J. Beecher, "Three Notes," *JBL* 8 (1888) 137-142. [III. Psa. 72, especially verses 9 and 17, pp. 140-142]

Psalm 73-83

*Crawford H. Toy, "On the Asaph Psalms," *JBL* 6 (1886) Part 1, 73-85. *[Psalms 73-83]*

Psalm 73

Talbot W. Chambers, "Studies in the Psalter, No. XXIV. The Seventh-third Psalm," *HR* 20 (1890) 542-545.

*James Oscar Boyd, "Psalms xxxvii., xlix., lxxxiii., as Theodicies," *CFL, N.S.,* 3 (1901) 115-119.

William Manson, "The Pure in Heart," *CJRT* 2 (1925) 308-309. *[Psalm 73]*

Norman Snaith, "The Prosperity of the Wicked. A Study of Psalm 73," *RL* 20 (1951) 519-529.

Donald Macleod, "Faith Beyond the Forms of Faith. *An Exposition of Psalm 73," Interp* 12 (1958) 418-421.

*E. Reim, "The Problem of Translation—Ps 71 and 73," *JTLC* 6 (1966) #3, 1-7.

Psalm 73:7

Anonymous, "Exegetical Notes. Psalm lxxiii. 7," *MQR, 3rd Ser.,* 45 (1919) 149-150.

Alexander Roifer, "Ps. LXXIII, 7," *Tarbiz* 32 (1962-63) #3, I.

Psalm 73:9

P. A. H. de Boer, "The Meaning of Psalm LXXIII 9," *VT* 18 (1968) 260-264.

Psalm 73:10

F. S. Marsh, "Psalm LXXIII 10," *JTS* 21 (1919-20) 265-266.

Psalm 73:15

James Moffatt, "Opera Foris. Materials for the Preacher," *Exp, 7th Ser.,* 5 (1908) 81-82. *[73:15]*

Psalm 73:17ff.

Harris Birklend, "The chief problems of Ps 73:17ff.," *ZAW* 67 (1955) 99-103.

Psalm 73:24

S. Jellicoe, "The Interpretation of Psalm LXXIII. 24," *ET* 67 (1955-56) 209-210.

(Book III)

Psalm 74

T. K. Cheyne, "Psalm LXXIV," *Exp, 4th Ser.,* 4 (1891) 398-399.

N. Liebschutz, "An Interpretation of Psalm 74," *AJSL* 40 (1923-24) 284-287.

N. Liebschutz, "On Psalm 74," *AJSL* 41 (1924-25) 279.

*M. Eliash, "The Cuthites and Psalm 74," *JPOS* 5 (1925) 55-57.

Psalm 74:1

*G. R. Driver, "Notes on the Psalms. II. 73-150," *JTS* 44 (1943) 12-23. *[74:1]*

Alfred Guillaume, "A Reply to Professor Driver," *JTS* 49 (1948) 55-56. [Reply by G. R. Driver, *JTS* 47 (1946) pp. 164-166] *[74:1]*

Psalm 74:4-5

F. H. Woods, "Notes on Ps. LXXIV. 4, 5," *AJSL* 3 (1886-87) 261-262.

Psalm 74:4

*P. R. Ackroyd, "Some Notes on the Psalms," *JTS, N.S.,* 17 (1966) 392-399. [I. *Psalm lxxiv. 4,* pp. 392-393]

Psalm 74:5

B. Halper, "The Reference to Trellis-Work in Psalm 74:5," *JQR, N.S.,* 2 (1911-12) 585-589.

J. Philip Hyatt, "A Note on *Yiwwāda‘* in Ps. 74:5," *AJSL* 58 (1941) 99-100.

*J. A. Emerton, "Notes on Three Passages in Psalms Book III," *JTS, N.S.,* 14 (1963) 374-381. [I. *Psalm lxxiv. 5,* pp. 374-377]

Psalm 74:9

John P. Peters, "How Long?" *JBL* 35 (1916) 324. *[74:9]*

Psalm 74:11

*J. A. Emerton, "Notes on Three Passages in Psalms Book III," *JTS, N.S.,* 14 (1963) 374-381. [II. *Psalm lxxiv. 11*, pp. 377-380]

Psalm 74:13-15

J. L. McKenzie, "A Note on Psalm 73 (74):13-15," *ThSt* 11 (1950) 275-282.

Psalm 74:14

Theodor H. Gaster, "Psalm lxxiv. 14 אַתָּה רִצַּצְתָּ רָאשֵׁי לִוְיָתָן תִּתְּנֶנּוּ מַאֲכָל
†וּלְעָם לְצִיִּים:," *ET* 68 (1956-57) 382.

Psalm 74:15

J. A. Emerton, "'Sprint and Torrent' in Psalm lxxiv 15," *VTS* 15 (1965) 122-133.

Psalm 74:19

*Joseph Reider, "Contributions to the Hebrew lexicon," *RDSO* 17 (1937-38) 103-110. [2. Ps. 74:19, pp. 104-106]

Psalm 74:23

X., "'In the Spirit'. Dominus Illuminato. Psalm lxxiii. 23," *Theo* 1 (1920) 38. *[74:23]*

Psalm 75:9

E. Weisenberg, "A Note on מזה in Psalm LXXV 9," *VT* 4 (1954) 434-439.

Psalm 76

*H. St. J. Thackeray, "Psalm LXXVI and Other Psalms for the Feast of Tabernacles," *JTS* 15 (1913-14) 425-431.

*W. E. Barnes, "Psalm LXXVI and Other Psalms for the Feast of Tabernacles," *JTS* 15 (1913-14) 431-432.

Psalm 76:3

*James Oscar Boyd, "'He Brake The Battle'," *CFL, N.S.,* 6 (1902) 298-300. *[76:3]*

Psalm 76:10

Benjamin Ralph, "'The Remainder of Wrath'," *ET* 28 (1916-17) 428. *[76:10]*

Psalm 77

Talbot W. Chambers, "Studies in the Psalter. No. XVI. The Seventy-seventh Psalm," *HR* 19 (1890) 360-364.

Helen G. Jefferson, "Psalm LXXVII," *VT* 13 (1963) 87-91.

Psalm 77:5

Yehoshua Blau, "On Two Biblical Expressions," *EI* 3 (1954) v. [II. שמורות in אחזת שמרות עיני (Ps. 77:5)]

Psalm 78:41

*J. A. Emerton, "Notes on Three Passages in Psalms Book III," *JTS, N.S.,* 14 (1963) 374-381. [III. *Psalm lxxviii. 41 and the Syriac verb* ܚܡܐ *, 'to be angry'*, p. 381]

Psalm 80:7

*A. A. Bevan, "Psalm XLIX. 15; L. 20; LXXX. 7; LXXXV. 14," *JP* 18 (1889-90) 143-144.

Psalm 80:13

Peddi Victor, "Note on Psalm LXXX. 13," *ET* 76 (1964-65) 294-295.

Psalm 80:14

D. Winton Thomas, "The Meaning of יזי in Psalm LXXX. 14," *ET* 76 (1964-65) 385.

Psalm 80:16-18

Alexander Roifer, "The End of Psalm 80," *Tarbiẓ* 29 (1959-60) #2, I-II. *[80:16-18]*

Psalm 81

*Adam C. Welch, "Psalm LXXXI.: A Sidelight into the Religion of North Israel," *ET* 38 (1926-27) 455-458.

*A. Guilding, "Some Obscured Rubrics and Lectionary Allusions in the Psalter," *JTS, N.S.,* 3 (1952) 41-55. [Psalm 81. A Psalm for New Year's Day, pp. 44-46]

William G. Braude, "Psalm Eighty-One From a forth-coming publication, מדרש תהלים," *CCARJ* #14 (1956) 18-21.

*S. E. Loewenstamm, "The Bearing of Psalm 81 upon the Problems of Exodus," *EI* 5 (1958) 88*.

Psalm 81:7

A. Cohen, "Psalm 81:7," *AJSL* 27 (1910-11) 191-192.

Psalm 81:16

*J. H. Eaton, "Some Questions of Philology and Exegesis in the Psalms," *JTS, N.S.,* 19 (1968) 603-609. [*Psalm lxxxi. 16* עתם, pp. 607-608]

Psalm 82

Adam C. Welch, "Some Misunderstood Psalms. II. Psalm LXXXII," *ET* 37 (1925-26) 128-130.

Julian Morgenstern, "The Mythological Background to Psalm 82," *HUCA* 14 (1939) 29-126.

G. E. Wright, "Psalm 82," *JBL* 68 (1949) viii.

Roger T. O'Callaghan, "A Note on the Canaanite Background of Psalm 82," *CBQ* 15 (1953) 311-314.

*A. T. Hanson, "John's Citation of Psalm lxxxii," *NTS* 11 (1964-65) 158-162.

*James S. Ackerman, "The Rabbinic Interpretation of Psalm 82 and the Gospel of John: John 10:34," *HTR* 59 (1966) 186-191.

*A. T. Hanson, "John's Citation of Psalm lxxxii Reconsidered," *NTS* 13 (1966-67) 363-367.

Matitiahu Tsevat, "God and the Gods in Assembly. An Interpretation of Psalm 82," *HUCA* 40 (1969) 123-137.

Psalm 82:5

F. I. Andersen, "A Short Note on Psalm 82, 5," *B* 50 (1969) 393-394.

Psalm 82:7

W. H. A. Learoyd, "An Emendation of Psalm LXXXII. 7," *ET* 39 (1927-28) 382.

Psalm 83

Harold W. Wiener, "The Historical Background of Psalm LXXXIII," *JPOS* 8 (1928) 180-186.

Psalm 84

Anonymous, "The Eighty-fourth Psalm," *ERG, 2nd Ser.,* 4 (1861-62) 176-182.

Anonymous, "Psalm LXXXIV," *BWR* 3 (1881) 347-349.

Talbot W. Chambers, "Studies in the Psalter. No. XI. The Eighty-fourth Psalm," *HR* 18 (1889) 446-449.

Talbot W. Chambers, "Studies in the Psalter. No. XII. The Eighty-fourth Psalm," *HR* 18 (1889) 536-540.

R. Balgarnie, "The Eighty-fourth Psalm," *TML* 6 (1891) 328-336.

*Lewis B. Radford, "Psalm LXXXIV. A Study in the History of Biblical Interpretation," *ET* 42 (1930-31) 556-562.

Edgar R. Somthers, "The Coverdale Translation of Psalm LXXXIV," *HTR* 38 (1945) 245-269.

Psalm 84:3

Anonymous, "Meaning of the Word Grace. Psalm lxxxiv. 3 Explained," *QTMRP* 4 (1814) 99-100.

G. G. Cameron, "Requests and Replies," *ET* 2 (1890-91) 137-138. *[84:3]*

Psalm 84:4-7

David Muir, "Psalm LXXXIV. 4-7," *ET* 40 (1928-29) 336.

Psalm 84:4-5

A. S. Laidlaw, "The Priest and the Pilgrim," *ET* 11 (1899-1900) 345-347. *[84:4, 5]*

Psalm 84:4

Taylor Lewis, "Exegetical Notes," *PR* 1 (1880) 366-368. *[84:4]*

Psalm 84:6-8

*J. P. Peters, "A Jerusalem Processional," *JBL* 39 (1920) 52-59. *[84:6-8]*

*J. P. Peters, "A Jerusalem Processional," *JPOS* 1 (1920-21) 36-41. *[84:6-8]*

*G. R. Driver, "Things Old and New in the Old Testament," *MUSJ* 45 (1969) 463-478. [II. 1. Psa. 84:6-8, pp. 469-477]

Psalm 84:7

*David Yellin, "Emek ha-bakha: Bekhaim," *JPOS* 3 (1923) 191-192. *[84:7]*

Psalm 84:10

H. Rose Rae, "The Doorkeeper: A Triple Parallel," *HR* 50 (1905) 280-281. *[84:10]*

*James Moffatt, "Opera Foris; Or, Materials for the Preacher. Second Series," *Exp, 8th Ser.,* 2 (1911) 182-192. *[84:10]*

Psalm 84:11

L. Grollenberg, "Post-Biblical חֲרוּת in Ps. LXXXIV 11?" *VT* 9 (1959) 311-312.

G. W. Buchanan, "The Courts of the Lord," *VT* 16 (1966) 231-232. *[84:11]*

Psalm 85

*[Daniel S. Gregory], "The International Lessons in Their Historical and Literary Setting," *CFL, 3rd Ser.,* 14 (1911-12) 357-371. [Psalm 85, pp. 362-363]

M[itchell] Dahood, "Enclitic *Mem* and emphatic *Lamedh* in Ps 85," *B* 37 (1956) 338-340.

Psalm 85:7

*A. A. Bevan, "Psalm XLIX. 15; L. 20; LXXX. 7; LXXXV. 14," *JP* 18 (1889-90) 143-144.

Psalm 85:9

*I. W. Slotki, "A Lost Selah, and Psalm LXXXV 9 [8]," *JTS* 20 (1918-19) 250-251.

A. E. Cowley, "The Emendation of Ps. LXXXV 9," *JTS* 20 (1918-19) 356.

Henry Bradley, "Psalm LXXXV 9," *JTS* 21 (1919-20) 243-244.

Psalm 85:14

*A. A. Bevan, "Psalm XLIX. 15; L. 20; LXXX. 7; LXXXV. 14," *JP* 18 (1889-90) 143-144.

Psalm 86

T. K. Cheyne, "Studies in Practical Exegesis: Psalm LXXXVI," *Exp, 3rd Ser.*, 10 (1889) 262-271.

Psalm 87

A. B. Bruce, "Zion the Spiritual Metropolis of the World. Psalm LXXXVII," *Exp, 1st Ser.*, 10 (1879) 134-148.

T. K. Cheyne, "Studies in Practical Exegesis: Psalm LXXXVII," *Exp, 3rd Ser.*, 10 (1889) 360-373.

Talbot W. Chambers, "Studies in the Psalter. No. X. The Eighty-seventh Psalm," *HR* 18 (1889) 358-362.

Alex. R. Gordon, "Psalm 87," *BW* 33 (1909) 102-106.

Psalm 87:1

Eb. Nestle, "'Those Holy Mountains'," *ET* 23 (1911-12) 478. *[87:1]*

Psalm 87:4-6

R. W. Stewart, "Every Man a Burgess," *ET* 40 (1928-29) 189. *[87:4, 5, 6]*

Psalm 88

Adam C. Welch, "Some Misunderstood Psalms. I. Psalm LXXXVIII," *ET* 37 (1925-26) 60-62.

Psalm 88:4

*J. W. Jack, "Recent Biblical Archaeology," *ET* 53 (1941-42) 367-370. [Archæology and the Biblical Text: 9. Going down to the Pit (Ps. 88:4), pp. 370]

Psalm 89

Jacob Neusner, "The Eighty-Ninth Psalm: Paradigm of Israel's Faith," *Jud* 8 (1959) 226-233.

Nahum M. Sarna, "Psalm 89: A Study in Inner Biblical Exegesis," *LIST* 1 (1963) 29-46.

Psalm 89:9

T. H. Hunt and W. E. Barnes, "Psalm LXXXIX 9," *JTS* 29 (1927-28) 398-399.

Psalm 89:10

J. H., "Note on Psalm LXXXIX. 10," *JSL, 5th Ser.,* 1 (1867) 484-485.

W. M. Valk, "The Labour and Sorrow and Life. A Note on Psalm lxxxix, 10," *Scrip* 5 (1952-53) 97-102.

Psalm 89:13

*J. P. Peters, "A Jerusalem Processional," *JBL* 39 (1920) 52-59. *[89:13]*

*J. P. Peters, "A Jerusalem Processional," *JPOS* 1 (1920-21) 36-41. *[89:13]*

(Book IV)

Psalm 90

A. B. Bruce, "The Ninetieth Psalm Reconciled with Christian Optimism," *Exp, 1st Ser.,* 9 (1879) 361-374.

T. K. Cheyne, "Cheyne's Translation of Psalm XC," *ONTS* 4 (1884-85) 321.

Talbot W. Chambers, "Studies in the Psalter. No. XVIII.—The Ninetieth Psalm," *HR* 19 (1890) 545-549.

Willis J. Beecher, "The Ninetieth Psalm," *HR* 50 (1905) 198-200.

Paul Haupt, "The Prayer of Moses the Man of God," *JBL* 31 (1912) 115-135 *[Psalm 90]*

Psalm 90:1-2

[Wilbert W. White], "Psalm xc. 1, 2," *BM* 1 (1913) 805-807. *(Editorial)*

Psalm 90:3

G. Gotthiel, "Psalm XC. 3," *ONTS* 2 (1882-83) 172.

S. C. Kirkpatrick, "Psalm XC. 3," *ET* 24 (1912-13) 334.

Psalm 90:5

D. Winton Thomas, "A note on זְרַמְתָּם שֵׁנָה יִהְיוּ in Psalm XC 5," *VT* 18 (1968) 267-268.

Psalm 90:9

Arthur T. Burbridge, "'A Tale that is Told'," *Exp, 9th Ser.,* 3 (1925) 308-310. *[90:9]*

Psalm 90:10

Israel W. Slotki, "Psalm XC. 10," *AJSL* 39 (1922-23) 195-196.

*Paul Haupt, "Philological and Archaeological Studies," *AJP* 45 (1924) 238-259. [6. Threescore and ten, pp. 249-252] *[90:10]*

Psalm 90:12

Anonymous, "Spiritual Arithmetic; or the numbering of our Days—A Calculation of the greatest importance," *MR* 6 (1823) 92-95 *[90:12]*

Anonymous, "The Great Text Commentary. The Great Texts of the Psalms," *ET* 22 (1910-11) 493-496. *[90:12]*

Psalm 90:17

Edward Beal, "Psalm XC. 17," *ET* 29 (1917-18) 475.

Psalm 91

Howard Crosby, "Light on Important Texts. No. XXV," *HR* 7 (1882-83) 529-530. *[Psalm 91]*

*W. O. E. Oesterley, "The Demonology of the Old Testament, Illustrated by Psalm XCI," *Exp, 7th Ser.,* 4 (1907) 132-151.

D. W. Lyon, "The Ninety-first Psalm: On Taking Refuge in Jehovah," *BRec* 8 (1911) 330-331.

Emery Barnes, "A Study of Psalm XCI," *Exp, 8th Ser.,* 10 (1915) 224-233.

*Wilfrid L. Hannam, "Psalms 91 and 94—A Study in Contrast," *LQHR* 167 (1942) 238-241.

Psalm 91:1-13

*S. Rosenblatt, "Notes on the Psalter," *JBL* 50 (1931) 308-310. *[91:1, 2, 3-8, 9a, 9b-13]*

Psalm 91:6

*Robert Gordis, "The Biblical Root ŠDY-ŠD: Notes on 2 Sam. i. 21; Jer. xviii. 14; Ps. xci. 6; Job v. 21," *JTS* 41 (1940) 34-43.

Psalm 91:14

X., "'In the Spirit'. Dominus Illuminato. Psalm xci. 14," *Theo* 1 (1920) 162.

Psalm 92

Nahum M. Sarna, "A Psalm for the Sabbath Day (Ps. 92)," *JBL* 81 (1962) 155-168.

Psalm 92:1-2

*Joseph Parker, "Notes on Scripture Passages," *ERG, 9th Ser.,* 3 (1887-88) 33-37. [II. Ps. 92:1, 2, pp 35-36]

Psalm 92:12

Thomas P. Hughes, "Saints Compared to Palm-Trees," *HR* 50 (1905) 438-440. *[92:12]*

Psalm 93

*Theodor H. Gaster, "The Battle of the Rain and the Sea: An Ancient Semitic Nature-Myth," *Iraq* 4 (1937) 21-32. *[Psalm 93]*

Helen Genevieve Jefferson, "Psalm 93," *JBL* 71 (1952) 155-160.

Psalm 93:1-2

*P. R. Ackroyd, "Some Notes on the Psalms," *JTS, N.S.,* 17 (1966) 392-399. [2. *The Text of Ps. xciii. 1,* pp. 392-393]

Psalm 93:4

*J. H. Eaton, "Some Questions of Philology and Exegesis in the Psalms," *JTS, N.S.,*19 (1968) 603-609. [*Psalm xciii. 4* אדירים, pp. 608-609]

Psalm 93:5

J. D. Shenkel, "An Interpretation of Psalm 93, 5," *B* 46 (1965) 401-416.

Psalm 94

Joseph M. Andel, "Psalm XCIV," *SS* 1 (1926) #1, 15-28.

*Wilfrid L. Hannam, "Psalms 91 and 94—A Study in Contrast," *LQHR* 167 (1942) 238-241.

Psalm 94:19

Samuel Cox, "Comfort in Cares. Psalm xciv. 19," *Exp, 2nd Ser.,* 6 (1883) 273-282.

Psalm 95

Anonymous, "The Psalms of Breviary. I. The Invitatory Psalm. Ps. 94 (Hebr. 95)," *AER* 46 (1912) 463-470.

John E. McFadyen, "The Messages of the Psalms: Psalm 95," *BW* 26 (1905) 336-340.

Joshua Finkel, "Some Problems Relating to Ps. 95," *AJSL* 50 (1934-35) 32-40.

Romanus Rios, "A Call to Worship (Psalm 94)," *Scrip* 1 (1946) 74-77. *[Psalm 95]*

Jack Riemer, "Psalm 95: The Prelude to Prayer," *CJ* 15 (1960-61) #1, 30-34.

Psalm 95:4

Arthur A. Dembitz, "ותועפת הרים לו" (Ps. 95:4)," *AJSL* 34 (1917-18) 139-141.

Psalm 95:6

*W. E. Barnes, "Two Psalm Notes," *JTS* 37 (1936) 385-387. *[95:6]*

Psalm 96

*H. L. Ginsberg, "A Strand in the Cord of Hebraic Hymnody," *EI* 9 (1969) 45-50. [Psalm 96, pp. 46-47] *[Non-Hebrew Section]*

Psalm 96:1

*G. W. H. Lampe, "The Exegesis of Some Biblical Texts by Marcellus of Ancyra and Pseudo-Chrysostom's Homily on Ps. XCVI. 1," *JTS* 49 (1948) 169-175.

Psalm 96:9

*P. R. Ackroyd, "Some Notes on the Psalms," *JTS, N.S.,* 17 (1966) 392-399. [3. The interpretation of הַדְרַת קֹדֶשׁ, pp. 393-396] *[96:9]*

Psalm 96:10

J. H. A. Hart, "The Lord Reigned from the Tree," *Exp, 6th Ser.,* 12 (1905) 321-335.*[Psalm 96 (95 - Vulgate): 10]*

Psalm 97:10

Anonymous, "'In the Spirit'. Dominus Illuminato. 'O ye that love the Lord, see that ye hat the thing which is evil.'—Psalm xcvii. 10," *Theo* 1 (1920) 346.

Psalm 97:11

W. E. Barnes, "Textual Criticism of the Old Testament. An Instance (Ps. xcvii. 11)," *JTS* 17 (1915-16) 152-156, 385-388.

N. McLean, "Textual Criticism of the Old Testament," *JTS* 17 (1915-16) 298-299. *[97:11]*

Shelomo Morag, "'Light is Sown' (Psalms XCVII, 11)," *Tarbiz* 33 (1963-64) #2, IV-V.

Psalm 98

John M'Carthy, "The Ninety-Eighth Psalm," *MQR, 3rd Ser.,* 53 (1927) 299-300.

*H. L. Ginsberg, "A Strand in the Cord of Hebraic Hymnody," *EI* 9 (1969) 45-50. [Psalm 98, p. 47] *[Non-Hebrew Section]*

Psalm 99

Talbot [W.] Chambers, "The Ninety-Ninth Psalm—An Echo of the Seraph's Trisagion," *HR* 30 (1895) 352-354.

Augustine, "On Psalm XCIX," *LofS* 3 (1948-49) 32-44. *(Trans. by Dominic Devas)*

*J. H. Eaton, "Proposals in Psalms XCIX and CXIX," *VT* 18 (1968) 555-558.

Psalm 99:8

R. N. Whybray, "'Their Wrongdoings' in Psalm 99:8," *ZAW* 81 (1969) 237-239.

Psalm 100

Charles Lee Feinberg, "'Old Hundredth'—Psalm C," *BS* 100 (1943) 53-66.

James L. Mays, "Worship, World, and Power. *An Interpretation of Psalm 100,*" *Interp* 23 (1969) 315-330.

Psalm 100:3

Joe O. Lewis, "An Assertive לֹא in Psalm 100:3?" *JBL* 86 (1967) 216.

Psalm 101

K. Budde, "Psalm CI," *ET* 8 (1896-97) 202-204.

Psalm 101:5

*E. Power, "A Study of the Hebrew Expression 'Wide of Heart'," *B* 1 (1920) 59-75. *[101:5, pp. 74-75]*

Psalm 102

Leslie Brandt, "Good Lord, Where are You? Paraphrase on Psalm 102," *TT* 24 (1967-68) 280-281.

Psalm 103

Talbot W. Chambers, "Studies in the Psalter. The One Hundred and Third Psalm," *HR* 19 (1890) 446-450.

Hermann Gunkel, "Psalm 103: An Interpretation," *BW* 22 (1903) 209-215.

N. H. Parker, "Psalm 103," *CJT* 1 (1955) 191-196.

Psalm 103:1-2

Anonymous, "The Great Text Commentary. The Great Texts of the Psalms," *ET* 22 (1910-11) 537-543. *[103:1, 2]*

Psalm 103:5

H. H. B. Ayles, "'Thy Ornament' in Psalm CIII. 5," *ET* 24 (1912-13) 47.

Psalm 104

Talbot W. Chambers, "Studies in the Psalter. No. XXVIII. The One Hundred and Fourth Psalm," *HR* 21 (1891) 361-364.

Anonymous, "Akhnaton and the One Hundred and Fourth Psalm," *MR* 93 (1911) 971-974.

*Paul Haupt, "Philological Studies," *AJP* 45 (1924) 47-63. [4. The Egyptian Prototype of Ps. 104, pp. 51-53]

Thomas E. Morrissey, "Psalm 104: A Survey of Criticism," *Focus* 4 (1967-68) #1, 87-96.

John H. Scammon, "Another Look at Psalm 104," *JHS* 1 (1969) 1-12.

Psalm 104:1

A. H. Shoenfeld, "The First Sentence of Psalm CIV," *OC* 42 (1928) 555-557. *[104:1a]*

Psalm 104:4

*J. J. Stewart Perowne, "Wind and Fire Ministers of God, Psalm civ. 4; Hebrews 1. 7," *Exp, 1st Ser.,* 8 (1878) 461-467.

Psalm 104:8

Edmund F. Sutcliffe, "A Note on Psalm CIV 8," *VT* 2 (1952) 177-179.

Psalm 104:10-30

H. F. D. Sparks, "A Textual Note on Psalm CIV. 16," *JTS* 48 (1947) 57-58.

G. R. Driver, "The Resurrection of Marine and Terrestrial Creatures," *JSS* 7 (1962) 12-22.

Psalm 104:16

Joseph Reider, "A Superfluous Emendation," *JJS* 1 (1948-49) 116. *[104:16]*

Psalm 104:25-26

*Leo Jung, "Mis-Translations a Source in Jewish and Christian Lore," *PAAJR* 5 (1933-34) 55-67. [V *Leviathan* (Ps. 104:25-26), pp. 62-63]

Psalm 104:26

G. Ernest Wright, "'There Go the Ships' (Ps. 104:26)," *BA* 1 (1938) 19-20.

Psalm 105

B. Margulis, "The Plagues Tradition in Ps 105," *B* 50 (1969) 491-496.

Psalm 105:11

J. F. McCurdy, "Light on Scriptural Texts from Recent Science and History. Psalm CV. 11.—The Land of Canaan, the Lot of Your Inheritance," *HR* 31 (1896) 505-508.

Psalm 105:23-25

J. F. McCurdy, "Light on Scriptural Texts from Recent Discoveries. The Silent Centuries in Egypt.—Ps. cv. 23-25," *HR* 31 (1896) 411-413.

Psalm 106

I. W. Slotki, "The Stichometry and Text of the Great Hallel," *JTS* 29 (1927-28) 255-268.

Psalm 106:15

James Moffatt, "Two Classical Parallels," *ET* 20 (1908-09) 184. *[106:15]*

(Book V)

Psalm 107

*Isaac Rabinowitz, "The Existence of a Hitherto Unknown Interpretation of Psalm 107 among the Dead Sea Scrolls," *BA* 14 (1951) 50-52.

Psalm 108:8

*Ch. R. North, "Psalm LX 8 // CVIII 8," *VT* 17 (1967) 242-243.

Psalm 109

†Anonymous, "Keate on the 109th Psalm," *BCQTR* 5 (1795) 157-159. *(Review)*

Joseph Hammond, "An Apology for the Vindictive Psalm. (Psalm CIX)," *Exp, 1st Ser.,* 2 (1875) 325-360.

W. J. Beecher, "The Hebrew Tenses in the Imprecations in the One Hundred and Ninth Psalm," *PR* 1 (1880) 731-734.

Talbot W. Chambers, "Studies in the Psalter. No. XX.—The One Hundred and Ninth Psalm," *HR* 20 (1890) 162-166.

F. G. Chomondeley, "A 'Vindictive' Psalm," *ET* 30 (1918-19) 183-184 *[Psalm 109]*

Harold L. Creager, "Note on Psalm 109," *JNES* 6 (1947) 121-123.

Edward J. Kissane, "The Interpretation of Psalm 108 (109)," *ITQ* 18 (1951) 1-8.

Psalm 109:6-19

W[illis J.] Beecher, "Use of the Hebrew Tenses in Ps. CIX. 6-19," *SBLP* June, (1880) 13-14.

W[illis J.] Beecher, "Use of the Hebrew Tenses in PS. 109^{6-19}," *JBL* 49 (1930) xxxiv-xxxvi. *[Reprint of the Proceedings of the first meeting of the Society of Biblical Literature (may be bound separately)]*

Psalm 109:10

A. Guillaume, "A Note on Psalm CIX. 10, ונוע ינועו בניו ושאלו ודרשו מחרבותיהם," *JTS, N.S.*, 14 (1963) 92-93.

Psalm 109:21-22

James Moffatt, "Opera Foris: Materials for the Preacher," *Exp, 7th Ser.*, 5 (1908) 186-188. *[109:21-22]*

Psalm 110

U. V., "Exposition of Psalm cx," *QCS* 2 (1820) 67-71.

*†Anonymous, "Translation of the Hebrew Psalter," *ERL* 7 (1847) 71-87. *(Review) [Psalm 110]*

Anonymous, "Expository: Psalm CX," *ERG, 1st Ser.*, 2 (1855-56) 1-16.

William Henry Simcox, "A Campaigner's Beverage," *Exp, 3rd Ser.*, 1 (1885) 226-232. *[Psalm 110]*

James Frame, "Christ Enthroned; Psalm CX, No. 1—The Welcome," *ERG, 8th Ser.*, 4 (1885-86) 193-201.

James Frame, "Christ Enthroned; Psalm CX, No. 2—The Prediction," *ERG, 8th Ser.*, 4 (1885-86) 297-302.

Thomas H. Rich, "Psalm 110," *JBL* 7 (1887) Part 2, 43-45.

Talbot W. Chambers, "Studies in the Psalter. No. XXIX.—The One Hundred and Tenth Psalm," *HR* 21 (1891) 457-460.

G. Margoliouth, "The Hundred and Tenth Psalm," *JRAS* (1892) 375-376.

E. Hastings, "Psalm CX," *ET* 7 (1895-96) 527.

*R. Balgarnie, "'Could Jesus Err?'" *ET* 8 (1896-97) 475. *[Psalm 110]*

*A. S. Carrier, "A Study of Psalms II, CX, LXV, and LXXII," *CFL, O.S.*, 3 (1899) 136-140.

G. C. M. Douglas, "Psalm Hundred and Tenth," *CFL, N.S.*, 3 (1901) 9-13.

*William C. Wilkinson, "Questions of Authorship: Psalm CX," *HR* 43 (1902) 308-311.

E. G. King, "Psalm CX," *JTS* 4 (1902-03) 338-344.

*David Smith "Our Lord's Reductio ad Absurdum of the Rabbinical Interpretation of Psalm CX. (Matt. xxii. 41-46 = Mark xii 35-37 = Luke xx. 41-44)," *ET* 16 (1904-05) 256-258.

G. C. M. Douglas, "Psalm CX," *LCR* 24 (1905) 39-44.

H. H. B. Ayles, "Psalm CX," *Exp, 8th Ser.,* 16 (1918) 286-290.

*Paul Haupt, "Zerubbabel and Melchizedek," *JSOR* 2 (1918) 76-82. *[Psalm 110]*

*Lawrence D. Murphy, "Messiah the Priest-King (Psalm CIX.)," *IER, 5th Ser.,* 21 (1923) 174-180. *[Psalm 110]*

W. Leonard, "Psalm Citation in the New Testament and Psalm CIX," *ACR* 14 (1937) 113-127. *[Psalm 110]*

Theodor H. Gaster, "Psalm 110," *JMUEOS* #21 (1937) 37-44.

*A. Guilding, "Some Obscured Rubrics and Lectionary Allusions in the Psalter," *JTS, N.S.,* 3 (1952) 41-55. [Psalm 110. A Psalm for Shabuoth, pp. 48-55]

Edward J. Kissane, "The Interpretation of Psalm 110," *ITQ* 21 (1954) 103-114.

Helen Genevieve Jefferson, "Is Psalm 110 Canaanite?" *JBL* 83 (1954) 152-156.

*O. Linton, "The Trial of Jesus and the Interpretation of Psalm CX," *NTS* 7 (1960-61) 258-262.

Roy A. Stewart, "Medieval Hebrew Interpretations of Psalm 110," *GUOST* 19 (1961-62) 63-73.

*M. Treves, "Two Acrostic Psalms," *VT* 15 (1965) 81-90. *[Psa. 110]*

J. W. Bowker, "Psalm CX," *VT* 17 (1967) 31-41.

John G. Gammie, "A New Setting for Psalm 110," *ATR* 51 (1969) 4-17.

Psalm 110:3

W. N., "Critical Remarks on Psalm cx. 3," *CongML* 5 (1822) 191-193.

Anonymous, "Illustration of Psalm CX. 3," *MR* 5 (1822) 301-302.

John   Taylor,   "Psalm   CX.   3,"   *ET*   6   (1894-95)   42.

J. A. Selbie, "A Suggested Emendation of Ps. CX. 3b," *ET* 11 (1899-1900) 217.

George   Farmer,   "Psalm   CX.   3,"   *ET*   28   (1916-17)   91-92.

*Paul Haupt, "Philological and Linguistic Studies," *AJP* 46 (1925) 197-212. [3. The Beauty of Holiness, pp. 202-205] *[110:3]*

Psalm 110:4

A.   S.   Carrier,   "Psalm   110:4,"   *BW*   13   (1899)   270.

Psalm 110:7

Michael J. Gruenthaner, "The Last Verse of Psalm 109," *AER* 115 (1946) 463-467. *[110:7]*

Thomas Plassman, "A Note to Psalm 109 Verse 7," *AER* 116 (1947) 452-455. *[110:7]*

Psalms 111 and 112

Talbot W. Chambers, "Studies in the Psalter No. XXX.—The 111th and 112th Psalms," *HR* 21 (1891) 550-553.

Psalms 113-118

Ed. G. King, "The Hallel," *Exp, 3rd Ser.,* 9 (1889) 121-135. *[Psalms 113-118]*

T. K. Cheyne, "Psalms CXIII-CXVIII," *Exp, 4th Ser.,* 1 (1890) 189-200.

Psalm 113

T. Torrance, "The First of the Hallel Psalms. Psalm CXIII," *EQ* 27 (1955) 36-64.

Psalm 113:2

*Samuel E. Loewenstamm, "'From this Time forth and for evermore'," *Tarbiz* 32 (1962-63) #4, I. *[113:2]*

Psalm 113:5-6

I. W. Slotki, "Omnipresence, Condescension, and Omniscience in Psalm CXIII 5-6," *JTS* 32 (1930-31) 367-370.

Psalm 114

Anonymous, "Expository Items. Psalm CXIV," *MQR, 2nd Ser.,* 2 (1880) 758-579.

W. Bacher, "The Mandaic Version of Psalm CXIV," *JQR* 4 (1891-92) 508.

Psalm 114:4-6

J. E. Hanauer, "Notes by Rev. J. E. Hanauer. I.—The Skipping of the Mountains and Little Hills (Psalm cxiv, 4 and 6, &c.)," *PEFQS* 30 (1898) 24-26.

*A[ngus] Crawford, "Exploration and Discovery," *PER* 12 (1898-99) 149-160. [The Skipping Mountains and Hills (Ps. CXIV, 4-6, pp. 150-152]

Psalm 115

K. Luke, "The Setting of Psalm 115," *ITQ* 34 (1967) 347-357.

Psalm 116:1-19

*E. H. Askwith, "Some Obscure Passages in the Psalms," *Exp, 8th Ser.,* 19 (1920) 313-320. [Psa. 116:1-19, pp. 317-320]

Psalm 116:6

Anonymous, "Psalm 116:6. The Simple," *ONTS* 10 (1890) 380.

Psalm 116:10-11

*John DeWitt, "Exegetical Notes on the Psalms," *PRR* 1 (1890) 106-110, 287-288, 476-479. [116:10-11, p. 479]

Psalm 116:11

A. F. Kirkpatrick, "Requests and Replies," *ET* 3 (1891-92) 69. *[116:11]*

Psalm 117

Jos J. Egan, "Ps. 117, A Liturgical Psalm," *SS* 3 (1929) 89-97.

Joseph L. Mihelic, "Praise Ye the Lord!," *TT* 14 (1957-58) 458-459.

Psalm 118

B. D. Eerdmans, "Foreign Elements in Pre-Exilic Israel," *OTS* 1 (1942) 126-138. *[Psalm 118]*

William Robinson, "Psalm CXVIII. A Liturgy for the Admission of a Prose-lyte," *CQR* 144 (1947) 179-183.

S. B. Frost, "Psalm 118: An Exposition," *CJT* 7 (1961) 155-166.

*P. R. Ackroyd, "Some Notes on the Psalms," *JTS, N.S.,* 17 (1966) 392-399. [4. *Psalm cxviii in 11QPs^a,* pp. 396-399]

Psalm 118:10

F. J. Briggs, "Psalm CXVIII. 10," *ET* 40 (1928-29) 237.

Psalm 118:15

K. G. Manz, "The Right Hand of God," *CTM* 8 (1837) 621. *[117 (118):15]*

Psalm 118:20

*E. B. Finlay, "Greek Inscription," *PEFQS* 7 (1875) 103. *[118:20 (117LXX)]*

Psalm 118:22-23

J. F. Denham, "The Cornerstone,"*JSL, 1st Ser.,* 2 (1848) 154-157.*[118:22-23]*

J. F. Denham, "The Corner Stone," *MR* 32 (1850) 668-670. *[118:22, 23]*

Psalm 118:24

Anonymous, "The Great Text Commentary, Psalm cxviii. 24," *ET* 23 (1911-12) 14-18.

Psalm 118:25

J. J. Petuchowski, "'Hoshi'an na' in Psalm CXVIII 25—A Prayer for Rain," *VT* 5 (1955) 266-271.

Psalm 118:27

George Farmer, "Two Expository Notes, Psalm cxviii. 27," *ET* 11 (1899-1900) 426-427.

Ed. König, "Psalm CXVIII. 27b," *ET* 11 (1899-1900) 565-566.

J. Meysing, "The Text-reconstruction of Ps CXVII (CXVIII) 27," *VT* 10 (1960) 130-137.

*G. R. Driver, "Things Old and New in the Old Testament," *MUSJ* 45 (1969) 463-478. [II. 2. Psa. 118:27, pp. 477-478]

G. Driver, "Psalm 118:27—חג אסורי," *Text* 7 (1969) 130-131.

Psalm 119

Anonymous, "Expository Items. Psalm CXIX," *MQR, 2nd Ser.,* 2 (1880) 756.

Talbot W. Chambers, "Studies in the Psalter. No. XXXI.—The 119th Psalm," *HR* 22 (1891) 68-71.

*W. E. Barnes, "Short Studies in the Psalter," *ET* 7 (1895-96) 166-169. [(A) Psa. cxix, pp. 166-168]

H. J. Heuser, "The Chant of the Captive—The Priest's Daily Prayer (Psalm CXVIII.)," *AER* 14 (1896) 511-518. *[Psalm 119]*

J. E. H. Thomson, "Criticism of Psalm CXIX," *GUOST* 2 (1901-07) 27-29.

J. E. H. Thompson*[sic]*, "Psalm CXIX," *CFL, N.S.,* 8 (1903) 205-220.

S. M. Vernon, "The Inspired Psalm of Law and Life. A Critique Upon Psalm CXIX.," *MQR, 3rd Ser.,* 29 (1903) 88-99.

Anonymous, "The Aleph of the 119th Psalm," *BRec* 9 (1912) 110-111.

Anonymous, "God's Golden Alphabet. Psalm 118. (Hebr. 119)," *AER* 76 (1927) 1-18.

*M. Meyer, "The Author of Psalm 118," *AER* 76 (1927) 19-27. *[Psalm 119]*

W. Leonard, "Sacred Scripture: Psalm 'Beati Immaculati' (118)," *ACR* 6 (1929) 314-322; 7 (1930) 37-44. *[Psalm 119]*

*P. J. Thompson, "Psalm 119: a possible Clue to the First Epistle of John," *StEv* 2 (1964) 487-492.

*J. H. Eaton, "Proposals in Psalms XCIX and CXIX," *VT* 18 (1968) 555-558.

Psalm 119:1-8

J. D[innen] Gilmore, "Studies in the Psalms," *HR* 61 (1911) 55. [Praise the Sovereign Law; or, The Christian's A B C of Praise.   Psalm 119] *[119:1-8]*

Psalm 119:9-16

J. Dinnen Gilmore, "Studies in the Psalms," *HR* 61 (1911) 138. [How to Maintain Practical Godliness, Psa. 119:9-16] *[Outline]*

Psalm 119:17-24

J. Dinnen Gilmore, "Studies in the Psalms," *HR* 61 (1911) 138. [How to Meet the Trials by the Way, Psa. 119:17-24] *[Outline]*

Psalm 119:25-32

J. Dinnen Gilmore, "Studies in the Psalms *(continued),*" *HR* 61 (1911) 308. [How to Overcome Spiritual Depression, Psa. 119:25-32] *[Outline]*

Psalm 119:28

William L Moran, "A Note on Ps 119:28," *CBQ* 15 (1953) 10.

Psalm 119:33-112

J. Dinnen Gilmore, "Studies in the Psalms," *HR* 62 (1911) 306-307. [How to Maintain Holy Living, Ps. 119:33-40; The Practical Outcome of Continued Mercy, Ps. 119:41-48; The Benefits of Obedience, Ps. 119:49-56; The Servant's Testimony to the Master's Goodness, Ps. 119:65-72; The Attractive Power of Personal Experience, Ps. 119:73-80; Faint: Yet Pursuing, Ps. 119:81-88; Where True Comfort is Found, Ps. 119:89-96; My Love for the Word, Ps. 119:97-104; The Believer's Candle, Ps. 119:105-112]

Psalm 119:83

*E. Power, "The meaning of קיטור in Ps. 148, 8 and 119, 83," *B* 7 (1926) 182-192.

Psalm 119:85

*R. H. Charles, "Two Passages in the Psalms," *ET* 32 (1920-21) 539-541. *[119:85]*

Psalm 119:96

Anonymous, "God's Perfect Law Our Despair and Our Comfort. Psalm cxix. 96," *Exp, 1st Ser.,* 4 (1876) 309-320.

Psalm 119:98-99

James Moffatt, "Opera Foris; Or, Materials for the Preacher. Second Series," *Exp, 8th Ser.,* 2 (1911) 182-192. *[119:98-99]*

Psalm 119:105

Anonymous, "The Great Text Commentary. The Great Texts of the Psalms," *ET* 23 (1911-12) 63-68. *[119:105]*

Psalm 119:113-128

J. Dinnen Gilmore, "Studies in the Psalms—Ps. 119," *HR* 63 (1912) 307. *[119:113-128 - Outline]*

Psalm 119:122

E. H. Sugden, "Critical Note on Psalm CXIX. 122," *Exp, 4th Ser.,* 3 (1891) 471-472.

Psalm 119:129-136

J. Dinnen Gilmore, "Studies in The Psalms—Ps. 119," *HR* 63 (1912) 392. *[119:129-136 - Outline]*

Psalm 119:137-144

J. Dinnen Gilmore, "Studies in the Psalms—Ps. 119," *HR* 63 (1912) 480. *[119:137-144 - Outline]*

Psalm 119:144

Beryl D. Cohon, "My Favorite Text—Bible: That I may Live," *YCCAR* 74 (1964) 216-220. *[119:144]*

Psalm 119:145-152

J. Dinnen Gilmore, "Studies in the Psalms—Ps. 119," *HR* 64 (1912) 57. *[119:145-152 - Outline]*

Psalm 119:161-176

J. Dinnen Gilmore, "Studies in the Psalms—Ps. 119," *HR* 64 (1912) 141. *[119:153-176 - Outline]*

Psalms 120-134 [The Songs of Ascents - See also: §385 ←]

David Smith, "The Songs of the Ascents," *ET* 12 (1900-01) 62-65, 161-164, 414-416. *[Psalms 120-134]*

T. C. Foote, "The Metrical Form of the Songs of Degrees," *JAOS* 27 (1906) 108-122. *[Psalms 120-134]*

E. W. Askwith, "The Song of Ascents," *Exp, 8th Ser.,* 23 (1922) 69-75. *[Psalms 120-134]*

B. D. Eerdmans, "The Songs of the Ascents. The Psalms Hamma'aloth," *OTS* 1 (1942) 139-161. *[Psalms 120-134]*

*Leon J. Liebreich, "The Songs of Ascents and the Priestly Blessing," *JBL* 74 (1955) 33-36. *[Psalms 120-134]*

Psalms 120-123

Herbert H. Gowen, "An Old Testament 'Pilgrim's Progress'," *ATR* 7 (1924-25) 438-450. *[Psalms 120-123]*

Psalms 120 and 121

David Smith, "The Songs of the Ascents," *ET* 13 (1901-02) 118-120, 500-503. *[Psalms 120 and 121]*

Psalm 120

Henry Woodward Hulbert, "A Pilgrim Psalm—Psalm CXX," *HR* 36 (1898) 450-452.

Psalm 120:3

W. Aldis Wright, "Psalm CXX $_{3m}$," *JTS* 11 (1909-10) 568.

Psalm 120:5-6

Eb. Nestle, "Psalm CXX. 5, 6," *ET* 28 (1916-17) 284.

Psalm 120:7

*Chr. A. W. Brekelmans, "Some Translation Problems," *OTS* 15 (1969) 170-176. *[120:7]*

Psalm 121

W. J. Cunningham Pike, "Psalm 121: A Circuit of Praise," *HR* 64 (1912) 139-141.

H. E. Maddox, "The Hundred and Twenty-first Psalm," *ICMM* 10 (1913-14) 430-434.

D[avid] S. K[ennedy], "The One Hundred and Twenty-first Psalm," *CFL, 3rd Ser.,* 33 (1927) 189-190.

J[ulian] Morgenstern, "Psalm 121," *JBL* 58 (1939) xvi.

Julian Morgenstern, "Psalm 121," *JBL* 58 (1939) 311-324.

P. Hewison Pollock, "Psalm 121," *JBL* 59 (1940) 411-412.

Psalm 121:1-2

E. H. Blakeney, "Psalm CXXI. 1-2," *ET* 59 (1947-48) 111.

Psalm 121:1

Dean A. Walker, "Note on Psalm 121:1," *JBL* 17 (1898) 205-206.

T. H. Weir, "Psalm CXXI. 1," *ET* 27 (1915-16) 90-91.

James   Kennedy,   "Psalm   CXXI.   1,"   *ET*   27   (1915-16)   138-139.

H.   G.   Grey,   "Psalm   CXXI.   1,"   *ET*   27   (1915-16)   185-186.

W.   T.   Whitley,   "Psalm   CXXI.   1,"   *ET*   27   (1915-16)   186.

Psalm 121:5-6

Rayner Winterbotham, "The Terrors of the Sun and of the Moon," *Exp, 6th Ser.*, 2 (1900) 355-368. *[121:5, 6]*

Psalm 121:5

Anonymous, "Questions and Answers. 4.," *AJSL* 1 (1884-85) 21. *[Grammatical construction in Psa. 121:5]*

Psalm 122

John E. McFadyen, "The Messages of the Psalms: Psalm 122," *BW* 26 (1905) 184-187.

Psalm 123

David Smith, "The Songs of the Ascents," *ET* 15 (1903-04) 39-42. *[Psalm 123]*

Psalm 123:2

T. K. Cheyne, "On Psalm CXXIII. 2," *Exp, 3rd Ser.*, 4 (1886) 80.

Psalm 124

*I. W. Slotki, "The Text and the Ancient Form of Recital of Psalm 24 and Psalm 124," *JBL* 51 (1932) 214-226.

Psalm 126

זָמַר, "The CXXVIth Psalm, Illustrated from the History of Livy," *CongML* 18 (1835) 273-281.

David Smith, "The Songs of the Ascents," *ET* 14 (1902-03) 163-166. *[Psalm 126]*

John E. McFadyen, "The Messages of the Psalms: Psalm 126," *BW* 26 (1905) 258-261.

Psalm 126:1

John Strugnell, "A Note on Ps. CXXVI. 1, בשוב יהוה את־שיבת ציון היינו כחלמים," *JTS, N.S.,* 7 (1956) 239-243.

Psalm 126:5-6

Maurice A. Canney, "'Sowing with Tears'," *ET* 37 (1925-26) 44-45. *[126:5, 6]*

F. Chilton, "'Sowing with Tears'," *ET* 37 (1925-26) 382. *[126:5, 6]*

Alan P. Anger, "Psalm 126:5-6 Sow and Reap," *CCBQ* 11 (1968) #2, 10-16.

Psalm 126:6

Anonymous, "The Great Text Commentary.   The Great Texts of the Psalms," *ET* 23 (1911-12) 124-128. *[126:6]*

Psalm 127

W. E[mery] Barnes, "A Fresh Interpretation of Psalm CXXVII," *Exp, 5th Ser.,* 7 (1898) 303-307.

James Robertson, "The Hebrew 'Cotter's Saturday Night'. (Psalm CXXVII)," *Exp, 5th Ser.,* 7 (1898) 414-423.

Samuel Daiches, "Psalm CXXVII. 2. A New Explanation," *ET* 45 (1933-34) 24-26.

A. G. McL. Pearce Higgins, "A Metrical Version of Psalm 127," *CQR* 166 (1965) 425.

Psalm 127:2

F. Bussby, "A Note on שֵׁנָא in Psalm CXXVII 2," *JTS* 35 (1934) 306-307.

Edward Edwards, "A New Interpretation of כֵּן יִתֵּן לִידִידוֹ שֵׁנָא (Psalm CXX-VII 2ᵇ)," *ET* 54 (1942-43) 25-26.

C. Lattey, "A New Interpretation of Psalm CXXVII 2ᵇ (כֵּן יִתֵּן לִידִידוֹ שֵׁנָא)," *ET* 54 (1942-43) 223.

*Mitchell Dahood, "Philological Notes on the Psalms," *ThSt* 14 (1953) 85-88. *[127:2]*

Psalm 127:5

*Mitchell Dahood, "Philological Notes on the Psalms," *ThSt* 14 (1953) 85-88. *[127:5]*

Psalm 129:6

Anonymous, "Biblical Illustrations. From Jowett's Christian Researches," *SP* 3 (1830) 106-108. [Psa. 129:6, pp. 106-107]

Psalm 130

Paul Haupt, "On the Penitential Psalm 'De Profundis'," *AJSL* 2 (1885-86) 98-106. *[Psalm 130]*

Talbot W. Chambers, "Studies in the Psalter. No. XXXII.—The 130th Psalm," *HR* 22 (1891) 160-162.

John Adams, "De Profundis—Psalm 130," *HR* 63 (1912) 221-224.

E. G. King, "Psalm CXXX," *ICMM* 11 (1914-15) 161-168.

Herbert H. Gowen, "Psalm CXXX," *JRAS* (1922) 576.

Robert C. Dentan, "An Exposition of an Old Testament Passage," *JAAR* 15 (1947) 158-161. *[Psalm 130]*

Psalm 130:1

X., "'In the Spirit'. Dominus Illuminato. 'Out of the deep have I called unto Thee O Lord.'—Psalm cxxx. 1," *Theo* 1 (1920) 284.

M.-L. Martin, "Psalm 130: Out of the depth I cry to Thee," *Min* 4 (1963-64) 64-65. *[130:1]*

Psalm 130:5-6

Štefan Porúbčan, "Psalm CXXX 5-6," *VT* 9 (1959) 322-323.

Psalm 131:2

P. A. H. de Boer, "Psalm CXXXI 2," *VT* 16 (1966) 287-292.

Psalm 131:3

*J. A. Montgomery, "Two Notes on the Kalamu Inscription," *JBL* 47 (1928) 196-197. *[131:3]*

Psalm 132

Talbot W. Chambers, "Studies in the Psalter. No. XXVI.—One Hundred and Thirty-second Psalm," *HR* 21 (1891) 163-166.

*Paul Haupt, "Zerubbabel and Melchizedek," *JSOR* 2 (1918) 76-82. *[Psalm 132]*

*J. R. Porter, "The Interpretation of 2 Samuel VI and Psalm CXXXII," *JTS, N.S.,* 5 (1954) 161-173.

*Terence E. Fretheim, "Psalm 132: A Form-Critical Study," *JBL* 86 (1967) 289-300.

*Delbert R. Hillers, "Ritual Procession of the Ark and Ps 132," *CBQ* 30 (1968) 48-55.

Psalm 132:6

Caius, "Psalm CXXXII. 6," *JSL, 3rd Ser.,* 7 (1858) 194.

Psalm 133

S. Fyne, "Psalm CXXXIII," *JQR* 19 (1906-07) 396-398.

W. K. Lowther Clarke, "Note. The 133rd Psalm," *Theo* 13 (1926) 334.

Psalm 133:3

*Eric Burrows, "The Dew Cult of Mount Herman," *JSOR* 11 (1927) 76-77. *[133:3]*

Psalm 134

*W[illiam] F[oxwell] Albright, "Notes on Psalms 68 and 134," *NTTO* 56 (1955) 1-12.

Psalm 134:1

Anonymous, "Night Watches in the Temple.—Psalm cxxxiv. 1," *ONTS* 2 (1882-83) 118-119.

Psalm 135

*Edward J. Kissane, "'Who Maketh Lightnings for the Rain'," *JTS, N.S.,* 3 (1952) 214-216. *[135:7]*

Psalm 137

Anonymous, "A Rhetorical Praxis on the cxxxvii. Psalm," *QCS* 4 (1822) 294-297.

*†Anonymous, "The Book of Psalms," *BCQTR, N.S.,* 23 (1825) 252-255. *(Review) [Psalm 137]*

Charles Short, "Greek Translation of Psalm CXXXVII," *BS* 5 (1848) 375-378. *(Subjoined notes are anonymous)*

*W. E. Barnes, "Short Studies in the Psalter," *ET* 7 (1895-96) 166-169. [(B) Psa. cxxxvii, pp. 168-169]

Anonymous, "Current Criticism and Interpretation of the Old Testament. A Study of Psalm cxxxvii," *CFL, O.S.,* 3 (1899) 147-148.

W. Emery Barnes, "A Study of Psalm CXXXVII," *Exp, 5th Ser.,* 9 (1899) 205-209.

Hermann Gunkel, "Psalm 137: An Interpretation," *BW* 22 (1903) 290-293.

Howard Osgood, "Dashing the Little Ones Against the Rock," *PTR* 1 (1903) 23-37.

John E. McFadyen, "The Messages of the Psalms: Psalm 137," *BW* 26 (1905) 96-100.

*John Hendrick de Vries, "Higher Criticism and the Sunday School," *CFL, 3rd Ser.,* 8 (1908) 209-212. *[Psalm 137]*

J. Closs Mantripp, "The Peril of Disciple: A Study of Psalm CXXXVII," *ICMM* 17 (1920-21) 222-227.

Psalm 137:3

Alfred Guillaume, "The Meaning of תולל in Psalm 137:3," *JBL* 75 (1956) 143-144.

Psalm 137:5

I. Eitan, "An Identification of tiškaḥ yĕmīnī, Psa. 137:5," *JBL* 47 (1928) 193-195.

Psalms 138-144

*John P. Peters, "Another Folk Song," *JBL* 40 (1921) 81-85.

Psalm 139

George Matheson, "Psalm CXXXIX," *Exp, 2nd Ser.,* 4 (1882) 356-368.

Talbot W. Chambers, "Studies in the Psalters. No. XXVII.—The One Hundred and Thirty-ninth Psalm," *HR* 21 (1891) 264-267.

G. G. Findlay, "God the Inevitable: A Study of Psalm CXXXIX," *Exp, 8th Ser.,* 17 (1919) 161-174.

W. Emery Barnes, "The Fugitive Wander's Psalm," *Exp, 8th Ser.,* 21 (1921) 329-337. *[Psalm 139]*

G. A. Danell, "Psalm 139," *UUÅ* (1951) #1, 1-37.

Aug C. Rehwaldt, "The God of the Universe and I. A Devotional Study of Psalm 139," *CTM* 27 (1956) 776-786.

S. B. Frost, "Psalm 139: An Exposition," *CJT* 6 (1960) 113-122.

E. J. Young, "The Background of Psalm 139," *BETS* 8 (1965) 101-110.

J. Vandevalle, "Psalm 139 and the Atharva-Veda," *IES* 8 (1969) 83-105.

Psalm 139:7

Anonymous, "The Great Text Commentary. The Great Texts of the Psalms," *ET* 23 (1911-12) 161-166. *[139:7]*

Psalm 141

F.   E.   Williams,   "Psalm   CXLI,"   *HR*   34   (1897)   353.

Psalms 143-144:6

*C. Taylor, "A New Septuagint Fragment," *JTS* 4 (1902-03) 130. *[143:1-144:6]*

*J. H. A. Hart, "The New Septuagint Fragment," *JTS* 4 (1902-03) 215-217. *[143:1-144:6]*

Psalm 145

John   A.   Bain,   "Psalm   145,"   *ET*   26   (1914-15)   94-95.

*Leon J. Liebreich, "Psalms 34 and 145 in the Light of Their Key Words," *HUCA* 27 (1956) 181-192.

Psalm 146

*John Carmody, "The Theology of Psalm 145," *BibT* #43 (1969) 2972-2979. *[Psalm 146]*

Psalm 148

Talbot W. Chambers, "The Universal Hallelujah. Psalm cxlviii," *HR* 31 (1896) 57-59.

E. B. Christie, "The Strophic Arrangement of the Benedicite," *JBL* 47 (1928) 188-193. *[Psalm 148]*

Psalm 148:8

*E. Power, "The meaning of קִישׁוֹר in Ps. 148, 8 and 119, 83," *B* 7 (1926) 182-192.

Psalm 149

Hermann Gunkel, "Psalm 149: An Interpretation," *BW* 22 (1903) 363-366.

Psalm 149:5

*Julius Boehmer, "כָּבוֹד a Divine Name? A Note on Ps. CXLIX. 5," *ET* 14 (1902-03) 334-336.

C. Taylor, "Further Notes on Psalm CXLIX. 5. I," *ET* 14 (1902-03) 382-383.

Ed. König, "Further Notes on Psalm CXLIX. 5. II," *ET* 14 (1902-03) 383-384.

Julius Boehmer, "Psalm CXLIX. 5," *ET* 14 (1902-03) 478-479.

Ed. König, "Psalm CXLIX. 5," *ET* 14 (1902-03) 526-527.

Julius Boehmer, "A Closing Word on Psalm CXLIX. 5," *ET* 15 (1903-04) 144.

Psalm 150

Giles Black, "The Last Psalm of All," *LofS* 6 (1951-52) 92-94. *[Psalm 150]*

Psalm 151 LXX

(   ) Baring-Gould, "Psalm CLI," *ONTS* 1 (1882) #1, 14. *[English Translation]*

Patrick W. Skehan, "The Apocryphal Psalm 151," *CBQ* 25 (1963) 407-409.

*J. A. Sanders, "Ps. 151 in 11QPSS," *ZAW* 75 (1963) 73-86.

*R. Y. Ebied, "A Triglot Volume of the Epistle to the Laodiceans, Psalm 151 and other Biblical Materials," *B* 47 (1966) 243-254. *[Psalm 151, pp. 253-254]*

Psalm 151:1-5

*W. H. Brownlee, "The 11Q Counterpart to Psalm 151, 1-5," *RdQ* 4 (1962-63) 379-388.

§646 *3.5.4.1.4 Studies on Manuscripts of the Book of Psalms*

†Anonymous, "Baber's Psalter, from the Alexandria Manuscript," *BCQTR* 42 (1813) 1-6. *(Review)*

L. Lund, "An Ethiopian Manuscript in the Astor Library," *CR* 36 (1881) 189-212. *[Volume may be listed as No. 135]*

Cyrus Adler, "Some Peculiarities of a Hebrew Manuscript of the Fourteenth Century of the Christian Era," *PAPA* 16 (1884) xxxiii-xxxiv. *[MSS of Psalms]*

*Cyrus Adler, "Notes on the Johns Hopkins and Abbott collections of Egyptian antiquities, with the translation of two Coptic inscriptions by Mr. W. Max Müller," *JAOS* 15 (1893) xxxi-xxxiv. *[Psa. 2:3-5]*

Anonymous, "A Fragment of the Greek Psalter," *MR* 77 (1895) 645-646.

*John E. Gilmore and P. le Page Renouf, "Coptic Fragments (Gen. xiii and xiv, and Psalm cv)," *SBAP* 17 (1895) 251-253.

F. E. Brightman, "The Sahidic Text of the Psalter," *JTS* 2 (1900-01) 275-276.

*J. D. Prince, "Two Versions of the Coptic Psalter," *JBL* 21 (1902) 92-99.

*C. Taylor, "A New Septuagint Fragment," *JTS* 4 (1902-03) 130. *[143:1-144:6]*

*J. H. A. Hart, "The New Septuagint Fragment," *JTS* 4 (1902-03) 215-217. *[143:1-144:6]*

F. C. Burkitt, "The Syriac Psalter," *JTS* 6 (1904-05) 286-290. *(Review)*

*W. O. E. Oesterley, "A Lost Uncial Codex of the Psalms," *ET* 17 (1905-06) 353-358.

W. E. Barnes, "The 'Nicene' Creed in the Syriac Psalter," *JTS* 7 (1905-06) 441-449.

P[atrick] V. Higgins, "The Psalms in the Vulgate," *IER, 4th Ser.,* 22 (1907) 372-379.

William H. Worrell, "A Coptic Biblical Manuscript in the Freer Collection," *AJA* 13 (1909) 63-64.

Henry A. Sanders, "The Freer Psalter," *BW* 33 (1909) 343-344.

Arthur Stanley Pease, "Fragments of a Latin Manuscript in the Library of the University of Illinois," *TAPA* 42 (1911) 147-156.

F. C. Burkitt, "The Monte Cassino Psalter, " *JTS* 14 (1912-13) 433-440.

Max L. Margolis, "A New Uncial of the Greek Psalter," *AJSL* 36 (1919-20) 84-86.

Robert L. Ramsay, "The Latin Text of the Paris Psalter: A Collation and Some Conclusions," *AJP* 41 (1920) 147-176.

F. C. Burkitt, "The First Book of Psalms in the Text of G. *I*," *JTS* 22 (1920-21) 165-172. *(Review)*

E. Power, "Corrections from the Hebrew in the Theodulfian MSS. of the Vulgate," *B* 5 (1924) 233-258. [Omitted passages or words supplied: 5:3; 29:8; 37:40; 42:11; 45:5; 50:6; 55:22; 59:18; 78:70-71; 80:19; 82:6; 83:2; 83:6; 116:2; 139:6; 142:7; Corrections in agreement with Hexaplar readings: 7:8; 7:10; 32:4; 32:6; 40:3; 68:18; 69:7; 71:20; 75:3; 77:7; 87:6; 89:3; 89:8; 102:29; 140:10; 142:8; 145:3; 147:16; Corrections at variance with Hexaplar readings: 22:31; 35:2; 46:5; 49:19; 50:23; 68:15; 87:7; 89:48; 91:6; 96:10; 111:2; 132:18; 138:3; Corrections where Hexaplar readings are unknown: 2:6; 18:14; 31:7; 34:22; 35:17; 37:13; 37:38; 40:10; 46:10; 48:15; 52:10; 54:9; 59:11; 77:6; 79:11; 89:11; 89:18; 90:2; 94:8; 96:13; 104:10; 105:43; 109:11; 109:29; 119:28; 125:1; 135:5; 135:7; 136:18; 140:5; 145:12; Some peculiar erroneous Corrections: 50:11; 78:42; 84:3; 78:69; 104:18; 106:39; Corrections agreeing with Old Latin Readings: 7:18; 8:3; 19:2; 36:8; 37:18; 38:14; 46:6; 48:9; 53:6; 64:6: 68:9; 73:23; 76:13; 78:7; 83:16; 98:3; 104:4; 104:11; 121:5; 136:14; 140:3; 140:11]

Henry A. Sanders, "A Newly Discovered Leaf of the Freer Psalter," *HTR* 22 (1929) 391-393.

F. Zimmermann, "The Text of the Psalms in the Peshitta," *JTS* 41 (1940) 44-46.

H. E. W. Turner, "Psalm Prologue Contained in MS. Bodl. Baroccianus 15," *JTS* 41 (1940) 280-287.

W. R. Taylor, "Syriac Mss. Found in Peking, *ca.* 1925," *JAOS* 61 (1941) 91-97. *[Liturgy on Psalms]*

*Allen Wikgren, "Two Ostraca Fragments of the Septuagint Psalter," *JNES* 5 (1946) 181-184.

*Charles M. Cooper, "Jerome's 'Hebrew Psalter' and the New Latin Version," *JBL* 69 (1950) 233-244.

J. A. Gaertner, "Latin Verse Translations of the Psalms 1500-1620," *HTR* 49 (1956) 271-305.

J. W. B. Barnes and G. D. Kilpatrick, "A New Psalm Fragment," *PBA* 43 (1957) 229-232. *[Psalms 48(49) and 49(50)]*

Henry Ashworth, "The Psalter Collects of Pseudo-Jerome and Cassiodorus," *BJRL* 45 (1962-63) 287-304.

*R. Y. Ebied, "A Triglot Volume of the Epistle to the Laodiceans, Psalm 151 and other Biblical Material," *B* 47 (1966) 243-254. *[Psalm 151, pp. 253-254]*

§647 **3.5.4.1.5 Exegetical Studies on the Book of Proverbs**

Talbot W. Chambers, "Misquoted Scripture. No. VII," *HR* 7 (1882-83) 112-113. *[4:23; 5:16; 6:11; 6:1-4; 6:22; 8:12]*

Talbot W. Chambers, "Misquoted Scripture. No. VIII," *HR* 7 (1882-83) 175-176. *[9:7; 10:9; 11:16; 12:4, 26]*

Talbot W. Chambers, "Misquoted Scripture. No. XVII," *HR* 8 (1883-84) 765-766. *[12:25; 13:15; 13:21; 13:23: 14:9; 14:24]*

A. B. Davidson, "The Book of Proverbs in the Revised Version," *Exp, 3rd Ser.,* 6 (1887) 381-396.

George R. Berry, "Some Textual notes on Proverbs," *AJSL* 19 (1902-30) 53-54. *[6:26a; 13:23a; 19:27; 30:31]*

G. R. Driver, "Problems in 'Proverbs'," *ZAW* 50 (1932) 141-148. *[7:11; 7:17; 7:22; 13:1; 13:11; 15:7; 17:4; 21:28; 22:23; 24:11; 27:19; 28:23]*

D. Winton Thomas, "Notes on Some Passages in the Book of Proverbs," *JTS* 38 (1937) 400-403. [Note by G. R. Driver on 3:35, p. 403] *[19:10; 24:14; 29:7; 25:17; 25:27; 39:4]*

*G. R. Driver, "Hebrew Notes on Prophets and Proverbs," *JTS* 41 (1940) 162-175. [Proverbs 9:13; 12:23; 13:1; 20:2; 21:26; 22:11; 26:28; 27:6; 27:16, pp. 173-175]

Steven T. Byington, "Some Bits of Hebrew. V. Texts in Proverbs," *ET* 57 (1945-46) 137-138. *[12:12; 13:5; 14:25; 18:19; 18:8; 21:8]*

G. R. Driver, "Problems in the Hebrew Text of Proverbs," *B* 32 (1951) 173-197. *[1:17; 1:23; 1:27; 2:9; 3:8; 3:13; 3:34; 3:35; 4:34; 7:2; 8:29; 9:13; 10:3; 10:28; 11:16; 11:31; 12:27; 13:9; 13:15; 14:9; 14:18; 15:2; 17:5; 17:14; 18:17; 18:18; 18:24; 20:26; 21:4; 21:8; 21:24: 22:5; 22:10; 22:11; 23:6; 23:31; 24:11; 24:22; 24:28; 25:4; 25:8; 25:27; 26:7; 26:23; 28:2; 28:17; 28:12 & 28:28; 29:6; 29:10; 30:31; 31:4; 31:8]*

D. Winton Thomas, "Textual and philological notes on some passages in the Book of Proverbs," *VTS* 3 (1955) 262-279. *[1:4; 1:11; 1:17; 3:35; 6:26; 7:21; 10:32; 14:8; 14:17; 15:30; 19:17; 19:18; 19:26; 22:4; 30:16; 30:31; 31:11]*

D. Winton Thomas, "Notes on some passages in the Book of Proverbs," *VT* 15 (1965) 271-279. *[1:9; 8:26; 9:17; 19:24 (=26:15); 23:17; 25:4; 26:11; 27:7; 27:9; 30:27; 31:8; 31:11; 31:28]*

J. A. Emerton, "Notes on Some Passages in the Book of Proverbs," *JTS, N.S.,* 20 (1969) 202-220. [a. Prov. 14:31; b. Prov. 19:16; c. Prov. 24:21; d. Prov. 26:9; e. Prov. 28:12]

Proverbs Chapters 1-9

Patrick W. Skehan, "The Seven Columns of Wisdom's House in Proverbs 1-9," *CBQ* 9 (1947) 190-198.

Proverbs 1:1-8

P. E. Kretzmann, "Pedagogical Hints from Prov. 1, 1-8," *CTM* 8 (1937) 709-710.

Proverbs 1:20

*Karl J. Grimm, "The Form , Prov. i 20, viii 3," *JBL* 21 (1902) 192-196.

Proverbs 1:22-23

J. A. Emerton, "A Note on the Hebrew Text of Proverbs i. 22-23," *JTS, N.S.,* 19 (1968) 609-614.

Proverbs 2:17

P. L. Hedley, "Proverbs II 17, הַעֹזֶבֶת אַלּוּף נְעוּרֶיהָ וְאֶת־בְּרִית ... שָׁכֵחָה:," *JTS* 31 (1929-30) 395-397.

Proverbs 3:11-12

Ross G. Murison, "God's Education of Men: Proverbs 3:11, 12," *BW* 24 (1904) 278-282.

Proverbs 3:17

Anonymous, "The Wisdom Whomse Ways are Ways of Pleasantness. (Prov. iii. 17.)," *ERG, 3rd Ser.,* 2 (1863-64) 255-260.

Proverbs 3:19-20

*C. F. Kraft, "The Concept of Wisdom in Proverbs 3:19-20 and 8:22-31," *JBL* 69 (1950) xiv.

Proverbs 3:20

H. F. W., "Proverbs III. 20," *JSL, 3rd Ser.,* 7 (1858) 465-466.

Proverbs 5:6

D. W. Thomas, "A Note on תדע לא in Proverbs V 6," *JTS* 36 (1936) 59-60.

Proverbs 5:15-20

*Paul Haupt, "Well and Field = Wife," *JAOS* 36 (1916) 418-420. *[5:15-20]*

Proverbs 5:15-19

*Patrick Skehan, "Proverbs 5:15-19 and 6:20-24," *CBQ* 8 (1946) 290-297.

Proverbs 6:6-8

Anonymous, "Postils," *MQR, 2nd Ser.,* 3 (1881) 553-556. *[6:6-8]*

Proverbs 6:10

*C. Rabin, "לשכב ידים חבק מעט (Proverbs vi, 10; xxiv, 33)," *JJS* 1 (1948-49) 197-198.

Proverbs 6:16-19

James Edward Hogg, "Prov. 6:16-19 ('Six Things,' etc.)," *AJSL* 44 (1927-28) 264-267.

Proverbs 6:20-24

*Patrick Skehan, "Proverbs 5:15-19 and 6:20-24," *CBQ* 8 (1946) 290-297.

Proverbs 7:22-23

James T. Hudson, "Proverbs VII. 22, 23," *ET* 55 (1943-44) 277.

Proverbs 7:22

A. A. Bevan, "Note on *Proverbs* VII. 22," *JP* 28 (1903) 287-288.

Israel Eitan, "The Crux in Prov. 7:22," *AJSL* 43 (1926-27) 60-63.

Proverbs Chapter 8

*J. Rendel Harris, "Christ the Firstborn," *Exp, 8th Ser.,* 14 (1917) 321-329.
[Chapter 8]

Proverbs 8:3

Karl J. Grimm, "The Form תִּלְנָּה,Prov. i 20, viii 3," *JBL* 21 (1902) 192-196.

Proverbs 8:22-31

F. A. Gast, "Wisdom Personified," *RChR* 25 (1878) 411-424. *[8:22-31]*

C. F. Burney, "Christ as the ΑΡΧΗ of Creation. (Prov. viii 22, Col. i 15-18, Rev. iii 14)," *JTS* 27 (1925-26) 160-177.

*C. F. Kraft, "The Concept of Wisdom in Proverbs 3:19-20 and 8:22-31," *JBL* 69 (1950) xiv.

C. F. Kraft, "Poetic Structure and Meaning in Proverbs 8:22-31," *JBL* 72 (1953) vii-viii.

*P. A. H. de Boer, "The counsellor," *VTS* 3 (1955) 42-71. [Prov. 8:22-31, pp. 69-70]

William A. Irwin, "Where Shall Wisdom be Found?" *JBL* 80 (1961) 133-142. *[8:22-31]*

Lou H. Silberman, "Farewell to O AMHN. A Note on Rev 3 14," *JBL* 82 (1963) 213-214. *[8:22-31]*

R. N. Whybray, "Proverbs VIII 22-31 and its supposed Prototypes," *VT* 15 (1965) 504-514.

Mitchell Dahood, "Proverbs 8,22-31. Translation and Commentary," *CBQ* 30 (1968) 512-521.

Proverbs 8:30

R. B. Y. Scott, "Wisdom in Creation: the ʾāmôn of Proverbs VIII 30," *VT* 10 (1960) 213-223.

Proverbs Chapter 9

*Murray Lichtenstein, "The Banquet Motif in Keret and in Proverbs 9," *JANES* 1 (1968-69) #1, 19-31.

Proverbs 9:1

Samuel Daiches, "Note on the word חצבה in Proverbs IX. 1," *ET* 55 (1943-44) 277.

Proverbs 9:13

D. Winton Thomas, "Note on בַּל־יָדְעָה in Proverbs 9¹³," *JTS, N.S.,* 4 (1953) 23-24.

Proverbs 10:16

D. Winton Thomas, "The Meaning of חַטָּאת in Proverbs X. 16," *JTS, N.S.,* 15 (1964) 295-296.

Proverbs 10:23

†Peter Tompson, "Various Readings in different Editions of the Bible," *MMBR* 56 (1823-24) 515. *[10:23]*

Proverbs 12:3

*Duncan B. Macdonald, "Notes Critical and Lexicographical," *JBL* 14 (1895) 57-62. [IV. Prov. 12:3b, p. 58]

Proverbs 12:26

J. A. Emerton, "A Note on Proverbs xii. 26," *ZAW* 76 (1964) 191-193.

Proverbs 12:28

M[itchell] Dahood, "Immortality in Prv 12, 28," *B* 41 (1960) 176-181.

Proverbs 13:8

*Francis M. Seely, "Notes on G'RH with Especial Reference to Proverbs 13:8," *BTr* 10 (1959) 20-21.

Proverbs 15:8-9

James Moffatt, "Opera Foris; Or, Materials for the Preacher. Second Series. —II.," *Exp, 8th Ser.,* 2 (1911) 380-384. *[15:8-9]*

Proverbs 16:4

E., "Illustration of Proverbs XVI. 4," *MR* 6 (1823) 380-381.

Proverbs 18:1

F. J. G., "Proverbs XVIII:1," *ONTS* 1 (1882) 72-73.

Proverbs 18:10

G. H. Whitaker, "Proverbs XVIII. 10," *ET* 27 (1915-16) 521.

Proverbs 18:13

James Moffatt, "Opera Foris; Or, Materials for the Preacher. Second Series," *Exp, 8th Ser.,* 2 (1911) 182-192. *[18:13]*

Proverbs 18:18

W[illiam] F[oxwell] Albright, "The Copper Spatula of Byblos and Proverbs 18:18," *BASOR* #90 (1943) 35-37.

Proverbs 18:24

†*S. R. Driver, "Requests and Replies. The Word להתרועע in Prov. xviii. 24," *ET* 11 (1899-1900) 230-231.

Proverbs 19:22

James B. Johnston, "The Measure of a Man," *ET* 42 (1930-31) 174-175. *[19:22]*

Proverbs 19:23

Melville Scott, "Proverbs XIX. 23," *ET* 29 (1927-28) 526-527.

*D. Muir, "Three Obscure O.T. Passages," *ET* 41 (1929-30) 44-45. *[19:23]*

Proverbs 19:26

G. R. Driver, "Proverbs xix. 26," *TZ* 11 (1955) 373-374.

Proverbs 20:13

*Paul Haupt, "Mistranslated Lines in Proverbs," *JBL* 45 (1926) 354-356. *[20:13]*

Proverbs 20:26

D. Winton Thomas, "Proverbs XX 26," *JJS* 15 (1964) 155-156.

Proverbs 20:27

E. C. Dargan, "The Lamp of Jehovah, the Spirit of Man," *R&E* 13 (1916) 476-479. *[20:27]*

H. W. Sheppard, "Note on Proverbs XX. 27. נֵר יְהוָה נִשְׁמַת אָדָם חֹפֵשׂ כָּל־חַדְרֵי־בָטֶן׃," *ET* 29 (1917-18) 45.

Proverbs 21:4

*E. Power, "A Study of the Hebrew Expression 'Wide of Heart'," *B* 1 (1920) 59-75. *[21:4, pp. 70-74]*

Proverbs 21:9

*W[illiam] F[oxwell] Albright, "b) Hebrew *bêth-ḥeber* in Proverbs and Canaanite *bêtu ḫubûri*, 'Granary'," *JBL* 62 (1943) vi. *[21:9]*

*S. B. Gurewicz, "Some Examples of Modern Exegeses of the OT," *ABR* 11 (1963) 15-23. [4. "BETH ḤOVER", Prov. xxi:2*[sic]* טוב לשבת על פנת גג מאשת מדינית ובית חבר, pp. 22-23]

Proverbs 22:6

Howard Crosby, "Light on Important Texts. No. XX," *HR* 6 (1881-82) 585. *[22:6]*

Anonymous, "Exegetical Suggestions and Opinions. Prov. xxii., 6," *CFL, O.S.,* 1 (1897) 23.

Proverbs 22:10

*H. A. Wolfson, "Notes on Proverbs 22:10 and Psalms of Solomon 17:48," *JQR, N.S.,* 37 (1946-47) 87.

Proverbs 22:12

D. Winton Thomas, "A Note on דַּעַת in Proverbs XXII. 12," *JTS, N.S.,* 14 (1963) 93-94.

Proverbs 22:17-21

W. K. Lowther Clarke, "Studies in Texts," *Theo* 10 (1925) 160-161. [(b) Proverbs xxii. 17-21, p. 161]

Proverbs 23:21

*Paul Haupt, "Mistranslated Lines in Proverbs," *JBL* 45 (1926) 354-356. *[23:21]*

Proverbs 23:26

W. H. Evans, "Exegesis of Proverbs xxiii. 26, with Special Reference to the Phrase לִי,תְּנָה בְנִי לִבְּךָ," *BQ* 6 (1872) 93-105.

Anonymous, "Expository Items. Proverbs XXIII. 26," *MQR, 2nd Ser.,* 2 (1880) 756.

Anonymous, "Proverbs XXIII. 26," *MQR, 2nd Ser.,* 4 (1882) 533-534.

Proverbs 23:29-35

Anonymous, "Proverbs XXIII. 29-35, Philologically Examined, and Translated," *JSL, 4th Ser.,* 8 (1865-66) 75-80.

Proverbs 23:34

A. H. W., "Proverbs XXIII. 34," *JSL, 4th Ser.,* 8 (1865-66) 459-460.

Proverbs 24:16

M. D., "Twenty Misused Scripture Texts," *ET* 6 (1894-95) 200-201. [II 24:16, p. 201]

Proverbs 24:27

James Moffatt, "Opera Foris. Materials for the Preacher," *Exp, 7th Ser.,* 5 (1908) 79-81. *[24:27]*

Proverbs 24:30-34

Samuel Cox, "The Sluggard's Garden. Proverbs xxiv. 30-34," *Exp, 2nd Ser.,* 6 (1883) 401-416.

Proverbs 24:33

*C. Rabin, "חבק ידים לשכב מעט (Proverbs vi, 10; xxiv, 33)," *JJS* 1 (1948-49) 197-198.

Proverbs 25:2

E. E. Kellett, "On Proverbs XXV. 2," *ET* 35 (1923-24) 226-227.

Proverbs 25:11

*T. K. Cheyne, "Old Testament Notes," *JBL* 18 (1899) 208-211. [1. "Apples of Gold," Prov. 25:11, pp. 208-209]

Proverbs 25:15

J. M. Rife, "A Note on Prov. 25:15," *JBL* 56 (1937) 118-119.

Proverbs 25:19

W. R. Hutton, "Textual Emendation in the Old Testament," *ET* 63 (1951-52) 93. *[25:19]*

W. R. Hutton, "Textual Emendation in the Old Testament," *BTr* 4 (1953) 13-14. *[25:19]*

Proverbs 25:21-22

A. T. Fryer, "'Coals of Fire'," *ET* 36 (1924-25) 478. *[25:21, 22]*

A. T. Fryer, "Studies in Texts," *Theo* 10 (1925) 160-161. [(a) Proverbs xxv. 21, 22; Rom. xii. 20]

Proverbs 25:22

A. S. Tritton, "Proverbs XXV 22," *JTS* 21 (1919-20) 172-173.

John Steele, "Heaping Coals on the Head (Pr. XXV. 22; Ro. XII. 20)," *ET* 44 (1932-33) 141.

Proverbs 25:23

*G. R. Driver, "Things Old and New in the Old Testament," *MUSJ* 45 (1969) 463-478. [2. Prov. 25:23, pp. 466-469]

Proverbs 25:24

*W[illiam] F[oxwell] Albright, "b) Hebrew *bêth-ḥeber* in Proverbs and Canaanite *bêtu ḫubûri,* 'Granary'," *JBL* 62 (1943) vi. *[25:24]*

Proverbs 26:4-5

P. J. Gloag, "Requests and Replies," *ET* 2 (1890-91) 42. *[26:4, 5]*

Proverbs 26:8

Hugh Macmillan, "Throwing a Stone at an Idol," *ET* 8 (1896-97) 399-400. *[26:8]*

W. Govan Robertson, "Proverbs XXVI. 8," *ET* 35 (1923-24) 428.

W. D. Morris, "כִּצְרוֹר אֶבֶן בְּמַרְגֵּמָה (Proverbs XXVI. 8)," *ET* 36 (1924-25) 332-333.

Proverbs 26:11

*Edward King, "Ἷς λουσαμένη εἰς κυλισμὸν βορπόρου," *JP* 7 (1876-77) 134-137. *[26:11]*

Proverbs 26:23

*R. Laird Harris, "A Mention of Pottery Glazing in Proverbs," *JAOS* 60 (1940) 268-269. *[26:23]*

W[illiam] F[oxwell] Albright, "A New Hebrew Word for 'Glaze' in Proverbs 26:23," *BASOR* #98 (1945) 24-25.

Proverbs 27:6

James Moffatt, "Opera Foris; Or, Materials for the Preacher. Second Series. —III," *Exp, 8th Ser.,* 2 (1911) 563-568. *[27:6]*

Proverbs 27:10

W. J. Masson, "Proverbs XXVII. 10," *ET* 47 (1935-36) 431.

Proverbs 27:13

*M[itchell] Dahood, "'To pawn one's cloak'," *B* 42 (1961) 359-366. *[27:13]*

Proverbs 27:16

Israel Eitan, "The Crux in Proverbs 27:16," *JQR, N.S.,* 15 (1924-25) 420-422.

Proverbs 27:21-22

*Eb. Nestle, "Ps. XXI. 6 and Prov. XXVII. 21, 22," *ET* 8 (1896-97) 287-288.

*T. K. Cheyne, "On Proverbs XXVII. 21, 22; Psalm XII. 7 (6)," *ET* 8 (1896-97) 335-336.

*Eb. Nestle, "Ps. XII. 7 and Prov. XXVII. 21, 22," *ET* 8 (1896-97) 379.

*G. M. Mackie, "The Pestle and the Mortar," *ET* 8 (1896-97) 521-522. *[21:21, 22]*

G. M. Mackie, "Prov. 27:21-22. The Pestle and the Mortar," *CFL, O.S.,* 1 (1897) 240.

Proverbs 27:22

T. K. Cheyne, "Prov. XXVII. 22," *ET* 8 (1896-97) 480.

Proverbs 28:22

*T. K. Cheyne, "On 2 Ch. xiv. 9; Job i. 15; Prov. xxviii. 22," *ET* 8 (1896-97) 431-432.

Proverbs 29:5

D. Winton Thomas, "The Interpretation of Proverbs XXIX. 5," *ET* 59 (1947-48) 112.

Proverbs 29:18

Anonymous, "Two Misapplied Phrases of Scriptures," *CTM* 14 (1943) 291-292. *[29:18]*

*Alfred Guillaume, "Is Episcopacy a Jewish Institution?" *BSOAS* 13 (1949-51) 23-26. *[29:18]*

Proverbs Chapter 30

*S. R. Driver, "'Sceptics of the Old Testament'," *ContR* 69 (1896) 257-269. *[Agur, Chapter 30](Review)*

George F. Genung, "An Old-Time Philistine," *BW* 28 (1906) 319-333. *[Chapter 30]*

Charles C. Torrey, "Proverbs, Chapter 30," *JBL* 73 (1954) 93-96.

Proverbs 30:8

*Paul Haupt, "Mistranslated Lines in Proverbs," *JBL* 45 (1926) 354-356. *[30:8]*

Proverbs 30:11-14

George Augustus Simcox, "Agur," *Exp, 5th Ser.,* 9 (1899) 148-150. *[30:11-14]*

Proverbs 30:15-16

J. M. Grintz, "The Proverbs of 'Aluqa," *Tarbiz* 28 (1958-59) #2, I. *[30:15-16]*

F. S. North, "The Four Insatiables," *VT* 15 (1965) 281-282. *[30:15f.]*

Proverbs 30:15

J. F. Denham, "The Horse-leech," *JSL, 1st Ser.,* 2 (1848) 158-159. *[30:15]*

Anonymous, "Remarks on Proverbs xxx, 15.—The Horse-Leech," *MR* 32 (1850) 165-166.

*T. K. Cheyne, "Notes on Gen. VI , 16, Isa. XVIII, 1, and Prov. XXX, 15," *SBAP* 23 (1901) 141-144. [III.—Prov. xxx, 15, pp. 143-144]

*Eric Burrows, "Cuneiform and Old Testament: Three Notes," *JTS* 28 (1926-27) 184-185. [II. The two *ardat liliῑ* (Prov 30:15), p. 185]

J. J. Glück, "Proverbs XXX 15a," *VT* 14 (1964) 367-370.

Proverbs 30:17

D. W. Thomas, "A Note on לְיִקֲּהַת in Proverbs XXX. 17," *JTS* 42 (1941) 154-155.

Proverbs 30:18-20

Edmund F. Sutcliffe, "The Meaning of Proverbs 30:18-20," *ITQ* 27 (1960) 125-131.

Proverbs 30:29-31

P. Haupt, "Four Strutters," *JBL* 45 (1926) 350-354. *[30:29-31]*

Proverbs 30:31

S. Feigin, "וּמֶלֶךְ אַלְקוּם עִמּוֹ (Proverbs 30:31)," *AJSL* 41 (1924-25) 138-139.

*Julius A. Bewer, "Two Suggestions on Prov 30:31 and Zech 9:16," *JBL* 67 (1948) 61-62.

Proverbs Chapter 31

M[argaret] B. Crook, "Program for a School of Home Economics in Proverbs 31," *JBL* 71 (1952) ix.

Proverbs 31:1

A. Aldis Wright, "Dr. Davidson's Introduction," *JSL, 4th Ser.,* 3 (1863) 185. *[31:1]*

Proverbs 31:4

D. Winton Thomas, "אַ in Prov. xxxi 4," *VT* 12 (1962) 499-500.

Proverbs 31:10-31

Margaret B. Crook, "The Marriageable Maiden of Prov. 31:10-31," *JNES* 13 (1954) 137-140.

Margaret B. Crook, "The marriageable maiden of Prov. 31:10-31," *TD* 5 (1957) 72. *[Synopsis]*

Proverbs 31:19

*A. Boissier, "A Sumerian Word in the Bible," *SBAP* 35 (1913) 159-160. *[kisurru (kišurru)] [31:19]*

Proverbs 31:21

G. R. Driver, "On a Passage in the Baal Epic (IV AB iii 24) and Proverbs XXXI 21," *BASOR* #105 (1947) 11.

Proverbs 31:27

M. Jastrow, "Notes on the Targum as a Commentary," *ONTS* 3 (1883-84) 52-53. *[31:27]*

(§648) **3.5.4.1.6 Studies on Manuscripts of the Book of Proverbs**

(§649) *3.5.4.2 Exegetical Studies on Several Books of the Megilloth*

§650 *3.5.4.2.1 Exegetical Studies on the Song
of Solomon (Canticles)*

George J. Walker, "Translations in the Solomon's Song," *JSL, 1st Ser.,* 2 (1848) 162-164. *[1:4, 7; 2:1, 5, 7, 14, 17; 3:6, 7, 9, 10; 4:1, 3, 16; 5:1, 8, 11, 13, 14, 15; 6:13; 7:5, 6, 9; 8:1, 2, 3, 5, 6, 7, 12]*

I. Horner, "The Song of Solomon. Translated, Arranged, and Annotated," *MR* 44 (1862) 391-409.

Charles E. Corwin, "The Song of Songs: An Exposition," *HR* 40 (1900) 446-449.

Paul Haupt, "The Book of Canticles," *AJSL* 18 (1901-02) 193-245.

Paul Haupt, "Difficult Passages in the Song of Songs," *JBL* 21 (1902) 51-73.

Paul Haupt, "The Book of Canticles," *AJSL* 19 (1902-03) 1-32.

Joshua Bloch, "A Critical Examination of the Text of the Syriac Version of the Song of Songs," *AJSL* 38 (1921-22) 103-139.

Grainger Tandy, "The Song of Songs. Annotated as a Dramatic Poem," *ICMM* 19 (1922-23) 131-145.

H. Speckard, "Summary Interpretation of the Song of Solomon," *WLQ* 62 (1965) 48-68, 135-151, 206-216, 264-274; 63 (1966) 127-135, 215-223, 272-281.

Chapter 1

Anonymous, "The Song of Love. A Commentary on the First Chapter of the Canticle," *LofS* 7 (1952-53) 268-273.

Canticles 1:4

Theodor H. Gaster, "Canticles I. 4 נַזְכִּירָה דֹדֶיךָ מִיַּיִן מֵישָׁרִים אֲהֵבוּךָ," *ET* 72 (1960-61) 195.

Canticles 1:5

*S[tephen] Langdon, "The 'Shalamians' of Arabia," *JRAS* (1927) 529-533. [Song of Solomon 1:5, pp. 530-531]

Canticles 2:3-5

*W. Robertson Smith, "Old Testament Notes," *JP* 13 (1884) 61-66. [III. חפות Canticles ii 3, 5, vii 9, pp. 65-66]

*[W. Robertson Nicoll], "Old Testament Notes," *Exp, 3rd Ser.,* 1 (1885) 160. *[2:3,5]*

Canticles 2:7

*T. K. Cheyne, "New God Names," *JBL* 30 (1911) 104-105. *[2:7]*

Canticles 2:11

Paul Haupt, "The Rose of Sharon," *JBL* 26 (1917) 147. *[2:11]*

Canticles 2:17

*Buchanan Blake, "'Until the Day Break, and the Shadows Flee Away'," *ET* 47 (1935-36) 45. *[2:17]*

*George Gifford, "Song of Songs II. 17 (IV. 6) and Isaiah XL. 3," *ET* 47 (1935-36) 381.

*D. Winton Thomas, "'Until the Day Break, and the Shadows Flee Away'," *ET* 47 (1935-36) 431-432. *[2:17]*

Canticles 3:5

*T. K. Cheyne, "New God Names," *JBL* 30 (1911) 104-105. *[3:5]*

Canticles 4:1-3

*E. H. Blankeney, "A Note on the Word σιώπησις: Canticles IV. 1, 3; VI. 6," *ET* 55 (1943-44) 138.

Canticles 4:4

*T. K. Cheyne, "Solomon's Armoury, Canticles, iv. 4," *ET* 9 (1897-98) 423-424.

*A. M. Honeyman, "Two Contributions to Canaanite Toponymy," *JTS* 50 (1949) 50-52. [II. 'Talpioth', pp. 51-52] *[4:4]*

B. S. J. Isserlin, "Song of Songs IV, 4: An Archaeological Note," *PEQ* 90 (1958) 59-60.

Canticles 4:6

*Buchanan Blake, "'Until the Day Break, and the Shadows Flee Away'," *ET* 47 (1935-36) 45. *[4:6]*

*George Gifford, "Song of Songs II. 17 (IV. 6) and Isaiah XL. 3," *ET* 47 (1935-36) 381.

*D. Winton Thomas, "'Until the Day Break, and the Shadows Flee Away'," *ET* 47 (1935-36) 431-432. *[4:6]*

Frederick H. Pickering, "'Until the Day Break and the Shadows Flee Away'," *ET* 48 (1936-37) 44. *[4:6]*

Canticles 4:7

Francis X. Curley, "The Lady of the Canticle. 'Thou art all fair, O my love, and there is no blemish in thee' (4:7)," *MH* 11 (1954-55) #3, 1-9.

Canticles 4:16

Joseph R. Sizoo, "The Winds of God," *JRT* 10 (1952-53) 149-154. *[4:16]*

Canticles 5:6

*H. S. Gehman, "Philological Notes on Two Hebrew Words," *JBL* 58 (1939) vi. *[5:6]*

Canticles 5:13

*T. K. Cheyne, "Canticles V. 13 and VII. 1," *JQR* 12 (1899-1900) 380.

Canticles 6:2

George Henslow, "The Song of Songs, Chap. vi. 2 (R.V.)," *ET* 8 (1896-97) 381.

Canticles 6:6

*E. H. Blankeney, "A Note on the Word σιώπησις: Canticles IV. 1, 3; VI. 6," *ET* 55 (1943-44) 138.

Canticles 6:10

S. D. Goitein, "Ayummā Kannidgālōt (Song of Songs vi. 10) 'Splendid like the Brilliant Stars'," *JSS* 10 (1965) 220-221.

Canticles 6:12

*T. K. Cheyne, "Has Amminadib in Canticles any Existence?" *Exp, 5th Ser.,* 9 (1899) 145-147. *[6:12]*

Canticles 7:1-2

*T. K. Cheyne, "Has Amminadib in Canticles any Existence?" *Exp, 5th Ser.,* 9 (1899) 145-147. *[7:2(1)]*

Canticles 7:1

*T. K. Cheyne, "Canticles V. 13 and VII. 1," *JQR* 12 (1899-1900) 380.

Canticles 7:3

*T. K. Cheyne, "The Text of Cant. VII. 3, 5-7," *JQR* 11 (1898-99) 404-407.

Canticles 7:5-7

*T. K. Cheyne, "The Text of Cant. VII. 3, 5-7," *JQR* 11 (1898-99) 404-407.

Canticles 7:6

T. K. Cheyne, "Note on Cant. VII. 6," *JQR* 11 (1898-99) 237-238.

*Joseph Reider, "Contributions to the Hebrew lexicon," *RDSO* 17 (1937-38) 103-110. [5. Cant. 7:6, pp. 109-110]

Canticles 7:7

*T. K. Cheyne, "Has Amminadib in Canticles any Existence?" *Exp, 5th Ser.,* 9 (1899) 145-147. *[7:7]*

Canticles 7:9

*W. Robertson Smith, "Old Testament Notes," *JP* 13 (1884) 61-66. [III. חמפה Canticles ii 3, 5, vii 9, pp. 65-66]

*[W. Robertson Nicoll], "Old Testament Notes," *Exp, 3rd Ser.,* 1 (1885) 160. *[7:9]*

Canticles 8:6-7

Samuel Cox, "The Praise of Love. Solomon's Song VIII. 6, 7," *Exp, 1st Ser.,* 10 (1879) 386-389.

Canticles 8:11-12

*Leon J. Liebreich, "Midrash Lekah Tob's Dependence upon Targum to the Song of Songs 8:11-12," *JQR, N.S.,* 38 (1947-48) 63-66.

§651 *3.5.4.2.2 Studies on Manuscripts of the Song of Solomon (Canticles)*

*Raphael Hai Malamed, "The Targum to Canticles according to Six Yemen MSS. compared with the 'Textus Receptus' (Ed. de Lagarde)," *JQR, N.S.,* 10 (1919-20) 377-410.

*Raphael Hai Malamed, "The Targum to Canticles according to Six Yemen MSS. compared with the 'Textus Receptus' (Ed. de Lagarde), Chapters II-IV," *JQR, N.S.,* 11 (1920-21) 1-20.

*Raphael Hai Malamed, "The Targum to Canticles according to Six Yemen MSS. compared with the 'Textus Receptus' (Ed. de Lagarde), concluded," *JQR, N.S.,* 12 (1921-22) 57-117.

*J. A. Emerton, "The Printed Editions of the Song of Songs in the Peshiṭta Version," *VT* 17 (1967) 416-429.

W. Baars, "The Peshitta Text of Song of Songs in Barhebraeus' Auṣar rāzē," *VT* 18 (1968) 281-289.

§652 **3.5.4.2.3 Exegetical Studies on the Book of Ruth**

S. Cox, "The Book of Ruth. Introduction," *Exp, 1st Ser.,* 2 (1875) 1-17.
[Introduction and Translation]

*A. F. Kirkpatrick, "The Revised Version of the Old Testament:—The
Books of Judges and Ruth," *Exp, 3rd Ser.,* 3 (1886) 109-127. [Ruth, pp.
126-127] *[1:15, 19; 2:3; 3:16; 4:3, 5, 15]*

Ruth 1:1-22

S. Cox, "The Book of Ruth," *Exp, 1st Ser.,* 2 (1875) 81-103. [I. The Sojourn
in Moab (1:1-5); II. The Return to Bethlehem (1:6-22)]

Ruth 1:8

*Claude R. Conder, "Notes on New Discoveries," *PEFQS* 41 (1909) 266-
275. [Widows (Ruth 1:8), pp. 272-273]

Ruth 1:14-22

*I. G. Matthews, "Expository Studies in the Old Testament: XI. Ruth and
Samuel," *BW* 30 (1907) 361-368. *[1:14-22]*

Ruth 1:14-15

*Anonymous, "Orpah. A Study in Internationalism," *ET* 28 (1916-17) 508-
512.

Ruth 1:16-17

Z., "A Paraphrase of Ruth i. 16, 17," *QCS* 2 (1820) 250.

Ruth 1:17

Anonymous, "Ruth's Oath," *R&E* 9 (1912) 557. *[1:17]*

Ruth 2:1-23

S. Cox, "The Book of Ruth. III. In the Harvest-Field," *Exp, 1st Ser.,* 2
(1875) 165-176. *[2:1-23]*

Ruth 2:8-9

Isaac H. Hall, "The Syriac reading of Ruth 2:8, 9," *JBL* 6 (1886) Part 1, 121.

Ruth 2:8

Morris Jastrow Jr., "On Ruth 2:8," *JBL* 15 (1896) 59-62.

Ruth 2:19

W. F. Stinespring, "Note on Ruth 2:19," *JNES* 3 (1944) 101.

Ruth 2:20

*W. E. Staples, "Notes on Ruth 2:20 and 3:12," *AJSL* 54 (1937) 62-64.

Ruth Chapter 3

Herbert Gordon May, "Ruth's Visit to the High Place at Bethlehem," *JRAS* (1939) 75-78. *[Chapter 3]*

Ruth 3:1-18

S. Cox, "The Book of Ruth. IV. In The Threshing-Floor," *Exp, 1st Ser.*, 2 (1875) 257-268. *[3:1-18]*

Ruth 3:12

*W. E. Staples, "Notes on Ruth 2:20 and 3:12," *AJSL* 54 (1937) 62-64.

Ruth 3:13

H. W. Sheppard, "Ruth III 13 b. An Explanation of B's inserted Words," *JTS* 19 (1917-18) 277.

Ruth 3:15

F. S. Rens, "שעורים שש וימד: Ruth III. 15," *ONTS* 2 (1882-83) 23.

Luther Poellot, "'He' or 'She' in Ruth 3:15b?" *CTM* 23 (1952) 600-601.

Ruth 4:1-22

S. Cox, "The Book of Ruth, V. In the Gate," *Exp, 1st Ser.*, 2 (1875) 360-374. *[4:1-22]*

Ruth 4:5

*Th. C. Vriezen, "Two Old Cruces," *OTS* 5 (1948) 80-91. *[4:5]*

Ruth 4:7-8

Ernest R. Lacheman, "Note on Ruth 4:7-8," *JBL* 56 (1937) 51-56.

Ruth 4:11

C. J. Labuschagne, "The Crux in Ruth 4:11," *ZAW* 79 (1967) 364-367.

Ruth 4:14-15

Julius A. Bewer, "The Goël in Ruth 4:14, 15," *AJSL* 20 (1903-04) 202-206.

§653 *3.5.4.2.4 Studies on Manuscripts of the Book of Ruth*

*Raymond Thornhill, "The Greek Text of the Book of Ruth: A Grouping of Manuscripts According to Origen's Hexapla," *VT* 3 (1953) 236-249.

§654 *3.5.4.2.5 Exegetical Studies on the Book of Lamentations*

Theodore H. Robinson, "Notes on the Text of Lamentations," *ZAW* 51 (1933) 255-259. *[1:1, 7, 12; 2:1, 3, 4, 6, 13, 20, 22; 3:11, 16, 19, 26, 36, 45, 47, 58, 63; 4:1, 7, 9, 15, 20; 5:10, 13, 19]*

G. R. Driver, "Notes on the Text of 'Lamentations'," *ZAW* 52 (1934) 308-309. (Notes by T. H. Robinson, pp. 309-310) *[2:22; 3:6, 47; 4:9, 15; 5:10]*

*Theophile James Meek, "Old Testament Notes," *JBL* 67 (1948) 233-239. [5. Compounds with Suffixes (Isa. 2:20; Lam 1:7, 5:15, p. 239)]

Robert Gordis, "A Commentary on the Text of Lamentations," *JQR 75th* (1967) 267-286.

Robert Gordis, "Commentary on the Text of Lamentations (Part Two)," *JQR, N.S.,* 58 (1967-68) 14-33.

Lamentations 1:1-22

*Paul Haupt, "Maccabean Elegies," *JBL* 38 (1919) 157-170. [Lam. 1:1-22, pp. 164-170]

Lamentations 1:4

James Moffatt, "Opera Foris. Materials for the Preacher," *Exp, 7th Ser.,* 5 (1908) 568. *[1:4]*

Lamentations 1:12

J. T. S. Stopford, "Notes on Lamentations I. 12," *ET* 18 (1906-07) 526.

James Moffatt, "Opera Foris: Materials for the Preacher," *Exp, 7th Ser.,* 5 (1908) 188-189. *[1:12]*

Lamentations 1:14

Solomon B. Freehof, "Note on Lam. 1:14,"*JQR, N.S.,* 38 (1947-48) 343-344.

Lamentations Chapter 2

*G. A. Smith, "The Desolate City," *Exp, 7th Ser.,* 1 (1906) 320-336. *[Chapter 2]*

Lamentations 2:13

Samuel Daiches, "Lamentations II. 13," *ET* 28 (1916-17) 189.

Lamentations 2:17

*T[heophile] J. Meek, "Hebrew Poetic Structure as a Translation Guide," *JBL* 57 (1938) viii. *[2:17b]*

Lamentations Chapter 3

S. B. Gurewicz, "The Problem of Lamentations III," *ABR* 8 (1960) 19-23.

Lamentations 4:1

J. A. Emerton, "The Meaning of אַבְנֵי־קֹדֶשׁ in Lamentations 4:1," *ZAW* 79 (1967) 233-236.

Lamentations 4:9-12

A. Shaffer, "The Mesopotamian Background of Lamentations 4:9-12," *EI* 8 (1967) 75*.

*A. Shaffer, "New Light on the 'Three-Ply Cord'," *EI* 9 (1969) 138-139. *[English Summary] [4:9-12]*

Lamentations 4:9

A. Cohen, "Lamentations 4:9," *AJSL* 27 (1910-11) 190-191.

A. Guillaume, "A Note on Lam. iv 9," *ALUOS* 4 (1962-63) 47-48.

Lamentations 4:20

B., "Lamentations IV. 20 in the Latin Vulgate," *JSL, 4th Ser.,* 6 (1864-65) 181.

Lamentations Chapter 5

*Samuel Tobias Lachs, "The Date of Lamentations V," *JQR, N.S.,* 57 (1966-67) 46-57.

(§655) *3.5.4.2.6 Studies on Manuscripts of the Book of Lamentations*

§656 *3.5.4.2.7 Exegetical Studies on the Book of Ecclesiastes (Qoheleth)*

Enoch Pond, "Remarks, Exegetical and Practical, on the Book of Ecclesiastes," *BRCR, 3rd Ser.,* 2 (1846) 421-444.

George W. Gilmore, "The Book of Ecclesiastes, in a New Arrangement and Translation," *BW* 22 (1903) 268-283.

Paul   Haupt,   "Ecclesiastes,"   *AJP*   26   (1905)   125-171.

James A. Montgomery, "Notes on Ecclesiastes," *JBL* 43 (1924) 241-244. [(1) 3:1; (2) הבל ורעות רוח; (3) 3:18; (4) 9:15; (5) 10:1; (6) 1:5; (7) 2:8; (8) 3:15; (9) 5:10; (10) 8:10; (11) 9:3; (12) 9:12; (13) 10:9; (14) 11:2; (15) 11:3; (16) 12:11]

H. J. Flowers, "Ecclesiastes, a Translation and Commentary," *R&E* 27 (1930) 421-437.

H. J. Flowers, "The Book of Ecclesiastes—Second Section," *R&E* 28 (1931) 52-74.

Ecclesiastes Chapter 1

C. E. Stowe, "A Lecture on the First Chapter of Ecclesiastes," *BRCR, 3rd Ser.*, 6 (1850) 274-283.

Ecclesiastes 1:1-11

J. J. Stewart Perowne, "Ecclesiastes. Chapter i Verses 1-11.," *Exp, 1st Ser.*, 9 (1879) 409-420.

Ecclesiastes 1:12-18

J. J. Stewart Perowne, "Ecclesiastes. Chapter I. Verses 12-18," *Exp, 1st Ser.*, 10 (1879) 61-74.

Ecclesiastes 1:17

Robert Gordis, "Ecclesiastes 1:17—Its Text and Interpretation," *JBL* 56 (1937) 323-330.

Ecclesiastes 2:1-3

J. J. Stewart Perowne, "Ecclesiastes. Chapter II. Verses 1-3," *Exp, 1st Ser.*, 10 (1879) 165-172.

Ecclesiastes 2:3

Anonymous, "Ecclesiastes II: 3," *ONTS* 11 (1890) 247.

Alan D. Corré, "A reference to Epispasm in Koheleth," *VT* 4 (1954) 416-418. *[2:3]*

Ecclesiastes 2:4-11

J. J. Stewart Perowne, "Ecclesiastes. Chapter II. Verses 4-11," *Exp, 1st Ser.*, 10 (1879) 313-320.

Ecclesiastes 2:8

*George Margoliouth, "Notes on Some Difficult Passages in Qoheleth," *Exp, 8th Ser.*, 26 (1923) 326-335. *[2:8]*

*Leo Jung, "Mis-Translations a Source in Jewish and Christian Lore," *PAAJR* 5 (1933-34) 55-67. [III. *Ashmedia* (Koheleth 2:8), pp. 60-61]

Ecclesiastes 2:12-26

J. J. Stewart Perowne, "Ecclesiastes. Chapter II. Verses 12-26," *Exp, 1st Ser.,* 12 (1880) 70-82.

Ecclesiastes 3:1-8

Anonymous, "Illustration of Ecclesiastes iii. 1-8," *MR* 4 (1821) 18-21.

Ecclesiastes 3:2-8

J. A. Loader, "Qohelet 3:2-8— A Sonet*[sic]* in the Old Testament," *ZAW* 81 (1969) 240-242.

Ecclesiastes 3:5

Edmund F. Sutcliffe, "Questions and Answers. What times had the author of Ecclesiastes in mind when he wrote that there is 'a time to scatter stones and a time to gather' (iii, 5)?" *Scrip* 5 (1952-53) 126-127.

Ecclesiastes 3:11

C. Taylor, "On some verses of Ecclesiastes," *JP* 2 (1869) 269-310. *[3:11]*

T. K. Cheyne, "'He hath set the world in their heart' (Eccles. III. 11)," *ET* 10 (1898-99) 422-423.

*Duncan B. Macdonald, "Old Testament Notes," *JBL* 18 (1899) 212-215. [1. Eccl. 3:11, pp. 212-213]

*George Margoliouth, "Notes on Some Difficult Passages in Qoheleth," *Exp, 8th Ser.,* 26 (1923) 326-335. *[3:11]*

David Max Eichhorn, "The Meaning of Kohelet 3:11," *CCARJ* 9 (1961-62) #3, 33-38.

Virgil H. Todd, "Note on Ecclesiastes 3:11," *CS* 9 (1961-62) #1, 4.

Ecclesiastes 3:18

C. Taylor, "On some verses of Ecclesiastes," *JP* 2 (1869) 269-310. *[3:18]*

W[illiam] A. Irwin, "Eccles. 3:18," *AJSL* 56 (1939) 298-299.

Frank Zimmermann, "On Eccles. 3:18," *AJSL* 58 (1941) 100.

W[illiam] A. Irwin, "A Rejoinder," *AJSL* 58 (1941) 100-101. *[3:18]*

Ecclesiastes 4:4-6

James Moffatt, "Opera Foris. Materials for the Preacher," *Exp, 7th Ser.,* 8 (1909) 187-188. *[4:4-6]*

Ecclesiastes 4:4

*H. Torczyner, *"Semel Ha-qin'ah Ha-maqneh,"* *JBL* 65 (1946) 293-302. [1. Eccl. 4:4, pp. 293-294]

Ecclesiastes 4:10

M[itchell] Dahood, "Scriptio Defectiva in Qoheleth 4, 10a,"*B* 49 (1968) 243.

Ecclesiastes 4:12

*A. Shaffer, "New Light on the 'Three-Ply Cord'," *EI* 9 (1969) 138-139. *[English Summary] [4:12]*

Ecclesiastes 4:13-16

William A. Irwin, "Eccles. 4:13-16," *JNES* 3 (1944) 255-257.

Charles C. Torrey, "The Problem of Ecclesiastes IV 13-16," *VT* 2 (1952) 175-177.

Ecclesiastes 5:19

George A. Barton, "A Text and Interpretation of Ecclesiastes 5:19," *JBL* 27 (1908) 65-66.

Ecclesiastes 6:6-7

*P. R. Ackroyd, "Two Hebrew Notes," *ASTI* 5 (1966-67) 82-87. [(2) מָקוֹם אֶחָד in Ecclesiastes 6:6 and the interpretation of 6:7, pp. 84-86]

Ecclesiastes 7:7

G. Margoliouth, "Studies in Texts. Qoheleth (Ecclesiastes) vii. 7," *Theo* 8 (1924) 228-229.

Ecclesiastes 8:2-9

William A. Irwin, "Ecclesiastes 8:2-9," *JNES* 4 (1945) 130-131.

Ecclesiastes 8:10

G. Margoliouth, "Ecclesiastes viii. 10," *Exp, 9th Ser.,* 1 (1924) 94-102.

J.J.Serrano,"I Saw the Wicked Buried(Eccl 8, 10),"*CBQ* 16(1954) 168-170.

Ch. W. Reines, "Koheleth VIII, 10," *JJS* 5 (1954) 86-87.

Ecclesiastes 9:14

*George Margoliouth, "Notes on Some Difficult Passages in Qoheleth,"
    Exp, 8th Ser., 26 (1923) 326-335. *[9:14]*

Ecclesiastes 10:15

MichaelLeahy,"The Meaning of Ecclesiastes10:15,"*ITQ* 18 (1951) 288-290.

Ecclesiastes 10:20

*George Margoliouth, "Notes on Some Difficult Passages in Qoheleth,"
    Exp, 8th Ser., 26 (1923) 326-335. *[10:20]*

D. WintonThomas, "A Note on בְּמַדָּעֲךָ in Eccles. x. 20," *JTS* 50 (1949) 177.

M[itchell]Dahood,"CanaaniteWordsinQoheleth10,20,"*B*46(1965) 210-212.

Ecclesiastes 11:1-6

Benevolus, "Exposition of Ecclesiastes, XI. 1-6," *QCS* 1 (1819) 119-121.

Ecclesiastes 11:1

Anonymous, "Comparative Translation: Ecclesiastes 11:1. A Study in
    Modernizing the English Bible," *BW* 22 (1903) 139.

Percy P. Stoute, "Bread Upon the Waters," *BS* 107 (1950) 222-226. *[11:1]*

Ecclesiastes 11:5

*James A. Montgomery, "Notes on the Old Testament," *JBL* 31 (1912) 140-
    146. [7. הכל, Eccles 11:5, etc., pp. 143-144]

Ecclesiastes Chapter 12

Tyron Edwards, "Ecclesiastes; Chapter XII," *HR* 20 (1890) 261-262.

Ecclesiastes 12:1-7

Anonymous, "Translation of Ecclesiastes XII. 1-7; with a Brief Explanation of the Nature of the Imagery Employed, and the Sentiment Conveyed by it," *QCS* 8 (1826) 563-565.

W. C. Green, "Ecclesiastes XII. 1-7," *Exp, 5th Ser.*, 2 (1895) 77-80.

Ecclesiastes 12:1

*T. K. Cheyne, "Notes on מַבּוּל, נְפִילִים, etc.," *AJSL* 3 (1886-87) 175-176. [2. Eccl. 12:1, p. 176]

*Paul Haupt, "Well and Field = Wife," *JAOS* 36 (1916) 418-420. *[12:1]*

Ecclesiastes 12:2-5

Michael Leahy, "The Meaning of Ecclesiastes," *ITQ* 19 (1952) 297-300. *[12:2-5]*

Ecclesiastes 12:4-5

Anonymous, "An Explanation of Eccl. 12, 4. 5," *CTM* 5 (1934) 135-136.

Ecclesiastes 12:4

*Paul Haupt, "Critical Notes. III. Assyr. *lam iççûri çabâri* 'Before the birds cheep," *AJSL* 32 (1915-16) 143-144. *[12:4]*

H. L. Ginsberg, "Koheleth 12:4 in the Light of Ugaritic," *Syria* 33 (1956) 99-101.

Ecclesiastes 12:5

John E. Todd, "Caper-berry, Eccles. 12:5," *JBL* 6 (1886) Part 2, 13-26.

George F. Moore, "The Caper-plant and its edible products, with reference to Eccles. XII. 5," *JBL* 10 (1891) 55-64.

Paul Haupt, "Critical Notes. I. Heb. *evyônâ*, 'Soul'," *AJSL* 32 (1915-16) 141-142. *[12:5]*

Ecclesiastes 12:6

A. Marmorstein, "Ecclesiastes XII. 6," *Exp, 8th Ser.,* 20 (1920) 203-207.

J. Edgar Bruns, "The Imagery of Eccles 12:6a," *JBL* 84 (1965) 428-430.

Ecclesiastes 12:8-14

G. Margoliouth, "Ecclesiastes XII. 8-14," *ET* 35 (1923-24) 121-124.

Ecclesiastes 12:11

*Kurt Galling, "The Scepter of Wisdom, A Note on the Gold Sheath of Zendjirli and Ecclesiastes 12:11," *BASOR* #119 (1950) 15-18.

(§657) 3.5.4.2.8 Studies on Manuscripts of the Book of Ecclesiastes (Qoheleth)

§658 3.5.4.2.9 Exegetical Studies on the Book of Esther

Paul Haupt, "Critical Notes on Esther," *AJSL* 24 (1907-08) 97-186.

Esther Chapters 1-3

Jacob Hoschander, "The Book of Esther in the Light of History, Chapters I to III," *JQR, N.S.,* 9 (1918-19) 1-41.

Esther 1:22

Theodor H. Gaster, "Esther 1:22," *JBL* 69 (1950) 381.

Esther 2:19-20

E. E. Kellett, "A Note on Esther II. 19, 20," *ET* 35 (1923-24) 380.

Esther 3:8-9

*Samuel Krauss, "Imprecation Against the Minim in the Synagogue," *JQR* 9 (1896-97) 515-517.

Esther Chapters 4-5

*[Daniel S. Gregory], "The International Lessons in Their Historical and Literary Setting," *CFL, 3rd Ser.,* 14 (1911-12) 357-371. [Esther, chaps. 4-5, pp. 363-364]

Esther Chapter 4

Jacob Hoschander, "The Book of Esther in the Light of History, Chapter IV," *JQR, N.S.,* 10 (1919-20) 81-119.

Esther 4:13-14

Thomas Pryde, "Queen Esther, or the Feast of Lots. Esther 4:13, 14," *ONTS* 13 (1891) 264-269.

Esther 4:14

*Peter R. Ackroyd, "Two Hebrew Notes," *ASTI* 5 (1966-67) 82-86. [(1) אַחֵר מָקוֹם in Esther 4:14, pp. 82-84]

Esther Chapter 5

Jacob Hoschander, "The Book of Esther in the Light of History, Chapter V," *JQR, N.S.,* 11 (1920-21) 307-343.

Esther Chapters 6-7

Jacob Hoschander, "The Book of Esther in the Light of History, Chapters VI, VII," *JQR, N.S.,* 12 (1921-22) 35-55, 151-194.

Esther Chapter 10

David Daube, "The Last Chapter of Esther," *JQR, N.S.,* 37 (1946-47) 139-147.

§659 *3.5.4.2.10 Studies on Manuscripts of the Book of Esther*

Carey A. Moore, "A Greek Witness to a Different Hebrew Text of Esther," *ZAW* 79 (1967) 351-358.

Herbert J. Cook, "The *A* Text of the Greek Versions of the Book of Esther," *ZAW* 81 (1969) 369-376.

(§660) **3.5.5 Exegetical Studies on Several Historical Books**

§661   **3.5.5.1 Exegetical Studies on the Book of Daniel**

*N. N. W., "Version of Daniel ii vii viii ix," *ASRB* 1 (1844-45) 167-180.

Eugene C. Caldwell, "A Kingdom That Shall Stand Forever. Outline Study of the Book of Daniel," *USR* 33 (1921-22) 89-124.

Daniel Chapters 1-6

W. Sibley Towner, "The Poetic Passages of Daniel 1-6," *CBQ* 31 (1969) 317-326.

Daniel Chapters 1-2

L., "On the Apparent Discrepancies in Exodus IX and Daniel I, and II. In reply to the Queries of M. at page 369," *CongML* 2 (1819) 408-409.

Daniel Chapter 1

*[Daniel S. Gregory], "The International Lessons in Their Historical and Literary Setting," *CFL, 3rd Ser.,* 14 (1911-12) 357-371. [Daniel 1:1-21, pp. 357-359]

Daniel 1:1

*T. Nicklin, "Two Chronological Enigmas in the Old Testament," *ET* 35 (1923-24) 168-170. [II. Daniel 1:1 and the reign of Jehoiakim, pp. 169-170]

Daniel 1:3

Michael Stone, "A Note on Daniel i. 3," *ABR* 7 (1959) 69-71.

Daniel Chapter 2

Anonymous, "The Revelation, Daniel II., respecting the Four Great Empires," *TLJ* 13 (1860-61) 276-310.

Edward F. Siegman, "The Stone Hewn from the Mountain (Daniel 2)," *CBQ* 18 (1956) 364-379.

Daniel 2:5

Howard Crosby, "Nebuchadnezzar's Dream," *HR* 18 (1889) 452-453. *[2:5]*

Daniel 2:20

Thos. Laurie, "An Assyrian Precative in Dan. II., 20," *AJSL* 2 (1885-86) 249.

Daniel 2:23

*C. R. Brown, "Note on כְּעַן (Dan. II., 23; Ezra V., 16) כְּעֶנֶת (Ezra IV., 10, 11; VII., 12) כְּעֶת (Ezra IV., 17)," *AJSL* 1 (1884-85) 251.

Daniel 2:25

*Ben Zion Bergman, "*Han'el* in Daniel 2:25 and 6:19," *JNES* 27 (1968) 69-70.

Daniel 2:28

*T. Francis Glasson, "'Visions of Thy Head' (Daniel 2^{28}) The Heart and the Head in Bible Psychology," *ET* 81 (1969-70) 247-248.

Daniel 2:40-43

O. S. Stearns, "The Fourth Kingdom.—Dan. II. 40-43.," *DTQ* 3 (1877) 135-149.

Daniel 2:44

Anonymous, "Who are 'These Kings?'" *BWR* 1 (1877) 305-306. *[2:44]*

Daniel Chapters 3 and 4

Anonymous, "The Golden Image, Daniel III. Nebuchadnezzar's Vision of the Tree, Daniel IV.," *TLJ* 13 (1860-61) 475-511.

Daniel Chapter 3

*Frederic Gardiner, "Various Topics III. The Jew and the Greek," *JBL* 8 (1888) 150-151. *[Chapter 3]*

*John P. Peters, "Notes on the Old Testament," *JBL* 15 (1896) 106-117. [2. The Three Children in the Fiery Furnace (Dan 3; Jer 29:22), pp. 109-111]

*Stanley A. Cook, "The articles of dress in Dan. III.," *JP* 26 (1898-99) 306-313.

*[Daniel S. Gregory], "The International Lessons in Their Historical and Literary Setting," *CFL, 3rd Ser.,* 14 (1911-12) 357-371. [Daniel 3:1-30, p. 358]

Rayner Winterbotham, "The Third Chapter of Daniel," *ET* 28 (1916-17) 167-169.

Max Eichhorn, "Sanhedrin 93a and the Third Chapter of Daniel," *CCARJ* 16 (1969) #2, 24-25.

Daniel 3:5

*John E. H. Thomson, "Dan. III. 5 (7, 10, 15)," *ET* 5 (1893-94) 180-181.

Owen C. Whitehouse, "Daniel III. 5, etc.,"*ET* 5 (1893-94) 284-286, 474-475.

J. E. H. Thomson, "Daniel III. 5," *ET* 5 (1893-94) 382-384.

Phillips Barry, "Daniel 3:5 Sūmpōnyāh," *JBL* 27 (1908) 99-127.

*Phillips Barry, "Psanterin According to Daniel III. 5," *Monist* 20 (1910) 402-413.

Daniel 3:7

*John E. H. Thomson, "Dan. III. 5 (7, 10, 15)," *ET* 5 (1893-94) 180-181.

Daniel 3:10

*John E. H. Thomson, "Dan. III. 5 (7, 10, 15)," *ET* 5 (1893-94) 180-181.

Daniel 3:15

*John E. H. Thomson, "Dan. III. 5 (7, 10, 15)," *ET* 5 (1893-94) 180-181.

Daniel 3:16-18

Donald C. Cox, "An Interpretation of Daniel 3:16-18," *CCBQ* 11 (1968) #1, 20-27.

Daniel 3:21-24

M. Sprengling, "Daniel 3:21-24," *AJSL* 37 (1920-21) 132-135.

Daniel 3:51b-52

*W. Baars, "An Ancient Greek Fragment of Daniel 3:51b-52," *Text* 6 (1968) 132-133. *[Munich, Bavarian State Library, MS Gr. 610, Nr. 7.]*

Daniel 4:14

*J. J. Rabinowitz, "A Legal Formula in the Susa Tablets, in an Egyptian Document of the Twelfth Dynasty, in the Aramaic Papyri, and in the Book of Daniel [4, 14]," *B* 36 (1955) 223-226.

Daniel 4:30

*H. L. Ginsberg, "Notes on Some Old Aramaic Texts," *JNES* 18 (1959) 143-149. [I., B. "Eagles' Hair and Birds' Claws" - Dan. 4:30, p. 145]

Daniel Chapters 5 and 6

C. Boutflower, "The Historical Value of Daniel V and VI," *JTS* 17 (1915-16) 43-60.

Daniel Chapter 5

Anonymous, "The Handwriting on the Wall, Daniel V.," *TLJ* 13 (1860-61) 529-538.

H. H. Rowley, "The Historicity of the Fifth Chapter of Daniel," *JTS* 32 (1930-31) 12-31.

Daniel 5:1-31

*[Daniel S. Gregory], "The International Lessons in Their Historical and Literary Setting," *CFL, 3rd Ser.,* 14 (1911-12) 357-371. [Daniel 5:1-31, p. 364]

Daniel 5:1

Charles Boutflower, "'Belshazzar the King' (Dan. V. 1)," *ET* 36 (1924-25) 526-527.

Daniel 5:2-3

*Claude R. Conder, "Notes on New Discoveries," *PEFQS* 41 (1909) 266-275. [Shegal (Psalm 45:9; Dan. 5:2, 3, 23), p. 275]

Daniel 5:5ff.

J[ohn] D. Prince, "Assyro-Babylonian Parallels to Dan. v. 5ff.," *JBL* 22 (1903) 32-40.

Daniel 5:12

J. A. Emerton, "The Particles in Daniel v. 12," *ZAW* 72 (1960) 262-263.

Daniel 5:23

*Claude R. Conder, "Notes on New Discoveries," *PEFQS* 41 (1909) 266-275. [Shegal (Psalm 45:9; Dan. 5:2, 3, 23), p. 275]

Daniel 5:25-28

*Solomon Gandz, "Mene Mene Tekel Upharsin, a chapter in Babylonian mathematics," *Isis* 26 (1936) 82-94. *[5:25-28]*

Daniel 5:25f.

Frank Zimmerman*[sic]*, "The Writing on the Wall: Dan. 5.25f.," *JQR, N.S.,* 55 (1964-65) 201-207.

Daniel 5:25

William Aldis Wright, "On the inscription in Daniel v. 25," *JP* 7 (1876-77) 138-139.

Francis Brown, "Daniel, v, 25," *AJA, O.S.* 2 (1886) 431.

A. H. Sayce, "Requests and Replies," *ET* 4 (1892-93) 80. [Daniel 5:25 - "Mene, mene, tekel, upharsin"]

John D. Prince, "On the writing on the wall at Belshazzar's feast (Daniel v. 25)," *JAOS* 15 (1893) clxxxii-clxxxix.

*John P. Peters, "Notes on the Old Testament," *JBL* 15 (1896) 106-117. [4. Mene, Mene, Tekel, Upharsin (Dan. 5:25), pp. 114-117]

W. D. Morris, "'Mene, Mene, Tekel, Upharsin' (Dan. v. 25)," *ET* 35 (1923-24) 226.

Antonie De Guglielmo, "Dan. 5:25—An Example of a double Literal Sense," *CBQ* 11 (1949) 202-206.

Daniel 5:30-31

†P. P. Saydon, "The Interpretation of Daniel v, 30-31," *Scrip* 4 (1949-51) 362-363.

Daniel 5:30

*Howard Crosby, "Light on Important Texts. No. XVIII," *HR* 6 (1881-82) 472. *[5:30]*

Andrew Craig Robinson, "The Fall of Babylon and Daniel v. 30," *JTVI* 46 (1914) 9-20, 29-30. (Discussion pp. 20-26) (Communications by J. J. Lias, pp. 26-27; John Schwartz Jr., p. 27; E. Walter Maunder, pp. 28-29)

Daniel 5:31

*I. W. Bosanquet, "Who was Ahasuerus of the Seed of the Medes, whose Son Darius was set over the realm of the Chaldeans, when about sixty-two years old? *Dan.* v. 31; ix. 1," *JSL, 3rd Ser.,* 4 (1856-57) 452-462.

H. F. D. Sparks, "On the Origin of 'Darius the Mede' at Daniel v. 31," *JTS* 47 (1946) 41-47.

Daniel Chapter 6

*[Daniel S. Gregory], "The International Lessons in Their Historical Setting," *CFL, 3rd Ser.,* 14 (1911-12) 357-371. [Daniel 6:1-28, p. 359]

James A. Montgomery, "The 'two youths' in the LXX to Dan. 6," *JAOS* 41 (1921) 316-317.

Daniel Chapters 7-12

R. G. Finch, "The Apocalypses of Daniel vii.-xii.," *IJA* #48 (1917) 5-8.

Daniel Chapter 7

Edward Winthrop, "The Papal Power identified with the Little Horn of the Fourth Beast. Daniel VII," *TLJ* 4 (1851-52) 116-133.

J. Oswald, "Notes on Prophecy. Daniel 7th Chap.," *ER* 4 (1852-53) 254-267.

J. Oswald, "Notes on Prophecy. *Daniel—Seventh Chapter.*," *ER* 5 (1853-54) 564-578.

C. Lattey, "The Beasts of Dan. vii," *ET* 30 (1918-19) 281.

*A. T. Cadoux, "The Son of Man," *ICMM* 18 (1921-22) 202-214. [Dan. chap. 7, pp. 202-203]

Millar Burrows, "Daniel 7 and the Vocabulary of Jesus," *JBL* 55 (1936) ix.

Ziony Zevit, "The Structure and Individual Elements of Daniel 7," *ZAW* 80 (1968) 385-396.

Daniel 7:1-14

Arnold B. Rhodes, "The Kingdoms of Men and the Kingdom of God. *A Study of Daniel 7:1-14,*" *Interp* 15 (1961) 411-430.

Daniel 7:5

J. Oswald, "Notes on Prophecy. *Notes on the kingdom referred to in verse fifth of Daniel, seventh chapter,*" *ER* 4 (1852-53) 369-385. *[7:5]*

LeRoy Waterman, "A Gloss on Darius the Mede in Daniel 7:5," *JBL* 65 (1946) 59-61.

Richard M. Frank, "The Description of the 'Bear' in Dn 7,5," *CBQ* 21 (1959) 505-507.

Daniel 7:7

J. Oswald, "Notes on Prophecy. *Notes on the kingdom referred to in verse seventh of Daniel, seventh chapter,*" *ER* 4 (1852-53) 568-574. *[7:7]*

Daniel 7:8

J. Oswald, "Notes on Prophecy. *Notes on the kingdom or power signified by the 'little horn' in verse 8, &c.,*" *ER* 5 (1853-54) 49-60. *[7:8]*

J. Oswald, "Notes on Prophecy. *The kingdom, or power signified by the 'little horn' in verse 8, Dan., chap. 7.,*" *ER* 5 (1853-54) 324-337.

Daniel 7:13f.

Julian Morgenstern, "The 'Son of Man' of Daniel 7:13f.: A New Interpretation," *JBL* 80 (1961) 65-77.

Daniel 7:14

J. Oswald, "Notes on Prophecy. *Daniel—Seventh Chapter. The Kingdom spoken of in verse fourteen, &c.*," *ER* 6 (1854-55) 194-209.

Daniel Chapters 8-12

*Frank Zimmermann, "The Aramaic Original of Daniel 8-12," *JBL* 57 (1938) 255-272.

Daniel 8:2

Leroy Waterman, "A Note on Daniel 8:2," *JBL* 66 (1947) 319-320.

Daniel 8:5ff.

Samuel Krauss, "Some Remarks on Daniel 8:5ff.," *HUCA* 15 (1940) 305-311.

Daniel 8:9-14

George F. Moore, "Daniel 8:9-14," *JBL* 15 (1896) 193-197.

Daniel 8:11-12

J. Dyneley Prince, "On Daniel 8:11, 12," *JBL* 17 (1898) 203-204.

Daniel 8:12

*C. G. Ozanne, "Three Textual Problems in Daniel," *JTS, N.S.,* 16 (1965) 445-448. [I. Dan. 8:12, pp. 445-446]

Daniel Chapter 9

Anonymous, "The Seventy Weeks of Daniel," *BWR* 1 (1877) 318-320. *[Chapter 9]*

C. E. Lindberg, "The Seventy Weeks (Dan. IX.)," *TTKF* 3 (1901) 53-62.

Cornelius Walker, "A Chapter in Prophecy: The Seventies and Sevens," *CFL, 3rd Ser.,* 4 (1906) 10-23. *[Chapter 9]*

R. G. Finch, "The Seventy Years and Seventy Weeks of Dan. ix," *IJA* #47 (1916) 59-61.

B. W. Jones, "The Prayer in Daniel IX," *VT* 18 (1968) 488-493.

Daniel 9:1

I. W. Bosanquet, "Who was Darius the Son of Ahasuerus of the Seed of the Medes?—Daniel IX. 1," *JSL, 3rd Ser.,* 2 (1855-56) 393-403.

*I. W. Bosanquet, "Who was Ahasuerus of the Seed of the Medes, whose Son Darius was set over the realm of the Chaldeans, when about sixty-two years old? *Dan.* v. 31; ix. 1," *JSL, 3rd Ser.,* 4 (1856-57) 452-462.

Daniel 9:24-27

Anonymous, "Daniel's Seventy Weeks Prediction. Dan. ix. 24-27," *ATG* 3 (1836-37) 1-8.

Anonymous, "*Identification of the Historical Periods comprised within the 'Seventy Weeks' in Daniel* ix, 24-27," *MR* 32 (1850) 498-510.

Josiah Pratt, "Prophecy of the Weeks in Daniel IX. 24-27," *JSL, 4th Ser.,*10 (1866-67) 462-468.

Franke Parker, "Prophecy of the Weeks in Daniel IX. 24-27," *JSL, 5th Ser.,* 1 (1867) 476-481; 2 (1867-68) 438-455.

Anonymous, "Note on Dan. IX. 24-27," *BWR* 3 (1881) 341-347.

Frederic Gardiner, "The Revised Version of Dan. 9:24-27," *JBL* 5 (1885) 75, 76.

Theo. Graebner, "The Seventy Weeks of Daniel. (Dan. 9, 24-27.)," *TTD* 5 (1903) 105-118.

John Theodore Mueller, "Notes on the Seventy Weeks in Daniel's Prophecy 9:24-27," *CTM* 17 (1946) 368-371.

Daniel 9:26

A. Van Hoonacker, "Daniel IX. 26. וְאֵין לֹו," *ET* 20 (1908-09) 380-381.

*C. G. Ozanne, "Three Textual Problems in Daniel," *JTS, N.S.*, 16 (1965) 445-448. [II. Dan. 9:26, pp. 446-447]

Daniel 9:27

Anonymous, "Who shall 'Confirm Covenant'?" *BWR* 1 (1877) 354-355. *[9:27]*

Daniel 11:30-12:10

*H. L. Ginsberg, "The Oldest Interpretation of the Suffering Servant," *JBL* 72 (1953) xxii. *[11:30-12:10]*

Daniel Chapter 11

*A. M. Gazov-Ginzberg, "The Structure of the Army of the Sons of Light. Appendix," *RdQ* 5 (1964-66) 176. *[The Kittim and the influence of Daniel Chapter 11 on the scroll col. 1]*

Daniel 11:4

William Duff McHardy, "The Peshitta Text of Daniel XI. 4," *JTS* 49 (1948) 56-57.

Daniel 11:18

*C. G. Ozanne, "Three Textual Problems in Daniel," *JTS, N.S.*, 16 (1965) 445-448. [III. Dan. 11:18, pp. 447-448]

Daniel 11:22

H. H. Rowley, "The 'Prince of the Covenant' in Daniel, XI. 22," *ET* 55 (1943-44) 24-27.

Daniel 12:1-3

R. H. Altus, "Daniel 12:1-3," *AusTR* 10 (1939) 65-70.

Daniel 12:1-2

J. F. Boerger, "Once More Dan. 12, 1. 2.," *CTM* 4 (1933) 784-785.

Daniel 12:2-3

Willis J. Beecher, "Daniel 12:2, 3," *BW* 14 (1899) 54-57.

Daniel 12:2

Anonymous, "National Resurrection," *BWR* 1 (1877) 289-291. *[12:2]*

Nathaniel West, "Daniel and the First Resurrection," *PR* 5 (1884) 134-153. *[12:2]*

Daniel 12:3

Robert Dick Wilson, "The Word הַזֹּהִיר in Daniel xii. 3.," *PTR* 17 (1919) 128-133.

Daniel 12:4

C. W. Emmet, "'Many Shall Run To and Fro' (Dan. XII. 4)," *ET* 20 (1908-09) 278-279.

Edward C. Porter, "A Remarkable Prophecy," *CFL, 3rd Ser.,* 31 (1925) 355-356. *[12:4]*

D. Winton Thomas, "Note on הַדַּעַת in Daniel XII. 4," *JTS, N.S.,* 6 (1955) 266.

*L. C. Allen, "Isaiah LIII. 11 and its Echoes," *VE* 1 (1962) 24-28. *[12:4]*

Daniel 12:11-12

B. Hunt, "A Short Note on Daniel 12:11-12," *Scrip* 9 (1957) 84-85.

§662 *3.5.5.2 Studies on Manuscripts of the Book of Daniel*

J. A. Montgomery, "The Hexaplaric Strata in the Greek Texts of Daniel," *JBL* 44 (1925) 289-302.

C. D. Benjamin, "Collation of Holmes-Parsons 23(Venetus) - 62 -147 in Daniel from Photographic Copies," *JBL* 44 (1925) 303-326.

H. S. Gehman, "The 'Polyglot' Arabic Text of Daniel and its Affinities," *JBL* 44 (1925) 327-352.

H. S. Gehman, "The Sahidic and the Bohairic Versions of the Book of Daniel," *JBL* 46 (1927) 279-330.

*W. Baars, "An Ancient Greek Fragment of Daniel 3:51b-52," *Text* 6 (1968) 132-133. *[Munich, Bavarian State Library, MS Gr. 610, Nr. 7.]*

§663   *3.5.5.3 Exegetical Studies on the Book of Ezra*

*A. F. Kirkpatrick, "The Revised Version of the Old Testament:—The Book of Ezra," *Exp, 3rd Ser.,* 4 (1886) 117-118. *[1:3 marg.; 4:2, 8 marg., 10ff., 14; 5:4; 7:12; 10:15]*

Ezra 1:1-4:24

George S. Goodspeed, "The Return of the Exiles," *BW* 1 (1893) 40-48. *[1:1-4:24]*

Ezra Chapters 1-4

*[Daniel S. Gregory], "The International Lessons in Their Historical and Literary Setting," *CFL, 3rd Ser.,* 14 (1911-12) 357-371. [Ezra, Chaps 1-4, pp. 360-362]

Ezra Chapters 1 and 2

*[Daniel S. Gregory], "The International Lessons in Their Historical and Literary Setting," *CFL, 3rd Ser.,* 14 (1911-12) 357-371. [Ezra 1-2, pp. 360-361]

Julius A. Bewer, "The Gap Between Ezra, Chapters 1 and 2," *AJSL* 36 (1919-20) 18-26.

Ezra Chapter 1

*C[harles] C. Torrey, "Old Testament Notes," *JBL* 16 (1897) 166-170. [2. The Missing Conclusion of Ezra i, pp. 168-170]

Elias J. Bickerman, "The Edict of Cyrus in Ezra 1," *JBL* 65 (1946) 244-275.

Ezra 1:4

M. D. Goldman, "Lexicographic Notes on Exegesis. The True Meaning of Ezra I, 4," *ABR* 1 (1951) 58.

H. L. Ginsberg, "Ezra 1:4," *JBL* 79 (1960) 167-169.

Ezra Chapter 2

*Kurt Galling, "The 'Gōlā list' According to Ezra 2 // Nehemiah 7," *JBL* 70 (1951) 149-158.

*A. L. Allrik, "The Lists of Zerubbabel (Nehemiah 7 and Ezra 2) and the Hebrew Numeral Notation," *BASOR* #136 (1954) 21-27.

*Ralph Walter Klein, "Old Readings in I Esdras: The List of Returnees from Babylon (Ezra 2 // Nehemiah 7)," *HTR* 62 (1969) 99-107.

Ezra Chapters 3 and 4

*[Daniel S. Gregory], "The International Lessons in Their Historical and Literary Setting," *CFL, 3rd Ser.,* 14 (1911-12) 357-371. [Ezra 3-4, pp. 361-362]

Ezra 4:4

R.J.Coggins, "The Interpretation of Ezra IV. 4,"*JTS, N.S.,* 16 (1965) 124-127.

Ezra 4:6-7

Edward Biley, "On Ahasuerus and Artaxerxes of Ezra IV. 6, 7," *JSL, 4th Ser.,* 9 (1866) 410-422.

Ezra 4:9

N. H. Torczyner, "Aryans and Non-Aryan Persians in the Bible *(Ezra IV, 9),*" *BIES* 14 (1947-48) #1/2, I.

Ezra 4:1-11

*C. R. Brown, "Note on כְּעַן (Dan. II., 23; Ezra V., 16) כְּעֶנֶת (Ezra IV., 10, 11; VII., 12) כְּעֶת (Ezra IV., 17)," *AJSL* 1 (1884-85) 251.

Ezra 4:12

*G. C. Tuland, "'Uššayyă' and 'Uššarnâ: A Clarification of Terms, Date, and Text," *JNES* 17 (1958) 269-275. *[4:12]*

Ezra 4:17

*C. R. Brown, "Note on כְּעַן (Dan. II., 23; Ezra V., 16) כְּעֶנֶת (Ezra IV., 10, 11; VII., 12) כְּעֶת (Ezra IV., 17)," *AJSL* 1 (1884-85) 251.

Ezra 5:3

*G. C. Tuland, "'Uššayyă' and 'Uššarnâ: A Clarification of Terms, Date, and Text," *JNES* 17 (1958) 269-275. *[5:3]*

*Sigmund Mowinckel, "אֲשַׁרְנָא Ezr. 5:3, 9," *ST* 19 (1965) 130-135.

Ezra 5:8

T. Witton Davies, "'Stones of Rolling'," *ET* 21 (1909-10) 283. *[5:8]*

Ezra 5:9

*G. C. Tuland, "ʾUššayÿaʾ and ʾUššarnâ: A Clarification of Terms, Date, and Text," *JNES* 17 (1958) 269-275. *[5:9]*

*Sigmund Mowinckel, "אֲשַׁרְנָא Ezr. 5:3, 9," *ST* 19 (1965) 130-135.

Ezra 5:16

*C. R. Brown, "Note on כְּעַן (Dan. II., 23; Ezra V., 16) כְּעֶנֶת (Ezra IV., 10, 11; VII., 12) כְּעֶת (Ezra IV., 17)," *AJSL* 1 (1884-85) 251.

*G. C. Tuland, "ʾUššayÿaʾ and ʾUššarnâ: A Clarification of Terms, Date, and Text," *JNES* 17 (1958) 269-275. *[5:16]*

Ezra Chapter 6

*G. G. Garner, "*Writing and the Bible:* Gods Stolen and Restored," *AT* 2 (1957-58) #4, 8-10. *[Chapter 6]*

Ezra 6:3

*G. C. Tuland, "ʾUššayÿaʾ and ʾUššarnâ: A Clarification of Terms, Date, and Text," *JNES* 17 (1958) 269-275. *[6:3]*

Ezra Chapter 7

*[Daniel S. Gregory], "The International Lessons in Their Historical and Literary Setting," *CFL, 3rd Ser.,* 14 (1911-12) 357-371. [Ezra 7:1-28, p. 365]

Ezra 7:12

*C. R. Brown, "Note on כְּעַן (Dan. II., 23; Ezra V., 16) כְּעֶנֶת (Ezra IV., 10, 11; VII., 12) כְּעֶת (Ezra IV., 17)," *AJSL* 1 (1884-85) 251.

Ezra 7:26

Z. W. Falk, "Ezra VII 26," *VT* 9 (1959) 88-89.

Ezra 8:17

*Laurence E. Browne, "A Jewish Sanctuary in Babylonia," *JTS* 17 (1915-16) 400-401. *[8:17]*

Ezra 10:6

J. R. Porter, "Son of Grandson (Ezra X. 6)?" *JTS, N.S.,*17 (1966) 54-67.

Ezra 10:27

*Joseph Offord, "Arza and Aziza, and other Archæological Notes," *SBAP* 23 (1901) 244-247. [Ezra 10:27, p. 245]

(§664) *3.5.5.4 Studies on Manuscripts of the Book of Ezra*

§665 *3.5.5.5 Exegetical Studies on the Book of Nehemiah*

A. F. Kirkpatrick, "The Revised Version of the Old Testament:—The Book of Nehemiah," *Exp, 3rd Ser.,* 4 (1886) 118-119. *[3:8; 4:2; 4:23; 6:11; 9:17]*

Nehemiah Chapter 1

*[Daniel S. Gregory], "The International Lessons in Their Historical and Literary Setting," *CFL, 3rd Ser.,* 14 (1911-12) 357-371. [Neh. 1:-11, pp. 365-366]

Nehemiah Chapters 2-4

*[Daniel S. Gregory], "The International Lessons in Their Historical and Literary Setting," *CFL, 3rd Ser.,* 14 (1911-12) 357-371. [Neh. 2-4, p. 367]

Nehemiah 2:8-10

*Millar Burrows, "Notes on Judges 3:8, 10; Neh. 2:8, 10; 3:26," *JBL* 53 (1934) xii.

Nehemiah 2:12-15

Theodore F. Wright, "Nehemiah's Night Ride (Neh. 2:12-15)," *JBL* 15 (1896) 129-134.

T. F. Wright, "Notes by Professor T. F. Wright, Ph.D. I. Nehemiah's Night Ride (ii, 12-15)," *PEFQS* 28 (1896) 172-173. (Note by Geo. St. Clair, pp. 262-263)

Millar Burrows, "Nehemiah's Tour of Inspection," *BASOR* #64 (1936) 11-21. *[2:12-15]*

Nehemiah 2:13-15

George St. Clair, "Nehemiah's Night-Ride," *PEFQS* 20 (1888) 46-48. *[2:13-15]*

Nehemiah 2:13

C. Schick, "The Dragon Well," *PEFQS* 30 (1898) 203-232. *[2:13]*

Ph. Baldensperger, "The Dragon Well," *PEFQS* 31 (1899) 57. *[2:13]*

John Thomas, "Note on the 'Dragon Well'," *PEFQS* 31 (1899) 57-58. *[2:13]*

Nehemiah 2:19

*Frank M. Cross Jr., "Geshem the Arabian, Enemy of Nehemiah," *BA* 18 (1955) 46-47. *[2:19]*

*Anonymous, "Geshem the Arab," *AT* 1 (1956-57) #3, 13. *[2:19]*

Nehemiah Chapter 3

*W. F. Birch, "Nehemiah's Wall and David's Tomb," *PEFQS* 11 (1879) 176-179. [The Course of the Wall. (Neh. iii.), pp. 177-179]

Nehemiah 3:8

C. G. Tuland, "ʿzb in Nehemiah 3:8," *AUSS* 5 (1967) 158-180.

Nehemiah 3:15-16

*W.F.Birch,"The Pool that was Made,"*PEFQS* 22 (1890) 204-208.*[3:15-16]*

Nehemiah 3:15

*Theodore F. Wright, "Stairs of the City of David, Neh. 3:15; 12:37," *JBL* 16 (1897) 171-174.

*Caleb Hauser, "Mizpeh and Mizpah," *PEFQS* 42 (1910) 126-131. [(4) Mizpeh (Neh. iii, 15), pp. 130-131]

Nehemiah 3:19

*Stanley A. Cook, "Notes on I Kings X. 25; Neh. III. 19," *ET* 10 (1898-99) 279-281.

Nehemiah 3:26

*Millar Burrows, "Notes on Judges 3:8, 10; Neh. 2:8, 10; 3:26," *JBL* 53 (1934) xii.

Nehemiah 3:33-37

Millar Burrows, "The Origin of Neh. 3:33-37," *AJSL* 52 (1935-36) 235-244.

Nehemiah 4:6

*Joseph Parker, "Notes on Scripture Passages," *ERG, 9th Ser.,* 3 (1887-88) 33-37. [III. Neh. 4:6, pp. 36-37]

Nehemiah 4:23

H. J. Warner, "A Simple Solution of Nehemiah IV. 23 (Heb. Verse 17) שֶׁלְחוֹ הַמָּיִם," *ET* 63 (1951-52) 322.

Nehemiah 5:11

*[Daniel S. Gregory], "The International Lessons in Their Historical and Literary Setting," *CFL, 3rd Ser.,* 14 (1911-12) 357-371. [Neh. 5, pp. 367-368]

*E. Neufeld, "The Rate of Interest and the Text of Nehemiah 5.11," *JQR, N.S.,* 64 (1953-54) 194-204.

Nehemiah 5:13

J. De Zwaan, "Shaking out the Lap. Nehemiah v. 13," *Exp, 7th Ser.,* 5 (1908) 249-252.

Nehemiah 6:1ff.

*Frank M. Cross Jr., "Geshem the Arabian, Enemy of Nehemiah," *BA* 18 (1955) 46-47. *[6:1ff.]*

Nehemiah 6:2

R. Schiemann, "Covenanting with the Princes: Neh VI 2," *VT* 27 (1967) 367-369.

Nehemiah Chapter 7

*Kurt Galling, "The 'Gōlā list' According to Ezra 2 // Nehemiah 7," *JBL* 70 (1951) 149-158.

*A. L. Allrik, "The Lists of Zerubbabel (Nehemiah 7 and Ezra 2) and the Hebrew Numeral Notation," *BASOR* #136 (1954) 21-27.

*Ralph Walter Klein, "Old Readings in I Esdras: The List of Returnees from Babylon (Ezra 2 // Nehemiah 7)," *HTR* 62 (1969) 99-107.

Nehemiah Chapters 8-10

Victor C. Frank, "Ezra's Bible School. Nehemiah 8-10," *CTM* 21 (1950) 129-132.

Nehemiah Chapters 8-10:33

*[Daniel S. Gregory], "The International Lessons in Their Historical Setting," *CFL, 3rd Ser.,* 14 (1911-12) 357-371. [Neh. 8-10:33, pp. 368]

Nehemiah Chapter 9

Adam C. Welch, "The Source of Nehemiah IX," *ZAW* 47 (1929) 130-137.

Nehemiah 12:31-43

Millar Burrows, "The Topography of Nehemiah 12:31-43," *JBL* 54 (1935) 29-39.

Nehemiah 12:31-39

Kemper Fullerton, "The Procession of Nehemiah. Neh. 12:31-39," *JBL* 38 (1919) 171-179.

Nehemiah 12:36

N. H. Snaith, "Nehemiah XII 36," *VT* 17 (1967) 243.

Nehemiah 12:37

*Theodore F. Wright, "Stairs of the City of David, Neh. 3:15; 12:37," *JBL* 16 (1897) 171-174.

§666 *3.5.5.6 Studies on Manuscripts of the Book of Nehemiah*

H. H. Howorth, "Some Unconventional Views on the Text of the Bible IV. *The Septuagint Text of the Book of Nehemiah*," *SBAP* 24 (1902) 332-340.

H. H. Howorth, "Some Unconventional Views on the Text of the Bible V. *The Septuagint Text of Nehemiah*," *SBAP* 25 (1903) 15-22, 90-98.

*Charles C. Torrey, "Portions of First Esdras and Nehemiah in the Syro-Hexaplar Version," *AJSL* 23 (1906-07) 65-74.

(§667) *3.5.5.7 Exegetical Studies on the Books of Chronicles*

§668   *3.5.5.7.1 Exegetical Studies on 1 Chronicles*

*A. F. Kirkpatrick, "The Revised Version of the Old Testament:—The First Book of Chronicles," *Exp, 3rd Ser.,* 4 (1886) 112-115. *[2:23; 3:17; 4:17, 18, 41; 6:28, 57; 11:11; 12:14; 16:7; 21:1; 26:18, 20; 27:32; 28:12; 29:7]*

1 Chronicles Chapters 1-7

Henry L. Gilbert, "The Forms of the Names in 1 Chronicles 1-7 compared with Those in Parallel Passages of the Old Testament," *AJSL* 13 (1896-97) 279-298.

1 Chronicles 1:43-50

*J. R. Bartlett, "The Edomite King-List of Genesis XXXVI. 31-39 and I Chron. I. 43-50," *JTS, N.S.,* 16 (1965) 301-314.

1 Chronicles 2:55

S. Talmon, ""המה הקינים הבאים מחמת אבי בית רכב"" (1 Chr. 2:55)," *EI* 5 (1958) 90*.

S. Talmon, ‫"ביתרכב‬ ‫אבי‬ ‫מחמת‬ ‫הבאים‬ ‫הקינים‬ ‫המה‬" 1 Chron. ii, 55,"
IEJ 10 (1960) 174-180.

*S. Abramsky, "The House of Rechab," *EI* 8 (1967) 76*. *[2:55]*

1 Chronicles 3:24

Eb. Nestle, "The 'Dictionary of the Bible': Abiud," *ET* 14 (1902-03) 334.
[3:24]

Eb. Nestle, "The 'Dictionary of the Bible.' Abiud," *ET* 19 (1907-08) 284.
[3:24]

1 Chronicles 4:9-10

*John Campbell, "Jabez," *BFER* 29 (1880) 291-313. *[4:9-10]*

1 Chronicles 4:12

*S. Abramsky, "The House of Rechab," *EI* 8 (1967) 76*. *[4:12]*

1 Chronicles 4:23

R. A. Stewart Macalister, "The Royal Potters. I Chron. IV. 23," *ET* 16
(1904-05) 379-380.

1 Chronicles 6:16-38

E. W., "Remarks on 1 Chron vi. 16-38," *JSL, 2nd Ser.,* 2 (1852) 195-202.

1 Chronicles 7:6ff.

*J. Marquart, "The Genealogies of Benjamin," *JQR* 14 (1901-02) 343-351.
[7:6ff.]

1 Chronicles 7:20ff.

*H. W. Hogg, "The Ephraim Genealogy," *JQR* 13 (1900-01) 147-154.
[7:20ff.]

1 Chronicles 7:24

*Anonymous, "Uzzen-Sherah; and Israel's Right to Canaan," *CongR* 1
(1861) 472-489. *[7:24]*

1 Chronicles 7:29

*B. D. Zaphrir (Frimorgen), "'Even Three Countries'," *BIES* 14 (1947-48) #3/4, II. *[7:29]*

1 Chronicles Chapter 8

*H. W. Hogg, "The Genealogy of Benjamin: A Criticism of 1 Chronicles VIII," *JQR* 11 (1898-99) 102-114.

1 Chronicles 8:1ff.

*J. Marquart, "The Genealogies of Benjamin," *JQR* 14 (1901-02) 343-351. *[8:1ff.]*

1 Chronicles 10:3-5

Albert A. Isaacs, "The Difficulties of Scripture. *1 Chronicles* x. 3-5," *EN* 2 (1890) 365-367.

1 Chronicles 10:10

*Claude R. Conder, "Notes on New Discoveries," *PEFQS* 41 (1909) 266-275. [Dagon (1 Chron. 10:10; see 1 Sam. 5:4), p. 274]

1 Chronicles Chapters 11 and 12

Willis J. Beecher, "The Added Section in I Chron. XI.-XII.," *CFL, 3rd Ser.,* 1 (1904) 247-250.

1 Chronicles 11:8-9

Q., "Various Versions of 1 Chronicles XI. 8, 9," *JSL, 4th Ser.,* 7 (1865) 220.

1 Chronicles Chapter 13

*N. H. Tur-Sinai, "The Ark of God at Beit Shemesh (1 Sam. VI) and Peres 'Uzza (2 Sam VI; 1 Chron. XIII)," *VT* 1 (1951) 275-286.

1 Chronicles 16:29

*P. R. Ackroyd, "Some Notes on the Psalms," *JTS, N.S.,* 17 (1966) 392-399. [3. The interpretation of קֹדֶשׁ הַדְרַת (*Ps. xxix. 2, xcvi. 9; I Chron. xvi. 29; 2 Chron. xx. 21*), pp. 393-396]

1 Chronicles 17:17

Shlomo Marenof, "A Note on I Chron. 17:17," *AJSL* 53 (1936-37) 47.

1 Chronicles Chapter 19

*John D. Davis, "Medeba or the Waters of Rabbah," *PTR* 20 (1922) 305-310. *[Chapters 19]*

1 Chronicles 19:2

*T. K. Cheyne, "Textual Criticism in the Service of Archaeology," *ET* 10 (1898-99) 238-240. [4. 1 Chron. 19:2, p. 240]

1 Chronicles Chapter 20

William H. Bates, "The Rabbah 'Atrocity'," *CFL, 3rd Ser.,* 27 (1921) 288. *[Chapter 20]*

1 Chronicles 20:3

Anonymous, "David's Character Vindicated," *CFL, 3rd Ser.,* 27 (1921) 356-357. *[20:3] (Editorial)*

1 Chronicles Chapter 21

*Luke Walker, "The Threshing Floor of Araunah," *NB* 9 (1928) 87-95. *[Chapter 21]*

1 Chronicles 21:1-17

James Walker, "David's Numbering the People. 1 Chron. XXI, 1 to 17," *ERG, 8th Ser.,* 4 (1885-86) 279-285.

1 Chronicles 22:2

*Henry Preserved Smith, "Old Testament Notes," *JBL* 24 (1905) 27-30. [IV. 1 Chronicles 22:2, p. 29]

1 Chronicles Chapters 23-26

*M. Berlin, "Notes on Genealogies of the Tribe of Levi in 1 Chron. XXIII—XXVI," *JQR* 12 (1899-1900) 291-298.

1 Chronicles 28:31

*H. J. Katzenstein, "The Royal Steward (*Asher al ha-Bayith*)," *IEJ* 10 (1960) 149-154. *[28:31]*

1 Chronicles 29:11

J. Coert Rylaarsdam, "The Recovery of Relevance," *Crit* 5 (1965-66) Winter, 13-16. *[29:11]*

1 Chronicles 29:22

Willis J. Beecher, "Note on the proper paragraph division in 1 Chron. 29:22," *JBL* 5 (1885) 73-75.

§669 **3.5.5.7.2 Exegetical Studies on 2 Chronicles**

A. F. Kirkpatrick, "The Revised Version of the Old Testament:—The Second Book of the Chronicles," *Exp, 3rd Ser.*, 4 (1886) 115-117. *[1:5, 13; 2:13; 11:15; 19:8; 20:1, 2, 25, 34; 24:27; 33:11, 19]*

*A. Kelber, "The chronology of 3 and 4 Kings and 2 Paralipomenon," *B* 2 (1921) 3-29, 170-205.

2 Chronicles 1:7-12

Holland Jones, "Sermon Study on 2 Chron. 1:7-12 for the Eighteenth Sunday After Trinity," *CTM* 22 (1951) 592-599.

2 Chronicles 1:10

*J. W. Jack, "Recent Biblical Archaeology," *ET* 53 (1941-42) 367-370. [Archæology and the Biblical Text: 4. The Land of Ḳuë (2 Chron. 1:10), p. 369]

2 Chronicles 1:11

*B. Dinaburg, "The Story of the Capture of Jerusalem in the Time of David and its Historical Significance," *Zion* 11 (1945-46) #1, I. *[1:11]*

2 Chronicles 1:13

B. Maisler, "Miscellanea," *BIES* 13 (1946-47) #1/2, IV. [Gibeon—Jerusalem in 2 Chron 1:13]

2 Chronicles 1:16f.

*William B Arnold, "Solomon's Horse-trade," *JAOS* 26 (1905) 104. *[1:16f.]*

2 Chronicles 6:8

Anonymous, "The Great Text Commentary. The Great Texts of Chronicles," *ET* 24 (1912-13) 155-159. *[6:8]*

2 Chronicles 6:13

*J. W. Jack, "Recent Biblical Archaeology," *ET* 53 (1941-42) 367-370. [Archæology and the Biblical Text: 6. Solomon's Copper Platform (2 Chron. 6:13), p. 369]

2 Chronicles 9:1-12

*Stewart Perowne, "Note on I Kings, Chapter X, 1-13 (II Chronicles, Chapter IX, 1-12)," *PEQ* 71 (1939) 199-202.

2 Chronicles 9:18

*J. A. Montgomery, "Notes on I Kings," *JBL* 55 (1936) xi. *[9:18]*

2 Chronicles 13:4-12

James L. Bigger, "The Battle Address of Abijah, 2 Chronicles XIII., 4-12," *ONTS* 3 (1883-84) 6-16.

2 Chronicles 13:19

*W[illiam] F[oxwell] Albright, "New Identifications of Ancient Towns," *BASOR* # 9 (1923) 5-10. [The Site of Jehanah, pp. 7-8] *[13:19]*

2 Chronicles 14:9

*Fritz Hommel, "Serah the Cushite," *ET* 8 (1896-97) 378-379. *[14:9]*

*T. K. Cheyne, "On 2 Ch. xiv. 9; Job i. 15; Prov. xxviii. 22," *ET* 8 (1896-97) 431-432.

2 Chronicles 14:10

E. Flecker, "The Valley Zephathah at Mareshah (2 Chron. xiv, 10)," *PEFQS* 18 (1886) 50-52.

2 Chronicles 20:21

*P. R. Ackroyd, "Some Notes on the Psalms," *JTS, N.S.,* 17 (1966) 392-399. [3. The interpretation of קֹדֶשׁ הַדְרַת (*Ps. xxix. 2, xcvi. 9; 1 Chron. xvi. 29; 2 Chron. xx. 21*), pp. 393-396]

2 Chronicles 20:35-36

*S. B. Gurewicz, "Some Examples of Modern Exegeses of the OT," *ABR* 11 (1963) 15-23. [4. "BETH ḤOVER", Prov. xxi:2*[sic]* טוב לשבת על פנת גג מאשת מדינית ובית חבר, pp. 22-23] *[20:35-36]*

2 Chronicles 21:16-19

*Paul Haupt, "Biblical Studies," *AJP* 43 (1922) 238-249. [2. Jehoram's Fatal Illness, p. 239] *[21:16-17, 19]*

2 Chronicles 24:15ff.

H. L. Ginsberg, "The Reported Enormities of Athaliah and Joash," *JBL* 70 (1951) xv. *[24:15ff.]*

2 Chronicles 25:2

*Anonymous, "The Great Text Commentary. The Great Texts of Chronicles,"*ET* 23 (1911-12) 492-497. *[25:2]*

2 Chronicles 26:1-23

*Daniel S. Gregory, "Introductory View to the Subsequent Lessons," *CFL, 3rd Ser.,* 14 (1911-12) 283-289. [i. 'Uzziah, King of Judah, Humbled' (2 Chron. XXVI. 1-23, pp. 290-292]

2 Chronicles 26:7

James Oscar Boyd, "'The Meunim'," *CFL, N.S.,* 2 (1900) 173-174. *[26:7]*

2 Chronicles 26:15

Yiga'el Sukenik, "'Engines invented by cunning men'," *BIES* 13 (1946-47) #1/2, II-III. *[26:15]*

2 Chronicles Chapter 28

E. G. Selwyn, "Studies and Texts. (a) 2 Chron. xxviii.: Oded and the Ruhr," *Theo* 7 (1923) 102-103.

*Peter R. Ackroyd, "Historians and Prophets," *SEÅ* 33 (1968) 18-54. [2 Chron. 28, pp. 33-37]

*B. Oded, "The Historical Background of the War between Rezin and Pekah against Ahaz," *Tarbiz* 38 (1968-69) #3, I-II. *[Chapter 28]*

2 Chronicles 28:1-15

*Frank H. Wilkinson, "Oded: Proto-type of the Good Samaritan," *ET* 69 (1957-58) 94. *[28:1-15]*

2 Chronicles 29:32-34

*W. Baars, "Papyrus Barcinonenis, Inv. No. 3 and Egerton Papyrus 4," *VT* 15 (1965) 528-529. *[29:32-34]*

2 Chronicles 30:3-5

*W. Baars, "Papyrus Barcinonenis, Inv. No. 3 and Egerton Papyrus 4," *VT* 15 (1965) 528-529. *[30:3, 5]*

2 Chronicles 30:20-25

*Walter T. McCree, "Josiah and Gadd's Babylonian Tablet," *CJRT* 1 (1924) 307-312. [B.M. 21,901] *[30:20-25]*

2 Chronicles 30:21

M. Buttenwieser, "2 Chronicles 30:21," *JBL* 45 (1926) 156-158.

2 Chronicles 31:21

*Anonymous, "The Great Text Commentary. The Great Texts of Chronicles,"*ET* 23 (1911-12) 492-497. *[31:21]*

2 Chronicles 33:11

Howard Crosby, "Light on Important Texts. No. XVI," *HR* 6 (1881-82) 361-362. *[33:11]*

J. F. McCurdy, "Light on Scriptural Texts from Recent Discoveries. Transition from Hezekiah to Manasseh," *HR* 32 (1896) 505-508. *[33:11]*

2 Chronicles 35:25

†Anonymous, "Concerning a Hebrew Dirge," *MMBR* 12 (1801) 219-220. *[35:25]*

2 Chronicles 36:11-21

*Peter R. Ackroyd, "Historians and Prophets," *SEÅ* 33 (1968) 18-54. [2 Chron. 36:11-21, pp. 50-54]

2 Chronicles 39:18-31

*Daniel S. Gregory, "The International Lessons in Their Literary and Historical Setting," *CFL, 3rd Ser.,* 1 (1904) 725-733. [Hezekiah Reopens the Temple (2 Chron. 39:18-30), pp. 725-729]

§670 *3.5.5.8 Studies on Manuscripts of the Books of Chronicles*

John F. Stenning, "Chronicles in the Peshitta," *ET* 9 (1897-98) 45-47. *(Review)*

*W. Baars, "Papyrus Barcinonenis, Inv. No. 3 and Egerton Papyrus 4," *VT* 15 (1965) 528-529.

§671 *3.6 Studies on the Apocrypha and Pseudepigrapha*
- General Studies

F. C. Porter, "The Jewish Literature of the New Testament Times: Why Should it be Studied?" *ONTS* 9 (1889) 71-78.

F. C. Porter, "The Jewish Literature of the New Testament Times: How Should it be Studied?" *ONTS* 9 (1889) 142-151.

J. A. Quarles, "The Apocryphal Scriptures," *PQ* 4 (1890) 370-388.

Allan Menzies, "Popular Books Among the Jews in the Time of Our Lord," *ET* 3 (1891-92) 21-23.

Frederic Relton, "Requests and Replies," *ET* 3 (1891-92) 67-68. *[Distinguishing between the Apocrypha and Pseudepigrapha]*

*F. H. Wallace, "Relation of Extra-Canonical Jewish Literature to the New Testament," *MR* 79 (1897) 697-711.

G. Margoliouth, "Some remarks on the Son of Sirach," *IJA* #11 (1907) 11-12.

Abram S. Isaacs, "What is Jewish Literature?" *BS* 66 (1909) 171-177.

*H. Maldwyn Hughes, "The Apocrypha and Pseudepigrapha and Christian Ethics," *IJA* #19 (1909) 77-79.

*George A. Barton, "The Origin of the Names of Angels and Demons in the Extra-Canonical Literature to 100 A.D.," *JBL* 31 (1912) 156-167.

*S. A. B. Mercer, "The Cosmology of the Apocrypha and Pseudepigrapha," *IJA* #32 (1913) 3-5.

Israel Abrahams, "The Oxford Apocrypha and Pseudepigrapha," *IJA* #35 (1913) 62-66. *(Review)*

*William Watson, "Paradise: according to the Apocrypha and Pseudepigrapha," *IJA* #38 (1914) 74-78.

Anonymous, "The Old Testament Apocrypha and Pseudepigrapha," *HR* 69 (1915) 143.

*Hewlett Johnson, "The Editor's Notes," *ICMM* 12 (1915-16) 1-20, 111.
[The Literature Between the Testaments; Religious Advance Between
the Testaments; Grounds for the Pre-Eminence of the Old Testament;
Recent Works on the Period Between the Testaments; The Great
Assize; Jewish and Pagan conceptions of retributive justice; The Jewish
Struggle Favoured in the Doctrine of Assize; Literature During the
Struggle; The Wane of Apocalypses; Christianity and Apocalypses; The
General Message of Enoch; Between the Testaments; Prophetic and
Apocalyptic Views of the Future; Authorship of the Apocalypses;The
Kingdom of God among Prophets and Apocalyptists; National and Indi-
vidual Hope; The Heavenly Kingdom; The Messianic Kingdom in
Prophecy and Apocalyptic; The Messiah; The Rise in Israel of the Doc-
trine of a Future Life; The Logical Consequences of Belief in One God;
Steps to Belief in a Resurrection; The Revolt of Job and Ecclesiastes;
Immature Conceptions of the Next Life in Apocalypses and Christian-
ity; The Development of Man's forgiveness of his neighbour]

*S. A. B. Mercer, "The Pre-existence of the Soul in the Apocrypha and
Pseudepigrapha," *IJA* #45 (1916) 19-22.

*T. Witten Davies, "The Priestly Code in the Historical Writings of the Old
Testament and also in the Apocrypha and Pseudepigrapha," *IJA* #49
(1917) 18-25.

*Robert Dick Wilson, "Use of the Words for God in the Apocryphal and
Pseudepigraphal Literature of the Jews," *PTR* 18 (1920) 103-122.

*R. Marcus, "Ancient Jewish Propaganda," *JIQ* 4 (1927-28) #2, 19-23.

*R. Marcus, "Ancient Jewish Propaganda (Part II)," *JIQ* 4 (1927-28) #3, 21-
27.

*Ralph Marcus, "Divine Names and Attributes in Hellenistic Jewish Litera-
ture," *PAAJR* 3 (1931-32) 43-120. [Concordance, pp. 50-120]

A. T. Olmstead, "Intertestamental Studies," *JAOS* 56 (1936) 242-257.

Sherman E. Johnson, "Notes and Comments," *ATR* 21 (1939) 313. *[Apocry-
phal and Pseudepigraphal Sources]*

Abraham Cronbach, "The Social Ideals of the Apocrypha and Pseudepigrapha," *HUCA* 18 (1944) 119-156.

Hugh Pope, "What are the 'Apocrypha'?" *AER* 114 (1946) 176-187.

*Solomon Zeitlin, "The Apocrypha," *JQR, N.S.,* 37 (1946-47) 219-248. [I and II Maccabees; The Book of Judith; The Book of Jubilees; The Fourth Maccabees; The Fourth (Second) Ezra and Apocalypse (Second) Baruch]

G. R. Beasley-Murray, "Doctrinal Developments in the Apocrypha and Pseudepigrapha," *EQ* 19 (1947) 178-195.

L. Wallach, "Rationalization and Historization in Post-Biblical Hebrew Literature," *JBL* 66 (1947) vii-viii.

Solomon Zeitlin, "Jewish Apocryphal Literature," *JQR, N.S.,* 40 (1949-50) 223-250.

*‡Raymond F. Surburg, "Intertestamental Studies 1946—1955," *CTM* 27 (1956) 95-114. [I. Apocrypha, Pseudepigrapha, Apocalypses, pp. 95-99]

*S. H. Hooke, "Life After Death: VI. The Extra-Canonical Literature," *ET* 76 (1964-65) 273-276.

Michael E. Stone, "The Apocryphal Literature in Armenian Tradition," *PIASH* 4 (1969-70) 59-77.

§672 *3.6.1 Studies on the Old Testament Apocrypha*

H. M. M., "On the Apocryphal Books," *MR* 10 (1827) 213-216.

Anonymous, "Canonical and Apocryphal Books," *JSL, 3rd Ser.,* 12 (1860-61) 182-183.

J. Radcliffe, "The Apocrypha," *BFER* 21 (1872) 561-589.

Hyman Hurwitz, "The Merits of the Uninspired Literature of the Hebrews," *DTQ* 3 (1877) 481-505.

*A. G. Laurie, "The Book of Enoch and the Apocrypha," *UQGR, N.S.,* 15 (1878) 339-348.

Anonymous, "The Apocrypha," *CQR* 11 (1880-81) 327-358.

J. A. Broadus, "The Old Testament Apocrypha," *BQR* 3 (1881) 107-123.

Milton S. Terry, "The Old Testament Apocrypha," *MR* 63 (1881) 77-103.

F. W. Farrar, "The Books of the Apocrypha," *Exp, 3rd Ser.,* 7 (1888) 321-341.

†Anonymous, "The Apocrypha," *QRL* 166 (1888) 274-308. *(Review) [Revised Version of 1881]*

Anonymous, "The Apocrypha," *CQR* 27 (1888-89) 138-153.

Anonymous, "The Apocrypha," *LQHR* 71 (1888-89) 1-21. *(Review)*

G. H. Schodde, "The Inter-Testament Literature," *ONTS* 11 (1890) 217-222.

Coker Adams, "The Apocrypha and the Gospel," *CM, 3rd Ser.,* 2 (1891) 222-235, 287-300.

Anonymous, "Neglect of the Apocrypha," *ONTS* 13 (1891) 122.

Thomas R. Slicer, "'Between the Testaments'," *NW* 1 (1892) 106-124.

Paul Carus, "The Apocrypha of the Old Testament," *OC* 9 (1895) #45, 4700-4702.

Frank C. Porter, "The Apocrypha," *BW* 8 (1896) 272-279.

James O. Murray, "The Study of the Apocrypha by the Preacher," *HR* 32 (1896) 109-114.

Anonymous, "The Revised Version of the Apocrypha," *LQHR* 86 (1896) 1-17. *[Revised Version of 1881]*

Joh Hudson, "The Neglect of the Apocrypha," *CM, 3rd Ser.,* 14 (1897) 171-184.

D. P. McGearchy, "The Old Testament Apocrypha," *USR* 9 (1897) 107-113.

John C. Bowman, "The Apocrypha in the Light of Biblical Criticism," *RChR, 4th Ser.,* 3 (1899) 289-309.

Anonymous, "Episcopal Opinion of the Apocrypha," *IJA* #3 (1905) 4-5; #4 (1906) 15; #5 (1906) 1.

W. E. Boulter, "Doth the Church 'read the other Books'?" *IJA* #13 (1908) 10-12.

Anonymous, "The Apocrypha and the Press," *IJA* #14 (1908) 18-19.

Hewlett Johnson, "Editorial Notes. The Apocrypha," *ICMM* 5 (1908-09) 127-128.

*Herbert Pentin, "The Inspiration of the Apocrypha," *ICMM* 5 (1908-09) 310-315.

Henry E. Thomson, "Dr. Schürer on the Apocrypha—in the New Schaff-Herzog," *CFL, 3rd Ser.,* 10 (1909) 11-14. *(Editorial)*

*W. M. Patton, "Cosmogonies in the Apocrypha and in Genesis," *IJA* #17 (1909) 33-37.

W. L. Courtney, "Some thoughts on the Apocrypha," *IJA* #20 (1910) 20-22.

R. W. Moss, "Christian Thought and the Apocrypha," *LQHR* 113 (1910) 128-130.

George Fitch McKibben, "The Apocrypha Good and Useful to Read," *IJA* #24 (1911) 8-10.

Anonymous, "The Apocrypha and the Press," *IJA* #24 (1911) 57-60.

*Anonymous, "The Deutero-Canonical Books and the Tridentine Decree," *IJA* #25 (1911) 23-24.

Alfred Plummer, "A Note on the Apocrypha," *IJA* #26 (1911) 52-53.

William Wallace Everts, "The Apocrypha, a Source of Roman Catholic Error," *R&E* 8 (1911) 234-247.

Herbert Pentin, "Apocrypha of the Old Testament," *AAOJ* 34 (1912) 193-200.

*J. E. Compton, "The Preacher's Use of the Apocrypha," *HR* 65 (1913) 138-140.

Milton S. Terry, "Books of the Maccabean Age," *IJA* #33 (1913) 22-24.

James Thompson Bixby, "The Apocrypha and its Narratives," *IJA* #35 (1913) 78-80.

Anonymous, "The Apocrypha," *MR* 95 (1913) 474-479.

Andrew C. Zenos, "The Bible, the Apocrypha, and Modern Scholarship," *HR* 68 (1914) 234-235.

*Andrew C. Zenos, "Apocryphal Literature and Bible Study. I. Eschatology," *HR* 68 (1914) 451-453.

*Andrew C. Zenos, "Apocryphal Literature and Bible Study. II. God, Sin, and Salvation," *HR* 69 (1915) 22-23.

*Andrew C. Zenos, "Apocryphal Literature and Bible Study. III. Literary Form," *HR* 70 (1915) 58-59.

J. W. Hunkin, "The Books of the Apocrypha," *JTS* 16 (1914-15) 429-430. *(Review)*

Anonymous, "The Apocrypha," *IJA* #40 (1915) 17-18.

H. S. Milner, "The Other Books," *IJA* #41 (1915) 29-31.

W. F. Howard, "A Wesleyan Methodist on the Re-instatement of the Apocrypha," *IJA* #42 (1915) 43.

*H. McLachlan, "The Apocrypha and the New Testament," *IJA* #42 (1915) 44-45.

W. E. Boulter, "The other Books the Church doth read," *IJA* #43 (1915) 65-67.

Charles C. Torrey, "A New Era in the History of the 'Apocrypha'," *Monist* 25 (1915) 286-294.

F. G. Vial, "What we owe to Alexandria," *IJA* #44 (1916) 7-9.

*J. E. Compton, "The Preacher's Use of the Apocrypha," *IJA* #46 (1916) 41-42.
Samuel Holmes, "Jewish Apostacy[sic]* according to the Apocrypha," *IJA* #48 (1917) 3-4.

* Sidney S. Tedesche, "Prayers of the Apocrypha and their Importance in the Study of Jewish Liturgy," *YCCAR* 26 (1916) 376-398.

*T. Herbert Bindley, "Canon and Apocrypha," *ICMM* 19 (1922-23) 252-260.

Edward C. Unmack, "Why We Reject the Apocrypha," *EQ* 1 (1929) 361-366.

George F. Hall, "Luther's Prefaces the Old Testament Apocryphal Books," *AQ* 13 (1934) 195-207.

*T. H. W. Maxfield, "The Evolution of Judaism in the Post-Exilic Period with special reference to its literature," *MC* 24 (1934-35) 275-294.

H. H. Kumnick, "The Study of the Apocrypha by the Preacher," *CTM* 7 (1936) 899-906.

Charles Arthur Hawley, "The Apocrypha," *RL* 6 (1937) 561-573.

K. G. Matz, "The Opinions of Modern Scholars on the Origins of the Various Apocryphal Books," *CTM* 12 (1941) 658-687, 744-768.

J. Coert Rylaarsdam, "The Apocrypha and the Bible," *JAAR* 17 (1949) 175-180.

Floyd V. Filson, "The Apocrypha," *McQ* 8 (1954-55) #5, 3-6.

*William Schneirla, "The Orthodox Old Testament Canon and the So-Called Apocrypha," *StVTQ, N.S.,* 1 (1957) #3, 40-46.

*Manfred R. Lehmann, "Ben Sira and the Qumran Literature," *RdQ* 3 (1961-62) 103-116.

*David Winston, "The Iranian Component in the Bible, Apocrypha, and Qumran: A Review of the Evidence," *HRel* 5 (1965-66) 183-216.

*Marvin E. Tate, "The Old Testament Apocrypha and the Old Testament Canon," *R&E* 65 (1968) 339-356.

(§673) **3.6.1.1 Textual Criticism on the Apocrypha - General Studies**

§674   **3.6.1.1.1 Textual Criticism on the Books of Esdras**

*H. H. Howorth, "Some Unconventional Views on the Text of the Bible. III. *The Hexapla and Tetrapla of Origen, and the light they throw on the books of Esdras A and B,*" *SBAP* 24 (1902) 147-172.

*Charles C. Torrey, "Portions of First Esdras and Nehemiah in the Syro-Hexaplar Version," *AJSL* 23 (1906-07) 65-74.

§675   **3.6.1.1.1.1 Textual Criticism on the Book of 1 Esdras / 3 Ezra**

Harry Clinton York, "The Latin Versions of First Esdras," *AJSL* 26 (1909-10) 253-302.

E. C. Dewick, "The Vocabulary and Style of Esdras A. Considered with Special Reference to the date of the Greek Version," *IJA* #33 (1913) 33-34.

H. L. Allrik, "I Esdras according to Codex B and Codex A as appearing in Zerubbabel's List in 1 Esdras 5:8-23," *ZAW* 66 (1954) 272-292.

§676   ***3.6.1.1.1.2 Textual Criticism on the Book of 2 Esdras / 4 Ezra / The Apocalypse of Ezra (Esdras)***

J. S. Wood, "The missing fragment of the Fourth Book of Esdras," *JP* 7 (1876-77) 264-278. *[Latin MSS]*

Richard J. H. Gottheil, "An Arabic Version of the 'Revelation of Ezra'," *AJSL* 4 (1887-88) 14-17.

Robert P. Blake, "The Georgian Version of Fourth Esdras from the Jerusalem Manuscript," *HTR* 19 (1926) 377-375.

Robert P. Blake, "The Georgian Text of Fourth Esdras from the Athos Manuscript," *HTR* 22 (1929) 57-105.

Bruce M. Metzger, "The 'Lost' Section of II Esdras (=IV Ezra)," *JBL* 76 (1957) 153-156.

Michael Stone, "Some Remarks on the Textual Criticism of IV Ezra," *HTR* 60 (1967) 107-115.

M. E. Stone, "Manuscripts and Readings of Armenia IV Ezra," *Text* 6 (1968) 48-61.

§677 ***3.6.1.1.2 Textual Criticism on the Book of Tobit***

†M. Gaster, "Two Unknown Hebrew Versions of the Tobit Legend. (Text)," *SBAP* 19 (1897) I-XV. *(following page 124)*

J. Rendel Harris, "The Double Text of Tobit. Contribution toward a Critical Inquiry," *AJT* 3 (1899) 541-554.

D. C. Simpson, "The Chief Recensions of the Book of Tobit," *JTS* 14 (1912-13) 516-530.

Hugh G. Bevenot, "The Primitive Book of Tobit. An Essay in Textual Reconstruction," *BS* 83 (1926) 55-84.

§678 *3.6.1.1.3 Textual Criticism on the Book of Judith*

M. Gaster, "An unknown Hebrew Version of the History of Judith," *SBAP* 16 (1893-94) 156-163.

Frank Zimmermann, "Aid for the Recovery of the Hebrew Original of Judith," *JBL* 57 (1938) 67-74.

(§679) *3.6.1.1.4 Textual Criticism on the Additions to Esther / The Rest of Esther*

§680 *3.6.1.1.5 Textual Criticism on the Book of the Wisdom of Solomon*

D. P. Buckle, "The Seventeenth Chapter of the Book of Wisdom. A Translation of the Coptic (Sahidic) Version, with textual and lexical notes," *IJA* #39 (1914) 70-72.

D. P. Buckle, "Boharic Lections of *Wisdom* from a Rylands Library MS," *JTS* 17 (1915-16) 78-98.

A. Marx, "Aramaic Fragment of the Wisdom of Solomon," *JBL* 40 (1921) 57-69.

Patrick W. Skehan, "Notes on the Latin Text of the Book of Wisdom," *CBQ* 4 (1942) 230-243.

Patrick W. Skehan, "The Text and Structure of the Book of Wisdom," *Tr* 3 (1945) 1-12.

C. S. C. Williams, "Armenian Variants in the Book of Wisdom," *JTS, N.S.,* 7 (1956) 243-246.

§681 *3.6.1.1.6 Textual Criticism on the Book of Ecclesiasticus / The Wisdom of Jesus the Son of Sirach / Ben Sira*

D. S. Margoliouth, "The Language and Metre of Ecclesiasticus. A Reply to Criticism," *Exp, 4th Ser.,* 1 (1890) 295-320, 381-387. [Notes by S. R. Driver, pp. 387-390; T. K. Cheyne, pp. 390-391]

Th. Nöldeke, "The Language and Metre of Ecclesiasticus," *Exp, 4th Ser.,* 2 (1890) 350-356.

D. S. Margoliouth, "The Language and Metre of Ecclesiasticus," *Exp, 4th Ser.,* 2 (1890) 356-359.

Margaret D. Gibson, "The Ecclesiasticus Discovery," *ET* 7 (1895-96) 564.

S. Schechter, "A Fragment of the Original Text of Ecclesiasticus," *Exp, 5th Ser.,* 4 (1896) 1-15.

D. S. Margoliouth, "Observations on the Fragment of Ecclesiasticus Edited by Mr. Schechter," *Exp, 5th Ser.,* 4 (1896) 140-151.

Hope W. Hogg, "Ecclesiasticus in Hebrew," *ET* 8 (1896-97) 262-266. *(Review)*

C. Taylor, "Studies in Ben Sira," *JQR* 10 (1897-98) 470-488. [III. The Lewis-Gibson folio, pp. 476-488]

W. Bacher, A. Cowley, A. Neubauer, S. R. Driver, and G. Buchanan Gray, "The Hebrew Text of Ecclesiasticus," *JQR* 9 (1896-97) 543-567.

R. B. Woodworth, "The Ecclesiasticus Discovery," *USR* 8 (1896-97) 156-165.

Hope W. Hogg, "The Hebrew Ecclesiasticus. Some of Its Additions and Omissions," *AJT* 1 (1897) 777-786.

W. Tayler Smith, "The Hebrew Ecclesiasticus," *BW* 10 (1897) 58-63.

Anonymous, "'The Original Hebrew of a Portion of Ecclesiasticus'," *CFL, O.S.,* 1 (1897) 215-216.

*Geo. H. Schodde, "Biblical Research Notes," *ColTM* 17 (1897) 371-384. [New Finds (Hebrew Ecclesiasticus), pp. 377-378]

Th. Nöldeke, "The Original Hebrew of a Portion of Ecclesiasticus," *Exp, 5th Ser.,* 5 (1897) 347-364.

S. Schechter, "Genizah Specimens, The Original Text of Ecclesiasticus XLIX 12 - L 22," *JQR* 10 (1897-98) 197-206.

N. Herz, "The Hebrew Ecclesiasticus," *JQR* 10 (1897-98) 719-724.

Joseph Bruneau, "Biblical Research. IV. Textual Criticism and Exegesis. 1.," *AER* 18 (1898) 281-282. *[Hebrew MS. of Ecclesiasticus]*

[James Hastings], "The Hebrew Ecclesiasticus," *ET* 10 (1898-99) 66-67. *(Review)*

Ed. König, "Professor Margoliouth and the 'Original Hebrew' of Ecclesiasticus," *ET* 10 (1898-99) 512-516, 564-566; 11 (1899-1900) 31-32, 69-74.

D. S. Margoliouth, "The Hebrew Ecclesiasticus," *ET* 10 (1898-99) 528; 11 (1899-1900) 46.

*D. S. Margoliouth, "The Hebrew Ecclesiasticus, I.," *ET* 10 (1898-99) 567-568.

S. Schechter, "The Hebrew Ecclesiasticus, II.," *ET* 10 (1898-99) 568.

J. A. Selbie, "The Hebrew Ecclesiasticus," *ET* 11 (1899-1900) 43-44.

D. S. Margoliouth, "The External Evidence Against the Cairene Ecclesiasticus," *ET* 11 (1899-1900) 90-92, 191-192.

J. A. Selbie, "The Sirach Controversy," *ET* 11 (1899-1900) 127-128, 446-447, 494, 550-551.

Ed. König, "Is The External Evidence Really Against the Cairene Ecclesiasticus? I.," *ET* 11 (1899-1900) 139-140.

S. Schechter, "Is the External Evidence Really Against the Cairene Ecclesiasticus? II.," *ET* 11 (1899-1900) 140-142.

I. Abrahams, "Is the External Evidence Really Against the Cairene Ecclesiasticus? III.," *ET* 11 (1899-1900) 142-143.

Ed. König, "The Origin of the New Hebrew Fragments of Ecclesiasticus," *ET* 11 (1899-1900) 170-176.

Ed. König, "The External Evidence is Not Against the Cairene Ecclesiasticus," *ET* 11 (1899-1900) 234-235.

S. Schechter, "The Hebrew Sirach. I.," *ET* 11 (1899-1900) 285-287.

D. S. Margoliouth, "The Hebrew Sirach. II," *ET* 11 (1899-1900) 287.

D. S. Margoliouth, "The Non-Biblical Literature of the Jews," *ET* 11 (1899-1900) 331-333. *[Ecclesiasticus]*

S. Schechter, "The Hebrew Sirach," *ET* 11 (1899-1900) 382-383, 522-523.

C. Taylor, "The Wisdom of Ben-Sira," *ET* 11 (1899-1900) 423.

*D. S. Margoliouth, "The Date of the Talmud and the Cairene Ecclesiasticus," *ET* 11 (1899-1900) 427-428.

G. Margoliouth, "The Original Hebrew of Ecclesiasticus XXXI. 12-31 and XXXVI. 22 - XXXVII. 26," *JQR* 12 (1899-1900) 1-33.

W. Bacher, "An Hypothesis about the Hebrew Fragments of Sirach," *JQR* 12 (1899-1900) 92-108.

A. Cowley, "Notes on the Cambridge Texts of Ben Sira," *JQR* 12 (1899-1900) 109-111.

A. Cowley, "The Old Latin Version of Ecclesiasticus," *JQR* 12 (1899-1900) 168-171. *(Review)*

S. Schechter, "The Hebrew Text of Ben Sira. The British Museum Fragments of Ecclesiasticus," *JQR* 12 (1899-1900) 266-272.

W. Bacher, "Notes on the Cambridge Fragments of Ecclesiasticus," *JQR* 12 (1899-1900) 272-290. [I. On the Hebrew Text; II. The Greek and Syriac Translations; III. The Ancient Quotations from Bar-Sira, in Their Relation to the Genizah Fragments]

S. Schechter, "A Further Fragment of Ben Sira," *JQR* 12 (1899-1900) 456-465. [Parts of Chs. IV, V, XXV, XXVI, and XXXI]

Elkan Nathan Adler, "Some Missing Chapters of Ben Sira (with four facsimiles)," *JQR* 12 (1899-1900) 466-480. [VII. 29 — XII. 1]

M. Gaster, "A New Fragment of Ben Sira (With two facsimiles)," *JQR* 12 (1899-1900) 688-702. [Parts of Chs. XVIII, XIX, and XX]

C. Taylor, "On the Wisdom of Ben Sira," *JTS* 1 (1899-1900) 571-583.

B. B. Warfield, "The Hebrew Ecclesiasticus," *CFL, N.S.,* 1 (1900) 291.

P. P. Flournoy, "A Leaf from the Hebrew Ecclesiasticus," *CFL, N.S.,* 2 (1900) 33-37.

D. S. Margoliouth, "The Cairene Ecclesiasticus," *ET* 12 (1900-01) 45-46.

Crawford H. Toy, "Remarks on the Hebrew Text of Ben-Sira," *JAOS* 23 (1902) 38-43.

Stanley A. Cook, "An Arabic Version of the Prologue to Ecclesiasticus," *SBAP* 24 (1902) 173-184.

W. O. E. Oesterley, "Ecclesiasticus in Greek," *IJA* #20 (1910) 19-20. *(Review)*

Max L. Margolis, "Mr. Hart's 'Ecclesiasticus'," *JQR, N.S.,* 1 (1910-11) 403-418. *[Review of: Ecclesiasticus. The Greek Text of Codex 248"]*

Joseph Marcus, "The Fifth Manuscript of Ben Sira," *JQR, N.S.,* 21 (1930-31) 223-240.

Max L. Margolis, "Notes on 'A Fifth MS. of Ben Sira'," *JQR, N.S.,* 21 (1930-31) 439-440.

*Felix Perles, "Ben Sira 33.5 (Comp. *JQR.,* N.S., XXI, 231)," *JQR, N.S.,* 22 (1931-32) 117.

M. H. Segal, "The Evolution of the Hebrew Text of Ben Sira," *JQR, N.S.,* 25 (1934-35) 91-149.

G. R. Driver, "Ecclesiasticus: A New Fragment of the Hebrew Text," *ET* 49 (1937-38) 37-39.

William Duff McHardy, "The Arabic Text of Ecclesiasticus in the Bodleian MS. Hunt. 260," *JTS* 46 (1945) 39-41.

W[illiam] D[uff] McHardy, "Ben Ze'eb's Edition of the Peshitta Text of Ecclesiasticus," *ZAW* 61 (1945-48) 193-194.

H. L. Ginsberg, "The Original Hebrew of Ben Sira 12:10-14," *JBL* 74 (1955) 93-95.

J. Schirmann, "A New Leaf from the Hebrew 'Ecclesiasticus' (Ben-Sira)," *Tarbiz* 27 (1957-58) #4, II-III.

J. Schirmann, "Some Additional Leaves from Ecclesiasticus in Hebrew," *Tarbiz* 29 (1959-60) #2, II-III.

M. Z. Segal, "'Additional Leaves from Ecclesiasticus in Hebrew'," *Tarbiz* 29 (1959-60) #4, I-II.

Alexander A. Di Lella, "Authenticity of the Geniza Fragments of Sirach," *B* 44 (1963) 171-200.

Alexander A. Di Lella, "The Recently Identified Leaves of Sirach in Hebrew," *B* 45 (1964) 153-168.

W. Baars, "On a Latin Fragment of Sirach," *VT* 15 (1965) 280-281.

*Solomon Zeitlin, "The Ben Sira Scroll from Masada," *JQR, N.S.,* 56 (1965-66) 185-190.

*Joseph M. Baumgarten, "Some Notes on the Ben Sira Scroll from Masada," *JQR, N.S.,* 58 (1967-68) 323-327.

§682 *3.6.1.1.7 Textual Criticism of the Book of Baruch*

Edward König, "The Rest of the Words of Baruch. *Translated from the Ethiopic and Illustrated with Notes,*" *DTQ* 3 (1877) 426-435. *(Trans. to English by Jessie Young)*

§683 *3.6.1.1.8 Textual Criticism of the Letter of Jeremiah / The Epistle of Jeremy*

W. Baars, "Two Palestinian Syriac Texts identified as parts of the Epistle of Jeremy," *VT* 11 (1961) 77-81.

§684 *3.6.1.1.9 Textual Criticism of the Prayer of Azariah and the Song of the Three Young Men / The Song of the Three Holy Children*

W. H. Daubney, "The Song of the Three," *ET* 18 (1906-07) 287.

§685 *3.6.1.1.10 Textual Criticism of the Story of Susanna*

M. Gaster, "The Unknown Aramaic Original of Theodotion's Additions to the Book of Daniel II. Text," *SBAP* 16 (1893-94) 280-290, 312-317.

Anonymous, "The Coptic Version of the Greek Homily on Susanna," *IJA* #25 (1911) 35-36. *(Review)*

R. A. F. MacKenzie, "Susanna the Martyr," *Scrip* 9 (1957) 15-20.

R. A. F. MacKenzie, "Susanna the Martyr," *TD* 6 (1958) 174-175. *[Synopsis]*

M. Wurmbrand, "A Falasha Variant of the Story of Susanna," *B* 44 (1963) 29-45.

*Leona G. Running, "Peshiṭta Communications VIII, The Problem of the mixed MSS of Susanna in the Seventeenth Century," *VT* 19 (1969) 377-383.

(§686) *3.6.1.1.11 Textual Criticism of the Bel and the Dragon / Additions to the Book of Daniel*

§687 *3.6.1.1.12 Textual Criticism of the Prayer of Manasseh*

George Wilkins, "The Prayer of Manasseh," *Herm* 16 (1910-11) 167-178. *[Syrian MSS]*

§688 *3.6.1.1.13 Textual Criticism of the Books of Maccabees*

Margaret D. Gibson, "Four Remarkable Sinai Manuscripts," *ET* 13 (1901-02) 509-511. [IV. Syriac Maccabees, pp. 510-511]

Eb. Nestle, "Note on the Syriac Manuscript Described on PP. 510, 511," *ET* 13 (1901-02) 563.

Dom Hugh Bevenot, "The Armenian Text of Maccabees," *JPOS* 14 (1934) 268-285.

§689 *3.6.1.1.13.1 Textual Criticism of the Book of 1 Maccabees*

Charles C. Torrey, "Schweizer's 'Remains of a Hebrew Text of I Maccabees'," *JBL* 22 (1903) 51-59.

J. W. Hunkin, "An Emendation of the Text of I Macc. III 48," *JTS* 29 (1927-28) 43-46.

§690 *3.6.1.1.13.2 Textual Criticism of the Book of 2 Maccabees*

Charles C. Torrey, "The Letters Prefixed to Second Maccabees," *JAOS* 60 (1940) 119-150.

Peter Katz, "The Text of 2 Maccabees reconsidered," *ZNW* 51 (1960) 10-30.

§691 *3.6.2.1 Literary Criticism of the Apocrypha - General Studies*

*C. E. Stowe, "The Apocryphal Books of the Old Testament, and the Reasons for Their Exclusion from the Canon of Scripture," *BS* 11 (1854) 278-305.

Eb. Nestle, "Coverdale on the Apocrypha," *ET* 15 (1903-04) 335.

W. H. Daubney, "Coverdale on the Apocrypha," *ET* 15 (1903-04) 383.

Christopher Wordsworth, "Some Notes on the Apocrypha," *IJA* #6 (1906) 6-8.

*W. O. E. Oesterley, "The Demonology of the Apocrypha," *IJA* #7 (1906) 8-9.

*W. O. E. Oesterley, "Messianic Teaching in the Apocrypha," *IJA* #9 (1907) 7-9.

*Anonymous, "The use of the Apocrypha in the New Testament," *IJA* #13 (1908) 4-6.

Allan Menzies, "Why the Apocrypha is absent from the English Bible," *IJA* #14 (1908) 16-18.

*W. J. Oldfield, "Marriage in the Apocrypha," *IJA* #16 (1908) 14-17.

(   ) Dodson, "The Missionary Outlook in the Apocrypha," *IJA* #16 (1909) 8-10.

*M. Gaster, "The Ethics of Jewish Apocryphal Literature," *IJA* #20 (1910) 17-19. *(Review)*

*Robert Roberts, "Almsgiving in the Apocrypha, Talmud and Qoran," *IJA* #21 (1910) 28-30.

*W. V. Hague, "The Eschatology of the Apocryphal Scriptures," *JTS* 12 (1910-11) 57-98.

H. E. Ryle, A. W. Streane, W. Fairweather, R. G. Moulton, W. B. Stevenson, J. A. F. Gregg, Crawford Toy, H. T. Andrews, G. Milne Rae, and H. F. Henderson, "They Say," *IJA* # 24 (1911) 55-57. *[Short Quips on the importance of the Apocrypha]*

Anonymous, "The Wisdom-Books of the Apocrypha. Some Hints to Students," *IJA* #27 (1911) 74-76.

*E. Walter Maunder, "The Astronomy of the Apocrypha," *IJA* #30 (1912) 46-52.

James Thompson Bixby, "The Wisdom-Books of the Apocrypha," *IJA* #36 (1914) 12-15.

D. Frew, "The Origin, Teaching and Contents of the Books of the Apocrypha," *IJA* #40 (1915) 6-9. *(Review)*

Andrew C. Zenos, "The Value of the Critical Study of the Apocrypha," *IJA* #40 (1915) 11-12.

H. Maldwyn Hughes, "The Apocrypha and its Value," *IJA* #40 (1915) 13-16.

*G. H. Box, "The Doctrine of God in the Jewish Apocryphal and Apocalyptic Literature," *IJA* #41 (1915) 37-39. *(Review)*

H. J. Wicks, "The Apocrypha: its Place and Value," *IJA* #42 (1915) 51-53.

*H. J. Wicks, "The Doctrine of the Messiah in Jewish Apocrypha and Apocalyptic," *IJA* #46 (1916) 34-36.

*Andrew C. Zenos, "Apocryphal Literature and Bible Study," *IJA* #47 (1916) 58-59.

Samuel Holmes, "Jewish Apostacy[sic]* according to the Apocrypha," *IJA* #48 (1917) 3-4.

*C. Ryder Smith, "The Social Teaching of the Apocryphal and Apocalyptic Books," *ET* 37 (1925-26) 505-508.

*George E. Ladd, "The Kingdom of God in the Jewish Apocryphal Literature," *BS* 109 (1952) 55-62.

Abraham A. Neuman, "Josippon and the Apocrypha," *JQR, N.S.,* 43 (1952-53) 1-26.

§692 *3.6.2.1.1 Literary Criticism on the Books of Esdras*

H. St. John Thackeray, "An Examination paper on I and II Esdras," *IJA* #4 (1905) 2.

H. St. John Thackeray, "Professor Torrey's 'Ezra Studies'," *IJA* #22 (1910) 48-50. *(Review)*

Anonymous, "A Roman Catholic View of the Books of Esdras," *IJA* #41 (1915) 27-29.

§693　　　　*3.6.2.1.1.1 Literary Criticism on the Book of I Esdras / 3 Ezra*

E. C. Bissell, "The First Book of Esdras," *BS* 34 (1877) 209-228.

*Henry H. Howorth, "Some Unconventional Views on the Text of the Bible. I. *The Apocryphal Book Esdras A and the Septuagint*," *SBAP* 23 (1901) 147-159.

*Henry H. Howorth, "Some Unconventional Views on the Text of the Bible. II. *The Chronology and Order of Events in Esdras A, compared with and preferred to those in the Canonical Ezra*," *SBAP* 23 (1901) 305-325, 328-330. (Remarks by R. B. Girdlestone, Paul Ruben, and M. Gaster, pp. 325-328)

[H. Petin], "The First Book of Esdras," *IJA* #1 (1905) 1.

*Henry H. Howorth, "The Modern Roman Canon and the Book of Esdras A," *JTS* 7 (1905-06) 343-354.

Hugh Pope, "Why does the Catholic Church reject III. Esdras?" *IJA* #6 (1906) 5-6.

Henry H. Howorth, "The Modern Roman Canon and Esdras A," *IJA* #7 (1906) 6-8.

C[harles] C. Torrey, "The Nature and Origin of 'First Esdras'," *AJSL* 23 (1906-07) 116-141.

C[harles] C. Torrey, "The Story of the Three Youths," *AJSL* 23 (1906-07) 177-201. *[1 Esdras]*

*H. Pope, "The Third Book of Esdras and the Tridentine Canon," *JTS* 8 (1906-07) 218-232.

Charles C. Torrey, "First Esdras," *IJA* #37 (1914) 24-27; #38 (1914) 69-71. *(Review)*

*Edward J. Kissane, "The Historical Value of Esdras I.-III.," *ITQ* 15 (1920) 126-138.

A. Shallit, "The Date and Place of the Story about the Three Bodyguards of the King in the Apocryphal Book of Ezra," *BIES* 13 (1946-47) #3/4, VI.

Frank Zimmermann, "The Story of the Three Guardsmen," *JQR, N.S.,* 54 (1963-64) 179-200.

*Ralph Walter Klein, "Old Readings in I Esdras: The List of Returnees from Babylon (Ezra 2 // Nehemiah 7)," *HTR* 62 (1969) 99-107.

§694 *3.6.2.1.1.2 Literary Criticism on the Book of 2 Esdras / 3 Ezra The Apocalypse of Ezra (Esdras)*

H. Petin, "The Second Book of Esdras," *IJA* #2 (1905) 1.

*Lewis A. Muirhead, "The Eschatology of 4 Esdras," *ET* 18 (1906-07) 406-409.

C. G. Montefiore, "The Fourth Book of Ezra," *IJA* #10 (1907) 6-7.

*W. O. E. Oesterley, "The Messianic Teaching of IV Esdras," *IJA* #11 (1907) 8-10; #12 (1908) 11-13.

*W. O. E. Oesterley, "The Messianic Teaching of IV. Esdras," *IJA* #17 (1909) 29-31.

David Frew, "Divergent Ideas in the Teaching of Fourth Esdras," *IJA* #24 (1911) 2-4.

G. H. Box, "A Contribution to the Study of II. Esdras," *IJA* #26 (1911) 53-54.

W. Sanday, "The Ezra-Apocalypse," *IJA* #30 (1912) 43-46. *(Review)*

Phillips Barry, "The Apocalypse of Ezra," *JBL* 32 (1913) 261-272.

David Frew, "The Ezra-Apocalypse," *IJA* #36 (1914) 18-20. *(Review)*

Arthur C. Headlam, "The Ezra Apocalypse," *CQR* 79 (1914-15) 288-317.

*C. W. Emmet, "The Fourth Book of Esdras and St. Paul," *ET* 27 (1915-16) 551-556.

M. R. James, "Ego Salathiel qui et Ezras," *JTS* 18 (1916-17) 167-169; 19 (1917-18) 347-348. *[On the Authorship of 4 Esdras]*

C. G. Montefiore, "An Ancient Arraignment of Providence," *HJ* 17 (1918-19) 261-271.

*Robert A. Bartels, "Law and Sin in Fourth Esdras and Saint Paul," *LQ, N.S.,* 1 (1949) 319-330.

Joshua Block, "Was There a Greek Version of the Apocalypse of Ezra?" *JQR, N.S.,* 46 (1955-56) 309-320.

Joshua Block, "The Ezra-Apocalypse was it Written in Hebrew, Greek or Aramaic?" *JQR, N.S.,* 48 (1957-58) 279-294.

Joshua Block, "Some Christological Interpolations of the Ezra-Apocalypse," *HTR* 51 (1958) 87-94.

Frank Zimmermann, "Underlying Documents in IV Ezra," *JQR, N.S.,* 51 (1960-61) 107-134.

§695 *3.6.2.1.2 Literary Criticism on the Book of Tobit*

G. B., "The Apocryphal Book of Tobit," *JSL, 3rd Ser.,* 4 (1856-57) 59-71.

Denis Hallinan, "The Book of Tobias," *IER, 3rd Ser.,* 7 (1886) 589-606, 898-911.

*I. Abrahams, "Tobit and Genesis," *JQR* 5 (1892-93) 348-350.

M. Gaster, "Two Unknown Hebrew Versions of the Tobit Legend," *SBAP* 18 (1896) 208-222, 259-271.

M. Gaster, "Two Unknown Hebrew Versions of the Tobit Legend *(concluded),*" *SBAP* 19 (1897) 27-38.

*George A. Barton, "The Story of Aḥiḳar and the Book of Daniel," *AJSL* 16 (1899-1900) 242-247.

J. H. Moulton ,"The Iranian Background of Tobit,"*ET* 11 (1899-1900) 257-260.

*W. H. Kent, "Rabbinical Studies. III," *AER* 27 (1902) 173-184. [XXI. The Chaldee Book of Tobias, pp. 178-180]

*J. H. A. Hart, "Primitive Exegesis as a Factor in the Corruption of the Texts of Scripture Illustrated from the Versions of Ben Sira," *JQR* 15 (1902-03) 627-631.

Robert Sinker, "The Book of Tobit," *IJA* #3 (1905) 1-2.

J. T. Marshall, "The Book of Tobit. Suggestions for Study," *IJA* #3 (1905) 2.

R. E. Warner, "Tobit and the Legend of Achiacharus," *IJA* #10 (1907) 9-10.

John Taylor, "Tobit and Ahikar," *ET* 19 (1907-08) 453-454.

D. C. Simpson, "The Literary and Religious Affinities of the Book of Tobit," *OSHTP* (1911-12) 28-32.

*Agnes Smith Lewis, "Achikar and the Elephantine Papyri," *Exp, 8th Ser.,* 3 (1912) 207-212.

M. Gaster, "Tobit and Ahikar," *IJA* #40 (1915) 4-6. *(Review)*

Albert J. Edmunds, "The Book of Tobit and the Hindu-Christian Marriage Ideal," *OC* 33 (1919) 336-344.

D. S. Margoliouth, "The Name Achikar," *ET* 31 (1919-20) 329-330.

*P[aul] Haupt, "Asdmodeus," *JBL* 40 (1921) 174-177.

Paul Haupt, "Tobit's Blindness and Sara's Hysteria," *PAPS* 60 (1921) 71-95.

C. C. Torrey, "'Nineveh' in the Book of Tobit," *JBL* 41 (1922) 237-245.

*J. Rendel Harris, "Tobit and the New Testament," *ET* 40 (1928-29) 315-319.

Michael J. Gruenthaner, "The Book of Tobias and Contraception," *CBQ* 8 (1946) 98-100.

F. Zimmermann, "Original Language of the Book of Tobit," *JBL* 71 (1952) v.

T. Francis Glasson, "The Main Source of Tobit," *ZAW* 71 (1959) 275-277.

*Joseph L. Mihelic, "An Analysis of the Books of Tobit and Judith," *DSJ* 2 (1967) 5-14.

§696 *3.6.2.1.3 Literary Criticism on the Book of Judith*

G. B., "The Book of Judith," *MQR* 10 (1856) 589-608.

G. B., "The Book of Judith," *JSL, 3rd Ser.,* 3 (1856) 342-363. [Note, *JSL, 3rd Ser.,* 4 (1856-57) 175-176]

B. Harris Cowper, "The Book of Judith, and its Geography," *JSL, 3rd Ser.,* 12 (1860-61) 421-440.

T. K. Cheyne, "On the Book of Judith," *Exp, 3rd Ser.,* 4 (1886) 79.

James A. Duncan, "A Hebrew Political Romance," *BW* 3 (1894) 429-434.

*Charles C. Torrey, "The Site of 'Bethulia'," *JAOS* 20 (1899) 160-172.

A. H. Sayce, "The Book of Judith," *IJA* #4 (1905) 1.

John Ruskin, "Judith," *IJA* #4 (1905) 2.

Herbert Pentin, "The Tragedy of Judith," *IJA* #8 (1907) 7-9.

*F. J. Knecht, "The Character of Judith and Susanna," *IJA* # 24 (1911) 15-16.

J. M. Grintz, "Cities of Nabhrakhta," *Zion* 12 (1946-47) #1, I.

*J. Edgar Bruns, "Judith of Jael?" *CBQ* 16 (1954) 12-14.

David Granfield, "Judith, Woman of Praise," *C&C* 7 (1955) 22-29.

J. Edgar Bruns, "The Genealogy of Judith," *CBQ* 18 (1956) 19-22.

*Richard L. Twomey, "Human Authorship in the Bible — The Book of Judith," *MH* 13 (1957-58) #1, 1-10.

Patrick W. Skehan, "Why Leave Out *Judith?*" *CBQ* 24 (1962) 147-154.

Roland J. Faley, "The Message of Judith," *BibT* #8 (1963) 505-510.

Patrick W. Skehan, "The Hand of Judith," *CBQ* 25 (1963) 94-110.

*Joseph L. Mihelic, "An Analysis of the Books of Tobit and Judith," *DSJ* 2 (1967) 5-14.

§697 *3.6.2.1.4 Literary Criticism on the Additions to Esther / The Rest of Esther*

*W. B. Stevenson, "Esther in the Apocrypha," *IJA* #5 (1906) 1-2.

Isidore Harris, "Apocryphal Additions to the Book of Esther," *IJA* #26 (1911) 50-52.

A. W. Streane, "The Additional Chapters of the Book of Esther," *IJA* #36 (1914) 6-8. *(Review)*

§698 *3.6.2.1.5 Literary Criticism on the Book of the Wisdom of Solomon*

Anonymous, "Who Wrote the Wisdom?" *MMBR* 16 (1803) 221-224, 305-307.

Anonymous, "Further Elucidations of Who Wrote the Wisdom?" *MMBR* 19 (1805) 326-329.

E. H. Plumptre, "The Life and Writings of Apollos. I. An Attempt to Fix the Authorship of the Wisdom of Solomon and the Epistle to the Hebrews," *Exp, 1st Ser.,* 1 (1875) 329-348.

E. H. Plumptre, "The Writings of Apollos. II. An Attempt to Fix the Authorship of the Wisdom of Solomon and the Epistle to the Hebrews," *Exp, 1st Ser.,* 1 (1875) 409-435.

Anonymous, "The Book of Wisdom," *CQR* 8 (1879) 77-98.

Reginald Lane Poole, "The Book of Wisdom," *ModR* 3 (1882) 441-461. *(Review)*

*E. R. Pope, "The Book of Wisdom and Ecclesiasticus," *ONTS* 4 (1884-85) 314-316.

D. S. Margoliouth, "Was the Book of Wisdom written in Hebrew?" *JRAS* (1890) 263-297.

J. Freudenthal, "What is the Original Language of the Wisdom of Solomon?" *JQR* 3 (1890-91) 722-753.

Moncure D. Conway, "'The Wisdom of Solomon'," *OC* 13 (1899) 21-27.

*F. R. Tennant, "The Teaching of Ecclesiasticus and Wisdom on the Introduction of Sin and Death," *JTS* 2 (1900-01) 207-223.

H. St. J. Thackeray, "Rhythm in the Book of Solomon," *JTS* 6 (1904-05) 232-237.

A. W. Streane, "The Book of Wisdom," *IJA* #6 (1906) 1.

Anonymous, "The Book of Wisdom," *IJA* #6 (1906) 2.

Crawford H. Toy, "Is the Book of Wisdom a unit?" *IJA* #10 (1907) 12-14.

*Frank Chamberlin Porter, "The Pre-Existence of the Soul in the Book of Wisdom and in the Rabbinical Writings," *AJT* 12 (1908) 53-115.

Anonymous, "The Book of the Wisdom of Solomon," *IJA* #12 (1908) 4-8.

D. C. Simpson, "The Book of Wisdom," *IJA* #17 (1909) 37-39.

*Richard Roberts, "St. Paul and the Book of Wisdom," *IJA* #18 (1909) 58-62; #19 (1909) 74-76.

*H. Bulcock, "The possible relation between the Pauline 'Christ' and the figure of Wisdom in the 'Wisdom of Solomon'," *IJA* #22 (1910) 61-63.

M. J. B. Bennett, "The Wisdom of Solomon," *IJA* #23 (1910) 67-69.

C. G. Montefiore, "An Analysis of the Contents of the Book of Wisdom," *IJA* #26 (1911) 41-43.

*Frank Porter Chamberlin, "The Pre-Existence of the Soul in the Book of Wisdom and in the Rabbinical Writings," *IJA* #29 (1912) 33-34. [Note by W. B. Stevenson, p. 34]

*H. McLachlan, "Was St. Luke influenced by the Book of Wisdom?" *IJA* #30 (1912) 60.

D. S. Margoliouth, "The Book of Wisdom in the Oxford Church Bible Commentary," *IJA* #34 (1913) 53-55. *(Review)*

A. T. S. Goodrick, "The Wisdom of Solomon," *IJA* #36 (1914) 4-5. *(Review)*

Anonymous, "A Quaker Translation of Ecclesiasticus and Wisdom, 1827," *IJA* #36 (1914) 17-18.

(   ) Nairne, "The Wisdom of Solomon," *IJA* #51 (1917) 50-52.

E[phraim] A. Speiser, "The Hebrew Origin of the First Part of the Book of Wisdom," *JQR, N.S.,* 14 (1923-24) 455-482.

T. Herbert Bindley, "The Book of Wisdom," *Theo* 11 (1925) 122-129.

*C. E. Purinton, "Translation Greek in the Wisdom of Solomon," *JBL* 47 (1928) 276-304.

May Waddington, "The Book of Wisdom," *ACM* 30 (1931) 272-277, 374-379.

*Herbert Lee Newman, "Influence of the Book of Wisdom on Early Christian Writings," *CQ* 8 (1931) 361-372.

*O. H. E. Burmester, "The Bohairic Pericopae of Wisdom and Sirach," *B* 15 (1934) 451-465.

*O. H. E. Burmester, "The Bohairic Pericopae of Wisdom and Sirach (II. III.)," *B* 16 (1935) 25-57, 141-174.

Stella Lange, "The Wisdom of Solomon and Plato," *JBL* 55 (1936) 293-302.

*Patrick Skehan, "Isaias and the Teaching of the Book of Wisdom," *CBQ* 2 (1940) 289-299.

*John J. Weisengoff, "Death and Immortality in the Book of Wisdom," *CBQ* 3 (1941) 104-133.

R[obert] H. Pfeiffer, "The Religious Teaching of the Wisdom of Solomon," *JBL* 64 (1945) viii.

Patrick W. Skehan, "Borrowings from the Psalms in the Book of Wisdom," *CBQ* 10 (1948) 384-397.

F. J. Yetter, "'The Wisdom of Solomon'," *RL* 17 (1948) 70-81.

Thomas Finan, "Hellenistic Humanism in the Book of Wisdom," *ITQ* 27 (1960) 30-48.

H. McKeating, "The Preacher and the Apocrypha," *PQL* 10 (1964) 353-359. *[The Wisdom of Solomon]*

James M. Reese, "Plan and Structure of the Book of Wisdom," *CBQ* 27 (1965) 391-399.

‡J. A. Emerton, "Commentaries on the Wisdom of Solomon," *Theo* 68 (1965) 376-380.

*R. M. Grant, "The Book of Wisdom at Alexandria. Reflections on the History of the Canon and Theology," *StP* 7 (1966) 462-472.

Frank Zimmermann, "The Book of Wisdom: Its Language and Character," *JQR, N.S.,* 57 (1966-67) 1-27, 101-135.

A[ddison] G. Wright, "The Structure of the Book of Wisdom," *B* 48 (1967) 165-184.

Addison G. Wright, "Numerical Patterns in the Book of Wisdom," *CBQ* 29 (1967) 524-238.

§699 **3.6.2.1.6** *Literary Criticism on the Book of Ecclesiasticus / The Wisdom of Jesus the Son of Sirach / Ben Sira*

†S. R., "Proverbs of Ben Sira," *MMBR* 2 (1796) 709-711.

†Anonymous, "Author of Ecclesiasticus; Who compiled the Ecclesiasticus?" *MMBR* 40 (1815-16) 407-410.

†Anonymous, "On Jesus, the Son of Sirach," *MMBR* 44 (1817-18) 35-37.

Anonymous, "Autobiographic Particulars of the Son of Sirach, continued," *MMBR* 44 (1817-18) 313-315.

Anonymous, "Autobiographic Particulars of the Son of Sirach, concluded," *MMBR* 44 (1817-18) 505-506.

Anonymous, "Autobiographic Particulars of the Son of Sirach," *MMBR* 46 (1818-19) 36-37, 405.

T. K. Cheyne, "Jesus the Son of Sirach," *Exp, 1st Ser.,* 11 (1880) 341-351.

W. J. Deane, "The Book of Ecclesiasticus: Its Contents and Character," *Exp, 2nd Ser.,* 6 (1883) 321-349.

*E. R. Pope, "The Book of Wisdom and Ecclesiasticus," *ONTS* 4 (1884-85) 314-316.

Aaron Bernstein, "Jesus, Son of Sirach," *TML* 2 (1889) 349-354.

Anonymous,   "Ecclesiasticus,"   *ONTS*   11   (1890)   55.

*S. Schechter, "The Quotations from Ecclesiasticus in Rabbinic Literature," *JQR* 3 (1890-91) 682-706.

F. C. Porter, "The Religious Ideas of the Book of Ecclesiasticus," *ONTS* 13 (1891) 25-34, 89-97.

A. Neubauer, "Hebrew Sentences in Ecclesiasticus," *JQR* 4 (1891-92) 162-164.

A. B. Davidson, "Sirach's Judgment of Women," *ET* 6 (1894-95) 402-404.

*Anonymous, "Ecclesiasticus and Philo," *MR* 78 (1896) 646-647.

*Moncure D. Conway, "Solomonic Literature," *OC* 12 (1898) 556-564. [(Ecclesiasticus) Wisdom, pp. 560-564]

Hope W. Hogg, "Another Edition of the Hebrew Ecclesiasticus," *AJSL* 15 (1898-99) 42-48.

*Samuel Krauss, "Notes on Sirach," *JQR* 11 (1898-99) 150-158. [1. The name Sirach; 2. The Author; 3. The Sayings of Sirach in Rabbinic Literature; 4. The word תחליף.]

Anonymous, "The Hebrew Ecclesiasticus," *MR* 81 (1899) 306-308.

J. A. Selbie, "The Sirach Controversy," *ET* 11 (1899-1900) 350-352.

Thomas Tyler, "Ecclesiasticus: The Retranslation Hypothesis," *JQR* 12 (1899-1900) 555-562.

*D. S. Margoliouth, "Lines of Defence of the Biblical Revelation. 4. The Argument from Silence," *Exp, 6th Ser.,* 2 (1900) 129-154. *[Evidence in Ecclesiasticus for the Canonicacy of Daniel]*

Anonymous,   "Ecclesiasticus,"   *MR*   82   (1900)   480-482.

Robert Dick Wilson, "Ecclesiasticus," *PRR* 11 (1900) 480-506. [I. Genuineness and Form of the Fragments; II. The Versions; III. Name and Author; IV. The Date; V. Relation to the Canon]

*F. R. Tennant, "The Teaching of Ecclesiasticus and Wisdom on the Introduction of Sin and Death," *JTS* 2 (1900-01) 207-223.

D. S. Margoliouth, "Some Notes on Ben-Sira," *ET* 14 (1902-03) 47-48.

C. Taylor, "The Wisdom of Ben Sira," *JQR* 15 (1902-03) 440-474, 604-626.

William Griffiths, "Ecclesiasticus. An Appreciation," *ET* 16 (1904-05) 44-48.

S. Schechter, "The Destruction of the Original Ecclesiasticus," *ET* 16 (1904-05) 185-186.

W. Bacher, "The Destruction of the Original of Ecclesiasticus," *ET* 16 (1904-05) 236-237.

D. S. Margoliouth, "Note on the Word 'Gānaz'," *ET* 16 (1904-05) 237. *[Ref. Previous two articles]*

C. Taylor, "The Alphabet of Ecclesiasticus," *JQR* 17 (1904-05) 238-239.

D. S. Margoliouth, "Ecclesiasticus," *IJA* #7 (1906) 1-2.

D. S. Margoliouth, "Ecclesiasticus in Arabic Literature," *ET* 18 (1906-07) 467-477.

C. Taylor, "The Alphabet of Ben Sira," *JP* 30 (1906-07) 95-132.

J. H. A. Hart, "The Prologue to Ecclesiasticus," *JQR* 19 (1906-07) 284-297. [The Composition of the Wisdom of Ben Sira; The Translation of the Wisdom of Ben Sira; Address to the Readers]

R. G. Moulton, "The Personality of the Son of Sirach," *IJA* #8 (1907) 13-14.

Allan F. Gardiner, "The Transmission of the Wisdom of Ben-Sira," *IJA* #10 (1907) 14-15.

N. Herz, "Dr. Ryssel on the Origin of the Doublets in the Hebrew 'Ben Sira'," *ET* 19 (1907-08) 189-190.

*D. S. Margoliouth, "Ecclesiastes and Ecclesiasticus," *Exp, 7th Ser.,* 5 (1908) 118-126.

Anonymous, "The Political Wisdom of Ben-Sira," *IJA* #13 (1908) 6-7.

H. F. B. Compston, "Word-Play in Ben Sira," *IJA* #18 (1909) 53-55.

Anonymous, "Ecclesiasticus," *IJA* #21 (1910) 27-28.

W. O. E. Oesterley, "The Date of Ecclesiasticus," *IJA* #21 (1910) 40-41.

J. H. A. Hart, "The Date of Ecclesiasticus," *IJA* #23 (1910) 69-71.

*Kemper Fullerton, "Studies in the Psalter," *BW* 37 (1911) 48-58. *[Title from Table of Contents:* "The Testimony of Ecclesiasticus as to the Psalter"*]*

W. O. E. Oesterley, "Ben-Sira on Men and Women," *IJA* #28 (1912) 3-10.

*E. H. Holthouse, "Dante and Ben Sira: A Comparison," *CQR* 75 (1912-13) 395-415.

M. Gaster, "Ecclesiasticus in the Cambridge Bible," *IJA* #32 (1913) 16-17. *(Review)*

*Anonymous, "A Quaker Translation of Ecclesiasticus and Wisdom, 1827," *IJA* #36 (1914) 17-18.

A. C. Benson, "Ecclesiasticus," *IJA* #43 (1915) 70-71.

*Robert Dick Wilson, "The Silence of Ecclesiasticus Concerning Daniel," *PTR* 14 (1916) 448-474. [Objections; Assumptions, Discussion of the Assumptions, Summary; Conclusions]

A. Buchler, "Ben Sira's conception of Sin and Atonement," *JQR, N.S.,* 13 (1922-23) 303-335, 461-502; 14 (1923-24) 53-83.

H. Biddulph, "The Date of Ecclesiasticus," *JTVI* 62 (1930) 117-128, 132-133. (Discussion, pp. 129-131)

*O. H. E. Burmester, "The Bohairic Pericopae of Wisdom and Sirach," *B* 15 (1934) 451-465.

*O. H. E. Burmester, "The Bohairic Pericopae of Wisdom and Sirach (II. III.)," *B* 16 (1935) 25-57, 141-174.

*W. B. Stevenson, "A Mnemonic Use of Numbers in Proverbs and Ben Sira," *GUOST* 9 (1938-39) 26-38.

Carl Semler, "Traces of the 'Sayings of the Seven Sages' in the *Liber Ecclesiasticus,*" *CBQ* 5 (1943) 264-274.

Emile Marmorstein, "A Note on the 'Alphabet of Ben Sira'," *JQR, N.S.,* 41 (1950-51) 303-306.

*Cecil Roth, "Ecclesiasticus in the Synagogue Service," *JBL* 71 (1952) 171-178.

Henry J. Cadbury, "The Grandson of Ben Sira," *HTR* 48 (1955) 219-225.

*P. Winter, "Ben Sira and the Teaching of 'Two Ways'," *VT* 5 (1955) 315-318.

H[enry] J. Cadbury, "The Grandson of Ben Sira," *BTr* 7 (1956) 77-81.

*Menahem Haran, "Problems of the Canonization of Scripture," *Tarbiz* 25 (1956-57) #3, I-III. [1. The place of *Ben Sira* in the History of the Canonization of the Bible; II. The Scriptures as 'Defiling the Hands'; III. The Holiness of Books and Their Consignment to Storage in *Genizoth.*]

A. Acrostic Foster, "The Date of Ecclesiasticus," *ATR* 41 (1959) 1-9.

*Robert T. Siebeneck, "May Their Bones Return to Life!—Sirach's Praise of the Fathers," *CBQ* 21 (1959) 411-428.

Louis F. Hartman, "Sirach in Hebrew and in Greek," *CBQ* 23 (1961) 443-451.

*Alexander A. Di Lella, "Qumrân and the Geniza Fragments of Sirach," *CBQ* 24 (1962) 245-267.

John G. Snaith, "The Importance of Ecclesiasticus (The Wisdom of Ben Sira)," *ET* 75 (1963-64) 66-69.

H. McKeating, "The Preacher and the Apocrypha," *PQL* 10 (1964) 219-225. *[Ecclesiasticus]*

James D. Purvis, "Ben Sira' and the Foolish People of Shechem," *JNES* 24 (1965) 88-94.

J[ohn]. G. Snaith, "Biblical Quotations in the Hebrew of Ecclesiasticus," *JTS, N.S.,* 18 (1967) 1-12.

§700 *3.6.2.1.7 Literary Criticism of the Book of Baruch*

George H. Schodde, "The Ethiopic Book of Baruch," *LQ* 8 (1878) 333-352.

J. M. Rodwell, "The Abyssinian or Aethiopic Book of Baruch," *SBAP* 1 (1878-79) 43-44.

W. B. Stevenson, "The Book of Baruch," *IJA* #9 (1907) 4-5.

H. Temple Robins, "The Complexity of the Book of Baruch," *IJA* #20 (1910) 4-7.

H. Temple Robins, "The Peculiarities of the Book of Baruch," *IJA* #21 (1910) 30-33.

W. B. Stevenson, "The Book of Baruch—I. Baruch," *IJA* #38 (1914) 79-80. *(Review)*

*M. R. James, "Notes on Apocrypha. I. Pseudo-Philo and Baruch," *JTS* 16 (1914-15) 403-405.

R. R. Harwell, "The Composition and Date of the Book of Baruch," *IJA* #45 (1916) 24-27.

§701 *3.6.2.1.8 Literary Criticism of the Letter of Jeremiah / The Epistle of Jeremy*

Wm. B. Stevenson, "The Epistle of Jeremy," *IJA* #38 (1914) 80. *(Review)*

§702 *3.6.2.1.9 Literary Criticism of the Prayer of Azariah and the Song of the Three Young Men / The Song of the Three Holy Children*

M. Gaster, "The Unknown Aramaic Original of Theodotion's Additions to the Book of Daniel. I. *Introduction*," *SBAP* 16 (1893-94) 280-290.

Eb. Nestle, "The Song of the Three Holy Children in Greek Bibles," *ET* 12 (1900-01) 527-528.

*F. A. Blackburn, "The Use in Old English Literature of the Apocryphal Passage in the Third Chapter of the Book of Daniel," *IJA* #19 (1909) 69-73. [Vulgate - 3:24-90; Chap. 13 and 14 from Theodotion]

§703 *3.6.2.1.10 Literary Criticism of the Story of Susanna*

W. H. Daubney, "The History of Susanna," *IJA* #14 (1908) 11-12.

*F. J. Knecht, "The Character of Judith and Susanna," *IJA* #24 (1911) 15-16.

M. Gaster, "The Story of the daughter of Amram: The Samaritan Parallel to the apocryphal story of Susanna," *IJA* #34 (1913) 45-49.

*E. H. Blakeney, "Julius Africanus: A Letter to Origen on the Story of Susanna," *Theo* 29 (1934) 164-169.

R. A. F. MacKenzie, "Susanna the Martyr," *Scrip* 9 (1957) 15-20.

R. A. F. MacKenzie, "The Meaning of the Susanna Story," *CJT* 3 (1957) 211-218.

Frank Zimmermann, "The Story of Susanna and Its Original Language," *JQR, N.S.,* 48 (1957-58) 236-241.

§704 *3.6.2.1.11 Literary Criticism of the Bel and the Dragon / Additions to the Book of Daniel*

*H. F. Talbot, "The Fight between Bel and the Dragon, and the Flaming Sword which turned Every Way (Gen. iii, 24.) *Translated from a Chaldean Tablet,*" *SBAT* 5 (1876-77) 1-21.

*William Hayes Ward, "Bel and the Dragon," *AJSL* 14 (1897-98) 94-105. *[Background]*

*T[heophilus] G. P[inches], "Talmudische und Midraschische Parallelen zum Babylonischen Weltschöpfungsepos," *JRAS* (1904) 369-370. *[English Text]*

A. W. Streane, "Bel and the Dragon," *IJA* #16 (1909) 3-6.

W. H. Daubney, "The History of Bel and the Dragon," *IJA* #25 (1911) 28-30.

W. H. Daubney, "The Three Additions to Daniel," *IJA* #37 (1914) 39-40. *(Review)*

T. Witton Davies, "The Three Additions to Daniel: Bel and the Dragon," *IJA* #39 (1914) 74-75.

A. H. Sayce, "The History of the Destruction of Bel and the Dragon," *IJA* #43 (1915) 58-59.

F. Zimmermann, "Bel and the Dragon," *VT* 8 (1958) 438-440.

§705 *3.6.2.1.12 Literary Criticism of the Prayer of Manasseh*

Anonymous, "The Prayer of Manasseh extant in Hebrew," *MMBR* 14 (1802) 414-415.

A. W. Stearne, "The Prayer of Manasses," *IJA* #14 (1908) 3-5.

*Henry H. Howorth, "Some Unconventional Views on the Text of the Bible. VIII. *The Prayer of Manasses and the Book of Esther*," *SBAP* 31 (1909) 89-99, 156-168.

H. F. B. Compston, "The Prayer of Manasses," *IJA* #37 (1914) 29-31. *(Review)*

†R. C. Fuller, "The Prayer of Manasses, King of Juda," *Scrip* 2 (1947) 49-50.

§706 *3.6.2.1.13 Literary Criticism of the Books of Maccabees*

I. Abrahams, "Niese on the Two Books of the Maccabees," *JQR* 13 (1900-01) 508-519. *(Review)*

William Fairweather, "I. and II. Maccabees," *IJA* #36 (1914) 10-11. *(Review)*

*Paul Haupt, "Maccabean Elegies," *JBL* 38 (1919) 157-170.

*R. B. Steele, "Notes on the Book of Job and Maccabees I. and II.," *MQR, 3rd Ser.*, 48 (1922) 148-150.

P. R. Ackroyd, "Criteria for the Maccabean Dating of the Old Testament Literature," *VT* 3 (1953) 113-132.

*S. Stein, "The Liturgy of Hanukkah and the First Two Books of Maccabees," *JJS* 5 (1954) 100-106, 148-155.

H. McKeating, "The Preacher and the Apocrypha," *PQL* 10 (1964) 264-270. *[I and II Maccabees]*

§707 *3.6.2.1.13.1 Literary Criticism of the Book of 1 Maccabees*

Anonymous, "A Biblical Fragment," *MMBR* 5 (1798) 129-130. *[1 Maccabees]*

R. Kraetzschmar, "The Original Name of the First Book of Maccabees," *ET* 12 (1900-01) 93-95.

Julius Boehmer, "Sarbeth Sabanaiel," *ET* 16 (1904-05) 191-192.

W. Fairweather, "The First Book of Maccabees," *IJA* #8 (1907) 4-5.

W. Fairweather, "Was I. Maccabees Written by a Sadducee?" *IJA* #11 (1907) 12-13.

Harry W. Ettelson, "The Integrity of I Maccabees," *CAAST* 27 (1925) 249-384.

Felix Gryglewicz, "Paradoxes in the First Book of Maccabees," *Scrip* 4 (1949-51) 197-205.

*Felix Gryglewicz, "Traces of the First Book of Maccabees in the Epistles of St Paul," *Scrip* 5 (1952-53) 149-152.

Solomon Zeitlin, "A Reply to a Reviewer," *JJS* 4 (1953) 85-90. *[1 Maccabees]*

§708 *3.6.2.1.13.2 Literary Criticism of the Book of 2 Maccabees*

W. Fairweather, "The Second Book of Maccabees," *IJA* #12 (1908) 8-9.

*Moses Hadas, "Aristeas and II Maccabees," *HTR* 42 (1949) 175-184.

M. B. Dagut, "II Maccabees and the Death of Antiochus IV Epiphanes," *JBL* 72 (1953) 149-157.

P. Katz, "Eleazar's Martyrdom in 2 Maccabees: The Latin Evidence for a Point of the Story," *StP* 4 (1961) 118-124.

§709 *3.6.3.1 Exegetical Studies on the Apocrypha*

*W. E. Boulter, "Marginal References to the Apocrypha in the Bible of 1611," *IJA* #6 (1906) 8-9.

(§710)   *3.6.3.1.1 Exegetical Studies on the Books of Esdras*

§711   *3.6.3.1.1.1 Exegetical Studies on the*
Book of 1 Esdras

*Anonymous, "The Earlier Chapters of the First Book of Esdras, and the Eleventh Book of the Jewish Antiquities of Josephus," *JSL, 4th Ser.,* 3 (1863) 143-154, 413-423.

Anonymous, "A 16th Century Dramatic Rendering of I(III) Esdras iii. 18-iv. 40," *IJA* #13 (1908) 17.

Anonymous, "Zorababell's Speech in the Esdras-Play 'King Darius,' 1565," *IJA* #14 (1908) 5-6. *[Compare: 1(3) Esdras 4:13-40]*

§712   *3.6.3.1.1.2 Exegetical Studies on the Book*
of 2 Esdras / 4 Ezra / The
Apocalypse of Ezra (Esdras)

Arthur F. Taylor, "Meditations in the Apocrypha," *ET* 36 (1924-25) 565-567. *[1:27; 2:37; 4:10; 5:33; 8:41]*

Michael E. Stone, "Some Features of the Armenian Version of IV Ezra," *Muséon* 79 (1966) 387-400.

2 Esdras Chapters 3 and 4

(Mrs.) L. Lydia Acadia Panter, "The Riddle of Good and Evil," *IJA* #35 (1913) 72-73. *[II. Esdras, Chapters 3 and 4 in verse]*

2 Esdras 4:8

*M. Stone, "Paradise in 4 *Ezra* iv. 8 and vii. 36, viii. 52," *JJS* 17 (1966) 85-88.

2 Esdras 4:13-19

C. N. Bromehead, "A Note on IV Ezra," *PEQ* 79 (1947) 129. *[4:13-19]*

2 Esdras 6:38-45

W. H. Daubney, "A Paraphrase upon II. Esdras vi. 38-45," *IJA* #29 (1912) 23-24.

2 Esdras 7:36

*M. Stone, "Paradise in 4 *Ezra* iv. 8 and vii. 36, viii. 52," *JJS* 17 (1966) 85-88.

2 Esdras 8:52

*M. Stone, "Paradise in 4 *Ezra* iv. 8 and vii. 36, viii. 52," *JJS* 17 (1966) 85-88.

2 Esdras 10:60-12:35

G. H. Box, "The Eagle-Vision of the Ezra Apocalypse," *OSHTP* (1910-11) 35-45. *[10:60-12:35]*

2 Esdras 13:45

William Aldis Wright, "Note on the 'Arzareth' of 4 Esdr. XIII. 45," *JP* 3 (1871) 113-114.

§713 *3.6.3.1.2 Exegetical Studies on the Book of Tobit*

B. H. C., "The Book of Tobit," *JSL, 3rd Ser.,* 6 (1857-58) 373-382.

P. P. Saydon, "Some Mistranslations in the Codex Sinaiticus of the Book of Tobit," *B* 33 (1952) 363-365. *[3:17; 5:16; 6:5; 7:11; 7:13; 7:16; 12:6]*

Tobit 1:13

*Felix Perles, "A Misunderstood Hebrew Word," *JQR, N.S.,* 17 (1926-27) 233. *[1:13]*

Tobit 3:8

*Louis H. Gray, "The Meaning of the Name Asmodaeus," *JRAS* (1934) 790-792. *[3:8]*

Tobit 3:17

*Louis H. Gray, "The Meaning of the Name Asmodaeus," *JRAS* (1934) 790-792. *[3:17]*

Tobit 6:1(6:2)

I. Abrahams, "Tobit's Dog," *JQR* 1 (1888-89) 288. *[6:1(6:2)]*

Tobit 11:11-13

Anonymous, "A Medical Explanation of the Miracle recorded in Tobit xi. 11-13," *IJA* #31 (1912) 79.

Tobit 14:5

*Eb. Nestle, "'The Times of the Gentiles'," *ET* 20 (1908-09) 279-280. *[14:5]*

§714 *3.6.3.1.3 Exegetical Studies on the Book of Judith*

Judith 8:14

*Rendel Harris, "A Quotation from Judith in the Pauline Epistles," *ET* 27 (1915-16) 13-15. *[Judith 8:14 // 1 Cor. 2:10]*

Judith 8:27

Aage Bentzen, "*ΕΠΥΡΩΕΝ,* Judith 8, 27," *BO* 9 (1952) 174-175.

Judith 16:15

P. Jouon, "Judith 16, 15," *B* 4 (1923) 112.

§715 *3.6.3.1.4 Exegetical Studies on the Additions to Esther / The Rest of Esther*

A. W. Streane, "The Esther-Additions in the Apocrypha," *IJA* #8 (1907) 9-10. *[10:4-13; 11:2-11; 11:12-12:6; 13:1-7, 8-11]*

A. W. Streane, "The Esther-Additions in the Apocrypha," *IJA* #9 (1907) 5-7. *[14:1-19; 15:1-16; 16:1-24]*

§716 *3.6.3.1.5 Exegetical Studies on the Book of the Wisdom of Solomon*

Arthur F. Taylor, "Meditations in the Apocrypha," *ET* 37 (1925-26) 139-142. *[1:2; 1:13; 4:13; 15:2; 17:11, 12]*

Wisdom Chapters 1-5

*Crawford H. Toy, "The Future in Wisdom i.-v.," *IJA* #14 (1908) 13-14.

*R. J. Taylor, "The Eschatological Meaning of Life and Death in the Book of Wisdom I-V," *ETL* 42 (1966) 72-137.

Wisdom Chapter 2

John P. Weisengoff, "The Impious of Wisdom 2," *CBQ* 11 (1949) 40-65.

Wisdom 2:10-5

M. Jack Suggs, "Wisdom of Solomon 2:10—5: A Homily Based on the Fourth Servant Song," *JBL* 76 (1957) 26-33.

Wisdom 2:23-24

W. J. Deane, "The Identification of the Serpent with Satan in the Book of Wisdom," *Exp, 2nd Ser.,* 6 (1883) 54-61. *[2:23, 24]*

Wisdom 2:24

*J. A. F. Gregg, "The Identification of the Serpent with Satan in the Book of Wisdom," *IJA* #23 (1910) 77-78. *[2:24]*

*W. H. A. Learoyd, "The Envy of the Devil in Wisdom II. 24," *ET* 60 (1939-40) 395-396.

Wisdom Chapters 10-19

Robert T. Siebeneck, "The Midrash of Wisdom 10-19," *CBQ* 22 (1960) 176-182.

Wisdom 10:10

E.   Burrows,   "Wisdom   X   10,"   *B*   20   (1939)   405-407.

Wisdom Chapters 11-19

Addison G. Wright, "The Structure of Wisdom 11-19," *CBQ* 27 (1965) 28-34.

Wisdom 12:3-7

D. Gill, "The Greek Sources of Wisdom XII 3-7," *VT* 15 (1965) 383-386.

Wisdom 15:3

Roland E. Murphy, "'To know your might is the root of Immortality' (Wis 15,3)," *CBQ* 25 (1963) 88-93.

Wisdom Chapter 17

L. L. Barclay, "The Seventeenth Chapter of the Book of Wisdom on its linguistic side," *IJA* #31 (1912) 64-67.

Wisdom 18:13-20

Anonymous, "The Book of Wisdom in Greek Lyrics," *IJA* #15 (1908) 16. *[18:13-20 (Poetic form)]*

Wisdom 18:14

Allen Cabaniss, "Wisdom 18:14f.: An Early Christmas Text," *VC* 10 (1956) 97-102.

§717 *3.6.3.1.6 Exegetical Studies on the Book of Ecclesiasticus/The Wisdom of Jesus the Son of Sirach / Ben Sira*

*W. Bacher, "Four Quotations from the Hebrew ben Sira," *JQR* 11 (1898-99) 344.

Arthur F. Taylor, "Meditations in the Apocrypha," *ET* 37 (1925-26) 40-42, 91-93. *[1:1, 9, 10, 26; 2:2; 3:1-16; 5:6; 7:36; 19:22; 21:27; 26:29; 39:21; 39:27]*

G. R. Driver, "Hebrew Notes on the Wisdom of Jesus ben Sirach," *JBL* 53 (1934) 273-290. *[3:12; 4:6; 12:11; 13:21; 14:2; 20:12; 27:5; 30:20; 31:19(2); 31:29; 32:11; 35:16; 36:8; 36:18(2); 37:14; 37:18; 37:19; 38:14; 38:16; 38:25; 39:17; 40:13; 40:14; 41:2; 41:5; 42:7; 43:2; 43:4; 43:7; 43:8; 43:20; 43:21; 44:3; 46:5; 47:7; 47:11; 47:15; 48:8; 48:13; 50:8; 51:4]*

Ecclesiasticus 3:14

*G. D. Kilpatrick, "προσανοικοδομηθήσεται Ecclus. III. 14," *JTS* 44 (1943) 147-148.

Ecclesiasticus 4:26

Bernard G. Hall, "Ecclesiasticus IV. 26," *ET* 37 (1925-26) 526.

Ecclesiasticus 6:11

*T. Penar, "Job 19, 19 in the Light of Ben Sira 6, 11," *B* 48 (1967) 293-295.

Ecclesiasticus 6:18-37

Donald Mackenzie, "The Sin of Accidie," *RL* 1 (1932) 115-120. *[6:18-37]*

Ecclesiasticus 7:25

D. S. Margoliouth, "Note on Ecclus. VII. 25," *ET* 23 (1911-12) 234-235.

Ecclesiasticus 11:19

*T. K. Cheyne, "On Some Suspected Passages in the Poetical Books of the Old Testament," *JQR* 10 (1897-98) 13-17. *[11:19]*

Ecclesiasticus 11:30

*D. S. Margoliouth, "Some Explanations of Ecclesiasticus," *IJA* #16 (1909) 6-8. *[11:30]*

Ecclesiasticus 12:1

*P[atrick W.] Skehan, "Didache 1, 6 and Sirach 12, 1," *B* 44 (1963) 533-536.

Ecclesiasticus 12:8-18

*D. S. Margoliouth, "Some Explanations of Ecclesiasticus," *IJA* #16 (1909) 6-8. *[12:8-18]*

Ecclesiasticus 12:10-19

Carl Selmer, "A Study of Ecclus. 12:10-19," *CBQ* 8 (1946) 306-314.

Ecclesiasticus 12:10-11

Eb. Nestle, "Ecclus. XII. 10, 11," *ET* 11 (1899-1900) 143.

Ecclesiasticus 14:12

*D. S. Margoliouth, "Three Notes on Ecclesiasticus," *ET* 13 (1901-02) 331-332. *[14:12 (Greek 16)]*

Ecclesiasticus 14:15

*T. K. Cheyne, "Biblical Difficulties," *Exp, 6th Ser.,* 3 (1901) 110-118. [3. Ecclesiasticus 14:15, pp. 116-117]

Ecclesiasticus Chapter 24

Bernard J. LeFrois, "Our Lady and Wisdom Passage from Sirach," *AER* 135 (1956) 1-8. *[Chapter 24]*

*T. Francis Glasson, "Colossians I 18, 15 and Sirach XXIV," *NT* 11 (1969) 154-156.

Ecclesiasticus 24:14

*Conrad Schick, "Reports of Dr. Conrad Schick. II. The Rose of Jericho," *PEFQS* 32 (1900) 63-65. *[24:14]*

Ecclesiasticus 26:22

Patrick W. Skehan, "Tower of Death or Deadly Snare? (Sir 26,22)," *CBQ* 16 (1954) 154.

Ecclesiasticus 33:2-4

*Joseph Reider, "Miscellanea Hebraica," *JJS* 3 (1952) 78-86. [17. Ecclus 33:2; 18. Ecclus. 33:4]

Ecclesiasticus 33:4

G. R. Driver, "Ben Sira, XXXIII, 4," *JJS* 5 (1954) 177.

Ecclesiasticus 33:5

*Felix Perles, "Ben Sira 33.5 (Comp. *JQR.,* N.S., XXI, 231)," *JQR, N.S.,* 22 (1931-32) 117.

Ecclesiasticus 33:13

D. Winton Thomas, "The LXX's Rendering of שנות לב טיב in Ecclus. XXXIII, 13," *VT* 10 (1960) 456.

Ecclesiasticus 33:31

*D. S. Margoliouth, "Some Explanations of Ecclesiasticus," *IJA* #16 (1909) 6-8. *[33:31]*

Ecclesiasticus 34:16-17 LXX

*Max L. Margolis, "A Passage in Ecclesiasticus," *ZAW* 21 (1901) 271-272. *[34:16-17 LXX]*

Ecclesiasticus 38:24-39:11

J. Estlin Carpenter, "The Scribe and the Craftsman. (Ecclesiasticus 38:24-39:11)," *IJA* #15 (1908) 5-7.

Ecclesiasticus 38:33

Patrick W. Skehan, "They shall not be found in parables (Sir 38,33)," *CBQ* 23 (1961) 40.

Ecclesiasticus 40:12

*David Kaufmann, "Notes on Sirach XLIII. 20 and XL. 12," *JQR* 11 (1898-99) 159-162.

Ecclesiasticus 40:16

*D. S. Margoliouth, "Three Notes on Ecclesiasticus," *ET* 13 (1901-02) 331-332. *[40:16 (Syriac)]*

Ecclesiasticus 41:14

*D. S. Margoliouth, "Three Notes on Ecclesiasticus," *ET* 13 (1901-02) 331-332. *[41:14]*

Ecclesiasticus 41:19

G. Buchanan Gray, "A Note on the Text and Interpretation of Ecclus. XLI. 19," *JQR* 9 (1896-97) 567-572.

*G. Buchanan Gray, "Two Notes on the Hebrew Ecclesiasticus," *OSHTP* (1896-97) 36-40. [II. On the Text and Interpretation of Eccles. XLI. 19, pp. 39-40]

Ecclesiasticus 42:3

*T. K. Cheyne, "On Some Suspected Passages in the Poetical Books of the Old Testament," *JQR* 10 (1897-98) 13-17. *[42:3]*

Ecclesiasticus 43:4

*D. S. Margoliouth, "The Hebrew Ecclesiasticus, I.," *ET* 10 (1898-99) 567-568. *[43:4c]*

Ed. König, "Ecclus. XLIII. 4c. In Reply to Professor Margoliouth," *ET* 11 (1899-1900) 45-46.

Ecclesiasticus 43:17

*C. Levias, "Ecclesiasticus 43:17 and 49:9," *AJSL* 14 (1897-98) 129.

Ecclesiasticus 43:20

C. Taylor, "Studies in Ben Sira," *JQR* 10 (1897-98) 470-488. [I. Job xiii 28 and Ecclesiasticus xliii 20, pp. 471-472]

*David Kaufmann, "Notes on Sirach XLIII. 20 and XL. 12," *JQR* 11 (1898-99) 159-162.

*T. K. Cheyne, "Biblical Difficulties," *Exp, 6th Ser.,* 3 (1901) 110-118. [4. Ecclesiasticus 43:20, p. 118]

Ecclesiasticus 44:16

*C. Taylor, "Two Notes on Enoch in Sir. xliv 16," *JTS* 4 (1902-03) 589-590.

*J. H. A. Hart, "Two Notes on Enoch in Sir. xliv 16," *JTS* 4 (1902-03) 590-591.

Ecclesiasticus 45:25

*J. Priest, "*Ben Sira* 45, 25 in the Light of Qumran Literature," *RdQ* 5 (1964-66) 111-118.

Ecclesiasticus 46:4-5

*Michael J. Gruenthaner, "Two Sun Miracles of the Old Testament," *CBQ* 10 (1948) 271-290. [Ecclus 46:4, 5, pp. 283-284]

Ecclesiasticus 48:17

J. H. A. Hart, "Sir. xlviii 17, *a, b,*" *JTS* 4 (1902-03) 591-592.

Ecclesiasticus 49:8-10

*G. Buchanan Gray, "Two Notes on the Hebrew Ecclesiasticus," *OSHTP* (1896-97) 36-40. [I. The Reference to Job and the Canon in Eccles. XLIX. 8-10, pp. 36-39]

Ecclesiasticus 49:9

*C. Levias, "Ecclesiasticus 43:17 and 49:9," *AJSL* 14 (1897-98) 129.

Ecclesiasticus 50:1-3

C. Taylor, "Studies in Ben Sira," *JQR* 10 (1897-98) 470-488. [II.Ecclesiasticus l. 1-3, pp. 473-476]

Ecclesiasticus 50:5-8

D. Kaufmann, "Sirach L. 5-8," *JQR* 10 (1897-98) 727-728.

Ecclesiasticus 50:9

T. K. Cheyne, "Note on Sirach L. 9," *JQR* 12 (1899-1900) 554.

Ecclesiasticus 51:13-29

C. Taylor, "The Alphabet of Ben Sira," *JP* 30 (1906-07) 95-132. *[51:13-29]*

Ecclesiasticus 51:21

D. Winton Thomas, "A Note on Ecclus. 51:21a," *JTS, N.S.,* 20 (1969) 225-226.

§718 *3.6.3.1.7 Exegetical Studies on the Book of Baruch*

Baruch Chapters 1-5

H. Temple Robins, "The Book of Baruch," *IJA* #22 (1910) 52-59. *[Chaps. 1-5]*

Baruch 1:4

J. A. Bewer, "The River Sud in the Book of Baruch," *JBL* 45 (1924) 226-227. *[1:4]*

§719 *3.6.3.1.8 Exegetical Studies on Letter of Jeremiah*
*   / The Epistle of Jeremy*

Epistle of Jeremy Chapter 26

*John Wesley Rice, "On the Septuagint Text of I Samuel 20.3 and the Epistle of Jeremiah 26," *AJP* 21 (1900) 445-447.

§720 *3.6.3.1.9 Exegetical Studies on the Prayer of Azariah*
*   and the Song of the Three Young Men*
*   / The Song of the Three Holy Children*

*M. Gaster, "The Unknown Aramaic Original of Theodotion's Additions to the Book of Daniel. III. *Commentary*," *SBAP* 17 (1895) 75-94. *[Song of the Three Children]*

Anonymous, "The Canticle of the Three Children," *IJA* #10 (1907) 4. *[Translation in Metred Verse]*

Anonymous, "Sternhold and Hopkins' 'Benedicite'," *IJA* #12 (1908) 13-14. *[Early English Translation]*

(§721) *3.6.3.1.10 Exegetical Studies on the Story of Susanna*

§722 *3.6.3.1.11 Exegetical Studies on Bel and the Dragon*
*   / Additions to the Book of Daniel*

*M. Gaster, "The Unknown Aramaic Original of Theodotion's Additions to the Book of Daniel. III. *Commentary*," *SBAP* 17 (1895) 75-94. *[Bel and the Dragon]*

A. W. Streane, "Bel and the Dragon. Notes on individual words and Passages," *IJA* #16 (1909) 5-6.

(§723) **3.6.3.1.12 Exegetical Studies on the Prayer of Manasseh**

(§724) **3.6.3.1.13 Exegetical Studies on the Books of Maccabees**

§725   **3.6.3.1.13.1 Exegetical Studies on the
                                        Book of 1 Maccabees**

1 Maccabees 1:33

*W. F. Birch, "The Levelling of Akra," *PEFQS* 35 (1903) 353-355. *[1:33]*

1 Maccabees Chapters 2-5

Felix Perles, "The Name ΜΑΚΚΑΒΑῖΟΣ," *JQR, N.S.*, 17 (1926-27) 404-405.

H. Hirschfeld, "The Name ΜΑΚΚΑΒΑῖΟΙ," *JQR, N.S.*, 18 (1927-28) 57. *[Chapters 2-5]*

1 Maccabees Chapter 2

Wallace N. Stearns, "Notes on Acts xiii 9 and the Assuptio Mosis[sic]* ix," *JBL* 19 (1900) 53-54. *[Chapter 2]*

1 Maccabees 3:1-9

C. F. Burney, "An Acrostic Poem in Praise of Judas Maccabaeus," *JTS* 21 (1919-20) 319-325. *[3:1-9]*

1 Maccabees 3:48

A. F. Kirkpatrick, "1 Maccabees iii. 48," *JP* 14 (1885) 111-112.

1 Maccabees 9:15

*Charles C. Torrey, "Three Troublesome Proper Names in First Maccabees," *JBL* 53 (1934) 31-33. *[9:15]*

*S. Yeivin, "Topographic Notes (annotations to S. Klein, *The Land of Judah*)," *BIES* 8 (1940-41) #2, II. [1. Ἀζώτου ὄρους — 1 Macc. 9:15]

1 Maccabees 12:37

Howard Crosby, "Note on a Verse in the First Book of Maccabees," *OBJ* 1 (1880) 201. *[12:37]*

Howard Crosby, "Note on a Verse in the First Book of Maccabees," *AAOJ* 3 (1880-81) 127-128. *[12:37]*

*Charles C. Torrey, "Three Troublesome Proper Names in First Maccabees," *JBL* 53 (1934) 31-33. *[12:37]*

1 Maccabees 13:50

*W. F. Birch, "The Levelling of Akra," *PEFQS* 35 (1903) 353-355. *[13:50]*

1 Maccabees 14:28

A. R. S. Kennedy, "Saramel-Asaramel, I Mac. xiv. 28," *ET* 11 (1899-1900) 523-526.

A. J. Grieve, "Saramel-Asaramel, I Mac. xiv. 28," *ET* 11 (1899-1900) 564.

*Charles C. Torrey, "Three Troublesome Proper Names in First Maccabees," *JBL* 53 (1934) 31-33. *[14:28]*

§726   ***3.6.3.1.13.2 Exegetical Studies on the Book of 2 Maccabees***

2 Maccabees 4:30-38

*M. Stern, "The Death of Onias III," *Zion* 25 (1960) #1, I. *[4:30-38]*

2 Maccabees 12:39-45

Anonymous, "2nd Maccabees 12:39-45; and Purgatory and Prayers for the Dead," *SPR* 13 (1860-61) 296-324.

2 Maccabees 12:39-44

*J. W. Hunkin, "Judas Maccabaeus and Prayers for the Dead," *Exp 8th Ser.,* 9 (1915) 361-365. *[12:39-44]*

§727 *3.6.4.1 Textual Criticism on the Pseudepigrapha - General Studies*

J. S. Candlish, "On the Moral Character of Pseudonymous Books," *Exp, 4th Ser.*, 4 (1891) 91-107, 262-279.

J. Paton Gloag, "Deane's Pseudepigrapha," *TML* 6 (1891) 301-315.

*William Watson, "The New Heaven and the New Earth," *Exp, 8th Ser.*, 9 (1915) 165-179.

*[J.] Rendel Harris, "Woodbrooke Studies. Editions and Translations of Christian Documents in Syriac and Garshūni. Fasc. 2., Introductions," *BJRL* 11 (1927) 329-351. (Letter by W. R. Smith, pp. 338-339)

A. M. Denis and M. de Jonge, "The Greek Pseudepigrapha of the Old Testament," *NT* 7 (1965) 319-328.

§728   *3.6.4.1.1 Textual Criticism on the Apocalyptic Literature - General Studies*

Arie Rubinstein, "Hebraisms in the Slavonic 'Apocalypse of Abraham'," *JJS* 4 (1953) 108-115; 5 (1954) 132-134.

§729   *3.6.4.1.1.1 Textual Criticism on the Books of Enoch*

R. H. Charles, "The Ethiopic Manuscripts of Enoch in the British Museum," *ET* 3 (1891-92) 135.

George H. Schodde, "The New Greek Enoch Fragments," *BW* 1 (1893) 359-362.

Campbell Bonner, "Biblical Papyri at the University of Michigan," *HTR* 25 (1932) 205-206.

C. Kaplan, "Versions and Readings in the Book of Enoch," *AJSL* 50 (1933-34) 171-177.

S. P. Brock, "A Fragment of Enoch in Syriac," *JTS, N.S.,* 19 (1968) 626-631.

§730   **3.6.4.1.1.1.1 Textual Criticism on the Book of 1 Enoch**

Frank Zimmermann, "The Bilingual Character of I Enoch," *JBL* 60 (1941) 159-172.

G[unter] Zuntz, "Notes on the Greek Enoch," *JBL* 61 (1942) 193-204.

G[unter] Zuntz, "The Greek Text of Enoch 102:1-3," *JBL* 63 (1944) 53-54.

J. C. Hindley, "Towards a Date for the Similitudes of Enoch. An Historical Approach," *NTS* 14 (1967-68) 551-565.

Moshe Gil, "Enoch in the Land of Eternal Life," *Tarbiz* 38 (1968-69) #4, I-II. *[Aramaic Fragments of 1 Enoch]*

§731   **3.6.4.1.1.1.2 Textual Criticism on the Book of 2 Enoch / The Book of the Secrets of Enoch / Slavonic Enoch**

J. A. Selbie, "The Slavonic Enoch," *ET* 8 (1896-97) 383-384.

Nathaniel Schmidt, "The Two Recensions of Slavonic Enoch," *JAOS* 41 (1921) 307-312.

(§732) **3.6.4.1.1.2 Textual Criticism on the Books of Baruch**

§733   **3.6.4.1.1.2.1 Textual Criticism on the Book of 1 Baruch / The Rest of the Words of Baruch / Paralipomenon of Jeremiah**

*A. Mingana, "Woodbrooke Studies. Editions and Translations of Christian Documents in Syriac and Garshūni. Prefaces, Texts and Translations," *BJRL* 11 (1927) 352-437. [(i) A New Jeremiah Apocryphon - [M 240]]

§734   **3.6.4.1.1.2.2 Textual Criticism on the Book of 2 Baruch / The Apocalypse of Baruch (Syriac and / or Greek) / 3 Baruch**

B. P. Grenfell, "A Fragment of the *Apocalypse of Baruch* from Oxyrhynchus," *OSHTP* (1902-03) 41-43.

M. R. James, "Notes on Apocrypha. VI. Traces of the Greek Apocalypse of Baruch in other Writings," *JTS* 16 (1914-15) 410-413.

F[rank] Zimmermann, "Textual Observations on the Apocalypse of Baruch," *JTS* 40 (1939) 151-156.

Sherman E. Johnson, "Notes and Comments," *ATR* 21 (1939) 205-206; 22 (1940) 330-331. *[Sources of the Syriac Apocalypse of Baruch]*

(§735) *3.6.4.1.1.3 Textual Criticism on the Book of the Assumption of Moses / The Testament of Moses*

§736 *3.6.4.1.1.4 Textual Criticism on the Book of the Ascension of Isaiah / The Martyrdom of Isaiah*

George H. Schodde, "'Ascensio Isaiae'," *LQ* 8 (1878) 513-538.

(§737) *3.6.4.1.1.5 Textual Criticism on the Books of Legendary Works*

§738   *3.6.4.1.1.5.1 Textual Criticism on the Book of Jubilees / The Laws of Moses*

Geo. H. Schodde, "The Book of Jubilees," *BS* 42 (1885) 629-645. [Introductory Notes; Chaps. 1-2]

Geo. H. Schodde, "The Book of Jubilees," *BS* 43 (1886) 56-72. [Chapters III.-IV.]

Geo. H. Schodde, "The Book of Jubilees," *BS* 43 (1886) 356-371. [Chapters VII.-XI.]

Geo. H. Schodde, "The Book of Jubilees," *BS* 43 (1886) 455-486. [Chapters XII.-XXIII.]

Geo. H. Schodde, "The Book of Jubilees," *BS* 43 (1886) 727-745. [Chaps. 24-30]

Geo. H. Schodde, "The Book of Jubilees," *BS* 44 (1887) 426-459. [Chapters XXXI-XLV]

Geo. H. Schodde, "The Book of Jubilees (Chapters XLVI.—L.)," *BS* 44 (1887) 602-611. [Errata, p. 7 of "Contents of Vol. XLV"*[sic]* (in Vol. 44)]

R. H. Charles, "The Book of Jubilees, Translated from a Text Based on Two Hitherto Uncollated Ethiopic MSS.," *JQR* 5 (1892-93) 703-708.

R. H. Charles, "A New Translation of the Book of Jubilees. Part I," *JQR* 6 (1893-94) 184-217.

R. H. Charles, "A New Translation of the Book of Jubilees. Part II," *JQR* 6 (1893-94) 710-745.

R. H. Charles, "A New Translation of the Book of Jubilees. *(Concluded),*" *JQR* 7 (1894-95) 297-328.

Charles C. Torrey, "A Hebrew Fragment of Jubilees," *JBL* 71 (1952) 39-41.

W. Baars and R. Zuurmond, "The Project for a New Edition of the Ethiopic Book of Jubilees," *JSS* 9 (1964) 67-74.

(§739)   *3.6.4.1.1.5.2 Textual Criticism on the Book of the Lives of the Prophets*

§740   *3.6.4.1.1.5.3 Textual Criticism on the Book of 3 Maccabees*

J. Rendel Harris, "Metrical Fragments in III Maccabees," *BJLR* 5 (1918-20) 195-207.

§741   *3.6.4.1.1.5.4 Textual Criticism on the Book of 4 Maccabees*

W. Fairweather, "The Fourth Book of Maccabees," *IJA* #17 (1909) 28-29.

§742 *3.6.4.1.1.6 Textual Criticism on the Books of Psalmic Literature*

*John Strugnell, "Notes on the Text and Transmission of the Apocryphal Psalms 151, 154 (= Syr. II) and 155 (=Syr. III)," *HTR* 59 (1966) 257-281.

§743   *3.6.4.1.1.6.1 Textual Criticism on the Book of the Psalms of Solomon*

Bernhard Pick, "The Psalter of Solomon," *PR* 4 (1883) 775-812.

W. Baars, "An Additional Fragment of the Syriac Version of the Psalms of Solomon," *VT* 11 (1961) 222-223.

W. Baars, A New Fragment of the Greek Version of the Psalms of Solomon," *VT* 11 (1961) 441-444.

(§744) *3.6.4.1.1.7 Textual Criticism on the Testamental Literature*

§745   *3.6.4.1.1.7.1 Textual Criticism on the Testament of the Twelve Patriarchs*

M. Gaster, "The Hebrew Text of One of the Testaments of the Twelve Patriarchs," *SBAP* 16 (1893-94) 33-49, 109-117. *[Naphtali]*

James Marshall, "The Hebrew Text of One of the Testaments of the Twelve Patriarchs," *SBAP* 16 (1893-94) 83-86. *[Naphtali]*

*F. C. Conybeare, "A Collation of Sinker's Text of the Testaments of Reuben and Simeon with the Old Armenian Version," *JQR* 8 (1895-96) 260-268.

*F. C. Conybeare, "A Collation of Armenian Texts of the Testaments of (1) Judah; (2) Dan; (3) Joseph; (4) Benjamin," *JQR* 8 (1895-96) 471-485.

H. Leonard Pass and J. Arendzen, "Fragment of an Aramaic Text of the Testament of Levi," *JQR* 12 (1899-1900) 651-661.

*F. C. Conybeare, "The Testament of Job and the Testaments of the XII Patriarchs, According to the Text of Cod. Vatican. Graecus, 1238," *JQR* 13 (1900-01) 111-127.

R. H. Charles and A. Cowley, "An Early Source of the Testaments of the Patriarchs," *JQR* 19 (1906-07) 566-583.

J. W. Hunkin, "The Testaments of the Twelve Patriarchs," *JTS* 16 (1914-15) 80-97.

M. R. James, "The Venice Extracts from the Testament of the Twelve Patriarchs," *JTS* 28 (1926-27) 337-348.

K. H. Kuhn, "The Sahidic Testament of Isaac," *JTS, N.S.,* 8 (1957) 225-239. [Index of Loan-Words, pp. 238-239]

K. H. Kuhn, "An English Translation of the Sahidic Version of the Testament of Isaac," *JTS, N.S.,* 18 (1967) 325-336.

(§746)   **3.6.4.1.1.7.2 Textual Criticism on the Testament of Adam
/ The Books of Adam and Eve**

§747   **3.6.4.1.1.7.3 Textual Criticism on the Testament
of Abraham**

M. Gaster, "The Apocalypse of Abraham, *From the Roumanian Text, discovered and Translated by* Dr. M. Gaster," *SBAT* 9 (1886-93) 195-226.

N. Turner, "The 'Testament of Abraham': Problems in Biblical Greek,"
NTS 1 (1954-55) 219-223.

§748   **3.6.4.1.1.7.4 Textual Criticism on theTestament of Job**

*F. C. Conybeare, "The Testament of Job and the Testaments of the XII
Patriarchs, According to the Text of Cod. Vatican. Graecus, 1238," *JQR*
13 (1900-01) 111-127.

§749 **3.6.4.1.1.8 Textual Criticism on the Letter of Aristeas**

H. St. J. Thackeray, "Translation of the Letter of Aristeas," *JQR* 15 (1902-
03) 337-391.

§750 **3.6.4.1.1.9 Textual Criticism on the Sibylline Oracles**

Eva Matthews Sanford, "The Influence of the Sibylline Books," *PAPA* 71
(1940) l. *[Roman numeral]*

(§751) **3.6.4.1.1.10 Textual Criticism on the Zadokite Document
[See also: The Zadokite Document /
The Damascus Document under
Qumran Literature→]**

§752 **3.6.4.1.1.11 Textual Criticism on other Pseudepigraphal Books**

Richard J. H. Gottheil, "An Arabic Version of the 'Revelation of Ezra',"
AJSL 4 (1887-88) 14-17.

M. R. James, "The Apocryphal Ezekiel," *JTS* 15 (1913-14) 236-243.

*M. R. James, "Notes on Apocrypha. V. Tertullian's allusion to the Apoca-
lypse of Adam," *JTS* 16 (1914-15) 409-410.

M. R. James, "Some Coptic Apocrypha. II.," *JTS* 18 (1916-17) 164-165. *[The Apocalypse of Zephaniah]*

A. Marmorstein, "A Fragment of the Visions of Ezekiel," *JQR, N.S.,* 8 (1917-18) 367-378.

§753 *3.6.5.1 Literary Criticism of the Pseudepigrapha - General Studies*

*A. S. D. Maunder (Mrs. Walter), "Astronomical Allusions in Sacred Books of the East," *JTVI* 47 (1915) 181-226, 231-232. [(Discussion, pp. 226-228) (Communication by F. C. Burkitt, pp. 228-231)]

G. F. Hamilton, "The Odes of Solomon and the Pseudepigrapha," *IJA* #44 (1916) 12-14.

§754   *3.6.5.1.1 Literary Criticism of the Apocalyptic Literature - General Studies*

Anonymous, "Side-Lights. The Apocryphal Apocalypses," *DTQ* 1 (1875) 145-146.

F. C. Conybeare, "On the Apocalypse of Moses," *JQR* 7 (1894-95) 216-235. [Translation, pp. 219-235]

*K. Kohler, "The Pre-Talmudic Haggada, II. C. The Apocalypse of Abraham and its Kindred," *JQR* 7 (1894-95) 581-606.

E. Bevan, "Jewish and Christian Apocalypses," *JTS* 16 (1914-15) 274-277. *(Review)*

*K. Kohler, "The Essenes and the Apocalyptic Literature," *JQR, N.S.,* 11 (1920-21) 145-168.

*E. E. Flack, "Motives for Pseudonymity in the Apocalypses: A Study in the Continuity of Revelation," *LCQ* 9 (1936) 1-17.

George W. MacRae, "The Coptic Gnostic Apocalypse of Adam," *HeyJ* 6 (1965) 27-35.

§755   *3.6.5.1.1.1 Literary Criticism of the Books of Enoch*

Anonymous, "Remarks on the Book of Enoch," *MMBR* 11 (1801) 300-301.

M. J. Cramer, "Biblical Monographs. The Book of Enoch," *MR* 51 (1869) 424-431.

Paton J. Gloag, "The Book of Enoch," *BFER* 28 (1879) 538-560.

William J. Deane, "The Book of Enoch," *TML* 4 (1890) 1-16.

*Benjamin Wisner Bacon, "II. The Calendar of Enoch and Jubilees," *AJSL* 8 (1891-92) 124-131.

*R[obert] H[enry] Charles, "Messianic Doctrine in the Book of Enoch, and Its Influence on the New Testament," *ET* 4 (1892-93) 301-303.

T. K. Cheyne, "Mr. Charles's Edition of the Book of Enoch," *ET* 4 (1892-93) 507-509. *(Review)*

*H. J. Lawlor, "Early citations from the Book of Enoch," *JP* 25 (1897) 164-225.

*Henry Hayman, "The Book of Enoch in Reference to the New Testament and Early Christian Antiquity," *BW* 12 (1898) 37-46.

*M. Gaster, "The Logos Ebraikes in the Magical Papyri of Paris, and the Book of Enoch," *JRAS* (1901) 109-117.

*Carl Clemen, "The First Epistle of St. Peter and the Book of Enoch," *Exp, 6th Ser.,* 6 (1902) 316-320.

*C. Taylor, "Two Notes on Enoch in Sir. xliv 16," *JTS* 4 (1902-03) 589-590.

*J. H. A. Hart, "Two Notes on Enoch in Sir. xliv 16," *JTS* 4 (1902-03) 590-591.

*C. Taylor, "Enoch and Clement," *JP* 29 (1903-04) 185-198.

H. J. Lawlor, "The Book of Enoch in the Egyptian Church," *Herm* 13 (1904-05) 178-183. *[Ethiopic Enoch]*

*E. G. King, "Enoch and the Feast of Dedication. (A Study in Natural Religion)," *ICMM* 5 (1908-09) 287-295.

L. S. A. Wells, "The Historical Succession of the Books of Enoch," *IJA* #23 (1910) 72-76; #24 (1911) 10-15.

J. E. H. Thompson, "The Enoch Books," *IJA* #37 (1914) 32-34. *(Review)*

A. C. Bouquet, "Why is the Book of Enoch So Important?" *ICMM* 11 (1914-15) 206-211.

Nathaniel Schmidt, "Traces of Early Acquaintance in Europe with the Book of Enoch," *JAOS* 42 (1922) 44-52.

Adam C. Welch, "A Zealot Pamphlet," *Exp, 8th Ser.,* 25 (1923) 273-287. *[Enoch]*

G. H. Box, "The Hebrew Book of Enoch," *JQR, N.S.,* 20 (1929-30) 77-85. *(Review)*

H. Hamann, "The Book of Enoch," *AusTR* 10 (1939) 84.

*O. Neugebauer, "Notes on Ethiopic Astronomy," *Or, N.S.,* 33 (1964) 49-71.

*Geo Widengren, "Iran and Israel in Parthian Times with Special Regard to the Ethiopic Book of Enoch," *Tem* 2 (1966) 139-177.

§756   *3.6.5.1.1.1.1 Literary Criticism of the Book of 1 Enoch*

*M. Stuart, "Future Punishment, as exhibited in the Book of Enoch," *BRCR, N.S.,* 4 (1840) 1-35.

*M. Stuart, "Christology of the Book of Enoch; *With an account of the Book itself, and Critical Remarks upon it,*" *BRCR, N.S.,* 3 (1840) 86-137.

A. G. Laurie, "The Book of Enoch," *UQGR, N.S.,* 15 (1878) 163-177.

*A. G. Laurie, "The Book of Enoch and the Apocrypha," *UQGR, N.S.,* 15 (1878) 339-348.

James Conford, "The Book of Enoch," *CM* 23 (1886) 51-53.

William J. Deane, "The Book of Enoch. Date, Authorship, and General Results," *TML* 4 (1890) 229-244.

*F. C. Burkitt, "Four Notes on the Book of Enoch," *JTS* 8 (1906-07) 444-447. [1. On the name of the Angel Semiazas, pp. 444-445; 4. On the Ethiopic for 'the Son of Man', pp. 446-447]

*L. W. Grensted, "The Use of Enoch in St. Luke XVI. 19-31," *ET* 26 (1914-15) 333-334.

*Hewlett Johnson, "The Editor's Notes," *ICMM* 12 (1915-16) 1-20, 111. *[The Book of Enoch]*

R[obert] D[ick] Wilson, "The Origin of the Ideas in Daniel," *PTR* 21 (1923) 161-201. [II. Daniel and Enoch, pp. 177-194]

G. H. Dix, "The Enochic Pentateuch," *JTS* 27 (1925-26) 29-42. *[Ethiopic Enoch]*

Wallace Newton Stearns, "Some Scientific Views of a Cultured Jew in the First Century B.C.," *PAPA* 57 (1927) xxix. *[Book of Enoch]*

Wallace N[ewton] Stearns, "Scientific Views of a Cultured Jew, First Century, B.C.," *OC* 42 (1928) 503-507. *[Book of Enoch]*

*C[haim] Kaplan, "Angels in the Book of Enoch," *ATR* 12 (1929-30) 423-437.

*Chaim Kaplan, "The Flood in the Book of Enoch and Rabbinics," *JSOR* 15 (1931) 22-24.

*Leo Jung, "Mis-Translations a Source of Jewish and Christian Lore," *PAAJR* 5 (1933-34) 55-67. [II The "Watchers" of Enoch, pp. 59-60]

Grant McColley, "The Book of Enoch and Paradise Lost," *HTR* 31 (1938) 21-39.

Arnold Williams, "Milton and the Book of Enoch—An Alternative Hypothesis," *HTR* 33 (1940) 291-299.

F. Zimmerman*[sic]*, "Linguistic Composition of I Enoch," *JBL* 59 (1940) xv.

(Mrs.) Euphemia Van Rensselaer Wyatt, "Enoch and His Angels," *DR* 211 (1942) 134-140.

*George E. Ladd, "The Kingdom of God in I Enoch," *BS* 109 (1952) 318-331; 110 (1953) 32-49.

James Muilenburg, "The Son of Man in Daniel and the Ethiopic Apocalypse of Enoch," *JBL* 70 (1960) 197-209.

R. H. Altus, "Enoch," *AusTR* 34 (1963) 124-132; 35 (1964) 16-20.

S. Aalen, "St. Luke's Gospel and the Last Chapters of I Enoch," *NTS* 13 (1966-67) 1-13.

§757   ***3.6.5.1.1.1.2 Literary Criticism of the Book of 2 Enoch***
          / The Book of the Secrets of Enoch
          / Slavonic Enoch

*Eb. Nestle, "Eph. V. 14 and the Secrets of Enoch," *ET* 9 (1897-98) 376-377.

L. S. A. Wells, "The Historical Succession of the Books of Enoch: 'The Secrets of Enoch'," *IJA* #25 (1911) 30-34.

J. K. Fotheringham, "The Date and Place of the Writing of the Slavonic Enoch," *JTS* 20 (1918-19) 252.

R. H. Charles, "The Date and Place of Writing of the Slavonic Enoch," *JTS* 22 (1920-21) 161-164.

J. K. Fotheringham, "The Easter Calendar and the Slavonic Enoch," *JTS* 23 (1921-22) 49-56.

Kirsopp Lake, "The Date of Slavonic Enoch," *HTR* 16 (1923) 397-398.

Arie Rubinstein, "Observations on the Slavonic Book of Enoch," *JJS* 13 (1962) 1-21.

(§758) ***3.6.5.1.1.2 Literary Criticism of the Books of Baruch***

§759   ***3.6.5.1.1.2.1 Literary Criticism of the Book of 1 Baruch***
               / The Rest of the Words of Baruch
               / Paralipomenon of Jeremiah

Owen C. Whitehouse, "The Historic Background of the Book of Baruch," *ICMM* 9 (1912-13) 363-375.

J. Rendel Harris, "Woodbrooke Studies, Fac. 2, Introduction., (I.) A New Jeremiah Apocryphon," *BJRL* 11 (1927) 327-342.

§760   ***3.6.5.1.1.2.2 Literary Criticism of the Book of 2 Baruch***
               / The Apocalypse of Baruch (Syriac
               and / or Greek) / 3 Baruch

James T. Bixby, "The Apocalypse of Baruch," *URRM* 10 (1878) 585-595. *(Review)*

William J. Deane, "The Apocalypse of Baruch," *MI* 1 (1884-85) 451-461.

William J. Deane, "The Apocalypse of Baruch. II.," *MI* 2 (1885) 117-130.

*K. Kohler, "The Pre-Talmudic Haggada, I," *JQR* 5 (1892-93) 399-419. [B. The Second or Rather the Jeremiah Apocalypse, pp. 407-419]

J. Rendel Harris, "Mr. Charles' Apocalypse of Baruch," *Exp, 5th Ser.,* 5 (1897) 255-265.

§761 *3.6.5.1.1.3 Literary Criticism of the Book of the Assumption of Moses / The Testament of Moses*

*J. Estlin Carpenter, "The Epistle of Jude and the Prophecy and Assumption of Moses," *TRL* 5 (1868) 259-276.

T. W. Davids, "The Assumption of Moses," *DTQ* 4 (1878) 86-90.

William J. Deane, "The Assumption of Moses," *MI* 1 (1884-85) 321-348.

J. C. Carrick, "'The Assumption of Moses'," *ET* 9 (1897-98) 374-375. *(Review)*

*J. Rendel Harris, "On an Obscure Quotation in the First Epistle of Clement," *JBL* 29 (1910) 190-195. *[Quote from the Assumption of Moses]*

Henry Todd, "The Assumption of Moses," *IJA* #39 (1914) 73-74.

Cuthbert Lattey, "The Messianic Expectation in 'The Assumption of Moses'," *CBQ* 4 (1942) 9-21.

C[halres]C. Torrey, "'Taxo' in the Assumption of Moses,"*JBL* 62 (1943)1-7.

H. H. Rowley, "The Figure of 'Taxo' in *The Assumption of Moses," JBL* 64 (1945) 141-143.

Charles C. Torrey, "'Taxo' once More," *JBL* 64 (1945) 395-397.

*Solomon Zeitlin, "The Assumption of Moses and the Revolt of Bar Kokba," *JQR, N.S.,* 38 (1947-48) 1-45.

David H. Wallace, "The Semitic Origin of the Assumption of Moses," *TZ* 11 (1955) 321-328.

Jacob Light, "Taxo, or the Apocalyptic Doctrine of Vengeance," *JJS* 12 (1961) 95-103. *[Assumption of Moses]*

*Charles de Santo, "The Assumption of Moses and the Christian Gospel. *A Survey*," *Interp* 16 (1962) 305-310.

§762 *3.6.5.1.1.4 Literary Criticism of the Book of the Ascension of Isaiah / The Martyrdom of Isaiah*

William J. Deane, "The Ascension of Isaiah," *BFER* 37 (1888) 664-690.

V.Burch, "The Literary Unity of the *Ascensio Isaiae*," *JTS* 20 (1918-19)17-23.

*David Flusser, "The Connection between the Apocryphal *Ascensio Isaiae* and the Dead Sea Scrolls," *BIES* 17 (1952-53) #1/2, I-II.

*D[avid] Flusser, "The Apocryphal Book of *Ascensio Isaiae* and the Dead Sea Sect," *IEJ* 3 (1953) 30-47.

(§763) *3.6.5.1.1.5 Literary Criticism of the Books of Legendary Works*

§764   *3.6.5.1.1.5.1 Literary Criticism of the Book of Jubilees / The Laws of Moses*

W[illiam] J. Deane, "The Book of Jubilees. I.," *MI* 2 (1885) 264-280.

W[illiam] J. Deane, "The Book of Jubilees. II.," *MI* 2 (1885) 333-348.

*L. S. A. Wells, "The Book of Jubilees: The Earliest Commentary on Genesis," *IJA* #28 (1912) 13-17.

*James A. Montgomery, "Abraham as the Inventor of an Improved Plow," *MJ* 4 (1913) 55-56. *[Jubilees]*

*Louis Finkelstein, "The Book of Jubilees and the Rabbinic Halaka," *HTR* 16 (1923) 39-62. [1. The Calendar; 2. The Sabbath; 3. Other Festivals; 4. Tithes, and Fruit of the Fourth Year; 5. Laws of Sacrifice; 6. Soiling the Priestly Garments; 7. Covering the Blood; 8. Laws of Marriage; 9. Cases of Bilhah and Tamar; 10. Intermarriage; 11. Impurity after Childbirth; 12. Circumcision; 13. The Law of Retaliation; 14. The Noachic Laws]

Solomon Zeitlin, "The Book of Jubilees, Its Character and Its Significance," *JQR, N.S.,* 30 (1939-40) 1-31.

H. H. Rowley, "Criteria for the Dating of Jubilees," *JQR, N.S.,* 36 (1945-46) 183-187.

Solomon Zeitlin, "Criteria for the Dating of Jubilees," *JQR, N.S.,* 36 (1945-46) 187-189.

*William H. Brownlee, "Light on the Manual of Discipline (DSD) from the Book of Jubilees," *BASOR* #123 (1951) 30-32.

*George E. Ladd, "The Kingdom of God in Jubilees," *BS* 109 (1952) 164-174.

J. Morgenstern, "The Calendar of the Book of Jubilees, its Origin and its Character," *VT* 5 (1955) 34-76.

*E. T. Leach, "A Possible Method of Intercalation for the Calendar of the Book of Jubilees," *VT* 7 (1957) 392-397.

*Solomon Zeitlin, "The Book of 'Jubilees' and the Pentateuch," *JQR, N.S.,* 48 (1957-58) 218-235.

*Bent Noack, "Qumran and the Book of Jubilees," *SEÅ* 22&23 (1957-58) 191-207.

*B[ent] Noack, "The Day of Pentecost in Jubilees, Qumran, and Acts," *ASTI* 1 (1962) 73-95.

*Joseph M. Baumgarten, "The Calendar of the Book of Jubilees and the Bible," *Tarbiz* 32 (1962-63) #4, I-II.

§765   *3.6.5.1.1.5.2 Literary Criticism on the Book of*
                              the Lives of the Prophets

Isaac H. Hall, "Notes on 'Lives of the Prophets'," *JBL* 6 (1886) Part 2, 97-102.

Isaac H. Hall, "Lives of the Prophets," *JBL* 7 (1887) Part 1, 28-40; Part 2, 63, 64.

§766   **3.6.5.1.1.5.3 Literary Criticism of the Book
of 3 Maccabees**

I. Abrahams, "The Third Book of Maccabees," *JQR* 9 (1896-97) 39-58, 175-176.

H. F. Henderson, "III Maccabees," *IJA* #16 (1909) 10-11.

*Sterling Tracy, "III Maccabees and Pseudo-Aristeas: A Study," *YCS* 1 (1928) 241-252.

V.[A.] Tcherikover, "The Third Book of the Maccabees as a Historical Source of the Augustan Period," *Zion* 10 (1944-45) #1, I-II.

*Moses Hadas, "Third Maccabees and Greek Romance," *RR* 13 (1948-49) 155-162.

M[oses] Hadas, "III Maccabees and the Tradition of Patriotic Romance," *CdÉ* 24 (1949) 97-104.

*Moses Hadas, "Aristeas and III Maccabees," *HTR* 42 (1949) 175-184.

Alexander Fuks, "Dositheos Son of Drimylos: A Prosopographical Note," *JJP* 7&8 (1953-54) 205-209. *[3 Maccabees]*

V. A. Tcherikover, "The third book of Maccabees as a historical source," *SH* 7 (1961) 1-26.

§767   **3.6.5.1.1.5.4 Literary Criticism of the Book
of 4 Maccabees**

W. Emery Barnes, "The Fourth Book of Maccabees," *IJA* #36 (1914) 12. *(Review)*

[J.] Rendel Harris, "Some Notes on 4 Maccabees," *ET* 32 (1920-21) 183-184.

*William Metcalfe, "Origen's Exhortation to Martyrdom and 4 Maccabees," *JTS* 22 (1920-21) 268-269.

§768 **3.6.5.1.1.6 Literary Criticism of the Books of Psalmic Literature**

William Wright, "Some Apocryphal Psalms in Syriac," *SBAP* 9 (1886-87) 257-266.

*A. Mingana, "Woodbrooke Studies. Editions and Translations of Christian Documents in Syriac and Garshūni. Fasc. 2., Prefaces, Texts, and Translations,"*BJRL* 11 (1927) 492-498. [*(iii) Some Uncanonical Psalms]*

§769   **3.6.5.1.1.6.1 Literary Criticism of the Book of the Psalms of Solomon**

William J. Deane, "The Psalter of Solomon," *Exp, 2nd Ser.,* 8 (1884) 401-418.

Frank C. Porter, "The Psalms of the Pharisees," *BW* 4 (1894) 167-176.

Bernhard Pick, "The Psalter of Solomon," *IJA* #8 (1907) 15-16.

Bernhard Pick, "The Theological Contents of the Psalter of Solomon," *IJA* #9 (1907) 13-15.

M. R. James, "Les Psaumes de Salomon," *IJA* #25 (1911) 35. *(Review)*

‡R. H. Connolly, "The Odes and Psalms of Solomon," *JTS* 22 (1920-21) 76-84. *(Review)*

‡R. H. Connolly, "The Odes and Psalms of Solomon: An Amends," *JTS* 22 (1920-21) 159-160.

*Joshua Efron, "The Psalms of Solomon, The Hasmonean Decline, and Christianity," *Zion* 30 (1965) #1/2, I-II.

§770 **3.6.5.1.1.7 Literary Criticism of the Testamental Literature - General Studies**

F. C. Conybeare, "The Testament of Solomon," *JQR* 11 (1898-99) 1-45.

*Edward Chauncey Baldwin, "Jesus and the Testament of Solomon," *HR* 80 (1920) 189-190.

C. C. McCown, "Solomon and the Shulamite," *JPOS* 1 (1920-21) 116-121. *[Testament of Solomon]*

§771   **3.6.5.1.1.7.1** *Literary Criticism of the Testament of the Twelve Patriarchs*

*Samuel Davidson, "Irenæus, Polycarp and the Testaments of the Twelve Patriarchs, in Relation to the Fourth Gospel," *TRL* 7 (1870) 297-331.

Benjamin B. Warfield, "The Apologetic Value of the Testaments of the Twelve Patriarchs," *DTQ* 6 (1880) 270-287.

B[enjamin] B. Warfield, "The Apologetic Value of the Testaments of the Twelve Patriarchs," *PR* 1 (1880) 57-84.

B. Pick, "The Testaments of the Twelve Patriarchs," *LCR* 4 (1885) 161-186.

William J. Deane, "The Testament of the Twelve Patriarchs," *TML* 5 (1891) 322-342.

C. Conybeare, "On the Jewish Authorship of the Testaments of the Twelve Patriarchs," *JQR* 5 (1892-93) 375-398.

*K. Kohler, "The Pre-Talmudic Haggada, I," *JQR* 5 (1892-93) 399-419. [A. The Testament of the Twelve Patriarchs, pp. 400-406]

R. H. Charles, "The Testaments of the XII. Patriarchs," *HJ* 3 (1904-05) 558-573.

R. Sinker, "The Testaments of the XII. Patriarchs," *IJA* #9 (1907) 12-13.

R. Sinker, "The Contents of the Testaments of the XII Patriarchs," *IJA* #10 (1907) 16.

Anonymous, "Editorial Notes. The Testament of the Twelve Patriarchs," *ICMM* 4 (1907-08) 239-241.

*Anonymous, "Editorial Notes. Ethical Thoughts in Our Lord's Day," *ICMM* 4 (1907-08) 241-242. *[Testament of the Twelve Patriarchs]*

*Anonymous, "Editorial Notes. Teaching on Forgiveness in the Testament of Gad," *ICMM* 4 (1907-08) 242-243.

*Alfred Plummer, "The Relation of the Testaments of the Twelve Patriarchs to the Books of the New Testament," *Exp, 7th Ser.,* 6 (1908) 481-491.

R. H. Charles, "Notes on the Testaments of the XII. Patriarchs," *IJA* #12 (1908) 14-15.

W. F. Slater, "The Testaments of the Twelve Patriarchs," *LQHR* 110 (1908) 268-280. *(Review)*

F. C. Burkitt, "The Testaments of the Twelve Patriarchs," *JTS* 10 (1908-09) 135-141. *(Review)*

*R. H. Charles, "The Testaments of the Twelve Patriarchs in Relation to the New Testament," *Exp, 7th Ser.,* 7 (1909) 111-118.

*H. T. Andrews, "The Ethical Teaching of the Testaments of the XII Patriarchs," *IJA* #18 (1909) 63-65.

Ernest W. Parsons, "The Testaments of the Twelve Patriarchs," *BW* 37 (1911) 176-188.

*E. W. Winstanley, "The Testaments of the Twelve Patriarchs as a Guide to Conduct," *IJA* #43 (1915) 61-65.

*P. A. Munch, "The Spirits in the Testaments of the Twelve Patriarchs," *AO* 13 (1935) 257-263.

*G. R. Beasley-Murray, "The Two Messiahs in the Testament of the Twelve Patriarchs," *JTS* 48 (1947) 1-12.

Elias J. Bickerman, "The Date of the Testaments of the Twelve Patriarchs," *JBL* 69 (1950) 245-260.

*A. W. Argyle, "The Influence of the Testaments of the Twelve Patriarchs upon the New Testament," *ET* 63 (1951-52) 256-258.

*C. Rabin, "The 'Teacher of Righteousness' in the 'Testaments of the Twelve Patriarchs'," *JJS* 3 (1952) 127-128.

M. de Jonge, "The Testaments of the Twelve Patriarchs and the New Testament," *StEv* 1 (1959) 546-556.

M. de Jonge, "Christian influence in the Testaments of the Twelve Patriarchs," *NT* 4 (1960) 182-235.

M. de Jonge, "Once more: Christian Influence in the Testaments of the Twelve Patriarchs," *NT* 5 (1962) 311-319.

(§772)   **3.6.5.1.1.7.2 Literary Criticism of the Testament of Adam / The Books of Adam and Eve**

§773   **3.6.5.1.1.7.3 Literary Criticism of the Testament of Abraham**

G. H. Macurdy, "Platonic Orphism in the Testament of Abraham," *JBL* 61 (1942) 213-226.

(§774)   **3.6.5.1.1.7.4 Literary Criticism of the Testament of Job**

§775   **3.6.5.1.1.8 Literary Criticism of the Letter of Aristeas**

I. Abrahams, "Recent Criticism of the Letter of Aristeas," *JQR* 14 (1901-02) 321-342.

H. St. J. Thackeray, "The Letter of Aristeas," *IJA* #38 (1914) 73-74. *(Review)*

*Sterling Tracy, "III Maccabees and Pseudo-Aristeas: A Study," *YCS* 1 (1928) 241-252.

V. Tcherikover, "The Ideology of the Letter of Aristeas," *HTR* 51 (1958) 59-86.

G. Zuntz, "Aristeas Studies I: 'The Seven Banquets'," *JSS* 4 (1959) 21-36.

*G. Zuntz, "Aristeas Studies II: Aristeas on the Translation of the Torah," *JSS* 4 (1959) 109-126.

Sidney Jellicoe, "St. Luke and the Letter of Aristeas," *JBL* 80 (1961) 149-155.

*Sidney Jellicoe, "Aristeas, Philo, and the Septuagint *Vorlage*," *JTS, N.S.*, 12 (1961) 261-271.

*A. F. J. Klijn, "The Letter of Aristeas and the Greek Translation of the Pentateuch in Egypt," *NTS* 11 (1964-65) 154-158.

S. Jellicoe, "The Occasion and Purpose of the Letter of Aristeas: A Re-examination," *NTS* 12 (1965-66) 144-150.

J. J. Lewis, "The Table-Talk Section in the Letter of Aristeas," *NTS* 13 (1966-67) 53-56.

John E. Stambaugh, "Aristeas of Argos in Alexandria," *Aeg* 47 (1967) 69-74.

*Oswyn Murray, "Aristeas and Ptolemaic Kingship," *JTS, N.S.,* 18 (1967) 337-371.

§776 *3.6.5.1.1.9 Literary Criticism of the Sibylline Oracles*

Anonymous, "The Sibylline Oracles," *MR* 36 (1854) 489-526.

W. M. W. Call, "The Sibyl," *TRL* 7 (1870) 465-488.

*B. Pick, "The Sibylline Oracles in the Writings of the Church Fathers," *LQ* 15 (1885) 448-464.

W. J. Deane, "The Sibylline Oracles," *BFER* 36 (1887) 148-192.

S. A. Hirsch, "The Jewish Sibylline Oracles," *JQR* 2 (1889-90) 406-429.

Fred. J. Hillig, "The Sibylline Books in the Light of Christian Antiquity," *AER* 21 (1899) 489-512.

Anonymous, "The Sibylline Oracles," *IJA* #17 (1909) 42-44.

Milton S. Terry, "The Sibylline Oracles," *IJA* #36 (1914) 15-16. *(Review)*

A. W. Hands, "The Sibylline Oracles," *IJA* #43 (1915) 67-69; #46 (1916) 38-41.

H. C. O. Lanchester, "The Eschatology of the Sibylline Oracles," *IJA* #44 (1916) 3-7.

Bernhard Pick, "The Punishments in the Other World. As Described in the Apocalypse of Peter, the Sibylline Oracles, the Acts of Thomas, and the Apocalypse of Paul," *OC* 32 (1918) 641-662. [The Sibylline Oracles, II, 238ff., pp. 648-652]

J. P. Arendzen, "The Jewish Sibyl," *IER, 5th Ser.,* 29 (1927) 1-15.

J. P. Arendzen, "The Christian Sibyl," *IER 5th Ser.,* 29 (1927) 125-139.

*Bard Thompson, "Patristic Use of the Sibylline Oracles," *RR* 16 (1951-52) 115-136.

*Bent Noack, "Are the Essenes Referred to in the Sibylline Oracles?" *ST* 17 (1963) 90-102.

§777 *3.6.5.1.1.10 Literary Criticism of the Zadokite Document*
[See also: The Zadokite Document
/The Damascus Document
under Qumran Literature→]

*G. Margoliouth, "The Two Zadokite Messiahs," *JTS* 12 (1910-11) 446-450.

Kaufmann Kohler, "Dositheus, The Samaritan Heresiarch, and His Relations to Jewish and Christian Doctrines and Sects," *AJT* 15 (1911) 404-435.

William Hayes Ward, "The 'Zadokite' Document," *BS* 68 (1911) 429-456.

*G. Margoliouth, "The Calendar, the Sabbath, and the Marriage Law in the Geniza-Zadokite Document," *ET* 23 (1911-12) 362-365.

M. H. Segal, "Notes on 'Fragments of a Zadokite Work'," *JQR, N.S.,* 2 (1911-12) 133-141. *(Review)*

G. Margoliouth, "The Sadducean Christians of Damascus," *BS* 69 (1912) 421-437.

M. H. Segal, "Additional Notes on 'Fragments of a Zadokite Work'," *JQR, N.S.,* 3 (1912-13) 301-311. *(Review)*

G. Margoliouth, "Fragments of a Zadokite Work," *IJA* #37 (1914) 36-37. *(Review)*

J. W. Lightley, "The Recently Discovered Zadokite Documents," *LQHR* 123 (1915) 15-31.

‡H. H. Rowley, "Recent Foreign Theology. The Zadokite Work," *ET* 58 (1946-47) 54. *(Review)*

R. A. Soloff, "Toward Uncovering Original Texts in the Zadokite Documents," *NTS* 5 (1958-59) 62-67.

*R. F. Collins, "The Berîth-Notion of the Cario Damascus Covenant and its Comparision with the New Testament," *ETL* 39 (1963) 555-594.

Barbara Thiering, "The Teacher of Righteousness and the Messiah in the Damascus Document," *AJBA* 1 (1968-71) #4, 74-81.

§778   *3.6.5.1.1.11 Literary Criticism of other Pseudepigraphal Books*

Isaac H. Hall, "The Vision of Ezra the Scribe Concerning the Latter Times of the Ishmaelites," *PR* 7 (1886) 537-541.

B. Pick, "The Prayer of Aseneth," *HR* 24 (1892) 26-30.

*J. A. Selbie, "The Apocalypse of Zacharias and the Gospel of Luke," *ET* 7 (1895-96) 497.

M. Gaster, "The Sibyl and the Dream of One Hundred Suns: An Old Apocryphon," *JRAS* (1910) 609-623.

*Martin Rist, "The Common Source of Revelation 16:17-22:5 and the Apocalypse of Elijah," *IR* 12 (1955) #1, 27-34.

(§779) *3.6.6.1 Exegetical Studies on the Pseudepigrapha - General Studies*

(§780)   *3.6.6.1.1 Exegetical Studies on the Apocalyptic Literature - General Studies*

(§781)   *3.6.6.1.1.1 Exegetical Studies on the Books of Enoch*

§782   *3.6.6.1.1.1.1 Exegetical Studies on the Book of 1 Enoch*

Charles C. Torrey, "Notes on the Greek Texts of Enoch," *JAOS* 62 (1942) 52-60. [Chapters 1-5. Introduction; Chapters 6-36; Chapters 37-71; Chapters 72-82. The Laws of the Heavenly Bodies; Chapters 83-90, The Visions; Chapters 91-108]

Enoch 1:2

*J. Rendel Harris, "An Unobserved Quotation from the Book of Enoch," *Exp, 6th Ser.,* 4 (1901) 194-199. *[Enoch 1:2 = Matt. 13:9 // Luke 10:24; 1 Peter 1:12]*

*C. Taylor, "I Peter and Enoch," *ET* 13 (1901-02) 40. *[Enoch 1:2 & (9:1) // 1 Peter 1:12]*

1 Enoch Chapters 6-21

*Birger A. Pearson, "A Reminiscence of Classical Myth at *II Peter* 2.4," *GRBS* 10 (1969) 71-80. *[1 Enoch 6-21]*

1 Enoch Chapter 6

*L. H. Gray, "Iranian Miscellanies. c) The Iranian Name בגדראנ," *JAOS* 33 (1913) 285. *[1 Enoch chapter 6ff.]*

1 Enoch 9:1

*C. Taylor, "I Peter and Enoch," *ET* 13 (1901-02) 40. *[Enoch 1:2 & (9:1) // 1 Peter 1:12]*

1 Enoch 10:4-13

*J. Rendel Harris, "A Further Note on the Use of Enoch in 1 Peter," *Exp, 6th Ser.,* 4 (1901) 346-349. *[1 Peter 3:19, 20 = Enoch 10:4, 5, 12, 13]*

1 Enoch Chapter 22

*A. O. Standen, "The Parable of Dives and Lazarus, and Enoch 22," *ET* 33 (1921-22) 523.

1 Enoch 22:3

*F. C. Burkitt, "Four Notes on the Book of Enoch," *JTS* 8 (1906-07) 444-447. [2. 'Spirits of Souls', Enoch xxii 3, pp. 445-446]

1 Enoch 22:9ff.

*F. C. Burkitt, "Four Notes on the Book of Enoch," *JTS* 8 (1906-07) 444-447. [3. Enoch xxii 9ff., p. 446]

1 Enoch Chapters 37-71

Matthew Black, "The Eschatology of the Similitudes of Enoch," *JTS, N.S.,* 3 (1952) 1-10. *[Ethiopic Enoch]*

1 Enoch Chapter 38

*[J.] Rendel Harris, "Enoch and 2 Corinthians," *ET* 33 (1921-22) 423-424. *[Chapter 38]*

1 Enoch Chapter 42

*Arthur J. Prowse, "The Book of Enoch," *ET* 25 (1913-14) 379. *[Chapter 42]*

1 Enoch Chapter 49

*Arthur J. Prowse, "The Book of Enoch," *ET* 25 (1913-14) 379. *[Chapter 49]*

1 Enoch 59:13-21

Chaim Kaplan, "The Hidden Name," *JSOR* 13 (1929) 181-184. *[59:13-21]*

1 Enoch 62:5

*F. H. Borsch, "Mark xiv. 62 and I Enoch lxii. 5," *NTS* 14 (1967-68) 565-567.

1 Enoch Chapters 65 and 66

Anonymous, "Chapters 65 and 66 of the Book of Enoch," *ONTS* 3 (1883-84) 55. *[Translation]*

1 Enoch 102:1-3

G[unter] Zuntz, "Enoch on the Last Judgment (Ch. CII. 1-3)," *JTS* 46 (1945) 161-170.

(§783)   ***3.6.6.1.1.1.2 Exegetical Studies on***
                              the Book of 2 Enoch

(§784) **3.6.6.1.1.2 *Exegetical Studies on the Books of Baruch***

§785   **3.6.6.1.1.2.1 *Exegetical Studies on the Book of***
                            1 Baruch / The Rest of the
                            Words of Baruch
                            / Paralipomenon
                            of Jeremiah

1 Baruch 2:18

*D. Kaufmann, "What was the Word for 'Unhappy' in Later Hebrew," *JQR*
    1 (1888-89) 442-444. *[2:18]*

1 Baruch 9:3

*C. A. Phillips, "The Use of John I. 9 in the 'Rest of the Words of Baruch',"
    ET 47 (1935-36) 431. *[9:3]*

(§786)   **3.6.6.1.1.2.2 *Exegetical Studies on the***
                            Book of 2 Baruch / The
                            Apocalypse of Baruch
                            (Syriac and / or Greek)
                            / 3 Baruch

§787 **3.6.6.1.1.3 *Exegetical Studies on the Book of the***
        Assumption of Moses / The
        Testament of Moses

Assumption of Moses Chapter 9

*Wallace N. Stearns, "Notes on Acts xiii. 9 and on Assumptio Mosis ix,"
    JBL 19 (1900) 53-54.

Sigmund Mowinckel, "The Hebrew equivalent of Taxo in Ass. Mos. ix,"
    VTS 1 (1953) 88-96.

Assumption of Moses Chapter 10

*T. W. Manson, "Miscellanea Apocalyptica," *JTS* 46 (1945) 41-45. [II. Ass.
    Mosis, x. 1-10, pp 42-45]

§788 *3.6.6.1.1.4 Exegetical Studies on the Book of*
the Ascension of Isaiah
/ The Martyrdom of Isaiah

Vacher Burch, "Material for the Interpretation of the *Ascensio Isaiae,*" *JTS*
21 (1919-20) 249-265.

(§789) *3.6.6.1.1.5 Exegetical Studies on the Books of*
Legendary Works

§790   *3.6.6.1.1.5.1 Exegetical Studies on the Book*
of Jubilees / The Laws
of Moses

Jubilees 7:4

*George F. Moore, "Conjectanea Talmudica: Notes on Rev. 13:18; Matt.
23:35f., 28:1; 2 Cor. 2:14-16; Jubilees 34:4, 7; 7:4," *JAOS* 26 (1905)
315-333. [6. Jubilees 7:4, p. 333]

Jubilees Chapter 11

James A. Montgomery, "An Assyrian Illustration to the Book of Jubilees,"
JBL 33 (1914) 157-158. *[Chapter 11]*

Jubilees 16:30

Moses   Hadas,   "Jub.   16:30,"   *AJSL*   49   (1932-33)   338.

Jubilees 34:4-7

*George F. Moore, "Conjectanea Talmudica: Notes on Rev. 13:18; Matt.
23:35f., 28:1; 2 Cor. 2:14-16; Jubilees 34:4, 7; 7:4," *JAOS* 26 (1905)
315-333. [5. Jubilees 34:4, 7, Zarethan-Ṣarṭabeh, pp. 331-333]

Jubilees 50:9

Leon J. Liebreich, "Jubilees 50.9," *JQR, N.S.,* 44 (1953-54) 169.

(§791)   ***3.6.6.1.1.5.2 Exegetical Studies on the Book of
the Lives of the Prophets***

(§792)   ***3.6.6.1.1.5.3 Exegetical Studies on the Book of
3 Maccabees***

§793   ***3.6.6.1.1.5.4 Exegetical Studies on the Book of
4 Maccabees***

*William Metcalfe, "Origen's Exhortation to Martyrdom and 4 Maccabees,"
JTS 22 (1920-21) 268-269.

S. Lauer, "Eusebes Logismos in IV Macc.," *JJS* 6 (1955) 170-171

(§794) ***3.6.6.1.1.6 Exegetical Studies on the Books
of Psalmic Literature***

§795   ***3.6.6.1.1.6.1 Exegetical Studies on the Book of
the Psalms of Solomon***

Psalms of Solomon Chapter 3

*James Moffatt, "The Righteousness of the Scribes and Pharisees," *ET* 13
(1901-02) 201-206. *[Chapter 3]*

Psalms of Solomon Chapter 4

*M. Aberbach, "The Historical Allusions of Chapters IV, XI and XIII of the
Psalms of Solomon," *JQR, N.S.,* 41 (1950-51) 379-396.

Psalms of Solomon Chapters 5 and 6

*James Moffatt, "The Righteousness of the Scribes and Pharisees," *ET* 13
(1901-02) 201-206. *[Chapters 5 and 6]*

Psalms of Solomon Chapter 10

*James Moffatt, "The Righteousness of the Scribes and Pharisees," *ET* 13
(1901-02) 201-206. *[Chapter 10]*

Psalms of Solomon Chapter 11

*M. Aberbach, "The Historical Allusions of Chapters IV, XI and XIII of the Psalms of Solomon," *JQR, N.S.*, 41 (1950-51) 379-396.

Psalms of Solomon Chapter 13

*M. Aberbach, "The Historical Allusions of Chapters IV, XI and XIII of the Psalms of Solomon," *JQR, N.S.*, 41 (1950-51) 379-396.

Psalms of Solomon Chapter 16

John Taylor, "The Sixteenth of the Psalms of Solomon," *IJA* #17 (1909) 41-42.

Psalms of Solomon 17:10

*Frederick W. Danker, "II Peter 3:10 and Psalm of Solomon 17:10," *ZNW* 53 (1962) 82-86.

Psalms of Solomon 17:48

*H. A. Wolfson, "Notes on Proverbs 22:10 and Psalms of Solomon 17:48," *JQR, N.S.*, 37 (1946-47) 87.

Psalms of Solomon 18:6

*T. W. Manson, "Miscellanea Apocalyptica," *JTS* 46 (1945) 41-45. [I. Pss. Sol. xviii. 6, pp 41-42]

(§796) *3.6.6.1.1.7 Exegetical Studies on the Testamental Literature*

§797   *3.6.6.1.1.7.1 Exegetical Studies on the Testament of the Twelve Patriarchs*

Testament of the Twelve Patriarchs (Levi) Chapter 8

T. W. Manson, "Miscellanea Apocalyptica III, *Text. XII Patr.: Levi viii*," *JTS* 48 (1947) 59-61.

Testament of the Twelve Patriarchs (Levi) Chapter 18

*Matthew Black, "Contributions and Comments. The Messiah in the Testament of Levi xviii," *ET* 61 (1949-50) 157-158.

J. R. Porter, "The Messiah in the Testament of Levi XVIII," *ET* 61 (1949-50) 90-91.

Testament of the Twelve Patriarchs (Levi) Chapter 23

*Matthew Black, "The Messiah in the Testament of Levi xxiii," *ET* 60 (1948-49) 321-322.

(§798)   ***3.6.6.1.1.7.2 Exegetical Studies on the Testament of Adam / The Books of Adam and Eve***

(§799)   ***3.6.6.1.1.7.3 Exegetical Studies on the Testament of Abraham***

§800   ***3.6.6.1.1.7.4 Exegetical Studies on the Testament of Job***

Testament of Job Chapter 7

*Campbell Bonner, "Four Lexicographical Notes," *AJP* 62 (1941) 451-459. *[Chapter 7, pp. 455-457]*

(§801) ***3.6.6.1.1.8 Exegetical Studies on the Letter of Aristeas***

§802   ***3.6.6.1.1.9 Exegetical Studies on the Sibylline Oracles***

Sibylline Oracles 3:388-400

H. H. Rowley, "The Interpretation and Date of Sibylline Oracles III 388-400," *ZAW* 44 (1926) 324-327.

§803   ***3.6.6.1.1.10 Exegetical Studies on the Zadokite Document [See also: The Zadokite Document / The Damascus Document under Qumran Literature→]***

*P. Wernberg-Møller, "Some Passages in the 'Zadokite' Fragments and Their Parallels in the *Manual of Disciple*," *JSS* 1 (1956) 110-128. [Z, i. 19f; ii. 7f.; ii. 9f.; ii. 12f.; iii. 16; iii. 20; vii. 9; ix. 9f; xiii. 7f.; xiii. 11.]

Zadokite Document 4:20-21

*Paul Winter, "Sadoqite Fragments IV 20, 21 and the Exegesis of Genesis 1:27 in late Judaism," *ZAW* 68 (1956) 71-84.

Zadokite Document 9:6

N. Wieder, "'Sanctuary' as a Metaphor for Scripture," *JJS* 8 (1957) 165-176. *[9:6]*

§804 *3.6.6.1.1.11 Exegetical Studies on other Pseudepigraphal Books*

R. H. Connolly, "The Odes of Solomon: Jewish or Christian?" *JTS* 13 (1911-12) 298-309.

Arie Rubinstein, "A Problematic Passage in the Apocalypse of Abraham," *JJS* 8 (1957) 45-50. *[Chapter 23]*

§805 *3.7 Studies on the Life and Works of Philo*

Pelagius, "Of the Platoism of Philo," *TRep* 4 (1784) 408-420.

*†Anonymous, "Bryant on Philo Judæus," *BCQTR* 11 (1798) 13-17, 141-148. *(Review)*

Anonymous, "Translation from Philo Judæus," *CE* 4 (1827) 377-380. *[Passage from Philo's 'On the Formation of the World' compared with a passage from Akenside's 'Pleasures of Imagination']*

*H[osea] B[allou], "Αἰώνιος, as used by Philo Judæus," *UQGR* 2 (1845) 133-136.

*Anonymous, "Philosophy of Philo," *PRev* 23 (1851) 624-635.

Theophilus Rubinsohn, "Philo and His Opinions," *CRB* 18 (1853) 119-135.

*Churchill Babington, "St. Paul and Philo: a Passage in 1 Cor., illustrated from Philo Judæus," *JCSP* 1 (1854) 47-51.

H. Goodwin, "Prof. Jowett and Philo," *JCSP* 3 (1857) 230-235.

*John A. Reubelt, "The Logos of Philo Judæus and that of St. John," *MR* 40 (1858) 110-129.

*Franz Delitzsch, "The Logos in John and Philo," *AThR, N.S.,* 2 (1864) 506-515.

R. H., "Philo Judæus," *BFER* 17 (1868) 732-751. *(Review)*

James H. Worman, "Philo, the Jew," *MR* 60 (1878) 121-141.

K[eningdale] C[ook], "A Contemporary of Jesus," *DUM* 95 (1880) 392-410, 598-622, 728-746. *[Philo]*

A. Hilgenfeld, "Philo and the Therapeutæ," *BQR* 4 (1882) 36-56. *(Trans. by Alfred G. Langley)*

A. Hilgenfeld, "Philo and the Therapeutæ. Translated with Notes from the German of Professor Dr. A. Hilgenfeld, at Jena," *DTQ, N.S.,* 1 (1882) 356-369. *(Trans. by Alfred G. Langley)*

*Bernhard Pick, "Philo's Canon of the Old Testament and his mode of quoting the Alexandrian Version," *JBL* 4 (1884) 126-143.

*L. S. Potwin, "Philo and the ΔΙΔΑΧΗ," *BS* 43 (1886) 174-176.

Anonymous, "Critical Theology. Drummond's Philo," *URRM* 30 (1888) 263-270. *(Review)*

*Fred C. Conybeare, "Upon Philo's Text of the Septuagint," *Exp, 4th Ser.,* 4 (1891) 456-466.

*Paton J. Gloag, "The Logos of Philo and St. John," *PRR* 2 (1891) 46-57.

G., "Philo the Jew and the Bible," *ONTS* 15 (1892) 73-74.

L. Cohn, "The Latest Researches on Philo of Alexandria," *JQR* 5 (1892-93) 25-50.

*F. C. Conybeare, "The Philonean Text of the Septuagint," *JQR* 5 (1892-93) 246-280.

*C. G. Montefiore, "Florilegium Philonis," *JQR* 7 (1894-95) 481-545.

F. C. Conybeare, "Philo: Concerning the Contemplative Life," *JQR* 7 (1894-95) 755-769.

*F. C. Conybeare, "Philonean Text of the Septuagint," *JQR* 8 (1895-96) 88-122.

*Anonymous, "Ecclesiasticus and Philo," *MR* 78 (1896) 646-647.

W. E. Ball, "St. John and Philo Judæus," *ContR* 73 (1898) 219-234.

*Lawrence [H.] Mills, "Was Vohu Manah Philo's Logos?" *IAQR, 3rd Ser.,* 9 (1900) 351-352.

*Lawrence [H.] Mills, "The Philoian Logos," *IAQR, 3rd Ser.,* 12 (1901) 109-119.

*Lawrence [H.] Mills, "Philo's δυνάμεις and the Amesha Spenta," *JRAS* (1901) 553-568.

Walter Boughton Pitkin, "Philo Judæus," *HSR* 13 (1902-03) 304-311.

J. H. A. Hart, "Philo of Alexandria," *JQR* 17 (1904-05) 78-122.

J. H. A. Hart, "Philo of Alexandria," *JQR* 17 (1904-05) 726-746. [De Decem Oraculis; Quod Liber sit quisquis Virtuti Studet; De Cherubim]

J. H. A. Hart, "Philo of Alexandria, De Somniis, I," *JQR* 18 (1905-06) 330-346.

*Anonymous, "'Zarathushtra, Philo: The Achæmenids and Israel'," *IAQR, 3rd Ser.,* 21 (1906) 314-317. *(Review)*

J. H. A. Hart, "Philo of Alexandria, IV," *JQR* 20 (1907-08) 294-329. [Preface; Concerning Repentance; Concerning Nobility; Concerning Curses; Concerning Migration]

*W. Lock, "Philo's Interpretation of Leviticus XVIII 30," *JTS* 9 (1907-08) 300-301.

*G. S. Hitchcock, "Philo and the Day of Atonement," *NYR* 3 (1907-08) 52-55.

*J. H. A. Hart, "Philo and the Catholic Judaism of the First Century," *JTS* 11 (1909-10) 25-42.

J. T. Marshall, "The Odes and Philo," *Exp, 8th Ser.,* 1 (1911) 385-398, 519-536.

*Charles Johnston, "Paul and Philo," *ConstrQ* 1 (1913) 810-825.

*F. H. Colson, "Philo on Education," *JTS* 18 (1916-17) 151-162.

H. A. A. Kennedy, "Philo's Relation to the Old Testament," *Exp, 8th Ser.,* 17 (1919) 143-160.

H. A. A. Kennedy, "Philo's Conception of God's Approach to Man," *Exp, 8th Ser.,* 17 (1919) 275-294.

H. A. A. Kennedy, "Philo on Man's Yearning for God," *Exp, 8th Ser.,* 17 (1919) 198-218.

H. A. A. Kennedy, "Philo's Union with God," *Exp, 8th Ser.,* 17 (1919) 345-362.

*Francis Clarke, "Sources of St. John's Logos Doctrine," *IER, 5th Ser.,* 20 (1922) 390-397, 602-615; 21 (1923) 50-68, 481-502. *[Philo Judæus on Logos, 21 (1923) pp. 50-68]*

*J. Rendel Harris, "The Influence of Philo upon the New Testament," *ET* 37 (1925-26) 565-566.

Erwin R. Goodenough, "Philo and Public Life," *JEA* 12 (1926) 77-79.

*James Edward Hogg, "'A Virgin-Birth in Philo' (Exod. 2:21)," *AJSL* 44 (1927-28) 206-207.

R. Marcus, "Philo's Divine Comedy," *JIQ* 5 (1928-29) #1, 1-6.

R. Marcus, "The Armenian Translation of Philo's Quaestiones in Genesim et Exodum," *JBL* 49 (1930) 61-64.

*R. Birch Hoyle, "Philo on Inspiration," *BR* 15 (1930) 23-39.

*J. S. Boughton, "Conscience and the Logos in Philo," *LCQ* 4 (1931) 121-133.

*A. Marmorstein, "Philo and the Names of God," *JQR, N.S.,* 22 (1931-32) 295-306.

Erwin R. Goodenough, "A Neo-Pythagorean Source in Philo Judaeus," *YCS* 3 (1932) 115-164.

Erwin R. Goodenough, "Philo's Exposition of the Law and His De Vita Mosis," *HTR* 26 (1933) 109-125.

Ralph Marcus, "An Armenian-Greek Index to Philo's *Quaestiones* and *De Vita Contemplativa,*" *JAOS* 53 (1933) 251-282.

‡Ralph Marcus, "Recent Literature on Philo," *JBL* 53 (1934) ix.

*Louis Finkelstein, "Is Philo Mentioned in Rabbinic Literature?" *JBL* 53 (1934) 142-149.

*Mary E. Andrews, "Paul, Philo and the Intellectuals," *JBL* 53 (1934) 150-166.

Erwin R. Goodenough, "Problems of Method in Studying Philo Judaeus," *JBL* 58 (1939) 51-58.

F. R. Montgomery Hitchcock, "Philo and the Pastorals," *Herm* #56 (1940) 113-135.

W. L. Knox, "A Note on Philo's Use of the Old Testament," *JTS* 41 (1940) 30-34.

F. H. Colson, "Philo's Quotations from the Old Testament," *JTS* 41 (1940) 237-251.

W. Richardson, "Philo and His Significance for Christian Theology," *MC* 30 (1940-41) 15-25.

Harry Austryn Wolfson, "Philo on Free Will," *HTR* 35 (1942) 131-169.

*H. A. Wolfson, "Philo on Jewish Citizenship in Alexandria," *JBL* 63 (1944) 165-168.

*Grace Amadon, "Important Passover Texts in Josephus and Philo," *ATR* 27 (1945) 109-115.

*Harry A. Wolfson, "Synedrion in Greek Jewish Literature and Philo," *JQR, N.S.,* 36 (1945-46) 303-306.

*Erwin R. Goodenough, "Philo on Immortality," *HTR* 39 (1946) 85-108.

Ralph Marcus, "Azariah de Rossi (16th cent.) on Philo," *JBL* 65 (1946) x.

Curtis W. Larson, "Prayer of Petition in Philo," *JBL* 65 (1946) 185-203.

*Peter Katz, "Notes on the Septuagint, II. A Fresh Aquila Fragment recovered from Philo," *JTS* 47 (1946) 31-33.

*Warren C. Young, "The Logos Doctrine of Philo Judaeus," *PF* 4 (1946) 14-22.

Thurston Davis, "A New Appreciation of Philo," *ThSt* 7 (1946) 142-145.

Erwin R. Goodenough, "Wolfson's *Philo*," *JBL* 67 (1948) 87-109. *(Review)*

Ralph Marcus, "Notes on the Armenian Text of Philo's 'Quaestiones in Genesim,' Books I-III," *JNES* 7 (1948) 111-115.

Jean Danielou, "The Philosophy of Philo. *The Significance of Harry A. Wolfson's New Study,*" *ThSt* 9 (1948) 578-589. *(Review)*

Ralph Marcus, "Wolfson's Revaluation of Philo: A Review Article," *RR* 13 (1948-49) 368-381. *(Review)*

Leo Roberts, "Wolfson's Monument to Philo," *Isis* 40 (1949) 199-213. *(Review)*

*Ralph Marcus, "A Textual-Exegetical Note on Philo's Bible," *JBL* 69 (1950) 363-365.

Samuel Sandmel, "Did Philo Know Hebrew?" *JBL* 70 (1951) xi.

*Ralph Marcus, "Philo, Josephus and the Dead Sea *Yaḥad*," *JBL* 71 (1952) 207-209.

*Y. Baer, "The Ancient Hassidim in Philo's Writings and in Hebrew Tradition," *Zion* 18 (1953) #3/4, I.

*Samuel Sandmel, "Philo's Place in Judaism: A Study of Conceptions of Abraham in Jewish Literature," *HUCA* 25 (1954) 209-237.

Samuel Sandmel, "Philo's Environment and Philo's Exegesis," *JAAR* 22 (1954) 248-253.

Yoshua Gutman, "Philo the Epic Poet," *SH* 1 (1954) 36-63.

*A. W. Argyle, "The Logos of Philo: Personal or Impersonal?" *ET* 66 (1954-55) 13-14.

*Samuel Sandmel, "Philo's Place in Judaism: A Study of Conceptions of Abraham in Jewish Literature II," *HUCA* 26 (1955) 151-332.

Samuel Sandmel, "Philo and His Pupils: An Imaginary Dialogue," *Jud* 4 (1955) 47-57.

*‡Ramond F. Surburg, "Intertestamental Studies 1946—1955," *CTM* 27 (1956) 95-114. [V. Philo Studies, pp. 107-108]

*S. Lauer, "Philo's Concept of Time," *JJS* 9 (1958) 39-46.

*James H. Burtness, "Plato, Philo, and the Author of Hebrews," *LQ, N.S.,* 10 (1958) 54-64.

*P. Smulders, "A Quotation of Philo in Irenaeus," *VC* 12 (1958) 154-156.

*Z. Werblowsky, "Philo and the Zohar," *JJS* 10 (1959) 25-44, 113-136.

*H. A. Wolfson, "The Philonic God of Revelation and His Latter-Day Deniers," *HTR* 53 (1960) 101-124.

*Sidney Jellicoe, "Aristeas, Philo, and the Septuagint *Vorlage*," *JTS, N.S.,* 12 (1961) 261-271.

Lee Levine, "Philo: The Allegorical Interpretation of the Scriptures," *YR* 1 (1961) 17-28.

*Jean-Georges Kahn, "Did Philo Know Hebrew?" *Tarbiz* 34 (1964-65) #4, IV-V.

Joshua Amir, "Philo's Homilies on Fear and Love and Their Relation to Palestinian Midrashim," *Zion* 30 (1965) #1/2, II-III.

*Samuel Belkin, "Some Obscure Tradition Mutually Clarified in Philo and Rabbinic Literature," *JQR 75th* (1967) 80-103.

*A. T. Hanson, "Philo's Etymologies," *JTS, N.S.,* 18 (1967) 128-139.

*Samuel Sandmel, "The Confrontation Of Greek And Jewish Ethics: Philo, De Decalogo," *CCARJ* 15 (1968) #1, 54-63.

E. I. Watkin, "New Light on Philo," *DownsR* 86 (1968) 287-297.

*Albert Henrichs, "Philosophy, the Handmaiden of Theology," *GRBS* 9 (1968) 437-450. *[Philo]*

*David Rokeah, "A New Onomasticon Fragment from Oxyrhynchus and Philo's Exegesis," *JTS, N.S.,* 19 (1968) 70-82.

§806 *3.7.1 Pseudo-Philo*

Leopold Cohn, "An Apocryphal Work Ascribed to Philo of Alexandria," *JQR* 10 (1898) 277-322.

*M. R. James, "Notes on Apocrypha. I. Pseudo-Philo and Baruch," *JTS* 16 (1914-15) 403-405.

Guido Kisch, "A Note on the New Edition of Pseudo-Philo's *Biblical Antiquities,*" *HJud* 12 (1950) 153-158.

Guido Kisch, "Pseudo-Philo's *Liber Antiquitatum Biblicarum,* Prolegomena to the New Edition," *HUCA* 23 (1950-51) Part 2, 81-93.

Abram Spiro, "Samaritans, Tobiads, and Judahites in Pseudo-Philo," *PAAJR* 20 (1951) 279-355.

*Abram Spiro, "Pseudo-Philo's Saul and the Rabbis' Messiah ben Ephraim," *PAAJR* 21 (1952) 119-137.

§807 *3.8 Studies on the Life and Works of Josephus*

*Anonymous, "Remarks on Judah's Speech to His Father, as Given by Josephus," *CD* 1 (1813) 183-185.

†[Karl Gollieb(?)] Bretschneider, "The Testimony of Josephus respecting Christ," *QCS* 7 (1825) 126-130.

C. G. Bretschneider, "On the Testimony of Josephus Respecting Christ," *BRCR* 4 (1834) 705-711. *(Trans. by Edward Robinson)*

Anonymous, "The Life and Writings of Josephus," *BRCM* 1 (1846) 372-382.

*Anonymous, "Restoration of the Chronology of Josephus," *JSL, 1st Ser.,* 5 (1850) 60-81.

O. E., "Josephus and the Bible," *JSL, 1st Ser.,* 6 (1850) 292-324. (Notes by J. T. G., pp. 324-327) *(Review)*

J. F., "Did Josephus Adopt the Long or Short Chronology?" *JSL, 3rd Ser.,* 7 (1858) 178-181.

*Anonymous, "The Earlier Chapters of the First Book of Esdras, and the Eleventh Book of the Jewish Antiquities of Josephus," *JSL, 4th Ser.,* 3 (1863) 143-154, 413-423.

R. H., "Josephus as a Man and as a Historian," *BFER* 15 (1866) 458-476. *(Review)*

Humphrey Fitzroy Woolrych, "Illustrations of the Old and New Testaments from Josephus," *CM* 16 (1883) 321-332.

Bernhard Pick, "A Study of Josephus with Special Reference to the Old Testament," *LQ* 19 (1889) 599-616.

*H. B. Swete, "Requests and Replies," *ET* 3 (1891-92) 300. *[Alexander's visit to Jerusalem in Josephus and the Prophecies of Daniel]*

*J. A. Howlett, "Josephus and the Language of Palestine in the Days of Christ," *IER, 3rd Ser.,* 16 (1895) 735-750.

*Adolf Buchler, "The Sources of Josephus for the History of Syria," *JQR* 9 (1896-97) 311-349.

M. Simon, "On Josephus, *Wars*, V, 5, 7," *JQR* 13 (1900-01) 547-548.

J. S. Riggs, "Josephus and Luke as Historians," *CFL, N.S.,* 5 (1902) 196-202.

*W. F. Birch, "The Levelling of Akra," *PEFQS* 35 (1903) 353-355. *[Josephus; Antiq. XIII, vi, 7]*

W. R. Morfill, "Josephus in Slavonic," *ET* 17 (1905-06) 301. *(Review)*

Fred. C. Conybeare, "An Old Armenian Version of Josephus," *JTS* 9 (1907-08) 577-583.

A. Kampmeier, "Josephus and Tacitus on Christ," *Monist* 20 (1910) 109-119. (Comment by William Benjamin Smith, pp. 119-124; Comments and Addenda by A. Kampmeier, pp. 124-126]

William Benjamin Smith, "The Silence of Josephus and Tacitus," *Monist* 20 (1910) 515-550.

F. C. Burkitt, "Josephus and Christ," *TTL* 47 (1913) 135-144.

W. Emery Barnes, "The Testimony of Josephus to Jesus Christ," *ContR* 105 (1914) 57-68.

Anonymous, "A Long-disputed Passage in Josephus," *HR* 67 (1914) 196-197.

*Joseph Offord, "Archaeological Notes on Jewish Antiquities. XLIX. *The Alexandrian Jewish Albarches of Josephus,*" *PEFQS* 50 (1918) 136-137.

Solomon Zeitlin, "Sameias and Pollion," *JJLP* 1 (1919) 61-67.

James A Montgomery, "The Religion of Flavius Josephus," *JQR, N.S.,* 11 (1920-21) 277-305.

*Bernard Revel, "Some Anti-Traditional Laws of Josephus," *JQR, N.S.,* 14 (1923-24) 293-301.

*J. A. Bewer, "Josephus' Account of Nehemiah," *JBL* 43 (1924) 224-226.

Herbert Thurston, "The Testimony of Josephus to Christ," *AER* 75 (1926) 6-16.

J. P. Arendzen, "The Russian Josephus," *DR* 179 (1926) 86-106.

Clyde Pharr, "The Testimony of Josephus to Christianity," *AJP* 48 (1927) 137-147.

*Solomon Zeitlin, "Note on the Relation of the Slavonic Josephus to Josippon," *JQR, N.S.,* 19 (1928-29) 77-78.

W. E. Barnes, "*Ιησους βασιλευς ου βασιλευσας,*" *JTS* 30 (1928-29) 65-68. *(Review)*

H. St. J. Thackeray, "An Unrecorded 'Aramaism' in Josephus ('He began to say unto them')," *JTS* 30 (1928-29) 361-370.

*George Foot Moore, "Fate and Free Will in the Jewish Philosophies According to Josephus," *HTR* 22 (1929) 371-389.

Joshua Bloch, "Josephus and Christian Origins," *JSOR* 13 (1929) 130-154.

Edwyn Bevan, "Josephus," *QRL* 253 (1929) 85-100. *(Review)*

Herbert W. Magoun, "A Modernist Crux," *CFL, 3rd Ser.,* 37 (1931) 299-304.

P. Canon Boylan, "The Slavonic Josephus," *IER, 5th Ser.,* 37 (1931) 449-460.

Herbert W. Magoun, "A Further Word About the Josephus Passage," *CFL, 3rd Ser.,* 38 (1932) 593-599.

*J. St. John Thackeray, "On Josephus's Statement of the Pharisees' Doctrine of Fate (Antiq. xviii, 1, 3)," *HTR* 25 (1932) 93.

John Martin Creed, "The Slavonic Version of Josephus' History of the Jewish War," *HTR* 25 (1932) 277-319.

Arthur Darby Nock, "Thackeray's Lexicon to Josephus," *HTR* 25 (1932) 361-362.

P. E. Kretzmann, "The So-called 'Christian Interpolations' in Josephus," *CTM* 4 (1933) 274-281.

H. M. DuB[ose], "The Testimony of Josephus," *CFL, 3rd Ser.,* 40 (1934) 9-11.

H. W. Magoun, "Eisler on the Josephus Passages," *BS* 92 (1935) 77-94.

C. C. Torrey, "1) The Language of Josephus," *JBL* 54 (1935) ii.

A. C. Bouquet, "The References to Josephus in the Bibliotheca of Photius," *JTS* 36 (1935) 289-293.

Eva Matthews Sanford, "Propaganda and Censorship in the Transmission of Josephus," *TAPA* 66 (1935) 127-145.

R. J. H. Shutt, "Josephus," *DUJ* 29 (1935-36) 401-407.

*Guido Kisch, "A Talmudic Legend as a Source for the Josephus Passage in the *Sachsenspiegel*," *HJud* 1 (1938-39) 105-118.

Isaac Heinemann, "Josephus' Method in the Presentation of Jewish Antiquities," *Zion* 5 (1939-40) #2, X.

*S. Yeivin, "Topographical Notes (annotations to S. Klein, *The Land of Judah*)," *BIES* 8 (1940-41) #3, II. [2. The Mount of Olives—Bell. Jud. V, 12, 2]

G. C. Richards, "The *Testimonium* of Josephus," *JTS* 42 (1941) 70-71.

Philip E. Hughes, "The Value of Josephus as a Historical Source," *EQ* 15 (1943) 179-183.

*Grace Amadon, "Important Passover Texts in Josephus and Philo," *ATR* 27 (1945) 109-115.

*Sidney B. Hoenig, "Synedrion in the Attic Orators, the Ptolemaic Papyri and its Adoption by Josephus, the Gospels and the Tannaim," *JQR, N.S.*, 37 (1946-47) 179-187.

Spencer Kennard, "Gleanings from the Slavonic Josephus Controversy," *JQR, N.S.*, 39 (1948-49) 161-170.

Solomon Zeitlin, "The Hoax of the 'Slavonic Josephus'," *JQR, N.S.*, 39 (1948-49) 171-180.

Spencer Kennard, "Slavonic Josephus: A Retraction," *JQR, N.S.*, 39 (1948-49) 281-283.

M. Aberbach, "The Conflicting Accounts of Josephus and Tacitus Concerning Cumanus' and Felix' Terms of Office," *JQR, N.S.*, 40 (1949-50) 1-14.

*M. Avi-Yonah, "Samaria and the 'Marissa' of Antiquities XIII, 275," *BIES* 16 (1951) #3/4, IV-V.

*Ralph Marcus, "Philo, Josephus and the Dead Sea *Yaḥad,*" *JBL* 71 (1952) 207-209.

W. D. Davies, "A Note on Josephus, Antiquities 15:136," *HTR* 47 (1954) 135-140.

Roderic Dunkerley, "The Riddles of Josephus," *HJ* 53 (1954-55) 127-134.

*A. Dupont-Sommer, "On a Passage of Josephus Relating to the Essenes (Antiq. XVIII, §22)," *JSS* 1 (1956) 361-366.

A. Rubinstein, "The Essenes according to the Slavonic Version of Josephus' *Wars,*" *VT* 6 (1956) 307-308.

Arie Rubinstein, "Observations on the Old Russian Version of Josephus' *Wars,*" *JSS* 2 (1957) 329-348.

Hans Petersen, "Real and Alleged Literary Projects of Josephus," *AJP* 79 (1958) 259-274.

S. G. F. Brandon, "Josephus: Renegade or Patriot?" *HT* 8 (1958) 830-836.

*Morton Smith, "The Description of the Essenes in Josephus and the Philosophumena," *HUCA* 29 (1958) 273-313.

*John Strugnell, "Flavius Josephus and the Essenes: *Antiquities* XVIII. 18-22," *JBL* 77 (1958) 106-115.

*Louis H. Feldman, "The Identity of Pollio, the Pharisee, in Josephus," *JQR, N.S.,* 49 (1958-59) 53-62.

*Sidney B. Hoenig, "Maccabees, Zealots and Josephus," *JQR, N.S.,* 49 (1958-59) 75-80.

*J. B. Fischer, "The Term ΔΕΣΠΟΤΗΕ in Josephus," *JQR, N.S.,* 49 (1958-59) 132-138.

*Solomon Zeitlin, "The Account of the Essenes in Josephus and in the Philosophumena," *JQR, N.S.,* 49 (1958-59) 292-300.

*Ernest Best, "The Use and Non-Use of Pneuma by Josephus," *NT* 3 (1959) 218-225.

*Abraham Schalit, "The Letter of Antiochus III to Zeuxis Regarding the Establishment of Jewish Military Colonies in Phyrygia and Lydia," *JQR, N.S.,* 50 (1959-60) 289-318. *[Antiquities xii, 148-153]*

*Menaḥem Stern, "*Trachides*—Surname of Alexander Yannai in Josephus and Syncellus," *Tarbiz* 29 (1959-60) #3, II. *[Antiquities viii, 383]*

*Solomon Zeitlin, "Josephus and the Zealots: A Rejoinder," *JSS* 5 (1960) 388.

George Orvick, "The Importance of Josephus in Biblical Studies," *LSQ* 3 (1962-63) #4, 20-23; 4 (1963-64) #1, 7-14.

*Norman Walker, "The Riddle of the Ass's Head and the Question of a Trigram," *ZAW* 75 (1963) 225-227.

Naomi G. Cohen, "Josephus and Scripture," *JQR, N.S.,* 54 (1963-64) 311-332.

Jacob Neusner, "The Conversion of Adiabene to Judaism: A New Perspective," *JBL* 83 (1964) 60-66. *[Antiq. 20, 2, 1-4, 3]*

*F. F. Bruce, "Josephus and Daniel," *ASTI* 4 (1965) 148-162.

A. Schalit, "Evidence of an Aramaic Source in Josephus' 'Antiquities of the Jews'," *ASTI* 4 (1965) 163-188.

W. J. Malley, "Four Unedited Fragments of *de Universo* of the Pseudo-Josephus found in the *Chronicon* of George Hamartolus (Coislin 305)," *JTS, N.S.,* 16 (1965) 13-25.

C. G. Tuland, "Josephus, *Antiquities*, Book XI," *AUSS* 4 (1966) 176-192.

*Z. Kallai, "The Biblical Geography of Flavius Josephus," *EI* 8 (1967) 77*.

*Solomon Zeitlin, "The Slavonic Josephus and the Dead Sea Scrolls: An Expose of Recent Fairy Tales," *JQR, N.S.,* 58 (1967-68) 173-203.

*Louis H. Feldman, "Abraham the Greek Philosopher in Josephus," *TAPA* 99 (1968) 143-156.

*Solomon Zeitlin, "A Survey of Jewish Historiography: From the Biblical Books to the *Sefer Ha-Kabbalah* with special emphasis on Josephus," *JQR, N.S.,* 59 (1968-69) 171-214.

*Solomon Zeitlin, "A Survey of Jewish Historiography: From the Biblical Books to the *Sefer Ha-Kabbalah*," *JQR, N.S.,* 60 (1969-70) 37-68.

§808 **3.9 Studies on the Works and Life of Hillel**

Franz Delitzsch, "Jesus and Hillel with reference to Renan and Geiger," *LQ* 11 (1881) 530-557. *(Trans. by P. C. Croll)*

F[ranz] Delitzsch, "Jesus and Hillel compared, with Reference to Renan and Geiger," *AR* 2 (1884) 305-313, 502-515. *(Trans. by B. Pick)*

Moses Levene, "Hillel the Babylonian," *BOR* 9 (1901) 1-10.

*Irving M. Melam, "Some Facts Concerning the Controversy in the Halakah Between the Schools of Shammai and Hillel," *JIQ* 1 (1924-25) 12-16.

A[rmand] Kaminka, "Hillel and his Works," *Zion* 4 (1938-39) #3, IV.

Armand Kaminka, "Hillel's Life and Work," *JQR, N.S.,* 30 (1939-40) 107-122.

Judah Goldin, "Hillel the Elder," *JR* 26 (1946) 263-277.

Hans Kosmala, "A Cryptic Saying of Hillel," *ASTI* 2 (1963) 114-118.

Solomon Zeitlin, "Hillel and the Hermeneutic Rules," *JQR, N.S.,* 54 (1963-64) 161-174.

Solomon Zeitlin, "The Semikah Controversy Between the School of Shammai and Hillel," *JQR, N.S.,* 56 (1965-66) 240-244.

§809 *3.10 Rabbinical Studies and Writings*

†Anonymous, "Hurwitz's *Hebrew Tales,*" *QRL* 35 (1827) 86-114. *(Review)*

Isaac Nordheimer, "The Rabbies and Their Literature," *BRCR, N.S.,* 6 (1841) 154-177.

†Anonymous, "Ethridge on Hebrew Literature," *LQHR* 7 (1856-57) 119-141. *(Review)*

Hyman Hurwitz, "Hebrew Tales. *Selected and Translated from the Writings of the Ancient Hebrew Sages,*" *DTQ* 4 (1878) 117-130.

*[Moses] Mielziner, "Rabbinical Sayings concerning Marriage," *ONTS* 4 (1884-85) 180-181.

*Thomas Chaplin, "Translations of the Middoth, &c," *PEFQS* 19 (1887) 132-133.

*H. Friedlænder, "Rabbinical Preaching," *EN* 1 (1889) 130-133.

*W. Bacher, "Seventy-Two Modes of Exposition," *JQR* 4 (1891-92) 509.

*Elsie Davis, "Sympathy with Brute Creation," *JQR* 8 (1895-96) 714-715.

*Elsie Davis, "Human Sympathy," *JQR* 8 (1895-96) 716-718.

*Samuel Krauss, "Imprecation Against the Minim in the Synagogue," *JQR* 9 (1896-97) 515-517.

H. Hirschfeld, "Historical and Legendary Controversies between Mohammed and the Rabbis," *JQR* 10 (1897-98) 100-116. [Correction by W. Bacher on p. 383]

D. S. Margoliouth, "The Non-Biblical Literature of the Jews," *ET* 11 (1899-1900) 331-333; 13 (1901-02) 190-192.

*S. Schechter, "Some Rabbinic Parallels to the New Testament," *JQR* 12 (1899-1900) 415-433.

*C. G. Montefiore, "Rabbinic Judaism and the Epistles of St. Paul," *JQR* 13 (1900-01) 161-217.

*W. H. Kent, "Rabbinical Studies. I," *AER* 26 (1902) 297-308. [I. On the Growing Importance of Hebrew Scholarship; II. St. Jerome and the Jews; III. Critical Value of the Vulgate; IV. The Hebrew Bible and the Vulgate in Agreement; V. Enduring Validity of Rabbinical Literature; VI. The Rabbinical Bible; VII. The Biblical Cryptogram; VIII. Vulgate and Targum in Agreement; IX. The Babylonian Talmud; X. Mishna and Germara; XI. Historical Evolution of the Talmud]

*W. H. Kent, "Rabbinical Studies. II," *AER* 26 (1902) 659-667. [XII. The Talmud of Jerusalem; XIII. Abbreviations and 'Rashe Theboth'; XIV. Orders and Treatises; XV. The Talmud and the Bible; XVI. Halacoth and Haggadoth; XVII. The Talmud and Higher Criticism]

*W. H. Kent, "Rabbinical Studies. III," *AER* 27 (1902) 173-184. [XVIII. The Midrash Rabba; XIX. The 'Kabbala,' or Mystical Tradition; XX. Jewish Vernacular Literature; XXI. The Chaldee Book of Tobias; XXII. The Church and the Talmud; XXIII. Early Catholic Hebrists; XXIV. Judaism and the Monuments]

C. G. Montefiore, "Jewish Scholarship and Christian Silence," *HJ* 1 (1902-03) 335-346; 2 (1903-04) 141-142.

Allan Menzies, "'Jewish Scholarship and Christian Silence.' A Rejoinder," *HJ* 1 (1902-03) 789-792.

Peter Cook, "Introduction to Quotations from the Talmud and Kindred Jewish Literature," *BW* 22 (1903) 216-223, 294-300.

*T[heophilus] G. P[inches], "Talmudische und Midraschishe Parallelen zum Babylonischen Weltschöpfungsepos," *JRAS* (1904) 369-370. *[English Text]*

A. Cohen, "Arabisms in Rabbinic Literature," *JQR, N.S.,* 3 (1912-13) 221-233.

D. S. Margoliouth, "The Bible of the Jews," *TZTM* 3 (1913) 544-567.

*J. N. Epstein, "Notes on Post-Talmudic-Aramaic Lexicography I," *JQR, N.S.,* 5 (1914-15) 233-251.

*‡G. H. Box, "Survey of Some Recent Contributions to the Study of Judaism and the Rabbinical Literature," *RTP* 10 (1914-15) 437-456, 497-513.

*A. Marmorstein, "A Doctrine of the Resurrection of the Dead in Rabbinical Theology," *AJT* 19 (1915) 577-591.

Solomon Zeitlin, "Studies in Tannaitic Jurisprudence," *JJLP* 1 (1919) 297-311.

*J. N. Epstein, "Notes on Post-Talmudic-Aramaic Lexicography II," *JQR, N.S.,* 12 (1921-22) 299-390. [Index of Words, pp. 389-390]

B. Halper, "Descriptive Catalogue of Genizah Fragments in Philadelphia II, Talmud, Midrash, and Halakah," *JQR, N.S.,* 13 (1922-23) 9-52.

*Julius J. Price, "Kapporoth," *OC* 37 (1923) 176-180; 38 (1924) 499-503.

Julius J. Price, "The Sun in the Talmud," *OC* 37 (1923) 605-609.

Julius J. Price, "Arabic Parallels to Rabbinic Literature," *OC* 38 (1924) 696-704.

Harry Lewis, "A Masterpiece of Rabbinic Studies," *JIQ* 3 (1926-27) #4, 11-15. *(Review)*

*Louis Finkelstein, "Is Philo Mentioned in Rabbinic Literature?" *JBL* 53 (1934) 142-149.

*Solomon Gandz, "The Rōbeh רוֹבֶה or the Official Memorizer of the Palestinian Schools," *PAAJR* 7 (1935-36) 5-12.

*Rachel Wischnitzer-Bernstein, "The Messianic Fox," *RR* 5 (1940-41) 257-263.

Louis Finkelstein, "The Transmission of Early Rabbinic Tradition," *HUCA* 16 (1941) 115-135.

*Samuel Rosenblatt, "A Reference to the Egyptian God Re' in the Rabbinic Commentaries," *JBL* 60 (1941) 183-185.

*Paul Romanoff, "The Fox in Jewish Tradition," *RR* 6 (1941-42) 184-187.

*Rachel Wischnitzer-Bernstein, "A Reply to Dr. Romanoff," *RR* 6 (1941-42) 187-190.

*Saul Lieberman, "Roman Legal Institutions in Early Rabbinics and in the Acta Martyrum," *JQR, N.S.,* 35 (1944-45) 1-57.

*Isaiah Sonne, "The Use of the Rabbinic Literature and Historical Sources," *JQR, N.S.,* 36 (1945-46) 147-169.

H. Medalie, "'The Talmudical College of Pumbeditha'," *JMUEOS* #24 (1947) 60-65.

Robert Gordis, "'Homeric' Books in Palestine," *JQR, N.S.,* 38 (1947-48) 359-368.

*Robert Gordis, "Quotations as a Literary Usages in Biblical, Oriental and Rabbinic Literature," *HUCA* 22 (1949) 157-219.

John Wick Bowman, "Implements of Interpretation. XII. Rabbinic Writings," *Interp* 3 (1949) 435-449.

*John Bowman, "Prophets and Prophecy in Talmud and Midrash," *EQ* 22 (1950) 107-114, 205-220, 255-275.

*Alexander Guttmann, "Foundations of Rabbinic Judaism," *HUCA* 23 (1950-51) Part 1, 453-473.

F. Bowman, "A 'Megillat Setarim'(?)" *JJS* 2 (1950-51) 31-36.

*A. D. H. Fishlock, "The Rabbinic Material in the *Ester[sic]* of Pinto Delgado," *JJS* 2 (1950-51) 37-50.

Elias J. Bickerman, "The Maxim of Antigonus of Socho," *HTR* 45 (1951) 153-165.

*L. Morris, "The Passover in Rabbinic Literature," *ABR* 4 (1954-55) 57-76.

*G. B. Sarfatti, "Pious Men, Men of Deeds, and the Early Prophets," *Tarbiz* 26 (1956-57) #2, II-IV. (Corrections, #3, X)

Zvi Dor, "The Original Forms of Some Statements of the First Palestinian Amoraim," *Tarbiz* 26 (1956-57) #4, II-III.

Ernst Roth, "A Geonic Fragment Concerning the Oral Chain of Tradition," *Tarbiz* 26 (1956-57) #4, V.

*L. Jacobs, "The Concept of Hasid in the Biblical and Rabbinic Literatures," *JJS* 8 (1957) 143-154.

*Robert Gordis, "The Origin of the Masoretic Text in the Light of the Rabbinic Literature and the Dead Sea Scrolls," *Tarbiz* 27 (1957-58) #4, III-V.

P. Kykan, *"Piqquaḥ Hefesh* (Preservation of Life)," *Tarbiz* 27 (1957-58) #4, VI.

P. R. Weis, "The Controversies of Rab and Samuel and the Tosefta," *JSS* 3 (1958) 288-297.

*Sidney B. Hoenig, "The Age of Twenty in Rabbinic Tradition and 1QSa," *JQR, N.S.,* 49 (1958-59) 209-214.

*M.-R. Lehmann, *"1Q Genesis Apocryphon* in the Light of Targumim and Midrashim," *RdQ* 1 (1958-59) 249-263.

Jakob J. Petuchowski, "The *Mumar*—A Study in Rabbinic Psychology," *HUCA* 30 (1959) 179-190.

*O. H. M. Lehmann, "Religious Experience in the Gospels and in Contemporary Rabbinic Literature," *StEv* 1 (1959) 557-561.

*Joseph Heinemann, "Prayers of Beth Midrash Origin," *JSS* 5 (1960) 264-280.

*H. Jaeger, "The Patristic Conception of Wisdom in the Light of Biblical and Rabbinical Research," *StP* 4 (1961) 90-106.

*G. Nádor, "Some Numerical Categories in Ancient Rabbinical Literature: The Numbers *Ten, Seven* and *Four,*" *AOASH* 14 (1962) 301-315.

Morton Smith, "A Comparison of Early Christian and Early Rabbinic Tradition," *JBL* 82 (1963) 169-176.

Haiim B. Rosen, "Palestinian KOINH in Rabbinic Illustration," *JSS* 8 (1963) 56-72.

Richard L. Rubenstein, "Scribes, Pharisees, and Hypocrites. A Study in Rabbinic Psychology," *Jud* 12 (1963) 456-468.

Morton Smith, "Observations on *Hekhalot Rabbati,*" *LIST* 1 (1963) 142-160.

Ranon Katzoff, "The Apikoros in Rabbinic Literature," *YR* 3 (1963) 35-41.

*Roy A. Stewart, "The Parable Form in the Old Testament and in Rabbinic Literature," *EQ* 36 (1964) 133-147.

Anonymous, "God's Replenishment of Israel from Pesikta Rabbati," *Jud* 13 (1964) 467-470. *[Trans. by William G. Braude]*

*Roy A. Stewart, "The Parable Form in the Old Testament and in the Rabbinic Literature," *F&T* 94 (1965-66) 113-127.

*B. Salomonsen, "Some Remarks on the Zealots with Special Regard to the Term 'Qannaim' in Rabbinic Literature," *NTS* 12 (1965-66) 164-176.

*Jacob Neusner, "The Religious Uses of History: Judaism in First-Century A.D. Palestine and Third-Century Babylonia," *H&T* 5 (1966) 153-171.

*M. McNamara, "Some Early Rabbinic Citations and the Palestinian Targum to the Pentateuch," *RDSO* 41 (1966) 1-15.

*S[hmuel] Yosef Agnon, "Sacred Letters," *HA* 11 (1966-67) 9-12.

*Samuel Belkin, "Some Obscure Tradition Mutually Clarified in Philo and Rabbinic Literature," *JQR 75th* (1967) 80-103.

Nathan Schnaper, "The Talmud: psychiatric relevancies in Hebrew tradition," *JRH* 6 (1967) 171-187.

*Joseph L. Blau, "The red heifer: a Biblical purification rite in Rabbinic literature," *Numen* 14 (1967) 70-78.

*Isaac D. Gilsy, "Measurements as Rabbinical Ordinances," *Tarbiz* 37 (1967-68) #3, I-II.

*David B. Weisberg, "Some Observations on Late Babylonian Texts and Rabbinic Literature," *HUCA* 39 (1968) 71-80.

Ernst Bammel, "Gerim Gerurim," *ASTI* 7 (1968-69) 127-131.

*Sidney B. Hoenig, "The Sectarian Scrolls and Rabbinic Research," *JQR, N.S.,* 59 (1968-69) 24-70. *(Review and Commentary)*

Joshua Brand, "Concerning Greek Culture in Palestine during the Talmudic Period," *Tarbiz* 38 (1968-69) #1, II-III.

*Nathaniel L. Gerber, "The Wise Man in Rabbinic Judaism and Stoic Philosophy," *YR* 7 (1969) 40-62.

§810 *3.10.1 Halakah (Law)*

*F. W. Farrar, "The Halacha and the Hagada," *Exp, 1st Ser.,* 6 (1877) 266-284.

L. M. Simmons, "The Talmudical Law of Agency," *JQR* 8 (1895-96) 614-631.

*S. Schechter, "Genizah Fragments," *JQR* 16 (1903-04) 425-452. [II. Halakhic, pp. 443-445]

*Jacob Z. Lauterbach, "Midrash and Mishnah. A Study in the Early History of the Halakah," *JQR, N.S.,* 5 (1914-15) 503-527 *[Part I]*

*Jacob Z. Lauterbach, "Midrash and Mishnah. A Study in the Early History of the Halakah," *JQR, N.S.,* 6 (1915-16) 23-95, 303-323. *[Parts II and III]*

*Louis Finkelstein, "The Book of Jubilees and the Rabbinic Halaka," *HTR* 16 (1923) 39-62.

*Irving M. Melam, "Some Facts Concerning the Controversy in the Halakah Between the Schools of Shammai and Hillel," *JIQ* 1 (1924-25) 12-16.

L[ouis] Finkelstein, "Some Examples of the Maccabean Halaka," *JBL* 49 (1930) 20-42.

Hyman Klein, "Gemara and Sebara," *JQR, N.S.,* 38 (1947-48) 67-91.

Samuel I. Feigin, "*Haggārîm,* the Castrated One," *HUCA* 21 (1948) 355-364. *[Mekilta]*

Solomon Zeitlin, "The Halaka, Introduction to Tannaitic Jurisprudence," *JQR, N.S.,* 39 (1948-49) 1-40. [The Written and Unwritten Laws; The Halaka and Midrash; Sources of Tannaitic Law; Interpretation and Legal Fiction; The Schools of Shammai and Hillel; Tannaitic Jurisprudence; The Halaka as a Mode of Life]

Solomon Zeitlin, "The Takkanot of Erubin: A Study in the Development of the Halaka," *JQR, N.S.,* 41 (1950-51) 351-361.

*E. Neufeld, "The status of the male minor in Talmud," *RIDA, 1st Ser.,* 6 (1951) 121-140.

*Solomon Zeitlin, "Is a Revival of the Sanhedrin in Israel Necessary for Modification of the Halaka?" *JQR, N.S.,* 42 (1951-52) 339-376.

B. de Vries, "The Early Form of Certain *Halakhot,*" *Tarbiz* 24 (1954-55) #4, III-IV.

*David Weiss, "Halakhic Exegesis," *CJ* 10 (1955-56) #3, 52-58.

B. de Vries, "The Early Form of Certain *Halakhot,*" *Tarbiz* 24 (1955-56) #4, III-IV; 25 (1956-57) #4, II.

David W. Perlman, "Symposium: The Chain of Tradition and the Law of Change. I. The Halacha—as the Authority of the Past," *YCCAR* 66 (1956) 231-238.

Shalom Albeck, "The Development of the Concept of Transfer of Debts in the Talmud," *Tarbiz* 26 (1956-57) #3, III-IV.

*A. Ehrman, "Law and Equity in the Talmudic Concept of Sale," *JJS* 8 (1957) 177-186.

*S. Stein, "The Dietary Laws in Rabbinic and Patristic Literature," *StP* 2 (1957) 141-154.

*E. E. Hallewy, "The Entry of a Field in Sale,"*Tarbiz* 27 (1957-58) #1, IV-V.

Ephraim E. Urbach, "The Derasha as a Basis of the Halakha and the Problem of the Soferim," *Tarbiz* 27 (1957-58) #2/3, VI-VIII.

Jacob Katz, "'Though He Sinned, He Remains an Israelite'," *Tarbiz* 27 (1957-58) #2/3, IX.

*Ben Zion Wacholder, "Attitudes Towards Proselytizing in the Classical Halakah," *HJud* 20 (1958) 77-96.

Shalom Albeck, "Negligence and Remoteness of Damage in the Talmud," *Tarbiz* 28 (1958-59) #3/4, IV-VI.

*E. E. Urbach, "The Rabbinical Laws of Idolatry in the Second and Third Centuries in the Light of Archaeological and Historical Facts," *IEJ* 9 (1959) 149-165, 229-245.

Ernst Bammel, "Any Deyathiqi Partially Cancelled is Completely Cancelled," *JSS* 5 (1960) 355-358.

*Manfred R. Lehmann, "Gen 2:24 as the Basis for Divorce in Halakhah and New Testament," *ZAW* 72 (1960) 263-267.

Yehuda Feliks, "Ploughing in Talmudic Literature," *Tarbiz* 30 (1960-61) #1, III-IV.

E. E. Urbach, "*Halakhot* Regarding Slavery as a Source for the Social History of the Second Temple and the Talmudic Period," *Zion* 25 (1960) #3/4, I-III.

Emanuel Rackman, "The Dialectic of the Halakhah," *Trad* 3 (1960-61) 131-150.

I. F. Baer, "The Historical Foundations of the Halakha," *Zion* 27 (1962) #3/4, I-III.

B. de Vries, "The Ancient Form of *Halakhot* and their Development," *Tarbiz* 33 (1963-64) #1, I-II.

*Isaac D. Gilat, "Leaven Belonging to Gentiles or to the Sanctuary," *Tarbiz* 33 (1963-64) #1, II.

Abraham Goldberg, "Palestinian Law in Babylonian Tradition, as Revealed in a Study of *Perek Arvei Pesaḥim*," *Tarbiz* 33 (1963-64) #4, I-II.

*E. E. Urbach, "The Laws Regarding Slavery as a Source for Social History of the Period of the Second Temple, the Mishnah and Talmud," *PIJSL* 1 (1964) 1-94.

*Solomon Zeitlin, "Mar Samuel and Manumission of Slaves," *JQR, N.S.,* 55 (1964-65) 267-269.

Joseph Kalir, "The Minhag," *Trad* 7 (1964-65) #2, 89-95.

Zeev W. Falk, "On Talmudic Vows," *HTR* 59 (1966) 309-312.

Stephen M. Passamanek, "Some Medieval Problems in *Mamzeruth*," *HUCA* 37 (1966) 121-145.

*Z. E. Kurzweil, "Fundamental Principles of Jewish Education in the Light of Halachah," *Jud* 16 (1967) 176-185.

*Norman Lamm, "The Fourth Amendment and Its Equivalent in the Halachah," *Jud* 16 (1967) 300-312.

Sheraga Abramson, "The Halachic Works of *RABAD* (R. Abraham Ben David)," *Tarbiz* 36 (1966-67) #2, II-III.

*E. E. Hallewi, "The Oath (A Chapter in the History of the Halakha)," *Tarbiz* 37 (1967-68) #1, III-IV.

Zeev W. Falk, "New-Babylonian Law in the Halakha," *Tarbiz* 37 (1967-68) #1, IV.

*Joseph Heinemann, "The *Targum* of Ex. XXIII, 4 and the Ancient *Halakha*," *Tarbiz* 38 (1968-69) #3, V.

Meyer S. Feldblum, "The Impact of the 'Anonymous Sugyah' on Halakic Concepts," *PAAJR* 37 (1969) 19-28.

Bernard Septimus, "Obligation and Supererogation in Halakha," *YR* 7 (1969) 30-39.

*Alexander Guttmann, "Jerusalem in Tannaitic Law," *HUCA* 40&41 (1969-70) 251-275.

*Solomon Zeitlin, "Studies in Talmudic Jurisprudence: Possession, Pignus and Hypothec," *JQR, N.S.,* 60 (1969-70) 89-111.

*Samuel Belkin, "Levirate and Agnate Marriage in Rabbinic and Cognate Literature," *JQR, N.S.,* 60 (1969-70) 275-329.

§811 *3.10.2 Aggada (Legend)*

E. F., "Poetical Legends of the Talmud," *JSL, 1st Ser.,* 6 (1850) 42-74.

*S. I. L. Rapport, "Asmodai," *MQR* 7 (1853) 500-513. *(Trans. by H. Bear)*

*F. W. Farrar, "The Halacha and the Hagada," *Exp, 1st Ser.,* 6 (1877) 266-284.

F. W. Farrar, "Characteristics of the Hagada," *Exp, 1st Ser.,* 6 (1877) 334-353.

*H. Graetz, "Notes and Discussion. Historical Notices. I. Alexander and his gold-lettered Scroll," *JQR* 2 (1889-90) 102-104.

*S. Schechter, "The Riddles of Solomon in Rabbinic Literature," *Folk* 1 (1890) 349-358.

*Alexander Kohut, "Parsic and Jewish Legends of the First Man," *JQR* 3 (1890-91) 231-250.

W. Bacher, "The Origin of the Word Haggada (Agada)," *JQR* 4 (1891-92) 406-429.

*K. Kohler, "The Pre-Talmudic Haggada, I," *JQR* 5 (1892-93) 399-419. [A. The Testament of the Twelve Patriarchs; B. The Second Baruch or Rather the Jeremiah Apocalypse]

*K. Kohler, "The Pre-Talmudic Haggada, II," *JQR* 7 (1894-95) 581-606. [C. The Apocalypse of Abraham and its Kindred]

H. G. Enelow, "The Significance of the Agada," *YCCAR* 24 (1914) 263-300.

*Armand Kaminka, "The Origin of the Ashmedai Legend in the Babylonian Talmud," *JQR, N.S.,* 13 (1922-23) 221-224.

*V. Aptowitzer, "Asenath, the Wife of Joseph—A Haggadic, Literary Historical Study," *HUCA* 1 (1924) 221-238.

*V. Aptowitzer, "The Rewarding and Punishing of Animals and Inanimate Objects. On the aggadic View of the World," *HUCA* 3 (1926) 117-155.

A. Marmorstein, "The Background of the Haggadah," *HUCA* 6 (1929) 141-204.

*Sheldon H. Blank, "The Death of Zechariah in Rabbinic Literature," *HUCA* 12&13 (1937-38) 327-346.

Bernard J. Bamberger, "Revelations of Torah after Sinai, An Aggadic Study," *HUCA* 16 (1941) 97-113.

Bernard J. Bamberger, "The Dating of Aggadic Materials," *JBL* 68 (1949) 115-123.

*Leo Baeck, "Haggadah and Christian Doctrine," *HUCA* 23 (1950-51) Part 1, 549-560.

*Ephraim E. Urbach, "Homilies of the Rabbis on the Prophets of the Nations and the Balaam Stories," *Tarbiz* 25 (1956-57) #3, III-IV.

Robert L Katz, "Empathy in Modern Psychotherapy and in the Aggada," *HUCA* 30 (1959) 191-215.

Ovadia Camhy, "Introduction to the Aggadah," *Jud* 8 (1959) 68-72.

E. E. Hallewy, "The Writers of the 'Aggada and the Greek Grammarians," *Tarbiz* 29 (1959-60) #1, III-IV.

*Z. W. Falk, "Collective Responsibility in Bible and Aggada," *Tarbiz* 30 (1960-61) #1, III.

Samuel Karff, "The Agada as a Source of Contemporary Jewish Theology," *YCCAR* 73 (1963) 191-198.

*Paul Connors, "Haggadic History," *BC* 3 (1963-64) 162-167.

Etan B. Levine, "Haggadah in Jewish Bible Study," *CTM* 40 (1969) 92-96.

§812 *3.10.3 Talmudic Literature (including Mishnah)*

Isaac Nordheimer, "The Talmud and the Rabbies," *BRCR, N.S.,* 2 (1839) 261-292. *[pp. 261-266 misnumbered as 1-16]*

Anonymous, "Experiment in Translation of the Talmud—Valuable Things in the Talmud," *DQR* 4 (1864) 310-326.

( ) Michelsen, "The Jews and the Talmud after the Time of Christ," *JSL, 4th Ser.,* 5 (1864) 321-327.

B. Harris Cowper, "The Talmud," *JSL, 5th Ser.,* 2 (1867-68) 249-284.

†Anonymous, "The Talmud," *QRL* 123 (1867) 417-464. *(Review)*

Reginald Stuart Poole, "The Talmud," *ContR* 7 (1868) 108-124.

B. Harris Cowper, "The Talmud," *ThE* 5 (1868) 526-559.

E. H. Plumptre, "Marcus Aurelius and the Talmud," *ContR* 10 (1869) 81-95.

†Anonymous, "The Talmud," *ERCJ* 138 (1873) 28-64. *(Review)*

Joseph Barclay, "The Edinburgh Reviewer on the Talmud," *PEFQS* 6 (1874) 30.

B. Pick, "The Talmud," *BQ* 10 (1876) 66-82.

Anonymous, "Selections from the Talmud," *DTQ* 3 (1877) 186-198, 348-367. *(Trans. by H. Polano)*

F. W. Farrar, "Christians in the Talmud," *Exp, 1st Ser.,* 6 (1877) 412-429.

F. W. Farrar, "A Talmudic Cryptography," *Exp, 1st Ser.,* 7 (1878) 40-58.

*Josiah Miller, "The Talmud in Relation to Biblical Archaeology," *SBAP* 1 (1878-79) 38-39. (Remarks by A. Lowy, 39-40) *[pages misnumbered as 36-38]*

*Albert Lowy, "The Samaritans in Talmudical Writings," *SBAP* 2 (1879-80) 11-13.

Anonymous, "The Books of the Talmud," *DUM* 96 (1880) 72-96.

Felix Adler, "On the Talmud, considered in its relation to the Early History of Christianity," *JAOS* 10 (1880) c-ci.

Philip H. Wicksteed, "A Controversy on the Talmud," *ModR* 3 (1882) 168-172.

*I. Stern, "Beams from the Talmud. I. Mankind," *ONTS* 1 (1882) #1, 14.

I. Stern, "Beams from the Talmud. II. World and Life," *ONTS* 1 (1882) #2, 13.

P. A. Nordell, "The Study of the Talmud," *ONTS* 1 (1882) 47-48.

I. Stern, "Beams from the Talmud. III. Youth and Age," *ONTS* 1 (1882) 53.

I. Stern, "Beams from the Talmud. IV. Fortune and Misfortune, Sorrow and Care," *ONTS* 1 (1882) 53.

P. A. Nordell, "The Origin and the Formal Contents of the Talmud," *ONTS* 2 (1882-83) 15-18.

H. Oort, "The Talmud and the New Testament," *ModR* 4 (1883) 464-494, 728-752.

*C[harles] A. Briggs, "The Tract Baba Bathra of the Talmud and the Old Testament," *PR* 4 (1883) 417-420.

Anonymous, "The Study of the Talmud," *ONTS* 3 (1883-84) 57-58.

*S. Louis, "On the Handicrafts and Artizans mentioned in Talmudical Writings," *SBAP* 6 (1883-84) 117-119.

*S. Louis, "Handicrafts and Artizans mentioned in Talmudical Writings," *SBAT* 8 (1883-84) 398-411.

*B. Pick, "Talmudic Notices Concerning the Messiah," *PR* 5 (1884) 505-510.

Anonymous, "On the Study of the Talmud," *WR* 123 (1885) 20-53.

B. Pick, "The Talmud a Witness to Christ and Christianity," *LCR* 5 (1886) 122-141.

Moïse Schwab, "A Talmudic Question to Prof. J. Oppert," *BOR* 2 (1887-88) 292. [Abâda zara, chap. I. §2] *['Abod. Zar. 1:2]*

*K. Kohler, "Jastrow's Talmudic Dictionary," *AJSL* 5 (1888-89) 1-6. *(Review)*

I. H. Weiss, "The Study of the Talmud in the Thirteenth Century," *JQR* 1 (1888-89) 289-313.

*Albert A. Isaacs, "Charity in Talmudical Times," *EN* 1 (1889) 97-103.

W. Bacher, "The Date of the Composition of the Talmud," *ET* 11 (1899-1900) 520-521.

Alexander Kohut, "Talmudical Miscellanies," *JQR* 3 (1890-91) 546-554. [1. Sifre Homeros, Books of Entertainment; 2. Croesus; 3. Zeus in Mishnah, Talmud, and Midrash]

A[lexander] Kohut, "Talmudical Miscellanies, IV—Lakes of the Holy Land," *JQR* 4 (1891-92) 690-696.

*J. Snowman, "Medicine in the Talmud," *EN* 4 (1892) 184-185.

W. Bacher, "A Talmudic Proverb in Petronius," *JQR* 5 (1892-93) 168-170.

*I. M. Casanowicz, "Non-Jewish religious ceremonies in the Talmud," *JAOS* 16 (1894-96) lxxvi-lxxxii.

J. Rendel Harris, "The Blessed Virgin in the Talmud," *Exp, 5th Ser.,* 2 (1895) 191-199, 350-356.

G. A. Cooke, "The Blessed Virgin in the Talmud: A Criticism," *Exp, 5th Ser.,* 2 (1895) 316-320.

Moses Levene, "The Romantic Side of the Talmud," *BOR* 8 (1895-1900) 229-236, 241-248.

*C. Levias, "A Grammar of the Aramaic Idiom Contained in the Babylonian Talmud," *AJSL* 13 (1896-97) 21-78, 118-139, 177-208; 14 (1897-98) 17-37, 106-128, 195-206, 252-266; 15 (1898-99) 224-243; 16 (1899-1900) 83-109.

T. Witton Davies, "Two Works on the Talmud," *ET* 8 (1896-97) 445-447. *(Review)*

C. Levias, "A Curious Mistake," *AJSL* 13 (1896-97) 309. ['Arukh quoting Babylonian Talmud (Bekh. 8b)]

*Alexander Kohut, "The Talmudic Records of Persian and Babylonian Festivals Critically Illustrated," *AJSL* 14 (1897-98) 183-194.

George Alexander Kohut, "A Persian Custom in the Talmud," *AJSL* 15 (1898-99) 54-55.

George Alexander Kohut, "A Talmudic Saying in the Quran," *AJSL* 15 (1898-99) 55-56.

*D. S. Margoliouth, "The Date of the Talmud and the Cairene Ecclesiasticus," *ET* 11 (1899-1900) 427-428.

D. S. Margoliouth, "The Date of the Talmud," *ET* 12 (1900-01) 95-96.

A. S. Isaacs, "The Talmud in History," *JQR* 13 (1900-01) 438-445.

Bernard M. Kaplan, "The Apostate of the Talmud," *OC* 16 (1902) 467-474.

Albert J. Edmunds, "Jesus in the Talmud," *OC* 16 (1902) 475-477.

Ludwig Blau, "Methods of Teaching the Talmud in the Past and in the Present," *JQR* 15 (1902-03) 121-134.

J. G. Tasker, "The Talmud and Theology," *ET* 15 (1903-04) 187-189. *(Review)*

*Herbert Loewe, "Some Talmudic Fragments from the Cairo Genizah, in the British Museum," *JQR* 17 (1904-05) 456-474.

*W. Bacher, "The Talmudical Particle הולכך," *JQR* 17 (1904-05) 583.

G[eo.] S. Hitchcock, "A History of the Talmud," *IER, 4th Ser.,* 25 (1909) 337-349.

*Robert Roberts, "Almsgiving in the Apocrypha, Talmud, and Qoran," *IJA* #21 (1910) 28-30.

*Jacob Z. Lauterbach, "The Ancient Jewish Allegorists in Talmud and Midrash," *JQR, N.S.,* 1 (1910-11) 291-333, 503-531.

*J. D. Wynkoop, "A Peculiar Kind of Paronomasia in the Talmud and Midrash," *JQR, N.S.,* 2 (1911-12) 1-23.

Henry Malter, "A Talmudic Problem and Proposed Solutions," *JQR, N.S.,* 2 (1911-12) 75-95.

*Jacob Z. Lauterbach, "The Ethics of the Halakah," *YCCAR* 23 (1913) 249-287.

L. Grünhut, "Our Edition of the Palestinian Talmud Compared with the Leyden MS.," *JQR, N.S.,* 4 (1913-14) 107-110.

*Julius J. Price, "Babylon in the Talmud," *ET* 28 (1916-17) 325-326.

Anonymous, "Babylon in the Talmud," *HR* 74 (1917) 25.

*Samuel Daiches, "Babylonian Dog-Omens and some Talmudic and later Jewish Parallels," *SBAP* 39 (1917) 168-171.

Arthur S. Bruce, "The Yemenite MS. of Megilla," *ET* 29 (1917-18) 91-92. *(Review)*

D. S. Blondheim, "Tentative List of Existant Manuscripts of Rashi's Talmudical Commentaries," *JQR, N.S.,* 8 (1917-18) 55-60.

Julius J. Price, "The Talmud on Dreams," *OC* 33 (1919) 182-186.

G. H. Box, "The Babylonian Talmud: Tractate B^{e}rākot," *JTS* 24 (1921-22) 105-108. *(Review)*

Israel Abrahams, "The Lost 'Confessions' of Samuel," *HUCA* 1 (1924) 377-386.

Moses Marcus, "The Difficulties in Translating the Talmud," *JIQ* 1 (1924-25) 40-42.

*Emil Johnson, "The Ancient Hebrew Education. *A Study in Proverbs, Ecclesiastes, and Talmud,*" *AQ* 4 (1925) 215-227, 338-349; 5 (1926) 8-24.

Paul Rieger, "The Foundation of Rome in the Talmud," *JQR, N.S.,* 16 (1925-26) 227-235.

Solomon Zeitlin, "A Critical Edition of the Talmud," *JQR, N.S.,* 21 (1930-31) 61-73.

E. I. Szadzunski, "Addenda to Krauss, 'Talmudische Nachrichten über Arabien,' *ZDMG,* LXX, 325ff., *AJSL* 49 (1932-33) 336-338.

*Shlomo Marenof, "Digging in Talmudic Archeology," *AJSL* 50 (1933-34) 93-95.

*Israel Eitan, "Talmudic Syntax," *JQR, N.S.,* 24 (1933-34) 161-164. *(Review)*

*Jacob Z. Lauterbach, "Misunderstood Chronological Statements in the Talmudical Literature," *PAAJR* 5 (1933-34) 77-84.

*Guido Kisch, "A Talmudic Legend as a Source for the Josephus Passage in the *Sachsenspiegel,*" *HJud* 1 (1938-39) 105-118.

*A. H. Dirksen, "The Talmud and Anti-Semitism," *AER* 100 (1939) 33-44.

*Solomon Gandz, "The dawn of literature. Prolegomena to a history of unwritten literature," *Osiris* 7 (1939) 261-522. [Chapter XVII., §6. When were Mishnah and Talmud Reduced to Writing? pp. 449-454]

Jacob Z. Lauterbach, "Rashi the Talmud Commentator," *YCCAR* 50 (1940) 360-373. [Discussion by: Max Vogelstein, 374-375; Felix A. Levy, 375; Bernard J. Bamberger, 375; Samuel Thurman, 375-376; Max C. Currick, 376-377; David S. Jacobson, 377; Harry J. Stern, 378; Meir Lasker, 378]

Solomon Zeitlin, "Ginzberg's Studies on the Palestinian Talmud," *JQR, N.S.,* 33 (1942-43) 83-92, 419-434.

David Neiman, "Tannaitic Literature and Old Testament Studies," *JBL* 67 (1948) x.

P. R. Weis, "The Office of Mufla," *JJS* 1 (1948-49) 172-177.

*Harry M. Orlinsky, "Studies in Talmudic Philology," *HUCA* 23 (1950-51) Part 1, 499-514.

Alexander Guttmann, "Tractate Abot—Its Place in Rabbinic Literature," *JQR, N.S.,* 41 (1950-51) 181-193.

*J. J. Rabinowitz, "Section 7 of the Code of Hammurapi. Light of a Legal Preposition in the Talmud," *BIES* 16 (1951) #3/4, IV. *(Misprinted as VI)*

L. Jacobs, "Evidence of Literary Device in the Babylonian Talmud," *JJS* 3 (1952) 157-161.

*Emanuel Rackman, "Talmudic Insights on Human Rights," *Jud* 1 (1952) 158-163.

Hyman Klein, "Gemara Quotations in Sebara," *JQR, N.S.*, 44 (1952-53) 341-363.

A. Weiss, "The Confirmation of a Hypothesis," *EI* 3 (1954) XII. *[Gemara]*

*Jacob Z. Lauterbach, "The Talmud and the Gospels," *CCARJ* #12 (1956) 8-13, 17.

G. Zuntz, "Greek Words in the Talmud," *JSS* 1 (1956) 129-140.

Judah M. Rosenthal, "The Talmud on Trial," *JQR, N.S.*, 47 (1956-57) 58-76, 145-169.

Solomon Zeitlin, "The Tosefta," *JQR, N.S.*, 47 (1956-57) 382-399.

Zvi Karl, "Remarks on Some Mishnayot in B. Kama," *Tarbiz* 25 (1956-57) #1, V.

Isidore Warsky, "'Taking or Accepting the Right Hand' in Talmudic Phrasaeology," *Tarbiz* 26 (1956-57) #2, IV.

Zeev Falk, "The Expression 'Iron Sheep' (צאן ברזל), in the Talmud," *Tarbiz* 26 (1956-57) #3, VI.

Shraga Abramson, "R. Samuel b. Hofni's Introduction to the Talmud," *Tarbiz* 26 (1956-57) #4, V-VI.

*J. J. Rabinowitz, "The Aramaic Papyri, the Demotic Papyri from Geblen and Talmudic Sources," *B* 38 (1957) 269-274.

Zevi Karl, "Some Observations on the Tractate Rosh Hashana," *Tarbiz* 27 (1957-58) #4, V-VI.

*S. Lowy, "The Motivation of Fasting in Talmudic Literature," *JJS* 9 (1958) 19-38.

L. Jacobs, "Further Evidence of Literary Device in the Babylonian Talmud," *JJS* 9 (1958) 139-148.

H. Klein, "Some General Results of the Separation of Gemara from Sebara in the Babylonian Talmud," *JSS* 3 (1958) 363-372.

*M. R. Lehmann, "Talmudic Material Relating to the Dead Sea Scrolls," *RdQ* 1 (1958-59) 391-404.

B. de Vries, "The Problem of the Relationship of the Two Talmuds to the Tosefta," *Tarbiz* 28 (1958-59) #2, III-IV.

Hyman Klein, "Some Methods of Sebara," *JQR, N.S.,* 50 (1959-60) 124-146.

Benjamin de Vries, "The Mishna and Tosephta of Tractate Me'ila," *Tarbiz* 29 (1959-60) #3, IV-V.

Benjamin de Vries, "The Tractate *Me'ila* in the Babylonian Talmud," *Tarbiz* 30 (1960-61) #4, II-III.

*Hyman Klein, "The Significance of the Technical Expression אי אלא" "איתמר הכי איתמר in the Babylonian Talmud," *Tarbiz* 31 (1961-62) #1, V-VI.

Abraham Goldberg, "The Sources and Development of the *Sugya* in the Babylonian Talmud," *Tarbiz* 32 (1962-63) #2, III-V.

Isaac Bacon, "The *Sugya* שנים אוחזין בטלית," *Tarbiz* 32 (1962-63) #3, IX.

*S[hemuel] Safrai, "The Avoidance of Public Office in Papyrus Oxy. 1477 and in Talmudic Sources," *JJS* 14 (1963) 67-70.

Abraham J. Brachman, "Dating Back a Talmudic Section," *CCARJ* 11 (1963-64) #2, 43-46.

E. E. Hallevy, "The Derivation of the Obscure from the Obscure (A Chapter in Talmudic Methodology)," *Tarbiz* 34 (1964-65) #1, II-III.

Shemuel Safrai, "The Correct Interpretation of the talmudic Passage סנהדרי" "שראו כולן לחובה פיטרין אותו (Sanhedrin 17a)," *Tarbiz* 34 (1964-65) #1, III.

E. Oren, "Herodian Doves (יוני הרדסיאות) in Talmudic Literature," *Tarbiz* 34 (1964-65) #4, VII-VIII.

*Stephen M. Passamaneck, "The Talmudic Conception of Deformation," *RIDA, 3rd Ser.,* 12 (1965) 21-54.

*B. Salomonsen, "Some Remarks on the Zealots with Special Regard to the Term 'Qannaim' in Rabbinic Literature," *NTS* 12 (1965-66) 164-176.

B. De Vries, *"We' Hawaynan Ba* בה והוינן," *Tarbiz* 35 (1965-66) #3, IV.

E. Wiesenberg, "Observations on Method in Talmudic Studies," *JSS* 11 (1966) 16-36.

D. Sperber, "On Sealing the Abysses," *JSS* 11 (1966) 168-174.

Ch. Merchavia, "Talmudic Terms and Idioms in the Latin Manuscript Paris B.N. 16558," *JSS* 11 (1966) 175-201.

*E. E. Hallevy, "The Correct Interpretation of ' אותו פוטריו' (Sanhedrin 17a)," *Tarbiz* 36 (1966-67) #1, IV-V.

*Abraham I. Katsh, "Unpublished Geniza Talmudic Fragments from the Antonin Collection," *JQR, N.S.,* 58 (1967-68) 297-308.

B. De-Vries, "The Talmudic Formula מידי לא ותו," *Tarbiz* 37 (1967-68) #1, IV.

D. Sperber, "Bab Nahara," *IA* 8 (1968) 70-73.

Solomon Zeitlin, "Some Reflections on the Text of the Talmud," *JQR, N.S.,* 59 (1968-69) 1-8.

Samuel Tobias Lachs, "A 'Jesus Passage' in the Talmud Re-Examined," *JQR, N.S.,* 59 (1968-69) 244-247.

S. J. Bastomsky, "The Emperor Nero in Talmudic Legend," *JQR, N.S.,* 59 (1968-69) 321-325.

E. E. Urbach, "The Talmudic Sage—Character and Authority," *JWH* 11 (1968-69) 116-147.

Israel Francus, "The Original Location of Three Talmudic Discussions," *Tarbiz* 38 (1968-69) #4, III.

*Bernard Heller, "Masada and the Talmud," *Trad* 10 (1968-69) #2, 31-34.

A. Ben-David, "Ha-Middah ha-Yerushalmit: An Archaeological Solution of a Talmudic-Metrological Problem," *IEJ* 19 (1969) 158-169.

Jacob Neusner, "The Babylonian Talmud as a Historical Document," *CJ* 24 (1969-70) #4, 48-57.

§813 *3.10.3.1 Midrashim*

Charles R. Brown, "The Sections in the Midrash of Deuteronomy," *ONTS* 3 (1883-84) 207-209.

R[ichard] Gottheil, "An alphabet Midrash in Syriac," *ZA* 8 (1893) 86-99. (Note, pp. 219-220)

S. Schechter, "Fragment of the Sifre Zuta," *JQR* 6 (1893-94) 656-663. *[Rabbinic Commentary on Numbers - Codex Heb. C.18]*

*S. Schechter, "Agadath Shir Hashirim," *JQR* 6 (1893-94) 672-697. *[Midrash on the Song of Songs]*

S. Schechter, "Agadath Shir Hashirim. (*Concluded from* VOL. VI., p. 697).," *JQR* 7 (1894-95) 145-163.

S. Schechter, "Corrections and Notes to Agadath Shir Hashirim," *JQR* 7 (1894-95) 729-754.

S. Schechter, "Corrections and Notes to Agadath Shir Hashirim. (*concluded from Vol. VII,* p. 754.)," *JQR* 8 (1895-96) 289-320.

*Elsie Davis, "Woman in the Midrash," *JQR* 8 (1895-96) 529-533.

George Alexander Kohut, "A Turkish Tale in the Midrash," *AJSL* 15 (1898-99) 108-114.

*S. Schechter, "Genizah Fragments," *JQR* 16 (1903-04) 425-452. [III. מכילתא דברים, pp. 446-452]

*S. Schechter, "The Mechilta to Deuteronomy," *JQR* 16 (1903-04) 695-701. *[Cf. pp. 443-452]*

*Jacob Z. Lauterbach, "The Ancient Jewish Allegorists in Talmud and Midrash," *JQR, N.S.,* 1 (1910-11) 291-333, 503-531.

*J. D. Wynkoop, "A Peculiar Kind of Paronomasia in the Talmud and Midrash," *JQR, N.S.,* 2 (1911-12) 1-23.

*Jacob Z. Lauterbach, "Midrash and Mishnah. A Study in the Early History of the Halakah," *JQR, N.S.,* 5 (1914-15) 503-527 *[Part I]*

*Jacob Z. Lauterbach, "Midrash and Mishnah. A Study in the Early History of the Halakah," *JQR, N.S.,* 6 (1915-16) 23-95, 303-323. *[Parts II and III]*

M. Gaster, "Pirkê de Rabbi Eliezer," *IJA* #47 (1916) 55-57.

Jacob Z. Lauterbach, "The Name of the Mekilta," *JQR, N.S.,*11 (1920-21) 169-196.

Jacob Z. Lauterbach, "The Arrangement and the Division of the Mekilta," *HUCA* 1 (1924) 427-466.

H. Slonimsky, "On Reading the Midrash," *JIQ* 4 (1927-28) #2, 1-6.

Benjamin Schultz, "Universalism in the Midrash," *JIQ* 6 (1929-30) #2, 15-20.

Louis Finkelstein, "Prolegomena to an Edition of the *Sifre* on Deuteronomy," *PAAJR* 3 (1931-32) 3-42.

H. G. Enelow, "The Midrash of Thirty-two Rules of Interpretation," *JQR, N.S.,* 23 (1932-33) 357-367.

Louis Finkelstein, "Improved Readings in the *Sifre,*" *PAAJR* 4 (1932-33) 43-51.

Jacob Z. Lauterbach, "The Two Mekiltas," *PAAJR* 4 (1932-33) 113-129.

Louis Finkelstein, "Maimonides and the Tannaitic Midrashim," *JQR, N.S.,* 25 (1934-35) 469-517.

L. Rabinowitz, "Does Midrash Tillim Reflect the Triennial Cycle of Psalms?" *JQR, N.S.,* 26 (1935-36) 349-368.

Louis Finkelstein, "Fragment of an Unknown Midrash on Deuteronomy," *HUCA* 12&13 (1937-38) 523-557.

Louis Finkelstein, "The Oldest Midrash: Pre-Rabbinic Ideals and Teachings in the Passover Haggadah," *HTR* 31 (1938) 291-317. [I. The Date of M; II. The Propagandist Nature of M; III. The Theological and Political Views of the Midrash; IV. Conclusion; Appendix I: Other Teachings of M; Appendix II: The Relation of the Midrash to Rabbinic Literature]

Jacob Mann, "Some Midrashic Genizah Fragments," *HUCA* 14 (1939) 303-358.

Louis M. Finkelstein, "The Sources of the Tannaitic Midrashim," *JQR, N.S.*, 31 (1940-41) 211-243.

Alexander Guttmann, "Akiba, 'Rescuer of the Torah'," *HUCA* 17 (1942-43) 395-421. *[Sifre to Deut. 48]*

*Hyman Klein, "Mekilta on the Pentateuch," *JQR, N.S.*, 35 (1944-45) 421-434.

Max Kadushin, "Aspects of the Rabbinic Conception of Israel, a Study in the Mekilta," *HUCA* 19 (1945-46) 57-96.

R. M. Montgomery, "Midrash Genesis Rabbah on 'Death'," *JBL* 68 (1949) xvi.

*John Bowman, "Prophets and Prophecy in Talmud and Midrash," *EQ* 22 (1950) 107-114, 205-220, 255-275.

*S. K. Mirsky, "Allusions to Sabbath in the Ugaritic Texts in the Light of Midrashic Literature," *JBL* 69 (1950) viii.

William G. Braude, "Midrash to Psalms. *Some Sections Translated With Introduction by Wm. G. Braude,*" *Jud* 2 (1953) 75-79. *[From the Midrash to Psalm 18]*

Solomon Zeitlin, "Midrash: A historical study," *JQR, N.S.*, 44 (1953-54) 21-36.

Bernard Madelbaum, "Prolegomenon to the Pesikta," *PAAJR* 23 (1954) 41-58.

*Henry Slonimsky, "The Philosophy Implicit in the Midrash," *HUCA* 27 (1956) 235-290.

*Ephraim E. Urbach, "Homilies of the Rabbis on the Prophets of the Nations and the Balaam Stories," *Tarbiz* 25 (1956-57) #3, III-IV.

*R[aphael J.] Loewe, "The Jewish Midrashim and Patristic and Scholastic Exegesis of the Bible," *StP* 1 (1957) 492-514.

Abraham I. Katsh, "From the Moscow Manuscript of David ha-Nagid's Midrash on Genesis," *JQR, N.S.*, 48 (1957-58) 140-160.

*Z. M. Rabinowitz, "Yannay's *Qerova* to Lev. 15, 1 (Sources and Interpretation)," *Tarbiz* 28 (1958-59) #3/4, VII.

*Isadore Wartski, *"Mezuqqar* and the *Pi'el Ziqqer* in the Midrashim," *Tarbiz* 29 (1959-60) #4, II-III.

*Jacob Neusner, "History and Midrash," *Jud* 9 (1960) 47-54.

*Samuel Tobias Lachs, "An Egyptian Festival in Canticles Rabba," *JQR, N.S.,* 51 (1960-61) 47-54.

William G. Braude, "Overlooked Meanings of Certain Editorial Terms in the Pesikta Rabbati," *JQR, N.S.,* 52 (1961-62) 264-272.

*M. R. Lehmann, "Midrashic Parallels to Selected Qumran Texts," *RdQ* 3 (1961-62) 546-552.

*E. E. Hallewy, "Biblical Midrash and Homeric Exegesis," *Tarbiz* 31 (1961-62) #2, III-IV.

Z. M. Rabinowitz, *"Midreshe Halakha* in the Liturgical Poetry of Yannai (Sifra and Sifre—Deut.)," *Tarbiz* 31 (1961-62) #2, IV.

Anonymous, "'The Words of the Wise Are as Goads'," *Jud* 12 (1963) 98-100. *[From Pesikta Rabbati]*

*Neal Kozodoy *(Trans.),* "The Death of Moses. A Midrash," *Mosaic* 4 (1963) #2, 20-28.

Eugene Mihaly, "A Rabbinic Defense of the Election of Israel. An Analysis of Sifre Deuteronomy 32:9, Pisqa 312," *HUCA* 35 (1964) 103-143. [Appendix: "Midrash Tannaim to Deut. 14:2 (D. Hoffman), pp. 73—", pp. 136-143]

*A. Steinsalz, "Rhyming Techniques in the Proems of *Midrash Haggadol,"* *Tarbiz* 34 (1964-65) #1, VIII.

*Shelomo Morag, "The Rhyming Techniques in the Proems of *Midrash Haggadol* and the Authorship of the *Midrash,"* *Tarbiz* 34 (1964-65) #3, III-IV.

Yehuda Razhabi, "The Authorship of *Midrash Haggadol,"* *Tarbiz* 34 (1964-65) #3, IV.

Samuel Tobias Lachs, "The Proems of Canticles Rabba," *JQR, N.S.,* 56 (1965-66) 225-239.

Addison G. Wright, "The Literary Genre Midrash," *CBQ* 28 (1966) 105-138, 417-457.

*Isadore Wartski, "The Usage of the Greek words βία—βίος in Midrashic Literature," *Tarbiz* 36 (1966-67) #3, IV.

L. I. Rabinowitz, "The Study of a Midrash," *JQR, N.S.,* 58 (1967-68) 143-161.

Joseph Heinemann, "Chapters of Doubtful Authenticity in Leviticus Rabba," *Tarbiz* 37 (1967-68) #4, I.

W. D. Davies, "Torah and Dogma: A Comment," *HTR* 61 (1968) 87-105.

Ben Zion Wacholder, "The Date of the Mekilta De-Rabbi Ishmael," *HUCA* 39 (1968) 117-144.

§814 *3.10.3.2 Pirke Aboth*

John   Currie,   "Pirke   Aboth,"   *ONTS*   3   (1883-84)   259-260.

B. Pick, "Pirke Aboth: or, Sayings of the Fathers," *AJSL* 1 (1884-85) 119-123, 212-216. *(Trans. from the Hebrew Edition of H. L. Strack)*

C. Taylor, "Textual Criticism of Pirke Aboth," *IAQR, 2nd Ser.,* 2 (1891) 393-396.

David Feinberg, "An Analysis of the Pirke Aboth," *JIQ* 4 (1927-28) #1, 27-32.

Louis Finkelstein, "Introductory Study to *Pirke Abot,*" *JBL* 57 (1938) 13-50.

L. Wallach, "A Tannaitic Polemic of the Second Century against Gnosticism," *JBL* 65 (1946) ix. *[Pirke Abot iii, 9]*

§815 *3.10.4 Targumim (Versions)*

Anonymous, "A Brief Account of the Chaldee Targums. From the Latin of Leusden," *PRev* 6 (1834) 231-249.

Anonymous, "The Targum on Canticles," *CongML* 20 (1837) 494-496.

R. Y., "The Last Blessings of Jacob. Translated from the Chaldee Targums of Jonathan ben Uziel and Jerusalem," *JSL, 2nd Ser.,* 2 (1852) 432-444.

Anonymous, "The Targums on the Pentateuch," *CQR* 12 (1881) 48-84.

*F. J. Gurney, C. E. Crandall, and O. O. Fletcher, "A Translation of the Targum (Jonathan) of the Prophecy of Nahum," *ONTS* 2 (1882-83) 58-61.

*M. Jastrow, "Notes on the Targum as a Commentary," *ONTS* 3 (1883-84) 52-53. *[Prov. 31:27; Isa. 3:12]*

*J. Grape Jr., "The Temptation and Fall, according to the Targums," *UQGR, N.S.,* 23 (1886) 84-98.

*Henry Preserved Smith, "The Targum to Jeremiah," *AJSL* 4 (1887-88) 140-145.

George H. Schodde, "The Targums," *ONTS* 8 (1888-89) 262-266.

G. F. Moore, "Note on the Targum manuscripts in the British Museum," *JAOS* 14 (1890) xxxviii.

R. J. H. Gottheil, "A Manuscript containing parts of the Targūm," *JAOS* 14 (1890) xlii-li.

*Michael Alder, "A Specimen of a Commentary and Collated Text of the Targum to the Prophets (Nahum)," *JQR* 7 (1894-95) 630-657.

Geo. H. Schodde, "The Targums," *ColTM* 18 (1898) 267-274.

W. Bacher, "Notes on the Critique of the Text of the Targum of the Prophets," *JQR* 11 (1898-99) 651-655.

John Taylor, "A Targum Concordance," *ET* 17 (1905-06) 347. *(Review)*

*Raphael Hai Malamed, "The Targum to Canticles according to Six Yemen MSS. compared with the 'Textus Receptus' (Ed. de Lagarde)," *JQR, N.S.,* 10 (1919-20) 377-410.

*Raphael Hai Malamed, "The Targum to Canticles according to Six Yemen MSS. compared with the 'Textus Receptus' (Ed. de Lagarde), Chapters II-IV" *JQR, N.S.,* 11 (1920-21) 1-20.

*Raphael Hai Malamed, "The Targum to Canticles according to Six Yemen MSS. compared with the 'Textus Receptus.' (Ed. de Lagarde) concluded," *JQR, N.S.,* 12 (1921-22) 57-117.

J. Rendel Harris, "The Odes of Solomon and the Biblical Targums," *Exp, 8th Ser.,* 21 (1921) 271-291.

*R. A. Aytoun, "The Servant of the Lord in the Targum," *JTS* 23 (1921-22) 172-180.

Aapeli Saarisalo, "The Targum to the book of Ruth," *SO* 2 (1928) 88-104.

*L. P. Smith, "The Prophetic Targum as a Guide and Defence for the Higher Critic," *JBL* 52 (1933) 121-130.

*Pinkhos Churgin, "The Targum and the Septuagint," *AJSL* 50 (1933-34) 41-65.

*Alexander Sperber, "The Targum Onkelos in its Relation to the Masoretic Hebrew Text," *PAAJR* 6 (1934-35) 309-351.

*Salomon Speier, "The Targum of Jonathan on Genesis 24:56," *JQR, N.S.,* 18 (1937-38) 301-303.

Leon J. Liebreich, "The Benedictory Formula in the Targum to the Song of Songs," *HUCA* 18 (1944) 177-197.

*Allen Wikgren, "The Targum and the New Testament," *JR* 24 (1944) 89-95.

*Salomon Speier, "The Jerusalem Targum to Num. 18:12 and Deut. 34:3," *JBL* 65 (1946) 315-318.

E. W. Hammer, "Implements of Interpretation. X. The Onkelos Targum," *Interp* 3 (1949) 174-183.

J. L. Teicher, "A Sixth Century Fragment of the Palestinian Targum?" *VT* 1 (1951) 125-129.

*N. Weider, "The Habakkuk Scroll and the Targum," *JJS* 4 (1953) 14-18.

E. Z. Melamed, "A Targum Yehonathan and the Arabic Tafsir of the Song of Deborah," *EI* 3 (1954) XIII.

*W. H. Brownlee, "The Habakkuk Midrash and Targum of Jonathan," *JJS* 7 (1956) 169-186.

*G[eza] Vermes, "The Symbolical Interpretation of *Lebanon* in the Targums: The Origin and Development of an Exegetical Tradition," *JTS, N.S.,* 9 (1958) 1-12.

*A. Diez Macho, "'Onqelos Manuscript with Babylonian Transliterated Vocalization in the Vatican Library, (MS. Eb. 448)," *VT* 8 (1958) 113-133.

A. Diez Macho, "The recently discovered Palestinian targum: its antiquity and relationship with the other targums," *VTS* 7 (1960) 222-245.

*P. Wernberg-Møller, "Some Observations on the Relationship of the Peshitta Version of the Book of Genesis to the Palestinian Targum Fragments, Published by Professor Kahle, and to Targum Onkelos," *ST* 15 (1961) 128-180.

*W. Baars, "A Targum on Exodus XV 7-21 from Cairo Geniza," *VT* 11 (1961) 340-342.

*Geza Vermes, "The Targumic Versions of Genesis iv 3-16," *ALUOS* 3 (1961-62) 81-114.

Alejandro Diez-Macho, "The Palestinian Targum," *CNI* 13 (1962) #2, 19-25. *[Neofiti 1]*

*P. Wernberg-Møller, "Prolegomena to a Re-Examination of the Palestinian Targum Fragments of the Book of Genesis Published by P. Kahle, and Their Relationship to the Peshitta," *JSS* 7 (1962) 253-266.

P. Wernberg-Møller, "An Inquiry into the Validity of the text-critical argument for an early dating of the recently discovered Palestinian Targum," *VT* 12 (1962) 312-330.

*M. Z. Kadari, "Studies in the Syntax of Targum Onqelos," *Tarbiz* 32 (1962-63) #3, III-IV.

J. Pierron, "A New Biblical Discovery. The Neofiti Codex I," *IES* 2 (1963) 304-312.

Geza Vermes, "Haggadah in the Onkelos Targum," *JSS* 8 (1963) 159-169.

*Jose Ramon Diaz, "Palestinian Targum and New Testament," *NT* 6 (1963) 75-80.

M. Fizmaurice Martin, "The Palaeographical Character of Codex Neofiti 1," *Text* 3 (1963) 1-34. *[Palestinian Targum]*

*M. Z. Kadari, "The Use of ד‍-Clauses in the Language of Targum Onkelos," *Text* 3 (1963) 35-59.

*J. A. Emerton, "Mark XIV. 24 and the Targum to the Psalter," *JTS, N.S.,* 15 (1964) 58-59.

Jan van Zijl, "Errata in Sperber's Edition of Targum Isaiah," *ASTI* 4 (1965) 189-191.

M. C. Doubles, "Toward the Publication of the Existent Texts of the Palestinian Targums," *VT* 15 (1965) 16-26.

Martin McNamara, "Targumic Studies," *CBQ* 28 (1966) 1-19.

*Raphael J. Loewe, "Apologetic Motifs in the Targum to the Song of Songs," *LIST* 3 (1966) 159-196.

*M. McNamara, "Some Early Rabbinic Citations and the Palestinian Targum to the Pentateuch," *RDSO* 41 (1966) 1-15.

*J. Shunary, "Avoidance of Anthropomorphism in the Targum of Psalms," *Text* 5 (1966) 133-144.

S. Speier, "Pseudojonathan Exodus 10, 11," *B* 48 (1967) 115.

*J. W. Bowker, "Haggadah in the Targum Onqelos," *JSS* 12 (1967) 51-65.

A. Díez Macho, "A Yemenite Manuscript for the Edition of Babylonian Onqelos," *OA* 6 (1967) 215-220.

*Martin McNamara, "*Logos* of the Fourth Gospel and *Memra* of the Palestinian Targum (Ex 12[42])," *ET* 79 (1967-68) 115-117.

*Yehuda Komlos, "Etymological Elucidations in the Aramaic Targum of Isaiah," *Tarbiz* 37 (1967-68) #1, II-III.

Clyde M. Woods, "Special Studies in Judaism: The Targums," *RestQ* 11 (1968) 262-268. *(Review)*

*J. van Zijl, "Is. XLVIII 7 according to the Targum Br. Mus. Or. Ms 2211," *VT* 18 (1968) 560-561.

Jan van Zijl, "A Second List of Errata in Sperber's Edition of Targum Isaiah," *ASTI* 7 (1968-69) 132-134.

David Rider, "On the Targum Yerushalmi MS Neofiti I," *Tarbiz* 38 (1968-69) #1, VII.

Moses Aberbach, "Patriotic Tendencies in Targum Onkelos," *JHS* 1 (1969) 13-24.

§816 *3.11 Rabbinic Interpretation of the Bible
[See also Exegetical Studies on
individual passages: §§ 578-669 ←]*

F. W. Farrar, "Rabbinic Exegesis," *Exp, 1st Ser.,* 5 (1877) 362-378.

S. Schechter, "The Riddles of Solomon in Rabbinic Literature," *Folk* 1 (1890) 349-358.

*Alexander Kohut, "Parsic and Jewish Legends of the First Man," *JQR* 3 (1890-91) 231-250.

*S. Schechter, "The Quotations from Ecclesiasticus in Rabbinic Literature," *JQR* 3 (1890-91) 682-706.

*Marcus Jastrow, "Light thrown on some Biblical passages by Talmudic usage," *JBL* 11 (1892) 126-130.

*F. Jarratt, "Rabbinic Interpretation of the Vision of the Ephah in Zechariah v," *ET* 6 (1894-95) 566-567.

A. Neubauer, "The Hebrew Bible in Shorthand Writing," *JQR* 7 (1894-95) 361-364.

*Samuel Krauss, "Notes on Sirach," *JQR* 11 (1898-99) 150-158. [3. The Sayings of Sirach in Rabbinic Literature, pp. 155-156]

*Jacob Z. Lauterbach, "The Ancient Jewish Allegorists in Talmud and Midrash," *JQR, N.S.,* 1 (1910-11) 291-333, 503-531.

Moses Gaster, "Eliezer Crescas and His Ben Zebul, the Bible References in Talmud and Midrash," *HUCA* 6 (1929) 277-295.

*C. H. Gordon, "Rabbinic Exegesis in the Vulgate of Proverbs," *JBL* 49 (1930) 384-416.

*Chaim Kaplan, "The Flood in the Book of Enoch and Rabbinics," *JSOR* 15 (1931) 22-24.

*B. Weitzel, "The Year of the Exodus in the Talmud," *Miz* 8 (1938) 15-19.

*John J. Collins, "Rabbinic Exegesis and Pauline Exegesis," *CBQ* 3 (1941) 15-26, 145-158.

*Alexander Altmann, "The Gnostic Background of the Rabbinic Adam Legends," *JQR, N.S.,* 35 (1944-45) 371-391.

*Raphael Patai, "Note to the Gnostic Background of the Rabbinic Adam Legends," *JQR, N.S.,* 36 (1945-46) 416-417.

*J. Weingreen, "The Rabbinic Approach to the Study of the Old Testament," *BJRL* 34 (1951-52) 166-190.

*A. Levene, "Pentateuchal Exegesis in the Early Syriac and Rabbinic Sources," *StP* 1 (1957) 484-491.

*Z̲. M. Rabinowitz, "Yannay's *Qerova* to Lev. 14, 1 (Sources and Interpretation)," *Tarbiz̲* 28 (1958-59) #3/4, VII.

*J. Bowman, "An Interesting Leningrad Samaritan Manuscript," *ABR* 1 (1959-60) 73-78. *[Samaritan discussion of what constitutes the Commandments in the Torah]*

*Ephraim E. Urbach, "Rabbinic Exegesis and Origenes' Commentaries on the Song of Songs and Jewish-Christian Polemics," *Tarbiz̲* 30 (1960-61) #2, V-VI.

W. Gunther Plaut, "Contrasts and Comparisons—Ruminations of Seven Pairs of Sidrahs," *CCARJ* 11 (1963-64) #4, 23-26.

*Moshe Aberbach, "The Relations between Ira the Jairite and King David according to Talmudic Legend," *Tarbiz̲* 33 (1963-64) #4, III.

*S. Coleman, "Dialogue of Habakkuk in Rabbinic Doctrine," *Abr-N* 5 (1964-65) 57-85.

*James S. Ackerman, "The Rabbinic Interpretation of Psalm 82 and the Gospel of John: John 10:34," *HTR* 59 (1966) 186-191.

*A. Levene, "The Blessings of Jacob in Syriac and Rabbinic Exegesis," *StP* 7 (1966) 524-530.

*Moses Aberbach and Leivy Smolar, "Jeroboam and Solomon: Rabbinic Interpretations," *JQR, N.S.,* 59 (1968-69) 118-132.

§817 **3.12 Studies on the New Testament Apocrypha with Reference to the Old Testament**

E. H. Palmer, "The Eastern origin of the Christian pseudepigraphic writings," *JP* 3 (1871) 223-231.

James C. Marshall, "Was Barnabas Ignorant of Jewish Ritual?" *Exp, 2nd Ser.,* 4 (1882) 63-77.

*L. S. Potwin, "Philo and the ΔΙΔΑΧΗ," *BS* 43 (1886) 174-176.

*C. Taylor, "The Two Ways in Hermas and Xenophon," *JP* 21 (1892-93) 243-258.

*Eb. Nestle, "Gen. XIV. 14 in the Epistle of Barnabas," *ET* 17 (1905-06) 139-140.

*J. Rendel Harris, "Symposium on the Pith of Palm Trees (continued)," *BBC* 4 (1927) 16-17. *[Ref. Apocrypha of Jeremiah]*

A. Lukyn Williams, "Early Anti-Judaica: The Books of Testimonies," *JTVI* 61 (1929) 239-252. (Discussion, pp. 252-259)

J. Rendel Harris, "The Odes of Solomon and the Apocalypse of Peter," *ET* 42 (1930-31) 21-23.

*O. H. E. Burmester, "Egyptian Mythology in the Coptic Apocrypha," *Or, N.S.,* 7 (1938) 355-367.

*Luitpold Wallach, "The Origin of Testimonia Biblica in Early Christian Literature," *RR* 8 (1943-44) 130-136.

*L. W. Barnard, "Some Folklore Elements in an Early Christian Epistle," *Folk* 70 (1959) 433-439. *[Epistle of Barnabas and 'the Scapegoat']*

*Robert A. Kraft, "Barnabas' Isaiah Text and the 'Testimony Book' Hypothesis," *JBL* 79 (1960) 336-350.

*S. Lowy, "The Confutation of Judaism in the Epistle of Barnabas," *JJS* 11 (1960) 1-33.

*Robert A. Kraft, "Barnabas' Isaiah Text and Melito's *Paschal Homily,*" *JBL* 80 (1961) 371-373.

*P. Skehan, "Didache 1, 6 and Sirach 12, 1," *B* 44 (1963) 533-536.

*Søren Giversen, "The Apocryphon of John and Genesis," *ST* 17 (1963) 60-76.

*William H. Shea, "The Sabbath in the Epistle of Barnabas," *AUSS* 4 (1966) 149-175.

*L. W. Barnard, "Hermas and Judaism," *StP* 8 (1966) 3-9.

§818 *3.13 Studies on the Early Church Fathers*

Augustus Neander, "The Right Use of the Holy Scriptures," *CRB* 9 (1844) 127-138. *(Trans. by S. F. Smith) [Use by Early Church Fathers]*

*J. C. M., "The Writings of Origen," *BRCM* 3 (1847) 103-122. [I. Editions of the Old Testament, pp. 103-111]

B. H. C., "Analecta Syriaca," *JSL, 3rd Ser.,* 8 (1858-59) 345-359. [Select Sentences from the Book of the Holy Hippolytus, the Exposition of Daniel the Prophet, taken as by force only; Those things of Holy Hippolytus which are from the Exposition of Daniel, the Prophet, end; Holy Hippolytus also, Bishop and Martyr, thus speaks in the Fourth Discourse upon Daniel the Prophet; Again of the Same Holy Hippolytus: a Scholium on the Distinction of the Psalms] *(Review)*

*Anonymous, "The Book of Daniel: as viewed by Hippolytus, Prophyry and others," *JSL, 4th Ser.,* 4 (1863-64) 257-285.

*Samuel Davidson, "Irenæus, Polycarp and the Testaments of the Twelve Patriarchs, in Relation to the Fourth Gospel," *TRL* 7 (1870) 297-331.

W. Sanday, "The Value of the Patristic Writings for the Criticism and Exegesis of the Bible," *Exp, 1st Ser.,* 11 (1880) 1-20, 85-100, 161-178, 241-263, 352-372, 430-458.

W. Sanday, "The Value of the Patristic Writings for the Criticism of the Bible," *Exp, 1st Ser.,* 12 (1880) 123-143, 217-236, 304-324.

*William De Loss Love, "The Sabbath: Did the Early Fathers Hold that the Fourth Commandment is Abolished?" *BS* 38 (1881) 254-286.

*Newell Woolsey Wells, "The Ante-Nicene Fathers and the Mosaic Origin of the Pentateuch," *ONTS* 3 (1883-84) 186-191.

*Newell Woolsey Wells, "The Ante-Nicene Fathers and the Mosaic Origin of the Pentateuch," *JLTQ* 1 (1884) 465-472.

B. Pick, "The Sibylline Oracles in the Writings of the Church Fathers," *LQ* 15 (1885) 448-464.

E. A. Wallis Budge, "On a Coptic Version of an Encomium on Elijah the Tishbite attributed to Saint John Chrysostom," *SBAP* 8 (1885-86) 133-140.

*L. S. Potwin, "Philo and the ΔΙΔΑΧΗ," *BS* 43 (1886) 174-176.

*Peter C. York, "Biblical Chronology and Patristic Tradition," *AER* 4 (1891) 360-376.

G. Salmon, "The Commentary of Hippolytus on Daniel," *Herm* 8 (1891-93) 161-190.

*S. Krauss, "The Jews in the Works of the Church Fathers," *JQR* 5 (1892-93) 122-157; 6 (1893-94) 82-99, 225-261.

*J. A. Zahm, "The Mosaic Hexaemeron in the Light of Exegesis and Modern Science," *AER* 10 (1894) 161-227. [I. Moses and Science; II. Allegorism and Literalism; III. St. Gregory of Nyssa and the Nebular Hypothesis; IV. St. Augustine and Evolution (exegesis old and new); V. Modern Theories of Cosmogony]

*H. J. Lawlor, "Early citations from the Book of Enoch," *JP* 25 (1897) 164-225.

*F. C. Burkitt, "On Isaiah XIX 18: On St. Ephraim's Quotation of Matt. XXI 3," *JTS* 1 (1899-1900) 568-571.

Anonymous, "Greek Catanæ of the Old Testament," *CQR* 50 (1900) 29-48.

*H. H. Howorth, "Some Unconventional Views on the Text of the Bible. III. *The Hexapla and the Tetrapla of Origen, and the light they throw on the books of Esdras A and B,*" *SBAP* 24 (1902) 147-172.

*James A. Kelso, "Theodoret and the Law Book of Josiah," *JBL* 22 (1903) 50.

*C. Taylor, "Enoch and Clement," *JP* 29 (1903-04) 185-198.

*G. E. Price, "Allegorical and Literal in the Fathers," *IER, 4th Ser.*, 16 (1904) 201-221. [I. The method of allegorical interpretation applied by pagans to pagan literature; II. The method applied by Jewish writers to the Old Testament; III. The method applied by Christian writers to both Testaments; IV. The reaction to literal interpretation]

Eb. Nestle, "Remarks. *P.S.*," *ET* 19 (1907-08) 475. *[Tertullian on Ex. 32; Num. 25]*

*J. Rendel Harris, "Athanasius and the Book of Testimonies," *Exp, 7th Ser.*, 9 (1910) 530-537.

*J. Rendel Harris, "On an Obscure Quotation in the First Epistle of Element," *JBL* 29 (1910) 190-195. *[Ref. Assumption of Moses]*

George Holley Gilbert, "Interpretation of the Bible by the Fathers," *BW* 38 (1911) 151-158.

*Frank Egleston Robbins, "The Influence of Greek Philosophy on the Early Commentaries of Genesis," *AJT* 16 (1912) 218-240.

A. J. Wensinck, "Ephrem's Hymns on Epiphany and the Odes of Solomon," *Exp, 8th Ser.*, 3 (1912) 108-112.

*E. C. Selwyn, "An Oracle of the Lord in Isaiah xxxii," *Exp, 8th Ser.*, 5 (1913) 167-177.

*B. V. Miller, "The Greek Fathers and Original Sin," *IER, 5th Ser.*, 2 (1913) 113-132.

*J. Rendel Harris, "Christ the Firstborn," *Exp, 8th Ser.*, 14 (1917) 321-329. [Cyprian's *Testimonies against the Jews*]

*T. Herbert Bindley, "Concerning 'Testimony Books'," *ICMM* 14 (1917-18) 210-219.

A. Marmorstein, "Jews and Judaism in the Earliest Christian Apologies," *Exp, 8th Ser.*, 17 (1919) 73-80, 100-116.

*William Metcalfe, "Origen's Exhortation to Martyrdom and 4 Maccabees," *JTS* 22 (1920-21) 268-269.

E. J. Martin, "The Biblical Text of Firmicus Maternus," *JTS* 24 (1922-23) 318-325.

*E. F. Sutcliffe, "Some Footnotes to the Fathers," *B* 6 (1925) 205-210. *[Ref. Num. chaps. 22-24]*

*Leonard Prestige, "Paradise," *Theo* 10 (1925) 141-149.

*J. Rendel Harris, "Irenaeus and the Song of Moses," *ET* 37 (1925-26) 333-334.

*B. V. Miller, "St. Irenaeus and Original Sin," *IER, 5th Ser.,* 32 (1928) 138-146.

*Charles Roads, "The Witch of Endor," *MR* 112 (1929) 454-456. *[Eustathius]*

*F. C. Burkitt, "Justin Martyr and Jeremiah XI 19," *JTS* 33 (1931-32) 371-373.

*E. H. Blakeney, "Julius Africanus: A Letter to Origen on the Story of Susanna," *Theo* 29 (1934) 164-169.

*Robert P. Casey, "The Armenian Marcionites and the Diatessaron," *JBL* 57 (1938) 185-194.

*Patrick F. Cremin, "According to the Order of Melchisedech: IV. The Patristic Interpretation and Its Value," *IER, 5th Ser.,* 54 (1939) 385-391.

Fred Gladstone Bratton, "Origen, The First Christian Liberal," *JAAR* 8 (1940) 137-141.

Edward J. Young, "Celsus and the Old Testament," *WTJ* 6 (1941-42) 166-198.

*Eric Werner, "Notes on the Attitude of the Early Church Fathers Towards Hebrew Psalmody," *RR* 7 (1942-43) 339-352.

R. P. C. Hanson, "Origen's Interpretation of Scripture exemplified from his *Philocalia,*" *Herm* #63 (1944) 47-58.

*Walter J. Burghardt, "Cyril of Alexandria on 'Wool and Linen'," *Tr* 2 (1944) 484-486.

*Louis E. Knowles, "The Interpretation of the Seventy Weeks of Daniel in the Early Fathers," *WTJ* 7 (1944-45) 136-160.

Frederick A. Norwood, "Attitude of the Ante-Nicene Fathers Towards Greek Artistic Achievement," *JHI* 8 (1947) 431-448.

*Stanislaus J. Grabowski, "Spiritus Dei in Gen. 1:2 according to St. Augustine," *CBQ* 10 (1948) 13-28.

*G. W. H. Lampe, "The Exegesis of Some Biblical Texts by Marcellus of Ancyra and Pseudo-Chrysostom's Homily on Ps. XCVI. 1," *JTS* 49 (1948) 169-175.

*George Ogg, "The Year of the Exodus in the Pseudo-Cyprianic de Pascha Computus," *ET* 60 (1948-49) 226.

*H. R. Smythe, "The Interpretation of Amos 4^{13} in St. Athanasius and Diymus," *JTS, N.S.,* 1 (1950) 158-168.

Patrick J. Cornish, "The Fall in Greek Tradition," *ITQ* 18 (1951) 138-160. *[Marked as "continued" but was not]*

*Bard Thompson, "Patristic Use of the Sibylline Oracles," *RR* 16 (1951-52) 115-136.

*J. Barton Payne, "Biblical Problems and Augustine's Allegorizing," *WTJ* 14 (1951-52) 46-53.

Francis X. Curley, "'On the Seventh Day God Rested from All His Work.'," *MH* 10 (Winter, 1953-54) 30-39.

Jean Danielou, "The Fathers and the Scriptures," *Theo* 57 (1954) 83-89.

*St. Gregory of Nyssa, "Moses and the Vision of God (A commentary on Exodus ch. 33, v. 11-23)," *LofS* 9 (1954-55) 271-279.

*A. W. Argyle, "Joseph the Patriarch in Patristic Teaching," *ET* 67 (1955-56) 199-201.

*R. P. C. Hanson, "Interpretations of Hebrew Names in Origen," *VC* 10 (1956) 103-123.

P. D. Pahl, "The Use of Scripture in 1 Clement," *AusTR* 23 (1957) 107-111.

*Joshua Finkel, "A Link Between Ḥasidism and Hellenic and Patristic Literature," *PAAJR* 26 (1957) 1-24; 27 (1958) 19-41.

*P. Katz, "Justin's Old Testament quotations and the Greek Dodekapropheton Scroll," *StP* 1 (1957) 343-353.

*A. Levene, "Pentateuchal Exegesis in Early Syriac and Rabbinic Sources," *StP* 1 (1957) 484-491.

*D. Daube, "Origen and the Punishment of Adultery in Jewish Law," *StP* 2 (1957) 109-113.

*S. Stein, "The Dietary Laws in Rabbinic and Patristic Literature," *StP* 2 (1957) 141-154.

*Morton Smith, "The Description of the Essenes in Josephus and the Philosophumena," *HUCA* 29 (1958) 273-313.

James N. S. Alexander, "The Interpretation of Scripture in the Anti-Nicene Period. *A Brief Conspectus,"* *Interp* 12 (1958) 272-280.

*T. Jansma, "Investigations into the Early Syrian Fathers on Genesis. An Approach to the Exegesis of the Nestorian Church and to the Comparison of Nestorian and Jewish Exegesis," *OTS* 12 (1958) 69-181.

*P. Smulders, "A Quotation of Philo in Irenaeus," *VC* 12 (1958) 154-156.

Matthew Black, "The Patristic Accounts of Jewish Sectarianism," *BJRL* 41 (1958-59) 285-303.

*St. Gregory of Nyssa, "'I Know That My Redeemer Liveth' (Job XIX, 25) From St. Gregory's Commentary on Job, Bk. XIV," *LofS* 13 (1958-59) 461-465. *(Trans. by E[dmund] H[ill])*

*L. W. Barnard, "Some Folklore Elements in an Early Christian Epistle," *Folk* 70 (1959) 433-439. *[Epistle of Barnabas]*

*H. F. D. Sparks, "The Symbolical Interpretation of *Lebanon* in the Fathers," *JTS, N.S.,* 10 (1959) 264-279.

Albert C. Sundberg Jr., "On Testimonies," *NT* 3 (1959) 268-281.

Harold O. Forshey, "The Doctrine of the Fall and Original Sin in the Second Century," *RestQ* 3 (1959) 119-129.

F. M. M. Sagnard, "Holy Scripture in the Early Fathers of the Church," *StEv* 1 (1959) 706-713.

*William G. Braude, "The Church Fathers and the Synagogue," *Jud* 9 (1960) 112-119.

Walter J. Burghardt, "The Image of God in Man: Alexandrian Orientations," *CTSP* 16 (1961) 147-160.

*Robert A. Kraft, "Barnabas' Isaiah Text and Melito's *Paschal Homily*," *JBL* 80 (1961) 371-373.

*W. H. C. Frend, "Notes on Tertullian's Interpretation of Scripture," *JTS, N.S.,* 12 (1961) 273-284.

*Albert Wifstrand, "The New Edition of Gregory of Nyssa's Commentary on the Song of Solomon," *JTS, N.S.,* 12 (1961) 291-298.

William M. Green, "Patristic Interpretation of the Bible," *RestQ* 5 (1961) 230-235.

*H. Jaeger, "The Patristic Conception of Wisdom in the Light of Biblical and Rabbinic Research," *StP* 4 (1961) 90-106.

*O. Linton, "Interpretation of the Psalms in the Early Church," *StP* 4 (1961) 143-156.

*J. C. M. Van Winden, "In the Beginning. Some Observations on the Patristic Interpretation of *Genesis* 1:1," *VC* 17 (1963) 105-121.

L. W. Barnard, "The Old Testament and Judaism in the Writings of Justin Martyr," *VT* 14 (1964) 395-406.

T. J. Towers, "The Value of the Fathers," *CQR* 166 (1965) 291-302.

David E. Aune, "Justin Martyr's Use of the Old Testament," *BETS* 9 (1966) 179-198.

*R. M. Grant, "The Book of Wisdom at Alexandria. Reflections on the History of the Canon and Theology," *StP* 7 (1966) 462-472.

*V. Keisch, "The Antiocheans and the Temptation Story," *StP* 7 (1966) 496-502.

*A. Levene, "The Blessings of Jacob in Syriac and Rabbinic Exegesis," *StP* 7 (1966) 524-530.

*L. Thunberg, "Early Christian Interpretation of the Three Angels in Gen. 18," *StP* 7 (1966) 560-570.

R. E. Witt, "The Importance of Isis for the Fathers," *StP* 8 (1966) 135-145.

J. T. Brothers, "The Interpretation of παῖς θεοῦ in Justin Martyr's *Dialogue with Trypho*," *StP* 9 (1966) 127-138.

*A. Crepin, "The Names of God in the Church Fathers and in Old English Poetry," *StP* 9 (1966) 525-531.

L. W. Barnard, "The Old Testament and the Authorship of Athenagoras' *De Resurrectione*," *JTS, N.S.*, 18 (1967) 432-433.

*A. J. B. Higgins, "Jewish Messianic Belief in Justin Martyr's *Dialogue with Trypho*," *NT* 9 (1967) 298-305.

John McRay, "Scripture and Tradition in Irenaeus," *RestQ* 10 (1967) 1-10.

*Stanley Harakas, "The Relationship of the Church and Synagogue in the Apostolic Fathers," *StVTQ, N.S.*, 11 (1967) 123-138.

*Albert Henrichs, "Philosophy, the Handmaiden of Theology," *GRBS* 9 (1968) 437-450.

*E. Brønno, "Samaritan Hebrew and Origen's Secunda," *JSS* 13 (1968) 192-201.

John F. Callahan, "The Serpent and H PAXI A in Gregory of Nyssa," *Tr* 24 (1968) 17-41.

§819 *3.14 Studies on the Early Commentaries on the Old Testament (from Post-Nicea to the Reformation)*

Alexander Kohut, "Notes on a Hitherto Unknown Exegetical, Theological and Philosophical Commentary to the Pentateuch, composed by Aboomanzur al-Dhamâri (מנצור אלדׁמארׁי) with Appendices Containing Hebrew and Arabic Extracts. A Contribution to the Critical Study of Maimunis Writings," *PJTSA* 3 (1892) 1-56, *plus appendices (paged separately)*

George Kerber, ed., "A Commentary to Deuteronomy. Taken from the four German Manuscripts which comprise the أوﻗار اﻷﻧوﻧ of Gregory Abulfaraġ Bar-Hebraeus," *AJSL* 13 (1896-97) 89-117.

Sidney Adams Weston, "The Kitâb Masâlik an-Naẓar of Saʿid ibn Ḥasan of Alexandria. Edited for the first time and translated with Introduction and Notes," *JAOS* 24 (1903) 312-383. *[Moslem commentary on the O.T. from the 13th Cent.]*

*J. Rendel Harris, "Athanasius and the Book of Testimonies," *Exp, 7th Ser.,* 9 (1910) 530-537.

*Frank Egleston Robbins, "The Influence of Greek Philosophy on the Early Commentaries of Genesis," *AJT* 16 (1912) 218-240.

Henry Malter, "Saadia Gaon's Messianic Computation," *JJLP* 1 (1919) 45-59. *[Commentary on Daniel chap. 12]*

Frank Gavin, "Aphraates and the Jews," *JSOR* 7 (1923) 95-166.

*Henry Englander, "Rashi as Bible Exeget and Grammarian," *YCCAR* 50 (1940) 342-359.

T. Fish, "The 'Literal' Commentary on the Book of Joel the Prophet. By Dionysius Bar Ṣalîbi (+1171)," *JMUEOS* #24 (1947) 22-27.

*Leon Nemoy, "Did Salomon ben Jeroham Compose a Commentary on Ruth?" *JQR, N.S.,* 39 (1948-49) 215-216.

Beryl Smalley, "Some Thirteenth-Century Commentaries on the Sepiential Books," *DS* 2 (1949) 318-355; 3 (1950) 41-77, 236-274.

Jacob Bosniak, "The Commentary of David Kimhi on the Fifth Book of the Psalms, CVII-CL," *CJ* 6 (1949-50) #2/3, 1-19.

Arnold D. Ehlert and Gleason Archer Jr., "An Old Commentary on Job," *FLB* #5 (1950) 5-6.

M. L. W. Laistner, "Some Early Medieval Commentaries on the Old Testament," *HTR* 46 (1953) 27-46.

*St. Gregory of Nyssa, "Moses and the Vision of God (A commentary on Exodus ch. 33, v. 11-23)," *LofS* 9 (1954-55) 271-279.

Joseph Kafih, "A Fragment of Saadia's Commentary on Proverbs," *Tarbiz* 26 (1956-57) VI-VII.

*St. Gregory of Nyssa, "'I Know That My Redeemer Liveth' (Job XIX, 25) From St. Gregory's Commentary on Job, Bk. XIV," *LofS* 13 (1958-59) 461-465. *(Trans. by E[dmund] H[ill])*

S. Z. L. Skoss, "From Se'adya's Longer Commentary to Genesis 22:20-23:18; 25:21-26," *Tarbiz* 28 (1958-59) #3/4, VIII.

Anonymous, "From B. Jacob's Commentary on Genesis," *CJ* 15 (1960-61) #4, 7-21. [The Angels' Visit with Abraham: Genesis 18:1-33; Jacob and the Angel: Genesis 32:25-31; Judah and Tamar: Genesis 38:1-30]

*Ephraim E. Urbach, "Rabbinic Exegesis and Origenes' Commentaries on the Song of Songs and Jewish-Christian Polemics," *Tarbiz* 30 (1960-61) #2, V-VI.

*A. Levene, "Some Observations on the Commentaries of Isho'dad Bishop of Ḥadatta and of the Manuscript Mingana 535 on Genesis," *StP* 4 (1961) 136-142.

Meredith B. Handspicker, "Athanasius on Tradition of Scripture," *ANQ, N.S.,*3 (1962-63) #1, 13-29. [O.T. Refs., pp. 18-19]

*Ezra Shereshevsky, "The Significance of Rashi's Commentary on the Pentateuch," *JQR, N.S.,* 54 (1963-64) 58-79.

Shelomo Pines, "Four Extracts from Abu l-Barakat Al-Baghdadi's Commentary on Ecclesiastes," *Tarbiz* 33 (1963-64) #2, VII.

*M. Altbauer, "Traces of Hebrew Commentaries in the Slavonic Translations of the Bible," *Tarbiz* 34 (1964-65) #4, IX-X.

*Efraim Gottlieb, "The Significance of the Story of Creation in the Interpretation of the Early Cabbalists," *Tarbiz* 37 (1967-68) #3, IV-V.

D. N. MacKenzie, "An Early Jewish-Persian Argument," *BSOAS* 31 (1968) 249-269. *[Or. 8659]*

Paul Meyvaert, "A New Edition of Gregory the Great's Commentaries on the Canticle and I Kings," *JTS, N.S.,* 19 (1968) 215-225.

David C. Fowler, "A Middle English Bible Commentary (Oxford, Trinity College, MS 93)," *ManSL* 12 (1968) 67-78.

About the Author

William G. Hupper studied at Florida Beacon College and Gordon College. He has continued scholarly pursuits in Ancient Near Eastern studies and biblical languages, as an avocation, studying Hebrew under a private tutor. He has spent over twenty-two years compiling, collating and editing the articles included in his multi-volumed index, while continuing his full time profession as a traffic administrator for a leading multi-national corporation. He has developed software for the Macintosh™ computer to produce Egyptian hieroglyphics on screen and in print which is available commercially. He has authored articles in theological journals as well as official government documents related to his vocation. Mr. Hupper has also been a member of the Society of Biblical Literature for over twenty years.